PAUL THE APOSTLE
Jew and Greek Alike

A THEOLOGICAL AND EXEGETICAL STUDY

Volume 1

PAUL THE APOSTLE
Jew and Greek Alike

by

ROMANO PENNA

translated by

THOMAS P. WAHL, O.S.B.

A Michael Glazier Book
THE LITURGICAL PRESS
Collegeville, Minnesota

The Translator:
Thomas P. Wahl, O.S.B., S.T.L., The Catholic University of America, S.S.L., Pontifical Biblical Institute, Ph.D., Union Theological Seminary, New York City. Father Wahl taught Scripture at St. John's University, Collegeville, Minnesota, from 1967 to 1993. He is a member of St. Anselm's Benedictine Priory, Tokyo, Japan, a foundation of St. John's Abbey, Collegeville, Minnesota.

A Michael Glazier Book published by The Liturgical Press.

Cover design by David Manahan, O.S.B. St. Paul; detail of iconostasis beam, St. Catherine's Monastery, Sinai.

Paul the Apostle: Jew and Greek Alike is the authorized English translation of *L'apostolo Paolo: Studi di esegesi e teologia*, published by Edizioni Paolini, Turin, Italy, in 1991.

Manufactured in the United States of America.

Library of Congress Cataloging-in-Publication Data

Penna, Romano.
    [Apostolo Paolo. English]
    Paul the Apostle : a theological and exegetical study / by Romano
Penna ; translated by Thomas P. Wahl.
       p.   cm.
    "A Michael Glazier book."
    Originally published in Italian in a single vol.
    Includes bibliographical references and index.
    Contents: v. 1. Jew and Greek alike — v. 2. Wisdom and the folly
of the Cross.
    ISBN 0-8146-5835-0
    1. Bible. N.T. Epistles of Paul—Theology. 2. Paul, the
Apostle, Saint. 3. Bible. N.T. Epistles of Paul—Criticism,
interpretation, etc.   I. Title.
BS2651.P37513 1996
225.9′2—dc20   95-37825
                                                        CIP

PETRO ROSSANO

MAGISTRO INCOMPARABILI

in memoriam

Contents

Preface   ix

Abbreviations   xi

1   Introduction to Paulinism   1

Part One
HISTORY AND EXEGESIS

2   The Jews in Rome at the Time of the Apostle Paul   19

3   Jewish-Christian Structures of the Roman Church
     in the First Century   48

4   The Structural Function of 3:1-8 in the
     Letter to the Romans   60

5   Narrative Aspects of the Letter to the Romans   90

6   Romans 1:18-2:29: Between Missionary Preaching
     and Borrowing from the Environment   103

7   Paul's Detractors in Romans 3:8   111

8   Baptism and Participation in the Death of Christ in
     Romans 6:1-11   124

9   The Motif of the *'Aqedah* Against the Background
     of Romans 8:32   142

10   The Gospel as "Power of God"
     According to 1 Corinthians 1:18-25   169

11   Saint Paul and Diogenes the Cynic:
     1 Corinthians 7:29b-31a   181

12   Only Love Will Have No End.
     A Reading of 1 Corinthians 13 in Its Various Senses   191

13   Adamic Christology and Anthropological Optimism in
     1 Corinthians 15:45-49   206

14   The Apostle's Sufferings:
     Anthropology and Eschatology in 2 Corinthians 4:7–5:10 232

15   The Presence of Paul's Opponents in
     2 Corinthians 10–13: Literary Examination   259

16   The Evolution of Paul's Attitude Toward the Jews   290

Index of Subjects   323

Index of Scriptural Texts   325

Preface

There are two ways to present the theology of Saint Paul, or for that matter the thought of any brilliant and prolific writer. One is to offer as complete a picture as possible, inserting each component into a systematic whole. The other does specialized investigations, dwelling on the individual components, digging ever deeper into specific lines of research. The difference is evident. The former achieves a synthesis, which, however, is in danger of being excessively abstract. The latter, preferring analysis, reaches more profoundly into the author's mind, but with the risk of never achieving an overview.

This book chooses the second method, with its attendant danger. This choice can surely claim theoretical justification in the complexity of Paul's thought, which is scarcely amenable to an ironclad Aristotelian logic. For Paul's charism, as has been said, is more one of richness than of clarity. But this observation also accords with the purpose of this book, which is to gather the best things I have written on the Apostle over the past twenty years and present them in an organic structure.

Each chapter represents a different earlier publication of mine, revised here and there in text and notes alike. Most of these were prepared for specialized periodicals or miscellanies, thus meeting the demands of rigorous scientific research. Nevertheless, there are among them some slightly less meticulous articles, and even conferences, that betray their original oral character. I have omitted some less important pieces and also some works on Deutero-Paul, especially the Letter to the Ephesians. At any rate, the variety should make the present work accessible to a varied audience.

One thing is certain: An encounter with Paul, even if relatively superficial, cannot help but stir the waters of one's life of faith and witness. Paul has always found eloquent praise in the Church, from John Chrysostom:

> Can you name me a better possession [than Paul's faithfulness to the Cross]? Or an equal one? How many angels and archangels is he not worth who uttered this word? (*Paneg.* 7:3);

to Martin Luther:

Nothing has ever entered the world so daring as the preaching of Paul (*Tischreden* 2:277);

and on into our own day:

One who is an honor to humanity (Daniel Rops, 1951);
It is he who originated the completely modern sense of the scandal of faith (Mario Luzi, 1991).

Still, let us not be carried away by the rhetoric. The best way to escape this is simply to take his letters in hand and weigh them with one's own study and meditation, in order to recognize that from these letters there always flows clear, cool water, capable of quenching the thirst of even the most parched spirits.

In all simplicity I offer this volume to help with such an approach, with the wish that it may succeed.

ROMANO PENNA

Rome
29 January 1991

Abbreviations

AB	Analecta Biblica
ABR	American Benedictine Review
AJut	Acta Jutlandica
AnglThRev	Anglican Theological Review
ANRW	Aufstieg und Niedergang der Römischen Welt
AThANT	Abhandlungen zur Theologie des Alten und Neuen Testaments
BBB	Bonner Biblische Beiträge
BCM	Biblioteca di Cultura Moderna
BCR	Biblioteca di Cultura Religiosa
BET	Beiträge zur biblischen Exegese und Theologie
BEThL	Beiträge Ephemeridum Theologicarum Lovaniensium
B.G.U.	Aegyptische Urkunden aus den Koeniglichen Museen zu Berlin: Griechische Urkunden
BhTh	Beiträge zur historischen Theologie
Bib	Biblica
BiblArchRev	Biblical Archeology Review
BibKir	Bibel und Kirche
BibOr	Bibbia e Oriente
BibTrans	Bible Translator
BJ	Bible de Jérusalem
BJRL	Bulletin of the John Rylands Library
BOr	Biblica et Orientalia
BSR	Biblioteca di Scienze Religiose
BT	Biblioteca Teologica
BU	Biblische Untersuchungen

BUL	Biblioteca Universale Laterza
BZ (NF)	Biblische Zeitschrift (Neue Folge)
BzHTh	Beiträge zur historischen Theologie
BZNW	Beihefte zu der Zeitschrift für die neutestamentliche Wissenschaft
CB NTS	Coniectanea Biblica, New Testament Series
CBQ	Catholic Biblical Quarterly
CII	Corpus inscriptionum iudaicarum
CNT	Commentaire du Nouveau Testament
Conc	Concilium
CTNT	Commentario Teologico del Nuovo Testamento
EB	Etudes bibliques
EKK	Evangelisch-Katholischer Kommentar zum Neuen Testament
EstBibl	Estudios Biblicos
EThL	Ephemerides Theologicae Lovanienses
ETThRel	Etudes Théologiques et Religieuses
EvQ	Evangelical Quarterly
EvTh	Evangelische Theologie
ExpT	The Expository Times
FRLANT	Forschungen zur Religion und Literatur des Alten und Neuen Testaments
FzB	Forschung zur Bibel
GLNT	Grande Lessico del Nuovo Testamento
GNS	Good News Studies
GThA	Göttinger Theologische Arbeiten
HistRel	History of Religions
HNT	Handbuch zum Neuen Testament
HThKNT	Herders Theologischer Kommentar zum Neuen Testament
HThR	Harvard Theological Review

HUCA	Hebrew Union College Annual
HUTh	Hermeneutische Untersuchungen zur Theologie
ICC	The International Critical Commentary
Int	Interpretation
IrThQuart	Irish Theological Quarterly
JournBiblLit (JBL)	Journal of Biblical Literature
JournJewStud (JJS)	Journal of Jewish Studies
JournRomStud	Journal of Roman Studies
JournStudJud (JSJ)	Journal for the Study of Judaism
JQR	Jewish Quarterly Review
JSNT	Journal for the Study of the New Testament
JTSt (JThS)	Journal of Theological Studies
LAB	Pseudo-Philo, Liber Antiquitatum Biblicarum
LD	Lectio Divina
LOS	London Oriental Series
MBS	Message of Biblical Spirituality
MRB	Monographische Reihe von Benedictina
NA NF	Neutestamentliche Abhandlungen, Neue Folge
NEB	New English Bible
NHC	Nag Hammadi Codices
NIGTC	New International Greek Testament Commentary
NRT	Nouvelle Revue Théologique
NT	Novum Testamentum
NT Suppl.	Novum Testamentum, Supplements
NTD	Neues Testament Deutsch
NTOA	Novum Testamentum et Orbis Antiquus
NTS	New Testament Studies
NTTS	New Testament Tools and Studies
NVB	Nuovissima Versione della Bibbia
OBO	Orbis Biblicus et Orientalis

PG	J. Migne, Patrologia Graeca
PL	J. Migne, Patrologia Latina
PS	Patristica Sorboniensia
QD	Quaestiones Disputatae
RAC	Reallexikon für Antike und Christentum
RB	Revue Biblique
RechScRel	Recherches de Sciences Religieuses
RestorQuart	Restoration Quarterly
RevEtJuives	Revue des Etudes Juives
RHPhR	Revue d'histoire et de philosophie religieuses
RHR	Revue de l'Histoire des Religions
RivArchCrist	Rivista di Archeologia Cristiana
RivBibl	Rivista Biblica
RivStLettRel	Rivista di Storia e Letteratura Religiosa
RNT	Regensburger Neues Testament
RQ	Revue de Qumran
RSB	Ricerche Storico-Bibliche
RSPhTh	Revue de Sciences Philosophiques et Théologiques
RSR	Religious Studies Review
RSV	Revised Standard Version
RTP	Revue de Théologie et de Philosophie
RvSR	Revue de Sciences Religieuses
SB	Studi Biblici
SBEC	Studies in the Bible and Early Christianity
SBL DS	Society for Biblical Literature, Dissertations Series
SBM	Stuttgarter Biblische Monographien
SBTh SS	Studies in Biblical Theology, Supplementary Series
SC	Sources Chrétiennes
ScottJourTheol	Scottish Journal of Theology
SDB	Supplément au Dictionnaire de la Bible
SNT	Studien zum Neuen Testament

SNTS MS	Society for New Testament Studies, Monograph Series
SNTU	Studien zum Neuen Testament und seiner Umwelt
SOC	Scritti delle Origini Cristiane
SPAA	Spicilegium Pontificii Athenaei Antoniani
SPCIC	Studiorum Paulinorum Congressus Internationalis Catholicus
ST	Studia Theologica
StEv	Studia Evangelica
STh (StTh)	Studia Theologica
StiZt	Stimmen der Zeit
StPat	Studia Patavina
SUNT	Studien zur Umwelt des Neuen Testaments
SVF	Stoicorum Veterum Fragmenta
TAPA	Transactions of the American Philological Association
TB	Babylonian Talmud
TDNT	Theological Dictionary of the New Testament
TgJo	Targum Pseudo-Jonathan
TgN	Targum Neofiti
ThB	Theologische Beiträge
ThF	Theologische Forschung
ThHNT	Theologischer Handkommentar zum Neuen Testament
ThJb	Theologische Jahrbücher
ThLZ	Theologische Literatur-Zeitung
ThSK	Theologische Studien und Kritiken
ThSt	Theological Studies
ThZ	Theologische Zeitschrift
TrThZ	Trierer Theologische Zeitschrift
TU	Theologische Untersuchungen
TZ	Theologische Zeitschrift
TZTh	Tübinger Zeitschrift für Theologie
USQR	Union Seminary Quarterly Review

VT	Vetus Testamentum
WA	D. Martin Luther's Werke (Weimar Ausgabe)
WBC	World Biblical Commentary
WdF	Wege der Forschung
WMANT	Wissenschaftliche Monographien zum Alten und Neuen Testament
WUNT	Wissenschaftliche Untersuchungen zum Neuen Testament
ZAW	Zeitschrift für die Alttestamentliche Wissenschaft
ZNW	Zeitschrift für die Neutestamentliche Wissenschaft
ZThK	Zeitschrift für Theologie und Kirche
ZWTh	Zeitschrift für die Wissenschaftliche Theologie

Chapter 1

Introduction to Paulinism

Preliminaries

The term "Paulinism" originated in the nineteenth century with the Tübingen school, which coined the expression and used it polemically in contrast to Petrinism or else to "Jewish Christianity." It was meant to contrast both Pauline theology and the tradition deriving from it with these latter terms.[1] It is thus quite evident that the term was originally indebted to presuppositions that were both philosophical (Hegelian idealism) and confessional (anti-Catholic Lutheranism). Moreover, it was used in the attempt to systematize Paul's thought, which is today developed more objectively in all its complexity, rather than as the abstract product of ivory tower scholarship.[2]

Nevertheless, the term is now used as a shorthand reference to the fundamental points characteristic of Paul's theology and also to their continuation in the later literature. What is needed is a calm historical evaluation of the phenomenon. From this point of view, while personally holding to the brilliant Pauline hermeneutic of the gospel, I cannot help but consider the attitude tendentious which would maintain that it is "in the form it took with Paul" that Christianity "is truest."[3] This is a value

1. See the word "Paulinismus" in the index of W. G. Kümmel, *The New Testament: The History of the Investigation of Its Problems*, trans. S. M. Gilmour and H. C. Kee (Nashville, 1972) = *Das Neue Testament. Geschichte der Erforschung seiner Probleme* (Munich, 1970²), with the references, esp. 126f., 161-164, 224ff., 262-265). Especially notable is the study of O. Pfleiderer, *Paulinism: A Contribution to the History of Primitive Christian Theology*, trans. E. Peters (London, 1877) = *Der Paulinismus. Ein Beitrag zur Geschichte der urchristlichen Theologie* (Leipzig, 1873, 1890²).

2. See the observations of R. Morgan, "The Significance of 'Paulinism,' " in M. D. Hooker and S. G. Wilson, eds., *Paul and Paulinism: Essays in Honour of C. K. Barrett* (London, 1982) 320-338.

3. C. K. Barrett, *A Commentary on the Second Epistle to the Corinthians*, Black's New Testament Commentaries (London, 1976²) VII.

1

judgment which the believer certainly has the right to express but which the historian as such cannot share. For Christianity from the very beginning assumed various forms, which are attested even in the New Testament canon and which all deserve equal attention as witnesses to the fact that Christ and the gospel of Christ are greater than the interpretations made of them.[4] It is surely more fair, because based on incontrovertible literary evidence, to say that in Paulinism we have the most widely attested and perhaps also the most original form of the great vitality of early Christianity—not the only form but the most documented one, both because of the strong personality of the Apostle, which largely dominates first-century Christianity, and because of the reception that it enjoyed in the succeeding generations.

It is beyond our scope to study the formation of the Pauline corpus[5] or its canonization, while recognizing that the very collection and canonization have much to say about the attention and the veneration that the Apostle of Tarsus already attracted during the first and second centuries. We can agree with what Childs has recently written:

> The shape which the canonical collection has given the Pauline letters greatly extends the profile of Paul far beyond that of his historical ministry. Regardless of how one decides on the relationship between the redactional and canonical process of the collection, the present shape of the Pauline corpus has included letters which give the appearance of transmitting Paul's message within a variety of settings which cannot easily be identified with the known facts of his life. In sum, a profile of Paul has been shaped by the canon which transcends that of the historical apostle.[6]

But we can go a step further and say that the same process of transformation of the image of Paul (the "Paulusbild" in German) can later be recognized in the transition from the canonical writings to those of the so-called subapostolic literature and that of the early patristic period.[7]

But first we must define Paulinism itself, no easy task. This can be attempted by such methodological questions as whether it is possible to dis-

4. See E. Käsemann, ed., *Das Neue Testament als Kanon* (Göttingen, 1970), where the author seems to fall into "Tendenzkritik," as he would make the Pauline proclamation of the *justificatio impii* the "canon within the canon" (405); J. D. G. Dunn, *Unity and Diversity in the New Testament: An Inquiry into the Character of Earliest Christianity* (Philadelphia, 1977).
5. See most recently D. Trobisch, *Die Entstehung der Paulusbriefsammlung: Studien zu den Anfängen christlicher Publizistik*, NTOA 10 (Freiburg/Schweiz-Göttingen, 1989).
6. B. S. Childs, *The New Testament as Canon: An Introduction* (London, 1984) 426f.
7. See the excellent book of G. Barbaglio, *Paolo di Tarso e le origini cristiane* (Cittadella, Assisi, 1985).

cover a focal point in Paul's thought,[8] and if so, what is it? Or at least what are the characteristic, unmistakable, and exclusive elements in Paul's theology? In other words, what is the originality of Paul in the context of the first generations of Christianity? One thing is certain: However one answers these questions, to single out the specifically Pauline traits entails a critical reduction, if not the very denial, of the *theological* unity of the New Testament and of Christian origins in general. For one must then distinguish other blocks of literature and other authors who do not agree with the Apostle in the way they do theology.

I. Related areas

In fact, it is precisely in this perspective, in the contrast with the other expressions of earliest Christianity, that all the originality of Paulinism emerges and is delineated. We can actually sketch early Christianity both historically and theologically by taking the Apostle of Tarsus as a point of reference both in his personality and in his rich teaching, measuring and delimiting the other hermeneutical positions by his.

First of all, let us consider *pre-Paulinism*, meaning the period of the first post-Easter Christianity preceding the conversion and Christian formation of Saul the Pharisee. This is a relatively brief period of time, a matter of three to five years between the death of Christ and the event on the road to Damascus, and a few more years until the decisive sojourn in Syrian Antioch (see Acts 11:19-26).[9] It was at this period that the testimony of the first disciples began, and also that the first attempts were made in the various Churches to elaborate and formulate the common Christian faith. These attempts in one way or another influenced the very formation of Pauline thought; see, for instance, the two pre-Pauline confessions of faith to be found in 1 Cor 15:3-5 ("I hand on to you what I

8. For example, H. Räisänen, *Paul and the Law*, WUNT 29 (Tübingen, 1983) 11, accepts "contradictions and tensions" as "*constant* features of Paul's theology of the law."

9. On the importance of the Antiochene Church for Christian origins, see R. E. Brown and J. P. Meier, *Antioch and Rome, New Testament Cradles of Catholic Christianity* (New York, 1983) 11–86; and especially J. Becker, *Paulus: Der Apostel der Völker* (Tübingen, 1989) 87–131. This Church owes its existence to the dispersion that occurred after the death of Stephen in Jerusalem, and it is precisely Stephen's group that represents the matrix of Christianity closest to Paulinism. See M. Hengel, "Between Jesus and Paul," in *Between Jesus and Paul: Studies in the Earliest History of Christianity*, trans. J. Bowden (Philadelphia, 1983) = "Zwischen Jesus und Paulus. Die 'Hellenisten,' die 'Sieben' und Stefanus," ZThK 72 (1975) 151–206 (some basic elements of this study are found in Hengel, *Acts and the History of Earliest Christianity*, trans. J. Bowden [Philadelphia, 1980] 71–80; a little more restrictive is H. Räisänen, "The 'Hellenists'—A Bridge Between Jesus and Paul?" in *The Torah and Christ* (Helsinki, 1986) 242–306.

have received'') and in Rom 1:3b-4a, witnessing to two different approaches to the Christ-event.

In the second place, we can identify a whole area of early Christianity that does not seem to have been particularly touched by the theological personality of the Apostle Paul, whether by having been influenced by him or by having reacted in opposition to him. We could label this area as *a-Paulinism*. This stance developed according to its own lines of tradition, beginning independently (see the line that leads to the ''disciple whom Jesus loved'') and ending up in equally original theological and ecclesial positions. Such an independence from Paulinism is best represented in the New Testament canon by the writings of the Johannine corpus (a Gospel, three letters, and an apocalypse)[10] and the so-called Letter to the Hebrews (which, however, may have been acquainted with deutero-Paulinism; see below). Even into the second century this theological-ecclesial area will continue in varying degrees to influence the *Didache*, the *Letter of Barnabas*, the *Pastor of Hermas*, and the bishop Papias of Hierapolis.[11]

In the third place, we find the vast movement of *anti-Paulinism*, which reacted violently against Paul not only theologically but on the practical missionary level, especially against one of the central points of his thought, namely, the discrediting of the Torah.[12] We recognize this above all in the Judeo-Christian phenomenon, which combined two poles that Paul considered mutually exclusive: faith in Jesus' messiahship and observance of the Law. It is possible that in such stubborn opposition there was a certain distortion of Paulinism (see Rom 3:8: ''We are slandered''; see chap. 7 below). Even so, there is reason to believe that the basic Pauline themes were well understood, and rejected as such by that wing of the Church that was, from a Jewish perspective, the more traditionalist and orthodox. Indeed, the negative reaction not only goes back to the early testimony of the new convert (see Acts 9:22-25, 28-30), but it kept growing vigorously, as Paul himself witnesses in more than one letter, and consequently in more than one Church (see 2 Cor 11:13, 26: ''false apostles'' and ''false brothers''; Gal 2:4: ''false brothers''; Phil 3:2: ''evil workers'';

---

10. See R. Penna, ed., *Il giovannismo alle origini cristiane*, RSB III/2 (Bologna, 1991).
11. See A. Lindemann, *Paulus im ältesten Christentum: Das Bild des Apostels und die Rezeption der paulinischen Theologie in der frühchristlichen Literatur bis Marcion*, BhTh 58 (Tübingen, 1979) 158–160, 174–177, 233–240, 263–296.
12. See R. Penna, ed., *Antipaolinismo: reazioni a Paolo tra il I e il II secolo*, RSB I/2 (Bologna, 1989); G. Lüdemann, *Paulus, der Heidenapostel—Antipaulinismus im frühen Christentum*, FRLANT 130 (Göttingen, 1983); J. J. Gunther, *St. Paul's Opponents and Their Background*, NT Suppl. (Leiden, 1973).

Rom 16:17: "those who provoke divisions and obstacles").[13] Even the Church in Jerusalem, in fact, at least displayed understanding of such opposition (see Acts 21:18-24). Such aversion apparently manifests itself in the Letter of James as well (see vol. 2, chap. 22);[14] and continues among Jewish Christians in later centuries, as is evidenced especially by the Ebionites and even more so by the Pseudo-Clementines.[15]

II. The original Paulinism

Let us now look at the true, proper Paulinism. This abstract noun, derived, of course, from the name of Paul, is meant to designate a doctrine and attitude of life associated with the Apostle himself, who is thus understood to be the originator and guarantor of the whole system that he championed. But historically speaking, Paulinism represents a reality, the complexity of which is evidenced by the fact that the sources that document it give rise to serious debate about their historical usefulness.

Regarding the Acts of the Apostles, for instance, more than half of which is devoted to the figure of Saint Paul, no serious Pauline scholar today utilizes it to delineate the theology of the historical Paul.[16] But even concerning the thirteen letters associated with his name, there is now a wide consensus that accepts seven as authentic, that is, deriving directly from the Apostle (in the canonical order: Romans, 1 and 2 Corinthians, Galatians, Philippians, 1 Thessalonians, Philemon), and six as inauthentic, that is, deriving from his later disciples (Ephesians, Colossians, 2 Thessalonians, 1 and 2 Timothy, Titus).[17] It goes without saying that their lack of authenticity in no way impugns their canonical status.[18]

Sharing this evaluation of the letters, we consider the question of how to appraise the Paulinism of the two groups of letters. The first group, derived as they are directly from Paul himself, clearly reflect and docu-

13. According to R. E. Brown, *Antioch and Rome*, 124-127, see 184, the note in 1 Clem 5:2 (according to which Peter and Paul were put to death through "jealous zeal and envy") would allude to a betrayal by Jewish Christians in the capital.
14. In the Gospel According to Matthew (note especially Matt 5:17ff.), we probably have not an explicit opposition but simply a different theological pole: see G. Barbaglio, "Paolo e Matteo: due termini a confronto," in R. Penna, ed., *Antipaolinismo*, 5-22.
15. See G. Barbaglio, *Paolo di Tarso*, 390-410; L. Cirillo, "L'antipaolinismo nelle Pseudoclementine," in R. Penna, ed., *Antipaolinismo*, 121-137.
16. See G. Schneider, *Die Apostelgeschichte*, 2 vols. (Freiburg, 1980, 1982) 1:137-145; J. Becker, *Paulus*, 12-16.
17. Besides the introductions to the New Testament, see R. F. Collins, *Letters That Paul Did Not Write*, GNS 28 (Wilmington, Del., 1988); C. L. Stockhausen, *Letters in the Pauline Tradition*, MBS 13 (Wilmington, Del., 1989); J. Becker, *Paulus*, 6-11.
18. See R. Penna, "Anonimia e pseudepigrafia nel Nuovo Testamento: comparatismo e ragioni di una prassi letteraria," *RivBibl* 33 (1985) 319-344.

ment authentic Paulinism, the original system of thought proper to the Apostle himself. We shall therefore call it the "original Paulinism." But as for the other group, being the expressions of different disciples (though disciples indeed, even if in a broad sense) and of differing historical importance, they certainly no longer manifest Paulinism in its pure state, which is here mixed with new contributions (which are themselves extremely interesting and fruitful) derived from a theological enterprise in development. In this second group we can, then, identify a Paulinism of inspiration, a Pauline school, deutero-Paulinism, post-Paulinism, or better still, the "Paulinism of tradition."[19]

But it is now time to undertake a very summary explanation of the contents of what we mean by the original Paulinism (which, moreover, will be found even in the Paulinism of tradition, albeit in partial and fragmentary but still identifiable ways). There are several elements that, taken together, identify the phenomenon. Some of them are simply external characteristics that just provide a framework for the Pauline material. Others actually help to constitute the very essence of Paulinism.

Among the external elements, we list certain typical characteristics of the figure of Paul within the earliest Christianity. The most extrinsic, but also the most fundamental and incontrovertible, is that no other Christian figure of the first century enjoys so much credible documentation as the ex-Pharisee Saul/Paul of Tarsus. Thirteen letters (even if we can acknowledge only seven as authentic), a biographical account (about half of Acts), and a few scattered mentions (in 2 Pet 3:15-16 and 1 Clem 5) are more than enough, for his features appear all the more remarkably distinct in the very first generations of Christianity. For no other author is there so much information—for none of the twelve apostles,[20] nor for any of the other disciples. We know much more about Paul than about Mary of Nazareth, or even than we know on the strictly documentary level about Jesus himself, in the sense that for neither of these do we have any personal writing directly reflecting their authentic historical selves.[21] Note,

19. The "Paulinism of tradition" itself is expressed in various ways, whether within the New Testament canon (where one must distinguish even among the six deutero-Pauline letters, as well as the Book of Acts), or especially in the later history of theology (where Marcion and Luther are only the highest peaks of a long range of stimulating hermeneutical approaches to the Apostle).

20. Not even for Peter, about whom we have biographical notes dating to as early as the public life of Jesus and continuing to the Acts of the Apostles and some of Paul's letters (1 Corinthians, Galatians—note that the authenticity of 1 and 2 Peter is not conclusively determined); nor yet for John, even if one follows the traditional attribution to him (now widely denied) of all the writings of the Johannine corpus (wherein, in any case, precious little is said of the author); nor finally for the author of the Letter of James, whose identity is also much disputed.

21. Paul differs from Jesus, John the Baptist, and James, the "brother of the Lord" (note the allusions by Flavius Josephus in R. Penna, *L'ambiente storico-culturale delle origini cristiane*.

this does not in any way mean that Paul is the most important figure; over against Jesus Christ he considers himself and claims himself to be nothing but a "servant" (see Rom 1:1; Gal 1:10) and in comparison with the other apostles, a "miscarriage" (1 Cor 15:8). It is just that for him we have the most evidence as to what kind of a person he was, based on documents of others and his own writings.

It is from these that there emerge the features of a man, a missionary, a writer, and a theologian to which nothing can compare in the earliest Christian history. Paul can be described briefly as follows. He was a Jew of the Hellenistic diaspora, born in Tarsus in Cilicia about the beginning of the Common Era; educated in the Pharisaic interpretation of Judaism at the feet of Rabbi Gamaliel I at Jerusalem (see Phil 3:5-6; Acts 22:3; 26:5); of remarkable, complex temperament: very impetuous, both before his conversion and after it (see Gal 1:13-14 and then Gal 1:8; 3:1; 5:12; 6:17), yet capable of tenderness (see Gal 4:19; 1 Cor 4:15; 1 Thess 2:7-8); insistent upon working with his own hands (see 1 Thess 2:9; Acts 18:3) but suffering an ill-defined disease (see Gal 4:13; perhaps 2 Cor 12:7?). His missionary activity, which he based precisely on the experience of his conversion (see Gal 1:15-16; Rom 11:13; Acts 9:15; 22:21), was certainly unparalleled in the first century, and was to remain so for many centuries. Writing to the Romans, he records, "From the region of Jerusalem to Illyria I have finished preaching the gospel of Christ" (Rom 15:19), making his way as far as Rome and intending to go on even to Spain (see Rom 15:23-24). He refers to the various Churches that he raised up in Asia Minor and Greece as "our hope, our joy, and our crown to boast of" (1 Thess 2:19-20; see 2 Cor 11:28). His writings consist completely of letters written in a lively conversational style; such use of the genre was due, not to his rabbinic training (centered on oral tradition), but to the Hellenistic environment from which he came (cf. the Greek papyri) and especially to the pastoral necessity of continuing his relations with the various communities he had founded. This accounts for the occasional character of

---

Una documentazione ragionata [Bologna: Dehoniane, 1991³] 254–260), in that we have no extra-Christian source for Paul (unless perhaps in the Mishnah, *Ab.* 3:11?; see R. Penna, *L'ambiente,* 265f.) We must distinguish between Jews and pagans in attempting to understand the silence about Paul. The pagans simply were not interested in him, since he was not the initiator of the Christian movement, the members of which did not trace themselves back to him as they did to Jesus; he is, however, treated with distortions by the philosopher Celsus in the second half of the second century: see Origen, *C. Cels.* 1:13. As for the Jews, who had much more reason to be concerned about Paul because of their cultural and religious relationship, the silence of the rabbinic sources can only be interpreted as a *damnatio memoriae,* similar to their ignoring of the two great Hellenistic Jews Philo of Alexandria and Flavius Josephus. The later *Toledôt Yeshû* treat of him as one who led part of Israel astray (see R. Di Segni, *Il Vangelo del ghetto* [Rome: Newton Compton, 1985] 62–64). A recent book by the Jewish writer A. Chouraqui, *Jésus et Paul, fils d'Israël* (Aubonne, 1988), is actually too irenic in its treatment of Paul, but it is based more on Acts than on the Pauline letters.

the letters, the importance of which is to be found not so much in their literary character (rather modest, but certainly effective),[22] as in the invaluable documentation they provide concerning the Churches they were addressed to, and the human and theological personality of their author. Indeed, Paul is well aware that he is "unskilled in the words, but not in knowledge" (2 Cor 11:6; cf. 1 Cor 2:1-5). And it is precisely in his thought that we encounter his originality and the reason for his profound effect on the history of theology.

Let us, then, come to the specific constituents of Paulinism, that is, to Paul's typical thinking. Here it is that we discover how Paul's original hermeneutic of the gospel (though in continuity with the earthly Jesus, and especially with the faith of the early Church) comes into existence, giving a whole new meaning to theological reflection, which will lead A. Schweitzer to say, perhaps a bit dramatically, that "Paul vindicated for all time the rights of thought in Christianity."[23] Today the well-known saying of Wrede that would make Paul "the second founder of Christianity" is no longer taken literally;[24] but it remains true that "his charism is not clarity, but originality and richness."[25] It is, therefore, easy to understand the difficulty of systematizing his thought with rigid logical consistency.[26] Some recent attempts are unsatisfactory because they either stop short at the level of presuppositions[27] or become diffused in excessive vagueness.[28]

With a bit of simplification we could say that there are roughly two different positions in identifying the center of Pauline theology.

A first position, rather Protestant in tone, finds in the center of Paulinism the anthropological dimension of the salvific event, the impact of

22. See the still valid study of A. Brunot, *Le génie littéraire de Saint Paul*, LD 15 (Paris, 1955); also J. A. Fischer, "Pauline Literary Forms and Thought Patterns," CBQ 39 (1977) 209-223; B. Standaert, "La rhétorique ancienne dans Saint Paul," in A. Vanhoye, ed., *L'apôtre Paul: personnalité, style et conception du ministère*, BEThL 73 (Louvain, 1986) 78-92.

23. *The Mysticism of Paul the Apostle* (New York, 1968) 376 = *Die Mystik des Apostels Paulus* (Tübingen, 1933 [= 1954]) 365.

24. W. Wrede, *Paulus* (Halle, 1904) 104 (= K. H. Rengstorf, ed., *Das Paulusbild in der neueren deutschen Forschung*, WdF 24 [Darmstadt, 1969²] 96).

25. O. Kuss, *Paulus: Die Rolle des Apostels in der theologischen Entwicklung der Urkirche* (Regensburg, 1971) 278: "He is always 'in transit.' . . . His task is always to forge new paths, often leaving the task of road-building to others; he solves a good many problems, of course, but at the same time raises as many new ones."

26. See J. C. Beker, "Paul's Theology: Consistent or Inconsistent?" NTS 34 (1988) 364-377; H. W. Boers, "The Foundations of Paul's Thought: A Methodological Investigation. The Problem of a Coherent Center of Paul's Thought," STh 42 (1988) 55-68.

27. Thus J. C. Beker, "Paul the Theologian. Major Motifs in Pauline Theology," Int 43 (1989) 352-365. The author identifies the center on the subtextual level, and specifically in the apocalyptic substratum of Paul's thought.

28. Thus J. Plevnik, "The Center of Pauline Theology," CBQ 51 (1989) 461-478, who would include all the components of Paul's gospel in the center.

the redeeming work of Christ on the human being. And this position actually assumes two forms. (1) According to the classical Lutheran thesis, which still resonates in twentieth-century authors like R. Bultmann, E. Käsemann, P. Stuhlmacher, the center of Paulinism consists in the doctrine of justification by faith without the works of the Law, and the resulting gospel of freedom. (2) According to other writers of our century, such as W. Wrede, A. Schweitzer, and more recently E. P. Sanders, at the center stands the theme of the participation of the baptized in the very life of Christ—hence the Christian's tendency toward "mystical" experience.[29]

The two theses certainly witness to two typical components of Pauline theology, so much so that a deep understanding of the Apostle's thought demands that one grant them their due weight. But from a methodological point of view, one must distinguish that which is specific to Paul from that which constitutes the central propelling force of his ideas, for the former may simply be the effect of the latter. Both the "justification of the impious" (Rom 4:5) and "to be in Christ" (Rom 6:11, etc.) are the effect of Christ's death and the purpose of his resurrection (see Rom 3:21-26; 6:1-11), which means that the Christ-event has the primary and fundamental value with respect to the two aspects of its soteriological result.[30]

A second position, rather Catholic in tone, puts the emphasis on the objective dimension of the salvific event, its historical *extra nos* aspect, which stands behind whatever impact it has on the believer.[31] One can protest that this objective dimension can be perceived as such only by means of faith; even so, it is precisely the believer's faith that, reflecting on itself, goes in search of that which can be defined as its basis, its content, and its constant point of reference. It is, then, Christology that must occupy the foreground, and precisely the figure of Christ that is discerned as the organizing center of all of Paul's theological thought.

But here, too, there are two possible ways of approaching the theme. According to the well-known study of L. Cerfaux, Paul's basic intuition consists in the conception of the divinity of Christ, in the sense that "where Christ is, there is God," since it is only through Christ that God works and communicates himself (see 2 Cor 5:19: "In Christ God has reconciled the world to himself").[32] According to R. Schnackenburg, on the other

---

29. See vol. 2, chap. 23, n. 2, and chap. 29, sect. I.

30. See also J. Plevnik, "The Center," 476.

31. Let us note in passing that the *extra nos* is even for Luther "the fundamental formula for a theological grammar," but being meant in an anti-mystical sense: see V. Subilia, *La giustificazione per fede* (Brescia: Paideia, 1976) 150–159.

32. See *Christ in the Theology of St. Paul*, trans. G. Webb and A. Walker (New York, 1959) 6–7, 521 = *Le Christ dans la théologie de Saint Paul*, LD 6 (Paris, 1954²) 9 and 392. An explana-

hand, the basis on which the whole Pauline theology is built and in which it is centered is the primitive kerygma of the death and resurrection of Christ, which Paul takes up as the focal point of his system.[33] Here also, from the methodological viewpoint, we must emphasize that neither on the one hand can what is only one component be made into the center, nor on the other can what was only a historical point of departure be elevated to the center.

Rather, it is better to concentrate on the figure of Christ as such, prescinding from any more specific aspects thereof. If we wanted to compare the theology of Paul to a circle, we would have to say that Jesus Christ is the center, that the things said of him in various ways represent the multiplicity of radii, while the resulting totality on the soteriological level forms its circumference. Actually, everyone from a Saint Thomas[34] to a Luther[35] is in agreement about the figure of Christ and its centrality in Paul, even if in Lutheranism the soteriological cast is stronger. Actually, the figure of Christ is central in every New Testament author—a little less so with some (e.g., the Letter of James) and a little more so with others (especially the Johannine corpus).

But what distinguishes the centrality of Christ in the original Paulinism can be seen on three levels. First, there is no such documentation for any other New Testament author (not even in the vocation of the Twelve, whose obtuseness and cowardice are scarcely glossed over in the Gospels) of how deeply and irrevocably the person of Christ entered into the life of a human being, binding them to himself so totally and exclusively; the same Damascus event is repeatedly associated with this intensely personal encounter (see 1 Cor 9:1; Gal 1:15-16; Phil 3:7-12), and from that point

---

tion of this type is given by J. Becker, the Protestant author of the most recent and finest general monograph on Paul (cited above, n. 9); see ibid., 423: "It is not because Christ dies 'for us' that Jesus' death is our salvation; rather it is because Christ is God for us that his death is deliverance for humankind."

33. See section on Paul's Christology in "Christologie des Neuen Testaments," in *Mysterium Salutis*, Band III/1 (Einsiedeln-Zurich-Cologne, 1970) 309–337, esp. 323–325 = "La Christologie des Épitres de Paul . . .," in *Mysterium Salutis* X (Paris, 1974) 125–161, esp. 143–147. See H. Ridderbos, *Paul: An Outline of His Theology*, trans. J. R. de Witt (Grand Rapids, Mich., 1975) 43 = *Paulus. Ein Entwurf seiner Theologie* (Wuppertal, 1970) 34.

34. In the prologue to his *Super epistolas S. Pauli lectura*, he synthesizes the theology of the Pauline letters in a *doctrina tota de gratia Christi* (ed. Cai, I, 11), "a teaching that is wholly about the grace of Christ," which he expounds systematically through an outline he makes of the letters themselves.

35. In the "Introduction to the New Testament" of the *Septemberbibel* (1522), after affirming, "The Gospel, then, is nothing but the preaching about Christ," he specifies that this can be found in long form in the narrations of the evangelists and in short form in the letters of Paul, who "does not tell of Christ's works, but indicates briefly how by his death and resurrection he has overcome sin, death, and hell for those who believe in him" (*Luther's Works*, vol. 35, Word and Sacrament I, ed. E. T. Bachmann [Philadelphia, 1960] 360).

on it is Christ who becomes the defining element in the personal life of Paul (cf. Gal 2:20; Phil 1:21).

Secondly, it is evident Paul does not recount the story of Christ in the past of his earthly life, even though he does summarize it essentially in striking terms in the picture of the crucified and risen One, "a stumbling block to the Jews and foolishness to the gentiles, but . . . the power of God and the wisdom of God!" (1 Cor 1:23-24); it is doubtless the formulation of the primitive kerygma that is thus taken up (see 1 Cor 15:3-5), but he develops its content in forms and dimensions unknown in any other canonical author.

Thirdly, on the basis of his epistles we can document in detail how Paul plays the whole score of his theology on the keyboard of the person of Christ without separating ontology from function.

Let us now see, if only summarily, how *Christology* is the *fundamental structure* of Paul's thought.

The Apostle defines God's very self in relation to Christ as "the Father of our Lord Jesus Christ," in an exclusively Pauline formulation (see Rom 15:6; 2 Cor 1:3; 11:31; also Col 1:3; Eph 1:3; 1 Pet 1:3); God is the one who has "sent" Jesus (Rom 8:3; Gal 4:4).

The *Pneuma* is now identified Christologically as "the Spirit of Christ" (Rom 8:9), "of the Son" (Gal 4:6), "of Jesus Christ" (Phil 1:19)—a typically Pauline formulation, but otherwise very rare even in any future use in the New Testament (see Acts 16:7; 1 Pet 1:11).

The decisive *salvific event*, while having God for its first origin and principal agent, is indelibly identified with Jesus Christ (and his blood) as historical protagonist, whether this event is understood in terms of reconciliation, liberation, redemption, expiation, justification, or salvation (see below, vol. 2, chaps. 18, 19, 20).

That is why *the cross* is never understood in Paul in the ethical sense it has in Mark 8:34 and parallels ("take up his cross"), but always only as "the cross of Christ" (1 Cor 1:17; Gal 6:12, 14; Phil 3:18), and as such is the place and the symbol of the *extra nos* of salvation.

For Paul *the Church* is originally defined as the "body of Christ" (1 Cor 12:27; see Rom 12:4-5), to be understood in the sense of its identification with the personal Christ. The discourse on ministries (see 1 Cor 12) goes beyond juridical hierarchization and attributes the establishment and constant nurturing of faith more to the word of the gospel than to the administration of the sacraments (see 1 Cor 1:17; Rom 1:1, 16f.; 10:17; see chap. 17 below).

Even the *last day* is called "of Jesus Christ" (1 Cor 1:8; Phil 1:6), in that it is characterized by the "parousia of our Lord Jesus" (1 Thess 3:13; 5:23); in this context Paul also speaks of the "judgment seat of Christ" (2 Cor

5:10), and the whole life to come is summarized as "being always with the Lord" (1 Thess 4:17).

Moreover, the whole *existence of the Christian* is typically considered as living "in Christ Jesus" (1 Thess 2:14; 2 Cor 5:17; Rom 8:1, etc.) in such a dimension as makes of the Christian a "new creation" (2 Cor 5:17; Gal 6:15): see vol. 2, chap. 29 (II, 4 and III, 1). This life according to the Spirit is understood as walking in the strength and the light of the Spirit of Christ (see Rom 8 and Gal 5).

Another absolutely characteristic aspect of Paulinism concerns the relationship of *Christ and Torah*. For Paul, unlike Jewish Christianity, Christ is not simply added to the Law to help the Christian to observe it but substituted for it in order to confer the justice that the Law intends but is unable to bring about (note Rom 10:4: "The end of the Law is Christ, so that justice be given to everyone who believes").[36] Typical aspects intimately correlated to the theme are those of pure grace (see Rom 5:6-8; 8:31-39), of faith that justifies (see Rom 3:28; Gal 2:16), and of Christian freedom (see Rom 6:18; 8:2; Gal 4:31–5:1).

Related to Christological faith is that other great component of Paulinism that makes Paul the theologian and the apostle most open culturally to the great pagan world. Precisely the *"gentiles"* (a distancing term as used by Israel [note Isa 40:17!]) enter and become a constitutive part of the Pauline gospel, directed as it is precisely toward those who are excluded from the enclosure of the sacred (consider the enclosure wall in the Jerusalem Temple precincts) and from the assurances of tradition (since they are not among the chosen of God). The gospel of Paul, on the other hand, carries the new conviction that in Christ "there is no distinction between Jew and Greek, for he himself is Lord of all, rich toward all who call upon him" (Rom 10:12). And thus, since there is no difference as far as sin is concerned, neither is there any difference in justification (see below, chaps. 4 and 6). Consequently, beyond all entrenched clichés, the Christian has the right to consider "all that is true, noble, just, pure, and deserving of love and honor" (Phil 4:8, sounding a typical stoic conceptualization).

Finally, no one develops the theme of *Christ's mediation* and its determining role for access to God the Father more than Paul. Two observations, at least, would lead to this conclusion. The one is the use of the Greek preposition *dia*, "by means of, through," which occurs in the context of various themes, from the death of Jesus (see Rom 7:4), to the present condition of the Christian (see Rom 5:1), to the Christian's prayer (see 2 Cor 1:20), and at last to the hope of eschatological salvation (Rom 5:9). The other is the use of the term *prosagōgē*, "access, entry, approach," which in the

---

36. Ever since Luther such a theme has become crucial to any discussion of Paulinism; but there is no way to resolve it till one again sees it as an aspect of Christology. For greater development, see vol. 2, chaps. 22, 23, 24.

whole New Testament is employed only by Paul (Rom 5:2) and by one work of the Pauline tradition (note Eph 2:18; 3:12) to signify the liberating access of the Christian face to face with God rendered possible precisely by Jesus Christ.

All these various aspects contribute to make of Paulinism, if not exactly a system, at least a very characteristic whole in its original setting and perennially fruitful in vivifying the theology of successive generations of Christians.[37]

III. The Paulinism of tradition

This volume of ours contains no developed study of the Paulinism of tradition, but we do present here some general considerations.

The important thing is to note that the Apostle's thought had a very important succession, that it originated a tradition (some prefer to speak of a school), leaving a considerable heritage, which was to be articulated by certain disciples of considerable note, anonymous though they be.[38] And it is interesting to note how enormously varied are the many schools and movements that claim this single Apostle.

While the forces of anti-Paulinism cannot be said to present a monolithic front, they certainly are relatively homogeneous in the explicit content of their polemic. In contrast, the tradition that begins with Paul displays so many different facets as to surprise us that such diverse ecclesial camps could have their origin in this one figure, Paul. Such, for instance, are the environments that gave rise to the Letter to the Ephesians, the Pastoral Letters, and a Marcion, with their diverse and sometimes contrasting hermeneutical or institutional solutions (note the varying conceptions of Church in these writings). Thus Paulinism after Paul shows itself to be a phenomenon of extraordinary vitality, as A. Harnack already noted: "Paulinism has proved to be a ferment in the history of dogma: a basis it has never been."[39] But it must be self-evident that our fundamentally historical approach to the question certainly precludes our dismissing the

---

37. On this whole treatment, see also J. Ziesler, *Pauline Christianity* (Oxford, 1983) 23–121.

38. For the canonical environment, see the citations of n. 17 above and also K. Kertelge, ed., *Paulus in den neutestamentlichen Spätschriften. Zur Paulusrezeption im Neuen Testament*, QD 89 (Freiburg-Basel-Vienna, 1981); further: A. Lindemann, *Paulus*, 36–91, 113–173, 177–232, 297–343; E. Dassmann, *Der Stachel im Fleisch. Paulus in der frühchristlichen Literatur bis Irenäus* (Münster i. W., 1979); G. Barbaglio, *Paolo di Tarso*, 276ff. See also D. R. McDonald, *The Legend and the Apostle: The Battle for Paul in Story and Canon* (Philadelphia, 1983), which attempts to establish a relationship between the Pastoral Letters and the "Acts of Paul."

39. A. Harnack, *History of Dogma*, I, trans. N. Buchanan (London 1896) 136 = *Lehrbuch der Dogmengeschichte*, I (Tübingen, 1909) 155.

Paulinism of tradition as a phenomenon of degeneration or corruption.[40]
We cannot, of course, help but recognize from time to time two apparently antinomian elements—on the one hand that which is in direct continuity with Paul (and which can even take the form of assuming his name
in order to guarantee a work), and on the other that which is in discon-
tinuity with his original historical-ecclesial situation. It is actually this second type that reveals the great fecundity of Paul's genius. But in 2 Tim
1:14 the exhortation to "preserve the good deposit" is completed with
the instrumental phrase "with the help of the Holy Spirit," and, as Paul
had indicated, "Where there is the Spirit of the Lord, there is freedom"
(2 Cor 3:17).

Let us therefore undertake our survey of the power of the message and
the personality of Paul with objectivity but also with the joy aroused by
the vitality of our subject, recognizing how it reverberates now more, now
less in succeeding generations. It would surely not be at all out of place
to hypothesize for the first two centuries a specifically Pauline (rather
than Petrine) charism in favor of a widespread Church unity, considering
how very different Churches and even contrary forms of Christianity all
trace their origin to the Apostle. A small but significant indication, we
might suggest, could be the constant association of Paul with Peter, already known from the end of the first century (see 1 Clem 5), which will
undergo a notable transformation when, in the episcopal succession of
the Church of Rome, the office will be seen to be in relation to Peter and
no longer to Paul (perhaps toward the end of the second century with
the anti-Marcionite polemic).[41]

In the "thick green forest" of Pauline tradition we encounter the difficult problem of finding a path or paths that will give a better view of the
countryside, that is, to gather the great complex of the Pauline heritage
into more homogeneous groups and trends. To speak of a single line of
evolution, for instance, as does J. Gnilka,[42] can be done only if one restricts oneself to the limits of the canon, and even then only if one sweeps
some of the data under the rug.

---

40. In this sense the Protestant historiography of the late nineteenth and early twentieth
centuries coined the expression and the idea of "early Catholicism," *Frühkatholizismus* (see
J. D. G. Dunn, *Unity and Diversity*, 341–366); but today this term is abandoned or understood
favorably (see V. Fusco, "Sul concetto di protocattolicesimo," RivBibl 30 (1982) 401–434;
L. Goppelt, *Apostolic and Postapostolic Times*, trans. R. A. Guelich (London, 1970) esp. 149ff.
41. See A. Harnack, *Geschichte der altchristlichen Litteratur bis Eusebius*, II/1, 703, cited in
E. Hennecke, W. Schneemelcher, *New Testament Apocrypha*, trans. A. J. B. Higgins et al.
(Philadelphia, 1963–66) II, 73–74 = *Neutestamentliche Apokryphen*, II (Tübingen, 1964³) 41.
42. *Der Kolosserbrief*, HThKNT 10 (Freiburg-Basel-Vienna, 1980) 11, n. 12.

It seems to me more enlightening to identify a "bifurcation"[43] and distinguish at least two paths: one will begin with the Letter to the Colossians and, passing through the Letter to the Ephesians, and will end up in the Gnosticism of the second century; another begins with the Pastoral Letters (or perhaps already with the Acts of the Apostles) and develops into the succeeding Church order of the Great Church. One path thus leads to heresy, the other to orthodoxy. This does not mean that the original Paulinism was something neutral, something antecedent to heresy and orthodoxy alike; even less is this to espouse the well-known thesis of W. Bauer,[44] which understood heresy as the original form of Christianity, from which orthodoxy emerged at a later date. We only want to take note of the historical fact that Paul was read in differing ways, some of which achieved canonical status.

At least one explanation for this consists not just in the unsystematic character of his thought, which was thus open to different elaborations, but especially in the intrinsic spiritual density of one who with good reason considered himself to know "the mind of Christ" (1 Cor 2:16; cf. 7:20). On this subject, note the incisive paradox formulated by A. Harnack, according to whom Paul "had only one disciple who understood him, Marcion, who, however, grossly misunderstood him."[45] Thus both the above-mentioned paths are explained by the rich complexity of the original Paulinism, which the derived Paulinism develops into divergence and so inevitably into conflict. Thus, for example, among the Nag Hammadi texts, alien though they are to the Great Church, we find an orthodox "Prayer of the Apostle Paul" (placed right at the beginning of a manuscript collection) and an "Apocalypse of Paul," which invites him to join the twelve apostles;[46] Tertullian, on the other hand, long an exponent of the Great Church, labels Paul directly *haereticorum apostolus*,[47] without even distinguishing among the various positions of the presumed heretics.

It would surely be fair to ask where Paul now survives with his authentic features most intact. Even today all the Christian Churches pay him great

---

43. R. Morgan, "The Significance," 327; the idea was in fact already expressed by J. M. Robinson in H. Köster, J. M. Robinson, *Trajectories Through Early Christianity* (Philadelphia, 1971) 10 = *Entwicklungslinien durch die Welt des frühen Christentums* (Tübingen, 1971) 10.

44. *Orthodoxy and Heresy in Earliest Christianity*, ed. R. A. Kraft and G. Krodel (Philadelphia, 1971) = *Rechtgläubigkeit und Ketzerei im ältesten Christentum* (Tübingen, 1934, 1964²; see now the criticism of T. A. Robinson, *The Bauer Thesis Examined: The Geography of Heresy in the Early Christian Church*, SBEC 11 (Lewiston, N.Y., 1988).

45. *History*, 88 = *Lehrbuch*, I, 100.

46. Note respectively NHC I A:1–B:11 and NHC V 19:15-17.

47. *Adv. Marc.* 3:5:4. Irenaeus, on the other hand, completely vindicated his orthodoxy: see *Adv. haer.* 4:41:4.

veneration, even though in some he is always a troublesome witness. But interesting as this question is, it is something we are really unable to answer now. What is most important is to revive his living presence before us not only as a strong moral missionary example (mostly a result of the Acts of the Apostles) but even more so as a thinker who in Christ's name will break through our present ways of thinking and force us ever anew to examine to what extent we live up to our Christian identity. We can do this only by again poring over his letters. And that is what we now propose to do.

I

HISTORY AND EXEGESIS

Chapter 2

The Jews in Rome at the Time of the Apostle Paul

Preliminaries

The New Testament mentions the Roman Jews in two places, Romans and Acts. The more explicit text of the two is the final section of the Acts of the Apostles (28:16-31), depicting Paul's two-year residence in Rome under military guard. Now it is interesting that Luke here completely ignores the Christian community, which must surely have been leading an energetic existence, as is evidenced by the great letter that the Apostle had earlier sent to them. All of Luke's attention is on the Jews of the City. Besides this, already in the Letter to the Romans the terms Ἰουδαῖος ("Jew" eleven times) and Ἰσραήλ ("Israel" eleven times) were used more frequently than in any other Pauline work, and certain typical themes are treated, dealing with problems raised concerning the encounter of Judaism with the new message of the gospel.[1] In this we see an indication of particular attention on Paul's part not only to the people of Israel as a whole but specifically to that part of the Christian community of Rome that was of Jewish origin, if not to the Roman Jews themselves.

But Luke even more than Paul, having scarcely mentioned the Christians, οἱ ἀδελφοί ("brethren"), who went to meet Paul "as far as the Forum of Appius and the Three Taverns" (Acts 28:15; outside Rome!), directs all his own interest toward the Jews of Rome, before whom Paul must appear again as a missionary (23:11); evidently Luke does this to show that the Jews, as earlier at Pisidian Antioch (13:46) and then at Corinth (18:6), closed themselves off to the gospel, thus justifying Paul's reorientation to the gentiles (28:28).[2]

---

1. See H. Schlier, "Von den Juden: Römerbrief 2:1-29," in *Die Zeit der Kirche* (Freiburg, 1956) 38–47; L. De Lorenzi, ed., *Die Israelfrage nach Röm 9–11*, MRB 3 (Rome, 1977).

2. This is the interpretation (correct, I think) of E. Haenchen, *The Acts of the Apostles: A Commentary*, trans. B. Noble and G. Schinn (Philadelphia, 1971) 724 = *Die Apostelgeschichte*

Concerning these, Luke recounts two meetings with Paul. In the first he assembles τοὺς ὄντας τῶν Ἰουδαίων πρώτους, "the leading Jews" (28:17-22), while in the second the number is larger, though not specified precisely (πλείονες, "many": 28:23). Their division over Paul's preaching is indicated by the adjective ἀσύμφωνοι, "in disagreement" (28:25). Which means that in any case some of them "believed what was said," (οἱ μὲν ἐπείθοντο τοῖς λεγομένοις: 28:24). Still, not only do they all take their leave of Paul together, but Paul levels an accusation of obstinacy against them all without distinction, quoting the harsh text of Isa 6:9-10 (Acts 28:25b-27). Now, the Jews of Rome even for Luke represent all Israel, and even if Paul addresses them as comrades, ἄνδρες ἀδελφοί, "men, brothers" (28:17), he ultimately renounces any responsibility for them, abandoning them to their unbelief.[3]

However, Luke's narrative is not historical in the strict sense. That is confirmed even in 28:22, where the Jews of Rome say that they know nothing of Christianity (περὶ τῆς αἱρέσεως ταύτης, "about this faction") except that it "runs into opposition everywhere" (πανταχοῦ ἀντιλέγεται). This profession of ignorance contradicts at least two historical data. The first is the fact that in Rome not only did Christians and Jews live elbow to elbow, but also this Christian community had experienced (as a result of the Letter to the Romans) the influx of a good number of Jews, surely coming largely from the Jewish groups present in the capital even though some of them may have originally come from elsewhere.[4] The second is the fact that no more than twenty years earlier the Roman Jews had experienced terrible disturbances on account of "Chrestus," as we read in Suetonius, *Claudius* 25 (about which we will speak later).

But setting aside the Lukan and Pauline texts, though they do provide us with a useful point of departure, we wish to study the historical socio-religious situation of Roman Jewry at the time of Saint Paul. Now, our Christian sources actually report only the situation of the Christian community in the City. And as for pagan Rome, we shall not detail the countless literary, epigraphic, and artistic sources that illustrate it in remarkable detail. Rather, we ask about the Jewish Rome, trying to answer these ques-

(Tübingen, 1965³) 652f. In Acts 21-28 Paul's journey to Rome "leads not to the imperial tribunal but to the Jews of Rome" (G. Schneider, *Die Apostelgeschichte*, I, HThKNT V/1 [Freiburg-Basel-Vienna, 1980] 144).

3. See H. J. Hauser, *Strukturen der Abschlusserzählung der Apostelgeschichte (Apg 28:16-31)*, AB 86 (Rome, 1979); B. Prete, "L'arrivo di Paolo a Roma e il suo significato secondo Atti 28:16-31," RivBibl 31 (1983) 147-187.

4. It was the opinion of F. Chr. Baur that the Letter to the Romans was addressed to a Christian community of entirely Jewish origin to emancipate it from its particularity: *Über Zweck und Gedankengang der Römerbriefes*, ThJb 16 (1857) 66-108.

tions: (1) How many Jews were there? And how many Jewish communities? (2) How were they organized? (3) Where did they originally come from? (4) Where were they distributed in the City? (5) What was their social level? (6) What can we reconstruct of their beliefs?

There is no lack of studies on the question,[5] but some are dated and some are too vast in scope or too restricted in topic. What is missing at present is a comprehensive overview of the subject done with rigorous methodology, limiting itself to the first century, gathering together all the most useful data, and making use of the most recent studies. This present contribution, however, more modestly proposes to present the *status quaestionis*.[6] Its main characteristic must be above all the identification and classification of the sources (I), and then a documented treatment of the subject by means of responses to the questions formulated above (II).

I. The sources

What sources are there on the basis of which one can reconstruct the situation of Judaism in Nero's Rome during the fifties and sixties of the first century? Before answering this question we must clarify our methodology, emphasizing that the Jewish War, which dominated the end of

---

5. See especially H. Vogelstein and P. Rieger, *Geschichte der Juden in Rom*, I–II (Berlin, 1895) = *Rome*, trans. Moses Hadas (Philadelphia, 1940); J. B. Frey, "Les communautés juives à Rome aux premiers temps de l'Eglise," RechScRel 20 (1930) 269–297; 21 (1931) 129–168; H. J. Leon, *The Jews of Ancient Rome* (Philadelphia, 1960); W. Wiefel, "Die jüdische Gemeinschaft im antiken Rome und die Anfänge des römischen Christentums," *Judaica* 26 (1970) 65–88 ("The Jewish Community in Ancient Rome and the Origins of Roman Christianity" in K. P. Donfried, ed., *The Romans Debate* [Minneapolis, 1977] 100–119); M. Simon, "Les Juifs à Rome au 1er siècle," *Le monde de la Bible* 18 (1981) 33–34.

6. Regarding the exact dating of Paul's stay in Rome, this fluctuates between two extremes. The earliest date for his arrival in the capital is spring of the year 56; this was already suggested by Jerome, *De vir. ill.* 7 (according to him, the account of Acts "continues up to the two years Paul spent in Rome, that is, to Nero's fourth year"; and Nero ascended the throne on the first of October in 54) and by the *Latin Passion of Peter and Paul* 13 (ca. 580), which sets his martyrdom when the consuls were "Nero for the second time, and Piso" (57 A.D.), and today is preferred by Haenchen, *The Acts*, 68–71 = *Die Apostelgeschichte*, 60–64; C. K. Barrett, "Pauline Controversies in the Post-Pauline Period," NTS 20 (1974) 229–245, 234; S. J. Dockx, *Chronologies néotestamentaires et vie de l'Eglise primitive* (Paris: Gembloux, 1976) 64–87; G. Lüdemann, *Paul, Apostle to the Gentiles*, trans. F. Stanley Jones (Philadelphia, 1984) 192, n. 104 = *Paulus, der Heidenapostel, I: Studien zur Chronologie*, FRLANT 123 (Göttingen, 1980) 197, n. 101. The latest date for his death in Rome is the fourteenth year of Nero, 67–68 A.D. (thus Eusebius of Caesarea, *Chronicon* 2; St. Jerome, *De vir. ill.* 5 and 12, speaks of the second year after the death of Seneca, that is, 67); Clement of Rome, *Ep. ad Cor.* 5, would seem to associate the martyrdom with Nero's persecution from 64 to 65; many contemporary authors, however, fluctuate between 60 and 63 (see H. M. Schenke and K. M. Fischer, *Einleitung in die Schriften des NT, I: Die Briefe des Paulus und Schriften des Paulinismus* [Berlin, 1978] 61; see also R. Jewett, *Dating Paul's Life* [London, 1979] dating to 62). In any case, accepting Luke's notice of a διετίαν ὅλην, "whole two years" (Acts 28:30), the Apostle was in Rome for at least two years, which at any rate must be set within a fairly restricted period of time: in the Rome of Nero between the late fifties and early sixties.

the sixties, was to bring about a certain transformation of the character of this Roman Judaism. According to Flavius Josephus,[7] a hundred thousand Jewish slaves were sold in the year 70 at cheap prices, and it is logical to suppose that a large portion of this human merchandise ended up in the capital of the empire, augmenting the lowest classes of the Roman population.[8] Consequently, the number of Jews in Rome (see below) increased considerably, thus bringing about a notable change from the days of Paul's sojourn. Even so, it would seem that the change was only one of numbers, and there is no reason to believe that it brought about other substantial changes.

Only with this presupposition can we justify the use of certain sources that are some decades later, even as much as a century after the Neronic age. I believe that their use is methodologically correct. Now, it is true that the end of the first and especially the beginning of the second century brought a remarkable improvement in the standard of living in Rome, first under the Flavii and then under Trajan, and consequently a considerable modification of the habits of the Romans.[9] But even so, we must suppose that the Jewish community, traditionally closed and substantially impervious to the pagan surroundings, maintained its own basic characteristics throughout the period. We see an indication of the consistency of the status of the Jewish community by simply comparing references to them in the *Sermones* of Horace (died 8 B.C.) with those of Juvenal (died ca. 130 A.D.), and noting how they both evidence the same atmosphere. We can, then, assume that when Paul was in Rome, exactly midway between these dates, he encountered the same kind of Judaism that we see reflected in these two very different authors separated from one another by more than a century. We see, then, that research into the Jews of Rome at the time of Saint Paul should not be just a matter of the "two years"— διετία of Acts 28:30—but entails the whole first century and even the beginning of the second.

So let us now list the sources available to us, which we will divide into four categories.[10]

---

7. *Bell.* VI 420.

8. For example, in Petronius, *Satyr.* 68, there is already mention of a *recutitus* ("circumcised," that is, Jewish; see *fragmenta* 37) servant bought for 300 denarii. And in the obscene verse of Martial, *Epigr.* VII 55,7, is an allusion to the destruction of Jerusalem (*quae de Solymis venit perustis:* "she came from Jerusalem destroyed by fire").

9. One may consult the highly interesting volume of J. Carcopino, *Daily Life in Ancient Rome,* trans. E. O. Lorimer (London, 1947) = *La vie quotidienne à Rome à l'apogée de l'Empire* (Paris, 1939); for more documentation see L. Friedländer, *Darstellungen aus der Sittengeschichte Roms in der Zeit von August bis zum Ausgang der Antonine,* I–IV (Leipzig, 1910, 1921–23[10]).

10. For biographical data of the ancient writers, check *The Oxford Classical Dictionary* (Oxford, 1962[2]). Their texts can be found in Th. Reinach, *Textes d'auteurs grecs et romains relatif*

A. *Latin and Greek writers before Paul's sojourn in Rome*

1. M. Tullius Cicero (106–43 B.C.) is the first to speak of the Jews of Rome, who were present in October, 59 B.C., at his speech *Pro Flacco*, in which he dealt with the proconsul of Asia, a matter of considerable importance to them: *Pro Flacco* 66; the tone is disparaging.[11]

2. Q. Horatius Flaccus (65–8 B.C.) refers to the Jews of Rome and their religious customs three times in the first book of *Satires*, published in 35 B.C.: I 4, 138–144; 5, 97–104; 9, 60–73; the tone is irenic.

3. P. Ovidius Naso (43 B.C.–ca. 17 A.D.) provides only one notice in *Ars Amatoria*, I 76[12] (cf. I 416; *Rem. am.* 220), published after the year 1 B.C.; the tone is completely indifferent.

4. Valerius Maximus (period of Tiberius) after 31 A.D. (year of the fall of Seianus), *Factorum ac dictorum memorabilium libri IX*, a compendium that contains a report of the earliest presence of Jews in Rome dating to 139 B.C.: I 3, 3 (under the title *De superstitionibus*).

5. Philo of Alexandria (ca. 30 B.C.–45 A.D.), who came to Rome in the year 40 at the head of a delegation to the emperor Caligula, surely had contacts with his co-religionists, and in a speech praising the behavior of Augustus toward the Jews also reports their settlement in the district of Trastevere already at the time of that emperor: *Leg. ad C.* 154–158.

B. *Latin authors contemporaneous with Paul*

1. L. Annaeus Seneca (ca. 5 B.C.–65 A.D.): A judgment of his concerning the Jews, about whom he surely knew from observation in the capital, is reported by Saint Augustine, *De Civ. Dei* VI 11; it is a sharp denunciation of the Sabbath.[13]

---

au Judaïsme (Paris, 1893), and especially in M. Stern, *Greek and Latin Authors on Jews and Judaism*, I: *From Herodotus to Plutarch*; II: *From Tacitus to Simplicius* (Leiden, 1974 and 1980).

11. Also in *De provinciis consularibus* V 10, Cicero says, ". . . *Iudaeis et Syris, nationibus natis servituti*": "Jews and Syrians, nations born for slavery" (see T. Livius, XXXVI 17,5).

12. According to Ovid, the various cults are useful for the amorous encounters of Roman matrons: *Nec te praetereat Veneri ploratus Adonis / Cultaque Iudaeo septima sacra Syro, / Nec fuge linigerae Memphitica templa iuvencae*: "Nor let Adonis bewailed of Venus escape you, nor the seventh day that the Syrian Jew holds sacred. Avoid not the Memphian shrine of the linen-covered heifer."

13. Here is the lengthy text of Augustine, who wrote thus of Seneca: *Reprehendit etiam sacramenta Iudaeorum et maxime sabbata, inutiliter eos facere adfirmans, quod per illos singulos septenis interpositos dies septimam fere partem aetatis suae perdant vacando, et multa in tempore urgentia non agendo laedantur. . . . De illis sane Iudaeis cum loqueretur ait, "Cum interim usque eos sceleratissimae gentis consuetudo convaluit, ut per omnes iam terras recepta sit; victi victoribus leges dederunt"*: "He also condemned the mysteries of the Jews, especially the Sabbath, declaring their behavior unproductive in that through this one day out of seven they lost about a seventh of their life on holiday, and that they were harmed by neglecting many important things. . . .

2. A. Persius Flaccus (34–62 A.D.) in his *Six Satires* offers us a vivid description of the mysterious feast of "Herod's Day" (Sabbath: *Herodis dies*) in V 176–184.

3. Petronius Arbiter: It is generally thought that the author of the novel *Satyricon* from the age of Nero was identical to the person mentioned by Tacitus (*Ann.* XVI 18: *elegantiae arbiter*, "arbiter of elegance"). From him we have two texts alluding to the Jews, both in a very sarcastic tone: *Satyr.* 68[14] (cf. 102) and *fragmenta* 37.[15]

4. M Fabius Quintilianus (born 35–40 A.D., died about 100): In his *Institutio oratoria*, published about 95, there is a very negative judgment of the Jews, whom he knows from Rome: III 7, 21.[16]

5. M. Valerius Martial (approximately 40–104 A.D.), in three different places of his *Epigrammaton libri XIV*, gives us a report of Jews, who make up part of the variegated humanity of the capital, with a tone that is somewhere between mocking and hostile:[17] VII 30; XI 94; XII 57; of the three books in which these texts appear, the first two were published in the 90s, the third in 99–102 (see also IV 4; VII 55).

6. D. Junius Juvenal (approximately 50–130 A.D.), author of the famous sixteen *Satyrae*, deemed the greatest Roman satirical poet, knew the life of the poor from experience; three of his *Satires* contain interesting reports about the Jews of Rome: III 10–16 and 296 (published at the end of the first century or the beginning of the second); VI 542–547 (published after 115); XIV 96–106 (published about 127).

Speaking of these Jews he said, 'Meanwhile, since the custom of this disgusting nation has triumphed, and has been accepted in all lands, the conquered have made laws for the conquerors.' " However, this same Seneca permitted himself in his youth to be influenced by the practice of *alienigena sacra* ("foreign religion") in his decision to avoid the meat of animals (*Ep.* 108,22). Judaism may have contributed to this decision.

14. Trimalchio says of a slave, *Duo tamen vitia habet, quae si non haberet, esset omnium numerum: recutitus est et stertit. Nam quod strabonus est, non curo. . . . Illum emi trecentis denariis:* "He has only two faults, and if he were rid of them he would be simply perfect. He is circumcised and he snores. I do not mind his being cross-eyed. . . . I bought him for three hundred denarii."

15. *Iudaeus licet et porcinum numen adoret et caeli summas advocet auriculas, ni tamen et ferro succiderit inguinis oram . . . .:* "Even though the Jew worship his pig-god and call on the exalted ears of heaven, unless he also cut back his foreskin with a knife [he will be excluded from his people]."

16. *Et parentes malorum odimus: et est conditoribus urbium infame contraxisse aliquam perniciosam ceteris gentis, qualis est primus Iudaicae superstitionis auctor:* "The vices of children bring hatred on their parents; founders of cities are hated for concentrating a race which is a curse to others, as for example the founder of the Jewish superstition."

17. But always with a vivid realism in Martial's typical style (see X 4,10: *hominem pagina nostra sapit:* "Our page tastes of humanity"; X 33,10: *parcere personis, dicere de vitiis:* "to spare persons but describe faults").

7. Flavius Josephus (born in 37–38 A.D., died after 100); besides several reports of events of the Jewish community of Rome from the past (especially from 4 to 19 A.D.: *Ant.* XVII 299–303; XVIII 81–84) and the preservation of a considerable dossier of official documents concerning privileges granted to the Jews from Julius Caesar on (contained esp. in *Ant.* XIV 215–246, 256–267, 312; see also XII 120; XVI 162–165), we are also indebted to him for some quite detailed information about certain personages who belonged to the Jewish milieu of Rome during Nero's time, such as the actor Alityros (*Vita* 3) and possibly Poppaea (*Ant.* XX 189–196; *Vita* 3).

C. *Latin and Greek writers later than Paul, authors of historiographic works; their information about the Jews of Rome is mostly secondhand, even when they are treating the first century.*

1. Cornelius Tacitus (55—later than 115): In the *Historiae* and the *Annales* alike he offers us texts on Judaism in general or specifically on events of Roman Jewry (the events of 19 A.D.: *Ann.* II 85; Poppaea's burial: ibid. XVI 6; see XV 61).

2. C. Suetonius Tranquillus (ca. 69–ca. 140), in his *De Vita Caesarum*, records two expulsions of the Jews from Rome, that of the year 19 under Tiberius (*Tib.* 36) and the better-known but undated one under Claudius (*Cl.* 25; his report here seems to conflict with that of Dio Cassius, see below). He also informs us of the love of Titus for Berenice, sister of Agrippa II (*Tit.* 7) and of the excessive severity of Domitianus in collecting the *fiscus Iudaicus,* "Jewish levy" (*Dom.* 12).[18]

3. Dio Cassius (born in Nicaea, praetor in Rome in 193, and consul there for the second time in 229): In his *Roman History* in eighty books he informs us about the decree of Claudius (LX 6, 6: not an expulsion but a prohibition of meetings); the *fiscus Iudaicus* imposed by Vespasian (LXVI 7, 2); the relationship between Titus and Berenice (LXVI 15, 3-4); and the persecution of Domitian (LXVII 14).

D. *Jewish epigraphic sources*

In the six or seven Jewish catacombs found thus far just outside the Aurelian Walls[19] it has been possible to collect a great mass of tomb inscrip-

---

18. In him we also find a report of the celebrated case of Flavius Clemens and his wife Domitilla; on this see also Dio Cassius, LXVII 14. See below, n. 144.

19. The first discovery occurred in 1602 on the Via Portuense. This was the catacomb of Monteverde, regular excavations of which were begun only in 1904–1905; it collapsed in 1928, and scarcely any of it still exists; but it did provide 204 inscriptions. The second catacomb, called the "Vigna Randanini," between the Appia Antica and the Appia Pignatelli, was discovered in 1859 and yielded several inscriptions besides three painted cubicles; it can be visited. The catacomb of "Vigna Cimarra," not far from the previous one, was discovered in 1866, but revealed only five inscriptions; today it is inaccessible. The catacomb of Via Appia

tions, which for many reasons are of the greatest interest.[20] Now these are firsthand witnesses for us, since they come directly from the milieu in which we are interested, thus obviously providing a completely faithful reflection of it. From these we come to know the names of many Roman Jews, their family attitudes, the organization of their community on the basis of various titles of public office, their social condition from the type of tomb and inscription, their speech, and finally their hopes or their pessimism about the next world. We can thus penetrate within Roman Judaism, know it authentically from inside, and despite death get a vivid impression of its specific human, social, and religious identity.[21]

But there is a problem in dating these inscriptions. Do they date back to the Neronic period or are they later? Granted, the major development of these catacombs, like that of their Christian parallels, is particularly characteristic of the third century, and includes the fourth as well.[22] And earlier? Some scholars, especially on the basis of brick stamps found in the excavations, have thought that the discoveries may go back to the first century. And this may be true at least for the Monteverde catacomb, if not for the

---

Pignatelli, discovered in 1885, is of little interest and is now inaccessible. The catacomb of Via Labicana (now Via Casilina) was found in 1882 with five inscriptions; no longer visitable. The double catacomb of Villa Torlonia on the Via Nomentana was discovered in 1918 and furnished more than sixty-five inscriptions and five painted cubicles; a new excavation season in 1973–74 furnished almost fifty new inscriptions. See esp. N. Müller, *Die jüdische Katakombe am Monte Verde zu Rom* (Leipzig, 1912); H. J. Leon, "The Jewish Catacombs and Inscriptions of Rome," in HUCA V (Cincinnati, 1921); D. Mazzoleni, "Le catacombe ebraiche di Roma," *Studi Romani* 23 (1975) 289–302; H. W. Beyer and H. Lietzmann, *Die jüdische Katakombe der Villa Torlonia in Rom* (Berlin, 1930); U. Fasola, "Le due catacombe ebraiche di Villa Torlonia," *RivArchCrist* 52 (1976) 7–62; on the generous use of perfumes in some tombs of Villa Torlonia, see idem, "Scoperte e studi archeologici dal 1939 ad oggi, che concorrono ad illuminare i problemi della Sindone di Torino," in *La Sindone e la Scienza. Atti del II Congresso Internazionale di Sindonologia 1978* (Turin, 1979) 59–83, 322–329, esp. 60–65; also L. Pitigliani, "A Rare Look at the Jewish Catacombs of Rome," *BiblArchRev* 6 (1980, 3) 32–43.

20. The critical edition of all these inscriptions except the most recent ones of Villa Torlonia was done by J. B. Frey, *Corpus inscriptionum Iudaicarum, Recueil des inscriptions juives qui vont du IIIᵉ siècle avant Jésus-Christ au VIIᵉ de notre ère*, I (Europe), II (Asie, Afrique) (Città del Vaticano, 1936 and 1952) (henceforth *CII*); see also A. Ferrua, "Addenda et corrigenda al *Corpus inscriptionum Iudaicarum*," *Epigraphica* 3 (1941) 30–46. A reedition of volume I of this *Corpus*, with a *Prolegomenon* by Baruch Lifshitz, was issued by KTAV in New York, 1975. In this first volume the first 534 inscriptions are the Roman collection. See also A. T. Kraabel, "Jews in Imperial Rome: More Archaeological Evidence from an Oxford Collection," *JournJewStud* 30 (1979) 41–58: what is most original here is the analysis of a jasper ring with the inscription *Iaō Saō Adōni* (pp. 50–55).

21. The broadest study of these inscriptions is still that of H. J. Leon, *The Jews of Ancient Rome* (Philadelphia, 1960–5721). According to this author, of the 534 Roman inscriptions, 405 are in Greek (76%), 123 in Latin (23%), 3 in Hebrew, 1 in Aramaic, 2 bilingual (1%; one Greek-Latin, the other Aramaic-Greek); but there are sometimes Latin inscriptions written in Greek characters (e.g. *ΦΕΚΙΤ* = fecit, "made"), more rarely vice versa. Even the inscriptions of Villa Torlonia are almost all in Greek; only two are in Latin.

22. See P. Testini, *Archeologia cristiana* (Bari, 1980²) 76–80. Originally neither Christians nor Jews used burial areas distinct from those of pagans. See also O. Marucchi, *Le catacombe romane* (Rome, 1933).

others. This catacomb is considered the oldest because it contains neither cubicles nor pictures, and it is there that the only Hebrew inscriptions were found.[23] Since this catacomb served the Jewish community of Trastevere, which is certainly the most primitive of those in Rome, as we shall see below, it is reasonable to suppose that it also has preserved the most archaic epigraphic material.[24] However, other authors, making no distinctions, prefer not to go back beyond the third century, maintaining that the brick stamps are a misleading criterion for dating, since bricks are frequently reused and so can at best indicate an earliest date for a site.[25] I should think an intermediate position would be reasonable; at least the second century cannot be apodictically excluded, as a recent author would prefer to maintain.[26]

In any case, in principle we cannot undervalue the use of these epigraphic sources even for the reconstruction of first-century Roman Judaism, which is reflected there, at least as its prolongation through a surely homogeneous process of development. Of course, prudence is always a valuable tool.

II. The Jewish communities of Rome

With the help of these sources, let us now try to answer the questions we proposed at the beginning of this chapter.

1. The first thing to be noted is that, as the title to this second section suggests, the Jews of Rome *were not united in a single community*. They did not form a πολίτευμα ("political unit"). And this, along with the lack of any real cultural tradition, is the most evident way in which they differed from the Jews of Alexandria, that other great diaspora population of Jews.[27]

23. See Frey, *CII*, I, 292, 293, 296, 319, 397, 499, perhaps also 283; these can also present the wish *šlwm*, "peace," or in the more developed form *šlwm ʿl yśr'l*, "peace upon Israel." For the thirty or so first-century brick stamps, see pp. 211–214; also T. Helen, *Organization of Roman Brick Production in the First and Second Centuries A.D.: An Interpretation of Roman Brick Stamps* (Helsinki, 1975), though this author does not treat the Jewish catacombs.
24. See N. Müller, *Il cimitero degli antichi Ebrei posto sulla via Portuense*, Dissertazioni della Pont. Accad. Rom. di Arch., ser. II, 121 (1915) 205–318; Frey, *CII*, I, LV; Leon, *The Jews*, 66.
25. See A. Ferrua, "Sulla tomba dei Cristiani e su quella degli Ebrei," *La Civiltà Cattolica* 87 (1936) IV, 309–310; Mazzoleni, *Le catacombe*, 289 and 294.
26. See U. Fischer, *Eschatologie und Jenseitserwartung im hellenistischen Diasporajudentum*, BZNW 44 (Berlin-New York, 1978) 216 and 233; M. Hengel (see n. 32 below), 172: "ab dem Ende des 1. Jh.s." Professor Umberto Fasola, rector of the Pontifical Institute of Christian Archeology and director of the 1973–74 excavations in the Jewish double catacomb of Villa Torlonia, has confessed his uncertainty to me, and the consequent theoretical possibility of a dating before the third century.
27. See J. Juster, *Les Juifs dans l'Empire Romain. Leur condition juridique, économique et sociale*, I–II (Paris, 1914): I, 402–405; especially: S. Safrai and M. Stern, eds., *The Jewish People in the First Century. Historical Geography, Political History, Social, Cultural and Religious Life and Institutions*, Compendia Rerum Judaicarum ad NT, 1, I–II (Assen, 1974 and 1976), I, 160–168, 473–476.

There, according to Strabo as cited by Flavius Josephus, "There is an ἐθνάρχης ('ethnarch': ruler of the nation) who governs the nation, deals with contracts and decrees, as if he were head of an autonomous government."[28] He may also have the title of γενάρχης ("genarch": ruler of the people.)[29] There is nothing like this in Rome.[30] On the contrary, the Jews are dispersed in various communities, some of them very ancient, as evidenced in the tomb inscriptions.[31] The common name for such groups, which were something like so many parishes, is always συναγωγή, "synagogue," which in Rome never stands for the place of worship. This latter is called (in a pagan text in Juvenal, for it is never attested in a Jewish inscription) by a metonymous Greek name transliterated into Latin, *proseucha*, "prayer," "place of prayer."[32] No architectural remains of an ancient synagogue have yet been found in Rome.[33]

To date at least eleven communities or "synagogues" of Roman Jews are known, namely:

—of the Hebrews or Ἑβρέων, present in four inscriptions.[34]
—of the *Vernaculi* or Βερναϰλησίων or Βερναϰλώρων;[35]

28. Fl. Josephus, *Ant.* XIV 117; on the existence of a true πολίτευμα in Alexandria, see Josephus, *Ant.* XII 108, and even earlier *Aristeas* 410. Already Caesar had given Hyrcanus II the title ἐθνάρχης τῶν Ἰουδαίων, "ethnarch of the Jews" (Josephus, Ant. XIV 194, 196f., 226), and that not only for those of Palestine; however, this does not mean that the title was also for his successors.

29. Philo of Alexandria, *In Fl.* 74 (where the γερουσία [council of elders] over which he presided is also mentioned). The two titles were probably synonymous; see id., *Rer. div. her.* 279.

30. Only in the fourth century is the title ἀρχιγερουσιάρχης (archigerousiarch: principal ruler of the council of elders) attested (see n. 55).

31. See Juster, *Les Juifs,* II, 177, n. 3; J. B. Frey, "Les communautés juives à Rome," Rech-ScRel 20 (1930) 282–297. Only at Ostia is a term like *[universitas] Iudeorum* ("totality of the Jews") possibly recognized, but even there the abstract noun is supplied by the editor to fill a mutilation of the stone: Frey, *CII,* no. 533).

32. Juvenal, *Sat.* III 296 (*in qua te quaero proseucha?*: "In which *proseucha* shall I look for you?"); see also *Corpus inscriptionum Latinarum, consilio et auctoritate Academiae litterarum regiae Borussicae editum* (henceforth *CIL*), 16 vols. (Berlin, 1863–1930) VI 9821 (Frey, *CII,* I, no. 531); the Greek name is attested eighteen times by Philo of Alexandria (e.g., *Leg. ad C.* 23). See M. Hengel, "Proseuche und Synagoge. Jüdische Gemeinde, Gotteshaus und Gottesdienst in der Diaspora und Palästina," in *Tradition und Glaube. Festgabe für Karl Georg Kuhn zum 65. Geburtstag* (Göttingen, 1971) 157–184.

33. The hypothesis proposed by S. Collon, "Remarques sur les quartiers Juifs de la Rome antique," *Mélanges d'Archéologie et d'Histoire de l'École Française de Rome* 57 (1940) 72–94, 83f., which identifies a marble remnant (Frey, *CII,* I, no. 289) as coming from a synagogue in Trastevere near the *Pons Agrippae* (present Ponte Sisto), has no serious foundation (see Leon, *The Jews,* 141). The case is quite different in Ostia, where the synagogue found in 1961 is moreover the only one of its kind in all Western Europe, excluding Greece. See M. Floriani Squarciapino, "La sinagoga recentemente scoperta ad Ostia," *Rendiconti della Pont. Accad. Rom. di Arch.* 34 (1961–62) 119–132; idem, "Ebrei a Roma e Ostia," *Studi Romani* 11 (1963) 2, 129–141.

34. Frey, *CII,* I, nos. 291, 317, 510, 535.

35. Ibid., 318, 383, 398, 494.

—of the *Augustenses* or 'Αὐγουστησίων (named after its patron, the Emperor Augustus), witnessed in six inscriptions;[36]

—of the *Agrippenses* or 'Αγριππησίων (named after M. V. Agrippa, son-in-law of Augustus, 62–12 B.C.), of which we have three inscriptions;[37]

—of the *Volumnenses* or Βολουμνησίων (from the name of Volumnius, legate in Syria in 8 A.D. and friend of Herod), with four inscriptions;[38]

—of the *Campenses* or Καμπησίων (from its location), with at least three inscriptions;[39]

—of the *Suburenses* or Σιβουρησίων (idem), with at least five inscriptions;[40]

—of the *Calcarenses* or Καλκαρησίων (idem), with at least five inscriptions;[41]

—of *Elaia* or 'Ελαίας (probably named after their city of origin in Mysia), with two inscriptions;[42]

—of the Τριπολειτῶν (those originating in Tripoli in Libya), with two inscriptions.[43]

—of the Σεκηνῶν, with only one inscription.[44]

Two other communities, each documented by only one inscription, are contested.[45]

Some of these communities certainly existed by Paul's time, and specifically by the time of his sojourn in Rome. The first two ("of the Hebrews" and "of the Vernaculi") "perhaps designate the oldest Jewish groupings in Rome."[46] Indeed, the explicit identification of one of the associations as "of Hebrews" would lead us to think of it as the only one of the kind, and hence the oldest, whereas the designation "of the Vernaculi" is strictly correlative to the preceding, distinguishing itself as grouping the Jews born

36. Ibid., 284, 301, 338, 368, 416, 496.
37. Ibid., 365, 425, 503.
38. Ibid., 343, 402, 417, 523. On Volumnius, see Fl. Josephus, *Ant.* XVI 277–281, 332, 354; *Bell.* I 535 (στρατοπεδάρχης), 538 (ὁ ἐπίτροπος).
39. Frey, *CII*, I, nos. 88, 319, 523, perhaps 433.
40. Ibid., 18, 22, 67, 140, 380, and perhaps 37 as well.
41. Ibid., 304, 316, 384, 504, 537, perhaps also 433.
42. Ibid., 281, 509; the city of Elaia was between Smyrna and Pergamum (hypothesis of Reinach and Frey); other hypotheses (Schürer's "synagogue of the olive" and Juster's "synagogue of Elijah") seem less plausible.
43. Ibid., 390, 408.
44. Ibid., no. 7; Frey hypothesizes the city of Scina, a port on the Libyan coast, today Medinet es-Sultan.
45. The first, by the name of *POΔIΩN* (rodiōn) is maintained by Frey to be mutilated, and he reconstructs it as "of the Herodians," while Leon (*The Jews*, 160, n. 2) prefers to read "of Rhodes," or still better, to see in it the name of a person, whether of a deceased person or of a relative doing the dedication. The second is witnessed in two manuscripts, (*CII*, I, no. 501); there we read the name of a deceased person with the identification Ἄρχης Λιβάνου ("Arca of Lebanon"), but while the one manuscript specifies this as συναγωγή (synagogē: the variant accepted by Frey), the other testifies only πόλις (polis: the variant accepted by Leon; see the discussion in *The Jews*, 163–165.
46. Frey, *CII*, I, LXXVII.

in Rome. In any case, the three communities of the *Augustenses*, the *Agrippenses*,[47] and the *Volumnenses* are evidently contemporaneous with the personages for whom they are named, and so their establishment must be dated during the first century before and the first century of the present era, being formed according to the system of *patronatus*, "patronage," which is also known from other, pagan inscriptions.[48] Specifically, the foundation of the *Augustenses* is fully reported in the great elegy by Philo of Alexandria (*Leg. ad C.* 154–158), lauding this emperor and the favors he had granted the Roman Jews.

The enumeration of Jewish groups leads us to the question of the number of Jews themselves. How many were there in first-century Rome? Scattered throughout the then known world,[49] in the capital they mixed in with the variegated oriental population who for some time had immigrated or been deported there, according to the Juvenal's clever verse, *Iam pridem Syrus in Tiberim defluxit Orontes:* "Long has the Syrian Orontes flowed into the Tiber."[50] Their number is calculated on the basis of two reports. First, eight thousand Jews accompanied a Jewish delegation from Palestine on their visit to Augustus in 4 B.C.[51] Second, four thousand young Jews of military age were exiled to Sardinia by Tiberius in the year 19.[52] Now, if we take into account the relationship of each of these persons to their respective families and the passage of the years, it is fair to deduce that before the new influx after the year 70, during the Neronic age the number may have been about twenty thousand.[53] Since it seems that at least

47. Honesty requires that we note that certain authors attribute the name of this "synagogue" not to M. Vipsanius Agrippa but to one of the two Jewish rulers Agrippa I or Agrippa II (see Müller, *Jüd. Kat.*, 108; Hengel, *Proseuche*, 160, n. 14); but while nothing is known of the relations between these kings and the Roman Jews, we have documentation of many favors granted them by the pagan Agrippa (Fl. Josephus, *Ant.* XII 125–126; XVI 14–15, 60, 160–173); see Leon, *The Jews*, 141.

48. H. Dessau, *Inscriptiones Latinae Selectae*, II/2 (Berlin, 1955²) 737–747 (chap. XV, "Tituli collegiorum"): nos. 7211–7215a ("Leges collegiorum"), 7216–7222 ("Tabulae patronatus"). See B. Lifshitz, *Donateurs et fondateurs dans les Synagogues juives*, Cahiers de la Revue Biblique 7 (Paris, 1967). Italy is excluded from this work.

49. "There is not a community in the whole world which does not have its share of our people," says King Agrippa II in Fl. Josephus, *Bell.* II 398. (Philo, of course, is exaggerating when he claims, *Leg. ad C.* 31, that they constituted half of the human race.) In Egypt alone there were one million, about an eighth of the population (Philo, *In Fl.* 6). According to the estimate of Juster, *Les Juifs*, I, 210, before the year 70 Jews accounted for 6 to 7 million in the empire out of a total population of about 55 million. According to the Mishna, *Meg.* I 3 (*Tos. Meg.* V 14), in a city the minimum number required for the reading of the Megillah of Esther is "ten disengaged men," that is, persons who can attend the synagogue.

50. *Sat.* III 62.

51. Thus Fl. Josephus, *Ant.* XVII 299–303, cf. *Bell.* II 80.

52. Suetonius, *Tib.* 36; Fl. Josephus, *Ant.* XVIII 81–84. Tacitus, on the other hand, identifies them as being "of the Egyptian and Jewish superstition" (*Ann.* II 85).

53. This number seems reasonable, whereas Juster, *Les Juifs*, I, 209, exaggerates in estimating 50–60,000, as does S. Collon, "Remarques," 78, with his calculation of 30–40,000 Jews

five of the eleven communities listed above already existed by 70 A.D., each of them counted about four thousand members.

2. What was the *organization of the Roman "synagogues"*? As we have pointed out, with the present state of research there is no reason to believe that Roman Judaism had central direction. And this is true despite two attested uses, in Latin and in Greek, of the title *exarchon* and ἐξάρχων τῶν Ἐβρέων, "exarchon of the Hebrews," evidenced by the catacomb of Monteverde. "In the first case, the man is only twenty-eight years old, which represents too young an age to wield supreme authority in a Jewish community of the importance of that of Rome. In the second, the exarchon exercised the office in a particular community, that of the *Hebrews*, which is known from other inscriptions; the name is simply a synonym of ἄρχων.''[54] A more recent discovery has documented the title ἀρχιγερουσιάρχης, but this dates from a rather late period, the fourth century, and is of uncertain significance.[55] Other titles are irrelevant to the present question.[56]

The closest model to the Roman συναγωγαί *(synagogae)* is that of the Greek θίασοι *(thiasoi)* and the Latin *collegia*, which all have certain parallel elements in their inner structure.[57] And we know that Julius Caesar dis-

---

(see also R. Brown and J. P. Meyer, *Antioch and Rome* [London, 1983] 94); it is implausible that the Jewish population of Rome (as distinguished from that of Alexandria in Egypt) approached that of Jerusalem, which, according to J. Jeremias, *Jerusalem in the Time of Jesus*, trans. F. H. and C. H. Cave (Philadelphia, 1969) 83 [but see the additional note on p. 84, dated 1966, lowering the estimate to 25-30,000] = *Jérusalem au temps de Jésus* (Paris, 1976²) 122, reached 55,000 in the first century (while M. Broshi, "La population de l'ancienne Jérusalem," RB 82 [1975] 5-14, calculates 82,500). The *Encyclopedia Judaica*, vol. 14 (Jerusalem, 1971), in the article "Rome," col. 242, proposes a number "probably nearer 10,000," but in my opinion this is too low and does not give enough weight to the figures attested by Josephus and Suetonius. The total population of Rome at the time of Augustus and Tiberius is estimated by Carcopino, *Daily Life* (Harmondsworth, Middlesex, 1967) 29, at about one million (but under the Antonines it will rise to about a million and a half: p. 31). But for a criticism of present criteria for determining the population of Imperial Rome, with a marked pessimism about the possibility of obtaining precise figures, see F. G. Maier, "Römische Bevölkerungsgeschichte und Inschriftenstatistik," *Historia* 2 (1953-54) 318-351. N.B.: In 1983 there were no more than 15,000 Jews in Rome out of a total population of 2,825,000.

54. Frey, *Les communautés juives à Rome*, 163; see the discussion of the whole question, pp. 161-168.

55. The complete inscription reads: *ΕΝΘΑΔΕ ΚΙΤΕ ΑΝΑCΤΑCΙΟΥC ΑΡΧΙΓΕΡΟΥCΑΡΧΗC ΥΙΟC ΑΝΑCΤΑCΙΟΥ . . .:* "Within, the bed of Anastasius, Archigerousiarch, son of Anastasius." It has been published by U. Fasola, "Le due catacombe ebraiche di Villa Torlonia," 36, who comments, "Did the archigerousiarch have complete authority over the entire Jewish community of Rome? Or was this simply a honorific title for a gerousiarch of a specific synagogue who fulfilled his duties in an extraordinary manner?" (p. 37); but we cannot know the person's age, since the marble stone is mutilated.

56. At a late period in some Latin-language communities there appear the titles of *patriarchae* and *primates*: see Juster, *Les Juifs*, I, 394, n. 4, and 403, n. 1.

57. See F. Poland, *Geschichte des griechischen Vereinswesen* (Berlin, 1909); J. P. Waltzing, *Étude historique sur les corporations professionnelles chez les Romains depuis les origines jusqu'à la*

solved *cuncta collegia praeter antiquitus constituta*, "all the *collegia* except those that had been founded in antiquity," and that in this he spared only the Jews.[58]

The structure and organization of the various Jewish societies can be reconstructed on the basis of their internal offices as evidenced in the catacomb inscriptions.[59] The known community functions are as follows:

—the γεϱουσίαϱχης (sixteen times in different forms, and with various specifications, of the *Augustenses*, of the *Agrippenses*, of the *Tripolitani*): this was the president of a *gerousia* or "council of elders"; even though this latter expression is not attested,[60] surely each "synagogue" must have had its own council in charge of the administration of the community and the protection of its religious, judicial, and financial interests;

—the πϱεσβύτεϱοι, "elders" (once in the singular): the members of the *gerousia;*[61]

—the ἄϱχοντες, "rulers" (at least fifty times, often in reference to a specific "synagogue"): formed the executive committee of the *gerousia;* elected for one year, they could be reelected (δὶς ἄϱχων, "twice a ruler," is found about ten times), perhaps even for life;[62] the institution of the "acting archon," the μελλάϱχων, certainly existed, since the former title is attributed even to children; these officers in practice had control of the community;[63]

—the ἄϱχων πάσης τιμῆς, "archon of all honor" (three times in Greek and once in an approximate Latin transliteration: *archon pases tessimen*) was the collector general, charged with collecting the monies designated for the common fund, which was used to pay various expenses;[64]

chute de l'Empire d'Occident, I–IV (Brussels, 1895–1900); idem, art. "Collegia," in D. Cabrol, *Dictionnaire d'Archéologie Chrétienne*, III/2 (Paris, 1914), cols. 2107–2140.

58. One should compare Suetonius, *Caes.* 42 and 84 with Fl. Josephus, *Ant.* XIV 215. This undertaking was completed by Augustus, since *plurimae factiones titulo collegi novi ad nullius non facinoris societatem coibant:* "Several factions under the name of new *collegia* gathered to cooperate in nothing but crime" (Suetonius, *Aug.* 32).

59. See E. Schürer, *Die Gemeindeverfassung der Juden in Rom in der Kaiserzeit, nach den Inschriften dargestellt* (Leipzig, 1879) and especially J. B. Frey, "Les communautés juives à Rome aux premiers temps de l'Église," RechScRel 21 (1931) 129–168 ("III. Leur organisation intérieure").

60. It is, however, apparently attested for nearby Ostia, though the reading is dependent on reconstruction from a sole remaining initial ΓΕ (Frey, *CII*, I, no. 533).

61. The extreme rarity of their attestation perhaps depends on the fact that they "were not, properly speaking, officials, and were so numerous that the dignity was not considered worth mentioning" (Schürer, *Die Gemeindeverfassung*, 19).

62. Even though it is not specified, it is probably this which is meant by the expression διά βίου ("for life") and its numerous variants—διὰ βίο, ζαβίου, diabiu—since the archonship was "the most frequent office" (Frey, "Les communautés," 140). A new inscription supposedly referring to a δὶς ἄϱχων is noted by Fasola, "Le due catacombe," 57.)

63. On the function of the archons in Judaism of the period, see M. Pesce, *Paolo e gli arconti a Corinto* (Brescia, 1977) 277–320.

64. The Jews were expressly authorized to do such collections by Julius Caesar (see Fl. Josephus, *Ant.* XIV 215).

—the φροντιστής, "guardian" (twice): the administrator of the goods of the community;

—the γραμματεύς, "scribe" (twenty-five times in Greek or in Latin transliteration, six of them being identified with a certain "synagogue"):[65] the function of this person is probably not only that of teacher of the law but approaches that of "secretary" or "chancellor" (cf. the γραμματεύς of Ephesus in Acts 19:35);

—the προστάτης, "assistant" (twice): the equivalent of an advocate and the legal protector of the community (see Rom 16:2);

—the πάτηρ (nine times) and the μήτηρ (twice) συναγωγῆς, "father" or "mother of the synagogue": an honorific title reserved for men and women who are outstanding benefactors of one or more communities;

—the ἀρχισυνάγωγος (five times) was responsible for the building and presided at the religious assemblies;[66]

—the ὑπηρέτης, "servant" (once): performed the most humble functions of synagogal service;

—ἱερεύς, "priest" (three times, and once ἱερίσσα, "priestess"): a simple honorific title alluding to levitical ancestry, since there was not a temple at Rome (unlike the situation in Leontopolis in Egypt), nor could the priesthood after 70 A.D. confer any cultic function.

Thus, it is clear that the administration of the community "is in itself a lay function: neither do those who bear the purely decorative title of 'priests,' nor do cultic ministers necessarily have a role in it. Its competence extends to religious questions as well as civil, financial, and judicial matters. As for the 'clergy,' their role is, so to speak, restricted to the sacristy."[67]

There is no reason to doubt that these functions were characteristic of the Jewish communities in Rome in the age of Nero, and thus at the time of Paul's residence there. If, then, we wish to identify the persons whom Luke in Acts 28:17 calls τοὺς ὄντας τῶν Ἰουδαίων πρώτους, "the leading Jews,"

65. The twenty-fifth occurrence of the title comes from the catacomb of the Villa Torlonia and is reported by Fasola, "Le due catacombe," 19–20; the person is a certain Γαιάνος, who is also typified by two singular epithets, ψάλμωδος (psalmodos: the only example of the expression, with its allusion to the chanting of psalms in liturgy) and φιλόνομος ("lover of the Law": the only parallel to which is in Frey, CII, I, no. 111).

66. This title recurs frequently in pagan associations of the Greek world and is equivalent to "president of the assembly": see Poland, Geschichte, 247f., 355–357; Juster, Les Juifs, I, 450–453. Moreover, almost all the titles that we have seen are also attested for these organizations.

67. Frey, "Les communautés," 157f. There is one reference to two brothers ἄρχοντες καὶ ἱερεῖς, "priests and rulers," but here the distinction indicates that priesthood gave no right to governance of the community (cf. ibid., 141). For a brief, negative comparison between these offices and those of the early Church, see ibid., 159–161.

we would have to include the ἄρχοντες of the various communities,[68] perhaps the γραμματεῖς, the γερουσιάρχης, and some πρεσβύτεροι (scribes, presidents of the councils, elders), while the others would not be included.[69] Assuming that there were at least five "synagogues," and that not all had sent their own representatives, one may suppose that on arriving at Rome the Apostle received a delegation of about fifty persons.

3. *Origin and history* before Paul. According to the report of Valerius Maximus, the earliest presence of Jews in Rome dates back to 139 B.C., and is witnessed by their expulsion from the city.[70] But the earliest direct information we owe to M. Tullius Cicero; in his oration *Pro Flacco*, given in October, 59 B.C., the orator speaks explicitly of the Jews present at the trial, in which they had their personal interests, and which was affected simply by their presence. Turning to his adversary, the accuser of Flaccus, he speaks thus: *Ob hoc crimen hic locus abs te, Laeli, atque illa turba quaesita est; scis quanta sit manus, quanta concordia, quantum valeat in contionibus:* "You procured this place and that crowd, Laelius, for this trial. You know how many hands are here, how they stick together, how influential they are in informal assemblies."[71] The terms *turba* and *manus*, "crowd" and "hands," indicate that the people are both numerous and capable of intervening.

The established date of their arrival in Rome corresponds to the conquest of Palestine and Jerusalem by Gnaeus Pompey in 63 B.C.[72] The ori-

68. It is impossible to determine how many *archontes* were responsible for a community, since the number varied from one city to another; perhaps they numbered about ten (see Frey, "Les communautés," 139).

69. Among the commentators, H. H. Wendt, *Die Apostelgeschichte* (Göttingen, 1913⁹; reported by E. Haenchen, *The Acts*, 722 = *Apostelgeschichte*, ad loc.), spoke of "presbyters, rulers, synagogue leaders, patrons," while A. Wikenhauser, *Die Apostelgeschichte* (Regensburg, 1956³), ad loc., estimates only "surely the gerousiarchs, that is, the presidents of the various synagogues"; but the terminology is imprecise.

70. *Factorum ac dictorum memorabilium*, I 3, 3 (see M. Stern, *Greek and Latin Authors*, I, no. 147b, cf. 147a). The *praetor peregrinus* ("praetor for foreigners") Gnaeus Cornelius Hispalus (or Hispanus) expelled from Rome the astrologers and Chaldeans, and moreover *idem Iudaeos, qui Sabazi Iovis cultu Romanos inficere mores conati erant, repetere domos suas coegit:* "sent back home the Jews who had tried to corrupt Roman customs with the cult of Sabazi Jove." This cult *Sabazi Iovis* can be interpreted in various ways: as a corruption of *Yahweh Ṣᵉbaot* or as an allusion to the Sabbath festival (thus Leon, *The Jews*, 3), or perhaps as a witness to a syncretistic Judaism originating in Asia Minor, land of origin of the god Sabazius (thus M. Hengel, *Judaism and Hellenism*, trans. John Bowden [Philadelphia, 1974], I, 263f. = *Judentum und Hellenismus* [Tübingen, 1969] 478f.). See also E. N. Lane, "Sabazius and the Jews in Valerius Maximus," *JournRomStud* 69 (1979) 35-38. It is not clear whether these Jews belonged to the embassy of Simon Maccabee (1 Macc 14:24) or perhaps remained in Rome after the embassy of Judas (ibid., 8) and Jonathan (12:1-4).

71. *Pro Fl.* 66; but Cicero suddenly adds that he wants to speak sottovoce so as to be heard only by the judges and not by the Jews present, for there are those who would stir the judges up against him.

72. See Philo, *Leg. ad C.* 155 (αἰχμάλωτοι ἀχθέντες εἰς Ἰταλίαν, "driven as prisoners of war to Italy"); Fl. Josephus, *Ant.* XIV 71 and 120; *Bell.* I 154 and 180; VII 154 and 154-157f.; VIII

gin of the Roman Jews is, then, due to their forced immigration. At least for this we have documentation; but we do not know whether there were business motives as well, and if so to what extent.[73]

The legislation of Julius Caesar in their favor is well known; it was to remain in force for more than three centuries.[74] We also are acquainted with the favors granted them by Augustus.[75] But the same cannot be said for Tiberius nor for Claudius.[76] The former deported a certain number to Sardinia in 19 A.D.[77] And the latter took severe measures against them, the date and very nature of which are subject to dispute because of discrepancies in the sources. This is not the place to discuss the question.[78] I do believe, however, that the account of Suetonius (*Cl.* 25: *expulit,* "expelled") and that of Dio Cassius (LX 6, 6: ἐκέλευσε μὴ συναθροίζεσθαι, "forbade them to gather together") refer to a single event rather than two, and that this must have taken place rather near the beginning of Claudius's reign.[79] It would seem that "the Emperor expelled the people who were directly involved in the disturbances involving Chrestos in a Roman Jewish synagogue. Fearing political implications, he denied the other mem-

---

168, 171, and 173f. Again, Cicero in his previously cited oration *Pro Flacco,* after having designated Jerusalem as *suspiciosa ac maledica civitas,* "suspicious and evil-speaking city" (68), says contemptuously of the Jews, *Illa gens quid de nostro imperio sentiret, ostendit armis; quam cara dis immortalibus esset docuit, quod est victa, quod elocata, quod serva facta:* "This nation has shown by arms how it feels about our empire; how dear it is to the immortal gods we learn from the fact that it has been conquered, exiled, and reduced to servitude" (69).

73. From Acts 18:2 we know that the Jew Aquila, Ποντικὸν τῷ γένει, "a native of Pontus," σκηνοποιός, a "tentmaker" like Paul, had lived in Rome for some years. We may imagine that such commercial reasons were behind the origin of the Jewish communities at Pozzuoli (see Fl. Josephus, *Ant.* XVII 328; *Bell.* II 104) and at Ostia (see Frey, *CII,* I, no. 533), both of which were commercial centers.

74. See Fl. Josephus, *Ant.* XIV 185–216; among the privileges these are fundamental: complete liberty of association and of cult; permission to collect money and send the tax to the Jerusalem Temple (later amended by Vespasian to the *fiscus iudaicus* for the Temple of Capitoline Jove); exemption from military service (to protect observance of the Sabbath and abstention from forbidden foods); permission for their own tribunals for their own cases. See also E. M. Smallwood, *The Jews under Roman Rule, from Pompey to Diocletian,* Stud. in Jud. and Late Ant. 20 (Leiden, 1976); C. Saulnier, "Lois romaines sur les Juifs selon Flavius Josèphe," RB 88 (1981) 161–198.

75. See Philo, *Leg. ad C.* 154–158.

76. Nor do we know how the Jews of Rome reacted to Caligula's proposal to erect a statue of himself in the Jerusalem Temple.

77. Surely at the instigation of the powerful Seianus (see Philo, *Leg. ad C.* 159). The occasion was that the matron Fulvia, wife of the Senator Saturninus and "Jewish sympathizer" (προσεληλυθυῖαν τοῖς Ἰουδαϊκοῖς), got involved with four Jewish charlatans, who extorted money from her under the pretext of giving her instructions about Moses (Fl. Josephus, *Ant.* XVIII 81–84); see also Suetonius, *Tib.* 36; Tacitus, *Ann.* II, 85; Dio Cassius, LVII 18.

78. See, for example, S. Safrai, "The Problem of the Expulsion of the Jews from Rome in the Time of Claudius," in Safrai-Stern, eds., *The Jewish People,* I, 180–183.

79. That is, in 41 rather than 49; see the discussion in Lüdemann, *Paul,* 164–171 = *Paulus,* 183–195.

bers of the synagogue the right to meet together, and thus retracted the right of association."[80]

In any case, the notice of Acts 18:2 that Claudius expelled πάντας τοὺς Ἰουδαίους ἀπὸ τῆς Ῥώμης, "all the Jews from Rome," is exaggerated and implausible, especially since Flavius Josephus, as well as Tacitus, ignores the episode completely, even though it should have appeared to be of quite considerable proportions. As for the name *Chrestus*, though it is theoretically possible that it belonged to a Jewish troublemaker,[81] it is more easily understood as a reference to Jesus Christ. And this not only on linguistic grounds[82] but for historical reasons, for in 64 A.D., after the great fire of Rome, the Christians *(chrestianos)* alone were blamed,[83] a fact which would indicate that in the City they were already clearly distinguished from the Jews; now it would, of course, have taken several years to develop such a distinct identity in the popular mind.

At any rate, under Nero the Jews were again to enjoy full freedom. In fact, a Jewish actor was a friend of the Emperor (see below). It is less clear whether his wife Poppaea, who according to Josephus was "God-fearing" (θεοσεβὴς γὰρ ἦν),[84] was at a stage close to being a proselyte[85] or whether she was just a "religious or superstitious" person in a general sense, at most a "sympathizer," as seems probable, considering the non-technical use of the terms θεοσεβής, *metuens deum* ("god-revering") as distinguished from φοβούμενος/σεβόμενος τὸν θεόν ("revering" or "fearing God").[86]

---

80. Lüdemann, *Paul*, 166 (see 186, n. 68) = *Paulus*, 188 (see 185, n. 67). But the hypothesis of E. Haenchen (*The Acts*, 65, n. 3, and 533–534 = *Apg.*, 68, n. 3, and 544) seems improbable; according to him, the order of Claudius reported by Dio Cassius would have been to prevent the Roman Jews from meeting as one community; however, they were already divided into different "synagogues" (the *Augustenses*, the *Agrippenses*, and the *Volumnenses*). The opinion of Wiefel, *Die jüdische Gemeinschaft*, 77–81 (according to whom the Christian community before the imperial edict was of Jewish origin, while the "new community," established with the installation of Nero, was primarily of pagan origin, and it was to them that the Letter to the Romans was addressed), is based on too many unproved suppositions: the date and content of the edict, the intervention of Nero against the restrictive measures of Claudius, and the existence of many anti-synagogal and so anti-Jewish "house churches."

81. The name is attested by Martial in the pagan world, *Epigr.* VII 55,1.

82. See Lüdemann, *Paul*, 169 = *Paulus*, 193.

83. Tacitus, *Ann.* XV 44,2; see 44,4: "a huge number," *ingens multitudo*! Furthermore, the silence of Dio Cassius about Chrestus in this report would suggest that this name has something to do with the Christians, since in his work there is a systematic (and therefore intentional) omission of anything concerning Christianity.

84. *Ant.* XX 195; cf. *Vita* 3.

85. B. Lifschitz, "Du nouveau sur les 'Sympathisants,'" *JournStudJud* 1 (1970) 77–84, 79. The issue may be confirmed by the fact that at her death (65 A.D.) her body was embalmed in the oriental manner rather than being cremated (Tacitus, *Ann.* XVI 6; cf. XV 61).

86. Still fundamental on this issue is the study of F. Siegert, "Gottesfürchtige und Sympathisanten," *JournStudJud* 4 (1973) 109–164, which clearly distinguishes the two kinds of persons (see pp. 160f. for his treatment of Poppaea; quite different he considers the case of

4. As for the distribution of Jews in the city of Rome, they were neither enclosed in a ghetto nor concentrated in a single quarter.[87] However the *Trastevere* was probably the oldest area to have been settled by Jews, and the one where they were most concentrated; in fact, this is the only one mentioned by Philo for the time of Augustus,[88] and the Monteverde catacomb, which served this area, is the one that has furnished the earliest and the most abundant inscriptions (see above).

But there were Jews living in at least four other residential areas. One is the Suburra, a lower-class district of ill repute squeezed into the hollows between the Quirinal, the Viminal, and the Esquiline; indeed, at least five catacomb inscriptions attest to a community of the *Siburenses* or *Σιβουρησίων* (see above). Another area is the Campo Marzio, as evidenced by the inscriptions that speak of the *Campenses* or *Καμπησίων*.[89] This area, located outside the ancient republican walls was first inhabited from the first century before Christ (with public buildings like the Theater of Pompey and later that of Marcellus, the *Saepta Iulia*, the Pantheon, the Baths of Agrippa).

Harder to locate is the community of the *Calcarenses* or *Καλκαρησίων* (from *calcaria*, "lime furnace"); this is probably located in the area in which Diocletian was to have his baths built, near the ancient *Porta Collina* (this location is suggested by two pagan inscriptions found there).[90] Moreover, it seems that the pagan epitaph of the fruitseller P. Corfidius Signinus from the late first century refers to this area; it says that he lived *de aggere a proseucha*, that is, "alongside the *agger* near the synagogue."[91]

Juvenal, *Sat.* XIV 96–106, where the term *metuens* designates a "Gottesfürchtig": 153–155). Therefore nos. 5, 285, 524, 529 should probably be omitted from the *CII*; but nos. 202, 222, 256, 523, and perhaps 21, 68, 462, are clear examples of proselytes (see Leon, *The Jews*, 253–256).

87. On the other hand, we know that in Alexandria two of the five residential quarters consisted of Jews, but they were also scattered in other quarters (Philo, *In Fl.* 55).

88. *Leg. ad C.* 155: τὴν πέραν τοῦ Τιβερέως ποταμοῦ μεγάλην τῆς 'Ρώμης ἀποτομήν οὐκ ἠγνόει κατεχομένην καὶ οἰκουμένην πρὸς 'Ιουδαίων: "[Augustus] was not ignorant that the great section of Rome beyond the River Tiber was settled and inhabited by Jews." The Trastevere is the XIV, that is, the last of the fourteen quarters into which Augustus divided the city (Dio Cassius, LV 8:7).

89. The *Campus* corresponded exactly to the Campo Marzio: see Titus Livius, XL 52:4; Cicero, *Cat.* II, 1:1; Juvenal, *Sat.* II 132.

90. *CIL* VI 9223–9224; thus Collon, "Remarques," 89–90. But according to Frey, *CII*, I, LXXIV, it should be the area of the Circo Flaminio (near the present ghetto); but use of the name *Calcaria* for this district is unknown till the Middle Ages. In either case, the name does not seem to designate a corporation of lime workers, since there would hardly be enough Jews of this one profession, nor do such professionally defined communities seem to have been customary to Jews (see Leon, *The Jews*, 143).

91. *CIL* VI 9821 (Frey, *CII*, I, no. 531). The *agger* (rampart) had been built in the sixth century B.C. by Servius Tullius or by Tarquinius the Proud to protect the city on the east, which was more level, and thus more exposed (see the notice of Strabo, V 3:7; Dionysius of Halicarnassus, IX 68; Pliny, *Hist. nat.* III 5:9.

Juvenal reports another place of Jewish settlement (but perhaps in the form of a squatters' camp) near the Porta Capena, immediately to the southeast of the Circus Maximus, from which the Via Appia originated before the present Aurelian walls. Here, says the satirical poet, who regrets the degradation of certain sacred sites, the grove with the spring of the nymph Egeria and the sanctuaries "are leased to Jews, who own no more than a basket and a pile of straw."[92]

Not far from this area lived a certain Jew named Alexander, whose inscription in the catacomb identifies him as *de macello* ("market of meat and other goods," "emporium").[93]

5. We know the *social level of the Jews* from characteristics of their tombs, but especially from contemporaneous literary sources. Their catacombs would already indicate prevailing poverty. Very few cubicles belong to them (and these are late), and even fewer of these are painted. Even sarcophagi are few and are not very elaborate. Many tombs have no epitaph, and what epitaphs there are, are more often than not of quite rudimentary work and not infrequently contain obvious grammatical errors (though, indeed, the phenomenon does provide us with an interesting insight into popular speech.)[94] All this would indicate that persons of some rank, who certainly existed, must have been very few.

But it is especially the literary sources that provide various features of the picture of their social standing. Philo of Alexandria explicitly informs us that "the greater part were 'emancipated Romans' ('Ρωμαῖοι . . . ἀπελευθερωθέντες); brought to Rome as prisoners of war, 'they had then been freed by their masters' (ὑπὸ τῶν κτησαμένων ἠλευθερώθησαν)."[95] On the basis of this text (and considering the total lack of epigraphic evidence), we cannot say that among the Roman Jews of the first century (at least before 70 A.D.) there were many slaves.[96] Nor do we have a single report

92. Juvenal, *Sat.* III 11-14: . . . *ad veteres arcus madidamque Capenam.* / *Hic, ubi nocturnae Numa constituebat amicae,* / *nunc sacri fontis nemus et delubra locantur* / *Iudaeis, quorum cophinus faenumque supellex.*

93. Frey, *CII*, I, no. 210: Since it does not specify, it probably refers to the *macellum magnum* (upon which now stands the church of Santo Stefano Rotondo) rather than the *macellum Liviae* (under the present Santa Maria Maggiore); see Collon, "Remarques," 90-94.

94. On this last matter, see Leon, *The Jews*, 75-92 ("IV. The Language of the Jews of Rome").

95. *Leg. ad C.* 155.

96. We do know that Julia (Livia), the wife of Augustus, had a Jewish slave by the name of Acme (see Fl. Josephus, *Ant.* XVII 134 and 141). For the years after 70 the sense of the obscene text of Martial, *Epigr.* VII 35, 2-3, is not clear. Still, the optimistic conclusion of Leon, *The Jews*, 237f. (which limits the allusions to Jewish slaves to "only two specific references," those just cited), must be corrected by the addition of Petronius Arb., *Satyr.* 68:8, which alludes to the circumcision of a *servus* ("slave") of Trimalchio (see above, n. 14); and this testimony comes from the Neronic age.

of any international business activity, as has sometimes been attributed to them.[97]

All we know for the time of Saint Paul is that there were among the Roman Jews σκηνοποιοί ("tentmakers") like Aquila, whom he met in Corinth (Acts 18:2-3); this craft probably consisted in working at tents in leather.[98] Also Josephus informs us about a certain Ἁλίτυρος who was a μιμόλογος, that is, an actor, who was very dear to Nero and who obtained a meeting with Poppaea for Josephus.[99] This type of work must have been popular also in the following years, for from Juvenal we know the name of another comic actor, Menophilus, who got a laugh out of his circumcision;[100] Juvenal attacks an anonymous Jewish poet, *Solymis natus in ipsis*, "born right in Jerusalem," accusing him of plagiarism and pederasty.[101] We know of other minor activities from Juvenal and Martial alike, representing the late first and early second centuries. "A walking salesman across the Tiber trades sulphur matches for broken glass";[102] a Jewish woman predicts the future: "For a few coins she'll sell you whatever dreams you could want";[103] the young mendicant daily "instructed by his mother to beg."[104]

From the catacomb inscriptions, the dating of which we have seen to be uncertain, we barely learn of the existence of a painter,[105] a butcher,[106]

97. See Leon, *The Jews*, 236f.; the author is very critical of this opinion: "It is a fallacy to attribute to the Jews of ancient Rome the mercantile activities that are associated with the Jews of the Middle Ages and of modern times" (237).

98. Actually, we know from Livy that tents were made of leather rather than textiles. See R. F. Hock, *The Social Context of Paul's Ministry: Tentmaking and Apostleship* (Philadelphia, 1980) 20–25.

99. Fl. Josephus, *Vita* 3: μιμόλογος κάλλιστα τῷ Νέρωνι καταθύμιος, "the actor most favored by Nero" (the encounter took place at Pozzuoli).

100. *Epigr.* VII 82.

101. Ibid., XI 94: in eight verses the mocking vocative *verpe poeta* ("circumcised poet") recurs four times; see also VII 55.

102. Martial, *Epigr.* I 41: *transtiberinus ambulator / qui pallentia sulphurata fractis / permutat vitreis*; cf. XII 57:14: *nec sulphuratae lippus institor mercis*: "nor the blear-eyed huckster of sulphur wares" [W. C. A. Ker, Loeb Classical Library]. It is not certain that the reference is to Jews, but this is generally accepted to be very probable, since it is proven that in the Mediterranean world of the time these were the principal glass workers (see H. J. Leon, "Sulphur for Broken Glass," TAPA 72 [1941] 233–236; F. Neuburg, *Glass in Antiquity* [London, 1949] 49).

103. Juvenal, *Sat.* VI 543 and 546f.: *arcanam Iudaea tremens mendicat in aurem / . . . aere minuto / qualiacumque voles Iudaei somnia vendunt*: "A trembling Jewish hag begs secretly in one's ear. . . . For a tiny coin Jews will sell whatever dreams you want."

104. Martial, *Epigr.* XII 57:13: *A matre doctus nec rogare Iudaeus [cessat]*, the child "never stops," and consequently, along with many other noisy disturbances (cf. v. 26: *et ad cubile est Roma*, "[In the city,] Rome is right by my bed"), drives the poet to take refuge in the tranquil villa *Nomentum* (Mentana).

105. Ζωγράφος named Eudoxius (*CII*, I, no. 109).

106. *Bubularus* named Alexander (*CII*, I, no. 210).

and a teacher.[107] A certain *Mniaseas* (Manasseh?) is described as having been μαθητὴς σοφῶν, "a disciple of the wise,"[108] meaning that he dedicated his life to the study of the scriptures and of Jewish tradition. Still, the Jewish community of Rome never did produce anyone of outstanding merit such as would testify to a noteworthy cultural level. Flavius Josephus can hardly be said to belong to Roman Jewry, since he was already fully formed before he took up residence in the capital.[109] In this sense there is no comparison between Alexandria and Rome.

6. Finally we ask *which religious practices or beliefs* of the Roman Jews can we reconstruct? We must here distinguish clearly between pagan literary sources and Jewish epigraphic sources. The former show us varied and superficial impressions produced by the Jews in their Roman milieu, while the latter is more accurate in presenting us with certain aspects— but only more specific aspects—of their religious world.

In the literary sources from Horace to Juvenal, most of the allusions refer to two practices that must have struck the citizens of the City: Sabbath[110] and circumcision.[111] They speak of these now indifferently, now ironically; the long text of Persius especially (*Sat.* V, 179-184), which is certainly contemporaneous with Paul's sojourn, gives evidence of a certain fear that the celebration of the Jewish Sabbath provokes among the superstitious Romans. There are also allusions to abstention from pork,[112]

107. Διδάσκαλος named Eusebius, identified also as νομομαθής, "learned in the Law" (Frey, *CII*, I, no. 333; see also 201).
108. Frey, *CII*, I, no. 508.
109. Moreover, in Rome he led a life of leisure: he resided as a guest in the house where Vespasian lived before becoming emperor, he was a Roman citizen and owned land in Judea (*Vita* 76, 423, 425, 428f.). Also Cecilius of Calatte (in Sicilia), a Jewish freedman, had a career in Rome under Augustus as an Atticist literary critic; it is he who is the object of the polemic of the anonymous author of *On the Sublime* I 1-2; IV 2; VIII 4; XXXII 1,8.
110. Horace, *Serm.* I 9:69 (*tricesima sabbata:* "the thirieth Sabbath"; perhaps the new moon); Ovid, *Ars Amat.* I 76 (*septima sacra:* "the holy seventh day"); Seneca, *Ep.* 95:47 (*lucernas sabbatis prohibeamus:* "Let us forbid lamps on Sabbaths"); idem, in Augustine's *De civ. Dei* VI 11 (*septenis interpositos dies:* "every seventh day"); Persius, *Sat.* V 180, 184 (*Herodis dies . . . recutita sabbata:* "Herod's day, the circumcised Sabbath"); Petronius, *fragmenta* 37 (*ieiuna sabbata:* "fasting Sabbath"); Martial, *Epigr.* IV 4:7 (*ieiunia sabbatarum:* "Sabbath fasts"); Juvenal, *Sat.* VI 159 (*mero pede sabbata:* "Sabbaths with bare feet"); XIV 96, 105f. (*metuentem sabbata . . . septima quaeque fuit lux / ignava:* "holding Sabbaths in awe").
111. Horace, *Serm.* I 9:70 (*curtis Iudaeis:* "the mutilated Jews"); Persius, *Sat.* V 184 (*recutita sabbata:* "the circumcised Sabbath"); Petronius, *Satyr.* 68:8 (*recutitus:* "circumcised"); 102 (*circumcide nos ut Iudaei videamur:* "Circumcise us so they'll think we're Jews"); idem, *fragmenta* 37 (*ni tamen et ferro succiderit inguinis oram:* "unless he cuts back his foreskin with a knife"); Martial, *Epigr.* VII 30:5 (*recutitorum . . . inguina Iudaeorum:* "the lecheries of circumcised Jews" [W. C. A. Ker, Loeb Classical Library]); VII 82:5 (*verpus:* "circumcised"); XI 94:2, 4, 6, 8 (*verpe poeta:* "circumcised poet"); Juvenal, *Sat.* XIV 99,104 (*praeputia ponunt . . . verpos:* "they circumcise the foreskin").
112. Petronius, *fragmenta* 37 (*Iudaeus licet et porcinum numen adoret:* "though the Jew worship his pig-god"); Juvenal, *Sat.* VI 160 (*vetus indulget senibus clementia porcis:* "long-standing

and to fasting, which they wrongly associate with the Sabbath,[113] though in fact the Mishna forbids fasting on the Sabbath.[114] Pagan Romans must also have been perplexed by the idea of a deity who could not be represented if Juvenal must write that the Jews *nil praeter nubes et caeli numen adorant*, "adore nothing but the clouds and the heavenly Deity."[115] As for places of cult, as we have already said, archeology has yet to discover any traces,[116] but there must have been several, since in Juvenal an anonymous tippler asks openly, *In qua te quaero proseucha?*: "In which *proseucha* should I look for you?"[117] (where presumably he would be begging or praying).

The epigraphic sources, of uncertain date, document a theme we should like to pursue. Since we are dealing with burial inscriptions, these necessarily contain expressions about death and about the lot of the dead in the afterlife. But here we must acknowledge the methodological reservation of U. Fischer, who maintains it is an open question to determine to what extent their formulas represent living religious attitudes or merely reflect unexamined traditional concepts, or simply express the thought of the stoneworker rather than that of the client.[118] Actually no great theology emerges; rather, the absence of such is astonishing, as is even the reduction of the expressions to the canon of the surrounding society.

The same observation applies to the decorations; thus these represent only cultic objects on the tombs themselves (the *menorah* [sevenfold lampstand], the *aron* [ark] with its sacred scrolls, the *shofar* [ram's horn], the *ethrog*, the *lulab*), while on the walls they consist of really ornamental paintings. However, these latter are completely missing in the old catacomb of Monteverde, which is thus confirmed as the most archaic and conservative; in catacomb A of Villa Torlonia these paintings depict only cultic

---

clemency spares their elderly pigs"); XIV 98 (*nec distare putant humana carne suillam*: "nor do they consider pork much different from human flesh").

113. Suetonius, *Aug.* 76 (*Ne Iudaeus quidem, mi Tiberi, tam diligenter sabbatis ieiunium servat quam ego hodie servavi*: "Not even a Jew, Tiberius, keeps the Sabbath fast as well as I have kept it this day"); Petronius, *fragmenta* 37 (*ieiuna sabbata*: "fasting Sabbaths"); Martial, *Epigr.* IV 4:7 (*ieiunia sabbatariarum*: "Sabbath fasts").

114. *Ta'anit* 2:9; 4:3.

115. *Sat.* XIV 97; see also Petronius, *fragmenta* 37 (*Iudaeus licet . . . et caeli summas advocet auriculas*: "Though the Jew call upon the exalted ears of heaven"); Lucanus, *Pharsalia* II 593 (*incerti Iudaea dei*: "Judea of the indeterminate god"); Tacitus, *Hist.* V 13 (*nec quicquam prius inbuuntur quam contemnere deos*: "and the first thing they learn is to despise the gods"). Cf. the witness of Varro, who praises the aniconic beginnings of Roman religion (in Augustine, *De civ. Dei* IV 31:2).

116. But see above, n. 33.

117. *Sat.* III 296; see Philo, *Leg. ad C.* 156; on the meaning of the word see above, n. 32.

118. U. Fischer, *Eschatologie und Jenseitserwartung im hellenistischen Diasporajudentum*, BZNW 44 (Berlin-New York, 1978) 216.

objects, especially the *menorah* and the *aron*); but in the catacomb of Vigna Randanini we find figures that clearly derive from pagan symbolism (Fortune crowning a nude youth, Plenty, a ram with the caduceus, peacocks, birds, flowers).[119]

For strict methodological control we will restrict our consideration to the catacomb of Monteverde, which is generally considered the oldest,[120] and the contents of which will consequently lead us closest to Paul's stay in Rome. Here we frequently find the greeting of peace,[121] normally imperative in sense or form, whether in Hebrew or in Greek.[122] There is an interesting prayer of a father for his four-year-old son: νῦν δέσποτα, ἐν εἰρήνῃ κόμησιν (!) αὐτοῦ Ἰοῦστον νήπιον ἀσύγκριτον, ἐν δικαιώματί σου:[123] "Now, Lord, according to your just will, let the repose of him, Justus, an innocent child, be in peace." There are another two instances where the wish stands that the repose of the deceased be "with the just,"[124] so that we must perhaps see an allusion to a communion with the just in the afterlife.[125]

More pessimistic is the recurring formula: "Courage, no one is immortal!"[126] A saying probably of pagan origin,[127] this simultaneously expresses disconsolate resignation and seeks to give the deceased courage

119. On this aspect of the question still fundamental are the volumes of E. Goodenough, *Jewish Symbols in the Greco-Roman Period,* I–XIII (New York, 1953–65); for the material on Rome, see II, 3–45, and the corresponding illustrations in vol. III.

120. See nn. 23 and 24 above.

121. On the topic see E. Dinkler, "Shalom-Eirene-Pax, Jüdische Sepulkralinschriften und ihr Verhältnis zum frühen Christentum," *RivArchCrist* 50 (1974) 121–144.

122. The common formula is ἐν εἰρήνῃ (ἡ) κοίμησις αὐτοῦ (αὐτῆς-αὐτῶν); twice is found ἐν εἰρήνῃ κοιμάσθω (Frey, *CII,* I, nos. 365, 390). Various forms in Hebrew recur seven times: *šlwm yšr'l, bšlwm, šlwm* (nos. 292, 293, 296, 319, 397, 497, 499); for a discussion of no. 349, which shows a *menorah* that subdivides a series of variously read letters (*ysr'l:* "Israel" or else *y'r 'l:* "God will raise up"), see Fischer, *Eschatologie,* 222.

123. Frey, *CII,* I, no. 8. For the same noun δικαίωμα ("justice") see Rom 1:32; 2:26; 5:16, 18; 8:4 (furthermore in Rom 16:14 Ἀσύγκριτος ["Innocent"] is a personal name).

124. Frey, *CII,* I, no. 340 (μετὰ τῶν ὁσίων: "with the devout"), no. 370 (μνία διχαίου εἰς εὐλογίαν: "The memory of the just becomes a blessing").

125. Consider other similar formulas in other Jewish catacombs: Frey, *CII,* I, nos. 55, 78, 110, 118, 193, 526 (μετὰ τῶν δικαίων, μετά τῆ ὁσίων, *cum iustis:* "with the devout/just"; no. 210: *dormitio tua inter dicaeis:* "your repose with the righteous"!). Elements of an intermediate eschatology, which we recognize as spread throughout intertestamental Judaism (see C. C. Cavallin, *Life after Death—Part I. An Enquiry into the Jewish Background* [Lund, 1974]), appear in various forms, including burial inscriptions: in Rome (see Frey, *CII,* I, no. 527: *vita subit caelum corpus tellure tenetur:* "Life ascends to heaven, the body remains on earth"); in Cilicia (ibid., no. 788: "the One who has carried us into the sphere of the stars"; cf. 4 Macc 17:5); at Antinopolis in Middle Egypt (ibid., II, no. 442: "Lazarus, may the repose of his soul be in the treasury of life"; 1 Sam 25:29); among the inscriptions of Leontopolis (Tell-el-Yaoudiyeh), from the most impressive to the poorest, two from the early imperial period stand out, nos. 1510 and 1513 (see Fischer, *Eschatologie,* 237–242).

126. Frey, *CII,* I, nos. 314, 335, 380, 401, 450.

127. See M. Simon, "Θάρσει οὐδεὶς ἀθάνατος. Etude de vocabulaire religieux," *RevHistRel* 113 (1936) 166–206. This exclamation does not allow us to see there an enigmatic reference to an eschatological overturning of the situation (contra Goodenough, *Jewish Symbols,* II, 137).

and consolation, scanty though it be; at most the Jews could understand in it a concealed "commendation to the peace of God without thereby believing in a salvation in the afterlife."[128] In this sense we read the epitaph of a certain *Eupsychos*, which describes the tomb itself as an "eternal dwelling" (οἶκος αἰώνιος).[129]

As for the typical Jewish-biblical faith in the resurrection of the dead, the indications are rare indeed. True, the personal names "Anastasius" or "Anastasia" could suggest such a belief in the resurrection (*anastasis*),[130] but besides the fact that an express hope in resurrection is never associated with the name, we must note that the Roman Jews do not seem to put much weight on the literal meaning of proper names, since many refer to pagan deities.[131]

Very significant, on the other hand, is the famous long inscription in thirteen hexameters which a husband had carved on the tomb of a certain *Regina* and which is dated to the second century.[132] After the first four lines treating their past common life, the text continues as follows:

> 5 *rursum victura reditura ad lumina rursum*
> 6 *nam sperare potest ideo quod surgat in aevom*
> 7 *promissum quae vera fides dignisque piisque*
> 8 *quae meruit sedem venerandi ruris habere.*

> > Again she will conquer, again return to the light,
> > for she can hope to rise forever,
> > having merited to have the seat (true faith!)
> > promised to the worthy and devout in the venerable land.

The parallelism is evident between "return to the light" of our first line, accented as it is by a double *rursum*, indicating a resumption of full life, and the "rise forever" of the second line. This clearly refers to resurrection, which is thus described metaphorically as having "a seat in the

---

128. Fischer, *Eschatologie*, 224.

129. Frey, *CII*, I, no. 337; cf. 523, 527, and the caustic cynic Leontius at no. 32 (*Amici, ego vos hic exspecto:* "Friends, I await you here"); biblical analogies in Ps 49:12; Qoh 12:5; Tob 3:6. The expression is common in antiquity: see E. Stommel, art. "Domus aeterna," in RAC IV, 109–128. Since the expression οἶκος αἰώνιος stands by itself and is immediately followed by an *aron* or ark of the Law (see also *CII*, I, no. 515: οἶκος εἰρήνης: "house of peace"), one might think that this symbolizes the heavenly temple; but this is a "pure supposition" (contra H. Gressmann, see Fischer, *Eschatologie*, 253 and 244f.); see Frey, *CII*, I, no. 460: "place (λόκου) of Bessula," with an *aron* flanked by two *menorot*. See also n. 143.

130. See Frey, *CII*, I, no. 298 ('Αναστασία), 354 (*Anastasis*), 481 (*Anestase*, perhaps *Anastasius*).

131. E.g.: *Aphrodisia* (Frey, *CII*, I, no. 232), *Dionysias* (nos. 104, 256), *Hermogenes* (no. 324), *Asklepiodote* (nos. 91, 92); see Leon, *The Jews*, 233–235.

132. Frey, *CII*, I, no. 476; see Fischer, *Eschatologie*, 233–235.

venerable land," probably a reference to a heavenly paradise.[133] The concept is of a revivification limited to the "worthy and pious"; and precisely this material return to life stands at the center of the *speranda futura*, "future hopes," that appear in the following line 12. The last five verses then enumerate the merits (see line 9: *hoc tibi praestiterit*, "this you will be given by") that are the foundation of the *vera fides* of the resurrection: *pietas, vita pudica, amor generis* ("piety, chaste life, love of the nation [i.e., of the people of Israel]),[134] *observantia legis, coniugii meritum* ("observance of the Law, the merits of your marriage"). The motifs are partly Jewish and partly general values.[135]

On the whole, then, there is precious little evidence of hope in an afterlife, and even less of the resurrection. This near absence of interest in resurrection is typical of Judaism throughout the Western diaspora in contrast to that of the East (cf. Greek inscriptions at Bet Shearim and decorations of Dura Europos).[136] We must probably see in this phenomenon a syncretistic assimilation to the religious-cultural conceptions of the milieu. One could say that in general this only emphasizes the importance of the characteristics that in the Regina inscription are considered merits for the resurrection. Specifically, the *observatio legis*, "observance of the Law," becomes a preferred criterion to describe the religious identity of the deceased. In the Monteverde catacomb we find two deceased persons identified as δίκαιος, "righteous."[137] Moreover, in other catacombs we discover equivalent expressions: *iuste legem colenti*, "righteously keeping the Law";[138] φιλόνομος, "loving the Law";[139] φιλέντολος, "loving the commandments";[140] φιλοσυνάγωγος, "lover of the 'synagogue' ";[141] of a woman we are told that *bene vixit in iudaismo*, "she lived well in Judaism."[142]

133. This meaning is confirmed by the Jewish pseudepigraphon, probably contemporary, *Test. Job* 33:5, where Job declares that his throne ὑπάρχει ἐν τῇ ἀγίᾳ γῇ: "stands in the holy Land" (see 33:3: ἐν τῷ ὑπερκοσμίῳ . . . ἐκ δεξιῶν τοῦ πατρός: "in the upper world . . . at the right hand of the Father") and that his glory ἐν τῷ αἰῶνί ἐστιν τοῦ ἀπαραλλάκτου: "is in the endless ages of the unchangeable" (see the observations of B. Schaller, "Unterweisung in lebhafter Form. Das Testament Hiobs," *Jüdische Schriften aus hellenistisch-römischer Zeit*, III/3 [Gütersloh, 1979] 353, n. 5a). On the other hand, Fischer, *Eschatologie*, 235, n. 73, prefers to think with geographic realism of the land of Palestine (citing Wis 12:7; *En. et.* 89:40; 90:20).

134. See Frey, *CII*, I, nos. 203, 509: φιλόλαος, "lover of the people" (and no. 203: φιλοπένης, "lover of the poor").

135. And thus the husband concludes: [12] *horum factorum tibi sunt speranda futura* [13] *de quibus et coniux maestus solacia quaerit*: "A future corresponding to such things is to be hoped for you, and from this your sorrowing husband seeks comfort."

136. This is the conclusion of Fischer, *Eschatologie*, 236f.

137. Frey, *CII*, I, nos. 321, 363.

138. Ibid., no. 72.

139. Ibid., no. 111; and in Fasola, "Le due catacombe," 20.

140. Frey, *CII*, I, nos. 132, 509.

141. Ibid., no. 321.

142. Ibid., no. 537; cf. no. 240: *bona Iudaea*, "a good Jew."

III. Conclusions

On the basis of the documentation we have, Roman Judaism of the first century reveals a rather pale and flat panorama. Nothing stands out beyond the ordinary daily attachment to the most elementary components of their own identity. This is not to say that it was unable to provide a certain attraction both to the lower classes[143] and the aristocratic levels of Roman society;[144] but the same was happening with all the Oriental religions and the various philosophies present in Rome. This influence may be related to the presence in Rome from time to time of the Herodians—Agrippa I, Agrippa II, and Berenice; however, we do not know the relationship of each with the Roman Jewish communities, though we have the impression that during their stay in the capital they quite ignored these latter.[145]

In any case, there is no cultural intensity in Jewish Rome, no wisdom or apocalyptic traditions.[146] We have not a single report of any reaction

143. In this regard the catacomb inscriptions document at least six cases of proselytes (Frey, *CII*, I, nos. 68, 202, 222, 256, 462, 523, and perhaps 21). Two of these are slaves (nos. 256, 462); most are women (21, 202, 222, 462, 523), a fact that reflects a widespread tendency in Rome (see L. Friedländer, op. cit., I, 509; F. Cumont, *The Oriental Religions in Roman Paganism* (New York, 1954 = 1911) 44 = *Les religions orientales dans le paganisme romain* [Paris, 1929] 40). Also the question of Juvenal, *Sat.* III 296 (*In qua te quaero proseucha?*: "In which *proseucha* should I look for you?"), indicates the popularity of the Jewish cultic place; moreover, the same poet witnesses to the diffusion of the Sabbath, circumcision, abstinence from pork (*Sat.* XIV 96–106; note vv. 100f.: *Romanas autem soliti contemnere leges, / Iudaicum ediscunt et servant ac metuunt ius:* "Accustomed though they are to despise Roman laws, they learn the Jewish Law and revere it").

144. Concerning how this was reflected among the wealthy classes of Roman society (apart from the case of Poppaea, who is probably not to be subsumed under such ideas; see above, n. 86), we know only of the troubles of the matron Fulvia at the time of Tiberius (see above, n. 77), and later under Domitian the problematic case of the consul Flavius Clemens, cousin of the emperor, and his wife Flavia Domitilla, condemned for "the crime of atheism, on the basis of which many others were condemned for deviating to Jewish customs" (ἔγκλημα ἀθεότητος, ὑφ' ἧς καὶ ἄλλοι εἰς τὰ τῶν Ἰουδαίων ἤδη ἐξοκέλλοντες πολλοὶ κατεδικάσθησαν: Dio Cassius, LXVII 14; see Suetonius, *Dom.* 15; in a Christian sense: Eusebius of Caesarea, *Hist. eccl.* III 18,4). See also the case of the matron Pomponia Graecina, who in the year 57 was accused of *superstitionis externae*, "foreign superstition" (Tacitus, *Ann.* XII 32).

145. Flavius Josephus traces a sort of biography of Agrippa in *Ant.* XVIII 133–354: he spent his youth in Rome until 23 A.D. and returned in 36–37 and 40–41. He was a friend of Caligula and later of Claudius, in whose imperial election he played a decisive role. Regarding Berenice, Suetonius provides a report in *Tit.* 7, and Dio Cassius in LXVI 15:3-4, always concerning relations with the court, with no allusion to the Jewish communities of the capital. (Allusions to Berenice and Agrippa II in Juvenal, *Sat.* VI 156–160, refer to Palestine rather than Rome: note v. 159.)

146. But see R. Kabisch, *Das vierte Buch Esra auf seine Quelle untersucht* (Göttingen 1889), which would find Rome to be the place of composition of the so-called "Apocalypse of Salatiel" (4 Esdr 3:1-31; 4:1-51; 5:13b–6:10; 6:30–7:25; 7:45–8:62; 9:15–10:57); but R. H. Charles does not agree (II, 552: Palestine). Rabbinic sources will report the arrival and activity of noted Palestinian rabbis in a later period, during the reigns of Domitian (81–96), Hadrian (117–138), and Antoninus Pius (138–161); see R. E. Brown and J. P. Meier, *Antioch and Rome*, 96.

either to Caligula's threat to set up his own image in the Jerusalem Temple
or to the outbreak and prosecution of the Jewish War.[147] The impression
is that the links with the motherland have grown very loose (see Acts
28:21).

In this relatively stagnant situation, the only cause of agitation, according to Suetonius, was the arrival in the forties, we know not whence, of
news regarding *Chrestus*-Christ. But we can legitimately suppose that even
greater disturbance must have resulted—at least indirectly through the effect of the Christian community on the as yet very closely related Jewish
communities—by the arrival of Paul's letter "to the Romans." Against the
background of Roman Judaism this stands out in enormous relief simply
through its breadth and the elevation of its thought even before one considers the novelty and originality of its Christian character. And we can
surely suppose that for the Christians (and particularly the Jewish Christians) this writing served to clarify the relationship and to provoke discussion with the Jewish component of the City.[148] For example, Rom
1:18-32, which commentators usually identify as a denunciation of the
decadent moral and religious situation of the pagan world, applies to the
Jews as well, at least as included with the others. In fact, not only does
Paul himself in 2:1 include them (τά γάρ αὐτά πράσσεις ὁ κρίνων, "you who
judge do the same things"; cf. 2:3), but we also know an epigram of Martial engaged in controversy with an anonymous Jewish poetaster, in which
he explicitly charges him with two things, pederasty and taking oaths *per
templa Tonantis*, "by the temple of the Thunderer,"[149] a clear allusion to

---

147. This observation makes it inappropriate to think that the Roman Jews had a tendency
toward revolt against state authority, or to conclude that consequently some such tendency
was characteristic of the Christian community. Rom 13:1-7, consequently, is surely not to be
explained by any preoccupation of the sort. We wish, therefore, to offer a new critically based
interpretation of this text: the passage would indicate not a political dimension but only an
eschatologically oriented paraenesis on relations with the Law: P. F. Beatrice, "Il giudizio
secondo le opere della Legge e l'amore compimento della Legge. Contributo all'esegesi di
Rom 13:1-10," StPat 20 (1973) 491-545.

148. Wiefel's hypothesis, *Die jüdische Gemeinschaft*, 75, is not altogether convincing. According to him, the expansion of Christianity among Roman Jewry would have been favored
by the lack of a single supreme unifying authority. However, each one of the Jewish communities did have a a strict structure of its own; moreover, Horace in *Serm*. I 4:142-143 had already witnessed (in writing about poets, *Nam multo plures sumus, ac veluti te / Iudaea cogemus
in hanc concedere turbam:* "For there are many more of us, and like Jews we shall force you
to join our crowd") to their strong tendency toward proselytism. It is more plausible to say
that "it is likely that different synagogues would make different responses to the Christian
message" (J. W. Drane, "Why Did Paul Write Romans?" in *Pauline Studies: Essays Presented
to F. F. Bruce*, ed. D. A. Hagner and M. J. Harris [Exeter, 1980] 208-227, 216).

149. *Epigr.* XI 94; see VII 30:5; VII 55.

Jove.[150] Even so, we need not think that the family virtues were totally neglected; they are indeed well attested.[151]

In any case, Paul's bold theology of justification by faith and his consequent polemic against law must necessarily collide with the typical Jewish tradition worthily expressed with the various epigraphic expressions cited a little above, and illustrated in tenacious attachment to circumcision and Sabbath observance. Still, we must not forget that the very positive language used by Paul in Rom 9–11 not only reminds Roman Christians of the historical-theological reality of their being grafted into Israel (see 11:17),[152] but diverges markedly from and contrasts with the obvious antisemitic tendencies of the general Greco-Roman milieu.[153] And Paul himself, who not many years earlier in 1 Thess 2:15-16 had spoken severely against his compatriots, here gives evidence of a considerable change of attitude toward them (see below, chap. 16). We can, therefore, legitimately state that Christian ecumenism toward the ancient people of Israel, even though it was often to be forgotten, first really began with relations with the Jews of Rome.

---

150. See, for example, Ovid, *Fast.* 2,69; *Met.* 170; Suetonius, *Aug.* 29 and 91.

151. Besides the epitaph for *Regina*, see also the case in the Monteverde catacomb of an *Aelius Primitivus*, whom his wife considers a *marito incomparabili* and *coniugi dulcissimo*, "incomparable husband and sweetest spouse," who died after sixteen years of marriage *sine ulla querela*, "without a single complaint" (Frey, *CII*, I, no. 457). But at least in part we are dealing with a stereotyped formula characteristic of tomb inscriptions; see, e.g., C. Carletti, "Iscrizioni cristiane inedite del cimitero di Bassilla 'Ad S. Hermetem'," *Atti della Pontificia Accademia Romana di Archeologia*, Series III, "Memorie in 8°—Volume II" (Vatican City, 1976) nos. 33, 34, 70.

152. And one aspect of Paul's intention in this letter seems surely to be to exhort the Christians of Rome to live fraternally with the Jews of the same city (see Wiefel, *Die jüdische Gemeinschaft*, 81 and 88). But it is not a question of some exclusive purpose of the letter; other issues are to be found as well (see A. J. M. Wedderburn, *The Reasons for Romans*, Studies of the N.T. and Its World (Edinburgh, 1988).

153. On this theme (which, however, contrasts with the testimony of Jewish authors on the spread of Jewish practices: Philo, *Vita Mos.* II 20–23; Fl. Josephus, *C. Ap.* II 280–283; see also Juvenal, *Sat.* XIV 96–106), see Wiefel, *Die jüdische Gemeinschaft*, 83–88; especially J. N. Sevenster, *The Roots of Pagan Anti-Semitism in the Ancient World*, NT Suppl. XLI (Leiden, 1975); J. L. Daniel, "Anti-Semitism in the Hellenistic-Roman Period," JBL 98 (1979) 45–65; M. Simon, "Antisémitisme et Philosémitisme dans le Monde Romain," in his *Le Christianisme antique et son contexte religieux. Scripta Varia*, WUNT 23 (Tübingen, 1981), vol. II, 837–846.

Chapter 3

Jewish-Christian Structures of the Roman Church in the First Century

Preliminaries

This chapter fits into the broad category of those New Testament studies that come under the general label of "unity and diversity in the New Testament." While such studies have their roots in the characteristic positions of the so-called Tübingen school of the last century, it is only in the last decades that the theme has become a preferred locus in research on the earliest Christian origins. By considering the various ways of conceiving and living Christianity (of which Jewish Christianity and Hellenistic Christianity represent only the most macroscopic variants, the description of which is often not without a good dose of simplification!), it attempts to answer a question that also includes the problem of the relationship between orthodoxy and heresy in the first and second centuries.[1]

Here we concentrate our attention only on the Christian community of Rome. We wish to examine the first-century documents which are available and which are directly concerned with the Roman Church or are addressed to it (thus, the letter of Paul to the Romans and perhaps the so-called Letter to the Hebrews) or are sent from there to other destinations (the First Letter of Peter and then the Letter of Clement). In any of these cases we can make use not only of explicit reports but also of hints, allusions, and whispers that reveal a little about the internal situation of the community, showing us not only specific aspects of its life but also in the broadest view its ways of thinking.

To begin with, I adopt an appropriate methodological affirmation expressed by R. E. Brown in a study on the present subject.[2] He maintains

1. For a general outline of the studies on the issue, see P. Grech, "Unità e diversità nel NT. Lo stato della questione," RivBibl 30 (1982) 291–299.
2. See R. E. Brown and J. P. Meier, *Antioch and Rome: New Testament Cradles of Catholic Christianity* (New York, 1983) 2. This chapter is based on the theses of this book (esp. 87–210).

that despite all the attention paid by the New Testament to Paul's role among the gentiles, "we must adamantly resist the notion that there was only one theological approach (Paul's) adopted in preaching to the gentiles, and that therefore all gentile converts shared in the same outlook (Paul's)." This would be an unacceptable simplification simply because it does not correspond to the historical data.

Similar, and just as important for our purposes, is the observation that likewise among the Jews who had accepted the gospel there existed notable differences far beyond insignificant nuances.

For example, consider the differences among the following four groups. (a) Those Christians of Jewish (and specifically Pharisaic: Acts 15:5) origin, who set themselves in direct opposition to Paul, upholding full observance of the Law and circumcision (e.g., the "false brethren" of Gal 2:4 and also Phil 3). (b) Those Christians who do not insist on circumcision but require even pagan converts to accept certain Jewish observances, especially concerning food (cf. Acts 15; Gal 2:11-14; Peter and James may have belonged to this group). (c) Those Christians who require neither circumcision nor the Jewish ordinances in general, such as the dietary laws, even though they cite the Torah and attribute to it an enduring, albeit attenuated, value (such is the case of Paul, who while excluding the Law as *Heilsweg* [a means of salvation], respects it as *Lebensnorm* [norm of behavior][3] and, at least according to Acts 16:1-3; 18:19; 20:16; 21:26 respectively, has Timothy circumcised, has his hair cut at Cenchreae to fulfill a vow, celebrates the Jewish feast of Pentecost, and purifies himself in the Temple.) (d) Finally those Christians who no longer attach any significance to Jewish cult and feasts, perhaps not even to the Law, considering Judaism now to be a stage that has been passed in the history of salvation (thus probably the "Hellenists" of Acts 6:1-6, and especially the Letter to the Hebrews and John's Gospel).[4]

But let us now come to the Church of Rome and try to describe its theological physiognomy or identify the camp to which Roman Christians belong. We will proceed chronologically by four stages.

I. The thirties and forties

We have no document from this period, but we do know that these are the years when Christianity reached Rome and when a group of Chris-

---

3. See W. Schrage, *Die konkreten Einzelgebote in der paulinischen Paränese* (Gütersloh, 1961); see also M. Barth, "St. Paul—A Good Jew," *Horizons in Biblical Theology* 1 (1979) 7-45; J. D. G. Dunn, "The New Perspective on Paul," BJRL 65 (1983) 95-122.

4. In the subapostolic period this last pattern will appear in an even stronger form in the *Letter of Barnabas*, the *Letter to Diognetus*, and the apologist Aristides; and it will develop radically in abnormal forms in Marcion and in certain Gnostic trends.

tians began to take shape in the capital of the empire. The origins are obscure. They are not linked to any of the apostles, unless at a very late date to Peter (see Irenaeus, *Adv. haer.* 3:3:3, then Eusebius of Caesarea and Jerome), and any such linkage is of scant historical reliability. For example, it is significant that in writing to the Romans, Paul does not so much as mention Peter, while he names him repeatedly as someone well known in 1 Corinthians (1:12; 9:5; 15:5) and Galatians (1:18; 2:7-9, 11). Moreover, in the fourth century Ambrosiaster will write explicitly that the Romans accepted faith in Christ *nulla insignia virtutum videntes nec aliquem apostolorum,* "though they had seen no great wonders, nor any of the apostles" (*In ep. ad Rom.,* prologue).

Even though we are not able to establish who brought the gospel to Rome (but see Acts 2:10), we can suppose with relative security that it first took root among the Jewish communities that had already for some time belonged to the diverse ethnic and religious geography of the capital. This is not the place to dwell at length on Roman Jewry in the first century, recalling only that by the year 70 their number may have reached about twenty thousand (thirty thousand at the most) and that other Romans were much aware of their presence in the City.[5]

A fundamental text for this period is the report of C. Suetonius Tranquillus according to which the emperor Claudius *Iudaeos impulsore Chresto assidue tumultuantis Roma expulit,* "expelled the Jews from Rome when they were in great ferment at the instigation of a Chrestus" (*Cl.* 25). While unable to discuss this text here,[6] I should only want to say that of the two dates proposed, I am tempted to reject the later one (49 A.D.) and adopt the earlier (41). In either case, we observe that Christianity is already present in Rome in the forties and is even able to arouse lively discussions, provoking immediate disciplinary intervention by the emperor. Above all, we observe that the dissents about Christian issues affect none other than the Jews of the capital, a clear sign that as already in Palestine and then in several centers of the diaspora the source of Christianity and its cradle were the Jews of the City. We observe, moreover, that at this time there is no clear distinction between Jews and Christians (contrary to what will happen after the great fire of Rome in July 64: see Tacitus, *Ann.* 15:44).

---

5. See chap. 2.

6. See R. Penna, *L'ambiente storico-culturale delle origini cristiane. Una documentazione ragionata* (Bologna, 1991³) 277-279. [See now Dixon Slingerland, "Suetonius *Claudius* 25.4 and the Account in Cassius Dion," JQR 79 (1988-89) 305-322.—T.P.W.]

II. The fifties

The first document concerning the Roman Church dates to this decade. It is not something produced by this Church; rather, it comes to the Church from outside. It is, of course, the letter of Paul to the Romans, addressed "to all God's beloved in Rome, called to be holy" (1:7), datable between 55 and 58. From this letter we can recognize elements of judgment against the community. It is already significant to note that the Apostle is writing to a Church that he did not found; it is therefore not a Pauline community in the strict sense, and the discussion about justification on the basis of works or on the basis of faith was in all probability originally foreign to them. But it is precisely here that we encounter the problem of the "confessional" configuration of the Roman Church insofar as it can be perceived from what Paul writes.

No one today follows the old opinion of F. Chr. Baur[7] that the Roman Church in the fifties was entirely Jewish in origin, and that Paul wrote an anti-Jewish exposition of the gospel to emancipate it from its particularism. But equally unacceptable is the contrary opinion that this Church was composed completely of Christians of pagan origin.[8] Nor is there enough evidence to affirm, as does a frequently cited study of W. Wiefel,[9] that when the Jews returned to Rome from their expulsion (under Nero from 54 on), they found a Christian community organized as a gentile Christian group; such a historical reconstruction is in fact totally hypothetical.

Equally unfounded, in my opinion, is the position of U. Wilckens,[10] who would have the first Christians of Rome belonging to the group of "Hellenists" of Stephen (see Acts 6:1f.) and specifically to the "freedmen" of Acts 6:9 (descendants of the Jews enslaved by Pompei in 63 B.C. and later emancipated), who would have returned to Rome after the martyrdom of Stephen. Not only is this pure hypothesis, but the text of Acts says that the synagogue of the freedmen (along with that of the Cyrenians, the Alexandrians, the Cilicians, and the Asians) furiously opposed Stephen's position. Therefore, even in the hypothesis that Roman Christianity origi-

7. "Über Zweck und Veranlassung des Römerbriefes und der damit zusammenhängenden Verhältnisse der römischen Gemeinde," TZTh (1836) 59–178.
8. See J. Munck, *Paul and the Salvation of Mankind* (Atlanta, 1977) chap. 7, "The Manifesto of Faith," 196–209 = *Paulus und die Heilsgeschichte* (Copenhagen, 1954) 190–203, "Das Manifest des Glaubens."
9. "Die jüdische Gemeinschaft im antiken Rom und die Anfänge des römischen Christentums," *Judaica* 26 (1970) 65–88 ("The Jewish Community in Ancient Rome and the Origins of Roman Christianity," in K. P. Donfried, ed., *The Romans Debate* (Minneapolis, 1977) 100–119.
10. U. Wilckens, *Der Brief an die Römer (Röm 1-5)* EKK VI/1 (Einsiedeln-Neukirchen-Vluyn, 1978) 38.

nated with these freedmen, they cannot be understood in the liberal sense
of Stephen and his companions, but rather in the sense of conservative
Judaism.

It would thus be partly misguided to want to make Rom 14:1–15:13
(taking a position on the tension between the "strong" and the "weak";
see also 11:11-24) as the key to interpretation of the whole letter, in the
sense of discerning within the community a conflict between Christians
of Jewish origin and Christians of pagan origin[11] or a conflict within a community of completely pagan origin.[12] Actually, what right did Paul have
to solve a problem within a Church that he did not even know, if that
was the only purpose of the letter? And then why not hypothesize that
the conflict between the "strong" and the "weak" was completely within
the group of Jewish origin, describing two possible fundamental attitudes?
In point of fact, we must note that if in chapter 11 Paul addresses the gentiles, inviting them not to exalt themselves in comparison with the Jews,
he has in 2:12-29 similarly invited the Jews not to think themselves as
better than the pagans.

To be able to describe the physiognomy of this community, we must
state certain plain and simple facts.

1) The Christian community of Rome is of mixed composition. In Rom
9:24 the Apostle openly recognizes, though in general terms, that God
"has called us not only among the Jews but also among the pagans"; and
while in 2:1 he addresses "whoever you are that pass judgment," in 2:17
he turns in direct address to someone of Jewish origin ("if you boast of
yourself as a Jew and rely on the Law") and does the same in 11:13 for
the counterpart ("Now I am speaking to you gentiles"). How can one say
he's not evenhanded?

2) We must here formulate a principle: Even if the Christians of Rome
in the fifties were mostly of gentile origin, that does not mean that they
lived a liberal and anti-Jewish type of Christianity. It would indicate only
their ethnic, not their "confessional," identity. We must always consider
the possibility, by no means theoretical, of a conversion from paganism
that does not at all reject Judaism, at least in certain of its practices and
in the value of acknowledging the Law.[13] At Rome this is all the more

11. See H. W. Bartsch, "Die historische Situation des Römerbriefes," StEv 4 (1968) 282–291;
E. Käsemann, *Commentary on Romans* (Grand Rapids, Mich., 1980) 365–366 = *An die Römer*,
HzNT 8a (Tübingen, 1980⁴) 388f. (even though he adds the motif of the relationship to Jerusalem); C. E. B. Cranfield, *A Commentary on Romans*, I, ICC (Edinburgh, 1975) 18–21.
12. See U. Wilckens, *Der Brief*, 39f.
13. This is in fact attested toward the end of the first century by the satirical poet Juvenal
(*Sat.* XIV 96–106; cf. vv. 100f.: the Romans *Romanas autem soliti contemnere leges / Iudaicum*

plausible insofar as the Christian community is certainly not founded by Paul, nor even less by John (see 15:22-24).[14]

3) It is of utmost importance to put the letter in its historical context, and not to see it as an abstract dogmatic tract. Even if this letter bears more signs than the others of being reworked, we must still not neglect its occasional dimension, which sheds light on its concrete purpose. It is not written only to anticipate a planned journey to Spain and to ask the Romans for help in this (see 15:24-25); if that were the case, what would be the point of the whole theological and soteriological discussion so amply developed through so many pages?

We would have to say the same if Paul simply wanted to give the Romans his own point of view regarding the gospel, to provide a balanced synthesis of his own thought for no other purpose. Rather, the Apostle writes just as he is about to depart for Jerusalem rather than for Rome (15:25-27: to carry there the collection gathered in Macedonia and Achaia). He feels great trepidation on the eve of this voyage. And he asks the Romans directly to fight along with him through their prayers (15:30), "that I may be delivered from the disobedient in Judea and that my service for Jerusalem may be acceptable to the saints" (15:31). And Luke, who of course writes *post eventum*, has him say at Miletus, "I am on my way to Jerusalem. What will happen to me there I know not, but the holy Spirit . . . has been warning me that imprisonment and hardships await me" (Acts 20:22, 23).

Now, a consensus is finally developing regarding the precise intention of the Letter to the Romans: to anticipate for the Jews of Rome his own defense, which the Apostle would want to mount in Jerusalem before the conservative leaders of that Church (James and his elders), developing at some length his own thought about the Christian mystery.[15] To do this,

---

ediscunt et servant ac metuunt ius: "The Romans, who usually disdain Roman laws, learn, keep, and fear the Jewish Law") and by the historian Dio Cassius (*Hist.* LXVII 14: ἄλλοι εἰς τὰ τῶν Ἰουδαίων ἤθη ἐξοκέλλοντες πολλοί: "Many . . . drifted into Jewish ways"); also Suetonius (*Dom.* 12,2: qui vel[ut] inprofessi judaicam viverent vitam: "who lived a Jewish life without acknowledging it").

14. Unfortunately this is not sufficiently noted when the composition of the Roman community is treated; e.g., see G. Bornkamm, *Paul, Paulus*, trans. D. M. G. Stalker (New York, 1971) 88–89; H. Schlier, *Der Römerbrief*, HthKNT VI (Freiburg-Basel-Vienna, 1977) 5. On the other hand, see K. Kertelge, "Rechtfertigung" bei Paulus, NA NF (Münster i. W., 1967) 74: "It is completely possible to consider the Christian community in Rome to have had a very strong Judeo-Christian cast, in fact even predominantly so. . . . One is inclined to describe the earliest Christianity in Rome as an outstanding example of Jewish Christianity."

15. See J. Jervell, "The Letter to Jerusalem," in K. P. Donfried, ed., *The Romans Debate* (Minneapolis, Minn., 1977) 61–74 = "Der Brief nach Jerusalem. Über Veranlassung und Adresse der Römerbriefs," StTh 25 (1971) 61–73; G. Bornkamm, "Romans as Paul's Testament," *Paul*,

Paul revises and attenuates his previous polemical positions on the value
and function of the Law, positions previously expressed in the Letter to
the Galatians, when he had to confront ultraconservative Jewish-Christian
opponents. We cannot here do a comparative analysis, which has in any
case been done by others, to whose studies we refer the reader.[16] The
Apostle thus writes to Rome, but with an eye on Jerusalem. And he writes
to seek (and not in a very veiled manner) the support and favor of the
Roman Christians, as one could surmise from the long catalogue of friends'
names given in chapter 16, like a list of character references whom the
Church of Rome can consult to assure themselves of the true identity of
the writer and his trustworthiness—a practice never followed in letters to
Churches that he had founded himself.

Now the reason for such an appeal to the Roman Church for help can
only be the close relationship of this community with the Mother Church
of Jerusalem, by which it had most likely been founded, and with which
it must have maintained good relations (see Acts 28:21) of loyalty, if not
of obedience.[17] The provisional conclusion is, then, that the Christian community of Rome in the fifties conformed to a moderate Jewish Christianity,
to which the Apostle is in fact paying homage.

III. The sixties to the eighties

Unfortunately we have no direct information about any reaction to
Paul's document among the Christians (or the Jews) of Rome, nor about
the internal evolution of that Church in the next few decades. The only
document that can be attributed with relative security to this Church is
the so-called First Letter of Peter. I say "so-called" because many authors
consider this a pseudonymous writing by a Judeo-Christian disciple of
Peter, who knows Greek well and belongs to the last decades of the first

Paulus, 88–96 = "Der Römerbrief als Testament des Paulus," in *Gesammelte Aufsätze*, IV
(Munich, 1974) 120–139; [see also G. Bornkamm, "The Letter to the Romans as Paul's Last
Will and Testament," in *The Romans Debate*, 17–31—T. P. W.]; E. Käsemann, *Commentary on
Romans*, 403–406 = *An die Römer*, 389f.; U. Wilckens, *Der Brief*, 43–46.

16. The evolution of the theme is studied especially by H. Hübner, *Das Gesetz bei Paulus*,
FRLANT 119 (Göttingen, 1978) (see 129: the phrase of Rom 10:4, "Christ is the end of the
Law," could also serve as a title for Galatians but would mean: "Christ is the end of the
Mosaic Law," while in Romans it means only: "Christ is the end of the carnal abuse of
the Law"); U. Wilckens, "Zur Entwicklung des paulinischen Gesetzesverständnisses," NTS
28 (1982) 154–190; R. E. Brown, *Antioch and Rome*, 111–114; E. P. Sanders, *Paul, the Law, and
the Jewish People* (Philadelphia, 1983) 148f.

17. R. E. Brown, *Antioch and Rome*, 110f., reports the opinion of Ambrosiaster (ca. 375),
in his commentary on Romans, that the Romans had received the faith *ritu licet iudaico*: "though
with a Jewish bent" (PL 17:46).

century.[18] In any case, the letter is written from "Babylon" (5:13), which is in all probability a symbolic designation of the capital of the Roman Empire current particularly in apocalyptic after the disaster of 70 A.D., the destruction of the Temple.[19] This usage itself already suggests that the writer is of Jewish origin or influence and writes after this date. It is difficult to affirm that the addressees of the letter ("Pontus, Galatia, Cappadocia, Asia, and Bithynia" according to 1:1) shared the same type of Christianity with Rome, having its origins in Jerusalem.[20] Far more certain is the identification of the author as a Christian who is comfortable using two different kinds of speech, and in this is surely reflecting the character of the community, especially as the author writes as one having authority.

1) On the one hand we note a Judaizing perspective, albeit not very pronounced. See above for the use of the term "Babylon." Also the formula of the address (1:1: "to the chosen sojourners of the diaspora in Pontus . . .") has only one parallel, the analogous formula in the most Judaizing of the New Testament writings, the Letter of James (1:1). Moreover, especially in the first two chapters the writer works a kind of counterpoint, associating events and situations of the Old Testament with the Christian life, thus giving evidence not only of acquaintance with the earlier Scriptures but also an implied judgment concerning their enduring validity to illuminate various aspects of Christian identity (for example, compare the image in 1:13 of "girding the loins of one's mind" with Exod 12:11, and the description of Christ and his blood in 1:19 "as of a spotless unblemished lamb" with Exod 12:5-7; furthermore, in 1:16 we have the only New Testament use of the typical levitical command [Lev 11:44, 45; 19:2; 20:7], "Be holy because I am holy.")

2) But on the other hand it is surely important to recognize in this writing a typically Pauline legacy characterized by a moderate Paulinism. We recognize it even in certain expressions that are otherwise exclusive to the Apostle (such as ἐν Χριστῷ: 3:16; 5:10, 14; πνεῦμα Χριστοῦ: 1:11; the verb

18. See the treatment of the question in the commentaries, as well as the New Testament introductions, of A. George and P. Grelot (vol. 3 [Paris, 1977] 268–271) and A. Wikenhauser and J. Schmid (Freiburg-Basel-Vienna, 1973) 598–602. [Note that this 1973 revision by Schmid, unlike the 1958 English edition, no longer considers the letter contemporaneous with Peter.— T. P. W.]

19. See 4 Esdr 3:1-2, 28, 31; 2 Bar 11:1; 67:7; Syb. Or. 5:143; Rev 14:8; 16:19; 17:5f.; 18:2-24. The term can hardly represent Babylon in Mesopotamia (insignificant at the time and never visited by Peter) or the Roman military fortress of the same name near Memphis (today's Old Cairo; see Fl. Josephus, *Ant. Jud.* 2:315).

20. Thus R. E. Brown, *Antioch and Rome*, 130–132; however, to some extent these regions were evangelized by Paul.

καλεῖν to designate the fundamental divine call: 1:15; 2:9, 21; 3:9; 5:10),
but also in the similar way in which it conceives the salvific value of Christ's
death (2:24: "so that, living no longer for sin, we might live for righteousness"; the phrase recalls the text of Rom 6:11, 18 almost verbatim); in
the theme of confidence in God, who has raised Jesus from the dead
(1:21; cf. Rom 4:18-24); in the use of a certain spiritualized cultic-priestly
language (2:5, 9) that corresponds to the Letter to the Romans, the richest
among the Pauline letters in this sense (cf. Rom 1:9; 3:25; 12:1; 15:16);
and finally in the appeal to be subject to political authorities (2:13-17; cf.
Rom 13:1-7).[21]

Other possible documents of this period could be the Gospel according to Mark and the so-called Letter to the Hebrews; but their use for our
purposes is too problematic. In the first case, although Mark is probably
associated with the Church of Rome (see Papias in Eusebius, *Hist. eccl.*
3:39:15; Irenaeus, *Adv. haer.* 3:1:1; Clement of Alexandria in Eusebius, *Hist.
eccl.* 2:15:2; the anti-Marcionite prologue: *In partibus Italiae*); we cannot draw
much from his Gospel to understand the Roman Church, and this is further complicated by the difficulty of distinguishing tradition from redaction.[22] As for Hebrews, while it may have been written from Rome or
addressed to Rome, the hypothesis is too uncertain. Besides this, we must
consider the poor reception the letter had precisely in Rome till the end
of the fourth century (while known to Clement of Rome [1 Clem 36], it
was not mentioned in the Roman Muratorian Canon, and it is only Pope
Damasus who will include it in the biblical canon; in the East it will have
better luck).[23]

Therefore the conclusion we reach even from 1 Peter alone is that the
letter of Paul to the Romans did in certain ways resonate positively with
the Romans, but that the community on the whole and especially its leaders
remained partially faithful to its own moderately Judaizing tradition (see
even in 1 Peter the absence of the typical Pauline opposition between faith
and works.)[24]

21. R. E. Brown's observation is interesting; he notes that the only two personal names
occurring in the letter ("Sylvanus" in 5:12 and "Mark" in 5:13) are both associated in the
New Testament with Jerusalem and with Paul alike (*Antioch and Rome*, 134–135).
22. Still, see R. E. Brown, *Antioch and Rome*, 191–201.
23. Still, see R. E. Brown, *Antioch and Rome*, 139–158. I find his opinion stimulating. According to this, the letter was addressed to the Church of Rome but was never accepted there
with much enthusiasm because of the radical separation from levitical cult that it advocates,
whereas Rome, in accord with its own original Jewish origin, would tend to want somehow
to salvage this cult. See also M. Mees, "Die Hohepriester-Theologie des Hebräerbriefes im
Vergleich mit dem ersten Clemensbrief," BZ 22 (1978) 115–124.
24. On the persistence of Paulinism, see A. Lindemann, *Paulus im ältesten Christentum.
Das Bild des Apostels und die Rezeption der paulinischen Theologie in der frühchristlichen Literatur
bis Marcion*, BhTh 58 (Tübingen, 1979) 72–82, 252–261 (on 1 Clement and 1 Peter respectively).

IV. The nineties

At the end of the first century the Roman Church produces a long, authoritative document, of immense significance, revealing this Church's theological and ecclesial character; this is the Letter to the Corinthians, attributed to Clement.[25] The writer is culturally if not ethnically of Hellenistic Jewish origin; various scholars have identified him more with the Hellenism or the Judaism.[26] In any case, for scientific honesty we must observe that the author never uses the personal name nor speaks on personal authority, but hides anonymously behind a community; in fact, the sender is thus identified in the *incipit:* "The Church of God that dwells as a guest (παροικοῦσα) at Rome to the Church of God that dwells as a guest at Corinth," and invariably uses the first person plural in the text.

Moreover, the letter implies a practical and theoretical equivalence between priests and bishops (especially in 44:4-5; cf. 42:4; 54:2), and the position of R. Brown seems quite secure to me when he suggests that the three-part hierarchical order bishops-priests-deacons was not yet practiced at the end of the first century in Rome, where the double division, priests (bishops)-deacons was already implied some years before in 1 Pet 5:1-5.[27] This in no way detracts from the fact that the Church of Rome, heir to Peter and Paul alike (see 1 Clem 5), considered itself obliged to intervene in another Church with fraternal authority, exercising a function that we should describe not so much in the juridical terms of a later understanding of primacy as in the pastoral terms of naturally assuming a responsibility to show the apostolic care proper to Peter and Paul, who had both died at Rome, addressing both the Jewish and pagan sides of the first Christian mission.

In developing these observations on ecclesial structure, it is important to note the elements of continuity and especially of evolution from what

25. Current dating would put it in 96–98, after the death of Emperor Domitian (see, for example, P. F. Beatrice, "Clement of Rome," in *Encyclopedia of the Early Church*, I (Cambridge, 1992) 181. The attribution to "Clement" goes back to Dionysius, bishop of Corinth, around 170 A.D. (see Eusebius, *Eccl. Hist.* 4:23:11; also Irenaeus, *Adv. haer.* 3:3:3; and earlier but less precise, *Past. Herm.*, Vis. 2:4:3).

26. For Judaism alone, J. Daniélou, *Théologie du Judéo-christianisme* (Paris, 1958) 53–55; L. W. Barnard, "The Early Roman Church. Judaism and Jewish Christianity," *AnglThRev* 49 (1967) 371-384. For Hellenism, see L. Sanders, *L'Hellénisme de Saint Clément de Rome et le Paulinisme* (Louvain, 1943). For the use of the Bible, see D. A. Hagner, *The Use of the Old and New Testament in Clement of Rome* (Leiden, 1973).

27. *Antioch and Rome*, 163–164. Not even Ignatius of Antioch, *Ad Rom.*, mentions a single bishop; and also the Shepherd of Hermas speaks of the presbyters (Vis. 2:4:2) and bishops (Sim. 9:24:2) in the plural. "In speaking of Linus, Anacletus, and Clement as if they were single bishops of Rome, then, Irenaeus and later authors would simply have been assuming that a structure known in their own times was functional at an earlier period" (*Antioch and Rome*, 164).

we perceive in the earlier writings, Romans and 1 Peter. Setting aside for the moment the obvious references to both these letters,[28] which must therefore have been known to the author of our letter, we attend to the nature of the response that 1 Clement offers to the problem that has arisen in Corinth. There some presbyters-bishops had been removed from their ministerial, or more accurately, their liturgical office (ἐκ τῆς λειτουργίας: 44:6), which they had exercised honorably and blamelessly. Perceiving in this dismissal a sign and a risk of further instability within the Church, "Clement" intervenes, recalling his addressees not only to love (citing in 49:5 the text of 1 Cor 13) but above all to "peace and concord" (62:3), invoking the necessity of an "order" that must reign supreme. Precisely this concept of τάξις (40:1) or τάγμα (41:1) stands at the heart of the letter and, as the text proceeds, is propounded repeatedly and insistently by appealing to certain images: of the cosmos (19:2–20:12, with Stoic resonances), of political-military aspects of the empire (37:1-4), of the human body (37:5), and of the ancient levitical priesthood.

Recourse to this last pattern eloquently shows more than the others how far the Roman Church has gone beyond the terms of the Letter to the Romans and the First Letter of Peter (not to mention the Letter to the Hebrews!). This happens not only at the level of the conception of ministry, equating the dignity of the ecclesial functions with the honor of the functions of the Israelite priesthood,[29] but also in the very manner of understanding precisely the exercise of the ministry. This is now conceived on the basis of an ever less spiritualized conceptualization of cult. Affirmations like 40:2 ("We accomplish all the sacred ceremonies [προσφορὰς καὶ λειτουργίας, 'offerings and services'] that the Lord enjoined on us at the proper time and in orderly manner") and 44:4 (concerning those who have been promoted to the ἐπισκοπή, who "have *offered the oblations* [προσενεγκόντας τὰ δῶρα] with holiness and perfection") already stand at a good distance from texts like Rom 12:1 and 1 Pet 2:5 (not to say Heb 10:10-12, 18: "There is no longer offering for sin"!), which spoke only of "spiritual sacrifices." We here note the tendency that will gain ground, growing ever more explicit, to treat the ecclesial orders "bishop, priest, deacon," as parallel to the ancient Jewish "high priest, priest, levite" (see 40-42),

---

28. See Hagner, *The Use*, 214–220 and 239–248; Brown, *Antioch and Rome*, 167.

29. In 42:5 the text of Isa 60:17 is applied to the Christian ministers, not according to the Masoretic Text ("I shall make your sovereign peace, your governor justice"), but according to the LXX ("I shall establish their overseers [ἐπισκόπους] in justice, and their servants [διακόνους] in faith").

through which many Jewish cultic elements reappeared—and not just surreptitiously—within the Church, and not the Roman Church alone.[30]

These observations are of interest to us to verify once again how much the Church of Rome from its beginning remained tied to theological conceptions and religious institutions molded in Judaism. This is not the forum in which to discuss the legitimacy of historical selection and evolution, which, after all, demonstrate the profound incarnation (inculturation) of Christ and of the community of his disciples. Here we have merely established, with sufficient plausibility, I believe, the real but restrained Judeo-Christian character of the first-century Church of Rome. For our own days we can at least pose the following question: Has this Church been in the course of centuries, does it remain today, aware of and loyal to its original characteristic bond with Judaism? And this simply to remain faithful to Christ, who "became a minister of the circumcised . . . to confirm the promises to the ancestors" (Rom 15:8).

30. One could also insist on the vision of a well-ordered Church, which 1 Clement conceives in the style of the order and discipline that characterize the Roman Empire politically and militarily (cf. 37:1-4), going well beyond a simple loyalty to constituted authorities (see 61), but rather representing at least a tendency to appropriate the same patterns.

Chapter 4

The Structural Function of 3:1-8
in the Letter to the Romans

The letter of Saint Paul to the Romans contains certain passages whose boundaries can be clearly identified. These pertain to the epistolary form of the work or else to some obvious expository unity in the discourse. To the first class belong the opening (1:1-7), the initial thanksgiving (1:8-15), the final notices and greetings (15:14–16:23, with the probably inauthentic addition of 16:25-27). The latter is found in 12:1–15:13, in which, because of the subject matter as well as the initial formula (12:1: παρακαλῶ οὖν ὑμᾶς, ἀδελφοί, "so I beseech you"), there is universal agreement in identifying the paraenetic section of the letter. Thus, from the structural point of view, these present no problem.

Here we will be treating the great block 1:16–11:36, where the task of identifying the structure is considerably more difficult.

I. *Status quaestionis*

The structure of the first twelve chapters of Romans has been the object of numerous studies. Identification of the structure is determinative not only for stylistic-literary purposes, to recognize Paul's ability to outline and formally elaborate an epistolary text, but even more so for purposes of theme and content, to understand how the Apostle articulates his thought: where his *caesurae* are to be found, where his emphases, progressions, references, and correlations. The attempt is more difficult in Romans than in the other letters because of its extent, its richness, and even the calmness of its language, which owes less of its structuring to the polemic than do other Pauline letters.

This specific difficulty has even led certain authors to maintain that the letter reveals no logical structure, but only presents more or less unrelated

lines of thought following each other, perhaps only on the basis of fundamental theological themes, treating the great concepts of justice, divine
election, the cross of Christ, sin, faith, Spirit, *eschaton,* etc.[1] Similarly,
certain commentators fail to attribute a logical role to chapters 9-11 and
treat them as something independent, as an excursus not integrated with
the rest of the letter.[2] In the same line, certain scholars deny the original
literary unity of the epistle, seeing it rather as a redactional composition
of more than one Pauline writing[3] or else the result of a conflation already
done by Paul himself, joining two distinct homilies that he had pronounced
in different circumstances.[4]

On the opposite side stands anyone who would see in Romans an
organic structure according to a relatively systematic doctrinal point of
view. We have certain attempts of this type. Thus A. Feuillet, who subdivides Rom 1:16-11:36 into two parts: 1:16-8:39 presents God's saving
plan and the fate of the individual, while 9-11 presents God's saving plan
and the fate of the Israelite people.[5] Meanwhile, S. Lyonnet, who provided

1. See, in part, J. Jeremias, "Zur Gedankenführung in den paulinischen Briefen," *Studia
Paulina, in honorem J. de Zwaan* (Haarlem, 1953) 146-154, esp. 146-149, who does not propose
a true structure but correctly emphasizes the *Gesprächscharakter* ("conversational character")
of the letter; also J. Dupont, "Le problème de la structure littéraire de l'épître aux Romains,"
RB 62 (1955) 365-397, sees the treatment of the theme announced in 1:16-17 to be exhausted
by chapter 5, while in chapters 6-11 Paul is dealing with certain difficulties raised by his teaching: sin (6:1-7:6), the Law (7:7-8:39), Israel's destiny (9-11), appended as three supplemen-
tary explanations. See also F. Montagnini, *La prospettiva storica della Lettera ai Romani. Esegesi
su Rm 1-4*, SB 54 (Brescia, 1980) 27-28.
2. Thus C. H. Dodd, *The Epistle of Paul to the Romans,* The Moffatt New Testament (London,
1932; 1941[8] = 1959); also more recently, H. Schlier, *Der Römerbrief,* HThKNT VI (Freiburg-
Basel-Vienna, 1977) 282, maintains that 9:1-11:36 seems to have "almost no real continuity
with the argument of 1:18-8:39"; see also F. Refoulé, "Unité de l'Épître aux Romains et histoire
du salut," RSPhTh 71 (1987) 219-242.
3. Thus W. Schmithals, *Der Römerbrief als historisches Problem,* SNT 9 (Gütersloh, 1975);
in 5:1-11 he sees a fragment derived from the Thessalonian correspondence (and marginal
glosses of diverse provenance in 2:1, 13; 6:17b; 7:25b; 8:1; 10:17); when it comes to the body
of chapters 1-11, he identifies the theme enunciated in 1:16-17, which is then treated in three
sections (1:18-3:20; 3:21-4:25; 5:12-21), which are followed by two excursuses (6:1-23; 7:1-
16), an independent dogmatic compendium (7:17-8:39), and an appendix (9-11).
4. Thus R. Scroggs, "Paul as Rhetorician: Two Homilies in Romans 1-11," *Jews, Greeks
and Christians. Religious Cultures in Late Antiquity. Essays in Honour of W. D. Davies,* ed. R. G.
Hamerton-Kelly and R. Scroggs (Leiden, 1976) 271-298. The two homilies would be (1) chapters 1-4 + 9-11 on the meaning of the history of Israel (from the point of view of the justice
of God; 3:21-26 "reads almost like an intrusion into the context": 276, n. 16); and (2) chapters 5-8 on the new life in Christ (with a subdivision into nine small units). Paul would have
inserted the one in the other because if he had just put one after the other, the letter would
have had no unity, and because with the rabbinic technique of *gezerah shawah,* it must be
clear that the justification recognized for Abraham was recognized all the more for all Christians. On this proposal see a series of critical observations in Th. Schmeller, *Paulus und die
"Diatribe." Eine vergleichende Stilinterpretation,* NA NF 19; (Münster, 1987) 287, n. 6.
5. "Le plan salvifique de Dieu d'après l'Épître aux Romains," RB 57 (1950) 333-387, 489-529.
In the first part the author even discovers a Trinitarian perspective: in 1:18-5:11 he would
see that the justifying intervention of the Father follows the situation of the Fall; in 5:12-7:6

the division of the text of Romans in the *Bible de Jérusalem,* believes in a
thematic structure in two strictly corresponding parts: 1:16–4:25 treats
justification based on God's justice, and 5–11 treats salvation based on
God's love.[6] A. Descamps upholds a similar position, distinguishing two
antithetical centers of interest: in 1:18–3:20 the revelation of the wrath of
God, and in 3:21–11:36 the message of salvation.[7]

These proposals presuppose Paul to have the mentality of Aristotelian
or Scholastic logic, which would totally favor content over form; they do
not even question whether it may not be form that governs content. For
example, the rare Pauline expression δικαιοσύνη θεοῦ (αὐτοῦ), "God's righteousness," in Romans is found only in 1:17; 3:5, 21, 22, 25, 26 and then
twice in 10:3; how is it possible, then, to isolate a homogeneous block of
chapters 9–11 rather than recognize a correlation between the two places
where the phrase occurs? Systematic-doctrinal structures are no longer
accepted today, at least not in their grosser forms. But they still will be
proposed by some commentators, though in more modest and tentative
form. Thus E. Käsemann[8] builds his whole commentary on the concept
of *Gottesgerechtigkeit,* "the righteousness of God," to which in fact all the
sections of the letter get reduced: (1:18–3:20: the need for the revelation
of the righteousness of God; 3:21–4:25: the righteousness of God as the
righteousness of faith; 5:1–8:39: the righteousness of faith as a reality of
eschatological freedom; 9:1–11:36: the righteousness of God and the problem of Israel; 12:1–15:13: the righteousness of God in daily Christian life).
Meanwhile C. E. B. Cranfield[9] divides the letter organically on the basis
of the declaration of 1:16b-17 ("the righteous by faith": 1:18–4:25; "will
live": 5:1–8:39; "for the Jew first": 9–11).

The attempts of Ramaroson and Rolland move in the same direction.
The former[10] has the ingenuity to identify three outlines, allowing us to

---

the Son is protagonist as the mediator of salvation; in 7:7–8:39 the action of the Holy Spirit
comes to the fore.

6. "Note sur le plan de l'Épître aux Romains," *Mélanges J. Lebreton* = RSR 39 (1951–52)
I, 301–316; *Quaestiones in epistolam ad Romanos. Series altera: Rm 9–11,* ad usum privatum (Rome,
1975³) 7–12: each of the two parts is constructed on a thesis: (1:16-17 and 5:1-11 respectively),
which is followed by the exposition of an antithetic situation (1:18–3:20 and 5:12–7:25), the
development of the thesis (3:21-31 and 8:1-39), a scriptural proof (4:1-25 and 9:1–11:36).

7. "La structure de Rm 1–11," *Studiorum Paulinorum Congressus Internationalis Catholicus
1961,* AB 17 (Rome, 1963) 3–14: according to this, Rom 3:21–11:36 contains three dogmatic
declarations: (1) on God's justice (3:21-31), followed by a primarily biblical demonstration
(chap. 4); (2) a synthesis of Paul's gospel (chap. 5), followed by a primarily dialectical demonstration (chaps. 6–7); (3) on the spiritual condition of the Christian (chap. 8), followed by a
demonstration that is both biblical and dialectical (chaps. 9–11).

8. *Commentary on Romans* (Grand Rapids, Mich., ca. 1980) = *An die Römer,* HzNT 8a (Tübingen, 1973: 1980⁴).

9. *A Critical and Exegetical Commentary on the Epistle to the Romans,* I–II, ICC (Edinburgh,
1975–79).

10. "Un 'nouveau plan' de Rm 1:16–11:36," NRTh 94 (1972) 943–958.

articulate the letter from three different points of view. One outline identifies four categories of people, each of which provides the content of one section of the letter (Greeks and Jews in 1:18–3:31; Abraham in 4:1-22; we the believers in 4:23–8:39; and all Israel in 9–11). The second outline is at the base of the principal division of Romans: the situation without faith in 1:18–3:20, and the situation with faith in 3:21–11:36. The third outline is temporal and allows for a subdivision of the second part: the past in 4:1-22; the present in 4:23–8:39; the eschatological future in 9–11.

Rolland[11] sees the thesis of the letter in 1:16-17, according to which the power of God manifested in the gospel brings three fundamental benefits, presented in three sections of the letter corresponding to the third outline of Ramaroson: the gospel is at the origin of our righteousness in 1–4 (corresponding to the past time of the Law and the promise), of our life in 5–8 (corresponding to the present time of grace and adoption), of our salvation in 9–11 (corresponding to the future time of mercy and fullness); upon these, then, follows the ethical encouragement in 12:1ff.

These attempts, useful as they may be, are characterized by an excessive elaboration of the themes of Romans; while they bring to light certain basic aspects, we get the impression that their proponents are not sticking objectively to the Apostle's reasoning but actually attribute to him a discovery of their own, or at least their own need for, theological synthesis.[12]

More recently another type of approach to Romans has been tried, based on the study of ancient rhetoric, especially by W. Wuellner and R. Jewett.[13] They classify the letter in the genre of epideictic or demonstrative discourse, perceiving in it the structure assigned to this genre by classical rhetoricians as systematized by Quintilian. This would consist of six parts, the fifth of which, however, is apparently omitted by Paul: the

11. Ph. Rolland, " 'Il est notre justice, notre vie, notre salut.' L'ordonnance des thèmes majeurs de l'Épître aux Romains," Bib 56 (1975) 394-404; *Épître aux Romains. Texte grec structuré* (Rome, 1980).

12. Actually one could theoretically add more outlines to the three of Ramaroson: for example, a Trinitarian outline (cf. Feuillet), one on the relation between faith and ethic, or between word and sacrament, or between Law and Spirit, etc. As for Rolland, his subdivision is surely too rigid, since the theme of justice appears also in the third part (9:30–10:10), that of salvation in the second (5:9f.; 8:24), and that of life in the first (2:7; 4:17) as well.

13. See W. Wuellner, "Paul's Rhetoric of Argumentation in Romans," CBQ 38 (1976) 330-351; "Paul's Rhetoric of Argumentation in Romans: An Alternative to the Donfried-Karris Debate," *The Romans Debate*, ed. K. P. Donfried (Minneapolis, 1977) 152-174; R. Jewett, "Romans as an Ambassadorial Letter," Int 36 (1982) 5-20; "Following the Argument of Romans," *Word and World* 6 (1986) 382-389. In general, see U. Ruegg, "Paul et la Rhétorique ancienne," *Bulletin du Centre Protestant d'Etudes* 35 (1983) 5-35; B. L. Mack, *Rhetoric and the New Testament* (Minneapolis, 1990). The position of F. Siegert was original, *Argumentation bei Paulus, gezeigt an Röm 9–11*, WUNT 34 (Tübingen, 1985), distinguishing three levels: semantic, pragmatic, and syntactic (see 112ff.).

exordium, 1:1-12; *narratio*, 1:13-15; *propositio*, 1:16-17; *probatio*, 1:18–15:13 (this in turn consists here in a *confirmatio*, 1:18–4:25, which will be enlarged in three amplifications, 5:1–8:39; 9:1–11:36; 12:1–15:13; the equivalent of the *refutatio*, which is the fifth part of the rhetorical discourse, is represented in these sections); finally the *peroratio*, 15:14–16:23. However, we can raise three objections to such an analysis; these have already been made by H. D. Betz in his commentary on Galatians.[14]

1) First of all, there is no resolving the question whether Paul was actually educated in the laws of rhetoric, and hence whether he consciously modeled his letter on a contemporary rhetorical pattern. In fact, while born at Tarsus in Cilicia (which, according to Strabo 14:5:13, was then experiencing great excitement for philosophy and for every branch of learning), he was "brought up" and "educated" in Jerusalem (Acts 22:3) as "a Pharisee" (Phil 3:5). And although we must be aware that a Hellenization of Palestinian Judaism had taken place, it is just as true that there was a reaction against this already in the second century before Christ with the movement of *ḥasidîm* and that the first century of the present era was influenced more by Hellenistic exegetical methodology than by the technique of constructing discourse.[15] Furthermore, while not wanting to overemphasize 2 Cor 11:6, where the Apostle admits being ἰδιώτης τῷ λόγῳ, "unskilled at words," it is significant that the apocryphal "Letters between Seneca and Paul,"[16] a work showing great sensitivity to questions of form, should lament Paul's "unpolished speech" (*cultus sermonis . . . desit*, describing Paul explicitly as "one deprived of a proper education" (*non legitime imbutus: Epist. 7*). It would thus seem more reasonable to speak more generally of an unconscious absorption of typical categories of the time without technical training.[17]

14. H. D. Betz, *Galatians: A Commentary on Paul's Letter to the Churches in Galatia*, Hermeneia (Philadelphia, 1979), which assigns Galatians to the apologetic genre.

15. See, for example, R. Riesner, *Jesus als Lehrer*, WUNT 7 (Tübingen, 1981) 181f.

16. *Epistolae Senecae ad Paulum et Pauli ad Senecam "quae vocantur,"* Papers and Monographs of the American Academy in Rome, ed. C. W. Barlow (Rome-Horn, 1938); L. Bocciolini Pagali, *Epistolario apocrifo di Seneca e San Paolo*, Biblioteca Patristica 5 (Florence, 1985).

17. See the judgment of E. Norden, *Die antike Kunstprosa* (Darmstadt, 1974 = 1990²) II, 499, who finds the argumentation of Paul "strange, and not Greek." Saint Augustine also, who had been a teacher of rhetoric (*Confess.* 3:3; 4:2), stated, "Sicut ergo Apostolum praecepta eloquentiae secutum fuisse non dicimus, ita quod eius sapientiam secuta sit eloquentia non negamus" (*De doctrina christ.* 4:7, 11; PL 34:94); before him Origen had affirmed that the apostles did not have "the power of eloquence, nor the arrangement of phrases according to the dialectical or rhetorical doctrines of the Greeks" (*C. Cels.* 1:62). Moreover, in antiquity rhetoric belonged to higher education, which was undertaken after adolescence; where, then, could Paul have learned it? And did his parents have the means to obtain it for him, considering that between the first and second century a rhetorician like Quintilian charged two thousand sestertii per student (Juvenal, *Sat.* 7:186-187); also, this was for the most part considered an alternative to philosophy, and the one who undertook the latter tended to reject the former as a purely esthetic—and calculating—exercise (thus, again, Saint Augustine): see H.-J. Marrou,

2) In the second place, too rigid a rhetorical construction would violate the true genre of the letter. It is true that the ancient conventions of letter writing cannot by themselves resolve the problem of structure except with regard to the specifically epistolary framework.[18] But Paul is not detached from real life in an ivory tower, writing some sample letter constructed artificially after the rules of art! Not even Seneca in his *Letters to Lucilius* follows a predetermined, fixed rhetorical outline. Jewett's attempt to define Romans as an "ambassadorial letter," and therefore as an expression of missionary "diplomacy" to gain the aid of the Roman Church for Paul's mission to Spain,[19] attempts precisely to explain what is specifically characteristic of this letter; nevertheless, he acknowledges that his is only a suggestion, since the references he adduces simply do not amount to a real proof.[20] Moreover, despite the recognized deliberation of Romans as a work of reflection rather than of passion, unlike Galatians, we must still note a certain immediacy to Paul's exposition with two attendant results: a syntax marked by more than one anacoluthon[21] and a style employing the technique of diatribe.[22]

3) In the third place, and most importantly, it would be possible to risk losing sight of the specific content of the letter by emphasizing its supposed rhetorical form. Dunn properly observes that to classify Romans according to rhetorical categories "does not actually advance understanding of the letter very far . . . since the chief force of the letter lies in its distinctive Pauline art and content."[23] Even Wuellner himself subdivides the *confirmatio* (consisting of the body of the letter: 1:18–15:13) into two sections that have nothing to do with the articulation of classical rhetoric: the argumentation in 1:18–11:36 and the paraenesis in 12:1–15:13.[24] This means that Paul's treatment in Romans cannot be reduced to the closely defined trajec-

---

A History of Education in Antiquity, trans. G. Lamb (New York, 1956) 194–216, esp. 210–212 = *Histoire de l'éducation dans l'antiquité* (Paris, 1948) 268–296, esp. 288f. The problematic of this is confirmed by the disagreement among the proponents of rhetorical structure in Romans. The analysis above follows R. Jewett; but W. Wuellner uses different terms and finds only an *exordium* (1:1-15), a *transitus* (1:16-17), a *confirmatio* (1:18–15:13), and a *peroratio* (15:14–16:23); while B. Standaert, *L'évangile selon Marc. Composition et genre littéraire* (Bruges, 1984²) 45, n. 2, suggests seeing in Romans a *narratio* (1:18–4:25), a *probatio* (5–8), and a *refutatio* (9–11).

18. See Wuellner, "Paul's Rhetoric," 334. Note S. K. Stowers, *Letter Writing in Greco-Roman Antiquity* (Philadelphia, 1986): "The classification of letter types according to the three species of rhetoric only partially works. This is because the letter-writing tradition was essentially independent of rhetoric" (52); see also C. J. Classen, "Paulus und die antike Rhetorik," *ZNW* 82 (1991) 1-33.

19. See Jewett, "Romans," 9f.

20. Jewett, "Romans," 12.

21. See G. Bornkamm, "Paulinische Anakolute," *Das Ende des Gesetzes* (Munich, 1952) 76–92.

22. See S. K. Stowers, *The Diatribe and Paul's Letter to the Romans,* SBLDS 57 (Chico, Calif., 1981); Schmeller, *Paulus und die "Diatribe."*

23. J. D. G. Dunn, *Paul's Epistle to the Romans: An Analysis of Structure and Argument,* ANRW II 25/4 (Berlin, 1987) 2842–2890, 2845.

24. See Wuellner, "Paul's Rhetoric," 335–348.

tories of the rhetorical schools but rather blasts them apart. In some way *what* the Apostle wants to say is more important than *how* he says it. The newness of the message bursts open even the outline of a well-established *modus dicendi.*

In all this I certainly do not want to deny the presence in Romans of a framing rhetorical outline. It is perfectly obvious that 1:16-17 functions as a *propositio* (but without a *partitio*) and that there is a structural correspondence between 1:8-15 and 15:14-33. It is the intervening development of thought (1:18-11:36) that causes the problem. This does not conform to any predetermined rhetorical grid; rather, the mechanisms of this development arise from within the thought itself.

The structure of the body of Romans, then, is to be found in itself, prescinding from any preconceived plan. Not that the structure is unimportant—quite the contrary! Much of an author's strategy, whether conscious or unconscious, lies concealed in the construction of the discourse.[25] But this strategy is identified especially through two basic criteria: (1) that of semantics, i.e., the logical evolution of the theme being developed, and (2) that of macrosyntax or of the syntax of the text, i.e., the signs of articulation given by particles, certain stock expressions, form of discourse (direct or indirect), etc. The first of these is the easier—at least it has been done repeatedly by numerous authors, though with very different results! But we simply must note that the structural function of 3:1-8 has been for the most part neglected.[26]

Meanwhile the second standard has been widely ignored. Apart from a few sporadic attempts,[27] one overall proposal has been made in this direction by U. Vanni.[28] Depending on conjunctions (γάρ, διό, διὰ τοῦτο, "therefore," etc.), the use of person in the verb, the recurrence of certain complements, key words, and rhetorical questions (τί οὖν and τι οὖν ἐροῦμεν, "what then?" "what then shall we say?"), he arrives at a four-part structure: 1:16-2:16 (historical situation of sin); 2:17-5:11 (begins with the

25. See Siegert, *Argumentation,* 112.

26. I furthermore consider it to be of some importance in applying this standard to determine to whom this letter was addressed. Knowing whether Romans was addressed to a predominantly gentile-Christian or Jewish-Christian Church helps much to determine the semantic context of Paul's vocabulary. I am myself inclined to consider the Roman Church to have been primarily Jewish Christian rather than gentile Christian, as is commonly thought. See chap. 3 above.

27. See R. Wonneberger, *Syntax und Exegese. Eine generative Theorie der griechischen Syntax und ihr Beitrag zur Auslegung des Neuen Testamentes, dargestellt an 2. Korinther 5,2f und Römer 3:21-26,* BET 13 (Frankfurt a. M, 1979); Siegert, *Argumentation.* These authors address only very specific and limited sections of Romans (3:21-26 and 9:1-11:36 respectively).

28. U. Vanni, "La struttura letteraria della lettera ai Romani (Rm 1:16-11:36," *Parola e Spirito. Studi in onore de S. Cipriani,* I (Brescia, 1982) 439-455.

sin of the Jew, passing through free justification by God, and arriving at the new dimension of the Spirit); 5:12–8:39 (beginning again with the sinful situation, with the contrast of Adam-Christ, passes through baptism, and offers the Christian the possibility of realistically facing the problem of the Law, which is resolved with the alternative of the Spirit as new Law permitting a new way of acting); 9:1–11:36 ("monographic"[29] treatment of the problem of the Jews, still in continuity with the themes of sin and faith): the themes of the first three sections (sinfulness, justification, and appropriate behavior) are applied to the Jews in the fourth section.

This attempt is commendable for the special attention given to the grammatical elements of the speech; however, I am perplexed by the outcome of the structural proposal, which does not attribute to 1:16-17 an importance for the whole, nor does it recognize the change of subject between 3:20 and 3:21; and further it sees a new beginning in 5:12 (after Feuillet) rather than in 6:1 (or in 5:1). In any case, it does not attribute any structural function to 3:1-8, even while Vanni admits that precisely with 3:1 there begin to appear "expressions of transition that set the discourse in motion, making it advance forward."[30]

II. Opinions concerning the function of 3:1-8

More or less all authors observe that 3:1-8 somehow interrupts the logical sequence of the theme that Paul is treating. But they evaluate the meaning of this fact quite differently. For some the passage fits right into the context without interruption, as the Apostle attacks the privileges on which the Jews rely (election, 2:1-11; the Law, 2:12-24; circumcision, 2:25-29; the promises, 3:1-8) in order then to conclude with the equality of Jews and gentiles in sin (3:9-20).[31] But according to others, the pericope diverges far from the main point of the context (1:18–3:20), which is to establish the equality of gentile and Jew in sin; it is therefore a "digression,"[32] which will end with 3:9, where the speech finally gets back on track. But for this

---

29. Vanni, "La struttura," 454.
30. Vanni, "La Struttura," 446.
31. See S. Lyonnet, *Exegesis epistulae ad Romanos: Cap. I ad IV*, ad usum privatum (Rome, 1963³) 158; also the comments of M.-J. Lagrange (who, however, notes on p. 60 how very difficult it is to fit it in), J. Huby, A. Nygren, F.-J. Leenhardt, C. E. B. Cranfield, G. Torti, G. Barbaglio. However, these authors generally indicate a coupling of 3:2 with chapters 9–11.
32. O. Kuss, *Der Römerbrief*, I (Regensburg, 1957) 99; similarly W. Sanday and C. Headlam (75), and H. Lietzmann (45); meanwhile C. H. Dodd (46), while giving reference to 6:1ff. and 9–11, adds that "the argument of the epistle would go much better if this whole section were omitted"! E. Käsemann speaks of a pause for breath ("Atemholen": 78); see also H. Schlier (176: "Paul has rather strayed from the argument"; nevertheless, on p. 463 he indicates the connection with 9–11).

digression no structural justification is given; at most, one recognizes that it just formulates certain objections raised in the preceding chapter 2. However, one author maintains that Paul "never follows out to its conclusion the argument here begun."[33]

On the contrary, other authors perceive in 3:1-8 "something of a bridge between earlier and later parts of the letter, like a railway junction through which many of the key ideas and themes of the epistle pass."[34] Dunn, who expresses himself so well in these terms, never does really show clearly the role of the passage in the structure of Romans. A contradiction thus remains between the intuition that our text fills a decisive structural function and the failure to exploit the suggestion by developing an effective structural proposal for it in Rom 1-11 at least. Other authors there are who handle the passage in the same way, such as P. Althaus,[35] O. Michel,[36] U.Wilckens;[37] and far more coherently, R. Pesch.[38] In this line, besides the plain observations of J. Jeremias,[39] one important study is that of W. S. Campbell,[40] who, however, concentrates attention on 3:21-26 as the central point of Paul's theological argumentation in Romans, to which 3:1-8, 27-31 is subordinated as a formulation of the questions that must be answered, and to which in fact is addressed the solution of Christ's cross in 3:21-26 and in chapters 5 and 8.[41]

III. The relationship of 3:1-8 to the preceding text of the letter

In order to recognize the turning point realized in 3:1, we must see how the discussion develops in the first two chapters of Romans. The letter begins with a salutation in 1:1-7 combining typical elements of ancient epistolary form with an expansion that is quite abnormal with respect to the letter-writing canons of the age, but is on the other hand fully consis-

33. C. K. Barrett, *The Epistle to the Romans*, Black's New Testament Commentaries (London, 1984 = 1957) 62.

34. Dunn, "Paul's Epistle," 2852.

35. *Der Brief an die Römer* (Göttingen, 1932; 1949⁶), which indicates the link between 3:1-4 and 9-11 (pp. 24f.); and between 3:5-8 and 6:1f. (p. 49).

36. *Der Brief an die Römer*, Meyer Kommentar (Göttingen, 1966 = 1955) 221, who, however, establishes a link only with 9-11.

37. *Der Brief an die Römer*, I, EKK VI/1 (Einsiedeln-Neukirchen, 1978) 18-19; II, EKK VI/2 (1980) 181; more than the others he underlines the structural importance of 3:1-8.

38. *Römerbrief*, Neue Echter Bibel (Würzburg, 1983) 11, 37, 76.

39. "Zur Gedankenführung," 146-154; on p. 147 he writes that "the replies to the objections (formulated in 3:1-8) occupy most of the bulk of the first eleven chapters of Romans."

40. "Romans III as a Key to the Structure and Thought of the Letter," NT 23 (1981) 22-40; see p. 32: "The structure of the letter will become clearer to us when we observe the relationship between the questions Paul asks and the answers he gives to them."

41. See "Romans III," 34.

tent in style and themes with the Pauline writings (with the probable presence of traditional elements in 1:3b-4a). In 1:8-15 there follows another formal component typical of the Pauline letter, the initial expression of thanks (at least in vv. 8-9), to which has been smoothly grafted the expression of Paul's vivid desire to visit Rome (in vv. 10-15) for several reasons: to see and get to know the Christians of the capital (11a), to reinforce them in the Christian life (11b), to share their common faith (12), and to preach the gospel to the pagans of the city (13d-15). Linked to this section, then, is 15:14-33, which will add two requests for support for a projected missionary journey to Spain and for an imminent trip to Jerusalem to deliver the collection he has promoted.[42]

Verse 16a is a hinge between what precedes and what follows in vv. 16b-17. For by repeating the affirmation of v. 15 in the form of litotes, v. 16a logically continues the preceding autobiographical section and actually brings it to a head, since at the same time it introduces what follows. Specifically, the term εὐαγγέλιον, "gospel," is here used for the first time in unmodified form (Paul having already professed his personal dedication to the "gospel of God" in 1:1, 9), on the one hand reformulating as a noun the verb εὐαγγελίσασθαι, "preach the gospel," of v. 15, while on the other hand suggesting the need for a general definition of this gospel. This definition is then given in vv. 16b-17, centered on four fundamental concepts: δύναμις θεοῦ, σωτηρία, δικαιοσύνη θεοῦ, πίστις: "God's power," "salvation," "God's righteousness," and "faith."

Here we encounter an enunciation of principle, clearly breaking from the familiar, autobiographical tone of the preceding verses and passing abruptly *in medias res* into what the Apostle means to develop in the letter. Still, the development will go beyond what is here sketched out. Thus, for example, certain concepts that are affirmed of the gospel will describe other realities elsewhere: δύναμις, "power," has already been used in 1:20 to refer not to the gospel itself but to natural theology; and δικαιοσύνη θεοῦ, "God's righteousness," in 3:21-26 is associated not with the preaching of the gospel but with the objective historical event of Christ's sacrifice on the cross. This means that Paul does not adhere rigidly to the subject

42. These two sections (1:8-15 and 15:14-33) function just like two parentheses, containing the body of the letter (1:16–15:13) between their arms. Their function is of utmost importance in determining the purpose of Romans, and in Wuellner's rhetorical approach it is precisely these (the *exordium* or *narratio*, and the *peroratio*) that chiastically support the whole body of the epistle (see Wuellner, "Paul's Rhetoric," 160–161). Their fully concrete reference to the "situation" contravenes any attempt to consider the central block of Romans to be a purely theoretical treatment of the gospel, as if this block were an abstract theological exercise of Paul, with no regard to the internal condition of the Roman Church. See also chap. 5 below.

as he has announced it. Rather, he will proceed with the freedom typical of one who uses words of great semantic density, and as F. de Saussure would say,[43] pays attention more to the object signified than to the significance of the words.

At any rate, it is extremely hard to perceive in this enunciation of the theme any projected division of the development to come.[44] Surely, at least, its delineation of the theme applies only to the first eleven chapters and not to the following paraenetic section;[45] for this passage contains nothing about the paraenetic, and also because the four basic concepts mentioned are typical of the first four chapters. (Thus, the idea of a δύναμις εἰς σωτηρίαν, "power for salvation," is not used again in the letter, while the expression σωτηρία, "salvation," has four of its five recurrences in 1-11 [1:16; 10:1, 10; 11:11; 13:11]; the expression δικαιοσύνη θεοῦ (αὐτοῦ), "God's (his) righteousness," occurs only in 1:17; 2:13; 3:10, 26; 5:7, 19; 7:12; the noun πίστις, "faith," is found thirty-nine times in Romans, of which only six are in chapters 12-14, and moreover with meanings in these places that do not correspond with that of chapters 1-11, while the verb πιστεύειν, "believe," occurs eighteen times in 1-11 but only three times in 12-15.) The section 1:16b-17, therefore, refers to subject matter that is essentially all treated in the first eleven chapters, and thus amounts to a title of these chapters.

But the development takes place in quite an original way. In a first section, 1:18-2:29, Paul proceeds by means of antitheses, tracing a very negative picture of the situation, in which humankind stand completely outside the ambit of God's justice, so that this very justice will turn back upon them! The basic contention is that there is no difference between pagans and Jews when it comes to sin, which all human beings share in common. Still, Paul's intent is not so much to demonstrate the universal sinfulness of humanity; indeed, he is willing to concede honestly that some there are who "seek glory, honor, and immortality through perseverance in good works" (2:7; cf. 2:10: "glory, honor, and peace for everyone who does good, Jew first and then Greek"), even among the pagans, who are "a

43. See de Saussure, Cours de linguistique générale, (Paris, 1949³) 97ff.
44. See M.-J. Lagrange, Saint Paul: Epître aux Romains, EB (Paris, 1950 = 1916) XXXVI: "So Paul himself here reveals his theme in a true propositio according to the rules of ancient rhetoric [a footnote here cites Quintilian, Instit. orat. VII 1:4], but there is no partitio to indicate the division of the subject into its different parts." (However, he perceives two parts in the quotation from Habakkuk: justifying faith in 1-5 and new life in 6-8; but what of 9-11?)
45. Against A. Nygren, Commentary on Romans (Philadelphia, 1979 = 1949) = Romarbrevet (Stockholm, 1944): note table of contents; he divides thus: I. 1:18-4:25: He Who Through Faith Is Righteous; II. 5-8: He Who Through Faith Is Righteous Shall Live; III. 9-11: The Righteousness of Faith Is Not Against the Promise of God; IV. 12-15: The Life of Him Who Through Faith Is Righteous. See also Käsemann above.

law to themselves even though they do not have the Law" (2:14). Now, to assert the sinfulness of the gentiles is completely normal and traditional for the Jew,[46] a tradition that survives in various ways in the New Testament.[47] What Paul is forced to say, and what must have appeared unheard of, is that the Jews are not exempt from this condition, and that they therefore have no reason to set themselves up before God and other human beings as standing in a privileged religious situation (as having no need of Christ).

Hence Paul's discourse is even more theological than it is moral. Essentially what he is saying is that whatever the moral state of human persons, God is impartial in encounter with them; God plays no favorites. No one, not even the Jew, can boast, "O God, I thank you that I am not like the rest of humanity—greedy, dishonest, adulterous" (Luke 18:11); above all, the Jew cannot rely on the Law as a sign of privilege to claim a special consideration from God, and thus to boast, "Blessed are we, Israel, for to us is revealed what is pleasing to God" (Bar 4:4).[48]

The Apostle therefore develops his argument briefly.[49] First, in 1:18–2:11 he considers the condition of humanity in a universal light insofar as it is subject to the sovereign judgment of God, who is impartial both toward one who does evil (see the concept of ὀργή, "wrath," in 1:18; 2:5, 8) and toward one who does good (to whom are devoted only vv. 2:7, 10). At issue is a judgment according to works (see 2:6 = Ps 62:13; Prov 24:12), which equates all human beings, Jews and Greeks, the wicked and the good alike, in their common state both of exclusion from the "justice of God" and of equal subjection to the same divine judgment.

Then taking one further step (2:12-29) and unexpectedly employing the second person singular with the value of *enallage* (εἰ δὲ σὺ 'Ιουδαῖος . . ., "if you, a Jew . . ."), Paul restricts his argument to the theme of the Law, the basic boast of the Jew, to say that this cannot constitute a motive for any singular pride. The reasons for this equality are basically two: even the pagans observe "an unwritten law," a νόμον ἄγραφον (2:12-16); and the Jews in fact do not observe it, thus dishonoring God (2:17-24). Hence it follows that not even circumcision can be a reason for religious separation, since the transgression of the Law transforms circumcision metaphorically into uncircumcision (2:25-27). Paul does not mean to say that all

46. See K. H. Rengstorf, TDNT 1:323-327; Strack-Billerbeck, III 36ff., 156.
47. See Luke 24:7; John 18:28; Acts 10:28; Gal 2:15; Eph 2:12; 4:17-19.
48. See the ample documentation on the subject in Strack-Billerbeck, III 115-118, 126-133. Specifically, see *m. Jeb*, 11,2, where it is said of the pagan who enters Judaism that he enters into "holiness" (qᵉdushshâ).
49. For the analysis of the text, see J. M. Bassler, *Divine Impartiality. Paul and a Theological Axiom*, SBL DS 59 (Chico, Calif., 1982) 121-154.

the Jews are liable to such accusation; in Phil 3:6 he even holds himself exempt.[50]

In fact, thoughout the section "the group of those who do good is an essential element of the Pauline argument, since it allows him to level off identities and hence the deserved retribution, or to bring them into question: If God is a just judge, he must consider actions without yielding to be impressed by exemptions, advantages or privileges" of anyone (cf. 2:1: "whoever you are").[51] But there is then only one inevitable conclusion, namely, that a true "Jew" is one who practices circumcision of the heart (with allusion to Deut 30:6; Jer 4:4) through the Spirit and not on the basis of the Mosaic code; only to such comes praise from God (2:28-29). But such a "Jew" can be anyone, even a (baptized) pagan!

And such a conclusion to the argument would inevitably be shocking.

IV. Role and function of 3:1-8

After the reasoning of 1:18–2:29 it is as if Paul were himself surprised at the conclusion. A spontaneous objection arises: "What advantage [τὸ περισσόν, "the extra"] is there in being a Jew? Or what is the value of circumcision?" (3:1).

The beginning of chapter 3 actually marks a turning point[52] that can be verified in two ways. First of all, on the formal literary level we can make two observations. There appears here for the first time the question τί οὖν, "what then?" which then recurs several times in the first part of the letter (3:5, 9; 4:1; 6:1, 15; 7:7; 8:31; 9:14, 30; 11:7). This question serves the function of indicating a breathing place in the logic of the author and of instigating a step forward from what has been previously said; its structuring function is evident both within the macrostructure and within a microstructure.

50. J.-N. Aletti, "Rm 1,18–3,20: Incohérence ou cohérence de l'argumentation paulinienne?" Bib 69 (1988) 47–62, p. 50, correctly notes that "the Apostle avoids applying the adjective πᾶς to the Jew (2:17-29)," while already in 1:18ff. it applied to human actions rather than to the persons themselves—thus the phrase πᾶσαν ἀσέβειαν καὶ ἀδικίαν rather than παντῶν τῶν ἀνθρώπων: "every impiety and injustice" rather than "every human being."
51. Aletti, "Rm 1,18–3,20," 56; cf. 59: "The decisive point is not that all are sinners or culpable, but that in virtue of the criterion enunciated in Rom 2 [= the impartiality of God] all persons alike, and *without any distinction at all*, are exposed to wrath" if they violate the Law.
52. On 3:1-8 see especially the following studies: G. Bornkamm, "Theologie als Teufelkunst: Römer 3,1-9," *Geschichte und Glaube*, II (Munich, 1971) 140–148; J. Piper, "The Righteousness of God in Romans 3:1-8," TZ 36 (1980) 3–16; D. R. Hall, "Romans 3,1-8 Reconsidered," NTS 29 (1983) 183–197; S. K. Stowers, "Paul's Dialogue with a Fellow Jew in Romans 3,1-9," CBQ 46 (1984) 707–722; H. Räisänen, "Zum Verständnis von Röm 3,1-8," SNTU (1985) 93–108 (*The Torah and Christ: Essays in German and English on the Problem of the Law in Early Christianity* [Helsinki, 1986] 185–205); C. H. Cosgrove, "What If Some Have Not Believed? The Occasion and Thrust of Romans 3,1-8," ZNW 78 (1987) 90–105; see also chap. 7 of this volume.

Moreover, the whole section 3:1-8 is strongly characterized by a relentless series of questions; one can count nine, which averages more than one per verse! Now, this certainly is due to the lively style of the diatribe, which creates an interlocutor to provoke a dialogue of objection and defense.[53] But this explanation is not enough, since Romans offers other cases of an apostrophe addressed to an imaginary interlocutor (cf. 2:1-5, 17-24; 9:19-21; 11:17-24; 14:4, 10), but, excepting 9:19-21, we never have such an abundant and urgent amassing of questions. At any rate, the series in 3:1-8 is the first really surprising case, since in 2:1-5 we have only two questions (vv. 3, 4), and in 2:17-24 the anacoluthon of vv. 17-20 is followed by five questions that are really questions only in form, since in fact they are simply so many reproofs to the Jew who transgresses the Law, and might just as well have been expressed in so many affirmations. We can also note a couple of literary inconsistencies: in 3:1-2 we have an unexpected passage from a singular noun ($\tau o\tilde{v}$ $\,$'$Iov\delta a iov$, "the Jew") to a plural verb ($\grave{\epsilon}\pi\iota\sigma\tau\epsilon\acute{v}\theta\eta\sigma a\nu$, literally "they were considered trustworthy"); then in vv. 5-8 occurs a surprising alternation of personal pronouns (v. 5, "we"; v. 7, "I"; v. 8, "we") which lacks consistency (the "we" of v. 8 does not correspond to that of v. 5).

So probably besides the stylistic data we must also consider the interior emotional state of the writer, whose thinking has grown unexpectedly turbulent: questions crowding in on one another, following one another in a chain; we recognize that behind him something is seething, indeed at the point of exploding, to provoke and provide matter for new directions of thought.[54] It is as if Paul realizes that he has spoken rashly (the Jew is no different from the pagan!), and while not really wanting to renounce this unheard-of position but also uneasily sensing the disruptive effect, he tries further to rationalize his position by studying and enunciating its proper implications.

Some of the twelve questions in 3:1-8 actually have only rhetorical value (v. 3: $\tau\acute{\iota}\,\gamma\acute{a}\varrho$, "what?"; v. 5: $\tau\acute{\iota}\,\grave{\epsilon}\varrho o\tilde{v}\mu\epsilon\nu$, "what shall we say?"). Others with a logical value can actually be joined up together (thus the two of v. 1, $\tau\acute{\iota}$ and $\tau\acute{\iota}\varsigma$, "What . . .? What . . .?"; those of v. 5 are synonymous with the question of v. 7: see below). Formally, the structure of the progression of thought is as follows:

53. From this point of view, there is no need to ask whether Paul is pretending a debate between himself and a possible external Jewish objector (thus Stowers, "Paul's Dialogue"; see also *The Diatribe*, 176f.) or whether the Apostle is only describing a debate arising from himself (thus Hall, "Romans 3,1-8," who, however, denies the presence here of the diatribe— unconvincingly, we may add).

54. See A. Brunot, *Le génie littéraire de Saint Paul*, LD 15 (Paris, 1955) 51: "One who does not want to venture into this torrent with its many rapids and whirlpools will understand little of Saint Paul."

A) Objection (3:1)	What is the advantage of the Jew?
B) Reply (3:2)	Considerable: the Jew has God's word.
C) Objection (3:3)	But does not the infidelity of some nullify the fidelity of God?
D) Reply (3:4)	No, because God remains faithful in his judgments even if the human being is a liar.
E) Objection (3:5)	But perhaps God's wrath is unjust insofar as our wickedness allows God to show his mercy.
F) Reply (3:6)	No, because God is the universal judge.
G) Objection (3:7-8a)	But for the sake of God's glory are we not perhaps obliged to continue to do evil so that good will come of it, as some say that Paul himself maintains?
H) Reply (3:8b)	No, rather whoever attributes this teaching to me slanders me and is condemned.

As can be seen, this articulation of the text[55] presents four objections. Still, from the point of view of content, they can be reduced to two pairs: the first and second are mutually homogeneous, as are the third and fourth. In effect, the pericope 3:1-8, while it has a basic homogeneity as a whole,[56] formulates *two different problems.* To each is given a brief, provisional, preliminary reply. Since the line of thought begun in 1:18 must follow its course (see below), the detailed and extended reply to the two questions

55. This differs from the analysis proposed by Stowers, "Paul's Dialogue," which joins v. 3 to v. 2, seeing in both a single question raised not by an opponent but by Paul himself, who intends thereby to lead the interlocutor to a necessary response. Hence the following attribution of the text differing from that above: (A) Interlocutor (3:1); (B) Paul (3:2-3); (C) Interlocutor (3:4); (D) Paul (3:5); (E) Interlocutor (3:6); (F) Paul (3:7-8). Stowers unfortunately overemphasizes the figure of a distinct interlocutor, whereas it is actually Paul himself who raises for himself and his readers questions logically raised by his own exposition. But we must make two further observations. (1) Admitting that v. 3 does not represent Paul's thought, as we shall see in chapters 9–10, the text gives no indication that would justify claiming an alternation of roles. That being the case, why not attribute the other objections to Paul as well? (2) As even Stowers indicates ("Paul's Dialogue," 713), when the interlocutor in a diatribe is an outsider rather than a disciple, the questions come from the interlocutor rather than the master; in our case it is clear that the interlocutor would be a Jew (cf. 2:17) or at least a Judeo-Christian functioning as Paul's opponent, and so v. 3 would have to express the objection of another just like the following objections.

56. Note these correspondences, centered on the dialectical relationship of truth and lie:

3:4b: ὁ θεὸς ἀληθής	3:7a: ἡ ἀλήθεια τοῦ θεοῦ
"God is true"	"the truth of God"
3:4c: πᾶς ἄνθρωπος ψεύστης	3:7b: ἐν τῷ ἐμῷ ψεύσματι
"every man is a liar"	"by my lie"

and also on the concept of the divine judge:

3:4f: ἐν τῷ κρίνεσθαί σε	3:6: κρινεῖ ὁ θεός "God judges"
"when you are judged"	3:7: κρίνομαι "I am judged"
	3:8: τὸ κρίμα "the judgment"

must be dealt with later in the letter. Meanwhile, the first of these problems has developed directly from what is said in 1:18–2:29, while the second flows directly from the first.

1) Romans 3:1-4

The first question surfaces in 3:1-4. It concerns the περισσόν, "the extra," of the Jew. It was inevitable that it should emerge. Having just said that anyone, and hence even the pagan, can be a Jew simply through circumcision of the heart, Paul is evidently downgrading any special privilege for one who is circumcised in the flesh (cf. 2:28), and especially one who claims to possess the incarnation of truth in the Law (cf. 2:20). But at this point the problem of the very constitution of Israel arises, both in comparison with the other peoples and over against God. The problem in fact divides into two. In vv. 1-2 the history of salvation provides the primary perspective, namely, what is the "extra" (τὸ περισσόν) of the Jew compared with the pagan? Is it really true that there is no difference? Not at all, since "much" (πολύ) does distinguish the Jew, and as if beginning a list of special prerogatives (note πρῶτον, "first"), Paul alludes to the fact that the Jews are entrusted with "the word of God"; but he does not continue, and we must wait till 9:4-5 for a full enumeration of the characteristics proper to Israel.

Meanwhile, in vv. 3-5 the perspective becomes more properly theological. The problem is this: Does not the unbelief (or else the infidelity to the Law) of one part of Israel perhaps call into question the fidelity of God in their regard? The question is complex and demands to be developed more or less like this: If God's righteousness is henceforth revealed in the gospel, and if in great part Israel does not believe in it (or else transgresses the Law), do the ancient promises of God to the chosen people remain valid? May it not rather be that the stubbornness of Israel brings about either the failure of God's promises or the fall of Israel itself from its role as people of God? Evidently, then, the problem of Israel necessarily involves the problem of God. The essentially dogmatic answer is clearly negative: With the authoritative citation of Ps 50 (51):6 LXX ("That you may be declared just in your word, and may overcome when you are judged"), supported by an allusion to Ps 116:11 ("Everyone is a liar"), Paul affirms decisively that "God is true," that is, trustworthy, faithful, and "turns out to be so" (γινέσθω) in any judicial accusation against him.[57]

---

57. The thesis of Piper, "The Righteousness," according to whom 3:4b expresses the true Pauline concept of God's justice (which would involve not only merciful fidelity but also the judgment of punishment), while 3:5 expresses the concept proper to Paul's Jewish adver-

The Apostle therefore defends the fidelity of God despite the infidelity of Israel. Between the lines, then, he says that the very "incredulity" (ἀπιστία; cf. ψεύστης, "falsehood") of the Jews lets God cause the irresistible victory of his sovereign and generous fidelity to shine all the more brightly.

2) Romans 3:5-8

In 3:5-8, then, another question is posed concerning more generally the relationship between human sin and the saving righteousness of God. The initial εἰ δέ, "but if," of v. 5 (picked up in v. 7; see the earlier 2:17) signals a new step forward on the part of the imaginary interlocutor, indicating dissatisfaction with the preceding answer and broadening the problem. On Paul's horizon we no longer have the Jews alone but all humanity; indeed, the pronoun ἡμῶν, "our," of v. 5 does not refer to the Jews alone, since the recompense of the two antitheses δικαιοσύνη-ὀργή, "righteousness/wrath" (which themselves refer back to 1:17 and to 1:18; 2:5, 8 respectively) picks up the universalist view of the preceding text, in which they applied to Jew and Greek alike (cf. 1:16; 2:1, 9, 10).[58] Such a view is finally evidenced in v. 6 with the idea of κόσμος, "world," which certainly includes the pagans, but in context the Jews as well.[59]

The difficulty expressed here consists in this: If my injustice provides the occasion for God to manifest (saving) justice, is God perhaps not unjust to consider me a sinner? Ought one not, on the contrary, do evil so as to permit God to reveal the good of his own powerful mercy?[60] The issue, as is evident, is of the greatest importance. As if the objection were

---

saries (who would think only of a saving reality) is unconvincing for two reasons. (1) The citation of Ps 51:6 in responding to the objection of v. 3 deals with the possibility of a failure of God's fidelity in the face of the unbelief of the Jews, not about the question of punishment for this unbelief, which is formally considered not as sin but simply as a given fact. And thus Ps 51:6 is extrapolated from its original context only to assert the transcendent and unconquered superiority of God rather than to affirm that God condemns (this, however, does not mean I accept the thesis of Käsemann, *Römer*, 76f., according to whom Rom 3:4b should be understood as a *iustificatio impii*). (2) The "justice of God" of v. 5 expresses not only the conception of Paul's opponents but that of the Apostle himself, since the expression represents simply a repetition of 1:17, but also because here we do not have an explicit quotation of a group opposed to Paul (as we will have in 3:8); rather, the objection of v. 5 comes less from an external interlocutor than from within Paul himself, articulating the theological difficulties set off by his own reasoning.

58. See the preceding note on justice.
59. See Wilckens, *Römer*, I, 166.
60. Paul himself in 5:20 will make the straightforward claim, "Where sin increased, grace increased all the more."

not clear enough, Paul formulates it twice, in vv. 5 and 7, which correspond as follows:[61]

v. 5: "If our injustice	v. 7: "If the truth of God
shows forth	abounded
the justice of God,	in my lie
	for his glory,
is God not perhaps unjust	why am I still
to execute wrath?	judged as a sinner?"

And in v. 8 this question is transformed directly into a proposition ("Let us do evil that good may result"), which "some" attribute to Paul and which he rejects out of hand. The reply to a similar grave question is hastily formulated in v. 6 with the traditional assertion that maintains God's function as universal "judge" (eschatological: $\varkappa\varrho\iota\nu\epsilon\tilde{\iota}$), and in v. 8 as well, where the attribution of a similar attitude to Paul (note $\beta\lambda\alpha\sigma\varphi\eta\mu\sigma\acute{\upsilon}\mu\epsilon\theta\alpha$, "are slandered"), and whoever maintains this is condemned ($\varkappa\varrho\acute{\iota}\mu\alpha$ $\accent"0112\nu\delta\iota\varkappa\sigma\nu$, "their condemnation is deserved"). But is it really thinkable to give such a hasty and summary response to such a question, which involves the very nature of the Pauline gospel?

The reader of the Letter to the Romans must ask, in effect, whether Paul can be satisfied with furnishing such rapid responses to problems of such weight. Were he to do so, one would have to assume that the Apostle wished to avoid the difficulties that he himself had raised, and that he was bolder in asking questions than in answering them! This, however, is not the case. In the course of the epistle, in fact, we see that the two problems expressed in 3:1-8 are taken up again and treated fully, the one in chapters 9-11 and the other in chapters 6-8. The inverted order of the resumption (3:1-4 = 9:1-11:36; and 3:5-8 = 6:1-8:39) depends simply on the prosecution of the speech from 3:9 on (see below).

V. The development from 3:9 to 5:21

The exposition continues in two stages: one with a repetition of earlier themes (3:9-20) and the other moving forward (3:21-5:21).

1) Romans 3:9-20

With 3:9 we have a division over against 3:1-8, in the sense that it starts again almost from the beginning, returning the speech directly to the sec-

---

61. This synoptic comparison also shows the rhetorical value of "enallage personae," specifically of the pronouns "our" and "my," which (like the "I" of chap. 7) are neither autobiographical (Paul can speak neither of a sinful life of his in Judaism nor of his failure to believe the gospel!) nor limited only to the Jewish world (see above).

tion 1:18–2:29. In fact, on the level of vocabulary the expression τί οὖν, "what then?" reappears,[62] and on the level of content it returns to the same subject as 1:18–2:29. Only on the formal level is there a superficial continuity between vv. 1-8 and v. 9, since the series of questions does continue this far; in fact, we have two ("What then?" and "Are we any better?").[63] But these questions do not move the thought forward; on the contrary, they turn us almost directly backward, since they only repeat the question of v. 1: the προεχόμεθα, "are better," of 3:9 corresponds to τὸ περισσόν, "the extra," of 3:1.

Still, we must be careful not to credit Paul with two completely opposite replies to the same question. In 3:1-2 he affirms that the "extra" of the Jew and the usefulness of the circumcision are "much in every way," whereas here, according to the popular translations, the term οὐ πάντως has the negative meaning of "not at all,"[64] so that it would here radically deny any cause for distinguishing the Jews, whereas in the former passage it is generally affirmed. But literally the expression (which is identical to 1 Cor 5:10 and differs from the πάντως οὐκ, "not at all," of 1 Cor 16:12) implies a concession and is equivalent to "not entirely, not totally,"[65] and thus recognizes a particular position of advantage for the Jews.

Even so, if there is an "extra" for the Jew, this concerns if anything only the Jew's objective role in salvation history (cf. 3:2) but has no real value with regard to the soteriological problem, where "Jews and Greeks are all subject to sin" (3:9b). And the verb προῃτιασάμεθα, "we already demonstrated," confirms a logical relationship not with 3:1-8 but with 1:18–2:29. The relationship here, however, is one of crescendo. On the one hand, it reaffirms the basic equality between Jews and Greeks, which was already the central point of that section in relation to the impartiality of God; on the other, the human situation grows all the worse, for while at first the possibility was suggested that either pagans or Jews might do

62. Certain manuscripts (D*, G . . .) and Ambst read τί οὖν προκατέχομεν περισσόν, "then what advantage do we have?" so that the reappearance of the neuter περισσόν, "advantage/extra," links 3:9 even more with 3:1.

63. Contra Stowers, "Paul's Dialogue," 719f., who sees in 3:9 a single question, and further gives the term προεχόμεθα a passive meaning ("Are we at a disadvantage / Are we bettered?"); see the philological discussion in Cranfield, A Commentary on Romans, I, 188–189.

64. Thus RSV, NIV; cf. the general run of translations: "nequaquam" (Vg), "nient'affatto" (Cei), "pas du tout" (BJ), "no, not at all" (RSV, NEB), "durchaus nicht" (U. Wilckens), "todo considerado, ninguna [ventaja]" (J. Mateos and L. Alonso Schökel).

65. Thus NAB, M.-J. Lagrange ("pas entièrement"); C. E. B. Cranfield ("not altogether, not in every respect"); E. Käsemann ("nicht entscheidend" [the English edition here seems to misunderstand: "not in any respect"—T. P. W.]); H. Schlier ("nicht absolut"; the Italian translation of Schlier misunderstands: "in nessun modo"!); see also A. Feuillet, "La situation privilégiée des Juifs d'après Rm 3,9. Comparaison avec Rm 1,16 e 3,1-2," NRTh 105 (1983) 33–46.

good (see 2:7, 10, 14f.), now it is affirmed that they "are all under sin" (3:9b) and that "there is none who is righteous, not even one" (3:10: the text comes from Ps 13 (14):1 LXX; Qoh 7:20.) There then follows a patchwork of biblical quotations till 3:18 to confirm the exclusion of any exception. In fact, the decisive word ʼαμαϱτία, "sin," first appears in the letter in 3:9, and then recurs in 3:20, forming a kind of inclusion and imposing a strict unity on the new passage 3:9-20.

In any case, there is a thematic climax rather than a contrast between the two sections 1:18-2:29 and 3:9-20. It is not that Paul was first taken up with a theological idea (the impartiality of God) and then with an anthropological idea (the universality of sin). As J.-N. Aletti correctly recognized,[66] Paul's preoccupation is to maintain the equality of retribution of the Jew and of the Greek over against God, even if it is here considered negatively: the critical point is to underline, not that all are sinners and guilty, but that all are equally exposed to the ὀϱγή, "wrath," of God, including the Jews, seeing that vv. 19-20 demonstrate the ineffectiveness of the Law for salvation.

2) Romans 3:21-5:21

And it is here, as we reach 3:21ff., that we encounter a surprise.[67] After the dramatic crescendo from 1:18 to 3:20, the reader of Romans would expect a punitive pronouncement of God's justice. Instead, the δικαιοσύνη θεοῦ, "righteousness of God," is manifested through the redemptive act of the expiatory death of Christ, and through the faith of the believers appropriating it for themselves as an act of grace (see 3:21-26). Actually it was not a complete surprise, since this positive conception of a saving "righteousness of God" had already been presented in 1:17 with reference to the gospel, hence providing an alternative possibility in the whole treatment. In 3:21 the idea is simply taken up again and developed adequately.

What we want to note now is the extent of this section and its precise function. To put it briefly, we believe (1) that the passage opposes 1:18-2:29 + 3:9-20 in a form that is mirrorlike in its treatment of ideas; it means to say that all human beings are equal when it comes to salvation, that is, that God is impartial in granting to all without distinction the same justification through faith, and (2) that the section ends with 5:21.

As for the development of the thought, let us note briefly that it proceeds in three stages:

66. "Rm 1,18—3,20," 58-59.
67. Aletti, "Rm 1,18—3,20," 61.

First: 3:21-31. Returning to the motif of God's righteousness and the correlative theme of faith, Paul clarifies (with probable elements taken from the tradition in 3:25) where the revelation of the former is to be found, and simultaneously what is the content of the latter: the blood of Christ's sacrifice; before this all are equalized by the impartiality of the one sole God (3:29), who is just and justifies whoever believes in Jesus (3:26).

Second: 4:1-22.[68] Here the figure of Abraham appears (basic is the text of Gen 15:6 supported by Ps 32:1f., with the indication from two points of view that he was justified on the basis not of the Law but of faith in the promise (4:2-5, 9b, 10, 13, 15-16a, 17b, 19-22) and that his case is normative for both pagans and Jews equally (4:9a, 11-12, 14, 16b-17a, 18). This section is thus characterized by a recurring counterpoint between the past of Abraham and the present of "us" (4:12, 16; cf. 4:11: "all who believe"; 4:11-12: "uncircumcised . . . and circumcised"; 4:17, 18: "many nations"; 4:16: "all Abraham's offspring"), he thus being not only a progenitor according to the flesh (4:1, 16) but also and especially the father of all who rely upon faith (4:16).

Third: 4:23–5:21. The Christological motif of 3:21-31 returns enriched by a midrashic reflection on Abraham. The thought proceeds in two steps: in 4:23–5:11 the relationship with Christ is seen as deriving completely from faith in him, which characterizes the present life of the Christian as based on the gifts of peace, free access, hope, agape, pneuma, reconciliation; in 5:12-21, through an original counterpoint (but this time antithetic) with Adam, the motif of 1:18–2:29 + 3:9-20 is resumed in order thoroughly to confirm the same conclusions, anthropological (all have sinned) and theological (God is impartial in granting to all not his ὀργή, "wrath," but his χάρις, "grace," in Christ).

As for the disputed place of Rom 5 in the structure of the letter, we firmly maintain that this section, while pointing in some way toward what follows (see below), belongs fully to 1:18–5:21, and more specifically to its "evangelical" side, 3:21–5:21. This is surely not the place to discuss the whole question.[69] I intend only to call attention to certain important considerations.

In the first place, let us note that if 5:1-11 anticipates certain motifs to be treated in chapter 8, as certain authors rightly observe,[70] the section 5:12-

68. For the break after 4:22, see Ramaroson, "Un 'nouveau plan,' " 948f., 952f.

69. See the ample treatment in H. Paulsen, *Überlieferung und Auslegung in Römer 8*, WMANT 43 (Neukirchen-Vluyn, 1974) 12–21. Among the major commentaries published since this date, those of Cranfield, Käsemann, and Schlier prefer a break after chapter 4, while those of Wilckens, Morris, Dunn, and Stuhlmacher choose a break after chapter 5.

70. See especially N. A. Dahl, "Two Notes on Romans 5," STh 5 (1951) 37–48; S. Lyonnet, *Exegesis epistulae ad Romanos: cap. V ad VIII (Except. Rom. 5,12-21)* (Rome, 1966) 7–9; more re-

21, on the other hand, turns its sights directly on the first chapters, so that chapter 5 provides a thematic of crossed orientations: the first part looks forward (but not exclusively so: see below), while the second looks back. The authors who associate chapter 5 with chapter 8 give more structural importance to 5:1-11 and orient 5:12-21 also with the following section. But why not do the opposite, emphasizing 5:12-21 as a reprise of 1:18-2:29 + 3:9-20 (negative review of soteriology) and 3:21-5:11 (positive review of soteriology), thus orienting 5:1-11 to what precedes it? This is all the more possible in that although Rom 8:17-39 anticipates certain motifs that will be the material of chapters 9-11,[71] one need not link chapter 8 to these following chapters.

In the second place, while it is true that one or the other word recurs only in 5:1-11 and then in chapter 8 (thus ἀγάπη, "love," in 5:5-8), still others that are likewise characteristic of chapter 8 are also common to earlier chapters (thus δόξα, "glory," in 3:7; ἐλπίς, "hope," in 4:18; πνεῦμα, "spirit," in 2:29). In particular, one can note the use of the adjective-pronoun πᾶς, "each," in a personal sense, expressing universality whether of the sinful condition of humanity or of the object of the salvific event; this is typical of 1:16-4:25 (sixteen times) and 9-11 (fourteen times), while in 5-8 it occurs five times (5:12 [twice]; 5:18 [twice]; 8:32), four of them in the section 5:12-21, which connects much better to the previous chapter. Similar to this is the use of κόσμος, "world," which in chapters 5-8 is present only in 5:12-13 and relates better to the preceding chapters (seven times) than to chapters 6-8 (never). Analogously, the fundamental concept of πίστις, "faith," which in 1:16-4:25 recurs twenty-four times, in chapters 5-8 appears only twice (in 5:1-2), where it therefore best corresponds to the preceding sections. The same must be said for the lexical family δικ-, "just-/righteous-" (δικαιοῦν, δικαιοσύνη, δικαίωμα, δικαίωσις, δίκαιος), the infrequent use of which in chapters 5-8 suggests associating its recurrences in chapter 5 (nine times) with the preceding sections in which it is much more frequently attested (thirty times, against twelve times in chapters 6-8).

In the third place, we must pay special attention to the structural function of the rhetorical question τί οὖν, "what then," and τί οὖν ἐροῦμεν, "What then shall we say?" First appearing in the letter at 3:1, it was repeated in 3:5, 9; 4:1, and each time indicated a step forward and a turning point in the logical concatenation of Paul's argument. Chapter 5, on the other hand, never uses this question or any other question mark.[72] On the contrary,

---

cently P. Lamarche and C. Le Dû, *Épître aux Romains V-VIII: structure littéraire et sens* (Paris, 1980), esp. the criteria pp. 11-12.

71. See, e.g., Cranfield, *A Commentary on Romans*, II, 446f., and J.-N. Aletti, "L'argumentation paulinienne en Rm 9," Bib 68 (1987) 41-56, 43, n. 9, and 53-55.

72. Thus in the first part of the letter (chaps. 1-11), this along with chapter 1 is the only chapter that does not formulate a question.

chapter 5 is characterized by the conjunction οὖν, "then" (5:1, 9, 18) and by a polemic character (with: a form of sorites in 5:3-5; a comparison in vv. 7-8 and another repeated in vv. 15-16, 18, 19, 21; the use of the technique *qal wahomer* in 5:9, 10, 15, 17 with the quadruple repetition of πολλῷ μᾶλλον, "much more"), which gives to the whole passage more the sound of a conclusion than the opening of a new speech. To this we add that the question τί οὖν ἐροῦμεν reappears only in 6:1, indicating a new logical point of articulation.[73]

VI. Chapters 6–8 as reply to the problem formulated in 3:5-8

The first verse of chapter 6 resumes the question formulated in 3:5-8 exactly in both form and content.[74] The problem that had appeared there and was basically left dangling now receives a fully developed reply. The repetition, and hence the linkage of chapter 6 to 3:5-8, can be confirmed both in form and in content.

On the formal level, the same question returns, formulated each time on the same pattern:

3:5: . . . τί ἐροῦμεν; "What shall we say?"	6:1: τί οὖν ἐροῦμεν; "What then shall we say?"
3:7: . . . τί ἔτι . . .; "Why . . . still . . .?"	6:15: τί οὖν; . . . "What then?"

Then in each passage the same peremptory reply is given: μὴ γένοιτο, "never!": indeed, after 3:6 it is precisely in 6:2 that this expression first recurs, repeated in 6:15. We discover, moreover, that in 6:3 second person plural direct discourse, neglected since 1:16, resumes ("Don't you know?"). Since 1:16 the tone had become more theoretical and reflective, not really enlivened by the introduction of the second person singular in 2:1-5, 17-27, where it has only a literary-stylistic rather than conversational value. But in 6:3 direct contact is unexpectedly restored between the writer and the recipients, and in 6:11-22 this becomes a direct imperative ("Do not let sin reign in your mortal body . . ."). It is therefore only in chapter 6 that Romans returns to the typical familiarity of an epistle. Paul, then,

73. Two more arguments must be added to these and will be developed below: the reappearance in chapter 5 of two verbs that were already important in 3:5, 7, συνίστησιν, "demonstrates," and ἐπερίσσευσεν, "has abounded" (see below, section VI at the end); and the revival of direct discourse in the second person plural in chapter 6 (see below, VI at beginning).

74. Against I. J. Canales, "Paul's Accusers in Romans: 3:8 and 6:1," EvQ 57 (1985) 237–245, we must note that in the two passages we are not dealing with two different groups of adversaries (Judaizing Christians in 3:8; antinomian gentile Christians in 6:1), but are still treating the same opinion wrongly attributed to Paul by certain Roman Christians of Jewish origin (see 7:1) but of libertine tendency; see chap. 7 below.

is here anxious to correct among the Romans the calumny that "some" of these have spoken of him and his preaching. In chapter 6 he is actually refuting the opinion that τινες, "some," have attributed to him in 3:8, distorting his thought. Paul now explains clearly and directly to the Roman Church that "some" of its members have not understood that his announcement of freedom does not justify continuation in sin.

It is important to note that these modes of expression give form to the same logical content, which after 3:5-8 reappears precisely in chapter 6.

On the level of content the same problem is reformulated as was raised by the dialectical contrast between human injustice and the merciful fidelity of God. The text of 6:1 is brief and lapidary:

ἐπιμένωμεν τῇ ἁμαρτίᾳ, ἵνα ἡ χάρις πλεονάσῃ;
("shall we go on sinning, so that grace may increase?")

The question is repeated forcefully with a slight variation in 6:15: "Shall we sin because we are not under the Law but under grace?"[75] The opposition ἁμαρτία-χάρις, "sin/grace," only continues the outline of the antithesis first developed in 5:15-21. But the problem that this poses, namely, whether we must favor the former so that the latter may triumph, is exactly the problem formulated in 3:5-8. The terminological correspondence can be gathered as follows:

3:5: ἡ ἀδικία ἡμῶν "our unrighteousness"	6:1: ἐπιμένωμεν τῇ ἁμαρτίᾳ "Let us remain in sin"
3:7: ἐν τῷ ἐμῷ ψεύσματι "by my lie"	6:15: ἁμαρτήσωμεν "Let us sin"
. . . ὡς ἁμαρτωλός "as sinner"	
3:8: ποιήσωμεν τὰ κακά "Let us do evil"	

3:5: θεοῦ δικαιοσύνη "God's righteousness"	
3:7: ἡ ἀλήθεια τοῦ θεοῦ "God's truth"	6:1, 15: ἡ χάρις (πλεονάσῃ) "grace (may abound)"
. . . εἰς τὴν δόξαν αὐτοῦ "for his glory"	
3:8: ἔλθῃ τὰ ἀγαθά "good may come"	

The problem, which is theological and ethical at the same time, arises precisely from the fact that the second of these two poles is affirmed on the occasion of (or because of) the existence of the first. Now, that which

75. The repetition shows that not only does the problem remain in Paul's consciousness but that it is experienced in all its gravity.

must be sought at any cost is surely the second of the elements (identified variously as "justice," "truth," "glory," "good," "the grace of God"); but if there is, as it were, a relationship of cause and effect between the two, that is, if the latter depends on the former, then it seems necessary to indulge in the former (identified variously as "injustice," "lie," "evil," "sin"). And in each passage the relationship between the two poles is expressed with the same "final" conjunction ἵνα, "in order that," in 3:8 and in 6:1.

The reply formulated by Paul in chapters 6–8 is not speculative and metaphysical in character (e.g., the incompatibility between sin and God's holiness, or the continued existence of grace even if one prescinds from the historical fact of sin). Rather, the Apostle reasons on the basis of what has been concretely verified in the Christian in her or his adherence to Christ. His discourse is not even properly speaking ethical, even if it does include certain exhortations (especially in chapter 6). Paul's discourse is ontological, or of supernatural anthropology: in the Christian there is verified something that is incompatible with sin. Except for the parenthesis concerning the tragic situation of the human person (of the pagan? the Jew? the Christian? or more than one of these?) as slave of sin (7:7-25), he bases his theses substantially on two positive and fundamental components of the new Christian identity, the one linked to the other. The first is the fact of baptism understood as association with the death of Christ: "In the same way count yourselves dead to sin but alive to God in Christ Jesus" (6:11). The second is the gift of the Spirit: this "has set [you] free from the law of sin and death" (8:2)[76] and has made of Christians adopted children of God (see 8:14).

Both motifs are strictly connected to the common motif of "liberty" (6:18, 22; 7:3; 8:2, 21).[77] However, it is difficult to subdivide these pages precisely. At best we can isolate the intermediate passage, 7:7-25, and the final one, 8:31-39, each introduced by the customary rhetorical question

76. Let us note in passing that the general theme of Rom 6–8 as a reply to 3:5-8 does not allow us to understand the *nomos* in 8:2 in the specific sense of Torah, but requires recognizing it in the general sense of norm or principle (and at most interpreting the phrase as an epexegetical genitive). Indeed the general subject of the section is sin, specifically whether or not one ought to remain in sin; its contextual connection with the law is very important, but not to the extent that law is more central here than sin. At any rate, a purely statistical comparison of Galatians with Romans shows that while in the former the motif of law prevails over that of sin (32 times to 3 times), in Romans the motif of sin prevails comparatively over that of law (47 times to 72 respectively): now, considering the unequal length of the two letters, it turns out that in order to correspond to the frequency of *hamartia* (3 times in Galatians and 47 times in Romans), *nomos* would have to be found about 350 times in Romans (rather than 72)!

77. We must note that in the whole letter the root ἐλευθερ-, "free-," is found only in these passages: the verb in 6:18, 22; 8:2, 21; the adjective in 6:20; 7:3; the noun in 8:21.

τί οὖν ἐροῦμεν, "What then shall we say?" For the rest, the motif of baptism and of the Spirit can be articulated thus: baptism, 6:1-23; and Spirit, 7:1-6 + 8:1-30 or else 6:1–7:6 and 8:1-30, except that the passage 8:18-30 can also be set aside for its eschatological motif. But for now we need not emphasize the internal articulation of this section, but rather the fact that the whole section in its entirety resumes and develops the question posed in 3:5-8, as we have said.

But we must add a word about a fact that does not seem very logical: Why does Paul reverse the answer to the two questions posed in 3:1-8? For in chapters 6–8 he begins by answering the second question (3:5-8). The reason is simple and is due to the contingency of the development of Paul's speech. In 5:21 he reached the conclusion that where sin reigned, grace reigned as well, apparently establishing between the two realities a relationship not only of succession but also of causality, precisely such as to give rise to the objection about whether it was appropriate to cultivate the former to bring about the latter. Indeed, precisely chapter 5 proves to be further connected with what precedes it by the fact that two verbs that were decisive in 3:5-8 recur in this chapter, namely συνίστησιν (3:5) and ἐπερίσσευσεν (3:7), used in chapter 3 respectively with reference to the justice and to the truth/fidelity of God, and it is precisely these that have historically triumphed over human injustice and falsehood. Now, of the two verbs the one appears in 5:8 ("God demonstrates [συνίστησιν] his own love for us in this: while we were still sinners Christ died for us"), and the other recurs in 5:15 ("If the many died by the trespass of the one man, how much more *did* God's grace and the gift that came by the one man, Jesus Christ, *abound* [ἐπερίσσευσεν] for the many!"; cf. 5:20b: "But where sin increased, grace *increased all the more* [ὑπερεπερίσσευσεν]"). It is therefore as if in chapter 5 Paul again took up the terms of the question posed in 3:5-8, not in the form of an objection but of a theological affirmation, thus making his own the scandalous terms of the question itself, in that it is historically true that sin (of Adam and of his descendants) objectively made it possible for God to demonstrate love and multiply grace. At this point, then, a repetition of the objection and a direct response were inevitable, and that is precisely what chapters 6–8 provide.

VII. Chapters 9–11 as reply to the problem expressed in 3:1-4

As we have said, the argument of chapters 6–8 is actually a reply to the problem enunciated in 3:5-8. But while such a response is occasioned in the context by reflection on the merciful behavior of God (3:21–5:21), the formulation of the problem was occasioned by the behavior of the Jews,

86 *History and Exegesis*

that is, of Israel, and by the problem of their identity. Indeed, 3:3-8 is only an extension to the human person and to the Christian in general of that which according to 3:1-4 comes to pass in the relationship between (an unbelieving) Israel and God. At this level, as we have seen above, the problem becomes twofold: it begins with the question of what is special about the Jew as compared with the pagan (3:1-2), and goes on to the question raised by Israel's failure to believe the gospel, maintaining that this does not cancel the fidelity of God toward his ancient people, but rather makes it possible for God to triumph over human falsehood (cf. 3:3-4).

In actuality, vv. 1-4 of chapter 3, for all their leanness, suggest a whole series of weighty questions: What is the role of Israel in the history of salvation? How is the election of God understood in their regard? How does Israel differ from the pagans, whether in the pre-Christian past or in the present time of the gospel? Is their original uniqueness compromised by their failure to believe the news of Christ? Does such failure of belief perhaps have an historic-salvific role? And what will be the eschatological future of this people?

Paul probably began writing the letter with his mind full of these teeming questions precisely concerning Israel.[78] But until now this had not received specific and exhaustive treatment.[79] Chapters 9–11 constitute precisely a response to it.

It is true that we cannot establish any formal element indicating a direct link of these chapters to 3:1-4.[80] The nexus is one of logic and motif. But on this level it is unquestionable. Indeed, after the solemn opening oath of 9:1-3, the enumeration in 9:4-5 of the specific titles to Israel's identity responds to the question formulated in 3:1 concerning the "extra" of Israel, enlarging the first, provisory response of 3:2. For example, to the ἐπιστεύθη-

78. See J. Jeremias, "Zur Gedankenführung," 149; U. Luz, "Zum Aufbau von Röm. 1–8," *TZ* 25 (1969) 161–181, p. 169; see also below, chap. 16.

79. It is interesting that for Paul there is no Christian problem distinguished from the Jewish problem, and that the former is based on the latter, just as Rom 3:5-8 follows 3:1-4. Now, even if within the economy of the epistle the Apostle first treats the situation of baptized Christians and their relationship to sin and to the Spirit (chaps. 6–8) and then that of Israel (chaps. 9–11), still the fact that the Jews are treated second does not indicate a secondary worthiness; the fact indicates rather that Israel poses an inescapable problem, which must therefore be faced. This actually stands at the beginning and the end of Paul's exposition, so much so that it produces a kind of inclusion between the initial 1:16 (where the Jew is put in the first place among the recipients of the gospel) and the concluding 9–11 (with which the theological section of the letter ends).

80. To see a link between the dialectical concepts "truth-falsehood" in 3:4bc (γινέσθω δὲ ὁ θεὸς ἀληθής, πᾶς δὲ ἄνθρωπος ψεύστης, "God be true, but every man a liar"; see also 3:7a: ἀλήθεια-ψεῦσμα "truth/falsehood") and in 9:1 (ἀλήθειαν λέγω ἐν Χριστῷ, οὐ ψεύδομαι, "I speak the truth in Christ; I do not lie") would be to force the correspondence, since the two concepts have different meanings in the two passages—theological in the first, and only human-noetic in the second.

σαν τὰ λόγια τοῦ θεοῦ, "They were entrusted with the oracles of God," of 3:2 corresponds the reaffirmation of 9:6: οὐχ οἷον δὲ ἐκπέπτωκεν ὁ λόγος τοῦ θεοῦ, "It is not as though the word of God had failed." Still, the meaning is not altogether identical: the λόγια alluded to revelation in general, entrusted to Israel, whereas now the λόγος is specified in the context as elective (and hence selective) choice of God in the history of salvation.

And it is this initial response that provides the starting point of Paul's thought, which, according to the most current subdivision, can be articulated in three stages. (1) As formerly in the story of the patriarchs and that of the Exodus, God chooses by indisputable grace, so today the adherence to the gospel by only a part of Israel and especially by the gentiles is a gratuitous act of God (see 9:6-29). (2) Now the justice of God is revealed in Christ, surpassing the οἰκονομία based on the Law, and to this justice one is related only through faith in the hearing of the gospel, which is addressed to all (9:30–10:21). (3) Still, God remains faithful to his people; one cannot vaunt oneself over against the unbelieving Jews, since it is they who contribute to the gentiles' entry into the covenant, after which all Israel will be saved (see 11:1-32). The following verses, 11:33-36, finally, contain a concluding doxology that expresses amazement and adoration before God's unsearchable plan of salvation.

Beyond the internal structure of this remarkably homogeneous section, what I must emphasize is that the thematic richness developed here actually finds no other connection in the whole rest of the epistle except in 3:1-4. In fact, it does not build on the immediately preceding chapter 8 in any satisfactory way. Despite certain preparations that would invite us not to think of a purely extrinsic juxtaposition,[81] chapter 8 had already concluded a section with the final passage 8:31-39, which sang almost in the style of a hymn the victory of the Christian due to God's ἀγάπη in Christ. Other connections do not count—even the case of Abraham, treated in chapter 4 and now resumed according to another perspective in 9:7-9. In the former he is a shining paradigm of the one who is justified through faith, whereas here he is father of one son according to the flesh and another according to the promise, and hence is an almost secondary personage in the face of God's elective intervention on the part of only one of his sons.

So the relationship of chapters 9–11 to 3:1-4 should be even more evident than the nexus of chapters 6–8 with 3:5-8. Moreover, the passage 3:1-4 is only a summary of the whole section 1:18–5:21, the whole of which is presupposed by chapters 9–11 in its twofold affirmation of the impar-

---

81. See n. 71 above.

tiality of God both in the face of sin and in the event of justification, and consequently in the affirmation of the equality of Jews and gentiles before God (see 10:12: "For there is no difference between Jew and Greek; the same Lord is Lord of all and richly blesses all who call on him"). From this point of view, chapters 9–11 are as a whole linked to the first five chapters of the epistle. Still, it is only in 3:1-4 that the question of Israel was formally posed, and consequently it is with this passage that chapters 9–11 have a privileged relationship.

VIII. Conclusion

Our structural study, as we have proposed it here, concerns only the first eleven chapters of the Letter to the Romans.[82] And here we have discovered that everything holds together harmoniously, if not with the art of logically concatenated, fully consequent exposition—since the line of thought is irregular and at points is suspended, postponed, or resumed—at least with the technique of a homogeneous thematic development. The arguments treated may break apart and multiply, but the one always develops from the other, and we never see the addition or superimposition of something heterogeneous.[83]

In this organic whole we have defined and illuminated the specific structural function of 3:1-8, into which the brief preceding section flows (i.e., 1:16–2:29) and from which derive all the developments of the following corpus of the letter. This pericope acts like a prism refracting and breaking up a ray of light that enters it. The structure of Rom 1:16–11:36 can be clarified with the following chart:

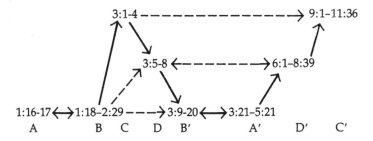

82. One could observe, however, that chapters 12–16 are not completely detached from what precedes them. One confirmation of their interconnection could be seen in the use of counterbalance between the abstract concepts "good-evil"; their appearance in 3:8 perhaps controls the passages 12:21 and 16:19b (see chap. 7 below).

83. I therefore do not consider the division of Romans proposed by B. Nowack justifiable, "Current and Backwater in the Epistle to the Romans," ST 19 (1965) 155–166, where he distinguishes the current (1:1-17; 3:9-20, 27-31; 4:1-25; 9:1-11, 36) from the backwater (1:18–3:8, 21-26; 5:1-8, 39), maintaining that only the former really represent the situation and prob-

As is evident, the thought develops always with new material till 3:8, but thereafter Paul simply resumes, develops, and deepens the rich ideas that have come before. To return to the analogy suggested above, the ray of light that enters the beginning of chapter 3 is the affirmation of the equality of Jews and Greeks before the gospel (A, developed in A', but underlying D' and C' as well) and especially before God, who judges both impartially (B, resumed in B'). Such a claim necessarily raised the problem of the specific identity of Israel (C, developed in C'), from which naturally proceeds the more general problem of the relationship of human sin and divine mercy (D, developed in D').

The delayed response to the questions of 3:1-4, 5-8 is motivated by the fact that Paul still has to finish the discourse begun in 1:18–2:29 (resumed at length in 3:9-20) concerning the equality of Jews and Greeks in sin, by saying antithetically in 3:21–5:21 that Jews and Greeks are likewise equal in justification by faith, that is, by grace. Still, the answers to the questions always presuppose the preceding treatments. Thus 6:1–8:39 answers 3:5-8 but develops logically from 3:21–5:21 by saying that not only can sin and grace not coexist but that one should not even sin in order to promote grace, for since sin is connected with the Law, the Christian is already free from them both on the basis of baptism and of the Spirit. Thus 9:1–11:36 answers 3:1-4 but presupposes all that has thus far been said, since the problem of Israel derives from the claim of the universal equality of humanity in sin and in justification, as well as from the treatment of God's mercy, which is not crushed by sin but even overcomes and destroys it (cf. the salvific eschatology of Israel.)

We therefore discover in the first eleven chapters of Romans three great complementary thematic patterns, characterizing three human groupings: (1) equal situation of sin and of justification for all human beings, *Jews and Greeks*, before God (A, B; B', A', i.e., 1:16–5:21); (2) new existence of *those baptized* in Christ and in the Spirit (D, D', i.e., 3:5-8 + 6:1–8:39); (3) the unbelief of *Israel* and God's fidelity (C, C', i.e., 3:1-4 + 9:1–11:36).

---

lems that caused Paul to write the letter. Still, the author is correct in maintaining that it was the new situation of salvation history that led Paul "to re-think the problem of Israel's rejection and salvation. And were it not for this problem and Paul's readiness to tackle it, we would never possess Romans v–viii" (164-165).

Chapter 5

Narrative Aspects of the Letter to the Romans

I. *Status quaestionis*

In recent times theological studies have fortunately rediscovered the narrative dimension.[1] And rediscovery it truly is. Indeed, what was originally a determining factor in the biblical way of talking about God and about human beings gave way little by little, at least in Christian tradition, to an abstract, speculative reasoning, so that finally within a faith in the Logos incarnate, "the Logos was not turned into a story, but instead the biblical stories were turned into logos, an argument."[2]

In the New Testament canon the writing that could best lend itself (at least apparently) to such treatment was the letter of Paul to the Romans, often considered (at least until F. Christian Baur) a quarry of systematic theological axioms. Significant examples of such an operation remain works of Saint Augustine, *Expositio quarumdam propositionum ex epistola ad Romanos,*[3] and of Philip Melanchthon, *Loci communes rerum theologicarum seu hypotyposes theologiae.*[4] But even in more recent times analogous attempts have not been lacking, something not illegitimate in itself but influenced by a prejudice favoring systematization, either by considering

1. The expression "narrative theology" goes back to H. Weinrich in Conc 5 (1973) no. 9, 46–56. We cite here several works purely by way of example: D. Ritschl and H. O. Jones, *"Story" als Rohmaterial der Theologie* (Munich, 1976); J. Navone and Th. Cooper, *Tellers of the Word* (New York, 1981); M. Goldberg, *Theology and Narrative: A Critical Introduction* (Nashville, 1982); R. Marlé, "La théologie, un art de raconter? Le projet de théologie narrative," *Études* 358/1 (1983) 123–137; S. Lanza, *La narrazine in catechesi* (Rome, 1985).
2. H. Weinrich, 51.
3. PL 35:2063-2088 (84 propositions are extracted, esp. from Rom 5-8); the work dates to 394.
4. The work dates to 1521 but was expanded in the editions of 1535 and 1543.

Romans as the mirror of the whole Pauline theology[5] or by attributing a structure of rather abstract doctrinal character to the epistle.[6]

It was precisely to deliver Romans from the dogmatizing tendencies into which it had fallen that just in the past century the Tübingen professor Ferdinand Christian Baur[7] began to emphasize the fundamental importance of the historical circumstances of the letter, and especially of its major theme concerning the relationship of Paul to Judaism.

But for all this, Baur did not yet succeed in taking into consideration the typical style of the letter as such, checking whether the letter treats questions from a cold, scholastic, purely argumentative point of view, or whether perhaps, and to what extent, it uses specific narrative techniques in presenting its message. On this latter point there are still no specific studies to this day. To my knowledge there is only a brief development in an article by G. Lohfink on narrative structure as the fundamental dimension of the New Testament.[8] He recognizes that while the narrative texts in Romans are far fewer than are the reasoning texts, they ''clearly supply a primary function.''[9] But he makes no detailed analysis. The study of Stowers, too, on the use of the literary genre of diatribe in Romans, limits itself to a brief treatment of the technique of the *exemplum* in the story of Abraham in chapter 4 of the epistle.[10] But is this all there is to it?

It is worth the trouble to try a broader analysis of Romans, doing a closer comparative study of the text to see if there are other narrative passages and proposing a list that includes their genres. But let us first try some methodological observations.

II. Clarifying the method

In the first place, I want to clear the field of some possible misunderstandings and say what I *do not understand* by ''narrative.''

5. Thus in the Protestant camp: see, for example, the treatment of R. Bultmann, *Theologie des NT* (Tübingen, 1965[5]) 187–353; G. Eichholz, *Die Theologie des Paulus im Umriss* (Neukirchen-Vluyn, 1972).

6. Thus in the Catholic camp: see, for example, the *Bible de Jérusalem* and specific studies such as those of A. Feuillet, A. Descamps, J. Dupont, K. Prümm.

7. ''Über Zweck und Veranlassung des Römerbriefs und die damit zusammenhängenden Verhältnisse der römischen Gemeinde,'' TZTh (1836), Heft 3, 59–178.

8. See G. Lohfink, ''Erzählung als Theologie. Zur sprachlichen Grundstruktur der Evangelien,'' StiZt 192 (1974) 521–532. On Galatians see rather R. B. Hays, *The Faith of Jesus Christ: An Investigation of the Narrative Substructure of Gal. 3:1–4:11*, SBL DS 56 (Chico, Calif., 1983): here will be found on pp. 37–83 an overview of how, in general, the narrative dimension of Paul had thus far been treated.

9. P. 524 (where he has the development of the first chapters depend on the text of Rom 3:21).

10. S. K. Stowers, *The Diatribe and Paul's Letter to the Romans*, SBL DS 56 (Chico, Calif., 1981) 171–173. The presence of *exempla* among the stylistic characteristics of the diatribe was already noted by H. Weber, *De Senecae philosophi dicendi genere Bioneo* (Marburg, 1895) 6–33.

a) I do not mean the *narratio* in the sense of ancient rhetoric. When they analyzed a developed discourse (in any of its three genres: deliberative, judiciary, and epideictic), they customarily distinguished six *partes orationis:* the *exordium,* the *narratio,* the *propositio,* the *argumentatio* or *probatio,* the *refutatio* or *reprehensio,* and the *peroratio* or *conclusio.* Of these the *narratio* constituted the entry into the material, involving the presentation of the facts or of the data to be discussed.[11] Now, some would like to divide Romans precisely according to these categories, proposing to find the *narratio* in the very brief initial section 1:13-15 (resumed then in the *peroratio* of 15:14-33).[12] But such a conception, apart from the fact that there is not enough certainty in attributing to Paul approaches proper to the rhetorical schools (see above, chap. 4, I), does not correspond to our conception of narration, which is much more broad and flexible. Indeed, we would like to verify in Romans the presence of narrative elements throughout the letter; in fact, it is theoretically possible that we should discover their presence in every section of the text, well beyond 1:13-15.

b) By narration I do not mean what is so for us but not for the original readers. The Letter to the Romans provides us with a good deal of information about the specific situation of the Christian community in Rome in the fifties of the first century of our era. For example, from the paraenetic part, and especially from 14:1–15:13, we can derive information directly concerning the internal life of this Church. From this point of view, the letter "tells us" certain aspects of the community experience of the Roman Christians. (And even this observation alone tells us that Paul has not written something purely doctrinal but alludes also to the concrete lived experience of his addressees.)

At any rate, this kind of information cannot be considered true narrative, since the first readers did not perceive it as such, but for them it was simply an allusion to experience. They must have considered "narrative" only what the author told them about third parties, or perhaps also that which did concern them but also involved their past. Indeed, a subject's present cannot be narrated to the person.

In the second place, we now ask just what is, properly speaking, a narrative or an account. Of course, we cannot develop the whole theory of the question here.[13] It is important at least to understand that narration

11. See H. Lausberg, *Handbuch der literarischen Rhetorik. Eine Grundlegung der Literaturwissenschaft* (Munich, 1960) 148f. H.-I. Marrou, *A History of Education in Antiquity,* trans. G. Lamb (New York, 1956) 194–205 = *Histoire de l'éducation dans l'antiquité* (Paris, 1948) 268–296.

12. Thus W. Wuellner, "Paul's Rhetoric of Argumentation in Romans," CBQ 38 (1976) 330–351; R. Jewett, "Romans as an Ambassadorial Letter," Int 36 (1982) 5–20.

13. We limit ourselves here to referring to R. Barthes, "Introduction a l'analyse structurale des récits," *Communications* 8 (1966) 1–27; H. Weinrich, *Literatur für Leser. Essays und Aufsätze zur Literaturwissenschaft* (Stuttgart, 1972); P. Ricoeur, *Temps et récit,* I–III (Paris, 1983–85).

has never been lacking in human history since its very origins, and that some of the greatest literary expressions of humankind are precisely narrative in form, from the epics of Homer and Virgil to the poem of Dante Alighieri, from the tragedies of Aeschylus to the dramas of Shakespeare, from the ancient Greek histories to the novels of Dostoevsky and Manzoni. Narrative has always been a fundamental mode of communication between human beings. It is also thus in the religious world (note the concept of the myth), from the ancient Mesopotamian poems to the Bible. Moreover, it is evident that narration takes place in quite diverse ways. It can, for instance, be done in prose and poetry alike. And the only thing in common to the report in a chronicle and a children's bedtime story is simply that each is a narration.

Narrative as such, then, is the common denominator of quite diverse literary forms. And the absolutely essential element of narrative will be its reference to life, to personages and what happens to them. It will be secondary to the definition of narrative whether the facts revealed are real or fictitious. What is important is that one or more subjects (usually human) be presented, to whom an action or a series of actions is attributed.

It is in this broad sense that we want to identify the presence of narrative aspects in Romans. Considering the various realizations of the concept of narration, we must expect it to be found at different levels. We can in fact identify various forms of narration in the Pauline epistle, which we must now pass in review without even trying to comment on each.

III. Forms of narration in Romans

Let us present here a selection of the narrative forms present in Romans, well aware of the fact that we are simply doing an attempt at identification, which is certainly subject to improvement. The basic guiding criterion has been to exclude sentences that have as grammatical or logical subject God (as a non-historical subject), or an abstract theological concept (e.g., the Law in 3:19 or hope in 5:5), or "man" generically in an axiomatic formulation. Positively, we have listed all those texts that have various human beings as subject, even when we are dealing with a similitude.

1) The most striking form in Romans is surely the *biblical narrative*, i.e., the representation of personages and events of Sacred Scripture.[14] The

---

14. We prefer this literary label to the theological term *Heilsgeschichte*, "history of salvation." This particular component has been amply studied: see esp. J. Munck, *Paulus und die Heilsgeschichte*, AJut 26.1 (Copenhagen, 1954) 190–203; O. Cullmann, *Heil als Geschichte. Heilsgeschichtliche Existenz im Neuen Testament* (Tübingen, 1965) 225–245; E. Käsemann, "Rechtfer-

reader meets these in two sections: chapter 4 and the block of chapters 9–11; both have places and functions of great importance in the structure of the epistle in developing the theme of justification by faith.

The personage whose story is most fully recounted is *Abraham* in 4:1-3, 10-11, 17-22. In these texts there re-echo various points of the old story about the great biblical patriarch, from the promise of descendants in Rom 4:13, 17, 18 (see in turn Gen 12:7; 15:5; 17:5), to the annunciation of the birth of Isaac despite old age in Rom 4:19-21 (see Gen 17:1, 17), to the acceptance of circumcision in Rom 4:11 (see Gen 17:11). But above all there is reference to his pure faith, according to Gen 15:6, which is cited three times, in Rom 4:3, 9, 22! It is for this attitude that Abraham is proposed as model of authentic faith, and so as father of all true believers (Rom 4:11b-12). The pivot of Paul's reasoning is the fact that according to the biblical account, faith was credited to Paul as righteousness when he was not yet circumcised (see Rom 4:10f.), and therefore before any work of the Law, i.e., prescinding from any merit. The whole narration serves to explain that the same pattern applies to the one who believes in Christ (see Rom 4:23-24), who therefore recognizes the necessity of conforming not just to abstract principles but to the story lived out by the most genuine "homo biblicus."

But there are other personages whose tales are told, if only in a few words. Such are *Isaac and Jacob* in Rom 9:7-13: each, with various references to Genesis (21:12; 18:10; 25:23; and also Mal 1:2-3), is contrasted with his brother (in turn, Ishmael—even though not named—and Esau) to underline the theological thesis that election is based not on works but on the free will of the One who calls (cf. Rom 9:11). The same thing—but in the opposite sense—is true of *Pharaoh* in Rom 9:14-17 (cf. Exod 9:16) to say that God sovereignly "has mercy on whom he wants to have mercy, and he hardens whom he wants to harden" (v. 18) and to explain that the obstinacy of Israel toward the gospel belongs to a divine plan.

The experience of the prophet *Elijah* is recorded as well in Rom 11:2b-4 (citing 1 Kgs 19:10, 14, 18), especially in reference to the fact that in Israel seven thousand persons had not bent the knee to Baal, in order to point out the existence of a "remnant" in Israel even at the present time, when despite everything Israel remains obstinate in unbelief.

---

tigung und Heilsgeschichte im Römerbrief," in *Paulinische Perspektiven* (Tübingen, 1969) 108–139; idem, "Der Glaube Abrahams in Römer 4," ibid., 140–177; O. Betz, "Die heilsgeschichtliche Rolle Israels bei Paulus," ThB 9 (1978) 1–21, etc. For this reason, in our treatment we will not review the question of Paul's use of the Old Testament in Romans; among the various studies on the subject, see most recently D. A. Koch, *Die Schrift als Zeuge des Evangeliums. Untersuchungen zur Verwendung und zum Verständnis der Schrift bei Paulus*, BzHTh 69 (Tübingen, 1986) esp. 302–321.

Other personages of the Old Testament remembered by Paul are Moses (in Rom 10:5, 19), David (Rom 4:6-8), Isaiah (Rom 9:27, 29; 10:16, 20; 15:12), Hosea (Rom 9:25), but not as protagonists in some story but rather as *hagiographi*, authors of texts cited by the Apostle. Still, apart from the fact that these names are mentioned explicitly in lieu of the more frequent impersonal formula "It is written" (Rom 1:17; 2:14; 3:4, etc.), the texts Paul reports of them stand out for *particularly concrete and imaginative language*, like the two macarisms of Ps 32:1-2, the veiled allusion to Hosea's singular marriage experience (Hos 2:1-25), the metaphor of the sands of the sea (Isa 10:22-23), the remembrance of Sodom and Gomorrah (Isa 1:9), the image of the stumbling block and the rock of offense (Isa 8:14; cf. 28:16), the double metaphor of going up to heaven and descending to the abyss (Deut 30:12f.), the image of jealousy (Deut 32:21), and the paradox of being found by one who was not seeking (Isa 65:1f.)

2) The absolutely decisive factor for Paul's discourse in Romans is *the narrative dimension of the Christological kerygma*. Not that this is a characteristic exclusive to Romans, belonging as it does to the Christian faith as such, as the ancient pre-Pauline confession of faith in 1 Cor 15:3-5 attests. But we must observe that it continues in importance, and is repeatedly recalled in our letter, where there are a dozen passages on the subject.

We encounter the first of these in the preface, where Paul offers a confession in truly original terms: "Who as to his human nature was a descendant of David, and who through the Spirit was declared with power to be the Son of God, by his resurrection from the dead" (1:3b-4a). Here we note only that in the New Testament there exists no other Christological formula that encompasses the whole earthly experience of Jesus in its two extremes, namely, the birth from the stock of David and the resurrection from death (cf. 2 Tim 2:8). The commentaries will of course have much more to say, but meanwhile it is worthwhile noting that the whole story of Jesus Christ is included between these extremes.

The other passages of Romans, on the other hand, always insist on or at least include the motif of the death or the blood, which is missing in this first text. The passages are these: "God presented him as a sacrifice of atonement through faith in his blood" (3:25); "He was delivered over to death for our sins and was raised to life for our justification" (4:25); "Christ died for the ungodly . . . Christ died for us . . . through the death of his Son" (5:6, 8, 10); "The death he died he died to sin once for all; but the life he lives he lives to God" (6:10); "raised from the dead" (7:4); "Christ Jesus, who died—more than that, who was raised to life—is at the right hand of God and is also interceding for us" (8:34); " 'Jesus is Lord' and . . . God raised him from the dead" (10:9); "For this very reason Christ died and returned to life" (14:9); "For even Christ did not please himself, but, as it is written, the insults of those who insult you have fallen on me" (15:3; cf. Ps 69:10); "Christ has become a servant of the Jews . . . to confirm the promises made to the patriarchs" (15:8); see also 7:4; 8:3, 32.

As we see, Paul does not tell in detail either the experiences of Jesus' birth (as do Matt 1-2 and Luke 1-2) or the story of his passion (like the four Gospels). His preoccupation is kerygmatic rather than biographical; or better, it is with reflection on the kerygma. But the kerygma remains intact in its narrative essentials, and its presence scattered throughout the Letter to the Romans indicates how much importance Paul attributes to it. One could, of course, question how far, according to modern sensibilities, the resurrection of Christ really belongs to a truly historical or at least historiographic dimension. But that in no way detracts from the fact that Paul "tells" it along with the death or from the fact that for his readers it was indivisibly united as an event with the death.

3) In Romans there are elements of the writer's autobiography: here and there Paul tells his own story. Already in the inscription he is not satisfied to give his own name, as was normal in ancient letter writing, but adds his specific apostolic identity (1:1: "called to be an apostle, and set apart for the gospel of God"), indicating also the origin of this call with Jesus (1:5: "through him . . . we have received grace and apostleship") and also its purpose (ibid.: "to call people from among all the gentiles to the obedience that comes from faith").

This last characteristic returns in 11:13b, where with a certain pride Paul emphasizes, "As apostle to the gentiles I do honor to my ministry." Even so, he does not forget, indeed he draws attention to, his own Jewish identity (see 11:1b: "I am an Israelite myself, a descendant of Abraham, from the tribe of Benjamin"), as elsewhere as well (2 Cor 11:21; Phil 3:5-6). But what is new in Romans is the explicitly declared anxiety concerning the salvation of his own people: "I speak the truth in Christ—I am not lying, my conscience confirms it in the Holy Spirit—I have great sorrow and unceasing anguish in my heart. For I could wish that I myself were cursed and cut off from Christ for the sake of my brothers, those of my own race" (9:1-3; cf. 11:14: "In the hope that I may somehow arouse my own people to envy and save some of them"). Here there comes powerfully to the foreground not only the apostle but the human person, with his consciousness of ethnic identity and his great interior sensitivity, which is a cause of suffering but also of generous altruistic forces.

We encounter specific autobiographical information in 3:8, where Paul says he has been slandered with the claim that he preached that one must do evil so that good will come from it (cf. 6:1). But he decisively denies such an accusation, which indicates a grave misunderstanding of his message if not simply deliberate detraction.[15]

But the longest autobiographical sections in Romans are those that provide the framework for the whole body of the letter and are found in the introduction (see 1:8-13) and the conclusion (see 15:16-32). Here more than anywhere the relationship to the readers is direct, conversational, personalized, and specifically narrative. Paul expresses the desire to see the Christians of Rome (and indeed his regret at not having been able to visit them earlier), the awareness that he has already traveled through all the regions from Jerusalem to Illyria, his plan to reach Spain, his fears for the imminent trip (from Corinth, where he probably wrote the letter) to Jerusalem to bring the collection for the poor of that Church, and finally the request for prayers of support for the trials that await him.

These two sections are surely important, not only from the simply historical point of view but also to establish the occasion that conditioned the sending of the letter to the Romans. But along with these, the other autobiographical fragments we have noted contribute to keeping Romans from being an impersonal and theoretical composition, immersing it rather in a living and dynamic situation.

4) Then there are passages we could call *theological biography of the recipients,* where the writer, using first or second person plural forms, describes a situation that regards the readers or involves them from the perspective of their new identity as Christians.

Thus we read, "Your faith is being reported all over the world" (1:8b; cf. 16:19a: "Everyone has heard about your obedience"); "I myself am convinced, my brothers, that you yourselves are full of goodness, complete in knowledge and competent to instruct one another" (15:14). More specifically at times he tells the spiritual journey or goal of the reader. In this case the basic theme is that of faith: "[We] believe in him who raised Jesus our Lord from the dead" (4:24; cf. 10:9); "Therefore, since we have been justified through faith, we have peace with God . . . we have gained access by faith into this grace in which we now stand . . ., we also rejoice in our sufferings . . ." (5:1-4).

But also baptism is recounted as the decisive turning point in one's biography: "Don't you know that all of us who were baptized into Christ

15. See below, chap. 7.

were baptized into his death? We were therefore buried with him through baptism into death in order that . . . we too may live a new life" (6:3-4; cf. 6:8, 11, 14, 17-18); "When you were slaves to sin . . . what benefit did you reap from the things you are now ashamed of? . . . But now . . . the benefit you reap leads to holiness . . ." (6:20-22). But everything leads back to the event of Christ's gift of self, through which the Christian life comes to be divided clearly into a "then" and "now": "When we were in the flesh . . . but now we are delivered from the law . . ." (cf. 7:4-6); the same pattern returns in 11:30: "As you who were at one time disobedient to God have now received mercy." Finally, the eschatological horizon is viewed as approaching: "Our salvation is nearer now than when we first believed" (13:11b).

So Paul does not speak abstractly about the gospel and its theological content but makes frequent reference to the story of Christians themselves, who not only can understand it better on the basis of their lived experience but can immediately recognize that it, so to speak, historicizes itself in their own existence.

5) A good part of the material in the Letter to the Romans could be labeled *theological narration.* These are the passages in which the speech is in the third person plural or even uses "I" or "you [singular]," but in a universal sense by means of *enallage,* the rhetorical use of one grammatical form for another. In all these cases the Apostle, rather than reasoning abstractly or just proclaiming fundamental truths, describes and so "narrates" moral or spiritual situations or experiences that concern not specific, defined persons (and hence are not biographical) but describe a general human condition.

There are principally five such passages. The first is in 1:18-32, where Paul describes the situation of those "who suppress the truth by their wickedness" (1:18b), that is, humanity without Christ and subject to God's wrath. Actually this passage is not written completely in narrative style, since we also find there statements of principle, which are found here and there within the description properly so called. But the text of 1:21-22, 25, 26b-32 certainly comes under our classification; its intent is to say that all have sinned and are deprived of the glory of God (cf. 3:23).

A second section of theological narrative consists of almost the whole of chapter 2 (with the exception of vv. 6-11, 16). But we note a stylistic variation, corresponding to two different groups of persons. In 2:12-15, where the subject is the unwritten law observed by pagans, the discourse proceeds normally in the third person plural. But in 2:1-5, 17-29, where it is the Law as Jewish patrimony that is treated, Paul uses the rhetorical device of direct address in the second person singular. In this case the "you" refers not to any single interlocutor but to the Jew in general (cf. 2:17), in the genre of diatribe, which tends thus to enliven the discourse. (But one can also hypothesize from this literary device that the recipients of Romans were for the most part Christians of Jewish origin.)

In the third place we can count 5:12-19 in this type of narration. Here the Apostle contrasts Adam and Christ each as universal ancestor, representing two different situations in human history. Applying to them what 1QS 4:15 says of the two spirits, we can say that "in these two is the history (*tôledôt*) of all human beings." And in effect, rather than speaking theoretically about sin and grace, Paul contrasts the disobedience of Adam and the obedience of Christ insofar as they resonate with all those who adhere to the behavior of one or the other and are led to death or to life.

In the fourth place is the celebrated passage 7:7-25. Despite its well-known difficulty, one thing is clear: it "tells" an experience of life. This is confirmed by the frequent use of the first person singular (the pronoun twenty-five times in nominative, dative, accusative, and genitive), thus forming a kind of match to the "you" of chapter 2. But as is the case there, so here the "I" is not autobiographical, unless very indirectly so. In the first place, the writer thinks in terms of a vast human totality, whether it be considered pagan, Jewish, or Christian (or some combination of these).

And then Paul also recounts the condition of Israel from the perspective of their inalienable religious patrimony (see 9:4-5 regarding Israel: "They are Israelites, and theirs is the adoption as sons, the glory, the covenants, the reception of the law, the cult and the promises. Theirs are the patriarchs, and from them comes Christ according to the flesh"); still, he notes that Israel as a whole has not achieved what the Law intended, faith in Christ (cf. 9:6b-7; 11:5, 7). He even personifies creation, humanizes it, as it were, in its longing for eschatological redemption (8:20-21).

6) In Romans there is another type of narrative, belonging to the genre of the *similitude*. It is not properly speaking a parable, nor is it introduced with any special formula; rather, these are examples which Paul draws from daily life to illustrate specific points of his doctrine with figurative language.

Here more than anywhere, even when the texts are brief the narrative character is especially evident, since it is expressed in concrete, tangible, effective, and memorable images. These have the double advantage of giving a shape to abstract concepts and bringing the matter of the discourse closer to the dimensions of daily life. They offer an *imagery* derived from various areas of human experience.

First: 4:4-5: "The wages of one who works are not considered a gift but an obligation. However, for the man who does not work but trusts in the God who justifies the wicked, his faith is credited as righteousness." As we see, the example is not developed autonomously; rather, it opens up a passage to the theological lesson to be imparted. In any case, the comparison derived from the practice of the laborer is unquestionably eloquent. And we can even recognize a thematic affinity to Jesus' parable about the laborers sent to the vineyard at different times (Matt 20:1-16).

Second: 5:7f.: "It is unlikely that anyone will die for a righteous man, though for a good man someone might dare to die. But God shows his own love for us in that while we were still sinners, Christ died for us." In fact, the example here is imperfect: it says that what is considered the greatest demonstration of friendship among human beings (cf. John 15:13) is surpassed by what God does in Christ, who thus shows the ability to forge new paths other than the human ways. But it is precisely the inadequacy of the comparison that puts in relief the fact and the meaning of the death of Christ.

Third: 7:2-3: "By law a married woman is bound to her husband as long as he is alive, but if her husband dies, she is released from the law that binds her to her husband. So if she goes over to another man while her husband is still alive, she is called an adulteress. But if her husband dies, she is released from that law and is not an adulteress, even though she goes over to another man. So, my brothers, you also died to the law through the body of Christ. . . ." Quite unlike a marriage catechesis is the use here. Paul inserts these lines as a comparison in the context of a reflection on the cessation of the validity of the Torah. The example is complex and apt, taking on the characteristics of an allegory. It is explained in the following vv. 4-6: the wife symbolizes the (Judeo-Christian?) recipients, the first husband is the Torah (or the old regime of the letter), the second is Christ (or the new regime of the Spirit). The example does not indicate how the first husband comes to die, but the explanation indicates that it happened "through the body of Christ." But we observe that while in the example it is the husband (the Torah) that dies, in the explanation it is the Christians themselves that die ("You also died to the law . . . that you might belong to another"; cf. v. 6). So the comparison limps here: on the level of salvation history Paul does not say that the Torah is to die, but that Christians are to die to it. Still, the image remains no less incisive.

Fourth: 9:20-21: "Who are you, O man, to talk back to God? Shall what is formed say to the one who formed it, 'Why did you make me thus?' Does not the potter have the right to make out of the same lump of clay one vessel for noble purposes and another for common use?" The Apostle here is clearly inspired by the prophetic texts of Isa 29:16; 45:9; Jer 18:6; and also Wis 15:7. But he reformulates the comparison in his own terms and especially applies it to the new situation of Israel in the face of the gospel. The example preserves the same effective tangibility that was characteristic of the old biblical texts.

Fifth: 11:16-24: This is the longest and perhaps the best known similitude of the whole letter; but Paul is well aware that it is a question of an example "against nature" (v. 24). It is the image of the wild olive shoot grafted onto the good olive, which in non-metaphorical reality refers to the insertion of pagan believers into the trunk of Israel. The extent of the text by itself already tells us that the Apostle attributes considerable importance to it. Its purposes are two: theological and paraenetic. On the one hand, Paul wants to make the Christians of gentile origin conscious that their new identity is intimately associated with the salvific-historic identity of the people of Israel; but on the other hand, he asks them not to boast over against Israel, not even against that Israel which remains unbelieving, since "it is not you that supports the root, but the root that supports you" (11:18). Moreover, there is still a component of hope regarding unbelieving Israel, which can always "be grafted back into their own olive tree" (11:24). It is no exaggeration to say that altogether this similitude recapitulates in itself the whole rich thematic of chapters 9–11.

Sixth: 13:12: "The night is nearly over; the day is near. So let us set aside the deeds of darkness and put on the armor of light." The beautiful image used here (cf. Eph 5:14; 1 Thess 5:6) follows on v. 11, "The hour has come for you to wake up from your slumber," a rather widely diffused image in Hellenism (see the commentaries). Night and day are understood here in an apocalyptic conceptual framework (this world and the beginning of the world to come; such images are found, for instance, in *Bar. syr.* 85:10). And we must at least note once again the effectiveness of this type of speech, in which the wave of imagery carries one immediately from the good news to the paraenesis.

IV. Conclusion

As we have seen, on the basis of our analysis Romans offers abundant narrative material that is not normally observed. By no means a speculative theological tract, the letter loves to tell a story. The narrative genre is included on various levels and following different types. We have counted six: biblical narrative, the narrative dimension of the Christological kerygma, elements of the writer's autobiography, passages of theological biography of the recipient, theological narration, and similitudes.

One could use different terms for these types, but each is formally distinct from any of the others.

The concept of narration, then, is concretely realized analogically. In any case, we are here dealing with an original dimension strongly attested precisely in the most mature and the most highly developed writing of the Apostle Paul, and making the Letter to the Romans (and indirectly its author) fresher, more concretely comprehensible, yes, more true to life and itself more full of life. Furthermore, the narrative dimension inserts our letter more deeply into the context of the whole Bible, which is itself precisely largely narrative in character.[16] In actual fact, if the Christian or for that matter the Jew had nothing to tell, they would have nothing new to say. But if there is anyone who really has something original to communicate, it is surely Saint Paul in the Letter to the Romans.

---

16. See N. Frye, *The Great Code. The Bible and Literature* (London, 1982).

Chapter 6

Romans 1:18-2:29: Between Missionary Preaching and Borrowing from the Environment

The pericope Rom 1:18-2:29 provides some notoriously interesting questions, not only on the level of detailed exegesis but especially with regard to its overall value, from the historical and theological as well as the literary point of view. Precisely on this question we want to consider two different and even opposing opinions. Some would have it that here stand reflected the praxis and content of Paul's missionary preaching, whereas for others these pages would be nothing but a reproduction of Jewish patterns and content, and so would represent a *pièce* that is neither Pauline nor Christian.

I. Missionary preaching of Paul?

The first developed exposition of this opinion is a study from the beginning of the century by E. Weber.[1] This author even establishes a parallel with the speech to the Areopagus of Acts 17 and maintains that Rom 1-3, more than any other Pauline letter, reflects the Apostle's missionary preaching or at least parts of it. He does make it clear that we do not have here simply a reproduction of such a missionary speech but the outline for the teaching preparatory to the missionary message properly so called.[2] In practice, Paul began with an appeal to the one only God and to openness to the truth present within the human person. Even the Jew was invited to overcome the resistance of self-assurance, since only if one breaks through this is there room for the gospel.

---

1. *Die Beziehungen von Röm. 1-3 zur Missionspraxis des Paulus,* Beiträge zur Forderung christlicher Theologie 9, 4 (Gütersloh, 1905).
2. See ibid., 81.

In the more recent literature this type of approach to our passage is favored in the commentaries of O. Michel[3] and O. Kuss,[4] while it is criticized by E. Käsemann.[5] The well-known Tübingen exegete acknowledges that "there is some truth in this thesis," but while admitting that "it is only the strength of this influence that is problematic" (note, for example, the diatribe style), he points out three problems: (1) reflections of missionary preaching are found in all the Pauline letters; (2) there is no need to dissolve the internal coherence of these pages by saying that here Paul would just be gathering fragments of sermons or of earlier disputes (in contrast to the speeches of Acts); and (3) we must bear in mind that Romans is a letter addressed to a solidly Christian community, and that consequently the accusations made in our passage are not directed toward this community, nor are they meant to bring about its conversion.

These observations of Käsemann are very pertinent. Still, it is possible to insist on the presence in Rom 1:18–2:29 of consistent echoes of Paul's missionary preaching, especially with regard to its pagan audience. In fact, despite the silence of the authors on the issue, one could recognize a thematic parallelism between Rom 1:18-32 and what the Apostle wrote to the Thessalonians in 1 Thess 1:9b: "You turned to God from idols to serve the living and true God." This sentence, which describes the effect of Paul's preaching at Thessalonica, and so indirectly also the content of it, can hardly help but resonate, for example, with Rom 1:25 ("They exchanged the truth of God for a lie, and worshiped and served the creature rather than the creator") and also with 2:4 (". . . not recognizing that God's kindness urges you to repentance"), not to speak of the contextual warning about the "wrath" of God on the last day, present also in 1 Thess 1:10 and Rom 1:18; 2:5, 8.

In such a case, however, we would be dealing only with partial echoes. Indeed, certain considerations allow us to say that Rom 1:18–2:29 has its own autonomy in function and content alike. Regarding the content, we recall above all the positive judgment given in 2:14-15 concerning the observance "by nature" of the law by the pagans; it is hard to understand such an affirmation as part of a missionary message, in which one should find oneself discredited rather than justified. The same is true for the Jews, concerning whom it is recognized paradoxically that "those who obey the law . . . will be justified" (2:13), even if in fact it is said that these on the contrary do not keep it. Besides, insofar as it concerns the Jews, the

3. *Der Brief an die Römer*, Meyer Kommentar (Göttingen, 1966⁴) 60.
4. *Der Römerbrief* I (Regensburg, 1957) 29-30.
5. *Commentary on Romans* (Grand Rapids, Mich., ca. 1980) 34 = *An die Römer*, HzNT 8a (Tübingen, 1973; 1980⁴) 30-31.

passage in 1 Thess 1:9b-10 is not comparable, for there it is attested that they have been converted to the gospel, whereas Rom 1:18–2:29 is concerned in large part, if not wholly, with the negative reaction of the Jews in relation to the announcement of the gospel.

From the perspective of function, our passage is meant to play a counterpoint to the theme of the "righteousness of God," which is something quite new in the context of the Pauline letters. Hence the whole section Rom 1:18–2:29 contains a smattering of reflection, formulated in new terms so as to illuminate by contrast such a crucial new way of conceiving the gospel.

II. Insertion of a synagogue sermon?

An opinion completely contrary to the preceding is maintained by E. P. Sanders,[6] who in Rom 1:18–2:29 would have Paul simply reproducing homiletic material from diaspora Judaism. Except for the little phrase 2:16b, nothing is distinctive of Paul's thought, which leaves no specific mark. The author affirms categorically that the best way to read our passage "is as a synagogue sermon. . . . The Christian viewpoint plays no role, and the entire chapter is written from a Jewish perspective."[7] He reasons thus not only from the polemic against idolatry in 1:18-32, typical of Hellenistic Jewry, but from several statements in chapter 2. Thus what is said in 2:4 about μετάνοια, "repentance," is completely atypical for Paul; in 2:13 it is surprising that the Apostle would recognize a justification on the basis of observance of the law; again in 2:13 the expression δίκαιος παρὰ τῷ θεῷ, "righteous before God," is Jewish and has no Pauline parallel; in 2:27 the affirmation that the pagans who keep the law will judge the Jews conflicts with 1 Cor 6:2, according to which it is the Christians who will judge the world; finally the πνεῦμα, "spirit," of 2:29 is not the Spirit of God but "the inner self," while the σάρξ, "flesh," of v. 28, to which it is opposed, is not a negative-alternative force but the physical body of circumcision.

But Sanders then decides that this passage is not a true interpolation, because of its being thematically adapted to Paul's intent: even though the Apostle did not compose the passage, he inserted it here because it treats salvation, and specifically salvation that depends on obedience to the law.[8]

6. *Paul, the Law, and the Jewish People* (Philadelphia, 1983) 123-135.
7. Ibid., 129.
8. Ibid., 131.

Such a position has the advantage of explaining in the clearest possible terms the fact that Rom 2 especially is out of accord with typical Pauline thought on the Law and on its observance, which is here treated too positively. The perception of this contrast is not new, as is already evidenced in the opposing sixteenth-century commentaries of Luther and Seripando.[9] Sanders resolves the question dramatically at the root, simply denying Paul the paternity of this passage. But this cannot be done without its own inconveniences, especially because of the interconnection with the context. If it is true that the passage does not square well with the general Pauline theology, it still fits perfectly into the specific context of Romans. It is here especially that Sanders is found wanting. According to him, the conclusion that should flow naturally from Rom 2 would be this: Repent and obey the Law from the depth of your heart in order that you may be a true Jew![10]

But in reality this is actually not the conclusion drawn by Paul. In fact, in 3:1ff. the Apostle asks himself what is the "advantage" (τὸ περισσόν) of the Jew in comparison with the pagan, thus supposing a type of reasoning that leads not to a call for conversion but to a posing of the problem of the place of Israel in the history of salvation, seeing that they are placed on a footing of equality with the gentiles, whether on the level of sin (all have sinned) or on that of divine retribution (all are judged impartially by God on the basis of their good or evil works). Therefore the role of Rom 1:18–2:29 in the epistle consists in scandalously leveling Jews and gentiles from a soteriological perspective (hence the rhetorical but ever so weighty question of Rom 3:1).[11] And this kind of discourse is surely not Jewish!

This conclusion is valid even if we accept the hypothesis (according to Sanders against Käsemann)[12] that Rom 2:29 represents not a thematic change to a Christian perspective but a continuing depiction of the true Jew, who is such "in the spirit" (circumcision of the heart in observance of the Torah: cf. Deut 30:6), "and not in the letter" (by the mere possession of the Torah). The basic intention remains to demonstrate, not that

9. For example the problematic text 2:13 is understood by Luther as referring to Christians (*factores . . . soli qui gratiam habent*, "the 'doers'. . . [are] only those who have grace": WA 56, 22–23), while Seripando notes a semantic variation in Paul's language (*iustificationis vocabula, quibus frequenter Paulus utitur, non eandem ubique hebent [sic!] rationem*, "the words for 'justification' often used by Paul do not always have the same meaning": *Hieronymi Seripandi . . . Commentaria . . .* [Naples, 1601] 38).

10. E. P. Sanders, *Paul, the Law*, 129. Nevertheless, he is right in maintaining that Rom 1:18–2:29 has no intention of demonstrating either that no one in fact keeps the Law or that the Law cannot be kept.

11. See chap. 4 above.

12. See E. P. Sanders, *Paul, the Law*, 127 and 131.

the good Jew is the one who obeys the Law (perhaps without circumcision), but that the Jew cannot claim any special status compared with the pagan, since the latter, when observing the law "by nature" (2:14; cf. 2:26-27), is equal to the former, and consequently they are both on a par. Very well, but neither is this kind of equalization exactly synagogal language.[13]

III. Inculturated theology

If neither of the two theses examined alone can explain the literary-thematic character of Rom 1:18-2:29, it is still true that each furnishes elements for an adequate understanding.

Our section surely describes the religious situation of humanity in general in terms that are negative only in part, and does so not simply to do cultural anthropology for its own sake, but for the purpose of announcing the gospel.[14] Now, it is theoretically possible that to do this Paul uses some elements of his missionary preaching. However, this is difficult to demonstrate beyond a generic, polemically exaggerated reproof of the moral degeneracy of paganism or of the unfounded boast of Judaism concerning its special status guaranteed by the Torah.

Above all, the anti-pagan polemic could be more completely documented in a missionary sense on the basis of contemporaneous Judeo-Hellenistic literature. This comparison has been attempted,[15] with all its attendant risks. Indeed, to what extent can the Hellenistic-Jewish literary production be considered technically missionary, even if dealt with selectively?[16] On the contrary, we can consider this more truly as a testimony

13. This cannot even be compared with what Philo of Alexandria writes when he says that "those who have an excellent character should not boast about the nobility of their race" (*Virt.* 206); nor would the "allegorists" (see *Migr.* 92; *Quaest. Ex.* 2, 2) have accepted Paul's position. Now, as Sanders himself admits, "We do not have a corpus of Diaspora synagogal sermons with which to compare Romans 2, and thus we can adduce no proof that Rom 2:12-15 is a non-Christian Jewish theme" (ibid., 130f.). Nor is any such proof afforded by the three homilies since published by F. Siegert, *Drei hellenisch-jüdische Predigten. Ps.-Philo, "Über Jona," "Über Simson" und "Über die Gottesbezeichnung "wohltätig verzehrendes Feuer.' "—I. Übersetzung aus dem Armenischen und sprachliche Erläuterungen,* WUNT 20 (Tübingen, 1980).

14. Correctly C. E. B. Cranfield, *The Epistle to the Romans,* I, ICC (Edinburgh, 1982 [= 1975]) 105, writes, "It is not Paul's judgment of his contemporaries that we have here, but the gospel's judgment of men, that is, of all men."

15. Thus Claus Bussmann, *Themen der paulinischen Missionspredigt auf dem Hintergrund der spätjüdisch-hellenistischen Missionsliteratur,* Europäische Hochschulschriften, Reihe 23: Theologie 3 (Bern-Frankfurt, 1971): on Rom 1:18-32: pp. 108-122); he resumes and corrects the study of P. Dalbert, *Die Theologie der hellenistischen-jüdischen Missionsliteratur unter Ausschluss von Philo und Josephus,* ThF 4 (Hamburg, 1954).

16. Against Dalbert, who is much more sanguine about the possibilities, Bussmann reduces the sources to the following: Aristoboulos, Eupolemos, Letter of Aristeas, Sibylline Oracles, Wisdom.

to the influence of the environment on Judaism, which simply rethinks itself with tools and categories derived from Greek tradition:[17] surely to enter into dialogue with the latter (even if this turned out to be fruitless), but purely defensively so, to mount an apologetic defense against external attacks.[18] But in fact, on a concrete practical level, it is a desperate enterprise to find real parallels to Paul's case, whether in the pagan world (where none is to be found with the consciousness of a specific vocation, and where the itinerants proceed with no clear plan of progress such as that witnessed in Rom 15:17-24), or in Jewry (where at most we can cite Fl. Josephus, *Ant.* 20, 34-38, who speaks of "a merchant named Ananias," τις ἔμπορος Ἀνανίας ὄνομα, who made proselytes in the course of his journeys).[19]

With regard to the themes of the possible missionary comparison, of the three central interests identified by Dalbert in the Hellenistic-Jewish literature (monotheism, spiritualized revelation, and the election of Israel), it is significant that the third not only is absent from Rom 1:18–2:29 but is explicitly reevaluated, if not refuted. And Bussmann in fact does not list it among the themes and concepts common to Paul and to the so-called Judeo-Hellenistic missionary preaching.[20]

The most evident thing about our passage is that Paul develops there a profoundly inculturated theological reflection, which, even if it considered human beings in general, treated them as culturally "situated." For that reason the Apostle is not satisfied to make accusations merely from a position of generic difference, but does so by making use of language and concepts proper to those whom he is addressing. It is for this reason that one finds here a "vorgeformtes Material." This can be more easily discovered in Rom 1:18-32, which has actually received the most scholarly attention. Here we identify: the apocalyptic motif of universal sinfulness, the (Judeo-Hellenistic) motif of the natural knowledge of God, the Stoic (and Judeo-Hellenistic) motif of immanent retribution, which considers vice itself to be its own punishment, and the pattern (both Hellenistic

17. On this subject there may be something symbolic in what Clearchos, a disciple of Aristotle, said of a Jew from Asia: "He was Greek (ἑλληνικός) not only in language but in soul (τῇ ψυχῇ) as well" (Fl. Josephus, *C. Ap.* 1, 180; cf. M. Stern, 15).

18. See H. Conzelmann, *Heiden-Juden-Christen. Auseinandersetzungen in der Literatur der hellenistisch-römischen Zeit*, BhTh 62 (Tübingen, 1981) esp. 121–218.

19. See P. Bowers, "Paul and Religious Propaganda in the First Century," NT 22 (1980) 316–323; 321: even Abraham in certain sources (*Gen. Rab.* 39, 40, 48; *Sifr. Deut.* 32) is considered the first proselyte, who in turn will bring other pagans to conversion (see also 2 Macc 3:34; 9:17; *Mek. Yitro*, Amalek 2).

20. These would be the following: foolishness of idolaters, relation between God and gods, the theme of error, that of judgment, the evaluation of idolatry, the "Lasterkataloge," conversion, the natural knowledge of God, titles given to God (living, true, only, creator, father), salvation (see *Themen*, 143–190).

and Jewish) of the "Lasterkatalog."[21] But Rom 2 also reveals clear traces of argumentation common to Paul's contemporaries: thus, the need for conversion (for Jews as well as pagans), the final judgment on the basis of works (idem), the Hellenistic concept of natural law, the Deuteronomic theme of circumcision of the heart, and the (rabbinic) Jewish idea of equivalence between the transgression of one precept and the transgression of the whole Law (along with the concept of Law as incarnation of God's will: 2:20b).

All these themes, of course, establish bridges between Paul and his contemporaries. But the whole discourse, rather than proclaiming the special election of Israel (as happens in Hellenistic Judaism), is subordinate to the Christological message of the gospel. The Apostle gathers Hellenistic and Jewish elements and fuses them together, but confers a specific orientation on them. Following Bussmann,[22] we perceive three steps in his argumentation. First, supporting himself on Hellenistic philosophy on the one hand and Jewish toralogy on the other, he surpasses them both, developing an accusation based on them both. Then it appears that contrary to the Jewish preaching of election and wrath, his accusation knows no exception, since all are subject to God's wrath. Finally, however, it turns out that the wrath of God is not the final purpose of the accusation, that it is only a background for the announcement of God's saving righteousness; it is with this that in 3:21 the whole section will reach its climax[23] as a reprise of the theme already developed in 1:17.

The whole discourse encompassed in Rom 1:18–2:29, then, contains very little that is specifically Christian, if we except the stray fragment 2:16b, which surely is not sufficient to put a Pauline stamp on the whole, and note that the meaning of $\pi\nu\varepsilon\tilde{\nu}\mu\alpha$, "spirit," in 2:29 is at least debatable. But as already indicated, the Christian character of the exposition consists properly not in the matter treated but in its context and its function. Still, this does not imply that the material was taken up whole from an earlier composition (whether pre-redactional or even non-Christian).

Paul here adopts a kind of approach to the human situation that is already determined from the start not just by Jewish (apocalyptic and sapiential) preconceptions, but especially by his understanding of the gospel (cf. 1:16-17), by his conception of the event of the Cross (cf. 3:21-26), and definitively by his faith in Jesus Christ (cf. 3:27-31). It is altogether true that Paul's

21. See C. Bussmann, *Themen,* 108–122; in addition to the commentaries, see G. Segalla, *L'empietà como rifiuto della verità di Dio in Romani 1,18-28,* StPat 34 (1987) 275–296.
22. See *Themen,* 121f.
23. On this last point see J.-N. Aletti, "Rm 1:18–3:20: Incohérence ou cohérence de l'argumentation paulinienne?" Bib 69 (1988) 47–62.

attitude is succinctly formulated by E. P. Sanders in a section title, "The solution as preceding the problem."[24] Indeed the explanation could be that it is the solution that reveals, and in some way even creates, the problem, for without the Cross of Christ understood as the *locus* of the eschatological manifestation of God's justice, the human situation of the Jew *as much as* that of the Greek would never have appeared in all its desperate gravity.

Still, the theological elaboration constructed by Paul shows that his gospel preaching does not come from a subjective indifference to culture, nor does it fall on an objective cultural void. The Apostle well knows human persons and assumes their concrete situation, discerning therein not only an extrinsic preparation for the gospel but a structural component corresponding to it, since if the gospel is the "power of God," it is so "for the salvation of everyone who believes, first for the Jew, then for the Greek" (1:16).

---

24. *Paul and Palestinian Judaism* (London, 1977) 442–447.

Chapter 7

Paul's Detractors in Romans 3:8

Ever since F. Christian Baur in the last century raised the question of the historical circumstances in which the Letter to the Romans was written,[1] the question has remained open as to what the reason was that moved Paul to compose such a substantial document and send it to a Christian community which had been established without him and which he did not yet know in person.[2] In particular there remains the question: Apart from other possible interests, in writing the Letter to the Romans did the Apostle also want to confront some situation within the Church? I believe the answer must be affirmative and that a bright ray of light to illuminate the situation can be found precisely in Rom 3:8, which we shall now consider first in isolation and then within its larger context in the epistle.

I. Syntactical, literary, and logical examination of Rom 3:8

The text offers no lexical problems.[3] More problematic could be the punctuation, and consequently the structure of the sentence, especially in relation to the preceding v. 7. The accurate analysis made of it by

1. See F. Chr. Baur, "Über Zweck und Veranlassung des Römerbriefs und die damit-zusammenhängende Verhältnisse der Römischen Gemeinde," TZTh (1836), Heft 3, 59–178.
2. For a *status quaestionis* on the subject, besides the introductions to the New Testament, see C. E. B. Cranfield, *The Epistle to the Romans*, ICC (Edinburgh, 1979), II, 814–823; J. W. Drane, "Why Did Paul Write Romans?" in D. A. Hagner and M. J. Harris, eds., *Pauline Studies, Presented to F. F. Bruce* (Exeter, 1980) 208–227; F. Montagnini, *La prospettiva storica della Lettera ai Romani*, SB 54 (Brescia, 1980) 28–40; and above all now A. J. M. Wedderburn, *The Reasons for Romans* (Edinburgh, 1989).
3. Neither are three textual variants (the omission of the second καί, "and," in B,K,326,629; the omission of the article τά before κακά, "evil," in D +; and the insertion of ἐφ' ἡμᾶς, "upon us," after the aorist subjunctive ἔλθῃ, "may come," in 0219, 81, cod. a of the Vetus Latina, and the Bohairic version) well enough attested, nor do they make any significant difference in the meaning.

Cranfield[4] supports the critical edition of Nestle-Aland, which separates v. 8 from v. 7, seeing them as two separate questions, the one distinguished by the first person singular, the other by the first person plural. Following his reasoning, we would read v. 8 literally, "And we do not say, do we, as we are slandered, and as some claim us to say that we must do evil in order that good may come from it? Their condemnation is just!"

The construction is hardly elegant! Especially, it is problematic whether the conjunction ὅτι (which in any case has a value of "that," introducing a quotation or making an affirmation) is connected with the immediately preceding verb λέγειν, "to say," (in which case the whole sentence is interrogative and depends on the initial μή, "not") or whether it goes directly with the initial questioning negation μή (in that case the parenthetic phrase "as we are slandered, and as some claim that we say" becomes isolated, and the interrogation would be only "and it is not, is it, . . . that [we say] we must do evil in order that good may come from it?"). Probably the first alternative is to be chosen, whether (1) because the supporters of the second (see Cranfield) must hypothesize the ellipsis of "we say" (λέγομεν or λέγωμεν) before ὅτι, even though there already is in the text the infinitive λέγειν, "saying/that we say," which it is useless to isolate in a supposed intermediate parenthetical phrase, or (2) because the relative ὧν, "whose/their," at the end of the verse makes better sense if the indefinite pronoun τινές, "certain ones," which is its antecedent, is an integral part of the one whole single preceding clause rather than only part of a parenthetical clause that would be farther away from the relative pronoun itself.

The whole of v. 8 is somehow in climactic parallelism with the question of v. 7b and, just like this, is dependent on the protasis of 7a ("But if God's truth has through my lie been abundantly revealed for his glory . . ."). That is, if human wickedness allows God to manifest the glory of his grace (3:7a), why must one still speak of the human being as God's enemy (3:7b)? Would it not be better, on the contrary, to live without moral constraints, since transgressions are the occasions for the affirmation of God's kindness (3:8)? Precisely here Paul informs us in a tone of indigna-

---

4. See Cranfield, *The Epistle to the Romans*, I, 137 and 185–187. He neglects, however, to consider a fifth possibility, represented by the Sixto-Clementine Vulgate, which reads v. 8 without any question mark, thus: *et non (sicut blasphemamur, et sicut aiunt quidam nos dicere) faciamus mala ut veniant bona: quorum damnatio iusta est*, or, in the obscurely literal Douay-Rheims-Challoner, "And not *rather* (as we are slandered, and as some affirm that we say) let us do evil that there may come good: whose damnation is just." Nevertheless, the stylistic and logical *ductus* of the whole section 3:1-9 does not allow v. 8 to be formulated as an affirmation (which in the present case would take on a paraenetic meaning that would not fit the context), but demands an interrogative, posing a question and thus confirming the question of v. 7.

tion (βλασφημούμεθα, "we are slandered") reflected even in the disorderly syntax of the text that "some persons" (τινές, not well defined) have attributed to him personally (on the meaning of this first person plural see below) the paternity of such a statement, concretized in the slogan Ποιήσω-μεν τὰ κακά, ἵνα ἔλθῃ τὰ ἀγαθά, "Let us do evil that good may come of it"!

But before trying to identify these "some persons," τινές, indeed in order to make this more possible, we must say a few words about the literary genre of our text. To do so we must broaden our sights, considering the whole section 3:1-20. Here we cannot but recognize a markedly lively style characterized by the technique of a concise dialogue (at least in 3:1-9) of attack and defense. We are doubtless witnessing the genre of diatribe; indeed we have here the most transparent example of the genre not only in Romans but in the whole Pauline correspondence.

From this specific point of view, the passage has recently been studied by Stowers, who had previously dedicated a monograph to the diatribe style in Romans.[5] He sees correctly that the passage is not so much an abstract theological discussion as a literary fiction representing an encounter between Paul and a Jewish opponent. This interlocutor is already evoked in 2:17 in the second person singular, after the diatribe style, there to be told that neither Law nor circumcision gives him reason for boasting unless he observes the former and practices the latter in the depth of the heart, so that the true "Jew" is the one who is so within (cf. 2:28-29), and a pagan could also be such, especially if such a one cleaves to Christ in the Spirit (2:14-16, 29). Such an affirmation, which in practice lowers the Jew to the level of the pagan, putting them both on the same footing of parity before the impartiality of God,[6] was bound to provoke an objection, which comes promptly in 3:1: "What is there extra [τὸ περισ-σόν, "the advantage"], then, for the Jew, or what is the value of circumcision?" Paul replies at once in 3:2: "Much in every way! First, they have been entrusted with the very words of God."

But from here on Stowers structures the dialogue in a way that I do not feel I can share. Subdividing 3:1-20 into eight parts, he articulates the text as follows:

5. See S. K. Stowers, "Paul's Dialogue with a Fellow Jew in Romans 3:1-9," CBQ 46 (1984) 707-722; idem, The Diatribe and Paul's Letter to the Romans, SBL DS 57 (Chico, Calif., 1981) 176-177. Against D. R. Hall, "Romans 3.1-8 Reconsidered," NTS 29 (1983) 183-197, according to whom Paul is not using diatribe style, since the interrogative formula that opens 3:1 introduces an internal debate within the Apostle rather than an external objection. On Paul's use of the diatribe, see now Th. Schmeller, Paulus und die 'Diatribe.' Eine vergleichende Stilinterpretation, NA NF 19 (Münster, 1987), which, however, has nothing to say on our passage.
6. See the excellent study by J. M. Bassler, Divine Impartiality: Paul and a Theological Axiom, SBL DS 59 (Chico, Calif., 1982), esp. 121ff.

A) Interlocutor: 3:1
B) Paul: 3:2-3
C) Interlocutor: 3:4
D) Paul: 3:5
E) Interlocutor: 3:6
F) Paul: 3:7-8
G) Interlocutor: 3:9a
H) Paul: 3:9b-20

The disagreement turns especially on v. 3, which Stowers attributes to Paul as if it were a question raised by the Apostle in order to lead the opponent to a necessary response. But to begin with, it is not appropriate to isolate the figure of an interlocutor too distinctly, since it is in fact Paul himself who raises for himself and for his hearers the questions that logically follow his own exposition. And we must note two further things. In the first place, v. 3 does not express Paul's thought, as we demonstrate in chapters 9-11 but merely expresses a problem that can only be fully answered after the partial answer furnished in v. 4. In the second place, as Stowers points out,[7] when the interlocutor of a diatribe is not a disciple of the master but a stranger, the questions are posed by the interlocutor and not by the master; in our case it is clear that the interlocutor is a Jew (cf. 2:17), or at most a Jewish Christian, who functions as an opponent of Paul, and so v. 3 must express the objection of someone other than Paul.

Furthermore, against Stowers we must say that the first person plural used in vv. 5, 8 cannot express sharing and association of Paul with the "fellow Jew" as interlocutor. Indeed:

Above all, the ἡμῶν of v. 5 ("But if *our* unrighteousness brings out God's righteousness . . .") absolutely cannot include Paul, who has fully accepted the justice of God (Phil 3:9), and so this is to be seen as an *enallage personae*, the rhetorical device substituting one grammatical form (here one grammatical person) for another, just like the singular ἐμῷ-κἀγὼ, "my, I," of v. 7; moreover, it has been said that this *enallage* does not limit the concept of ἀδικία, "unrighteousness," to Jews alone but extends it to the pagans as well, since precisely in v. 5 we have the resumption of the terms δικαιοσύνη, "righteousness," and ὀργή, "wrath," both of which bring the discourse back to a universalist horizon, just as these concepts have already been developed in turn in 1:16-17 (and then 3:21ff.) and in 1:18-2:29.

Furthermore, the plural first person forms βλασφημούμεθα . . . ἡμᾶς, "we are . . . us," in v. 8 cannot refer to the Jew in general, since it makes

---

7. See Stowers, "Paul's Dialogue," 713.

no sense for the Apostle to include in his own defamation his supposed
Jewish interlocutor, representative of all Jews; what we have is rather an
autobiographical plural, to be explained as a self-effacing plural, a *plurale
humilitatis*, or as a collective designation for Paul and his closest associates.

Finally, we must observe that v. 8 cannot be read exclusively as a question, since it also actually implies a response, even a twofold response:
in one part, indeed, Paul identifies what is said of him as calumny (and
this is already a reply, even though inserted in a long interrogative sentence); in the other, he concludes the verse with a curse against his slanderers ("Their condemnation is deserved"). So vv. 7-8 are divided and
an objection of the interlocutor can be recognized in 7-8a.

In conclusion we structure the section thus:

A) Objection (3:1):   What is the advantage of the Jew?
B) Reply (3:2):   Great! They have the Word of God.
C) Objection (3:3):   But does their lack of faith cancel God's fidelity?
D) Reply (3:4):   No, because God is faithful and righteous in his judgments (quoting Ps 51:6).
E) Objection (3:5):   But is his wrath perhaps unjust, since our wickedness allows God to manifest his mercy?
F) Reply (3:6):   No, because God remains the judge of all.
G) Objection (3:7-8a): But to promote God's glory should we not perhaps remain in sin, doing evil that good may come of it, as Paul himself seems to preach?
H) Reply (3:8b):   No! Indeed anyone who attributes this teaching to me slanders me and should be condemned.
I) Objection (3:9a):   Then the Jews are superior?[8]
J) Reply (3:9b-20):   No, because all, Jews and Greeks alike, are subject to sin, and the works of the Law do not justify anyone.

Our v. 8, then, is inserted into a chain of questions and answers, the
basic theme of which is the relationship between human behavior and
God's behavior—how are they related to each other? This question really

8. The sense of the present indicative προεχόμεθα is disputed. In any case, the understood subject is "we Jews" (cf. 31); it is normally read as a middle voice with the sense of an active (προέχομεν) and with the meaning already expressed in the Vulgate: *praecellimus?* "are we better?" (see the discussion in Cranfield, *The Epistle to the Romans*, I, 187–191); whereas Stower's "Paul's Dialogue," 719f., understands it as a passive: "are we bettered?" with the sense of "are we Jews at a disadvantage?" uniting it to the initial τί οὖν, "What then!" with a question mark only after the verb. The reading in the active is preferable in the context; however, in either case the basic sense does not change. But a certain variation of sense is possible in the answer of v. 9b, which could mean either "not at all" (most often, and perhaps correctly) or "not completely" (thus A. Feuillet, "pas entièrement" in "La situation privilégiée des Juifs d'après Rm 3,9. Comparaison avec Rm 1:16 et 3:1-2," in NRTh 105 [1983] 33–46).

becomes two, depending on whether it concerns the Jews alone or human beings in general.

In fact, in the framework of the literary genre of the diatribe, the basic questions that are to structure the first major part of the letter (1:8–11:36) are here. This was said some time ago by Campbell with reference to the whole of chapter 3.[9] Still, it is precisely the section 3:1-20 that governs the later developments. As the same author recognizes intuitively, "The structure of the letter will become clearer when we observe the relationship between the questions Paul asks and the answers he gives to them."[10] Well, then, in our verses we can discover three logical unities, which are crucial from the structural point of view.[11]

—3:1-4 poses the problem of the identity of Israel and of their role in salvation history: the replies barely sketched out here direct us to the more complete treatment, that will be done in chapters 9–11.

—3:9-20 returns to the themes of the universal situation of sin already developed in 1:18–2:29 and prepares that of the universal justification by grace and by faith, which will be developed in 3:21–5:21.

—3:5-8 poses another problem, which emerges from that of Israel but is more general: What is the relationship between my injustice and God's justice, that is, between sin and grace? Or to speak in the terms slanderously attributed to Paul: Ought we not do evil to give God the means to show the goodness of his grace? To this Paul here gives a hasty and provisional answer; it is simultaneously personal and theological, since the βλασ-φημούμεθα, "are slandered," implies a disparagement of God, a reduction of God's grace and wrath to the ridiculous, for all the seriousness of grace and wrath is lost if we eliminate all difference between the just and the sinner.[12] But the development of this response is delayed to chapters 6–8. And it is precisely on the basis of chapter 6 that we will be able to determine more precisely the identity of the τινές, "some," with whom the Apostle is disputing.

II. The relationship with 6:1, 15

The protasis found in 3:5a ("If our unrighteousness shows forth God's righteousness") and repeated in reverse terms in 3:7a ("If God's truth-

9. W. S. Campbell, "Romans III as a Key to the Structure and Thought of the Letter," in NT 23 (1981) 22-40.
10. Campbell, "Romans III," 32.
11. See above, chap. 4.
12. Regarding this, see above all the commentary of U. Wilckens, *Der Brief an die Römer*, EKK VI/1 (Zurich-Neukirchen, 1978) 167; also H. Schlier, *Der Römerbrief*, HThKNT (Freiburg-Basel-Wien, 1977) 97, speaks of the "calumnious doctrine" attributed to Paul, with the word βλασφημεῖν constructed personally. Still, this reading should not become exaggerated to the point of undervaluing the autobiographical component of the construction, since the word is used precisely in that sense in 1 Cor 10:30 (ἐγώ . . . βλασφημοῦμαι, "I am slandered").

fulness abounded through my falsehood") actually expresses a thesis that is central in the whole first part of the letter (1:16–5:21): Human injustice, rather than challenging or obscuring God's faithfulness to the promises of salvation, becomes as it were the prime matter that historically has furnished the fuel for the intervention of God's abundant mercy.

This concept returns in chapter 5, where the same verbs are reused for the first time in the letter, and that in the same grammatical forms. The first *(συνίστησιν)* recurs in 5:8 ("But God *demonstrates* his own love for us in this: while we were still sinners . . ."), while the second *(ἐπερίσσευσεν)* is used twice: 5:15b ("For if the many died by the trespass of the one man, how much more did God's grace and the gift that came by the grace of the one man Jesus Christ *abound* for the many") and 5:20b ("But where sin increased, grace *abounded* all the more"); see also the noun περισσεία, "abundance," in 5:17.

But besides the specific word, it is the idea itself which fills chapters 3–5 (see 3:35b; 4:5, 25; 5:6, 10, 15-20) and which reaches a climax in 5:21: "So that just as sin reigned in death, so also grace might reign through [God's] righteousness to bring eternal life through Jesus Christ our Lord." To the end of chapter 4 Paul does nothing but establish a strict connection between human unrighteousness and sin on the one hand and God's righteousness and grace on the other. When Luther writes in the *Scholia* to the Epistle to the Romans that in it the Apostle intends to *plantare ac constituere et magnificare peccatum*, "plant, build up, and magnify sin,"[13] he must be alluding to the first five chapters and the truly "evangelical" paradox of a God who, rather than punishing, redeems and justifies the sinner. For Paul, then, sin promotes and exalts grace.

But here is the problem: Can one perhaps also say the contrary, that grace promotes sin? "Some," τινές, attributed precisely this teaching to the Apostle. And it is precisely in 6:1 that he resumes the apodosis amply expressed in 3:5b, 7b-8 and condensed in the formula "Let us do evil that good may come of it." Resuming the diatribe style, the Apostle reformulates the question: "What shall we say, then? Shall we go on sinning, so that grace may increase?" and again in 6:15: "What then? Shall we sin because we are not under the law but under grace?" Each time he answers at once with an abrupt μὴ γένοιτο, "by no means!" (6:2, 15),[14] which till now he had used only in 3:4, 6, 31 and which also recalls the clear negative μή, "not," of 3:8. But that is not the end of it. Paul goes on to develop a broad discourse on the theological foundations of Christian ethic embracing chapters 6–8. It is articulated around these concepts: through

---

13. See J. Ficker, *Luthers Vorlesung über den Römerbrief 1515–1516* (Leipzig, 1908) II, 1.
14. See A. J. Malherbe, "*MH ΓΕΝΟΙΤΟ* in the Diatribe and Paul," HThR 73 (1980) 231-240 (the term "does not mark the termination of an argument, but rather a transition," 239).

baptism (chap. 6) and the Holy Spirit (chap. 8), the Christian is dead to the law and to the sin that it provokes (chap. 7). In any case, one is slave to someone, "whether to sin, which leads to death, or to obedience [faith], which leads to righteousness" (6:16b), but what is now important is "to walk in newness of life" (6:4; cf. 7:6). Therefore, even if the dominant principle is no longer law but grace, it is still unimaginable to continue in sin, whether because the Christian is ontologically dead to it (with baptism and with the Holy Spirit) or because the Christian is consequently free from any debt to the flesh, being called to live each day according to the Spirit.

With this precise clarification of his thought, Paul replies to these "some persons" (3:8) who maligned him in the eyes of the Church of Rome. Our opinion is, therefore, that the questions of 6:1, 15 simply restate the same question raised in 3:5-8.[15] But recently it has been suggested[16] that we see in the two texts an allusion to two different groups of adversaries: Judaizing Christians in 3:8 and gentile Christian antinomians in 6:1, because in chapter 6 (as distinguished from chapter 3) Paul has recourse not to terms and symbols from the Old Testament to support what he has to say but rather to baptism against a possible background of the mysteries. But this position is unacceptable for the following reasons:

> In general, it can no longer be held that criticism of the Law was characteristic only of gentile Christians; we actually know that some forms of partial antinomianism existed even among the Jews of the first century,[17] and even more so among Christians of Jewish origin, as demonstrated by Stephen and his group (cf. Acts 6–7), and Saint Paul himself.
>
> As for the use of the Old Testament, except for 8:36 (= Ps 44:23), it is never cited in Rom 6–8 (well, note also 7:7 = Exod 20:17; Deut 5:21); and yet in 7:1 Paul says, "I am speaking to people who know the law," assuming, therefore, in his readers a familiarity with the *nomos* which can be true only of Jewish Christians. Moreover, this address opens with the same formula as 6:3 ("Or do you not know that?"—ἢ ἀγνοεῖτε ὅτι), where the subject is baptism: a sign that the possible mystery categories are proper to Paul's hermeneutic of baptism rather than an accommodation to supposed gentile Christians.

15. Thus also the commentaries of Wilckens, *Der Brief*, EKK VI/2, 3-4; H. Schlier, *Der Römerbrief*, 190; also U. Luz, "Zum Aufbau von Röm I-VIII," TZ 25 (1969) 161-181, 169; R. B. Hays, "Psalm 143 and the Logic of Romans 3," JBL 99 (1980) 107-115, 112, n. 20; Campbell, "Romans III."

16. See I. J. Canales, "Paul's Accusers in Romans 3:8 and 6:1," EvQ 57 (1985) 237-245 (the author is introduced as "a Mexican-American pastor in California").

17. See the documentation in H. Räisänen, *Paul and the Law* (Tübingen, 1983) 93, 120-124, 234-235 (add LAB 25:13; 16:1).

Finally, we must take into account the fact that the question raised in 3:5-8 had not had an exhaustive answer till chapter 6; it is only now that the Apostle returns to the subject, and does so at some length, so that we cannot help but suppose that chapter 6 has the same persons as interlocutors as those we met in 3:8.

We must therefore recognize that the question raised in 3:8 "is in fact answered in vi 1–vii 6 and may also account for Paul's discussion of the law in vii 7f."[18]

III. Identification of the slanderers

The scarcity of data available to us depends on the typical polemic style of Paul, who always leaves his opponents anonymous. Nevertheless, this is not enough to keep us from reaching some conclusions sufficient to sketch the general traits of the physiognomy of the τινές who were slandering the Apostle.

1) In the first place, we determine that it concerns a *Jewish Christian*, not so much in the confessional as in the ethnic sense of the term.[19] When the label "Jewish Christian" is used, we must accurately distinguish between: (a) Christians of Jewish origin who maintain a permanent salvific value for the Law (such as the opponents in Galatians); (b) Christians of Jewish origin who maintain a nullification of the Torah in the economy of salvation (including Paul and his coworkers); (c) and Christians of pagan origin, but clinging to a legalistic hermeneutic of the gospel (this is not just a theoretical possibility, considering the report we have from Juvenal, *Sat.* 14:96-106).[20]

In our case, both the interlocutor of the diatribe in 3:1-9 and the explicit admission of Paul in 7:1 are sufficient indications to think that the calumny comes from the Jews (also because there is not a single direct reference to antinomians of pagan origin; cf. 2:14). Furthermore, the marked insistence of chapters 1-5 on the equality of Jews and pagans in sin and justification alike leads us to understand that Paul is writing the letter to Jewish Christians of the first or third group, to whom this teaching must have seemed difficult to accept (cf. 4:11-12!).

18. Campbell, "Romans III," 33.
19. See above, chap. 3.
20. Here Juvenal informs us that toward the end of the first century at Rome many pagans *Iudaicum ediscunt et servant ac metuunt ius*, "learn the Jewish Law, and keep it and revere it"; see also Suetonius, *Dom.* 12:2.

Still, we must immediately add that the specific anti-Pauline calumny (like the whole question raised in 3:5-8) is concerned not only with the Jew but with the human person in general. As we said above, the resumption of the concepts δικαιοσύνη-ὀργή, "righteousness-wrath," and the anticipation of the verbs συνίστησιν-ἐπερίσσευσεν, "demonstrates-abounded," takes place in a universal perspective that includes all together regardless of their religious differentiation. "To do evil that good may come from it," was, then, a slogan attributed to Paul and touted as applicable for all without distinction.[21]

2) In the second place, we must add that these Jewish Christians *maintained a libertine interpretation of the gospel* (placing themselves, so to speak, to the left of Paul). This becomes clear from the treatment of chapters 6-8, which correspond to 3:5-8 with a strong insistence on the fact that the Christian who has been freed from the Law now belongs to another lord and is subject to a new bond; the effective image for this is the analogy to marriage in 7:2-6. The affirmation that "we must do evil that good may come of it" is an intolerable caricature of the Pauline gospel of liberty, which the Apostle himself had already blunted in response to the enthusiasts of Corinth and their similar slogan, "Everything is permissible for me" (1 Cor 6:12; 10:23). Actually, as Käsemann notes, "Libertinism really could develop out of Paul's view of justification, and his adversaries claim that it is an unavoidable result."[22]

At any rate, we must assert that the slogan attributed to Paul comes not from orthodox Jewish Christians unable to bear his preaching against the Law but from a group of Jewish Christians, mistaken disciples of the Apostle, who to the nullification of the Torah add the revocation of all ethical limits.[23] The criticism of Paul that resulted from this, then, was based not on an accusation against him but on a misunderstanding of him that

21. This must be clarified against all those authors who speak too hastily of gentile Christian antinomians, like Campbell, "Romans III," 31f., 36. Not only are Paul's interlocutors not Christians of gentile origin and conditioning, but they are not even really antinomians, seeing that Paul himself in 6:14b and throughout chapter 7 theorizes the replacement of the Law and not a reinstitution. Actually the Apostle opposes his interlocutors not in "nomistic" but rather in "Christic" and "pneumatic" terms by saying that even alone Christ and the Spirit are the basis of Christian ethic.

22. E. Käsemann, *Commentary on Romans*, trans. and ed. G. W. Bromiley (Grand Rapids, Mich., 1980) 84 = *Der Brief an die Römer*, HzNT 8a (Tübingen, 1980⁴) 79; on a group of "libertarian extremists" in Rome, see also P. S. Minear, *The Obedience of Faith: The Purpose of Paul in the Epistle to the Romans*, SBTh SS 19 (Naperville, Ill., 1971) 61–63; the author identified them with those who according to Rom 14–15 considered themselves strong in faith and despised the weak.

23. It is, then, not a question of Jewish opponents' "hostile objection to the Apostle's . . . doctrine of grace" (Schlier, *Der Römerbrief*, 190).

all the more required a clarification in that it expressed not a contradiction, but a particularly unfortunate misinterpretation, by persons who wanted, perhaps, to be more Pauline than Paul.

3) Finally, we can demonstrate that not only do the τινές, "some," of 3:8 not represent a purely fictitious group, but neither should they be sought in other Churches, since *they are* rather *part of the Roman Church.* We come to this conclusion on the basis of the syntactical form of speech in the reply of 6:1–7:6. Decisive is the observation that direct second person plural discourse resumes here after not having been used since chapter 1 in the address (1:6) and in the autobiographical dialogue begun with the Romans in the thanksgiving after the address (1:8-13, 15). Beginning with 1:16, the tone became more theoretical and reflective,[24] with third person singular or plural forms becoming overwhelmingly prevalent.[25]

This type of exposition had been barely interrupted and enlivened by the introduction of the second person singular in 2:1-5, 17-27, which has, however, as we have seen, a purely literary significance entering into the fiction created by the diatribe style. Unexpectedly in 6:3 the second person plural reappears, this time reestablishing a direct and real relationship between sender and recipients: "Do you not know that all of us who were baptized into Christ were baptized into his death?" In 6:11-22 the interrogative immediately becomes an imperative (cf. 6:12-13: "Therefore let sin not reign in your mortal body so that you obey its desires. Do not offer the members of your body to sin as instruments of wickedness, but rather offer yourselves to God, as persons who have been brought from death to life . . ."). When the problem is posed anew in 6:15, we are reminded that Paul is still answering the question raised in 3:5-8 and then again in 6:1.

Use of the second person plural, then, while not being frequent (also present in 7:1, 4; 8:9-11, 13, 15)[26] is quite significant. It actually tells us clearly that the matter discussed is of direct interest to the recipients of the letter, since the "you" plural does not have the fictitious value of the

---

24. This does not mean that the arguments are abstract: see chap. 5 above.

25. Only in 1:16a do we have the first person singular (see also 2:16; 3:7); the first person plural appears several times with various values: in 3:5 (*enallage* of person, like first singular in 3:7); 3:8 (Paul himself, perhaps with co-workers); 3:9a (the Jews); 3:9b (Paul himself); 3:19 (Paul and the Jews); 3:29, 31 (Paul himself, perhaps with his co-workers); 4:1, 9 (rhetorical plural; thus in 6:1a); 4:16, 24f.; 5:1f., 5f., 8-11, 21 (all Christians; thus 6:1b-2, 4-6, 8, 15, 23; 7:5-6, etc.); but this never has a conversational value that would involve sender and recipients in something that concerns them alone.

26. In the section chapters 9–11 the plural "you" resurfaces in 10:19 (where Deut 32:21 is quoted, but with the addition of "you," ὑμᾶς, twice); 11:2 (with allusion to 1 Kgs 19:10, 14); 11:13 ("I am talking to you gentiles": here Paul turns explicitly to a different portion of the Roman Church); 11:25, 28, 30.

"you" singular of the diatribe. With the direct conversational style Paul shows his anxiety to correct among the Romans what "some" of them are calumniously saying about his preaching. This type of discourse is present again in the paraenetic section (see 12:1: "Therefore I urge you, brothers, in view of God's mercy, to offer your bodies as living sacrifices, holy and pleasing to God").

Above all, we find twice again the juxtaposition of the abstract concepts "good-evil," which recall the formula of the slogan in 3:8 *(κακά-ἀγαθά)*, though only with the intention of correcting it.²⁷ A first time is in 12:21, where at the end of a long series of exhortations Paul expresses himself in the form of a general principle: "Do not be overcome by evil *(μὴ νικῶ ὑπὸ τοῦ κακοῦ)*, but overcome evil with good *(ἀλλὰ νίκα ἐν τῷ ἀγαθῷ κακόν)*." The Apostle could not have contradicted his accusers in clearer terms, in this moral exhortation more or less turning on end the very terms of the teaching wrongly attributed to him.

The second time is in 16:19b: "I want you to be wise about what is good *(σοφοὺς εἶναι εἰς τὸ ἀγαθόν)* and innocent about what is evil *(ἀκεραίους δὲ εἰς τὸ κακόν)*." This is the last recommendation of the letter, and is joined directly to the warning *(παρακαλῶ σκοπεῖν . . . ἐκκλίνετε)* to "keep away" from "those who cause division and set up obstacles" (16:17), who "serve not our Lord Christ, but their own bellies [and] by smooth talk and flattery . . . deceive the minds of the simple" (16:18). Do we perhaps have here a different group of adversaries from those in 3:8? This is usually thought to be the case, since no commentary refers to that text.²⁸ But precisely the return of the antitheses ἀγαθόν-κακόν, "good-evil," along with the concept of serving the Lord recurring in the section replying to 3:8

27. The text of 14:16 *(μὴ βλασφημείσθω οὖν ὑμῶν τὸ ἀγαθόν,* "Let not your good behavior be *slandered")* probably does not echo 3:8 but is turning to another category of persons: those who maintain that Christian identity is not conditioned on questions of diet, and who are reproached for how much scandal they permit for the sake of this freedom. Here, unlike in 3:8, there is a question of internal accusations within the community and coming from its most conservative sectors.

28. Some think of the "strong" of 14:1–15:13 (H. Lietzmann, *An die Römer,* HzNT 8, 127; C. E. B. Cranfield, *The Epistle to the Romans,* ICC, II, 800–802, who, however, considers more than one group possible), while others are unsure whether it is Judaizers or gnostics (H. Schlier, *Der Römerbrief,* I, 448.) But E. Käsemann, *Commentary on Romans,* 418 = *Der Brief,* HzNT 8a, 402, cautions against the facile assumption that we have here an early anti-heretical position "directed against libertinizing and gnosticizing Jewish-Christians" (thus C. H. Dodd, *The Epistle of Paul to the Romans,* ad loc., and the study of W. Schmithals, "Die Irrlehrer von Röm, 16,17-20," in *Paulus und die Gnostiker,* ThF 35 (Hamburg, 1965) 159–173). And, U. Wilckens, *Der Brief,* EKK VI/3, 142, explicitly denies that they are libertines but sees them as Judaizing missionaries who passed themselves off as servants of Christ but actually were providing for their bellies (cf. 2 Cor 11:13ff.; Phil 3:18-19). Before finishing the letter, Paul would seem to have learned that some of these have been sent to Rome, and so is warning his readers. But Wilckens cites the text of 3 Macc 7:10, 11 (which speaks of "Jews who of their own will have acted against the holy God and God's Law, and for the sake of their stomach have trans-

(6:16–7:6), seems to me more than sufficient reason to conclude that Paul wants for the last time to dissociate himself from those who defame him, or at least to include them among those who represented a danger for the Church of Rome.

In conclusion, we can say that with the imperative use of the plural "you," the Apostle has no intention of reprimanding all the Christians of Rome; rather, he repeatedly praises their faith-obedience, as he notes everywhere (see the inclusion between 1:8 and 16:9). But neither can one imagine that he only wants to make generic edifying exhortations of universal value without specific reference to his recipients; that would be like treating them as innocent guinea pigs for his own moral expatiations. Rather Paul, taking a cue from the false slogan attributed to him by some Roman Christians, wants to clarify his gospel before the whole community, in order that there may be no doubt that the former teaching is not his at all, while the announcement of the Christian's liberty before the Law remains firm and untouchable.

The Roman Church, then, must have known perfectly well who the τινές, "some," were. The Apostle on his part is aware of having written to this Church "quite boldly on some points" (15:15); but he also was able to clear the field of certain prejudices against him that would have hindered his acceptance in the city on a future visit (cf. 1:10-13, 15; 15:22, 24).

---

gressed the divine commandments"), which actually goes against his Judaizing interpretation; moreover, the expression "to serve Christ" in 16:18 does not necessarily have the technical meaning of missionaries of Christ, since it (and also the literal parallel in 12:11; 14:18) recalls the discourse of 6:16–7:6, where in response to the objection of 3:8 Paul had used the same verb δουλεύειν and the noun δούλοι to say that Christians after baptism have all become "servants" of God, of justice, etc.

Chapter 8

Baptism and Participation in the Death of Christ in Romans 6:1-11

The subject we want to examine is found in a very specific passage of the Letter to the Romans, the structure of which we must carefully consider in order to focus its intent clearly.

I. Contextual and internal articulation of Rom 6:1-14

Even though our subject is limited to the first eleven verses of chapter 6, they are part of a slightly larger pericope that continues to v. 14.[1] It is actually possible to find a criterion of subdivision for the argument: the simultaneously logical and rhetorical interrogative, τί οὖν (ἐροῦμεν), "What then (shall we say)?" In Romans this always has in fact a structural function, as one can easily verify in the passages where it recurs (3:1, 5, 9; 4:1; 6:1, 15; 7:7; 8:31; 9:14, 30; 11:7), that is, it always signals a turning point in Paul's thought and its expression at either the macro- or the micro-structural level.[2] Now, this is typical of the reasoning procedure of Romans, since in practice it does not reappear again in the other Pauline letters except Gal 3:19 (see the weaker formulas in 1 Cor 10:19: τί οὖν φημί, "what then am I saying?"; and in Phil 1:18: τί γάρ, "what then?"), not

---

1. Among the major recent commentaries, the following agree on this division: C. E. B. Cranfield, *The Epistle to the Romans*, I-II, ICC (Edinburgh, 1975-79 and reprints); H. Schlier, *Der Römerbrief*, HThKNT (Freiburg-Basel-Vienna, 1977); U. Wilckens, *Der Brief an die Römer*, I-III, EKK VI/1-3 (Einsiedeln-Neukirchen, 1975-82); L. Morris, *The Epistle to the Romans* (Grand Rapids, Mich., 1988); W. Schmithals, *Die Römerbrief* (Gütersloh, 1988); P. Stuhlmacher, *Der Brief an die Römer*, NTD 6 (Göttingen, 1989). Only E. Käsemann, *Commentary on Romans* (Grand Rapids, Mich., 1980) 158ff. = *An die Römer*, HzNT 8a (Tübingen, 1980[4]) 150ff., and J. D. G. Dunn, *Romans 1-8*, WBC 38a (Dallas, Tex., 1988), divide 6:1-11 and 6:12-23; but this articulation does not account for the repetition of the rhetorical question in 6:15.
2. See, for example, F. Siegert, *Argumentation bei Paulus, gezeigt an Röm 9-11*, WUNT 34 (Tübingen, 1985) 115.

to speak of the other New Testament writings, where at any rate one could cite Heb 11:32: καὶ τί ἔτι λέγω, "What else shall I say?"[3]

Hence follows a tripartite articulation in chapters 6–7:

6:1-14: The subject discussed here is the relationship of the Christian to ἁμαρτία, "sin," which is referred to a dozen times (1, 2b, 6c [including "our old man," ὁ παλαιὸς ἡμῶν ἄνθρωπος], 7, 10, 11, 12, 13, 14); but 6:14b ("you are not under Law but under grace") already announces a transition of subject toward the concept of Law (absent in the preceding verses).

6:15–7:6: The central theme now becomes νόμος, "Law" (6:14b, 15; 7:1b, 2b, 3, 4, 5, 6), but joining it to what precedes we have the continuation of "sin" (6:15, 16, 17, 18, 19, 20, 22, 23; 7:5) in such a way as to suggest an equivalence between the two realities; this impression in turn raises a corresponding question, which is treated in the next section.

7:7-25: Here is discussed the relationship between ἁμαρτία and νόμος ("sin" and "Law") clarifying that it is not a matter of identity but a close relationship that is configured in two ways: (a) consecutively, i.e., in a line going from sin to Law (the one preexisting the other); and (b) causally, i.e., in a line going from Law to sin (the latter provoked by the former). Thus is revealed the twofold nature of sin as state and as act.

The formal unity of the first section is also shown by the inclusion between vv. 1 and 14 on the basis of recurrence of the expression χάρις, "grace" (then taken up again in v. 15, but otherwise missing in the next two chapters, since in 6:17 and 7:25 it reappears in a merely exclamatory formula).

We present the structure of the first section as follows:[4]

6:1: Initial question, presenting a grave problem.
6:2: Basic response proposed as a thesis: the original hypothesis is impossible because "we are dead to sin."
6:3-11: Demonstration of the thesis:
    6:3-4: Appeal to baptism as a fact known and experienced by everyone, insofar as it is essentially related to the death of Christ (with consequent resurrection).
    6:5-7: Development concerning the fact of the death of Christ.
    6:8-11: Development concerning the fact of the resurrection in and with Christ.

3. See the annotation of W. Sanday and A. C. Headlam, *The Epistle to the Romans*, ICC (Edinburgh, 1902⁵) 73.
4. Here we must note that vv. 8-10 form an exact parallel to vv. 5-7; see G. Bornkamm, "Taufe und neues Leben (Röm 6)," in *Das Ende des Gesetzes: Paulusstudien* (Munich, 1966) 34-50, 38-39.

6:12-13: Paraenetic consequences.

6:14: Inclusive conclusion, taking up the thesis and confirming it (v. 14a), and preparing the transition to the next section (v. 14b).

Within the section, we see, vv. 12-14 serve to develop the consequences, so that vv. 1-11 emerge as determinative for the argument. And here it is vv. 3-4 that carry most of the weight of the argument, the two parts of which are developed by vv. 5-7 and 8-11.

II. Structural location of 6:1-14 in the book

The initial question of 6:1 ("What shall we say? Shall we go on sinning, so that grace may increase?") clearly picks up the objection of 3:5-8 concerning the relationship in general between human sin and God's saving righteousness. The question that had been formulated and then left in suspense is now treated in chapters 6-8. Therefore 6:1 signals the beginning of a new section of the letter. Since we have already discussed this structural problem,[5] we touch on it only lightly here, making a few necessary observations.

The fact that 6:1 signals a new beginning does not mean that our passage has no links with the immediately preceding page concerning the Adam-Christ typology in 5:12-21. Indeed, as R. Schnackenburg rightly says, "The misunderstanding expressed in 6:1 became possible because a valid principle for the history of salvation in its universal dimension [human sin has occasioned the display of God's mercy] has been unjustifiably transposed to the level of the individual's pursuit of salvation."[6] Now, the reasoning behind the question is this: Seeing that God has answered the sin of Adam through God's own merciful intervention in the death of Christ, why should we not ourselves sin today in order to promote the display of God's mercy all the more?

This inappropriate transposition had already been posed as a question in 3:5-8, with the only difference that there the misunderstanding flowed only indirectly from the affirmation of universal sin (described in 1:18–2:29) through the consideration of the unbelief of Israel in 3:1-4. But here the enunciation of the question is directly related to the preceding passage 5:12-21, which treats what amounts to the protasis of the false reasoning reported in the preceding paragraph (note 5:20: "Where sin increased,

---

5. See above, chaps. 4 and 7.
6. R. Schnackenburg, "Die Adam-Christus-Typologie (Röm 5,12-21) als Voraussetzung für Taufverständnis in Röm 6:1-14," in L. De Lorenzi (ed.), *Battesimo e giustizia in Rm 6 e 8,* Serie Monogr. di Benedictina 2 (Rome, 1974) 37-55, 42.

grace increased all the more"). Even so, this direct contextual link does not prevent 6:1 from beginning a new section, precisely insofar as it finally resumes the problem expressed in 3:5-8.

In any case, our passage includes changes in language and concepts from what is found in chapter 5, such as to give evidence of a structural division.

These are of three types:

1) The lexical family δικ-, "just-," is substantially missing: well attested in 5:1, 9, 16, 17, 18, 19, 21, it then appears only in 6:7 (in an unusual aphoristic sense), 13 (in a metaphorical phrase), and then in the second section (6:16, 18, 19, 20).

2) Our passage, while speaking of baptism and assimilation to the death of Christ, presents no connection between this language and the concept of πνεῦμα, "spirit," as distinguished from earlier (5:5) and later (7:6) passages (and especially in chapter 8); note that such a connection is also found in 1 Cor 12:13; 2 Cor 1:22; Eph 1:13; 4:30.

3) Especially we notice a remarkable semantic leap in the concept of θάνατος, "death": while amply attested (6:2, 4, 5, 7, 8, 9, 10, 11), the idea of death has here completely lost the sense of consequence of sin, whereas it had been present in chapter 5 and, moreover, in a global, salvation-history dimension (5:12b, 14, 15, 17, 21; only 6:21, 23 is at all comparable), but while the former verses allude to sin as *caused by* sin, the latter to death *to* sin (or the death of Christ).

III. The three fundamental concepts sin-death-life and their semantic complexity

Each of these three concepts is employed with reference to different realities that are not always easy to distinguish.

1) Ἁμαρτία, "sin." The concept swings between two meanings: as state and as act. To speak of sin as a *state* means to consider it a basic condition, a superindividual fact, commonly expressed with the idea of power or "Machtsphäre," higher than and prior to single sinful acts. This hermeneutical position is common among the authors.[7] But recently such interpretation has been contested by B. N. Kaye[8] and by G. Röhser,[9] who always understand sin in reference to the act of the individual.

7. See, for example, S. Lyonnet, art. "Péché," in SDB VII, 503-509 ("Le Péché personnifié"); and also recently P. Stuhlmacher, *Der Brief an die Römer*, 80.
8. B. N. Kaye, *The Thought Structure of Romans with Special Reference to Chapter 6* (Austin, Tex., 1979); see 137: in the Letter to the Romans there is always the same concept of "sinful action," not of "power."
9. G. Röhser, *Metaphorik und Personifikation der Sünde. Antike Sündenvorstellungen und paulinische Hamartia*, WUNT 2.25 (Tübingen, 1987); see 177: the personification of sin means

In favor of the majority opinion we must note at least the following:

1) Already in the section 5:12-21 we must distinguish between the use of the verb and the use of the noun: while the former more easily refers to repeated behavior (see 5:12d: πάντες ἥμαρτον, "all have sinned"), the same cannot be said of the latter, especially since it has been made the subject of personifying verbs ("entered/ruled"—5:12a: εἰσῆλθεν; 5:21: ἐβασίλευσεν).

2) The two terms in 6:6 (ὁ παλαιὸς ἡμῶν ἄνθρωπος, "our old man" and τὸ σῶμα τῆς ἁμαρτίας, "the body of sin") surely do not refer to a single act.

3) The same can be said for the recurring verbs in 6:1 (ἐπιμένειν, "to remain"); 2a (ἀποθνῄσκειν, "die": one does not die to a single act); 6c (δουλεύειν, "be enslaved to"); 7 and 10 (as in 2a); 11 (idem), all of which refer to a perduring situation, considered from time to time as a remaining in place, a type of existence, and a governance to which one submits.

Sin as an *act* is certainly present in the use of verbs in 5:12, 14. Also the verb ἁμαρτήσωμεν, "sin," in 6:15 could have such a meaning in itself. And on the basis of parallelism between 6:15 and 6:1, one might think that even the expression ἐπιμένωμεν τῇ ἁμαρτίᾳ, "let us remain in sin," has an "actualistic" sense. But the opposite interpretation is recommended by these two observations: the one that the verb ἐπιμένειν, "remain," in Paul always indicates a stable permanence or at least duration (see Rom 11:22, 23; 1 Cor 16:7, 8; Gal 1:18; Phil 1:24; Col 1:23; 1 Tim 4:16); the other that the expression ζήσωμεν ἐν αὐτῷ, "let us live in it," of 6:1 (synonymous with ἐπιμένωμεν τῇ ἁμαρτίᾳ) has an antithetic parallel in the expression ζῶντας . . . ἐν Χριστῷ Ἰησοῦ, "living in Christ Jesus," of 6:11, which clearly indicates a transfer of dominion.

Moreover, we also note an implicit correlation of ἁμαρτία, "sin," with νόμος, "Law," in 6:14: the opposition in 6:1 of ἁμαρτία and in 6:14 of νόμος to χάρις, "grace," makes both expressions semantically very similar. The fact is all the more worthy of note in that each (as well as θάνατος, "death") is used as subject of the same verbs, namely, βασιλεύειν, "reign" (said of sin in 5:21 and 6:12; of death in 5:14, 17), and especially κυριεύειν, "dominate" (said of sin in 6:14, of the Law in 7:1, and of death in 6:9).

2) θάνατος, "death," has three basic meanings. In the first place it means *physical death*, but as such it has a secondary use: only in 6:9 is this sense clear, referring to the death of Christ (one can also add the modifier "from the dead" in 6:4, 9). More problematic is its weight in 6:7 ("Whoever has

---

nothing other than "der Inbegriff menschlicher Tatverfehlungen"; the author is right insofar as he opposes sin as a demoniacal power, but he neglects to take into consideration the Essene and apocalyptic hamartiology.

died has been freed from sin"), where it could be part of an aphorism in a universal sense with rabbinic resonance (thus E. Käsemann and H. Schlier), or else it could refer to the death of the Christian through Christ, according to the context (though acknowledging a re-use of the rabbinic principle; thus C. E. B. Cranfield, U. Wilckens, L. Morris, P. Stuhlmacher).

In the second place, we see that *the death of Christ* is much more concentrated on a theme, namely, its salvific value, as attested in the following expressions that have become classical for the Christian: εἰς τὸν θάνατον αὐτοῦ, "into his death" (6:3); συνετάφημεν οὖν αὐτῷ, "we were buried with him" (6:4a); τῷ ὁμοιώματι τοῦ θανάτου αὐτοῦ, "the likeness of his death" (6:5); συνεσταυρώθη, "was crucified together with" (6:6); ἀπεθάνομεν σὺν Χριστῷ, "we died together with" (6:8); ὃ γὰρ ἀπέθανεν, "insofar as he died" (6:10). In all these cases except the last,[10] it should be observed, however, that whenever there is allusion to the death of Christ, this is always in reference to the death of the Christian to sin.

In the third place, indeed, we note that the persistent datum is *the death of the Christian to sin*, yet conforming to the assumption enunciated from the very beginning in 6:2. This is, then, present in 6:2 (ἀπεθάνομεν, "we died"); 4a (συνετάφημεν, "were buried together with"); 5 (σύμφυτοι γεγόναμεν . . ., "we have been amalgamated"); 6 (συνεσταυρώθη, ἵνα καταργηθῇ, "were buried together so that the body of sin might be destroyed"); 7 (ὁ ἀποθανών, "the one who dies": probably); 8 (ἀπεθάνομεν, "we died"); 11 (εἶναι νεκρούς, "to be dead").

We therefore note the changed character of the vocabulary in comparison with the preceding section 5:12-21. Since there "sin" and "death" are almost interchangeable realities, at least in the sense that the one never stands without the other, here instead the Christian, since dead to sin, is also dead to death!

3) Also ζωή, "life," can function on any of three semantic levels: (a) *the life of the risen Christ* (thus in 6:4, 9, 10): like his death, this is the foundation of the two following components; (b) *the new moral life of the Christian* (thus in 6:2, 4, 6, 7, 10, 11), which is the aspect most developed in

---

10. To these texts we can add the expression of v. 4b, εἰς τὸν θάνατον, "to death," which according to most should be referred to Christ's death (Käsemann, Cranfield, Schlier, Wilckens, Schnackenburg; but it actually could refer to the death of the Christian: see G. Barbaglio, *Le lettere di Paolo*, II [Rome, 1980] 323, n. 20; B. Frid, "Römer 6,4-5. Ἐις τὸν θάνατον und τῷ ὁμοιώματι τοῦ θάνατον ["in the likeness of (his) death"] als Schlüssel zu Duktus und Gedankengang in Römer 6:1-11," BZ 30 [1986] 188-203, 194), even though it lacks the pronoun αὐτοῦ, "his," and is joined to the modifier διὰ τοῦ βαπτίσματος, "through baptism." Lacking any qualifying pronoun, the expression can probably be read in reference to either the death of Christ or the death of the Christian insofar as the latter is identified with the former.

terms of frequency; (c) *the eschatological life of the Christian,* in 6:5 (καὶ τῆς ἀναστάσεως ἐσόμεθα, "shall also be so of his resurrection") and 6:8 (καὶ συζήσομεν αὐτῷ, "shall also live with him").

But with regard to these last two verses, it is not actually evident to what they refer. The *status quaestionis* concerning the positions of the exegetes offers this diversity:

—Some understand both verbs of the two verses as a simple logical future, referring only to the moral life of the Christian in the present of one's historical existence: Thus Cranfield on the basis of the context, even though he concedes in v. 8 the presence of an eschatological horizon.[11]

—Others refer both verses to the present, but with an essential eschatological perspective.[12]

—Still others consider both verses eschatological, but with anticipatory reflections in the moral life of the Christian.[13]

—Others, finally, interpret our two verses as univocally eschatological.[14]

Faced with such a display of possibilities, which witness not so much to the subjectivity of interpreters as to the difficult semantic density of the text itself, we find it rather difficult to take a decisive stand. The third group, however, merits particular attention, even though this is not the place for a deeper investigation of the position.

IV. Baptism as a visible moment of union with Christ

Romans 6:1-11 unquestionably contains a discourse on Christian baptism, which is clearly attested in vv. 3-4a with two first person plural aorist indicatives, ἐβαπτίσθημεν, "we were baptized" (the first indicating the fact of baptism, the second giving its meaning), and with the noun βάπτισμα, "baptism," in a prepositional phrase indicating means. We will consider this datum, which is both lexical and theological, globally and analytically.

Essentially, what we want to establish is that the discourse on baptism is subsidiary in this passage, where the foreground is occupied rather by

11. C. E. B. Cranfield, *The Epistle to the Romans,* I, 308 and 312f.

12. A. Maillot, *L'épître aux Romains* (Paris-Geneva, 1984) 157: "Nous sommes toujours en train de ressusciter dans la vie nouvelle"; G. Barbaglio, *Le lettere di Paolo,* II, 324; L. Morris, *The Epistle to the Romans,* 250 and 254.

13. Otto Kuss, *Der Römerbrief,* I (Regensburg, 1957) 303–305; H. Schlier, *Der Römerbrief,* 195 ("V. 5 becomes primarily a reason for ἐν καινότητι ζωῆς περιπάτειν but in a broader sense for the whole declaration of v. 4"); 199 ("the eschatological meaning that expressions [in the future] with σὺν Χριστῷ habitually have": Rom 7:32b; 2 Cor 4:14; 13:4; Phil 1:23; 1 Thess 4:14, 17; 5:10; Col 2:13; 3:3); P. Stuhlmacher, *Der Brief an die Römer,* 86.

14. E. Käsemann, *Commentary on Romans,* 169 and 170 = *An die Römer,* 161 and 162; C. K. Barrett, *The Epistle to the Romans,* Black's New Testament Commentaries (London, 1984 = 1957) 124 and 126 ("Paul's view of baptism is primarily eschatological").

the motif of the death of Christ and the association of the Christian with this death, as a reality that both implies and transcends baptism itself. First of all we consider the extreme lexical scarcity with which the motif is expressed: the verb twice and the noun once. Käsemann[15] also notes the absence of the motifs of both πνεῦμα, "spirit," and σῶμα, "body," of Christ, as well as that of the filiation of the Christian. Actually we are here seeing a constant practice in Paul's letters, where the links to baptism are made almost furtively, left undeveloped, and standing complementary to a series of other motifs of greater weight, such as purification from sin (in 1 Cor 6:11; see Eph 5:26; Titus 3:5); the body of Christ (in 1 Cor 12:13); faith (in Gal 3:27); the old and uncircumcised man (in Col 2:11-12).

In none of these passages do we have a full development of the theme. Baptism for Paul is not a direct subject of catechesis; at most it is the occasion for catechesis on other aspects or components of the Christian identity. Indeed, when it once is the object of polemic (1 Cor 1:13-17), the point is to emphasize baptism as secondary to evangelization.[16] In various cases something that is related positively to baptism is not necessarily an effect thereof. Thus faith and the body of Christ are realities that preexist baptism.

Of particular interest is the passage of 1 Cor 12:13. Here the expression εἰς ἓν σῶμα ἐβαπτίσθημεν, "we were baptized into one body," according to the best exegesis, does not mean that it is baptism that makes the one body of Christ, as if the latter were the result of the former; but rather baptism simply inserts one to become part of the body of Christ as an already given, autonomous reality, which already has in itself its own reason for being, because it is Christ's own self.[17]

The same thing, but in still more evident terms, comes in Rom 6:3, where the same aorist passive ἐβαπτίσθημεν, "were baptized," governs two complementary phrases of "motion toward," εἰς Χριστὸν Ἰησοῦν, "into Christ Jesus," and εἰς τὸν θάνατον αὐτοῦ, "into his death." The new datum is not the first phrase (it recurs in Gal 3:27 and has a parallel in 1 Cor 10:2: εἰς τὸν Μωυσήν, "into Moses"; see also εἰς τὸ ὄνομα, "into the Name," in Acts 8:16; 19:5; Matt 28:19), but the second. What gives value to the act of baptism is none other than the death of Christ; indeed it is to this that baptism has its essential reference, and moreover it is with this that the

---

15. E. Käsemann, *Commentary on Romans*, 163 = *An die Römer*, 155.
16. On this text see M. Pesce, " 'Christ Did Not Send Me to Baptize but to Evangelize' (1 Cor 1,17a)," in L. De Lorenzi (ed.), *Paul de Tarse, Apôtre de notre temps* (Rome, 1979) 339–362.
17. See L. Cerfaux, *La théologie de l'eglise suivant Saint Paul*, Unam Sanctam 54 (Paris, 1965³) 229–232; H. Conzelmann, *Der erste Brief an die Korinther*, Meyer Kommentar (Göttingen, 1969) 249–250; Chr. Senft, *La première épître de Saint Paul aux Corinthiens*, CNT 7 (Paris, 1979) 161–162. For another understanding see Chr. Wolff, *Der erste Brief des Paulus an die Korinther*, ThHNT 7/2 (Berlin, 1982²) 108.

baptized is placed into close relation. Christ's death is the soteriologically preexisting datum, which has in itself its own reason for existing, and is therefore in some sense autonomous and self-sufficient.

Like the body of Christ, so the death of Christ precedes, establishes, and gives meaning to baptism. There is precisely a parallelism between 6:4a ("we were buried with him through baptism," συνετάφημεν αὐτῷ διὰ τοῦ βαπτίσματος) and 7:4a ("you also were put to death to the Law through the body of Christ," ἐθανατώθητε τῷ νόμῳ διὰ τοῦ σώματος τοῦ Χριστοῦ), where "baptism" and "body of Christ" (modifying "put to death") share the same grammatical construction.

When, then, is the Christian put to death as to sin and as to Law? Is it only at the moment of baptism (as 6:4a would suggest) or already at the moment of Christ's death (as 7:4a would suggest)? Well, it is precisely to this question that the thesis about the subsidiarity of baptism to the Cross should respond, a subsidiarity which is so not just in reality but which is embedded even in the structures and vocabulary of the Pauline text in question.

Our passage, as I have already noted, after the formulation of the problem in 6:1, opens in v. 2 with the pronouncement of a very concise axiom ("all we who have died to sin," οἵτινες ἀπεθάνομεν τῇ ἁμαρτίᾳ) that is not just a motif to develop, as if the following mention of baptism clarified where and when that death came, but even more refers back to a preceding event, of which baptism is only a part, and a subsidiary part at that.

What I want to say is that the frequent verb ἀποθνῄσκω, "die" (used in 6:2, 7, 8, 10 [twice]) and the substantive θάνατος, "death" (present in 6:3, 4, 5, 9) always in fact refer fundamentally to the death of Christ on the cross and the death of the Christian with Christ on the cross, and only reflexively and indirectly to a sacramental death.

In fact, in our passage Paul is simply applying by extension a terminology and a conceptualization that serve him elsewhere to express only the salvific sufficiency of the Cross of Christ. This occurs already in 2 Cor 5:14b: "One died for all, therefore all died" (εἰς ὑπὲρ πάντων ἀπέθανεν, ἄρα οἱ πάντες ἀπέθανον): under the first clause of the sentence (resumed in 5:15a) stands the proto-Christian confession of faith, "Christ died for our sins" (1 Cor 15:3; cf. Rom 5:8; 8:32; 1 Thess 5:10), which Paul precisely explains with the second clause, "therefore all died." There is here no reference to baptism,[18] and curiously there is no antithesis between the death of Christ and the life of human persons (as on the contrary we read in 1 Cor

---

18. Thus, correctly, R. Bultmann, *Der zweite Brief an die Korinther*, Meyer Kommentar (Göttingen, 1976) 153; against W. Mundle, *Der Glaubensbegriff des Paulus* (Leipzig, 1932 = Darmstadt, 1977).

15:22; Rom 5:18). But it is not enough to say that all receive the opportunity to appropriate for themselves the death of Christ through faith.[19] In fact, the context actually speaks of a "new creation" (2 Cor 5:17) and of the love of Christ that "holds us in its power" (2 Cor 5:14a).

There is an indispensable objective dimension to that death, at least in the sense that all without exception have come to participate in the sphere of influence of Christ's death as eschatological manifestation of God's saving power.[20]

In the Letter to the Galatians, then, the participation in the Cross of Christ is more than once affirmed, and this prescinding from the perspective of baptism: thus in Gal 2:19 ("I have been crucified with Christ," Χριστῷ συνεσταύρωμαι); 5:24 ("those who belong to Christ Jesus have crucified the flesh," οἱ δὲ τοῦ Χριστοῦ τὴν σάρκα ἐσταύρωσαν); 6:14 (through Christ "the world has been crucified to me, and I to the world," ἐμοὶ κόσμος ἐσταύρωται κἀγὼ κόσμῳ). There does exist among some exegetes the tendency to see the presence of a baptismal tradition in each of these passages,[21] but other scholars maintain rather that these texts have nothing to do with baptism[22] and that we see here testimony to the objective soteriological component of Christ's death on the cross.

For the rest, the whole context of Rom 6:1-11 is in the line of the historical-Christological foundation of Christian existence, in chapter 5 (where especially the opposition Adam-Christ places the salvific event in a macrohistorical and objective perspective) as well as in the dialectical relationship between chapters 7 and 8 (where the opposition Law-Spirit prescinds completely from any baptismal language). Indeed, the already noted expression διὰ τοῦ σώματος τοῦ Χριστοῦ, "through Christ's body," in 7:4 (cf. 7:6: κατηργήθημεν . . . ἀποθανόντες, "released . . . by dying") refers unequivocally to the sacrifice of Christ. Precisely on this subject Paul writes in 6:10 that Christ "died to sin once for all," in the sense that adherence to him deprives sin of any power over the human being[23] so as to establish the truth of 8:1, according to which "there is now no condemnation for those who are in Christ Jesus," and then the hymn of victory that ends chapter 8 (8:31-39).

This is confirmed on the evidence of 6:6, where we find the verb συνεσταυρώθη, "was co-crucified," said of "our old man." With regard

---

19. Thus still R. Bultmann, *Der zweite Brief*, 153.

20. See V. P. Furnish, *II Corinthians*, The Anchor Bible 32A (Garden City, N.Y., 1984) 327f.

21. See, e.g., F. Mussner, *Der Galaterbrief*, HThKNT 9 (Freiburg-Basel-Vienna, 1981⁴) 180, 390, 414.

22. See A. J. M. Wedderburn, *Baptism and Resurrection. Studies in Pauline Theology Against Its Graeco-Roman Background*, WUNT 44 (Tübingen, 1987) 49f.

23. Compare H. Schlier, *Der Römerbrief*, 199; U. Wilckens, *Der Brief an die Römer*, II, 19.

to this, R. Schnackenburg observes that "the rite and its symbolic content certainly do not stand in the foreground,"²⁴ just as "the opposition death/life in Rom 6 was derived not from the figurative nature of baptism," but "from the *salvation event* of the death and resurrection of Christ."²⁵ This consideration is reflected in the understanding of the phrase συνετάφη-μεν αὐτῷ, "we were buried with him," in 6:4a. It is only with the *Apostolic Constitutions* (3:17:3) that the rite of baptism is interpreted in the light of Romans 6 in symbolic terms: "Immersion signifies dying together, the emergence, rising together" (ἡ κατάδυσις τὸ συναποθανεῖν, ἡ ἀνάδυσις τὸ συναναστῆναι; the "descending-ascending" is found also in *Barn.* 11:11; *Hermas, Sim.* 9:16:4, but without the prefix συν-, which would make it improbable that it is a reference to Romans 6). But neither was the death of Christ by drowning, nor does baptism come by crucifixion.

In Pauline speech the verb of 6:4a simply underlines the reality of the death of Christ with a probable allusion to the ἐτάφη, "was buried," of the profession of faith of 1 Cor 15:3f. (cf. Col 2:12), but with the added idea of the participation of Christians in this completed death. The burial that is mentioned, then, has at most a metaphorical but not symbolic sense,²⁶ that is, it is not the ritual sequence of baptismal practice that is in the foreground but the content of Christological faith, extended to include the destiny of the Christian. Now, in the interpretation of the phrase σύμφυτοι γεγόναμεν τῷ ὁμοιώματι τοῦ θανάτου αὐτοῦ, "we have become connatural [with him] by the sharing of his death," in 6:5, we must also be careful not to distance ourselves from this hermeneutic. Actually, the present sentence corresponds to and in some sense repeats the preceding verse, συνετάφημεν αὐτῷ, "we were buried together with him," but with a minor change in syntactical emphasis, for while earlier we had had a principal clause, here we have only a subordinate clause, modifying the following affirmation of the resurrection (in 6:5b). But precisely this subordinate role suggests that it is simply a reprise of what has just been said in the verse before. Recognizing that σύμφυτος is a verbal adjective derived from συμφύειν ("cause to grow together, unite, amalgamate," rather than συμφυτεύειν, "plant together, graft") and means "congenital, connatural," we must understand the following phrase not as a *dativus sociativus* but as a dative of instrument or cause.²⁷ This means that ὁμοιώματι, "in the like-

24. R. Schnackenburg, *Baptism in the Thought of St. Paul* (Oxford, 1964) 54.
25. Schnackenburg, ibid., 58.
26. See L. Alvarez Verdes, *El imperativo cristiano en San Pablo. La tensión indicativo-imperativo en Rm 6. Aná lisis estructural* (Rome, 1980) 167.
27. See B. Frid (n. 10 above), "Römer 6:4-5," 195ff., who, however, by translating, "Wir mit ihm zusammengewachsen sind durch die Entsprechung zu seinem Tod (die Taufe)," 197, separates the death of Christ too much from baptism.

ness," should be thought of not as immediately connected to the adjective (as in the Vulgate: "complantati facti sumus similitudini mortis eius"; Douay: "we have been planted together in the likeness of his death"), but with an understood αὐτῷ, "with him," as in the preceding verse, and as in the logic of the use of σύν also in 6:6, 7 (twice), where the Christological reference is always determinative.

The decisive term here is the noun ὁμοίωμα, "likeness." Comparison with the other occurrences in Paul (Rom 1:23; 5:14; 8:3; Phil 2:7; cf. Rom 8:29; Phil 3:21) and with its use in the Septuagint[28] tends to exclude the purely extrinsic meaning of "abstract similarity" or "image, copy," and rather to support the meaning of "[ontological] affinity." In our case that does not intend to introduce a figurative mediation (rite of baptism) but expresses "the fact of the reality indicated in the genitival referent [Christ's death],"[29] so that the expression ὁμοίωμα τοῦ θανάτου αὐτοῦ ("likeness of his death") "indicates the form *(die Gestalt)* of the death of Christ and his dying, but in no case baptism."[30]

Thus, while in the two closest texts, Rom 5:14 and 8:3, the accent falls completely on transgression and the flesh, affirming the sharing of humans in the former and Christ in the latter, here what is proclaimed is real participation in the death of Christ: ὁμοίωμα, "likeness," indicates not baptism as an image or symbolic reproduction of that death, but the objective fact of the participatory insertion of the Christian in that very death. And such insertion, which already radically took place at the very moment of Christ's death on the cross (see 5:18-19), happens all the more, in actualized form, at the moment of baptism,[31] in which is concretized and applied to the individual the Christian's "co-crucifixion" (σνσταυροῦσθαι), which is then explained in the next verse.[32]

An interesting fact about Rom 6:1-11 is the absence of the motif of faith (except for v. 8b, where it is referred to the future resurrection), and along with this the absence of justification (except for ill-focused allusions in vv. 7 and 13c). Vice versa, in the Pauline texts that do speak of faith and of justification, there is an absence of expressions in "σνν-," and hence of the theme of unitive participation with Christ.

It seems to me that the only possible explanation with regard to our present text is to think that Paul intends to speak on the objective level, recalling to the Romans the concrete, external facts of the death of Christ

---

28. See U. Vanni, "'Ὁμοίωμα in Paolo," *Gregorianum* 58 (1977) 431–470.
29. L. Alvarez Verdes, *El imperativo cristiano*, 166.
30. N. Gäumann, *Taufe und Ethik. Studien zu Römer 6*, BhTh 47 (Munich, 1967) 78.
31. Also J. Schneider, art. ὁμοίωμα, TDNT 5:195.
32. See W. Grundmann, art. σνν-μετα κτλ., TDNT 7:789–792.

and of the baptismal event. These are the realities that permit the use of terms that are more corporeal and, so to speak, more verifiable in response to the provocative question of whether we still remain in sin (6:1). But if the subjective datum of personal faith and of justification is less evident in our text, it is still present in our context and provides the framework. In fact, 5:19 had already asserted that "through the obedience of the one man the many will be made righteous," and such righteousness is in turn explained on the basis of 5:17b, "[receiving] God's abundant provision of grace and of the gift of righteousness." Now, in Pauline logic such a reception of righteousness can come only through faith (see 1:17; 3:22-25, 26, 27, 28, 30; 4; 5:1-2), whereas δικαιοσύνη, "righteousness," is never connected with baptism.

But then a little later, 6:16b presents an alternative of slavery to sin leading to death or of obedience leading to righteousness, understanding this "obedience," ὑπακοή, as a synonym for πίστις, "faith," in conformity with Pauline semantics as seen in Rom 1:5; 10:16; 16:19, 26. (Note, the same expression for "obedience" was used twice in this same verse; the change in its meaning is seen in this paraphrase of the text: "You become slaves of the one to whom you offer obedience; so either obey sin or obey obedience!") And it is in this light that we can better understand the sentence of proverbial tone in 6:7: To die to sin with Christ in baptism, that is, to "be justified" in his death (note δεδικαίωται), is possible as an extension and concretization of a justification that comes essentially "through faith in his blood" (3:25) or more simply "by his blood" (5:9). Now, already in Gal 3:26 Paul had declared that faith is the basis of the Christian's relationship to God as child of God, while indicating in the following verse that it is through baptism that one clothes oneself in Christ.[33]

It is, then, not a matter of establishing artificial distinctions between a juridical and mystical dimension of Pauline soteriology,[34] since in fact there are only different aspects of one single anthropological reality, or better, there is the actualization and appropriation of a single foundational and soteriologically fruitful fact, which is the death of Christ and his resurrection. The whole Christ, then (since in 4:25 his resurrection also is viewed in function of our justification), not only is antecedent to faith and baptism but also is present in their realization, and further directs the Christian life toward new goals, ethical and eschatological alike.

---

33. See F. Mussner, *Der Galaterbrief*, 361-363.
34. See E. P. Sanders, *Paul and Palestinian Judaism* (London, 1977) 502-508; see 460, 472.

V. Further considerations

a) In his commentary on Rom 6:3-4, Origen affirms that Paul "in this passage certainly meant to examine not so much the nature of baptism as the nature of the death of Christ."[35] Now actually Origen's perspective is partially ethical: he means to say that one must first die to sin in order to be then buried with Christ in baptism. With this in mind, I maintain that we must share the distinction, or better the shift of emphasis, that he proposes.

This is, moreover, substantially the position of not a few contemporary authors.[36] This actually means not a depreciation of baptism but rather putting it in its proper place as the factor of mediation between the Christ-event and the person of the believer (as believer). But the Christ-event consists essentially in the death of Christ. It is with this that baptism puts one into direct relation. The resurrection of the Christian, both ethical and eschatological (see above), is a result of baptism, not a constitutive part of it, just as for Christ the resurrection is a result of his death.

Therefore, what baptism brings about directly is death to sin, even if this is the foundation for, and demands the positive component of, a new life. Baptism brings about a liberation (see 6:18a, 22a), as personal application of the liberation accomplished by Christ (Gal 5:1, 13). As such, baptism means the expulsion of sin, and so brings about a void,[37] which, however, disposes one to walk "in newness of life" (6:4), "in the newness of the Spirit" (7:6). But baptism is death only insofar as it assimilates one to the death of Christ. And it is this decisive reference to Christ that also gives it its own fullness. Death to sin derives not autonomously from the simple performance of the rite in its own nature but rather from the fact that this inserts the Christian "into the death of" Christ, εἰς τὸν θάνα-τον αὐτοῦ: "It means delivery to and transition into possession by the death of Christ."[38] And it is the saving efficacy of this death that is celebrated in the life of the baptized.

This aspect is particularly evidenced by the use of the preposition σύν, mostly in compound verbs. Its typical Pauline use to describe the union

35. Origen, *Commentarium in epistolam ad Romanos*, PG 14:1039D.

36. See K. Barth, *Kirchliche Dogmatik*, IV/4, 129; R. C. Tannehill, *Dying and Rising with Christ*, BZNT 32 (Berlin, 1967) 7f.; P. Siber, *Mit Christus leben: eine Studie zur paulinischen Auferste-hungshoffnung*, AThANT 61 (Zurich, 1971); R. Schnackenburg, in L. De Lorenzi, ed., *Battesimo e giustizia in Romani 6 e 8*, 54; B. N. Kaye, *The Thought Structure*, 62 and 64; A. J. M. Wedderburn, *Baptism and Resurrection*, 49-50. Against such a conception see U. Schnelle, *Gerechtigkeit und Christusgegenwart. Vorpaulinische und paulinische Tauftheologie*, GThA 24 (Göttingen, 1986²) 204, n. 386.

37. The same, according to Luther, is true of faith: *Qui credit in Christum evacuatur a seipso:* "Who believes in Christ is emptied of self" (WA 2:564).

38. H. Schlier, *Der Römerbrief*, 192.

of the Christian with Christ appears here five times in four of the five verses 6:4-8.[39] Four of these refer to death (6:4: συνετάφημεν, "we were buried"; 6:5: σύμφυτοι . . . τοῦ θανάτου αὐτοῦ, "aggregated"; 6:6: συνεσταυρώθη, "was crucified together with"; 6:8a: ἀπεθάνομεν σὺν Χριστῷ, "we died with Christ") and only one to life (6:8b: συζήσομεν αὐτῷ, "we shall live together with him").

Conformity to the death of Christ, indeed sharing in it, is therefore absolutely central; it is death rather than life that defines Christian life as a salvific event. And once again we confirm that the origin of Paul's reflection is not in the baptismal rite but in the historical-soteriological fact of Christ's death, to which the resurrection is accessory. Even the ethical dimension of the whole section 6:1-7:6 is primarily based on the datum of the death of Jesus rather than that of his resurrection. The whole section begins (6:2) and ends (7:6) with a clear reference to death to sin, which is revealed in the context as a participation in the death of Christ (see 6:3, 4a, 5, 7, 10a, 11a); and the whole marriage analogy in 7:1-6 presents the woman's liberty as rendered possible only by the death of the husband. Now, the resurrection of Christ also plays a role as an ethical foundation, but more as the somehow secondary and extrinsic subject of a comparison. It is not the resurrection of Christ but his death that entails death to sin; thus the moral life of the Christian can only reveal the radical overcoming of ἁμαρτία, "sin," that has already come about through its conformity to the death of Christ as confirmed in baptism. This is why the resurrection of the Christian is expressed only in the future.[40]

b) Given the determinative weight in our text of the language of participation, we might ask, What is its matrix, its original religious and cultural context, especially with regard to "dying with Christ"? Among the various proposals that have been made[41] today, it seems we must exclude the Hellenistic mystery cults, since they evidence no terminology similar to ours in this matter.[42] Other explanations derived from other texts of the New Testament itself are not convincing.[43]

---

39. Such use appears at least thirty-two times in the Pauline corpus either as preposition or as a prefix; ten of these uses are in Romans.

40. Quite different will be the situation in Eph 2:5-6 (see R. Penna, *La lettera agli Efesini*, SOC 10 [Bologna, 1988] 130f.).

41. See A. J. M. Wedderburn, *Baptism and Resurrection*, 342–356.

42. The present subjunctive συγχαίρωμεν, "rejoice with," of the cult of Isis (testified to in Firmicus Maternus, *Err. prof. rel.* 2:9) refers to the joyous experience of Isis on finding her dead brother, not to the violent death of Osiris.

43. See A. J. M. Wedderburn, *Baptism and Resurrection*, 346–348, which sketches the positions of U. Wilckens (who proposes a derivation from the synoptic language about following Jesus toward the cross), of E. Schweizer (who proposes language of eschatological fellowship with Christ), and of G. Wagner (who refers to the Adam-Christ parallel of Rom 5:12ff.).

For his part, Wedderburn[44] refers to the Jewish Passover tradition as attested in *m. Pes.* 10:5: "In each generation each person must consider self as having personally gone out from Egypt." The paschal *haggadah* then adds, "Not only our ancestors did the Holy One liberate, but also us did he liberate with them (*'immahem)*; therefore it is our duty to thank, praise, laud, glorify, exalt, magnify the One who did these wonderful works for our ancestors and for us; leading us out of slavery into freedom, from subjection to redemption, from grief to joy, from mourning to feasting, from darkness to the bright light."[45] It is possible that such a perspective was conflated with the Greco-Roman conception of the union between the sovereign and the people, as we read for instance in an acclamation of the crowd to Augustus: *Per illum se vivere, per illum navigare, libertate atque fortunis per illum frui,* "Living through him, through him sailing, enjoying freedom and good fortune through him."[46] Similarly, already in Gal 3:9 Paul had written that "those who have faith are blessed *with faithful Abraham* [σὺν τῷ πιστῷ 'Αβραάμ]," but there in the context the expression is equivalent to ἐν σοί, "in you," of the preceding verse (taken from Gen 12:3).

Still, what in Wedderburn's explanation does not square well with Saint Paul is that the rabbinic tradition is referring to a collective political and religious event (the liberation of Israel from Egypt), while the Apostle refers to an event interpreted with sacrificial categories and proper to a single person (the death of Christ on the cross). This last should rather, then, be related to the concept of victim offered to God, in which those who offer it and its beneficiaries somehow participate (see the rituals of Leviticus 4 to 16); even so, the fact remains that in such a case the participation is external and juridical, since it is only said that they are forgiven their sins, not that the sinner actually dies!

Perhaps despite everything the greatest affinity is on the side of the mystery cults, even if we must admit that in these "there is nothing as explicitly resounding as the passages in the New Testament, especially in Saint Paul. . . ."[47] It is actually here that we find the idea of a παθεῖν of the initiated in a mystical sense, and therefore the idea of the experience of a "voluntary death" in the celebration of cult.[48] In any case, the con-

44. *Baptism and Resurrection,* 343–345.
45. See also W. D. Davies, *Paul and Rabbinic Judaism* (London, 1965 = 1955²), 102f., where it is stated that this text was probably standardized by R. Gamaliel II, 80–120 A.D.
46. Suetonius, *Aug.* 98:2.
47. W. Burkert, *Ancient Mystery Cults* (London, 1987) 101.
48. See the texts recorded by Burkert, op. cit., 89–101 (with the corresponding notes): the concept of *pathein* as mystical experience (Aristotle, frag. 15); the declaration by an initiate, "I came out of the mystery hall feeling like a stranger to myself" (Sopatrus, *Rhet. Gr.* VIII 114f.); the following words: "Be happy that you have suffered the sufferings you had never

cepts of representation and even more of solidarity are fundamental. The destiny of Christians is linked to that of Christ, not only in the sense that the saving efficacy of his death is reflected on them, but especially insofar as they participate in that death, in which they come to find themselves inserted, as if it simply counted for them, indeed as if it were their own.⁴⁹

c) Finally, we can ask ourselves if all this dense thematic expressed by Paul concerning baptism in Rom 6:1-11 is an original creation of his theological genius or whether it was known and shared by the recipients of the letter. The initial formula of 6:3, ἢ ἀγνοεῖτε ὅτι, "Or do you not know that . . .?" would seem to presuppose a fact known to the readers. But how far is this knowing supposed to extend? Both Käsemann⁵⁰ and Cranfield⁵¹ think that even v. 3b ("[we] were baptized into his death") expresses a known tradition, and hence baptism in Christ as immersion in his death belonged to the common early Christian teaching. Wilckens,⁵² on the other hand, thinks that the tradition is limited to v. 3a ("All of us who were baptized into Christ Jesus"), since the declaration in v. 3b has no parallel in primitive Christianity. Schlier,⁵³ on the other hand, tends to consider this question formula to be rhetorical, so as to have only a pedagogical meaning, "in order to present certain theological ideas of the Apostle as obvious."⁵⁴ To resolve the question, a comparison with Gal 3:27 can be useful; there we find a sentence constructed just like this one. Their parallelism is as follows:

Rom 6:3	Gal 3:27

ἢ ἀγνοεῖτε ὅτι
"or are you unaware that"

ὅσοι ἐβαπτίσθημεν εἰς Χριστὸν Ἰησοῦν   ὅσοι γὰρ εἰς Χριστὸν ἐβαπτίσθητε
"all we who have been baptized   "For whoever has been baptized

---

suffered before" (found on a gold plate from Turi, even though it is not sure whether this refers to an initiation or to death); of the initiation mysteries of Isis, the priest says that they "make one to be reborn . . . in the manner of a voluntary death and salvation obtained by favor" (*ad instar voluntariae mortis et precariae salutis . . . renatos*: Apulaeius, *Metam.* 11.21.1 [see now Apulaeius, *Metamorphoses*, II, Loeb Classical Library (Cambridge, Mass., 1989) 334—T. P. W.]). If we then go to the later attestations concerning the *taurobolium* in the Mithras cult, it becomes even more pertinent.

49. See the soteriological value of the preposition ὑπέρ, "for. . .," first in 1 Cor 15:3 and then in Rom 5:6, 8; 8:32; 2 Cor 5:15, 21; Gal 2:20; 3:13; 1 Thess 5:10; etc. See H. Riesenfeld, art. ὑπέρ, TDNT 14:508–513, which examines the meanings "on behalf of" and "in place of."

50. E. Käsemann, *Commentary on Romans*, 165 = *An die Römer*, 157.

51. C. E. B. Cranfield, *The Epistle to the Romans*, I, 300: though not absolutely certain, it is considered highly probable.

52. U. Wilckens, *Der Brief an die Römer*, II, 11.

53. H. Schlier, *Der Römerbrief*, 192, following O. Kuss.

54. O. Kuss, *Der Römerbrief*, 297, who instead of depending on 7:1 cites Rom 6:16; 11:2; 1 Cor 3:16; 5:6; 6:2, 3, 9, 15, 16, 19; 9:13, 24.

Rom 6:3	Gal 3:27
into Christ''	into Christ''
εἰς τὸν θάνατον αὐτοῦ ἐβαπτίσθημεν	Χριστὸν ἐνδύσασθε
''have been baptized into his death.''	''has put on Christ.''

Galatians takes for granted the knowledge of a baptism εἰς Χριστόν ''into Christ'' (such, that is, as to put baptism in relation to belonging to Christ), and to this Paul adds the specification in metaphorical terms of clothing oneself in Christ (cf. Rom 13:14; Col 3:10; Eph 4:24), which only defines the datum of tradition. Thus by analogy we would do well to think of Rom 6:3b as a new Pauline explanation of the tradition reported in the first part of the verse. It is true that the introductory question would seem to suggest, as in 7:1, that the recipients would already be acquainted with this hermeneutic of baptism. But actually, given the tenor of the whole passage, what we can suppose to be already known is not so much the factor of the Christian's participation in Christ's death by being baptized as it is the saving dimension of the death of Christ itself as a past event with continuing resonance. That is, what the readers know is that ''Christ died for our sins,'' as the ancient confession of faith reported in 1 Cor 15:3 acknowledges.

Presupposing this soteriological principle common to early Christianity,[55] Paul extends it and applies it to baptism. From here on baptism is understood as the privileged moment when the believing sinner comes to participate through an objective and ritualized manner in the decisive event of Christ's death to sin, that is, in his expiatory sacrifice.[56] With this reintegration of the tradition of kerygma and of baptismal praxis with his own original rethinking, Paul has given us one of the most interesting pages of his epistles.

---

55. There does remain the problem of its absence from the confession of faith reported in Rom 1:3b-4a.

56. See R. Schnackenburg, *Baptism*, 33f.: ''It is possible that the baptismal instruction in the primitive Church set the first sacrament in relation to the death of Jesus in a general way only (cf. 1 Cor xv.3), while Paul, grasping more deeply the symbolism and significance of the bath, gave his own interpretation of it in v. 4. . . . Behind vv. 3-4 stands the early kerygma, taken over by Paul, that Christ died for our sins, was *buried*, and was raised.''

Chapter 9

The Motif of the *'Aqedah* Against the Background of Romans 8:32

It has now been over a century since the theme of the *'aqedah* became an object of specific attention in the fields of Jewish and New Testament studies alike.[1] The term (in the construct state *'qydt Yṣḥq*), the precise lexical equivalent of which is found in the Aramaic of TgN, Lev 22:27, for instance, means literally the "binding, tying" of Isaac. The noun derives ultimately from the Hebrew verb *wayya'aqod*, "and he bound," of Gen 22:9 MT (LXX: συμποδίσας), said of Abraham, who, arriving at the place of sacrifice, "bound his son Isaac, and laid him on the altar."

But if the meaning and origin of the expression present no difficulty, it is quite a different matter when attempting to define the concept, which is understood quite differently by various authorities. Some mean it only with reference to the biblical story and the events narrated in Gen 22:1-19 (thus J. Swetnam: see note 1), ignoring that in fact what is distinctive about

---

1. For the history of research see the good overview of J. Swetnam, *Jesus and Isaac: A Study of the Epistle to the Hebrews in the light of the Aqedah*, AB 94 (Rome, 1981) 4–22; add to the final bibliography of this volume: R. Hayward, "The Present State of Research into the Targumic Account of the Sacrifice of Isaac," JJS 32 (1981) 127–150, which dates the targumic substratum to the first century; C. Thoma, "Observations on the Concept and the Early Forms of Akedah Spirituality," in A. Finkel and L. Frizell, eds., *Standing Before God: Studies on Prayer in Scriptures and in Tradition with Essays in Honor of J. Oesterreicher* (New York, 1981) 213–222; idem, *Christliche Theologie des Judentums* (Aschaffenburg, 1978) 145–150; R. Martin-Achard, "La figure d'Isaac dans l'Ancien Testament et dans la tradition Juive ancienne," *Bulletin des facultés catholiques de Lyon* 106 (1982) 5–10; E. A. Coffin, "The Binding of Isaac in Modern Israeli Literature," *Michigan Quarterly Review* 22 (1983) 429–444; A. F. Segal, " 'He who did not spare his own son . . .': Jesus, Paul, and the Akedah," in P. Richardson and J. C. Hurd, eds., *From Jesus to Paul: Studies in Honour of F. W. Beare* (Waterloo, Ont., 1984) 169–184; J. Milgrom, *The Binding of Isaac: The Akedah—A Primary symbol in Jewish Thought and Art* (Berkeley, Calif., 1988). For the developments of the motif in the Middle Ages, see R. P. Schmitz, *Aqedat Jishaq. Die mittelalterliche jüdische Auslegung von Genesis 22 in ihren Hauptlinien*, JTSt 4 (Hildesheim-New York, 1979).

it is that it has become a *theologoumenon,* a true haggadic development growing out of the simple biblical data. But others (and they are more numerous, e.g., P. R. Davies and B. D. Chilton: see note 3) apply the term only to the Jewish interpretation of the Genesis passage. But here it grows ever more problematic with the difficulty of explaining and especially of dating the various stages of evolution, and hence the various semantic components of the concept itself: the connection of the sacrifice of Isaac with the Temple (and especially with the *tamîd* sacrifice), with the Passover festival, with the motif of blood, with the New Year festival, and most specifically with the theme of a vicarious expiation (and so with the theology of merit).

At this point we raise the problem of knowing what kind of relationship there is between the more mature rabbinic expression of the 'aqedah and the writers and theology of the New Testament (especially Rom 8:32). Some authors have, in fact, affirmed the dependence of the expiatory sense of the death of Christ, and specifically of the Pauline soteriology precisely upon the 'aqedah,[2] while others more recently have shown themselves more cautious or have actually maintained the opposite, an influence of the Christian message concerning the redemptive death of Jesus on the very development of the rabbinic concept of the 'aqedah.[3] And then another author would distinguish between the Targums on the one hand, which would reflect an archaic stage, even before the end of the Second Temple, and the midrashim and the Talmud on the other, which would reflect a later, more evolved age: the former would act as a bridge between the earlier Jewish traditions and the later rabbinic literature.[4]

It is certain on the basis of the available sources that the full maturation of the motif is later than the first century of the present era; on the other hand, we already see the motif of the 'aqedah clearly in process of formation, as evidenced by some Jewish texts of the period as well as

2. Thus I. Levi, "Le sacrifice d'Isaac et la mort de Jésus," *RevEtJuives* 64 (1912) 161–184; H.-J. Schoeps, *Paulus. Die Theologie des Apostels im Lichte der jüdischen Religionsgeschichte* (Tübingen, 1959) 144–152; in much more moderate terms, see also R. Le Déaut, *La présentation targumique du sacrifice d'Isaac et la sotériologie paulinienne,* SPCIC 2 (Rome, 1963) 563–574; *La nuit pascale. Essai sur la signification de la Pâque juive à partir du Targum d'Exode XII 42,* AB 22 (Rome, 1963, 1975²) 131–212.

3. See M.-L. Gubler, *Die frühesten Deutungen des Todes Jesu,* OBO 14 (Freiburg-Göttingen, 1977) 336–375; and especially P. R. Davies and B. D. Chilton, "The Aqedah: A Revised Tradition History," CBQ 40 (1978) 514–546; P. R. Davies, "Passover and the Dating of the Aqedah," JJS 30 (1979) 56–67; B. D. Chilton, "Isaac and the Second Night: A Consideration," Bib 61 (1980) 78–88.

4. Thus R. Hayward, "The Present State," 150; he picks up and develops an opinion of G. Vermes, *Scripture and Tradition in Judaism: Haggadic Studies* (Leiden, 1973²) 195–208. But A. F. Segal maintains that so far it is "almost impossible to develop consistent criteria for isolating the first century traditions in the targumim" (" 'He who did not spare . . .,' " 172).

certain passages of the Christian scriptures that belong in their origin to the same religious and cultural matrix. Precisely this evidence entitles us to use the term *'aqedah* at least in the somewhat fluid sense of a theological category on the way to full development.

Hence the four parts of our study, which intend to clarify the motif, at the same time respecting the stages of its formation: to the biblical text in its redactional meaning (I) we immediately juxtapose the complete rabbinic formulation of the *'aqedah* (II) in order to be able immediately to compare the two extreme ends; we then go on to scrutinize the texts situated in between, first treating the Jewish sources of the first century B.C. and the first of the new era (III); then we will inspect in the New Testament, and particularly in Rom 8:32, the material that belongs to this same stage, albeit from the Christian side (IV).

I. The testing of Abraham in Gen 22:1-19 (and in the biblical tradition)

The present story of Gen 22:1-19 is probably based on archaic traditions of different purposes. Worth mentioning would be especially the intention to condemn the ancient practice of child sacrifice, still attested in the monarchical period (see 1 Kgs 16:34; 2 Kgs 23:10; Lev 18:21; 20:25). It is quite possible that there was originally a preoccupation to explain the existence of a specific cultic place associated with "the territory of Moria" (v. 2), for which name there are two possible etymological explanations ("fear of Yah" or "Yah will provide"). But we will leave aside the questions concerning the preredactional basis of the text.[5] We limit ourselves rather to at least a summary treatment of the principal components of the present (postexilic) redaction.

Of utmost importance is the phrase of v. 1, "God tested (MT: *nissāh*; LXX: ἐπείραζεν) Abraham." This opening of the story announces, as it were, the musical key, making the reading and interpretation of the whole story possible and immediately revealing its sense. At the center of the narrative, then, is not so much the figure of Isaac as that of Abraham, not the son but the father. Isaac's role is, of course, coessential to that of Abraham, but only insofar as his being destined as sacrifice sheds light on the unswerving steadfastness of Abraham in accepting and executing the

---

5. On this matter in addition to the commentaries, see J.-L. Vesco, "Abraham: actualisation et relectures," RSPhTh 55 (1971) 33–80; G. W. Coats, "Abraham's Sacrifice of Faith. A Form-Critical Study of Genesis 22," Int 27 (1973) 389–400. On the literary attribution of the text to the sources E or J, see the differing positions in R. Kilian, *Isaaks Opferung zur Überlieferungsgeschichte von Gen 22*, Stuttgarter Bibelstudien 44 (Stuttgart, 1970); J. van Seters, *Abraham in History and Tradition* (New Haven-London, 1975).

divine command, unreasonable though it appears from the human perspective. This is confirmed by the word of the angel who intervenes as a *deus ex machina* to prevent the slaughter of Isaac: "Now I know that you fear God" (v. 12); and then follows the blessing of the patriarch and of his progeny (vv. 15-18).

This biblical passage, then, ought to bear not the current title of "sacrifice of Isaac" but rather "testing of Abraham," or at least "sacrifice of Isaac as test of Abraham." Actually there is no emphasis on any subjective attitude of the young heir; we only hear his naive but perfectly understandable question, "The fire and the wood are here, but where is the lamb for the burnt offering?" (v. 7). But rather than showing any participation of Isaac in what was about to happen, it shows him completely ignorant, and so a purely passive object in Abraham's hands, a victim—and that not only in the sacrificial sense!

Moreover, the whole biblical tradition has here developed only the aspect of the pure and unwavering faithfulness to the word of the Lord on Abraham's part: thus in Neh 9:8 ("You found *his heart faithful* [MT: *'et-lᵉbābô ne'ĕmān;* LXX: τὴν καρδίαν αὐτοῦ πιστήν] to you"); Sir 44:20 ("Abraham . . . in trial was found faithful"); 1 Macc 2:52 ("Was not Abraham found faithful in temptation, and was that not credited to him for justice?"); Wis 10:5 ("She recognized the just one, and preserved him before God without stain, and kept him strong despite his tenderness for his son"). As is evident, the accent is always on the attitude of Abraham; the figure of Isaac never enters into account (except indirectly in Wis 10:5). Only in Jdt 8:25-27, when the "trials of the ancestors" are remembered cumulatively, is Isaac explicitly recalled (see v. 26: "Remember how much [God] did with Abraham, what trials he caused Isaac to undergo, and what happened to Jacob in Mesopotamia"), but the plural "what trials" (ὅσα ἐπείρασεν) suggests that the writer does not intend to emphasize the attempted sacrifice, which is rather left together with other difficult times that he experienced (cf. Gen 25:1-5: famine; 25:21: the sterility of Rebekah), among which the importance of this event is tempered.[6]

Still, we absolutely must recognize that it was in relation to nothing other than his own son that the test of faith was given to Abraham. It is precisely Isaac, the son of the promise, that is demanded in sacrifice. And

---

6. The Vulgate text of Judith completely omits the clauses of Jdt 8:26 concerning Isaac and Jacob, while emphasizing Abraham all the more: *Memores esse debent quomodo pater noster Abraham tentatus est et per multas tribulationes probatus Dei amicus factus est. Sic Isaac, sic Iacob, sic Moyses et omnes qui placuerunt Deo, per multas tribulationes transierunt fideles:* "They must remember how our ancestor Abraham was tempted, and having been tested through many tribulations, became God's friend. Thus Isaac, thus Jacob, thus Moses and all who pleased God remained faithful through many tribulations" (Jdt 8:22-23).

in vv. 2-16 the word "son" (MT: *bēn*; LXX: υἱός, twice τέκνον, "child") recurs all of ten times (vv. 2, 3, 6, 7, 8, 9, 10, 12, 13, 16); and of these, three times (vv. 2, 12, 16) the noun is accompanied by the adjective "only" *(yaḥîd)*, which the LXX renders significantly with "beloved" *(ἀγαπητός)*, always in the mouth of God, as if to increase the weight of the request. It is precisely this circumstance (i.e., that the victim must be a son, indeed the son par excellence, the heir to the promise) that makes Abraham's test the supreme trial, and moreover makes his willingness—without the least hesitation—the supreme demonstration of total trust in God and in God's word.[7]

We can, then, say that it is precisely Isaac who makes Abraham great in our eyes. The willingness to sacrifice the son is actually the real sacrifice of the father. To paraphrase the text of John 3:15, we could say: "Abraham has so loved God as to give his only beloved son"! In the Genesis passage there is probably an edifying intention in addressing Jewish readers tested by various temptations to infidelity to God and to apostasy (consider the lateness of the biblical texts cited above), who were (and still are) thereby inspired to steadfast adherence to the Lord.

One motif explicitly present in Gen 22:1-19 is that of the promise, which is here not only repeated but emphasized with a crescendo of new formulations (vv. 16-18). Thus, in comparison with the earlier formulas of the promise (Gen 12:1-3, 7; 13:14-17; 15:7, 18), the solemn formulas are altogether new: "I swear by myself" (22:16); "oracle of the Lord" (ibid.); "Your descendants will possess the gates of their enemies" (v. 17). Only from here on will there be further allusions to an oath by God (in 24:7; 26:3f.), each time referring back to the oath of chapter 22; and in 26:24 God renews the promise to Isaac, but "for love of Abraham my servant."

Thus the tone is high-sounding and is contextually motivated precisely by Abraham's behavior. The motivation is clearly expressed: "Because you have done this, and have not refused your only son" (v. 16; MT: *kî ya'an 'ăšer 'āśîtā 'et-haddābār hazzeh wᵉlô ḥāśaktā 'et-binkā 'et-yᵉḥîdekā*; LXX: οὗ εἵνεκεν ἐποίησας τὸ ῥῆμα τοῦτο καὶ οὐκ ἐφείσω τοῦ υἱοῦ σου τοῦ ἀγαπητοῦ δι' ἐμέ); "because you have obeyed my voice" (v. 18b; MT: *'ēqeb 'ăšer šāma'tā b'qolî*; LXX: ἀνθ' ὧν ὑπήκουσας τῆς ἐμῆς φωνῆς). Between these two causal clauses is the whole blessing, "I will bless you with every blessing and multiply your descendants like the stars of heaven and the sands of the

---

7. The commentary of G. von Rad seems completely pertinent to me, showing two readings inherent in the Genesis story: on the one hand the obscurity and solitude in which Abraham moves, unaware that he is only being tested, and on the other the absurdity of God's request, asking if Abraham is able to return to God the gift of the promise ("God therefore poses before Abraham the question whether he understands the gift of promise as a pure gift": G. von Rad, *Genesis*, Old Testament Library, rev. ed. [Philadelphia, 1973] 244).

seashore; your descendants will possess the gates of your enemies; through your descendants will all the nations of the earth be blessed" (vv. 17-18a). This blessing appears here—and only here—as a reward for the obedient fidelity of Abraham.[8] I believe that we have here the origin of the bipolar pattern, simultaneously antithetic and climactic, of renunciation-reward, sacrifice-blessing, humiliation-exaltation, or in New Testament terms, death-resurrection. Hence all the more Gen 22:1-19 becomes important to understand a good part of the successive reflection, Christian as well as Jewish (see below).

Finally, we note that in the biblical text the idea of "binding" of Isaac is lexically secondary. It occurs only in v. 11: "He bound (waya'āqod) his son Isaac and placed him on the altar"; more expressive still is the LXX Greek aorist participle συμποδίσας, which evokes the image of an animal or a prisoner "with feet tied" to prevent any escape, completely controlled by the owner or the celebrant of the sacrifice.

II. The rabbinic concept of 'aqedat Yiṣḥāq

From the biblical text we pass immediately to the re-reading of it in the rabbinic tradition,[9] as it comes attested to us through the paraphrastic Aramaic versions of it (Targums), as well as through its treatment in the biblical interpretations (midrashim). To keep to a sure dating, we must say that the works we are interested in are all (at least redactionally) later than the first century of the present era, specifically from the second to the eighth century.[10] Let us first make a selection of texts in two stages in order then to be able to draw some systematic conclusions.

1. *The Aramaic versions.* We will first check two Targums of Gen 22:1-19 and then those of Exod 12:42 and Lev 22:27.

8. The idea of reward appears explicitly in the cited Hebrew text of v. 18b: 'ēqeb 'ăšer; this expression can be the equivalent of a simple causal conjunction, and the translation "because" already itself contains the idea of a consequent reward, the cause of which is indicated by the present clause. But the Hebrew 'ēqeb by itself means "price, payment, reward," and our text could be also be translated "in return for": "*en retour* de ton obéissance" (*Bible de Jérusalem*), or more clearly still, "in compensation for": "*In compenso del fatto che* tu hai obbedito alla mia voce" (E. Testa, *Genesi*, II [Turin, 1974] 393).

9. A broad examination of the motif in this area of Jewish literature was presented by Sh. Spiegel, *The Last Trial: On the Legends and Lore of the Command to Abraham to Offer Isaac as a Sacrifice: The Akedah*, translated from the Hebrew with an introduction by J. Goldin (Philadelphia-New York, 1967 [= 1950; 1979²]).

10. On the dating of the rabbinic material, see especially, e.g., E. P. Sanders, *Paul and Palestinian Judaism: A Comparison of Patterns of Religion* (London, 1977) 63–69; M. McNamara, *Palestinian Judaism and the New Testament*, GNS 4 (Wilmington, Del., 1983) 174–177. Specifically on the Targumîn see R. Le Déaut, *Introduction à la littérature targumique* (Rome, 1966) 73–181 (a new edition is in preparation); D. D. York, "The Dating of Targumic Literature," JSJ 5 (1974–75) 49–62.

a) The Palestinian Targum represented by codex Neofiti 1 (TgN) is perhaps the most ancient Targum on Genesis 22. "The basic text of the tradition that leads up to Neofiti goes back to the second-third centuries of our era and constitutes one reduction to writing of a much more ancient oral tradition."[11] We report the principal passages of the Aramaic version of the biblical text.[12] Verse 8 of chapter 22 is rendered thus: "Abraham said, 'Before Yahweh there has been prepared for him a lamb for the holocaust. Otherwise you are the lamb of holocaust.'" In Gen 22:10 an exhortation of Isaac to Abraham has been introduced in v. 10: "'My father, tie me tightly lest I kick you in such a way as to render your offering invalid . . . .' Abraham's eyes were (turned) to the eyes of Isaac, and the eyes of Isaac were turned toward the angels on high. At that moment a voice came down from heaven saying, 'Come, see two persons unique in my universe. The one sacrifices and the other is sacrificed: the one who sacrifices does not hesitate, and the one who is sacrificed offers his throat.'" In Gen 22:14 a prayer of Abraham to God is inserted that is very important for our purposes: "Then Abraham worshiped and prayed in the name of the Word of Yahweh saying, 'I beg you, by the love before you, Yahweh! All things are manifest and known before you. There has been no division in my heart from the first moment you told me to sacrifice my son Isaac, and to reduce him to powder and ashes before you. But at once, I rose early in the morning and rapidly have executed your words with joy and accomplished your decision. And now, when his sons shall be in a time of distress, remember the *ʿaqedah* of their father Isaac and hear the voice of their supplication! For the generations to come will say: On the mountain of the sanctuary of Yahweh, where Abraham offered his son Isaac, on that mountain there appeared to him the Glory of the Shekinah of Yahweh.'"

b) The Palestinian Targum known as "Pseudo-Jonathan" (TgJo) is redactionally late (no earlier than the eighth century) but as a whole, according to R. Le Déaut, contains material even older than the interpretation of the Mishna. Already in Gen 22:1 the trial asked of Abraham is anticipated by these words of Isaac addressed to Ishmael (who claims the inheritance, counting on the fact that he was circumcised at the age of thirteen, that is, with full consciousness): "Behold, today I am thirty-seven years old, and if the Holy One (blessed be he) asked for all my members I should not refuse him." Also here in Gen 22:10 Isaac asks to be bound

11. R. Le Déaut, *Targum du Pentateuque—I. Genèse*, SC 245 (Paris, 1978) 40.
12. The translations reported here are based on those of R. Le Déaut, *Targum du Pentateuque—II. Exode et Lévitique*, SC 256 (Paris, 1979).

tightly, "so that I may not struggle because of the anguish of my soul." The prayer of Abraham in Gen 22:14 is shorter than it is in TgN: "I beg you, by the love before you, Yahweh! It is manifested before you that there has been no reluctance in my heart, and that I have sought to accomplish your decision with joy. Therefore, when the children of my son Isaac will enter on the time of anguish, remember them, hear them, and save them. For all the generations to come will be saying: On this mountain Abraham bound his son Isaac, and the Shekinah of Yahweh appeared to him."

c) Concerning Exod 12:42 ("This was a night of watching for the Lord to cause them to leave the land of Egypt"), the TgN develops a very long text that goes under the name of the *Poem of the Four Nights:* the first is the night of creation, the third the night of the exodus, the fourth is the eschatological night. And the second is described thus: "The second night, when Yahweh appeared to Abraham, who was a hundred years old, and to Sarah, his wife, aged ninety, to accomplish what the Scripture said, "Will Abraham at the age of one hundred beget a child, and Sarah, his wife, at the age of ninety give birth? And Isaac was thirty years old when he was offered on the altar. The heavens bowed and came down, and Isaac saw their perfections, which clouded his eyes. And he called it the Second Night." As is evident, the second night consists of two moments: the announcement of a son to Abraham and the sacrifice of Isaac. The much shorter parallel text of TgJo alludes only to the first of these in rather succinct terms ("The second, when he appeared to Abraham").[13]

d) The biblical text of Lev 22:27 ("When a calf or lamb or kid is born . . .") is paraphrased in TgN with an explanation referring to the story of Abraham for each of the three animals. Concerning the lamb we read: "The lamb was chosen to recall the merit of the unique man who was bound like a lamb on the mountain, as a holocaust on the altar; but [God] delivered him in his merciful goodness. And a time [will come] when his sons will pray, and say in their hours of tribulation: 'Hear us in this hour, attend to the voice of our prayer, and remember for us the *'aqedah* of Isaac our father.' " The parallel text of TgJo is more abbreviated as usual ("The lamb was chosen, in the second place, to recall the merit of the just one, who was bound on the altar, and merited to have a lamb destined for holocaust in his place").

2. *Midrashic commentaries.* There are three midrashim that refer to the *'aqedah.* The most ancient is certainly the *Mekilta* on Exod 12:13. The work,

---

13. See R. Le Déaut, *La nuit pascale,* 133–153; the recension of TgJo is considered an abbreviation of the larger primitive text.

known also as "Mekilta of R. Išmael," dates in content to the Tannaitic period (R. Išmael ben Eliša died about 135 A.D.), though the redaction is of the fourth century.

a) The *Mek. Exod* 12:13, commenting on the biblical text, "I shall see the blood and will pass by," says:[14] "I see the blood of the sacrifice of Isaac. For it is said: 'And Abraham called the name of that place Adonai-jireh' (the Lord will see), etc. (Gen. 22.14). Likewise it says in another passage: 'And as He was about to destroy, the Lord beheld and He repented Him,' etc. (1 Chr. 21.15). What did He behold? He beheld the blood of the sacrifice of Isaac, as it is said: 'God will Himself see the lamb,' etc. (Gen. 22.8)."

b) The midrash *Genesis Rabba* in its present form dates to the fifth century. The biblical text of Gen 22:1-19 is amply treated with a whole series of significant explanations.[15] These elements are particularly developed: theme of the "third day" (Gen 22:4; *Gen. Rab.* 56:1 enumerates six biblical texts on the "third day"); the theme of merit (see *Gen. Rab.* 56:1: "through the merit of the third day of our father Abraham"; 56:2: "Abraham returned unscathed only through the merit of adoration"; 56:3: "Through the merit of that knife"; 56:5: "The merit of Abraham"; especially in an expiatory sense, 56:10: "Thus may it please you, Lord, our God, that when the descendants of Isaac are in trouble, this sacrifice may be remembered for them, and you may have mercy on them"); the ineffective temptation of the devil to dissuade either Abraham or Isaac (in 56:4); the theme of blood and of vicarious substitution (in 56:7: "And where was the knife? Three tears from the ministering angels had fallen and destroyed the knife. He said, 'Shall I strangle him?' He answered him, 'Do not lay your hand upon the boy." He said to him, 'Shall I shed a drop of his blood?' He answered him, 'Neither do anything to him'; in 56:9: "Lord of the world, consider the blood of this ram as the blood of Isaac my son; . . . as if I had offered my son Isaac first, and later this ram in his place"); the theme of Isaac the lamb, who offers himself freely (in 56:4: "*God will see to the lamb,* otherwise you are the lamb for the holocaust, my son. *And the two went on together,* the one to bind and the other to be bound"; in 56:8 Isaac, in order to avoid trembling with fear of the knife, asks: "Bind me well, and at once . . . Can a man bind someone thirty-

14. The translation is of J. Z. Lauterbach, *Mekilta de-Rabbi Ishmael,* I (Philadelphia, 1976) 57. See G. Stenberger, "Die Datierung der Mekilta," *Kairos* 21 (1979) 81–118.
15. The translations quoted here are based on A. Ravenna, *Commento alla Genesi (Berešit Rabbâ),* Classici delle religioni (Turin, 1978) [see also Midraš Rabba, I, ed. H. Freedman and M. Simon (London, 1939 = 1961)—T. P. W.].

seven years old without his consent?''); the theme of the *Tamîd* (in 56:9: ''like the lamb of daily sacrifice''); the theme of atonement during the New Year festival (in 56:9 commenting on Gen 22:13: ''All the days of the year Israel is enveloped in sin and is the victim of misfortunes, but at the New Year the Holy One, blessed is he, takes the šofar, blows it and remembers to pardon him; and in the end he will be freed with the ram's horn, as it is said: *The Lord sounds the šofar* = Zech 9:14.'' This alludes to the ram's horn sounded as a trumpet at the New Year).

c) The midrash *Lev. R.*, contemporaneous with the preceding, alludes more than once to the *'aqedah*. In 2:10 (on Lev 1:2) it is said that Isaac threw himself before his father like a lamb of sacrifice. Especially interesting is the text of 2:11 (on Lev 1:5):[16] ''AND HE SHALL KILL THE BULLOCK BEFORE THE LORD'' (1:5), while of the ram it says, *'and he shall kill it on the side of the altar northward (zafonah) before the Lord'* (ib. 11). The Sages said: When Abraham, our father, bound Isaac his son, the Holy One, blessed be He, instituted the sacrifice of two he-lambs, one in the morning and one in the evening. Why did he do this? — When Israel offered up the daily sacrifices on the altar, and read this verse, viz. 'Zafonah *before the Lord*' the Holy One, blessed be he, remembers the binding of Isaac.'' (The term ''north'' is explained with the word ṣafah, ''see''). In 29:9-10 (on Lev 23:24) the *'aqedah* is associated with the New Year: Abraham asks God to repress his claims to justice as Abraham repressed his instincts at the moment of the *'aqedah*, so that when the children of Isaac sin, God may have mercy on them because of the *'aqedah*; redemption is related to the horn of the ram of Genesis 22. Finally, 36:5 (on Lev 26:42) says that God saw the ashes of Isaac heaped on the altar (certainly in a proleptic sense).

d) We leave aside two other texts: Palestinian Talmud *Taan* 2:65d:2 (of the fourth century)[17] and the *Pesikta of R. Kahana* 40:6 (of the fifth century);[18] they both repeat the traditional motifs already observed. On the other hand, in *Pirqê of R. Eliezer* 38A (of the tenth century)[19] we are told that Abraham actually did kill Isaac, but it is quite plausible to suppose that the story is a rival claim against the Christian message of the death and resurrection of Jesus of Nazareth.

16. The translation is by J. Israelstam and J. J. Slotki, *Midrash Rabbah: Leviticus* (London, 1961).
17. See Strack-Billerbeck, III, 242, where it is seen as pertinent to Rom 8:13 *because it says that Abraham repressed his [evil] inclination (yṣry)* in order to do God's will.
18. See the edition edited by W. G. Braude (New Haven-London, 1968).
19. G. Friedländer, *Pirkê de Rabbi Eliezer (The Chapters of Rabbi Eliezer the Great)* (New York, 1971²).

3. *Conclusions.* On the basis of texts we have examined, we can now define the *ʿaqedah* in the final stage of its semantic development. We note above all that in contrast to the biblical account it is now Isaac who has achieved the center of attention, and with him the idea of sacrifice enters the foreground, so that within the story of 22:1-19 the institution of the *Tamîd* is now perceived (this is connected with the fact that since 2 Chr 3:1 Mount Moriah has been identified as the Temple Mount). The paradoxical allusion to the "blood" of Isaac (surely mentioned in a proleptic sense, since it was not shed, and in a substitutive sense with regard to that of the ram) relates the *ʿaqedah* strictly to a theology of merit (through which the sacrifice of Isaac becomes a thesaurus to draw on in seeking the mercy and aid of the Lord in times of trouble), and thus with the idea of a vicarious expiation for the sins of Israel.[20] From the liturgical point of view, while a relationship to the daily Temple sacrifice is clear, and even more so (after the destruction of the Temple) to the New Year festival, the same cannot be said for the Passover feast; the mention of the *ʿaqedah* in TgN Exod 12:24 and in *Mek. Exod* 12:13 has probably only an accessory value.[21]

From all the factors noted, we must conclude that the rabbinic *ʿaqedah* is in practice the Jewish rival corresponding to what Christians had been proclaiming for some time about the meaning of the death of Jesus. Even if it is difficult to deny that individual elements of detail have their roots in earlier times, the very chronological placement of the literature we have been examining must dissuade us from considering its characteristic motifs as causes that influenced the nature of the Christian message.

III. The preparation of the *theologoumenon* in the first century B.C. and the first century of the new era

We leave aside the texts of Philo the Ancient (early second century B.C.) and of Alexander Polyhistor (mid-first century B.C.) reported by Eusebius

---

20. In *Gen. Rab.* 56:3, commenting on Gen 22:6 ("Abraham took the wood for the holocaust and laid it on his son Isaac's shoulders"), we read: "like one who carries the pole on his shoulders." The Italian translator (op. cit., 445, n. 10) explains: "on which the infamous Haman will be hanged." This allusion is not pertinent, as Haman did not carry the pole on his shoulders (cf. Est 7:9-10). Much more plausible is that we perceive here a reaction to the Christian message of the Cross of Jesus (see J. Swetnam, *Jesus and Isaac*, 78 and n. 452), indeed Sh. Spiegel, *The Last Trial*, 77, translates, "Like one bearing his own cross." See also M. Maher, "The Merits of the Fathers and the Treasury of the Church," IrThQuart 46 (1979) 256–275.

21. J. Swetnam, *Jesus and Isaac*, 79 and n. 457. Still, see R. Hayward, "The Present State," 144–148, who notes that the pre-rabbinic sources give little importance to the feast of Rosh ha-Shanah (New Year) and maintains that in the Tannaitic period there were transferred to this feast events that in pre-Christian times were associated rather with Passover. For the

of Caesarea, *Praeparatio Evangelica,* IX 20:21 and IX 19:4; the former especially celebrates in emphatic terms the "immortal fame" of Abraham's
act, but neither of the two evidences much theological depth.[22] We address rather a series of five quite different writers belonging to the two
centuries marking the change of the era.

1) The apocryphal *Book of Jubilees* (commonly dated to the last years of
the reign of John Hyrcanus, 109–105 B.C.) in 17:15–18:19 offers us a
paraphrased version[23] of Gen 22. The major elements of originality are
the introduction of the diabolic "Prince Mastema" (17:16; 18:9, 12) who,
probably under the influence of the Book of Job, persuades God to try
the just man Abraham;[24] the identification of the place of sacrifice with
"Mount Zion" (18:13) and its consequent identification with Jerusalem
and the Temple; and especially the dating of the event. This last element
is deduced from the following indications: the order was given to Abraham "the twelfth day of the first month" (17:15); he "got up early in the
morning at dawn" (18:3a), that is, the thirteenth day; finally he arrived
at the place of sacrifice "on the third day" (18:3b), that is, the fourteenth
day. But since the first month is Nisan, it follows that the day of the sacrifice of Isaac was 14 Nisan, that is, the day of the celebration of the Passover.[25]

This conclusion could theoretically be important for New Testament
interpretation, but in practice it should not really be overvalued, both for
critical reasons internal to the book (which tends to associate various events
with specific festivals) and because the position of *Jubilees* is simply not

---

late association with the feast of Rosh ha-Shanah, see C. J. Liebreich, "Aspects of the New
Year Liturgy," HUCA 34 (1963) 125–176, 146.
22. See J. Swetnam, *Jesus and Isaac,* 29, 31, discussing the identity of the second writer
cited by Eusebius.
23. See the translation from the ancient Ethiopic (Ge'ez) by L. Fusella, in *Apocrifi dell'Antico
Testamento,* ed. P. Sacchi, Classici delle religioni (Turin, 1981) 298–301 [also *The Old Testament
Pseudepigrapha,* ed. J. Charlesworth, vol. 2 (New York, 1985) 90–91—T. P. W.].
24. The presence of "Mastema" doubtless serves the author to exculpate God—at least
partially—of having taken the initiative in an act of such cruelty. This appears especially in
the story of Moses (Jub. 48).
25. Some attempts to date the event either to Tabernacles (thus M. Testuz, *Les idées religieuses
du Livre de Jubilés* [Geneva-Paris, 1960] 162–163) or to the New Year (thus J. B. Segal, *The
Hebrew Passover from the Earliest Times to A.D. 70,* LOS 12 [London, 1963] 236–248) fail to take
account either of the precise chronological indication "the twelfth day of the first month"
(Jub. 17:15) or of the fact that the solar calendar of *Jubilees* can allude in this case only to Passover
(see J. Morgenstern, "The Calendar of the Book of Jubilees, Its Origin and Its Character,"
VT 5 [1955] 34–76). Therefore, "The paschal interpretation of the sacrifice of Isaac in *Jubilees*
constitutes the classic exegesis" (A. Jaubert, *La notion d'alliance dans le Judaïsme aux abords de
l'ère chrétienne,* PS 6 [Paris, 1963] 90, n. 5). It is quite another thing, however, to attribute
a historical-liturgical value to this dating, which is denied by P. R. Davies, "Passover and
the Dating of the Aqedah," JJS 30 (1979) 56–57; but see n. 21 above.

common to Judaism of the intertestamental period (perhaps because the book is of Essene origin? But surprisingly there is not a trace of the *'aqedah* in the Qumran manuscripts thus far known).[26]

2) The *Fourth Book of Maccabees* (datable to the first half of the first century of the present era and indebted to Pharisaic influence) refers three times to the sacrifice of Isaac as it recalls the great national figures of the past who were faithful to God even in trials: 13:12 ("Remember from whence you come, and which was the father by whose hand Father Isaac *endured being immolated* [σφαγιασθῆναι . . . ὑπέμεινεν]"); 16:20 ("For God also our Father Abraham hastened to immolate [σφαγιάσαι] his son Isaac, our first forebear, who, seeing the hand of his father descending on him armed with the knife, did not flee"); 18:11 (the father of the seven brothers "read to us of Abel killed by Cain and of Isaac *offered as a holocaust* [ὁλοκαρπούμενον] and of Joseph in prison").

Besides these recurrences, which are not so impressive in themselves, what should be noted is that they occur in a book that is characterized by the new and fertile motif of the expiatory value of the death of the martyrs (so much so that it avoids any mention of sacrifice in the Jerusalem Temple).[27] Any connection of this motif, which is clearly affirmed in 1:11; 6:29; 17:22; 18:3-4, with the sacrifice of Isaac is not explicit. But the supposition that the matter could be seen in this light rests on two considerations: (a) the offering of Isaac is presented in evident sacrificial terms (note the Greek verbs reported above); (b) it was chosen along with other examples of trial that foreshadow or explain the experience of the Maccabean martyrs. And while the fact that Isaac did not shed his blood tended to discourage the explicit designation of his story in an expiatory sense (note in contrast the sense of "ransom/redemption" attributed to the death of martyrs in 6:29; 17:22), still it is perhaps legitimate to read between the lines that implicitly the sacrifice of Isaac also shared this salvific signification, at least in an exemplary sense.[28]

26. The fragment 4Q180 (". . . journey of two days . . . Mount Zion Jerusalem . . .") noticed by J. T. Milik, *The Books of Enoch, Aramaic Fragments of Qumran Cave 4* (Oxford, 1976) 252, does not by itself permit secure deductions.

27. See A. P. O'Hagan, "The Martyr in the Fourth Book of Maccabees," *Liber Annuus* 24 (1974) 94-120; U. Breitenstein, *Beobachtungen zu Sprache, Stil und Gedankengut des Vierten Makkabäerbuchs* (Basel-Stuttgart, 1976) 171-173; and also R. Le Déaut, *Aspects de l'intercession dans le judaïsme ancien*, JSJ 1 (1970) 35-57; D. Flusser, "Das jüdische Martyrium im Zeitalter des Zweitens Tempels und die Christologie," *Freiburger Rundbrief* 25 (1973) 187-194.

28. See A. F. Segal, " 'He who did not spare . . .' " 175-177, who notes the absence of recourse to Isa 53; see also R. J. Daly, "The Soteriological Significance of the Sacrifice of Isaac," CBQ 39 (1977) 45-75, 57.

3) *Philo of Alexandria* (died ca. 45 A.D.) treats Gen 22 in *De Abrahamo* 167–207. We must say *at once* that in this long text he treats the material in completely original terms that distance him from the Palestinian traditions.[29] Certain omissions are particularly striking: the name of Mount Moriah is missing (par. 169); there is no talk of the "binding" of Isaac (par. 176); there is no mention of the substitute ram (ibid.); and even the motif of the "trial" of Abraham is missing, though compensated for by that of his complete and firm openness to the divine command (par. 170, 175). Philo probably means to respond to certain detractors of Abraham and his action, which would not be at all unusual (par. 178-183); to such persons he replies saying that the patriarch acted in obedience to God (par. 192) and only out of his love for God, who had given him his own "only beloved" son (μόνον . . . ἀγαπητόν: par. 196). Then, applying his typical allegorical method (and playing with the etymology of the Hebrew name Isaac), Philo makes of Abraham the perfect figure of the sage who sacrifices his joy to God (par. 201–202).

But we must observe in any case that the Alexandrine philosopher considers Abraham's action in clear sacrificial terms (σφαγιάσαι, "immolate": par. 169; ἱερουργεῖν, "sacrifice": par. 202),[30] and celebrating it as an "act most worthy of being known" (par. 167; cf. 196), recognizes it as "complete and perfect" (ὁλόκληρος καὶ παντελής), even if the expected conclusion was not accomplished (par. 177): as if to say that the interior dispositions (obedience and love) were decisive for the validity of the sacrifice. The fact remains that Philo's attention is all concentrated more on Abraham than on Isaac, on the "extraordinary piety," on the "sublimity and greatness of his soul" (par. 199).

4) *Flavius Josephus* treats Gen 22 in paragraphs 222–236 of the first book of the *Antiquitates Iudaicae* (published in Rome in 94 A.D.). His account has a definite apologetic intent, as one can conclude from 1:233: "It was not from desire for human blood that God called for Abraham to immolate his son, nor did he make him a father in order to take his son from him with such impiety, but to test his intention, whether he actually would obey even such a command" (in 1:222 it says that Abraham ὑπερηγάπα = "passionately loved" his son, since he was μονογενής = "only-begotten"); and also in 1:228-231 Abraham himself justifies his deed to Isaac (1:231:

---

29. See, e.g., S. Sandmel, *Philo's Place in Judaism: A Study of Conceptions of Abraham in Jewish Literature* (New York, 1971) 198, 210.

30. In *De sacrificiis Abelis et Caini* 110, Isaac is characterized as "a splendid example" of "the indivisible sacrifices, that is, the holocausts."

"You acquire God for me in your place" = τὸν θεὸν ἀντὶ σεαυτοῦ).³¹ In comparison with the biblical account, that of Josephus also makes room for a response by Isaac, who affirms that it would be better not to have been born than to disobey God and his own father (1:232). That the act had a sacrificial meaning appears in the words that appear repeatedly, θυσία, θῦμα, ἱερεῖον, all synonyms for "sacrifice," and also in the specific identification of the place with the Temple (see 1:226). No mention is made of "binding" properly speaking nor of any expiatory value. But as a reward God promises to show every care for Abraham and for his descendants (1:234).

5) A case apart for the original treatment of the subject is the *Liber Antiquitatum Biblicarum (LAB)* of Pseudo-Philo. Its date is disputed, varying from the end of the first century (before 70?) to the beginning of the second.³² But both the literary genre and many of the traditions contained in it would suggest putting it in the first century at least as its environment of origin if not of its final redaction.³³ Besides a secondary mention in 40:2 (where the daughter of Jephthah [Judg 11:36] is compared to Isaac), there are two texts that particularly support our case.

a) In 18:5, to prevent Balaam from cursing the Israelites, God reminds him (cf. Num 22–24) of their election in Abraham: *Et filium eius petii in holocaustomata . . . et, quia non contradixit, facta est oblatio eius in conspectu meo acceptabilis, et pro sanguine eius elegi istos:* "I asked for his son as a holocaust . . . and because he did not refuse, his offering was acceptable in my sight, and for his blood I chose them." From the popular Latin in which the translated text has been preserved, it becomes apparent how such rich and positive values as the obedience of Abraham and the blood of Isaac are becoming associated, and how the former procures God's benevolence, and the latter, God's act of election for Israel. Worthy of note is especially the "blood," which is here mentioned for the first time in connection with the sacrifice of Isaac. In reality, of course, if we base ourselves on the story of Gen 22, this was unbloody, and yet Pseudo-Philo writes *as if* the blood actually had been shed. This can mean two things: on the one hand, that the author places himself in the perspective of the official Jewish bloody sacrifice (cf. Heb 9:22); and on the other, that the will to sacrifice alone is already equivalent to the completed act, and that God accepts it as such.

31. See T. Franxmann, *Genesis and the "Jewish Antiquities" of Flavius Josephus*, BOr 35 (Rome, 1979) 161.
32. See the *status quaestionis* in J. Swetnam, *Jesus and Isaac*, 49, n. 205.
33. See Ch. Perrot and P.-M. Bogaert, *Pseudo-Philon. Les Antiquités Bibliques*, II, SC 230 (Paris, 1976) 22–74. The text we cite is that of D. J. Harrington, ibid., I, SC 229 (Paris 1976).

In any case, the *'aqedah* has an evident meritorious value on the basis of a completed sacrifice that combines external action and internal disposition.

b) In 32:2-4 (in the context of the hymn of Deborah: Judg 5), the author develops his reference to Gen 22 to major proportions. The most interesting passage concerns the words spoken by Isaac to his father in 32:3: *Si . . . pro iniquitatibus hominum pecora constituta sunt in occisionem, homo autem positus est in hereditatem seculi:* "If flocks have been destined to be killed for human iniquities, man on the other hand is destined to inherit the world," *et quomodo nunc dicis mihi: Veni et hereditare securam vitam et inmensurabile tempus?:* "And why do you now tell me, 'Come and inherit a secure life, and time without measure'?" *Quid si non essem natus in seculo, ut offerer sacrificium ei qui me fecit?:* "What would have happened if I had not been born in the world to be offered in sacrifice to the One who made me?" *Erit autem mea beatitudo super omnes homines, quia non erit aliud:* "But my joy will be above all human beings because there will be no other [sacrifice like this]."[34] Since the neuter *aliud*, "other," cannot refer grammatically to anything but *sacrificium*, "sacrifice," it follows that Pseudo-Philo recognizes for the offering of Isaac some unique prerogative, through which it will bring blessing to all humanity or at least to the people of Israel. It is possible that such a conception already represents "a reaction to Christian claims" concerning Jesus.[35]

Still, we cannot ignore the parallelism established by the author between the sacrifice of Isaac and the killing of animals *pro iniquitatibus hominum*, "for human iniquities," for while it is too implicit to be considered systematic and an anti-Christian counterclaim, it is nevertheless apposite, at least so much so that it cannot be passed over in silence. "There is here only a comparison—but a highly suggestive one—between the *'aqedah* and the expiatory sacrifices.[36]

6) *Conclusions.* In the period of the second Temple, in the environment of extrabiblical Jewish tradition, Gen 22 had certainly not yet taken on all

---

34. The translation of this last phrase corresponds to that proposed by L. H. Feldman, in M. R. James, ed., *The Biblical Antiquities of Philo* (New York, 1971) cxviii; P. R. Davies and B. D. Chilton, "The Aqedah," 525f.; J. Swetnam, *Jesus and Isaac,* 51, 53f. But the translation of J. Cazeaux, Ch. Perrot, and P.-M. Bogaert in SC 229:245-246 reads: "Aussi mon honneur l'emportera-t-il sur les autres hommes"; see also G. Delling, "Von Morija zum Sinai (Pseudo-Philo Liber Antiquitatum Biblicarum 32:1-10)," JSJ 2 (1971) 1-18, 5.

35. J. Swetnam, *Jesus and Isaac,* 54 and 55.

36. R. Le Déaut, *La nuit pascale,* 190 ("It is not claimed that the 'aqedah should be considered as having an expiatory value; but the text suggests that this sacrifice must remain present before God as an eternal *memorial* for all generations"). This conclusion, shared by J. Swetnam, *Jesus and Isaac,* 55, n. 241, strikes me as more balanced than the absolute denial maintained by P. R. Davies and B. D. Chilton, "The Aqedah," 525.

the theological meaning that it will have in the later rabbinic literature. But there are at least three elements to emphasize that do show how it is on the way to being recognized as having major importance.

First of all, the place of the sacrifice of Isaac, Mount Moriah, becomes identified (thus further specifying the indication of 2 Chr 3:1) with the Jerusalem Temple mount, which is not without significance whether for Abraham's act or for the sacrificial liturgies of the Temple itself: the former providing an archetype for the latter, and the latter identifying the former as a true sacrifice (see Jub. 18:13; Fl. Josephus, *Ant.* 1:226).

In the second place, the *'aqedah* comes to be understood also as a free and voluntary act of Isaac himself, who offers himself consciously to death, so that the figure of the son (Fl. Josephus, *Ant.* 1:232) is brought into the foreground, as well as that of the father (emphasized rather by Philo Al., *De Abr.* 167-207).

In the third place, we see the first hints of the attribution of an expiatory dimension to the sacrifice of Isaac, at least exemplary (indirectly indicated in 4 Macc: see above) if not directly so (implied attribution in Pseudo-Philo, LAB 18:5; 32:3). On the other hand, we ignore its association with Passover (cf. Jub. 17:15; 18:3; probably of secondary value).

IV. The Letter of Paul to the Romans 8:32

The New Testament writings substantially all belong to the first century of the new era. They therefore belong properly to the preparatory phase of the rabbinic haggadah concerning the *'aqedah*. This is certainly true at least from the simple chronological point of view. But we can and even must also ask, Up to what point can the New Testament be considered to be participating in the formation of the concept of the *'aqedah?* Or else, has it already been influenced by the developed concept? In other words, did the New Testament influence the *'aqedah*, or did the *'aqedah* influence the New Testament? This latter, if interpreted too rigidly, would apparently have to be excluded or at least sharply reduced for two simple reasons. In the first place, as we have seen, the concept of the *'aqedah* in its fullest evolution is later than the first century, even if a writing like the LAB brings us rather close (but with problems concerning its final redaction). In the second place, we should note that Gen 22 or parts of it will never be introduced in the New Testament with formulas of direct quotation. Explicit reference to the story of the sacrifice of Isaac appears in only two texts, Heb 11:17 and Jas 2:21; but in each case the figure who most interests the writer is Abraham, because of his unflinching faith (Heb) and faith-inspired deed, rather than Isaac the victim.

Nevertheless, in the history of research, contacts between Gen 22 and many New Testament texts have repeatedly been established with varying degrees of probability and proximity.[37] But it does seem inadmissible to me to totally deny the thesis, as do P. R. Davies and B. D. Chilton.[38] These two authors, indeed, make two methodological mistakes: in the first place they want to restrict the comparison only to the rabbinic concept, without taking adequate account of the passage of Gen 22 itself; and in the second they ultimately restrict the concept of the ʿaqedah only to its expiatory value, without including, for example, the components of Abraham's readiness and Isaac's obedience. Moreover, their exegetical treatment of the New Testament passages in question is superficial because their approach is a priori, since their point of departure is the final, fully developed state of the ʿaqedah rather than the New Testament itself.

We here limit our attention exclusively to the Pauline text of Rom 8:32 to see which elements we can extract by interpreting it against the background of both the biblical text of Gen 22 and the Jewish haggadah that grew out of it. There are two reasons for choosing this Pauline text: it is the only New Testament text, apart from Heb 11:17 and Jas 2:21, that seriously poses the problem of an allusion to the sacrifice of Isaac; and besides this, and unlike the other two, it is written in view of soteriology, since Abraham, if he is present there, is so not as a pure didactic example, since God himself is identified with him in sacrificing his only Son (see below). But let us continue a step at a time.

---

37. A maximalist position is represented by R. J. Daly, "The Soteriological Significance," 67–73, who distinguishes between sure allusions (Heb 11:17-20; Jas 2:21-23; Rom 8:32); probable ones (John 3:16; Mark 1:11 and 9:7 ‖; 1 Cor 15:4; Rom 4:16-25); and possible ones (thus, the use of the verb δίδωμι, "give," in Gal 1:4; 2:20; Eph 5:2, 25; Titus 2:14; 1 Tim 2:6; and the use of the adjective ἀγαπητός, "beloved," in Matt 12:18 ‖; also John 1:29; 19:17; 1 Pet 1:19-20; 1 Cor 11:24; and wanting if possible to add to the third category: Phil 2:8; Col 1:13f.; Eph 1:8. A more moderate position is espoused by M.-L. Gubler, *Die frühesten Deutungen*, 336–375, who divides up the typology of Isaac according to whether it is present in explicit terms (Rom 9:7-8; Gal 4:28; Jas 2:21; Heb 11:17-19) or implicit terms (Rom 8:32; John 3:16; Rom 3:24-26; the motif of the lamb in John 1:29; 1 Cor 5:7; 1 Pet 1:19; the title of "Son" in Mark 1:9-11; 9:2-8; 15:39 and parallels; the motif of the "third day" in 1 Cor 15:4 and the theme of the blessing of the descendants in Gal 3:12-14). But the first two texts (Rom 9:7-8 and Gal 4:28) do not refer properly to Gen 22.

38. See above, n. 3. R. Hayward, "The Present State," 136–137, opposes them with four critical observations: (1) the ʿaqedah of the Targums alone does not correspond to the definition proposed by the two authors; (2) the verb used for "bind" is kpt in the Targums, but ʿqd in the Mishnaic rules for the *Tamîd*, [which explicitly forbid the "tying," kpt, of the victim—T. P. W.], that is, the former do not depend on the latter; (3) the sacrifice of Isaac serves to validate not only the *Tamîd* but every type of sacrifice of the lamb; (4) it is strange that TgJo never uses the root ʿqd in its version of Gen 22, and yet, even according to Davies and Chilton, the theology of the ʿaqedah is present there. See also A. F. Segal, " 'He who did not spare . . .,' " 173f.

1) *The authors* who have written on the matter present *a variety of opinions.*[39] We can begin with two opposite attitudes. On the one hand, the well-known compilation of Strack-Billerbeck on the New Testament interpreted on the basis of Jewish tradition offers absolutely nothing on our passage. On the other hand, we have the contribution of N. A. Dahl,[40] dedicated to this passage alone; he elaborates a whole complex of correspondences between Rom 8:32 and Gen 22. The central thesis of this study is that Paul here takes up a primitive Jewish Christian tradition, according to which the redemption worked by Christ would be understood as a divine reward for Abraham's deed, actuating the blessing of Gen 22:16-17, an attempt of the earliest Christians to overcome the scandal of the Cross. The impression is that Dahl reads into our Pauline text much more than is written there.[41] Nevertheless, he deserves credit for having called attention to the possible hermeneutical implications of the passage deriving from the ʿaqedah.

The recent work of A. F. Segal (n. 1 above), which derives its title precisely from the words of Rom 8:32, is actually not an exegetical study of the Pauline passage but simply an underlining (opportune and pertinent indeed) of the original resonance of Gen 22 in Paul in relation to the contemporaneous Jewish exegesis, to which we now perceive the necessity of referring in order to explain the *new element* in the death of Jesus the Messiah, even though the figure of Isaac was never used in Judaism as an image of the messiah.

The positions of the commentaries on Romans are quite divergent. The complete silence of P. Althaus and F. Lehnhardt[42] is scarcely improved on by O. Kuss and H. Schlier,[43] who say only that "an allusion to the . . . generally repulsive legend of . . . the immolation of Isaac . . . is

---

39. See n. 37: for R. J. Daly the allusion to the sacrifice of Isaac in Rom 8:32 is *certain*, while for M.-L. Gubler it is *implicit*; but the two understandings are not in fact antithetical, since something that is implicit can be recognized as certain (and the author treats it first in her series).

40. "The Atonement—An Adequate Reward for the Akedah? (Ro 8:32)," in *Neotestamentica et Semitica*, Studies in Honour of M. Black, ed. E. E. Wllis and M. Wilcox (Edinburgh, 1969) 15-29.

41. In particular, we must note the methodological defect of using later rabbinic texts to explain not only the Pauline text but its preredactional form. Furthermore, we cannot resist the conclusion that Paul would have had to be more explicit if he were to propose a theological thesis of such importance. Not to mention that for Dahl the motif of the ʿaqedah would play a basically extrinsic role in Rom 8:32: in Jesus, God rewarded Abraham; the relation between the two would be only a matter of cause and effect, while the Pauline text, rather than separating them, would seem to read in the death of Jesus the same internal structure as in the deed of Abraham with regard to Isaac (see below). See also the criticisms of H. Paulsen, *Überlieferung und Auslegung in Römer 8*, WMANT 43 (Neukirchen-Vluyn, 1974) 165–168.

42. The former in NTD 6 (Göttingen, 1949) 82, the latter in CNT VI (Neuchâtel, 1957) 135.

43. O. Kuss, RNT III (Regensburg, 1978) 652; Schlier, HThKNT VI (Freiburg-Basel-Vienna, 1977) 277 (Schlier does not cite the study of Dahl, even in the bibliography).

hardly enlightening" (Kuss) or that simply "there is no allusion to Gen 22:16" (Schlier). A probable or at least possible allusion to the Genesis passage is briefly affirmed by U. Vanni, G. Torti, and G. Barbaglio.[44] Also for C. K. Barrett "Paul seems to allude to the story of Abraham and Isaac. . . . See especially Gen xxii.16. . . . This allusion is at least as likely as that to the Suffering Servant (Isa liii.12 (LXX))."[45] W. Sanday and A. C. Headlam already wrote that in Rom 8:32 "οὐκ ἐφείσατο ["did not spare"], the word which is used of the offering of Isaac in Gen. xxii. 16 . . . directly recalls that offering—the greatest sacrifice on record."[46] A somewhat more pronounced insistence on the parallelism of the two texts is offered by S. Lyonnet,[47] O. Michel,[48] E. Käsemann,[49] C. E. B. Cranfield,[50] U. Wilckens.[51] These writers claim to varying degrees the importance of Gen 22 (without its haggadic development: only S. Lyonnet, explicitly questioned by U. Wilckens); the idea of a resonance is considered certain (Lyonnet, Michel), incontestable (Wilckens), probably intentional (Cranfield), at least not to be excluded (Käsemann).

2) *Exegetical notes.* It is helpful methodologically to divide the Pauline text into three parts following the three clauses of which it is made up:

Rom 8:32

a) ὅς γε τοῦ ἰδίου υἱοῦ οὐκ ἐφείσατο

b) ἀλλὰ ὑπὲρ ἡμῶν πάντων παρέδωκεν αὐτόν,

c) πῶς οὐχὶ καὶ σὺν αὐτῷ τὰ πάντα ἡμῖν χαρίσεται;

a) He did not spare his own Son,

b) but handed him over for our sake:

c) how then should he not grant us everything along with him?

The text is governed by three verbs, each with God as subject; and God is indirectly described as Father through the explicit mention of "his Son" (but unnamed here; he will be named only in v. 34). The structure is: A, A', B; indeed v. 32b only repeats 32a, although in a grammatically posi-

---

44. Respectively NVB 40 (Rome, 1978) 164; SB 41 (Brescia, 1977) 182; II (Rome, 1980) 387. Thus also J. D. G. Dunn, *Romans 1–8*, 501.

45. *A Commentary on the Epistle to the Romans*, Black's New Testament Commentaries (London, 1957) 172.

46. *A Critical and Exegetical Commentary on the Epistle to the Romans*, ICC (Edinburgh, 1902⁵ = 1964) 220.

47. Both in the reedition of J. Huby, *San Paolo: Epistola ai Romani*, Verbum Salutis (Rome, 1961) 525, and especially in *Exegesis epistulae ad Romanos*, II (Rome, 1966²) 278–279.

48. *Der Brief an die Römer*, Meyer Kommentar (Göttingen, 1966⁴ [1955]).

49. *Commentary on Romans*, 247 = *An die Römer*, HNT 8a (Tübingen, 1973¹, 1980⁴) 239.

50. *The Epistle to the Romans*, ICC (Edinburgh, 1975) I, 436.

51. *Der Brief an die Römer*, EKK VI/2 (Zurich-Neukirchen-Vluyn, 1980) 173 and n. 772.

tive form, but a real advance of thought appears in v. 32c. Still, v. 32b forms a good transition between the first and third stich, for to the "Son" of 32a is now added the "us" as beneficiaries of the act of handing over to death, and then in 32c the ecclesial "us" represents the climax of a total gift of grace, in which are united all three personal factors of the text (i.e., God as subject of the new verb χαρίσεται, "grant"; the Son associated with him: σὺν αὐτῷ, "with him"; and the Christians: ἡμῖν, "us").

In substance we are dealing with a climactic parallelism that can be reformulated thus: (a) the sacrificial relationship between God and his Son (b) is put into effect for the sake of us all, (c) and this event implies and guarantees a cumulative and unrestricted gift giving. In the final analysis the relationship that governs all three actions is that between "God" and "us"; it is not without reason that Paul in 8:31 writes, "If God is for us, who can be against us?" But between these two terms there now is inserted, like a kind of bridge, "his Son" and all the tragic reality that took place in him. Indeed, the relationship of grace between "God" and "us" is based on God's behavior toward "his Son." But precisely this behavior is not a matter of grace; quite the contrary, it is abandonment, delivery to death, apparently condemnation. In a word, it is not paternal behavior! The verbs οὐκ ἐφείσατο, "did not spare," and παρέδωκεν, "handed him over," say it clearly. It seems that God, out of concern for "us," loses all concern for "his Son." In even more dramatic terms, God the Father shows his love for strangers (us) precisely *through* the handing over of the Son.

How not be surprised, I say, not of the fact itself but of the Pauline reasoning that expresses it? The fact could be downright scandalous, and a philosopher like E. Bloch has expressed this perplexity vividly.[52] But before judging things on the level of events, we must ask ourselves: How was it that Paul came to speak in these terms? The question is all the more legitimate in that Rom 8:32 is not the only Pauline passage to present this thematic; it also occurs in Rom 3:25; 4:25; 5:8-10; 2 Cor 5:21. But ours is the only text in which Paul combines God's deed with the identification of "Son" (further specified by "his," or better "his own") applied to Jesus; the action therefore appears all the more "repulsive."[53]

---

52. See E. Bloch, *Atheismus im Christentum: Zur Religion des Exodus und des Reichs* (Frankfurt a. M., 1980: "The ultimate source of the doctrine of sacrificial death is not only very bloody but also very archaic; it springs from the long suppressed human sacrifice of antiquity, which is actually even more ancient than Moloch. Indeed, it proceeds from whatever was most absolutely opposed to Christianity. . . . It is all the more strange, then, that behind the Pauline theology of the right of satisfaction there is hidden that heavenly cannibal who had long been all but forgotten!" (222–223); the theme is explicitly opposed to the case of Isaac, in which "the Lord rejects Abraham's sacrifice of Isaac" (122).

53. O. Kuss, *Der Römerbrief*, III, 652.

Precisely for this reason it is legitimate to ask oneself if Paul does not re-use ancient biblical patterns to serve him as guides in expressing his conception of the death of Jesus on the cross. In fact, scholars often have recourse to Isa 53:6, 12 and Gen 22:12, 16. There are those who prefer the former to the latter[54] or who place them on the same level.[55] In reality one must distinguish.

Only in Rom 8:32b is there resonance of the Isaiah Suffering Servant passage; indeed, Isa 53:6 LXX (καὶ κύριος παρέδωκεν αὐτὸν ταῖς ἁμαρτίας ἡμῶν, "And the Lord handed him over for our sins") is found partially in the παρέδωκεν αὐτόν, "handed him over," of Rom 8:32b (see also the double παρεδόθη, "was handed over," in Isa 53:12 LXX), but the adverbial phrase is already different (Isaiah: "for our sins"; Paul: "for us all"). In any case, it is evident that each of the texts attributes an expiatory dimension to the death of the Servant or of Jesus.

But the text of Gen 22:12, 16 LXX underlies Rom 8:32a, if it is not actually quoted. What Paul says of God (τοῦ ἰδίου υἱοῦ οὐκ ἐφείσατο, "He did not spare his own Son") finds a clear correspondence in God's address to Abraham in Genesis: (οὐκ ἐφείσω τοῦ υἱοῦ σου τοῦ ἀγαπητοῦ, "You did not spare your beloved Son" [N.B. The LXX text follows with a phrase δι' ἐμέ, "for me," which is missing in the MT]). It is true that we are not faced here with a direct citation. But the case can be compared to those many other passages where the Apostle uses the Old Testament as a direct linguistic medium, supplementing his own speech, perhaps unconsciously, with typical expressions from the ancient scriptures.[56]

Nevertheless, we must make two observations. On the one hand, Paul could not introduce the text of Gen 22 with a citation formula if he was to apply it to God, for in Genesis God is the goal of the sacrifice, not its subject, and the verb φείδεσθαι, "spare," is said of Abraham, not of God; and besides, Pauline typology is normatively applied to Christ, to the believer/unbeliever, or to specific ecclesial realities,[57] but not to God, and all the less so if the prefiguring should be supplied by some human behavior (even that of the patriarch Abraham). On the other hand, in the Greek of the Septuagint, Gen 22:12, 16 represents the only case where the negative verb οὐ φείδεσθαι, "not to spare," and the noun υἱός, "son,"

54. See K. Romaniuk, *L'amour du Père et du Fils dans la sotériologie de Saint Paul*, AB 15 (Rome, 1961) 230f.; H. Schlier, *Der Römerbrief*, 277.

55. See C. K. Barrett, *Romans*, 172. The Isaiah text is also mentioned by the previously cited commentaries: S. Lyonnet, C. E. B. Cranfield, and U. Wilckens; but it is ignored by all the others.

56. See vol. 2, chap. 24, last section.

57. See A. T. Hanson, *Studies in Paul's Technique and Theology* (London, 1974) 151–158; L. Goppelt, art. τύπος κτλ., TDNT 8:246–289.

are used together;[58] and this happens in a sacrificial context, just as in our passage.[59] We should moreover note that Paul does not refer to "the Son" by the name of Jesus, identifying him only as "Son," and so recalling more the relationship between Abraham and Isaac.[60]

It is true that Paul never describes Jesus as "beloved" *(ἀγαπητός)* Son of God; nevertheless, Rom 8:32 is precisely the only case in his letters where Jesus is called God's "own *(ἴδιος)* Son" (cf. the more attenuated *τοῦ υἱοῦ αὐτοῦ*, "his Son," of Rom 8:29), as if to underline the most special relationship between the two. It seems to me perfectly fair, then, and anything but hasty to conclude that in Rom 8:32a we have an allusion to the sacrifice of Isaac. Now, the line of comparison runs less from Isaac to Jesus than from Abraham to God. The underlying idea is this: As Abraham was ready to sacrifice everything to God, since by giving his only, his beloved son he showed he would give whatever was most dear to him, so God, by giving "his own Son" for our sake, showed willingness to give us "every thing along with him."[61]

But, then, we cannot exclude the possibility that in Rom 8:32c there re-echoes the motif of the blessing pronounced by God on Abraham in Gen 22:16-17 (see above: I), which expresses the fruitfulness of the sacrifice (see earlier Gal 3:14). But while the idea of merit and recompense is suggested in Gen 22, in that God rewards the obedience of Abraham (cf. Jas 2:21f. in this sense), still in Rom 8:32 grace rules undisputed, since the God who has offered his Son is also the same God who with him gives the gift of "every thing" (cf. Wis. 7:11).

The greatest novelty of Rom 8:32 over against Gen 22 stands, however, in the fact that the handing over of the Son by God has an expiatory value

---

58. The text of Prov 13:24 (ὃς φείδεται τῆς βακτηρίας μισεῖ τὸν υἱὸν αὐτοῦ, "One who spares the rod hates his child") obviously does not correspond to our case; note also the indeterminate νεανίσκος in the apocryphal 1 Esdr 1:50 (Vg: 3 Esdr 1:53): "The Chaldeans spared not the 'young man,' the virgin, the old . . . but [God] 'handed over all' [πάντας παρέδωκεν] into their hands."

59. That Paul's text refers to the passion rather than the sending of the Son into the world is demonstrated by W. Popkes, *Christus Traditus. Eine Untersuchung zum Begriff der Dahingabe im Neuen Testament*, AThANT 49 (Zurich-Stuttgart, 1967) 194–197; against W. Kramer, *Christos Kyrios Gottessohn*, AThANT 44 (Zurich, 1963) 144f. Actually the verb παραδίδωμι, "hand over," in every other Pauline context refers to the death of Jesus.

60. In Gen 22:1-17 LXX the term "son" recurs ten times (υἱός: vv. 2, 3, 6, 9, 10, 12, 13, 16, τέκνον: vv. 7, 8); moreover, the Hebrew *yaḥîd*, "only," in MT v. 2 is rendered in LXX as τὸν ἀγαπητόν, "beloved," to which both texts add "whom you love."

61. The phrase σὺν αὐτῷ, "with him," is understood not in the sense of association of Christ with God as subject of the act of giving (thus O. Michel, *Römer*, 215, n. 1; U. Wilckens, *Römer*, II, 173, n. 775), but in the sense that God, having handed Christ over, by that deed guarantees the extreme abundance of grace (thus E. Käsemann, *Romans*, 248 = *An die Römer*, 239; C. E. B. Cranfield, *Romans*, 436f. and n. 3).

for Paul.[62] The formula ὑπὲρ ἡμῶν πάντων, "for all of us," of v. 32b says it with sufficient clarity. Its outline, relatively frequent in the Pauline letters (note similar constructions in Rom 5:6, 8; 8:31; 14:15; 1 Cor 1:13; 2 Cor 5:15c, 21; Gal 1:4; 2:20; 3:13; 1 Thess 5:10), derives from the pre-Pauline traditions of the Last Supper (cf. 1 Cor 11:24) and the confessions of faith (cf. 1 Cor 15:3). Now if there is dispute about the possible influence of Isa 53 on the earliest Christian conception of the death of Jesus as an expiatory sacrifice,[63] still, the resonances of the Isaiah passage seem unquestionable to me in Rom 8:32b, for thematic as well as lexical reasons.[64] Indeed we find here several basic components of the prophetic text: the handing over of the servant by God (with the same vocabulary already noted; cf. even the passive παρεδόθη, "was handed over," in Isa 53:12b), his death in an expiatory sense (see the περὶ ἡμῶν, "for us," in Isa 53:4 and the many related expressions, with explicit references to ἁμαρτία, "sin," and ἀνομία, "offense," in vv. 4, 5, 6, 10, 11, 12), and the universal reference of the sacrifice (note the frequent recurrence of πολλοί, "many," in Isa 52:14; 53:11, 12b, and the explicit expression ἔθνη πολλά, "many nations," in 52:15).[65] But we must note that God's blessing of Abraham after the test ends with a universalist horizon: "All the nations of the earth *(πάντα τὰ ἔθνη τῆς γῆς)* will be blessed in your progeny."

Therefore the "God for us" (Rom 8:31) whom Paul presents is illuminated by two biblical passages which interpret this God for us and which

62. The fact is quite explicable from the perspective of *Religionsgeschichte*, in the light of which such presuppositions regarding Jesus become historically comprehensible. For, according to classical Hebrew tradition "each one shall die [only] for his or her own sin" (Deut 24:16; cf. Exod 18:20: "The one who sinned shall die, and none other"). But Isa 53 is actually a foreign body in this theological world. As M. Hengel rightly emphasizes, "The Expiatory Sacrifice of Christ," BJRL 62 (1979–80) 455ff., it is only from the Hellenistic period, specifically from that of the Maccabees, that the theology of martyrdom gains a foothold in Israel, i.e., that martyrs are recognized as having not only an exemplary value but also a dimension of vicarious expiation (see E. Lohse, *Märtyrer und Gottesknecht*, FRLANT 64, n. s. 46 [Göttingen, 1963²]); for the rest, as Hengel has documented, the expression "to die for," and less often "to give oneself for," is widely used in the Greek world. Thus, in 4 Macc 6:27-29 (prayer of Eleazar) we have the clearest Jewish counterpart to the expiatory value of the death of Jesus of Nazareth, although with no reference to Isa 53 and only a tenuous contextual link to Gen 22 (see above).

63. See the good *status quaestionis* in M.-L. Gubler, *Die früheste Deutungen*, 284–311 and 319–324.

64. Note that the same expression παρέδωκεν αὐτόν, "handed him over," is present in Isa 53 LXX. However, the preposition ὑπέρ, "for," is missing, replaced by two others of similar value, περί (vv. 4, 10) and διά (vv. 5 [twice], 12).

65. See J. Jeremias, πολλοί, TDNT 6:540-545. The only case of ὑπὲρ ἡμῶν πάντων, "for all of us," represents a sort of conflation between the more common "for us" (Rom 5:8; 8:31; 2 Cor 5:21; Gal 1:4; 3:13; 1 Thess 5:10) and the more rare "for all" (only 2 Cor 5:15 [twice]). It is not impossible that in πάντων, "all," there is a reference to the typical theological perspective of Rom 9 concerning the universal salvation of Jews and pagans without distinction (therefore C. E. B. Cranfield, *Romans*, I, 436, rightly refers to Rom 10:11, 12, 13; 15:33; cf. 1 Cor 1:2).

are here associated by allusion and, as it were, sewn together. Genesis 22 makes him a disinterested giver, and Isa 53 attributes to his deed a sacrificial and redemptive meaning with universal effects.

3) *Conclusions.* Even the New Testament, then, is a witness, albeit indirect, to the evolution of the motif of the *'aqedah*. But it is so in an original way. Actually, in Judaism the expiatory value of the sacrifice of Isaac appears tenuously in 4 Macc in the context of a reflection on the martyrs for the faith of the Maccabean age; it then is affirmed more clearly in Pseudo-Philo, LAB 18:5; 32:3, and imposes itself with evidence in the later, post-Christian rabbinic literature (see above: Targum and Midrash); but this is all understood intrinsically with regard to what took place on Mount Moriah.

However, in Paul[66] there is no explicit teaching of the expiatory value of the *'aqedah* in itself. In fact, Gen 22 is never explicitly cited; indeed it is found only in allusions, serving to express indirectly the value inhering in a new historical fact, the death of Jesus. Here we see God (the Father) handing his own Son over to death. The apparent cruelty of the deed is explicable precisely insofar as it is modeled in the paradigm of the sacrifice of Isaac by Abraham. Now of course the sacrifice was probably not physically consummated, but on the one hand the Jewish tradition always did consider it to have been formally completed, and on the other the case of Jesus does not fully correspond as a prototype because the relationship of Jesus to God is considered quite different from the relationship of human son and father.

In substance, the affirmation that God "did not spare his own Son" can be considered from two points of view: historically, this shows that the formulation is governed more by the text of Gen 22 (where the central figure is that of the father, Abraham) than by the later Jewish haggadah (which brings the figure of the son, Isaac, to the fore); theologically, then, this must be integrated into the whole of Pauline theology, especially with those passages that attribute to Jesus not just a passive attitude but a dynamic attitude of love (see a little further on, Rom 8:35, 37, 39; and Gal 2:20).

---

66. One can argue whether the author is already debtor to an earlier Christian tradition on the subject. The stark denial by E. Käsemann, *Commentary on Romans*, 247 = *An die Römer*, 239, perhaps calls for more shading. One ought, in fact, to reflect more on the fact that the motif of the handing over of Jesus by God is more ancient than that of the handing over of self by Jesus (see W. Popkes, *Christus Traditus*, 246–270), as well as the fact that even elsewhere in Paul there is never an explicit treatment of the *'aqedah*, which is rather simply assumed in a non-reflexive manner (see H. Paulsen, *Überlieferung und Auslegung*, 167).

The expiatory value of God's deed is deduced not from the sacrifice of Isaac but from that of the Isaian Suffering Servant[67] through an implicit association of two biblical texts that, so far as I can determine, are not associated in Jewish tradition. The reticence of the New Testament in general and of Paul in particular toward any greater and more explicit use of the 'aqedah can perhaps be explained by the fact that if we compare these with the death of Christ, the blade of Abraham never did really fall on the neck of Isaac, whereas the Isaian figure of the Suffering Servant offered more links with the historical truth of the paschal deeds.[68] So we can hardly accept the thesis of I. Levi and H.-J. Schoeps,[69] according to whom the rabbinic (!) motif of the 'aqedah "furnished the model for the formation of the Pauline soteriology." As we have seen, the text of Rom 8:32 and of the New Testament in general stands at an intermediate phase of the development of the Jewish *theolegoumenon* that grew on the text of Gen 22, before the teaching had reached its final form. But we do not venture here to claim that the later rabbinic motif was in its turn conditioned by the Christian message:[70] the principle *post hoc ergo propter hoc* is not in itself a critical principle; nevertheless, such a claim would be plausible enough, representing a very interesting example of reciprocal interaction between Judaism and Christianity in which neither does all the giving, nor does either do all the receiving.

The New Testament, then, here offers a reading of Gen 22 that is substantially independent with respect to the haggadic traditions, whether contemporaneous or later. In synthesis, what can we say of the 'aqedah motif in Rom 8:32? The motif is directly present in v. 32a with two complementary components: primarily through the act of offering by the father (but with different motives or goals between type and antitype: obedience to God for Abraham, and love of "us" for God), and secondarily through the special character of "son" as found in Isaac on the one hand or Jesus on the other.[71] But indirectly the motif of the 'aqedah is present as well

67. See W. Schmithals, *Die theologische Anthropologie des Paulus. Auslegung von Röm 7,17–8,39,* KT 1021 (Stuttgart, 1980) 181.

68. Thus does L. E. Wood rightly reason, "Isaac Typology in the New Testament," NTS 14 (1967–68) 583–589; but we should also remember that the New Testament recourse to Isa 53 is itself also always implicit and is problematic as concerns the soteriological interpretation of the death of Jesus. See the comment of Sh. Spiegel, *The Last Trial,* 82–84.

69. See above, n. 2.

70. See the studies of P. R. Davies and B. D. Chilton (n. 3 above), which should be counterbalanced by that of R. Hayward (nn. 4 and 37).

71. It will only be later in the patristic literature that, alongside the rabbinic development, the attention will turn from the father's deed to the attitude of the son, and Melito of Sardis (died ca. 195) will first make Isaac "the type of the Lord" (PG 5:1217). On the patristic age, see also T. Caruso, "Il sacrificio di Isacco," in *Sangue e antropologia biblica nella letteratura cristiana,* I, ed. F. Vattioni (Rome, 1983) 291–314.

in 32b with the theme of expiation, which is, however, derived not from the story of Abraham and Isaac but from the Isaian passage about the Suffering Servant, the relationship of which to Gen 22 is quite circumstantial indeed, occasioned as it is, not by the exercise of a method of biblical hermeneutic, but by the vital necessity of explaining the death of Jesus.[72] And in the framework of the historical evolution of the *'aqedah* motif, it is certainly this necessity that is original.

---

72. A. F. Segal is right in reminding us that there is no historical proof of the expectation of a crucified or even suffering messiah. But after Calvary "all discussions of suffering in the Bible thereafter take on a new meaning—as prophecies of Jesus' suffering. But no Jew would have seen them in this way before Jesus' crucifixion. Rather, like a magnet, everything dealing with 'sonship' or 'messiah' or 'suffering' or 'servant' is attracted to Jesus" ("'He who did not spare . . .,'" 182).

Chapter 10

The Gospel as "Power of God"
According to 1 Corinthians 1:18-25

The short Pauline pericope that we now intend to examine can be considered central in the first debate conducted by the Apostle with the Christian community in Corinth (1 Cor 1:10-14, 21).[1] The various motifs scattered throughout the section lead up to it: first of all the opposition between the σοφία τοῦ κόσμου, "wisdom of the world," and the σοφία τοῦ θεοῦ, "wisdom of God,"[2] then the insistence on Christ as the only point of reference of the ἐκκλησία, "church," rent by the sectarian spirit, and also the motif of faith, of the kerygma, of the divine εὐδοκία, "benevolence." This passage also proves to have a central value in the whole Pauline correspondence and in its most characteristic set of motifs; certain of these texts can, after all, be considered parallels to texts of the great Letter to the Romans (thus 1 Cor 1:18 = Rom 1:16; 1 Cor 1:21 = Rom 1:21-22).

But one expression in particular attracts our attention: the formula δύναμις θεοῦ ("power of God"), which in v. 18 has as subject ὁ λόγος τοῦ σταυροῦ ("the speech or language of the Cross," the kerygma), while in v. 24 it is attributed to Χριστόν, "Christ" (v. 23: ἐσταυρωμένον, "crucified"). We want to ask ourselves: What does it mean that both in Christ crucified and in the proclamation of the gospel the δύναμις, "power," of God is manifest? The answer to this question depends on the answer that can

---

1. The central role of our passage is evidenced especially by the hypothesis of the so-called threefold rhythm or cyclical pattern, according to which a specific subject enters at a given moment (1 Cor 1:10-17), is apparently forgotten in a subsequent digression (1:18–3:4), and then is definitively taken up again, enriched by the elements introduced in the second movement (3:5–4:21). See J. Weiss, *Der erste Korintherbrief*, Meyer Kommentar (Göttingen, 1910); also A. Brunot, *Le génie littéraire de saint Paul*, LD 15 (Paris, 1955) 41–51.

2. See U. Wilckens, *Weisheit und Torheit. Eine exegetisch-religionsgeschichtliche Untersuchung zu I. Kor 1 und 2* (Tübingen, 1959); H. Schlier, "Kerygma und Sophia," in *Die Zeit der Kirche* (Tübingen, 1956) 206–232.

be given to another question: How is it that in a section so theologically complex and rich there is not the least explicit linkage to the resurrection of Christ, but only to his crucifixion?

Now, we would think there is good reason to maintain that precisely the expression δύναμις θεοῦ, "power of God," applied to Christ, is essentially a reference to the resurrection, and that when applied to λόγος τοῦ σταυροῦ, "word of the Cross" it is equating the paschal intervention of God with God's action when the kerygma takes place.[3]

I. Δύναμις, "power," in the Greek world

In the Greek world the term δύναμις essentially connotes the idea of an attitude or capacity, that is, the possibility of acting in a given way. The following general principle of Aristotle is axiomatic: πᾶν σῶμα αἰσθητὸν ἔχει δύναμιν ποιητικὴν ἢ παθητικὴν ἢ ἄμφω, "Every sensible body has an active or passive capacity, or both" (*Cael.* 1:7 p. 275 b 5). For the human being, the affirmation is true on the level of spiritual, intellectual, and moral life as well as that of physical life.[4] But the δυνάμεις proper to human beings are only a part of that broader natural sphere where plants and animals as well, and even the stars, each possess their own "potentialities." There is, therefore, a δύναμις at work in all life. "This explains, then, how in the historical development of Greek and Hellenistic thought δύναμις gradually assumes the shape of a cosmic principle."[5] From the most ancient text on the subject, a fragment of the Pythagorean Philolaos,[6] through Plato,[7] Pseudo-Aristotle and the Stoa,[8] to Poseidonius, Greek reflection on the subject grows ever more organized, so that in the last of these it reaches its clearest formulation. Poseidonius speaks of ζωτική δύναμις, "life spirit," a primordial and cohesive energy of all being, which makes the whole cosmos the most perfect of all organisms.

Thus little by little is clarified the relationship between δύναμις and divinity. Since divinity is generally understood as an impersonal principle, the great philosophers of antiquity speak only rarely of a "potentiality of God." It will rather be the Stoics who will develop the idea of God paral-

---

3. See K. Müller, "1 Kor. 1,18-25. Die eschatologisch-kritische Funktion der Verkündigung des Kreuzes," BZ (NF) 10 (1966) 246–272; see also L. A. Rood, "Le Christ comme ΔΥΝΑΜΙΣ ΘΕΟΥ," in *Littérature et théologie pauliniennes*, Recherches bibliques V (Bruges, 1960) 93–108.

4. For instance, Plato identifies the senses of sight and hearing as δυνάμεις, "powers" (see *Resp.* 5. 477cd). See J. Souilhé, *La Dunamis dans les dialogues de Platon* (Alcan, 1919).

5. W. Grundmann, art. δύναμις, TDNT 2:285.

6. Ibid. The concept of δύναμις is here closely related to that of "number," which in the Pythagorean system gives form to everything.

7. See *Soph.* 247de.

8. The Stoics consider δύναμις the efficient cause of all phenomena: see J. von Arnim, *Stoicorum veterum fragmenta*, II, 112, 39ff.; III, 49, 12.

lel to that of δύναμις through their identification of "the cosmic principle and deity as the basis of being."[9] Alexander of Aphrodisia transmits to us a Stoic system whereby the "mixing" *(μέμικται)* of God-δύναμις with matter on the one side is seen as the equivalent of the fusion of the vital principle with the body in living beings on the other.[10] The normal Greek polytheism is clearly in great contrast to such an expression of pantheism. "The individual gods become δυνάμεις of the universal force. They are personifications of the capacities of a neutral deity."[11] In this thought world it remains Poseidonius who has made a fairly lengthy and systematic discourse on the subject.[12]

But a new component emerges in the evolution of Greek thought concerning δύναμις—magic. In fact, with the world defined as a system of forces in tension and constantly at work in it, there will naturally arise in the human being the desire to know them and to discover appropriate means to control them. The popular Hellenistic mind saw, then, in nature a complex of demonic forces, which are on the one hand merely emanations of the one supreme δύναμις, but are nevertheless closer to us and so impose upon us a whole study of magical techniques.[13]

Still, there is a quite different later semantic development when one speaks of δυνάμεις ("powerful actions") as signs of the marvelous intervention of a god on behalf of human beings (e.g., the cures of Aesclepius at Epidaurus).

The final stage of semantic evolution of δύναμις is represented by the context of soteriology, in which the concept came to be found within the mystery and gnostic environments. The condition of contingent matter calls forth an acute thirst for immortality and urges the search for a saving δύναμις. The *Corpus Hermeticum* offers us a characteristic example of the sort; in the first tract, the *Poimandres*, the initiate prays thus: "ἐνδυνάμωσόν με," "empower me" (1:32). The "dynamization" here requested is properly speaking divinization, that is, one's insertion as a δύναμις into the ensemble of divine forces.[14]

9. W. Grundmann, art. cit., 287; after citing specific texts, the author continues: "In these fragments deity is a universal pantheistic force, whereas in Platonic and Aristotelian philosophy it is a transcendent being," 287.

10. Ibid., 287-288.

11. Ibid., 287-288; the text of Diogenes Laertes quoted there is quite revelatory, as is also that of Plutarch in *De Iside et Osiride*, 67.

12. See the studies of K. Reinhardt, *Poseidonios* (Munich, 1921); idem, *Kosmos und Sympathie* (Munich, 1926).

13. See the incantation formulas and the speculations of Iamblicus cited in W. Grundmann, art. cit., 288-289.

14. The thirteenth tractate, however, gives us a slightly different meaning: in contrast to twelve τιμωρίαι ("punishments"), we find ten saving δυνάμεις entering one through the mystery and determining one's divinization (XIII, 7f.).

II. Δύναμις in the LXX Bible

In place of the four terms that the Hebrew text of the Old Testament used for the concept of "power," the LXX translators had only the Greek terms ἰσχύς, κράτος, and δύναμις.[15] The first is by far the most frequently used, indicating concretely strength at work: it puts the emphasis on the physical aspect of the manifestation of power. The second indicates domination, royal power, sovereign power in a rather static sense. But note that the New Testament will use these terms rather rarely, preferring the third.[16] Moreover, the New Testament usage will be found in the same line of meaning as δύναμις has in the LXX when translating ʿōz: out of twenty-one instances the translator of Psalms uses this word twenty times.[17] It is always a matter of the δύναμις of God manifesting itself in victory over the enemies, and thus it comes to be always the saving presence of God in favor of the one for whom it is put into action. In many of these texts the event that reveals it is the Exodus, as is true also in Neh 1:10: "These are your servants and your people, whom you have acquired with your great δύναμις and with your mighty hand" (see also Exod 9:16).

It is apparent just from these links how the Old Testament distances itself substantially from the Greek religious world by the particular relationship that the former intuitively senses between God and the world on the one hand (see Jer 32:17) and between God and history on the other (see Deut 3:24). Rather than a deity understood as cosmic δύναμις, we find here the personal God who governs the world and history not with an immanent law but with the freedom of God's will, that is, with God's grace. Thus δύναμις becomes simply an attribute of God, or else in some

15. The Hebrew terms are kōaḥ, ʿōz, gᵉbûrâ, ḥayil, which can all refer either to the physical force of the human being or animal or to the force of the soul, or else to the power of God, in either active or even passive sense (completed action as result of power). See F. Zorell, *Lexicon hebraicum et aramaicum* (Rome, 1940–55) under the various words. It is interesting to note that while the first three words are translated now by one Greek term and now by another, the Hebrew ḥayil is translated only by δύναμις. The semantic nuances of the three expressions in classical Greek can be defined as follows: ἰσχύς indicates physical "strength," which makes it possible to prevail over an adversary; κράτος means rather "power" of dominion, possessed by a human being or a god; and δύναμις, as we have seen, has the general meaning of power or (passively) potentiality, but generally in the former, active sense. Another similar word is the expression ἐξουσία, meaning physical or moral capacity, freedom, authority (see H. G. Liddell, R. Scott, and H. S. Jones, *A Greek-English Lexicon*, 5th printing of the 9th edition [Oxford, 1961]). For the analysis of the same words in the New Testament, see W. Bauer, *Griechisch-Deutsches Wörterbuch zu den Schriften des Neuen Testaments und der übrigen urchristlichen Literatur*, reprint of 5th edition (Berlin, 1963); in English: *A Greek-English Lexicon of the New Testament and Other Early Christian Literature* (Chicago, 1957).

16. To confirm this one need only glance at a concordance, such as that of W. F. Moulton and A. S. Geden, *A Concordance to the Greek Testament* (Edinburgh, 1957³).

17. Pss 21:2, 14; 46:2; 59:17; 63:3; 66:3; 68:29, 34, 35, 36; 74:13; 77:15; 89:11, 18; 93:1; 110:2; 138:3; 140:8; 145:6; 150:1.

instances is understood as God himself, meaning a manner in which he manifests himself.

And so on the basis of a free revelation of God's δύναμις toward the whole people or toward a single human person, the attempt is made to establish an original relationship between God and the petitioner, allowing the latter to cry, "Yahweh Lord, δύναμις of my salvation" (Ps 140:8).

III. Δύναμις θεοῦ, "power of God," and δύναμις Χριστοῦ, "power of Christ," in the Pauline correspondence

Simple statistics show us that our noun—even without considering derived adjectival and verbal forms—is used far more extensively by Paul than by any other New Testament writer.[18] It is evident that for him this is an essential term for the expression of his own thought.

In a first context the δύναμις characterizes God as creator of the visible world. The principal passage is Rom 1:19-20 (cf. Rev 4:11), closely connected with the theme of natural knowledge of God, rendered possible precisely through a type of cosmic revelation; God is thus reached in his attributes of ἀΐδιος δύναμις, "eternal power," and θειότης, "divinity."[19] This first aspect of God's δύναμις is not very much developed in the Pauline letters.[20] Hence it appears that in the text cited Paul does not just refer to pure physical causality (thus Huby), but already implicitly alludes to a communion of life which God means to prepare on a natural level but which must blossom into an interpersonal relationship on the basis of a new manifestation of his own δύναμις. This final salvific meaning is well attested even in Romans itself, where certain passages orient us toward a δύναμις manifested by God in history: in favor of his own ancient people (9:17), or again to win them to the Christian faith (11:23), but especially to fulfill his historic-salvific promises (4:21; 9:22; cf. 2 Cor 9:8; Heb 11:19).

Paul also uses the word in two other senses: in the singular in a prepositional expression (1 Thess 1:5; 2 Cor 1:8; 8:3), but without important theological significance; and in the plural in the already current sense of "miracles" (1 Cor 12:10, 28, 29; 2 Cor 12:12) or of "heavenly powers" (Rom 8:38; sing.: Eph 1:21).

18. He uses it forty-six times, not counting the Pastoral Epistles and the Letter to the Hebrews. After Paul comes Luke, who uses it twenty-two times in the Gospel and in Acts. The Fourth Gospel never uses the noun, always preferring the verb δύναμαι, "be able."
19. See A. Feuillet, "La connaissance naturelle de Dieu par les hommes d'après Rom 1:18, 23," *Lumière et Vie* (1954) 63–80.
20. But Rom 1:20, although an isolated text, does not resemble the cosmic δύναμις in the sense of the Stoic elaboration as much as it does the Jewish texts of the *Letter of Aristeas* 1:32; Flavius Josephus, *Contra Apionem* II, 167, following Wis 13; Apoc Bar 54:17-18; Test Naphtali 3:3-4.

But quite different is the Pauline use of δύναμις that most attracts our attention as being the most original. According to certain passages of his correspondence, Paul speaks of the δύναμις as a vivifying power proper to both God the Father and Christ at once. Such equalization between God and Christ is based on a uniquely original event, namely, the resurrection on the third day (see 1 Cor 15:4);[21] this, in fact, signals the moment of the greatest manifestation of the δύναμις θεοῦ, "God's power," and of the great potentiality transmitted to Christ of henceforth exercising a δύναμις of his own. Now, while there are not many texts that speak of this, we can count at least five of them with sufficient certainty: Rom 1:4; 1 Cor 6:14; 2 Cor 13:4; Phil 3:10; Eph 1:19. In substance, what results from these texts is that the "sovereign power displayed by the Father in the resurrection of Christ did not act on him only externally, but was communicated to him, permeated him intimately, thus making of him a principle of life and of resurrection for all of humanity that is saved."[22]

We cannot here subject each pericope to a minute exegetical examination (see the commentaries). But among all the others let us underline Rom 1:4, which treats Christ Jesus *"constituted Son of God in power (ὁρισθέντος υἱοῦ θεοῦ ἐν δυνάμει)* according to the spirit of sanctification by resurrection from the dead." With the greater number of commentators we join ἐν δυνάμει, "in power," to the adjoining words υἱοῦ θεοῦ, "Son of God," rather than to ὁρισθέντος, "constituted": with the resurrection Christ has been established as Son of God "in power," that is, invested even in his humanity with divine power, which thus reveals his being Son and makes possible his new activity as Savior.[23] The δύναμις θεοῦ, "power of God," thus becomes δύναμις Χριστοῦ, "power of Christ" (1 Cor 5:4; 2 Cor 12:9; cf. 1 Pet 1:16), who precisely "is raised up [as an] other priest, having become such not according to a carnal law but *according to a power of indestructible life (κατὰ δύναμιν ζωῆς ἀκαταλύτου)"* (Heb 7:15-16). Henceforth, "the power to save and deliver is grounded only in the omnipotence of God and must proceed from it. The disciples who looked to Jesus knew that he brought the saving power of God, and they could attain it in him. This is the New Testament and early Christian kerygma."[24]

21. "The New Testament, just like the Old, attributes omnipotence to God but sees the greatest proof of this quality in the victory over death accomplished with the resurrection of Christ" (W. Grundmann, art. cit., 304). See Matt 22:29; Acts 2:24; 1 Cor 15:43; cf. Heb 11:19.
22. P. Biard, *La puissance de Dieu*, Travaux de l'Institut catholique de Paris 7 (Paris, 1960) 149.
23. See the different thesis of M.-É. Boismard, *Constitué Fils de Dieu (Rom 1,4)*, RB 60 (1953) 5–17, and against this P. Biard, op. cit., 151–155.
24. W. Grundmann, art. cit., 309. We note in passing that the expression ἡ δύναμις τῆς ἁμαρτίας, "the power of sin" (1 Cor 15:56), is not strictly in opposition to the δύναμις Χριστοῦ; in fact, while the latter contains a subjective genitive, the former contains rather an objective genitive, where the true subject is the following ὁ νόμος, "the Law." The opposition is, then,

IV. The equivalent salvific presence of the δύναμις θεοῦ in Christ and in the kerygma according to 1 Cor 1:18-24

Lietzmann, Allo, Huby, Jacono, Osty, and Héring in their commentaries[25] are all so preoccupied with the opposition that Paul establishes between the σοφία τοῦ κόσμου, "wisdom of the world," and the σοφία τοῦ θεοῦ, "wisdom of God," that they lose sight of certain essential literary and theological points that we wish to note.

1) *Literary examination of the pericope.* We noted at the beginning of this study how our passage stands at the center of the discussion about the factions of Corinth. According to the "threefold pattern," which the author uses in his cyclical treatment of the problem, 1 Cor 1:18-24 is at the level of digression (in this case on the relationship of gospel to wisdom: 1:18-3:4). Paul here makes liberal use of the literary techniques of his semitic roots, like antithetical parallelism (vv. 18, 25) and synonymous parallelism (in the Isaiah citation, v. 19), and also elements of a chiastic construction in v. 21. But the most notable thing is an evident inclusion between v. 18 and vv. 23-24, which binds the whole section in a true literary unity. The inclusion can be thus analyzed in its extremities:[26]

1 Cor 1:18		1 Cor 1:23-24
ὁ λόγος γὰρ	A	ἡμεῖς δὲ κηρύσσομεν
ὁ τοῦ σταυροῦ		Χριστὸν ἐσταυρωμένον
τοῖς μὲν ἀπολλυμένοις	B	Ἰουδαίοις μὲν σκάνδαλον
μωρία ἐστιν		ἔθνεσιν δὲ μωρίαν
τοῖς δὲ σῳζομένοις ἡμῖν	C	αὐτοῖς δὲ τοῖς κλητοῖς
		Ἰουδαίοις τε καὶ Ἕλλησιν
<u>δύναμις θεοῦ</u> ἐστιν		Χριστὸν <u>θεοῦ δύναμιν</u> καὶ θεοῦ σοφίαν

For the word	A	But we preach
of the Cross,		Christ crucified,
to those who are perishing	B	a stumbling block to the Jews,

Christ-Law as two mutually exclusive saving principles (see P. Benoit, "The Law and the Cross according to St Paul," in *Jesus and the Gospel*, 2, trans. B. Weatherhead [London, 1974] 11–39 = RB 47 [1938]) 481–509).

25. H. Lietzmann, *An die Korinther I–II* (Tübingen, 1949⁴); E.-B. Allo, *Première épître aus Corinthiens* (Paris, 1935); J. Huby, *Saint Paul: première épître aux Corinthiens*, Verbum Salutis (Paris, 1946); V. Jacono, *Le epistole di S. Paolo ai Romani, ai Corinti e ai Galati* (Turin, 1951); E. Osty, *Les épîtres de Saint Paul aux Corinthiens* (Paris, 1953²); J. Héring, *The First Epistle of Saint Paul to the Corinthians*, trans. A. W. Heathcote and P. J. Allcock = *La première épître de saint Paul aux Corinthiens* (Neuchâtel, 1959²).

26. See K. Müller, art. cit., 268.

1 Cor 1:18	1 Cor 1:23-24
it is foolishness,	and foolishness to the gentiles,
but to us who are being saved	C but to those who are called
	Jews and Greeks alike
it is the Power of God	Christ, the power of God and
	the wisdom of God

We note a strict structural as well as lexical parallelism between the two columns: to a subject on the one hand and to a subjective clause on the other (A); there follow two phrases (B-C), which, while having predicative value in v. 18 but attributive value in 23b-24, on each side open respectively with the *contrastive particles* μέν (B) and δέ (C); the particles, then, underline quite markedly their thematic correlation.

We want to point out here a final parallel between 1 Cor 1:18, 23-24 and Rom 1:16, a text that also presents a construction and thematic completely corresponding to our passage. It lacks only the B element, that is, the element that stresses the negative echoes (but both "the Jew" and "the Greek" are present, in this case as addressees of the good news); for the rest, we find there an initial clause serving as principal subject: "Indeed, I am not ashamed of the *gospel (εὐαγγέλιον)*" (A), the "dynamic" value of which is then at once affirmed: "indeed it is the *power of God (δύναμις θεοῦ)* for the salvation of everyone who believes, first the Jew and then the Greek" (C).

Finally, the passage 1 Cor 1:25 adds nothing logically to the preceding verses. It is attracted to them only in the sense of a summarizing formula representing axiomatically what has already been developed.

2) *Theological examination.* It is impossible here to analyze the whole suggestive theological richness of our text, nor do we wish to do so. We only want to emphasize two things: the "paschal" value of the expression δύναμις θεοῦ as applied to Christ (v. 24) and its meaning in reference to the kerygma.

a) We recall what we said above about the δύναμις θεοῦ in the Pauline correspondence because it can throw light on our present passage. Initially we asked: How is it that in such a rich passage Paul makes no explicit mention of the resurrection of Christ? It would seem that here the ἐσταυρωμένος, "crucified" (v. 23; cf. v. 18), fills the whole foreground of Paul's thought and of our literary section. And yet we know the Apostle to be par excellence "the herald, the ambassador of the risen Christ. His message will always be the message of the risen Christ,"[27] saturating all that he writes.

Now, the five texts cited above have shown us that the δύναμις θεοῦ is essentially the display of the greatest possible salvific intervention of God with regard to Christ (see also 2 Cor 13:4a), in which then Christ himself is called to participate (cf. Rom 1:4). On the basis of this discovery, then, we will say that here also the crucified Christ is now announced by Paul as θεοῦ δύναμις (v. 24) insofar as it is precisely on him that this very δύναμις has broken in. We thus find the two aspects of the paschal mystery united more intimately than ever. In 2 Cor 13:4 we read that Christ "was crucified through [his] weakness, but [now] lives through the power of God *(ἐκ δυνάμεως θεοῦ)"*; indeed, it is in weakness that the δύναμις can reveal itself in its greatest brilliance.[28] This is the best commentary on our text. We thus understand how the Crucified is himself proclaimed δύναμις θεοῦ, no longer in the sense that this is communicated to him, but primarily because through his being destined to death, he has given God the possibility to display himself fully by means of the resurrection.[29]

Thus do we reach one of the most, if not *the* most fundamental of themes of all revelation: the story of Gideon, of David and Goliath, of Mary of Nazareth (see Luke 1:49a), and the Pauline theme of πίστις, "faith," all alike find their primordial analogue in Jesus Christ, who through the most profound self-denial permits God the Father henceforth to manifest his own saving δύναμις decisively, *in manu potenti et in brachio extento*, "with mighty hand and outstretched arm." Therefore in 1 Cor 1:24 the attribute θεοῦ δύναμις referred to Christ has above all a passive meaning: Christ is Christ insofar as this δύναμις has been exercised upon him.

---

27. L. Cerfaux, "La Résurrection du Christ dans la vie et la doctrine de saint Paul," *Lumière et Vie* 3 (1952) 61–82; see D. M. Stanley, *Christ's Resurrection in Pauline Soteriology*, AB 13 (Rome, 1963).

28. 2 Cor 12:9a: ἡ γὰρ δύναμις ἐν ἀσθενείᾳ τελεῖται, "Indeed the power is made complete in weakness." This famous Pauline saying absolutely cannot be enervated by a moralizing interpretation that would reduce the δύναμις to the Christian's faithfulness in tribulations. The context, remote as well as proximate, is consciously theological. Indeed, v. 9b itself clarifies the meaning of the expression, speaking explicitly of ἡ δύναμις Χριστοῦ, "the power of Christ"; therefore certain ancient manuscripts as well as Irenaeus and Ephrem remained faithful to its original meaning when in 9a, in the words spoken to Paul by the *Kyrios*, they read: ἡ γὰρ δύναμις "μου," "because *my* power."

29. "For the Apostle the Cross is, in its sense in the history of salvation, that high point where the God who raises the dead secretly demonstrated his own power. Consequently, the expression Χριστὸς ἐσταυρωμένος, 'Christ crucified,' identifies Jesus as the one who by the power of God was given to the death of the cross *and* was raised again. It is a formula that summarizes the saving event brought about by God in the death and in the resurrection of the *Christ (Χριστός)"*—K. Müller, art. cit., 268. The idea was already pointed out by Allo, op. cit., 18. See also Grundmann, art. cit., 309–310.

But we must at once add that this same attribute also has inseparably an active meaning: Christ himself exercises the δύναμις θεοῦ on an equal footing. This is so much true that he comes to stand as an eschatological-critical function (K. Müller) between those on the one hand who identify him as σκάνδαλον, "stumbling block," and μωρία, "foolishness" (v. 23), and those on the other who in clinging to him are κλητοί, "chosen" (v. 24a). So let us go on to the second theme we have proposed.

b) As we have already noted, v. 18 is strictly parallel to vv. 23-24. But the δύναμις θεοῦ here is found in a different, we might say new, context. It is no longer the paschal event but the announcing of the kerygma; better, it is still dealing with the same fact, but insofar as it is converted into speech: ὁ λόγος τοῦ σταυροῦ, "the word of the Cross." The two events are thus identified: just like the crucifixion (v. 23b), so also the kerygma (v. 21b) or "the word of the Cross" (18a) is identified as μωρία, "foolishness."[30] Well, even this "speech" in turn comes to be identified by Paul as δύναμις θεοῦ; moreover, the same is said in Rom 1:16 of the εὐαγγέλιον (see above). What does this mean? In short, we can express ourselves thus: the same formula, though in a different context, shows clearly that the genuine apostolic kerygma is none other than the prolongation, and in a certain sense a ritualization, of the divine work accomplished in the historical Christ. The Christian message, essentially centered in the paschal mystery, finally consummates the ineffectiveness of both the Mosaic Law (Rom 8:7-8; 1 Cor 15:56) and the Old Testament cult (Heb 10:11). The passage cited from Rom 1:16 makes more explicit the character of the δύναμις θεοῦ already present in 1 Cor 1:18, in the sense that by it the kerygma is made powerful εἰς σωτηρίαν παντὶ τῷ πιστεύοντι, "for the salvation of everyone who believes"; we can also compare Jas 1:21, writing about the "planted *word which can save (λόγον τὸν δυνάμενον σῶσαι)* your souls."

The Christian message, then, is no empty word but saving power, and this message is so in the sense of its content, which consists of a δύναμις already exercised by the Father upon Christ crucified, but also of its principal author, since here and now it is Christ who acts, who calls, who welcomes.[31] The part to be played by faith in such an event is evident. The

30. "The foolishness of the Christian message consists in the contention that a historically contingent event should have an absolute, definitive value" (W. G. Kümmel in the *Anhang* to H. Lietzmann, op. cit., 169).
31. See H. Schlier, "Vom Wesen der apostolischen Ermahnung," *Die Zeit der Kirche* (Freiburg, 1956) 74–89; "Die Eigenart der christlichen Mahnung nach dem Apostel Paulus," *Besinnung auf das Neuen Testament* (Freiburg-Basel-Vienna, 1964) 340–357; J. Murphy-O'Connor, *Paul on Preaching* (London and New York, 1964); S. Virgulin, "La croce come potenza di Dio in 1 Cor 1,18.24," in auct. pl., *La sapienza della croce oggi*, I (Turin, 1976) 144–150.

New Testament expression δύναμις θεοῦ actually does not mean to emphasize the salvific capacity of the gospel as a static privilege belonging to it or inhering in it as a hidden treasure; rather, the expression would indicate that the gospel, the kerygma, is δύναμις essentially when it is active, when it calls forth a response, provokes one to take a position. But only if this movement of the person is one of acceptance does the δύναμις of the kerygma achieve its purpose, which is to be "salvific"; indeed, 1 Cor 1:18 and Rom 1:16 alike make it clear that the message is δύναμις only "for those who are being saved" or "for everyone who believes"; about the one who does not accept it, Romans says nothing, while 1 Corinthians indicates: "For those who are perishing it is foolishness." Thus does the critico-eschatological function of the Word take effect.[32]

In conclusion, the parallelism noted between 1 Cor 1:24 and 1:18 reveals the presence of the precise identical *vivifying* δύναμις that we find first in the work of Christ and then in the believer; analogically, then, the act of faith at the moment of the kerygma is equivalent to the resurrection of Jesus. A text that is thematically close to ours confirms such an understanding, completing the argument: in 1 Cor 2:1-5 Paul remembers his arrival in Corinth, when he preached "not in persuasive words of wisdom"[33] but *in the manifestation of the spirit and of power (ἐν ἀποδείξει πνεύματος καὶ δυνάμεως)*, in order that your faith be not [based] on human wisdom *but on the power of God (ἀλλ᾽ ἐν δυνάμει θεοῦ)"* (vv. 4-5). If there can be some question in the first case, in the second recurrence it is clear that the δύναμις cannot be understood as thaumaturgic power. "As a witness of the Cross of Christ, [the Apostle] establishes his hearers on the δύναμις θεοῦ [power of God], not on the σοφίαν ἀνθρώπων [wisdom of men]. . . . This determines the form of his proclamation, [which] has the goal of exhibiting the presence of Christ in the Spirit, and therefore exhibiting the saving power of God, which is identical with Jesus Christ and which is the basis of the existence of believers."[34] This means only that faith is absolutely not a human work but the absolute and exclusive work of God.

32. "In the preaching of the cross present human judgment encounters divine eschatological judgment. At one moment, in one event, the λόγος τοῦ σταυροῦ [word of the Cross] melds together those who are being challenged in a situation of eschatological decisiveness determined by the judicial will of God. When the cross is announced, the hearers must face a separation into ἀπολλύμενοι [those being lost] and σῳζόμενοι [those being saved], according to an intervention of God equivalent to the final judgment. *To the λόγος τοῦ σταυροῦ [word of the Cross] belongs a critical-eschatological authority"* (K. Müller, art. cit., 247–248).
33. This passage is textually problematic. To the reading of Nestle and Merk we prefer that of Huby and Héring, who follow Origen, Eusebius, and Ambrosiaster along with certain ancient versions (Coptic and Syro-Peshitta).
34. W. Grundmann, art. cit., 312. In the Christian, therefore, bound to Christ by means of faith, the power of God shows its final effects. He is simply ἐν δυνάμει πίστεως, "in the

Thus is completed the circle of the process of salvation, which proceeds from Χριστὸς ἐσταυρωμένος, "Christ crucified" (1 Cor 1:23-24), through the λόγος τοῦ σταυροῦ, "word of the Cross" (1:18), onward to πίστις, "faith" (2:5; Rom 1:16), finding at every stage of the process a particular saving intervention of God at work, namely, the δύναμις θεοῦ. This is always a free, overwhelming initiative of resurrection, the constantly available display of which allows the Christian once more to sing with the Qumran poet:

> I give you thanks, O Adonai, because . . .
> according to your marvelous counsel
> you have manifested your *power* toward me. . . .
> what creature of clay has power to accomplish such marvels?
> . . . And I had said,
> "Because of my sins I am excluded from your covenant."
> But when I recalled the *power* of your hand
> and the immensity of your mercy,
> I was lifted up, and stood erect.[35]

power of faith" (Ignatius of Antioch, *Ad Eph.* 14:2-3); see the *Letter to Diognetus* 9:1 and 2: ". . . in order that we might clearly manifest the impossibility of entering the kingdom of God with our own forces alone, whereas we can do so with the divine δύναμις . . . to show forth his goodness and power."

35. I QH IV:5, 28, 29, 35-36 (after Dupont-Sommer, *Les écrits esséniens découverts près de la Mer Morte* (Paris, 1960²). For basic information on δύναμις in Judaism and at Qumran, see P. Biard, op. cit., 157-160. This short study deliberately neglected the pneumatological aspect of the δύναμις θεοῦ, about which, however, there would be much to say; see E. Schweizer, "The Spirit of Power. The Uniformity and Diversity of the Concept of the Holy Spirit in the NT," Int 6 (1952) 259-278.

Chapter 11

Saint Paul and Diogenes the Cynic: 1 Corinthians 7:29b-31a

The cultural background of 1 Cor 7:29-31 has always been grounds for research and interesting disputes. Its attractiveness is justified by its (certainly not marginal) theme concerning the relationship of the Christian to the world and likewise by its original literary formulation. In particular, here we meet one of the most characteristic points of encounter between Christianity and its original surrounding world, at the ethical level.

According to the common opinion of the commentators, from J. Weiss to H. Conzelmann, this passage seems ''to be the passage most strongly subject to stoic influence in all the Pauline epistles, and to commend the ideal of that ataraxy which is secured by dissociating oneself inwardly from one's outward fate.''[1] However, W. Schrage has sought to divert the exclusive attention to Stoicism, toward Jewish apocalyptic instead.[2] He has done so by calling attention to an interesting parallelism between this passage and 4 Esdr 16:42-45; and in effect in 1 Cor 7, vv. 29a and 31b act as an apocalyptic framework.[3] Nevertheless, this type of interpretation has recently been criticized by D. J. Doughty, who maintains that Schrage has not correctly perceived the hermeneutical significance of the constructions and of the linguistic relations developed by Paul in the section.[4] Indeed, the future eschatology proper to apocalyptic has here been radically trans-

1. H. Conzelmann, *1 Corinthians*, Hermeneia, trans. J. W. Leitch (Philadelphia, 1975) 133 = *Der erste Brief an die Korinther* (Göttingen, 1969) 158; see J. Weiss, *Der erste Korintherbrief* (Göttingen, 1910) 197-201.

2. W. Schrage, ''Die Stellung zur Welt bei Paulus, Epiktet und in der Apokalyptik,'' ZThK 61 (1964) 125-154.

3. See the explanation in G. Hierzenberger, *Weltbewertung bei Paulus nach 1 Kor 7,29-31. Eine exegetisch-kerygmatische Studie* (Düsseldorf, 1967) 67-100.

4. D. J. Doughty, ''The Presence and Future of Salvation in Corinth,'' ZNW 66 (1975) 61-90, 66-74.

formed into the present (note the verbal tenses and moods); furthermore (and consequently) in the ὡς μή ("as if not") phrases, what is expressed is not a tension between present and future but rather a dialectic relation between the person and the person's world; finally, such a relationship is understood as a dialectic between *Christians* and the world insofar as they are subject to the lordship of Christ. The conclusion is that "the destiny of those who belong to Christ, therefore, is discovered not from speculation about the future of salvation, but from the recognition that already in the present their lives are determined by the lordship of Christ (v. 22) and no longer therefore by the σχῆμα, "form," of this world (vv. 23, 31)."[5]

So we now turn to consider the Greco-Stoic background of our present passage, with all the rich implications of what we are doing.[6] The trouble is that in the specialized research scholars have almost always limited the comparison to Paul and Epictetus.[7] Surely, between the philosopher of Hierapolis and the Apostle of Tarsus there have been found precisely in 1 Cor 7 certain surprising affinities not only thematic (like the preference of celibacy to marriage) but also lexical (compare, for example, the adverb ἀπερισπάστως, "without distraction," in 1 Cor 7:35 with the adjective ἀπερίσπαστος, "undistracted," in Epictetus, *Diatr.* II 21, 22; III 22, 69, in the same kind of context. Still, a real Greek parallel with the original pattern of the five antithetic sentences of 1 Cor 7:29b-31a has not yet been proposed.

With this contribution of ours we wish, in fact, to point out a curious parallel of this type, drawn from the ethical philosophy of Diogenes the Cynic. We have come across it in the *Vitae philosophorum* in the philosopher of the same name, Diogenes Laertius in Book VI, paragraph 29. This is the text:[8]

---

5. Art. cit., 73; see ibid., 71, 72. "The worldliness of the Christian is not denied. Christians live in the world and continue to make use of the world. Whereas for apocalyptic it can perhaps be said that 'the present is nothing, but the future is nevertheless of great (worth),' Paul proclaims no such renunciation of worldly relationships. . . . Similarly, marriage is understood in a new way, as a relationship which is no longer determined by the 'passion of desire,' (1 Thess 4[4f.]); as a relationship in which 'love is not jealous or boastful, arrogant or rude, and does not seek to assert its own will' (1 Kor 13[5])."

6. But we must attend to two things: first of all, we do not intend to misinterpret the apocalyptic echoes in 1 Cor 7; secondly, we must finally recognize that the encounter with Stoicism was not abjectly accepted by Paul but corrected with his Christological faith.

7. Thus, e.g., A. Bonhöffer, *Epiktet und das Neue Testament* (Giessen, 1911); H. Braun, "Die Indifferenz gegenüber der Welt bei Paulus und bei Epiktet," in *Gesammelte Studien* (Tübingen, 1962) 159–167; thus the commentaries in general.

8. The citation follows the critical edition of H. S. Long, *Diogenis Laertii vitae philosophorum*, 2 vols. (Oxford, 1964).

ἐπῄνει τοὺς μέλλοντας γαμεῖν καὶ μὴ γαμεῖν,
καὶ τοὺς μέλλοντας καταπλεῖν καὶ μὴ καταπλεῖν,
καὶ τοὺς μέλλοντας πολιτεύεσθαι καὶ μὴ πολιτεύεσθαι,
καὶ τοὺς παιδοτροφεῖν καὶ μὴ παιδοτροφεῖν,
καὶ τοὺς παρασκευαζομένους συμβιοῦν τοῖς δυνάσταις καὶ μὴ προσιόντας.

We give our own translation of this, as literal as possible:

He praised those who intended to marry and not to marry,
and those who intended to sail and not to sail,
and those who intended to dedicate themselves to political life
    and not to dedicate themselves there,
and those who intended to raise children and not to raise them,
and those who prepared to live together with the powerful and
    who did not approach them.

Let us examine the text in two stages: first in itself and then in relation to Paul.

I. Some observations of textual and literary character on the text of Diogenes.

a) The old Greek-Latin edition of Laertius, edited in the seventeenth century by Henricus Wetstenius, reports in a note: "The most learned Turnebus thought this passage should read: ἐπῄνει τοὺς μέλλοντας γαμεῖν καὶ μὴ γαμοῦντας, . . . καὶ μὴ καταπλέοντας, . . . καὶ μὴ πολιτευομένους, . . . καὶ μὴ παιδοτροφοῦντας [He praised those who were going to marry but did not marry, . . . and did not sail, . . . and did not so dedicate themselves, . . . and did not raise them]. But I consider the earlier reading of these phrases more probable."[9] The changing of the four infinitives into present participles has all the air of being secondary, not only because there is no trace of it in the manuscript tradition but because it makes the style dull. (The reading was perhaps derived from the influence of the present participles in 1 Cor 7:29b-31a, or more simply due to the desire to harmonize the first four phrases with the fifth.) Therefore the editor Wetstenius did not accept it.[10]

b) The translation of the text is not obvious. We certainly get the impression that the author wants to condense a much longer discursive teaching into very concise, concentrated phrasing—hence the lack of immediate

9. *Diogenis Laertii de vitis, dogmatibus et apophtegmatibus clarorum philosophorum libri X graece et latine* . . . (Amsterdam, 1692) 329, n. 30.
10. Moreover, the critical edition of H. S. Long cited above does not so much as mention the conjecture.

clarity in meaning. However, it seems that we must reject an alternative to the attested text that would attribute the antithetic behavior of the two parts of each line to the same subject.[11] That the subject of the negative infinitive is not the same as that of the preceding infinitive can be gathered especially from the specific meaning of the negative μή, which, as distinct from the other negative particle οὐ, refers to the subjective rather than the objective level of the action expressed.[12] Thus the negative infinitive cannot indicate the decision not *actually to do* the action originally projected; rather, it is as if each phrase were structured with correlative conjunctions "both . . . and . . .," alluding to two different kinds of persons, and so to two opposite intentions, both of which are praised. Or one might also construe the negative infinitives as substantives (normally gerunds in English: he praised "not getting married," "not sailing," etc.).

More problematic is the sense of the fifth phrase, which ends with a participle (and at that, not the one we would have expected, i.e., συμβιοῦντας, "living together") rather than the infinitive that the first four had led us to expect, and so might refer to one category of persons in both members of the line; but again, because of the μή, "not," we must think of a new, opposite type of decision, attributed to persons different from the preceding παρασκευαζομένους, "preparing." The participle προσιόντας, "approaching," will be recognized, then, as an elegant stylistic variation to conclude the whole section (see n. 16 as well).

c) In the second line the verb καταπλεῖν, "sail," seizes our attention as the only one of the whole series that does not allude to interpersonal and social relationships, referring rather to an external and rather brief activity. However, the verb does not properly mean just "sail" in a general sense, but rather "navigate from high seas to the coast, follow the current, to land" (the antonym is ἀναπλεῖν, "take to the seas, go against the current, set sail"). It would fit the thematic context better if it carried the metaphorical sense "follow the current," meaning "do as the others do"; the praise for both those who practice and those who reject such an attitude would thus assume the sense of an axiomatic principle, spelled

---

11. I.e., the textual conjecture of the *most learned* Turnebus, which must be considered a *lectio facilior*, which is offered, for instance, in the Italian translation of M. Gigante in Diogene Laerzio, *Vite dei filosofi*, 2 vols. (Bari, 1976): "He praised those who were to marry, and did not marry; those who were to undertake a maritime journey, and did not do so; those who were to dedicate themselves to a political life, and did not dedicate themselves to it; those who wanted to begin a family, and did not begin it; and those who girded themselves to live with the powerful, and then abstained from it" (I 213–214). But the other vernacular citations we present from Diogenes Laertius will be based on this edition.

12. See Blass-Debrunner, 426ff.; also F. Marinelli and U. E. Paoli, *Grammatica greca* (Florence, 1952[10]) 390, erroneously numbered 460.

out more completely by the other lines. But this is only an hypothesis that, however attractive, cannot be based on documentation of any metaphorical sense of *καταπλεῖν*; nor does it help that the phrase, which in that case would have a general value, stands in the second place rather than the first.

d) One can hardly fail to recognize a certain rhythmic movement of the passage as a whole. This is emphasized both by the verb *ἐπαινέω*, "praised," placed alone at the beginning and so functioning as the key to the whole long sentence, and by the simple paratactic succession of the several objects of the initial verb. The result is a sort of litany, which surely favors memorization of what may have been the concise guide for the Cynic concerning social life.[13]

II. We now come to the *relationship* between the text of Diogenes and 1 Cor 7:29b-31a, *on the level of both form and content*.

a) In each of the two cases we have a series, indeed a list, of five propositions exemplifying five life-situations thought to symbolize the variety of human experience. Specifically, we note that from each side either the acceptance-refusal (Diogenes) or the reevaluation (Paul) of such experiences becomes the explicit object of praise or of urgent admonition, even though the grammatical techniques are formally different. For while in Diogenes the verb for "praise" *(ἐπήνει)* is clearly in evidence, in Paul we have only the stray *ἵνα*, "in order that," standing by itself and apparently not governed by any verb. But this conjunction certainly conceals an implicit paraenetic verb, and even by itself can have the value of an imperative.[14] In neither of the texts, then, do we have a mere catalogue of observed social behavior; on the contrary, each of the authors expresses involvement, thus revealing his own respective concerns, to be determined below.

b) Above all, we are to consider the related construction of the sets of five phrases. Now, each of the lists is centered on the opposition between two different ways of considering each of the five experiences. We see this in Diogenes and Paul alike through the use of a simple negative conjunction. Of course, the *ὡς μή*, "as if not," of Paul is not completely equivalent to the *καὶ μή*, "and . . . not," of Diogenes. Indeed, the former has an argumentative rather than a comparative sense, that is, it does not just juxtapose two terms as of equal value but envisions a second term

---

13. Diogenes Laertius himself, shortly after recording our passage, notes, "The boys [educated by Diogenes the Cynic] memorized many passages . . . of the works of Diogenes. And from time to time he reviewed for them the method of compiling the material concisely and committing it easily to memory" (op. cit., VI, 31).

14. See Blass-Debrunner, 387.3 ("vernacular" usage).

as modifying the first (in German it would be translated with "als" rather than "wie");[15] but the latter retains its simple value as a negative conjunction, acquiring, however, a typical copulative sense ("also") with a correlative connotation ("both . . . and"), even without the correlative καὶ, "both," before the first infinitive of the phrase.

The grammatical distinction suggests a perceptible thematic distinction: in Paul the opposition remains within a single life-situation that is not rejected, while in Diogenes it is expressed in terms of both divergence and indifference, so that the praise even of a refusal is just as detached as that of an acceptance (see below, d). Nevertheless, in both cases the negative μή is positioned right in the middle of every single phrase and thus fulfills a discriminating function as a kind of logical watershed distinguishing two different attitudes or behaviors in the face of the same human experience. The only difference is that for Paul the object that is recommended is the second member, that is, the negative member—yet only insofar as it implies neither exclusion nor alternative—while for Diogenes the object of evenhanded praise is equally acceptance of and abstention from the various experiences.[16]

c) While the five aspects of life listed by Diogenes are very specific, concrete, and tangible, those of Paul are substantially more hazy, generic, and universal. This is immediately evident from a glance at the following:

Diogenes	*Paul*
1 marriage	marriage
2 navigation	weeping
3 political commitment	rejoicing
4 raising children	purchasing
5 joining the rich	using the world

In Paul, as we see, at least 2, 3, and 5 are rather abstract (moreover, nos. 2–3 simply correspond to each other in antithetic parallelism); but precisely for that reason they are labels applicable to an infinity of possible situations. On the other hand, in Diogenes, setting aside no. 2 (see above: 1.c), the other four cases in effect represent only a reduplication of two basic themes, marriage (1 and 4) and public life (3 and 5).

---

15. In 1 Cor 7:29b-31a it is not only the μή but also the use of ὡς, "as," with the participle that moves the lived experience ("those who have a wife") to a subjective level ("like those who have none"); see Blass-Debrunner, 425.3; F. Marinelli and U. E. Paoli, op. cit., 402.

16. Were one to choose to understand the same subject for both participles of the fifth phrase (according to the Gigante translation: n. 11), then the praise of Diogenes would apply only to the μὴ προσιόντας, "those not approaching," and we would have in this phrase a case of internal antithesis more like the contrasts of 1 Cor 7:29b-31a.

d) There is another interesting difference between Diogenes and Paul. The casuistic presentation of the former, while based on the observation of real human experience, consists in certain situations presented only as possibilities (τοὺς μέλλοντες . . ., "those who intended to") or else indifferently (. . . καὶ μή . . ., "and not to"). The philosopher here shows his total neutrality before the possible choices that may be imposed or requested of humans in their life. What emerges is substantially a lack of ideals, making the Cynic a mere spectator of the experiences of others: for him these are all good. But this absolute indifference precludes him from any possibility of coming to the aid of his peers, rather leaving them alone with themselves, since their existential situation, whatever it may be, finds each person independently to be that person's own reason for validity. Consequently, the discourse here moves a bit on the level of coldly clinical scholastic-casuistic analysis, which betrays a disengaged detachment and in fact an unconcern for the needs of social life.[17]

But with Paul matters are quite different. He writes from a viewpoint not of purely philosophical ethics but of concrete pastoral intervention. Therefore he realistically counts the cost of marriage, mourning, rejoicing, etc. (five present participles!). That is, Paul speaks not out of presuppositions of incorporeal indifference; indeed, precisely because he typically enters *in medias res* in the lived experience of the life of his addressees, he is far from the abstraction of the mere teacher (cf. 1 Cor 4:15). Still, his willingness to take a position does not mean warning his hearers and putting them on guard against certain experiences judged to be negative in themselves; on the contrary, he builds on real experiences undergone naturally, and so indirectly approving their goodness or at least recognizing their obvious human dimension. The judgment passed on these, then, is basically optimistic: what the Apostle finds beneficial is not the egoistical individual ἀταραξία, "imperturbability," nor the flight from the concrete needs of others in their situations, but rather the improvement of the experience of these situations in one specific manner. His message is only an invitation not to absolutize specific spheres of life; he rather relativizes their passing σχῆμα, "form" (v. 31b; cf. Rom 12:2). Indeed, that which is not relative is outside these experiences, not in the self-sufficiency of the human subject but rather in the Κύριος, who has already made the time short (v. 29a; cf. 31b).

---

17. See Diogenes Laertius, VI, 24 ("He was expert at treating others with extreme insolence. . . . He never tired of repeating that in life one must choose between 'reason or the gallows' " = λόγον ἢ βρόχον); VI:71 ("His life's model, he said, was Heracles, who set nothing ahead of freedom"). Far are we, for example, from 1 Cor 8, where loving concern for the weakest brother or sister is placed ahead of personal freedom.

Therefore, while Diogenes is simply an exponent of indifference in relation to marrying or not marrying, engaging in political life or not, etc. (praising either alternative equally), Paul rather can perceive an antithesis right within marriage itself, or grief, or joy, etc. (which are, then, accepted per se as normal components of human life). The Apostle, then, proposes not the simplistic Cynic solution of accepting everything as right, which ultimately just sanctions the status quo, but the more engaged and complex solution of Christian dialectic, which, far from removing the individual from the world, inserts the individual there in a completely original kind of relationship (see 1 Cor 5:9-10; John 17:15-16).

There is no doubt, then, that it is Paul rather than Diogenes who is closer to human needs, since rather than distancing himself self-sufficiently from the situations of human life, Paul grasps hold of them through his sympathetic pastoral intervention, solicitous only to supple new and liberating dimensions of the absolute.

e) In Paul's text, and that of Diogenes as well, we find a distinct interest in marriage. Both put it at the beginning of the series (Paul: οἱ ἔχοντες γυναῖκας, "those who have wives," a somewhat periphrastic expression; Diogenes more simply, τοὺς μέλλοντας γαμεῖν, "those who were to marry."[18] Paul, moreover, has inserted this passage within the context of a discourse on the relationship between marriage and celibacy. But the text of Diogenes, though it stands by itself, does return to the theme with the verb of the fourth line: παιδοτροφεῖν, "raise children / set up a family," most likely alluding to the spouses generating children (though not excluding the task of training them).[19]

Still, there lies an abyss between the conceptions of marriage held by the two. This is what Diogenes Laertius reports about the attitude of our philosopher: "He allowed having women in common, *did not recognize marriage (γάμον μηδὲ ὀνομάζων)*, but man and woman getting together by agreement; consequently the children also had to be common."[20] It fol-

---

18. Whereas in the apocalyptic text of 4 Esdr 16:42-45 (noted by W. Schrage: see n. 2), marriage comes at the end of a series of eight sentences, the first six of which are all devoted to economic aspects of life *(qui vendit . . . qui emit . . . qui mercatur . . . qui aedificat . . . qui seminat . . . qui vineam putat . . .)*; then the last two allude to the married and the unmarried in the face of the end: *qui nubunt sic quasi filios non facturi, et qui non nubunt sic quasi vidui* (v. 45). This implies a pessimistic judgment of the uselessness of various endeavors of human life brought to nothing by the approaching end (see v. 46: *propter quod qui laborant sine causa laborant!*).

19. That the verb should be understood in the generative rather than the pedagogical sense is confirmed by the fact that Diogenes Laertius a little later informs us that our philosopher "educated the children of Xeniades" (VI, 30; see ibid., 74); see also VI, 63: "When certain parents were sacrificing to the gods to obtain a child, he addressed them, 'But do you not sacrifice to see what kind of a child will come forth?' "

20. Diogenes Laertius, VI, 72; see 54 and 69.

lows, then, that the praise of Diogenes the Cynic for "those who intended to marry, and not to marry" allows for a shade of preference for the latter, insofar as they avoided the juridically sanctioned but not the sexual union.

In any case, even here we see affirmed the basic indifference of our philosopher.[21] And once again we see the naturalistic oversimplification of the "cynic." After all, he had no particularly elevated ideals that could provide him with norms for his own existence or that of others, nor conformity to a Κύριος like the Crucified and Risen One, nor an eschatological expectation, nor self-surrender to a community like the Christian ἐκκλησία and its missionary expansion. Nothing, then, defined him better than the inscription placed by the citizens of his city, Sinope, on the statue dedicated to him: ". . . you alone taught mortals the doctrine that life by itself is enough, and pointed out the easiest way to live."[22] And the "way" of αὐτάρκεια ("self-sufficiency"), which goes well beyond simple private individualism, crossing over into egoism,[23] is the way of the "dog," excluded by definition from the social relations of human life, or simply choosing to reduce them to his own measure.[24] Finally, he himself admitted that "the only right political constitution is that which regulates the universe."[25]

In conclusion, we note that the text of Diogenes the Cynic, which we have cited (and which Diogenes Laertius reported), is the only passage yet discovered in the Greek world that offers a certain formal parallelism with 1 Cor 7:29b-31a, at least in its internal structure.[26] Now, it was precisely at Corinth that the philosopher spent the last years of his life as a slave-pedagogue, and there it was that he died and was buried,[27] doubtless leaving an echo of his teaching or at least of his example. But the diver-

21. For comparison, see the saying of Socrates reported by Eusebius, *Praep. Evangel.*, V, 29:6: "Asked by someone whether he should marry or not, Socrates replied, 'In either case you will be sorry' " (μετανοήσει ἀμφότερα). See also Stobaeus, *Anthol.* IV, 22:59: 520 Hense; the whole chapter 22 of Stobaeus's book IV is dedicated to the theme of marriage and contains quotations of ancient writers, sometimes canceling each other out; see, for example, no. 14: ἄριστον ἀνδρὶ κτῆμα συμπάθης γυνή, "For a man an excellent possession is a compatible wife," and no. 50: γυναῖκα θάπτειν κρεῖττόν ἐστιν ἢ γαμεῖν, "Better to bury a wife than to marry one."

22. Diogenes Laertius, VI, 78.

23. The *autarkeia* of Diogenes the Cynic goes well beyond that of Paul (see 1 Thess 4:12; 2 Cor 6:10; Phil 4:11f.) but also beyond that of Socrates and the Stoics, more dignified and more open to social relations (see, e.g., Diogenes Laertius, II, 24f., 27); not without reason did Plato call him "a Socrates gone mad" (ibid., VI, 54).

24. Diogenes Laertius, VI, 33, 45, 55, 60; for some of the strange episodes attributed to him, see VI, 32, 46.

25. Ibid., VI, 72.

26. In this sense the Pauline text is much nearer to that of Diogenes than it is to 4 Esdr 16:42-45 (see above, n. 18).

27. Diogenes Laertius, VI, 74-75, 77-78, 30-31.

gence between the content of his message and Paul's is irreconcilable, indeed it is implicitly polemical. If there has been an influence, it could have been mediated only from Stoicism, where Epictetus himself took "the Cynic" as an ideal of life,[28] but in a more rational and even more religious way.

28. In his works, Epictetus cites Diogenes the Cynic more often than any other philosopher (followed by Chrysippus); not counting the texts where he refers only to "the Cynic" as an ideal of life, he explicitly names Diogenes in the following passages: *Diatr.* I 24:6, 9; II 3:1; 13:24; 16:35; III 2:11; 21:19; 22:24, 57, 63, 80, 88, 91; 24:40, 64; 26:23; IV 1:30, 114, 152, 156; 7:29; 9:6; 11:21 *Man.* 15.

Chapter 12

Only Love Will Have No End.
A Reading of 1 Corinthians 13 in Its Various Senses

I wish at once to indicate the methodological intent that has governed my approach to 1 Cor 13: it consists of an exegetical reading of a syntagmatic character. I shall therefore not make a detailed analysis of the text but shall seek to perceive the overall meaning of this extraordinary passage, considered as a semantic whole.

Preliminaries

The first reaction I am conscious of on reading 1 Cor 13 is to ask, Why did Paul never write something like this on faith?

Since the Lutheran reformation, in fact, we habitually associate Paul and Paulinism to the absolute necessity, if not exclusivity, of faith in the occurrence of justification, so that now even Catholics admit that Luther was right when their German translation of Romans 3:28 adds the adverb *allein*, "alone," despite its absence in Greek, and the Italian Catholic version "Cei" does the same in the parallel, Gal 2:16. The appropriateness of my question is confirmed by a glance at a concordance to find the preference of Paul's vocabulary. The balance tips definitively toward faith. Indeed, taking the whole Pauline correspondence without trying to separate the inauthentic from the authentic, we find that the noun ἀγάπη, "love," recurs only 78 times, compared with 138 for πίστις, "faith," while the verb ἀγαπάω, "love," is present 32 times to 54 for πιστεύω, "believe." Then why on earth did Paul not write an encomium of faith as he did for love? Indeed, in 1 Cor 13:13 we actually read that faith is among the passing realities of Christian identity!

One first reply to the question could be derived from the missionary biography and theology of the Apostle. For the crucial theme of faith was actually fully formulated in Paul's mind only on the occasion of the crisis of the Church in Galatia, along with the formulation of the problem of the Law and its relationship to Christ. The idea was then fully developed in the later Letter to the Romans, which deepens the original tumultuous thought of Galatians. But this decisive stage of Paul's life came only after his sojourn in Corinth and his first letter to the Christians of that Church. But would it perhaps be legitimate to hypothesize that if Paul had had to write 1 Corinthians after Romans and Galatians, there would no longer have been such an ardent celebration of *agape?* Certainly not!

I firmly believe that the theological value of 1 Cor 13 remains intact and absolute, independently of the biographical and conceptual evolution of its author, unlike that of other elements of Paul's theology (as is probably the case with the concept of the Law, and especially of the delay of the parousia).

My assurance is based on two observations. One negative reason consists in the fact that even in the fervor of the antilegalistic polemic of Galatians and Romans, as we have said, Paul never wrote a literarily autonomous praise of the special character of faith. The other reason, positive, lies in the observation that even the Letter to the Romans uses the noun ἀγάπη and the verb ἀγαπάω just as much as the earlier letters. This is an evident indication that we are here dealing with a major, fundamental theme of Christian life and theology. *Agape* remained for Paul, and will always remain for us, that καθ' ὑπερβολήν ὁδός, "more excellent way" (1 Cor 12:31b) that he had wanted to show to his readers. And that remains true in the light of Gal 5:6 ("In Christ Jesus neither circumcision has any value nor uncircumcision, but faith, which works through *agape*"), where the exact relationship between the two entities is defined. From a Lutheran point of view there will be a tendency to point out that the works of love are not what define faith as a justifying faith, and that there remains a vast difference between the realm of God's free work on the one hand and that of moral works of humans on the other.[1] But surely Thomas Aquinas hit the mark when he put both together at the heart of the New Covenant, since on the one hand "through faith one belongs to the New Covenant" (ST I-II 106, 2 and 3), and on the other, "The Holy Spirit, when bringing about in us charity, which is the fullness of the law, is the New Covenant" (*Super 2 Cor 3:6*, ed. R. Cai 90).

1. See G. Ebeling, *Die Wahrheit des Evangeliums. Eine Lesehilfe zum Galaterbrief* (Tübingen, 1981) 333.

In any case, contrary to the criticism of L. Feuerbach,[2] for the Christian there is no such thing as faith without love, and love is not limited by faith but rather is powerfully nourished.

But for now let us leave off the comparison between faith and agape, necessary though it be in the general framework of Pauline theology, and attend to our specific passage.

While recognizing an intrinsic ability of 1 Cor 13 to speak incisively to any reader, no matter how ill-equipped, because of the innate, common pre-understanding of love, still we must not excuse ourselves from noting at least the principal historical-literary problems raised by this chapter.

I. Historical-literary problems

Text criticism does not have much to say, except that in v. 3 it is preferable (against BJ and the Italian Cei) to read καυχήσωμαι, "boast" (thus Nestle-Aland), rather than καυθήσωμαι, "be burned." Turning to lexical issues, especially on the basis of studies by C. Spicq, we know that the verb ἀγαπᾶν had undergone a change in meaning from classical Greek, where it has the vague meaning "revere with affection," "take care of," to the biblical Greek of the LXX and especially the New Testament, where it acquires the technical meaning "to love gratuitously and superabundantly." As for structure, this is not difficult to discern in 1 Cor 13; the articulation of the thought is not only evident but practically univocal, so that the judgment of Saint Thomas is still valid today: Paul wanted to show the preeminence of agape in three different ways: *quantum ad necessitatem* (vv. 1-3), *quantum ad utilitatem* (vv. 4-7), *quantum ad permanentiam* (vv. 8-13): "as to necessity, utility, and permanence" (see *Super 1 Cor.*, ed. R. Cai, 759).

A more problematic and even controversial issue is the present deployment of our passage. This exuberant section, which appears here quite unexpectedly and then leaves no trace on the following chapter, is supposed to be redactional; either it had originally been found elsewhere in the same letter,[3] or Paul has employed an already existing composition.[4] Now, in its present redaction, especially because of vv. 8-9, the passage does refer to its present context in chapters 12-14 and their treatment of

---

2. See L. Feuerbach, *The Essence of Christianity*, trans. G. Eliot (New York, 1957) 263–265.

3. Thus the commentaries of J. Weiss (Göttingen, 1910²); J. Héring (London, 1964 = Neuchâtel, 1959²); and the studies of W. Schmithals, *Gnosticism in Corinth*, trans. J. E. Steely (Nashville, 1971) 95, n. 23 = *Die Gnosis in Korinth*, FRLANT 48 (Göttingen, 1965) 89; W. Schenk, "Der 1 Korintherbrief als Briefsammlung," ZNW 60 (1969) 219ff.

4. Thus the commentaries of C. K. Barrett (London, 1971²), Chr. Senft (Neuchâtel, 1979).

the charismata that belong to the Corinthian community, especially glossolalia and prophecy. But noting the lack of any Christological reference,[5] we cannot help feeling that we see here the reutilization of a preredactional composition, belonging perhaps to the Jewish tradition or more likely to proto-Christian tradition, if not to Paul himself.

This last problem is intimately related to that of literary genre, to which we will now turn our attention more closely, since identifying the genre is important precisely for an understanding of the meaning of love for the Christian. What immediately strikes us in 1 Cor 13 is that the noun ἀγάπη always stands in the absolute form, with no grammatical modification either by adjective or phrase. Elsewhere Paul expresses himself quite differently: *agape* is termed "of God" (τοῦ θεοῦ: Rom 5:5; 8:39; 2 Cor 13:13); "of Christ" (τοῦ Χριστοῦ: Rom 8:35; 2 Cor 5:14; cf. John 15:9, 10); and even "of the Spirit" (τοῦ πνεύματος: Rom 15:30). Sometimes the Apostle speaks of *"my agape"* (1 Cor 16:24); of "your [sing.] *agape"* (Phlm 5:7); of "your [plur.] *agape"* (ὑμῶν: 2 Cor 8:24; Phil 1:9; 1 Thess 1:3; 3:6; τῆς ὑμετέρας: 2 Cor 8:8); "of each of you" (ἑνὸς ἑκάστου πάντων ὑμῶν: 2 Thess 1:3); of *agape* "toward one another" (εἰς ἀλλήλους: 1 Thess 3:12; cf. Gal 5:13); of *agape* "from us to you" (ἐξ ἡμῶν ἐν ὑμῖν: 2 Cor 8:7) or which is directed "to all the saints" (εἰς πάντας τοὺς ἁγίους: Eph 1:15; Col 1:4). At other times the term occurs in more abstract expressions, such as "the *agape* of truth" (2 Thess 2:10) or "the *agape* that is in Christ Jesus" (1 Tim 1:14; 2 Tim 1:13). And finally we point out two passages (Rom 13:8-9; Gal 5:14) in which it is compared to the Mosaic Law, which is completely summarized in the commandment of love of neighbor. As we see, then, in the Pauline discourse *agape* is richly described as belonging to various persons and as a characteristic mark of relations between persons.

Precisely in this we see the difference from 1 Cor 13, where *agape* is not modified in any way but is proposed in absolute form as a most precious value. Not that Paul never uses "agape" in unmodified grammatical form (Rom 12:9; 14:15; 1 Cor 4:21; 8:1; 2 Cor 2:4, etc.), but then we can immediately tell from the context how it is being understood; and at least it is never praised in itself, as in the present passage. Here it is raised to a unique and autonomous height, and actually personified: not only does it become the subject of a whole series of verbs (fifteen in vv. 4-7 alone), but three times in vv. 1-3 it expresses a hypothetical lack of love not with a simple verb, "If I do not love . . .," but periphrastically, "If I do not have love" (ἀγάπην δὲ μὴ ἔχω), thus isolating and emphasizing

5. Note the observation of H. Conzelmann, *1 Corinthians*, Hermeneia (Philadelphia, 1975) 220 = *Der erste Brief an die Korinther* (Göttingen, 1969) 261.

the concept of *agape* as a concept that can even be autonomous in reference to who it may be that possesses it, just as one might "have" or "not have" the Spirit of Christ (Rom 8:9), a treasure in vessels of clay (2 Cor 4:7), or someone in one's heart (Phil 1:7).

Now, it is completely inappropriate to identify our passage as a "paraenetic exhortation" or "didactic exposition,"[6] because the imperative (in contrast to the indicative) mode of the verb is never used, and also because there is nothing here of the epistolary style properly so called, understood as conversation with the recipients. Nor does the literary form of the text use the speech forms of canticle or hymn, as is often the case, since it lacks the techniques proper to poetic composition.[7] The literary genre of 1 Cor 13 is perceived especially through parallels to related passages of Greek and especially of Judeo-Hellenistic literature that sings the praises not of a personage but of the greatest virtue or of that which represents the greatest good for humanity. Thus, a fragment from Tyrtaeus celebrates manly ἀρετή as warlike "valor" placed at the service of the homeland (*Anth. lyr. gr.*, ed. E. Diehl, I, 15f.). The Alexandrine Book of Wisdom lauds Wisdom as of divine nature, more beautiful than the sun and superior to all riches (see Wis 7:7–8:1). In the apocryphal 1 Esdras LXX (3 Esdr Vg) we even read of competition among a series of eulogies of different realities: it begins with wine, passes on to the power of the sovereign, to that of woman, and ends with ἀλήθεια, "truth," which remains powerful forever, great and more powerful than any other thing (cf. 4:33-41). For his part, the great Alexandrian philosopher Philo offers praise to πόνος, that is, "hard labor," as "the first and greatest of goods, origin of every good and every virtue, . . . without which you will find nothing fine or beautiful in all that is done among mortals" (*De sacr.* 35; cf. 35-41).

Coming, then, more specifically to the subject of love, we note the eulogy of its various types. Plato celebrates ἔρως, or love of desire, "most beautiful and excellent . . . fairest and best leader . . . who bewitches the minds of all gods and mortals . . . midway between wisdom and ignorance," being the son of Expediency and Poverty (*Symp.* 197C, E, 203C, 204A; see also the middle-Platonic Maximus of Tyre, Or. 20:2; on the contrary, see the Jewish polemic in Pseudo-Phocylides, *Sent.* v. 194: "Eros is not a god but a passion that destroys all"). Aristotle, on the other hand, exalts φιλία, friendship or the love of benevolence, as "something not only necessary but also beautiful" (*Eth. Nic.* VIII 1:1155a), so much so that while

6. Thus C. Spicq, *Agapé dans le Nouveau Testament*, II (Paris, 1966³) 59.
7. We can say this even against an attempt to speak of "didactic rather than lyric poetry" (J. Héring, 135 [Engl.], 116 [Fr.]), considering the enormous formal difference from the didactic poem of Pseudo-Phocylides.

identifying δικαιοσύνη, "justice" (respect for law and equality), as "the most important of the virtues, more admirable than the morning star and the evening star" (ibid., V 1:1129b), he proclaims friendship to be still superior to this, since "when people are friends there is no need for justice, whereas when they are just, there is still need for friendship, and the highest level of justice is considered to consist in an attitude of friendship" (ibid., VIII 1:1155a; see its centrality in the thought of Empedocles, Epicurus, etc.; Plutarch, *Mor.* 478-492, wrote a tractate on fraternal love, *Peri philadelphias*).

Regarding *agape*, we know of only one brief encomium before the time of Paul; it is in the *Letter of Aristeas*, an apologetic piece expressing the Alexandrine Judaism of the second century before Christ; here it is defined as "God's gift" *(θεοῦ δόσις)*; if you possess it, "in it are included all other good things" (229: πάντα περιέχων ἐν αὐτῇ τὰ ἀγαθά; cf. Col 3:14).

Against this background, 1 Cor 13 is recognized precisely as a generous and solemn encomium of agape. But in addition to the form, we recognize all the importance of the love here celebrated. The first three verses underline the absolute necessity of agape; vv. 4-7, its intrinsic beauty and dignity; and vv. 8-13, its indomitable endurance. Truly, more could not have been said to proclaim the greatness of love. On this subject, surpassing the axiom of the Song of Songs 8:6 ("Agape is strong as death"), a rabbinic text can only add that this "brings freedom from death" (TB *Baba Batra* 10a).

II. The polysemeia of love: its various meanings

But here is the problem: Which love are we dealing with here? We will not yet reply exhaustively to the question, saying only that it is not the same as eros (the lexical root of which is totally absent from the New Testament) nor as simple friendship (of which the New Testament speaks in Jas 4:4, but in negative terms: "friendship with the world, which is enmity to God"). We can, of course, lament the absence in the New Testament canon of a positive evaluation of an authentic φιλία (but cf. John 15:15). Without a doubt, *agape* is much more. In Col 3:14 it is defined as σύνδεσμος τῆς τελειότητος, "bond of perfection," that is, not so much "perfect bond" but "bond that brings together all other virtues and so brings them to perfection."[8]

Now, regarding 1 Cor 13, it would be selling it far short to try to limit the reality of *agape* to the merely ethical concept of virtue, even the greatest virtue. It is true that the immediate context orients us to an understand-

---

8. See J. Gnilka, *Der Kolosserbrief,* HThKNT (Freiburg-Basel-Vienna, 1980) 197.

ing of *agape* as a relational attitude among the Christians of Corinth, and especially among the charisms possessed by that Church. Nevertheless, the literary genre of this passage, and consequently the tone that is so highly celebratory of *agape*, clearly breaks through the fabric of the context and raises the reality praised to a higher and universal value.

It is no exaggeration to say that here somehow all the threads of Paul's thought concerning love are pulled together. Now love, as we have observed, is proper to God and to Christ; it also goes out from Paul to his addressees and vice versa. If, then, *agape* is the absolute by which the Christian is identified, a phrase like that in v. 2b ("if I have not love I am nothing") does not refer only to horizontal love, so to speak, to love between humans. Indeed, a little earlier in the same letter the Apostle has assured, "The one who loves God is known by God" (1 Cor 8:3); and elsewhere he declares that the final root of what is new in Christians is the love with which God himself has loved us (see below), thus gathering in a theology like that of 1 John 4. And surely one cannot apply the concept of virtue to God!

The question, then, is now becoming clear: Who is the subject of the agape being praised, and who is the object? Expressed concisely, with no mystification, "Who loves whom?" It re-echoes the question posed by Socrates to his hearers, "When one loves another, who becomes the friend of whom? Does the lover become friend of the beloved? Or the beloved friend of the one who loves? Or is there no difference?" (Plato, *Lysis* 212AB). In our case the possibilities are greater, given precisely the rich theological (and not just human) complexity of what has become the object of praise.

There is an evident "polysemeia," ambiguity or variety of senses, in the Pauline concept of *agape*. And this is particularly true in our passage, rendering it not difficult but rich and profound. Borrowing a word from Paul Valéry, I would say that "the richness of a work consists in the number of senses or values it can assume while remaining itself."[9] The same can be said of 1 Cor 13: How many meanings or aspects or dimensions does this *agape* tolerate? Surely more than one. The very genre of encomium, which in some way absolutizes the value it celebrates, would lead us to this conclusion. Similarly, the wisdom extolled in the Book of Wisdom, the truth according to 1 Esdr LXX, hard labor in Philo of Alexandria, and Aristotle's friendship—all are values that are realized in various milieus and on different levels. Nor can one ever claim to have exhausted,

9. Paul Valéry, *Éloge de la virtuosité*, cited in R. Kieffer, *Le primat de l'amour. Commentaire épistémologique de 1 Corinthiens 13*, LD 85 (Paris, 1975) 9.

I don't say the intellectual understanding, but the profound existential commitment to such a reality. They are truly greater than we, since they touch the absolute. How much more is this true of the love of *agape*, which differs not only from eros, insofar as it is not moved by concupiscence, but also from friendship, since it is not motivated by any quality inherent in the one loved (which, according to Aristotle, can be what is good, what is pleasant, or what is useful).

But let us proceed in order. The text of 1 Cor 13 can be read on two major levels, the second of which will be the more complex.

III. Philosophical reading

In the first place, this passage could be read from a purely secular point of view, that is, prescinding from any confessional dimension. In more noble terms we could speak of a philosophical reading.

Now, unless one takes up the purely defensive position of solipsism, there is no one in the world but would join in the celebration of the fundamental value of love, which, according to the greatest of our Italian poets, "moves the sun and the other stars" (*Divina Commedia, Par.* XXXIII 145). And that, I should say, is from the point of view of the non-believer and from the perspective of a purely humanistic formation. According to L. Feuerbach as well, love is the secret essence of religion, if we take the latter as reduced to the moral; it unifies, heals wounds, and is the freedom that does not condemn.[10] And Eric Fromm, in his fine book *To Have or to Be?* explicitly attributes to love in the Pauline sense the characteristic of "giving up one's own ego," and so of freedom from all "egoboundedness" as the "condition for love and for productive being."[11]

Even the eschatological horizon of 1 Cor 13:8-13 could be reread in merely axiomatic terms (the ἔσχατον, "last thing," is the μέριστον, i.e., the "ultimate" in the perspective of becoming, and even "that which is greatest"), all the more so in that Paul, contrasting adulthood with childhood, and direct face-to-face vision with the indirect vision of the looking glass, exalts love as the ripe fruit in the development of the human individual, as the overcoming of all imperfect incompleteness (note ἐκ μέρους, "in part": vv. 9, 10, 12b), while elsewhere it is defined as the πλήρωμα, "fullness," of the law (Rom 13:10; cf. Gal 5:14). And indeed, according

10. See *The Essence of Christianity*, 247: but completely in antithesis to faith.
11. See Eric Fromm, *To Have or to Be*, 63, see 145–146: the Catholic Church, in contrast to Luther, has practiced the maternal principle of unconditioned love, as mercy and compassion, rather than the paternal principle of conditioned love, expressed by righteousness.

to Paul it is greater than hope (1 Cor 13:13). Love is not part of the *not yet* but of the *already;* already in this world it is the realized *eschaton.*

Finally, love can be understood only on the level of being, not of having, since it is not one possession among others but involves, defines, and realizes the person in his or her entirety.[12] And if Paul writes that one must "have" love, this means only that this makes "being" complete; indeed, if I don't have it, $οὐθέν εἰμι$ = "I am nothing" (13:2), where the indicative of $εἶναι$, "to be," is used not as a simple copulative but as a true verb in itself! And this formulation is formally even stronger than the already impressive declaration of 1 John 3:14: "One who does not love remains in death." Paul finds an equation like this convincing: Loving is equal to being; one who loves *is.* In comparison with Descartes, we could say that Paul's philosophical principle is not *Cogito, ergo sum,* but *Amo, ergo sum,* not "I think" but "I love, therefore I am" (cf. 1 Cor 8:3). But the axiom calls for further precision in view of the relational character of love, which can exist only between two or more persons. As R. Kieffer rightly suggests,[13] we should say, "I love, therefore we are." Constitutive of love, indeed, is lack of concern for self but concern for the other: "Love seeks not what is its own" (13:5b). It therefore not only gives consistency to me who loves, but gives substance and relief and importance to the one who is loved, and makes the other to exist fully before me. We see, then, that it supposes a relationship, but even more, it creates a communion; that is, it lives and prospers, and in fact simply exists in a community dimension.

However, all this reasoning is, from a Pauline viewpoint, still superficial. The Apostle is not philosophizing about love, and a secular approach to our passage would lose sight of the ultimate roots, and hence of the true motivations of *agape,* even if all we have thus far said remains valid.

IV. Christian reading

In the second place, and more properly, we must make a *specifically Christian reading,* which alone can fully account for the thematic content and for the author's intention. But on this level the density of the concept of agape is refracted more fully and offers us a much wider semantic spectrum. For as we have seen, the celebration of *agape* in absolute terms has left the field open to various applications. I intend now to define these, passing them one by one in review. To do so we must gather together

---

12. See Eric Fromm, *To Have or to Be,* 44–47.
13. See R. Kieffer, *Le primat de l'amour,* 7.

the various threads of the Pauline and the New Testament theology of love, recognizing that our passage has the authentic function of catalyzing the many theological components. So let us answer the earlier question, "Who loves whom?"

For clarity we distinguish the divine subject of *agape* from the human one.

1) To begin with, we must always remember that the *ultimate foundation of love* in a Christian perspective *is God*. In Johannine terms, indeed, "God is love" (1 John 4:8); in Pauline terms he is "God of love" (2 Cor 13:11). And before loving, Christians are loved: ἀγαπητοί θεοῦ, "beloved of God" (Rom 1:7), ἠγαπημένοι ὑπὸ κυρίου, "loved by the Lord" (2 Thess 2:13; cf. 1 Thess 1:4). Precisely this announcement constitutes the kernel of the *gospel* and causes it to be truly "good news"; indeed, "in all things we are more than victors because of the one who has loved us" (Rom 8:37). On the basis of this certainty the Apostle formulates a rhetorical question that already contains its own response: "If God is for us, who can be against us?" (Rom 8:31). And since "nothing can ever separate us from God's love" (Rom 8:39: subjective genitive!), it is surely in this context that we can understand the declaration of 1 Cor 13:8a: "Love never ceases." Only God's love is indefectible, always young, never unfaithful.

The love to which the Christian is called, then, has a strictly theological motivation, not psychological or even sociological. The Christian loves because urged and carried by a love much greater than self, by which he or she has already been invested, purified, empowered. As John writes, "If God has loved us, we also must love one another. . . . We love because he loved us first" (1 John 4:11, 19). It is the same thing that the king says to the pitiless servant: "Should not you also have had pity on your companion as I had pity on you?" (Matt 18:33). In point of fact, it is the love of God that brings the Christian into being. And if Paul in 1 Cor 13:2 writes, "If I have not *agape*, I am nothing," we cannot but think also, and above all, of the love with which God loves us, of that eternal affection with which God has had mercy on us (see Isa 54:8) and which calls into being what does not yet exist (see Rom 4:17).

From the point of view of faith, the philosophical principle enunciated above is changed into a passive formulation: *Cogitor*, indeed *Amor* [first person singular indicative present passive], *ergo sum*, "I am thought— I *am* loved, therefore I am!" (cf. Gal 4:9), or in the plural, *Amamur, ergo sumus*, "We are loved, therefore we are" (cf. Eph 2:4; 1 Pet 1:3). This love, which is displayed freely from above as a liberal overflowing of God's fullness (cf. Eph 2:4: "through his great love wherewith he has loved us") is the most extraordinary that one can conceive of, in comparison with the Greek eros, which is motivated by an emptiness that needs to be filled; note that A. Nygren has compared the two of them in a famous work, which despite some problems is always stimulating.[14]

At any rate, we are not talking about a love that is just vaguely divine; rather, love at this level is specifically Trinitarian. I do not intend here to consider the intra-Trinitarian relations of agape (cf. John 3:35; 17:24; Col 1:13), but those which the Trinity manifests *ad extra* and which become historical events. I shall do only a rough sketch. There are essentially two points at which the divine love becomes an event that touches our story: the Cross of Calvary and our baptism. The Apostle says, "God shows his love toward us because when we were still sinners Christ died for us" (Rom 5:8); and "The love of God has been poured out in our hearts through the Holy Spirit that is given to us" (Rom 5:5). From Calvary to our hearts it is the one God who acts, and God does so under the sign of one love in which there participate equally, though under different formal aspects, Christ and the Holy Spirit. And each of these three has something to do with love.

a) The expression "the *agape* of God" in 2 Cor 13:13, occurring in a Trinitarian formula, certainly means the *agape of God the Father* (and it is understood in such a sense in the alternative liturgical salutation at the beginning of Mass); whenever we read of the "agape of God in Christ Jesus" (Rom 8:39), it means the paternal love of God demonstrated through his Son.

b) But it is precisely the *love of Christ* that reveals the *agape* of God in history: it is Christ who concretely "has loved me and has given himself for me" (Gal 2:20). The subject of the fifteen verbs in 1 Cor 13:4-7, rather than *agape* personified, could rather be Christ himself: he is patient, is kind, is not envious, does not boast, etc., and has so demonstrated in the story of his passion. From this love of his nothing can separate us (see Rom 8:35), since it "holds us in its power" (συνέχει ἡμᾶς: 2 Cor 5:14; cf. *Letter of Aristeas* 229: above), and it "surpasses all understanding" (Eph 3:19).

c) Moreover, love is a *fruit of the Spirit*; indeed, it is the first of a whole series (Gal 5:22), and all the rest are contained in it. Also in Rom 15:30 Paul makes his exhortation to his addressees διὰ τῆς ἀγάπης τοῦ πνεύματος,

---

14. A. Nygren, *Eros and Agape* (Paris, 1962). It is Denis the Areopagite (*De divinis nominibus* IV, 12-14) who will make an interesting identification between Platonic eros and New Testament *agape*, attributing the former to God as well.

i.e., "through the love that comes from the spirit" (genitive of origin); *agape* thus has a pneumatic sense, and this is confirmed by the context of precisely the encomium of 1 Cor 13, which traces back all the manifestations of ecclesial life *to one and the same Spirit* (12:11).

And so as we read this passage we cannot restrict the viewpoint of our understanding to a purely human horizon, even the horizon of so-called supernatural anthropology. That would be to weaken, if not completely undermine, the roots of love, reducing to a single dimension a reality that by its nature rather shares the riches of God.

2) But if love is the greatest expression of life, it does not even exist unless it somehow demonstrates itself *on the level of daily experience*. The warning of 1 John 3:18 is a salutary warning: "Little children, let us not love with words nor with the tongue, but in deeds and in truth." Moreover, according to Paul this is the law of Christ: "Bear one another's burdens" (Gal 6:2; cf. John 13:34).

But here too we must proceed in order. For there are a variety of meanings also in the love of which the Christian is the subject—or better, a variety of directions.

a) In the first place, there is *love for God,* commonly called simply "love of God." But we must at once say that very little is said of this in the New Testament. Apart from the quotation of Deut 6:5 ("You shall love the Lord your God . . ."), cited by Jesus on the subject of the greatest of the commandments (Matt 22:37f. and parallels), there are not even ten appropriate texts to cite (see Rom 8:28; 1 Cor 2:9; 8:3; Jas 1:2; 2:5; 1 Pet 1:8; 1 John 5:3; cf. 2 Tim 4:8). It is not actually impossible that this type of love is present in 1 Cor 13; for in the phrase of v. 12b ("then I shall know just as I have been known") we perceive the typical nuance of the Hebrew verb *yāda',* which means "*to know* by personal experience"; moreover, there resounds in this the text of 8:3: "The one who loves God is known by God." But this love for God is scarcely presupposed at all times. In general, then, while the New Testament does not actually ignore this important aspect of Christian spirituality, which moreover belongs to every religion, there would almost seem to be a fear of the ambivalence. Indeed, though the so-called love of God can lead on the one hand to the highest mystical experiences,[15] it can also become an easy excuse either for savage fanaticism (see John 16:2) or for sluggish indolence.

No one has so clearly expressed this state of things as 1 John: "If one says, 'I love God' but hates one's brother, one is a liar; for if one does

---

15. See vol. 2, chap. 32.

not love the brother one sees, one cannot love God, whom one does not see'' (4:20). Therefore *love for others* is precisely the criterion by which to recognize love for God. Anyhow, this love for God is not the real reason for loving others but only a concomitant aspect, if not one that follows. The motive that attracts is quite other, as we read also in 1 John: ''In this is love, not that we loved God but that God loved us'' (4:10). And after writing ''If God loved us,'' John continues not that we must love God but that ''we also must love one another'' (4:11).

Thus we continually are *brought back to the original love proper to God,* which alone deserves our praise, indeed our thanksgiving and adoration. It is only this that stands at the origin of our identity as believers and as baptized. And God's demonstration of love in the life and death of Christ was, so to speak, the ''big bang'' that set the whole Christian universe in motion. Whatever we can do for others is only a sign of the propulsive force of what took place there, which will never dissipate through some phenomenon of entropy, unless it be only our lack of faith or our sloth. But if ''we believe in the love which God has for us'' (1 John 4:16), then truly nothing is impossible, and we will even be able to move mountains (cf. Matt 17:20).

Thus, the love that comes from God does not want so much to return where it was as to extend itself, to spread in every direction, like the rain which, according to the prophet, comes down from heaven and does not return there ''without having watered the earth and made it sprout and flourish, so as to give seed to the sower and bread to the eater'' (Isa 55:10).

Let us, then, pass to other aspects of *agape* of which the Christian is subject and which concern love of neighbor, according to the great commandment of Lev 19:18 (''You shall love your neighbor . . .''), which is cited far more often in the New Testament than the other commandment (Matt 5:43; 22:39 and parallels; Rom 13:9; Gal 5:14; Jas 2:8).

b) Christian love is called to be exercised especially *within the Church.* We must remember that 1 Cor 13 is inserted within a whole context that goes from chapter 8 to chapter 14 and that, having begun with an allusion to *agape* in 8:2 (''wisdom puffs up while love builds up''), deals with typical intra-ecclesial relationships, concerning offerings made to idols, and the Christian assembly.[16] Indeed, the neighbor who is closest to the Christian is the co-disciple, and it is these that Paul calls ''brothers in the faith'' (Gal 6:10: ''toward those of the household of the faith''). Here it is that the sincerity and magnanimity of love are in the first place measured, as the Apostle writes in Rom 12:9-13 and Phil 2:1-4, where the same

16. See C. Spicq, *Agape in the N.T.*, II, 56.

concepts as those of 1 Cor 13:4-7 re-echo in the form not of encomium but of direct paraenesis. But no New Testament writing so strongly insists as does the Letter to the Ephesians on the value and the need for agape for the sake of peace and unity in the Church.[17] And we have begun to ask whether the long and flourishing history of divisions among Christians does not depend essentially on a tragic deficiency of love on every side of the opposing fronts. The criterion of orthodoxy is perhaps not enough to keep the ecclesial community together, because it is a cold criterion and exactly the opposite of what *agape* demands (see 1 Cor 13:4-6), and so is likely to produce presumption and arrogance, and thus to ignore the exhortation to consider everyone else superior to oneself (Phil 2:4), as well as the example of Paul when he protests, "We do not want to lord it over your faith, but to cooperate with your joy" (2 Cor 1:24). We note, moreover, that the "nothing" about which 1 Cor 13:2 warns refers specifically to the Christian who has all faith so as to move mountains but has not love.

c) Finally the *agape* that Paul celebrates, which characterizes the behavior of the Christian, must *extend to all;* nor can it be otherwise, since it is surprisingly asked even for the enemies (see Matt 5:44; Rom 12:14). Here also the example and the stimulus come precisely from God, who "so loved the world as to give his only Son" (John 3:16). The lack of barriers or limits is already the measure of God's behavior, "who causes the sun to rise on the evil and the good and the rain to fall on the just and unjust" (Matt 5:45), and who above all, as we have noted, sent his Son for us while we were sinners (Rom 8:3; 5:8). After all, love for those who reciprocate it is not at all surprising (see Luke 6:32). But to love one who is different, distant, marginalized, who has nothing to give back—except perhaps curses—this is the love that bears the imprint of God, because this is exactly what God has done to us in Christ.

The Gospels are full of this kind of love: the publicans, the prostitutes, the unclean, the Samaritans, the children, the ill, the poor and with them the supposed rich—all are recipients of the love of Christ. And here more than ever love becomes attentive, concrete, particular, the opposite of all theory or ideology. Remember how Dostoyevsky's staretz Zosima cites the experience of a philanthropist: "The more I love humanity in general, the less I love men in particular,"[18] but Christ loved humanity in the individual.

---

17. See vol. 2, chap. 30.
18. F. Dostoyevsky, *The Brothers Karamazov*, trans. D. Magarshack (New York, 1982) 62 (I:2:4).

In conclusion, we can say that *agape* is the summary of the whole Christian mystery from its most deeply hidden theological foundations to its most tangible ethical fruits. From a certain point of view, it would not be inappropriate to seek to replace the Lutheran *sola fide*, ''by faith alone,'' with a more impartial *sola ἀγαπῇ* or *sola caritate*, ''by love alone,'' provided that this formula were exempt from any spiteful form of polemic or any extremism, which would be incompatible with love (cf. 1 Cor 13:4). After all, as our passage says, it is *agape* that ''believes all things and hopes all things'' (1 Cor 13:7).

Chapter 13

Adamic Christology and Anthropological Optimism in 1 Corinthians 15:45-49

The complexity of the Pauline passage 1 Cor 15:45-49 is well known. The lexicography, the literary structure, the pre-Pauline stage, the cultural background, the dialectical method of the Apostle, the various themes (cosmology, anthropology, Christology, eschatology), the level of the message are so many chapters that could demonstrate the originality and richness of this passage.[1] There is, of course, no lack of studies, even recent ones, though no comprehensive monograph exists dealing with all the problematic aspects.[2] Nor can this, obviously, be our intent in the present work. We limit ourselves to singling out an aspect of some importance concerning Pauline anthropology in vv. 45-49; but to do that let us allow some observations on the literary structure of the context, then passing on to the probable cultural background of Paul and of the Adam-Christ antithesis.

I. Observations on literary structure

In the whole long chapter 1 Cor 15 it is easy to perceive a first caesura after v. 34. It is evident from at least two things. First, we note with v.

---

1. Simply by way of example note what E. Norden (*Agnostos Theos. Untersuchungen zur Formengeschichte religiöser Rede* [Berlin, 1912; Darmstadt, 1971⁵]) admitted concerning the series of antithetic lines of equal length of the fragment vv. 42b-44a: "This suggests to me something similar in ancient classical prose" (356)!
2. Among the more recent offerings, see esp. B. Spörlein, *Die Leugnung der Auferstehung. Eine historisch-kritische Untersuchung zu 1 Kor 15* (Regensburg, 1971) esp. 103ff.; J. P. Versteeg, *Christus en de Geest* (Kampen, 1971) 43–96; K.-A. Bauer, *Leiblichkeit—das Ende aller Werke Gottes. Die Bedeutung der Leiblichkeit des Menschen bei Paulus* (Gütersloh, 1971) 89–106; L. Audet, "Avec quel corps les justes ressuscitent-ils? analyse de 1 Corinthiens 15,44" *Studies in Religion/Sciences Religieuses* 1 (1971) 165–177; R. Morissette, "La condition de ressuscité. 1 Corinthiens 15,35-39: structure littéraire de la péricope," *Bib* 53 (1972) 208–228; "L'expression 'sôma' en 1 Cor 15 et dans la littérature paulinienne," *RSPhTh* 56 (1972) 223–239; "L'antithèse entre le 'psychique' et le 'pneumatique' en 1 Corinthiens XV, 44 à 46," *RvSR* 46 (1972) 97–143.

35 an evident change of topic on the basic theme of the resurrection; if originally the author's interest was *the fact* (cf. v. 12), it now is the *modality* that takes the foreground (as underlined by the πῶς, "how," and the ποίῳ σώματι, "with what kind of body" of v. 35). Second, we note a change of style. The unexpected appearance of an interlocutor (τις, "someone"), who from the context does not seem very fictitious (see below) and raises the question at the beginning of the argument, closely recalls the procedure of the diatribe (cf. 1 Cor 6:12; 10:23; Jas 2:18) with the tone of its dialogue, rational and persuasive; an impressive parallel of similar questioning is found in *Apoc. Bar.* 49.[3]

A second caesura is evident after v. 49, no longer on the level of topic (which remains the modality of the resurrection) but rather on the literary procedure. We have now the solemn but obscure tone of apocalyptic (vv. 50-56): the formula τοῦτο δέ φημί, ἀδελφοί, "Now, this I say, brethren" (v. 50), was already used in 1 Cor 10:29 to introduce an important "revelation"; likewise suggestive of apocalyptic is the concept of μυστήριον, "mystery" (v. 51), now communicated (cf. 11:25; *I Hen.* 103:2), the "trumpet" (v. 52), and the midrash on death in vv. 54ff.[4]

The section of vv. 35-49 is, then, clearly isolable at both beginning and end. And it is precisely the literary structure that now interests us. Never thoroughly examined, it was first studied organically by R. Morissette in 1972.[5] He claims to find in our passage (and we think rightly so) an example of rabbinic argumentation *qal waḥômer*, i.e., *a minore ad maius*, "argumentation from the lesser to the greater," where the proof is based not on Scripture but on reason. The main texts called in for proof are *TB Sanh* 90b (two examples); *TB Kethubb* 111b; *Midr Qoh* 1:10 (27b), where we find the same comparison of a seed of grain as in 1 Cor 15:36-38.

The procedure has three stages: it begins with a question; then there is a response based on experiences of daily life; it ends *a fortiori* in favor of the article of faith under discussion. Thus in 1 Cor 15: v. 35 raises the question; vv. 36-38 and 39-41 propose two examples drawn from the world (the grain of wheat and then the different created bodies); finally vv. 42-49 conclude *a fortiori* that there exists a σῶμα πνευματικόν, "spiritual body"

3. "[1] Nevertheless, I will again ask of Thee, O Mighty One. . . .[2] In what shape will those live who live in thy day? Or how will the splendour of those who (are) after that time continue?[3] Will they then resume this form of the present, and put on these entrammelling members, which are now involved in evils, and in which evils are consummated? Or wilt thou perchance change these things which have been in the world as also the world?" (R. H. Charles, ed., *The Apocrypha and Pseudepigrapha of the Old Testament in English*, II [Oxford, 1913] 508).
4. R. Morissette, "Un midrash sur la Mort (1 Cor XV, 54c à 57)," RB 79 (1972) 161–188.
5. See the article cited: "La condition ressuscité . . ."

(v. 44b), and that we "will bear the image" of the heavenly man (v. 49). Now according to Morissette, "the *a fortiori* argument announced in v. 42a, the central statement of which is contained in 44b, is first of all prepared in a fragment of hymnic character through a gradation that culminates in the distinction and opposition of the two σώματα, 'bodies' (vv. 42b-44a); this is developed with the motif of the two men and groups of men under the form of a midrash on the basis of Gen 2:7 (vv. 45-48); and it is finally *resumed*, enriched by all the elements brought in the preceding lines (v. 49)."[6]

It is our opinion, however, that Morissette levels off the passage excessively, perceiving in it a grand and articulated argument *qal waḥômer*, and being satisfied with only pointing out "Christian retouches of the rabbinic material."[7] The author seems to bypass the importance of the biblical citation in v. 45, which marks vv. 45-49 off from the preceding vv. 35-44, introducing a new kind of *qal waḥômer*, no longer rational but rather biblical.

We therefore distinguish clearly:

1) *A rabbinic argumentation* qal waḥômer, *of rational character in vv. 35-44*, climaxing in v. 44b: "if there is a σώμα ψυχικόν, " 'psychic' body / 'soul' body," there is also a πνευματικόν, "pneumatic," one." With regard to this, all that Morissette writes is valid.

2) *An allegorizing based on Gen 2:7 in vv. 45-49*. The biblical text in the LXX reads thus:

καὶ ἔπλασεν ὁ θεὸς τὸν ἄνθρωπον χοῦν ἀπὸ τῆς γῆς
καὶ ἐνεφύσησεν εἰς τὸ πρόσωπον αὐτοῦ πνοὴν ζωῆς
καὶ ἐγένετο ὁ ἄνθρωπος εἰς ψυχὴν ζῶσαν

And God formed man, earth from the soil
and breathed into his face the breath of life
and the man became a living soul.

On the basis of this text it is easy to recognize in vv. 45-49 at least three differences compared with the preceding verses. In the first place, as al-

---

6. Art. cit., 224. [Translator's note: The general principle in this translation is to use language that is not gender specific in passages which integrate Pauline insights into our theology and spirituality, but to reflect Paul's own use of gender in describing Paul's thought. It hardly seemed honest in attempting to do a nuanced description of Paul's theology to use language which would suggest that the Apostle had thought through the issues to which our contemporaries have with justice forcefully called our attention.—T. P. W.]

7. Art. cit., 224–227: for vv. 35-44 the author studies various lexical elements, besides the supposed pre-Pauline hymnic fragment of vv. 42b-44a, whereas for vv. 45-49 the author limits himself to "the evidence itself" (224).

ready indicated, there is a difference of literary procedure: Paul no longer reasons by basing himself on facts of universal human experience but by appealing to Scripture (note the opening of v. 45: οὗτος καὶ γέγραπται, "Thus also it is written"), from which he derives (again through a passage *a minore ad maius*) the attributes of the final Adam, or the existence of a new type of humanity linked to him.[8] The literary technique can be variously identified as a "paraphrase after the manner of the targums"[9] (but this is true only of the technique of biblical citation—if at all) or better yet, as a "midrash,"[10] thus accounting for the peculiarity of the whole citation of vv. 45-49; indeed, the Genesis text, retouched as it is, stands at the beginning of a new logical development. The Pauline allegorizing manipulates the Old Testament past and makes it the foundation of three contrasts: (1) a "last Adam" corresponds to the "first man" (vv. 45-47: parallelism of the founder of the family); (2) all the "heavenly" correspond to all the "earthly" (vv. 48-49: parallelism of the descendants); (3) and the Christ who becomes a "life-giving spirit" refers to the θεός, "God," who breathes in the "breath of life" (v. 45: parallelism of the two agents, with a value more properly Christological than it has in Genesis; see below).

In the second place, there is a difference of vocabulary. In vv. 45-49 there emerge expressions that are absolutely new compared with vv. 35-44. Thus nouns: ἄνθρωπος, "man" (three times; in vv. 35-44 it occurs only in passing in v. 39, while σῶμα, "body," predominated with nine recurrences but is completely absent in vv. 45-49; for v. 46 see below); πνεῦμα, "spirit" (once in v. 45, in a Christological sense); εἰκών, "image" (twice in v. 49, referring to the two Adams); similarly with regard to the adjective χοϊκός, "earthly" (four times in vv. 47-49; *hapax legomenon* in the New Testament), contrasted with ἐπουράνιος, "heavenly" (three times in vv. 48-49, but see also ἐξ οὐρανοῦ, "from heaven," in v. 47). This last adjective was already used in neuter plural in v. 40 opposite ἐπίγεια, "earthly," but in a cosmological sense modifying σώματα, "bodies." But here it is used anthropologically and in a perspective of salvation history, where the pattern is not spatial (v. 40: heaven-earth) but rather temporal (v. 45:

---

8. The critics do not favor the opinion of C. F. Burney, *The Aramaic Origin of the Fourth Gospel* (Oxford, 1926) 43–48, according to which the whole v. 45 (therefore including the more directly Christological part) would be a quotation derived from a hypothetical pre-Pauline Christian collection of *testimonia* composed for dialogue with rabbinism. See W. D. Davies, *Paul and Rabbinic Judaism* (London, 1965³) 43–44; Gen 2:7 "was not a favorite [text] for discussion among the rabbis and the New Testament only makes use of it at this point" (ibid., 44). See also A. Feuillet, *Le Christ sagesse de Dieu* (Paris, 1966) 327–329.

9. Thus J. Jeremias, art. *Adam*, TDNT 1:142; K.-A. Bauer, op. cit., 98.

10. Thus R. Scroggs, *The Last Adam. A Study in Pauline Anthropology* (Philadelphia, 1966) 86; R. Morissette, art. cit., 224–228.

πρῶτος-ἔσχατος, "first/last"; v. 46: πρῶτον-ἔπειτα, "first/then"; v. 47: πρῶτος-δεύτερος, "first/second"; v. 49: ἐφορέσαμεν-φορέσομεν, "bore/will bear"). All this obviously means a change of theme.

Indeed, in the third place we must note a change of argument. If the "pointe" of the preceding section was to demonstrate the transfigured corporality of those who rise from the dead (note the σῶμα πνευματικόν, "spiritual body"), now this theme, which remains in the background, is enriched by a new and important refinement: the accent falls on the chronological succession rather than the qualities of the risen.[11] This is confirmed by the substitution of the term ἄνθρωπος, "man," for σῶμα, "body," explicable both with the citation of Gen 2:7 and with the new Christological perspective—elements that favor a shifting of attention simultaneously toward the human person globally understood according to nature and toward the totality of human beings with their collective destiny. This fact finds its axiomatic expression in v. 46, which will therefore be considered separately.

3) *The position of v. 46.* This has always been troublesome because of its position in the present text, which is, moreover, firmly attested in the manuscript tradition. Already J. Weiss[12] proposed placing v. 46 before v. 45; A. E. J. Rawlinson[13] rather considered v. 45 a parenthesis; and W. Schmithals[14] thinks that v. 46 is a simple gloss, attributable to an anti-Gnostic disciple of Paul; others finally are content to identify it as a *Zwischenbemerkung* "digression."[15] In fact, this does seem to break the logical train of thought of the discourse, which links v. 45 to vv. 47ff., and that on two bases, lexical and grammatical. The antithesis ψυχικόν-πνευματικόν, "psychic/pneumatic," actually belongs to v. 44, and so to the section vv. 35-44 (i.e., the *qal waḥômer* based on reason); v. 45 begins a new speech with the dominant use of the adjectives χοϊκός-ἐπουράνιους, "earthly/heavenly." Moreover, the two neuters τὸ ψυχικόν and τὸ πνευ-

11. Therefore we agree only in part with H. Conzelmann: "The corporeality of the future existence is not the point of the exposition [in vv. 35ff.], but its self-evident presupposition. It is not in itself theological; it *becomes* theological *in actu* at particular moments, e.g., against spiritualistic narrowing down of hope, against exclusion of the world from the realm of God's sovereignty and thus against every form of Gnosticism or fanaticism, against direct desecularization of the way of salvation, etc." (*1 Corinthians*, Hermeneia [Philadelphia, 1975] 280).
12. *Der erste Korintherbrief* (Göttingen, 1910) ad loc.; thus J. Jervell, *Imago Dei: Gen 1,25f im Spätjudentum, in der Gnosis und in den paulinischen Briefen* (Göttingen, 1960) 260, n. 311.
13. *The New Testament Doctrine of Christ* (London, 1926 [1949³]) 129, n. 1.
14. *Gnosis in Corinth*, trans. J. E. Steely (Nashville, 1971) 170, n. 81 = *Die Gnosis in Korinth. Eine Untersuchung zu den Korintherbriefen* (Göttingen, 1965) 160.
15. Thus E. Brandenburger, *Adam und Christus* (Neukirchen, 1962) 74; K.-A. Bauer, op. cit., 100.

ματικόν fit badly with the new reasoning of vv. 45, 47-49, where everything is in the masculine, whether singular or plural.[16]

Even so, v. 46 is attracted to the midrashic section of vv. 45ff. through the adverbial succession πρῶτον-ἔπειτα, "first/then," which conforms to every one of vv. 45, 47, 48, 49, where with more or less evidence the temporal order is regularly reasserted.

We can therefore say that v. 46 is characterized by elements that identify it as a literary transition. At the same time, though, it seems to be an axiomatic statement (note the neuter adjectives used as substantives), acting as a logical watershed between the sections vv. 35-44 and 45-49. This is all the more true in that v. 46 carries a clearly (and universally acknowledged) polemic coloring. This is evidenced by the double ἀλλά, "but rather," and the clear temporal concatenation πρῶτον-ἔπειτα, which would exclude τὸ πνευματικόν from first place to relegate it (with repetition of the same word) to a second period, making room for τὸ ψυχικόν as that which identifies the first stage of a succession, an order that is dear to Paul's heart. The polemic vein of the axiom then colors the whole section vv. 45-49. What is important is to identify to what the Apostle refers.

II. The cultural background of vv. 45-49

It is hard to believe that Paul is turning to opponents who are purely hypothetical or distant from those whom he is concretely addressing; 1 Corinthians is not an encyclical, nor does it deal with abstract general problems of the vast first-century world. Without a doubt it is at Corinth that we must seek his anonymous interlocutors. Now, as is evident especially in 1:18-3:3 (where we have the antithesis ψυχικός-πνευματικός), Paul is facing two fronts: on the one side the Greeks (for whom Christ is "foolishness"), and on the other the Jews (for whom Christ is a "scandal"; see 1:22-23). It seems that in 15:45-49 as well, both these religious-cultural contexts are understood, but now they are no longer distinct, because in some way on the anthropological level they both share a doctrine of πρῶτον τὸ πνευματικόν, "first the spiritual," as we shall see.[17]

16. Now, it hardly seems possible to associate the two adjectives with v. 44, giving the τό, "the," the value of an anaphoric article, considering the too great distance between the two verses; thus with W. Schmithals, op. cit., 149, and J. Jervell, op. cit., 260, we maintain that the two neuter words (adjectives used as substantives) do not refer to the σῶμα, "body," of v. 44, but rather have the broader value of identifying a sphere, time, way of being. See also B. Schneider, "The Corporate Meaning and Background of 1 Cor 15:45b," CBQ 29 (1967) 144-161, 150.

17. Since J. Weiss, op. cit., 345, it has been common to maintain that in chapter 15 Paul is opposed on two fronts: on one side the Greek denial of any resurrection of the dead favoring a misunderstood "spirituality," but on the other a rabbinism that is too crassly material

1) *Philo and Gnosticism.* The Pauline polemic is directed not so much against classical Greek anthropology (which in 2 Cor 4:16–5:8 the Apostle even seems partially to adopt; see below, chap. 14),[18] as primarily against certain contemporary Greek-speaking contexts that are, however, under Jewish influence. This is the case with Philo the Jew and, according to many authorities, Gnosticism in general.[19] Not only that, but Philo himself is not alien to certain "Gnostic affinities";[20] for this reason, while noting certain differences, we will consider them together.

As for Philo himself, it is probable that if not Paul himself[21] at least the Corinthians were aware of the general ideas of the Alexandrine philosopher, mediated through the preacher Apollo, who was also from Alexandria, "an eloquent man well-versed in Scripture" (Acts 18:24f; cf. 19:1; 1 Cor 3:4-5; 16:12).[22] Now, in Philo we find at least two texts in which, by comparing and contrasting Gen 1:26 and Gen 2:7, he proposes the distinction between two types of human beings:

> There are two types: the one is heavenly, the other earthly (διττὰ ἀνθρώπων γένη ὁ μὲν γάρ ἐστιν οὐράνιος ἄνθρωπος, ὁ δὲ γήϊνος). The heavenly one is made in the image of God, having no part of what is mortal and earthly. The earthly one, however, was made of scattered matter, which [Scripture] calls "earth" (χοῦν). But [Scripture] does not say that the heavenly one "was formed" (πεπλάσθαι) but that it was "modeled" (τετυπῶσθαι) in the image of God, while the earthly is "something formed" (πλάσμα) by the artist, but not a "creation" (γέννημα) (*Leg. all.* 1:31-32).

In this first text we see not so much the temporal succession of the two as the simple distinction between them. The other passage seems quite different:

---

concerning the manner of the resurrection. See also J. H. Wilson, "The Corinthians Who Say There Is No Resurrection of the Dead," ZNW 59 (1968) 90–107.

18. Still, Paul does pass judgment on that whole line of Greek thought that since Heraclitus (Diels-Kranz, frag. 62) so exalts the human person as to make of the human a "corporeal and mortal god" and correspondingly defines God as "an incorporeal and mortal man" (see also *Poimandres*, 25); see the definition of the historian Dio Cassius: "a product not earthly but heavenly" (φυτὸν οὐκ ἔγγειον ἀλλά οὐράνιον: Hist., fr. 28:3; but 1 Cor 15:47 explicitly denies that the human being is heavenly). See J. Pepin, *Idées grecques sur l'homme et sur Dieu* (Paris, 1971) esp. 34–51.

19. For this question see McL. R. Wilson, *Gnosis and the New Testament* (Oxford, 1968) 20f., 25–27. See also J. Jonas, *Lo gnosticismo* (Turin, 1973 = 1991).

20. M. Simon, "Éléments gnostiques chez Philon," in *Le origini dello gnosticismo. Colloquio di Messina 13-18 aprile 1966*, ed. U. Bianchi (Leiden, 1967) 359–376, 366.

21. For the relationship of Paul to Philo, see H. St. J. Thackeray, *St. Paul and Contemporary Jewish Thought* (London, 1900); J. Daniélou, *Philon d'Alexandrie* (Paris, 1958) 199–203.

22. "Certainly Corinthian Christians would be familiar with Philo's distinction between the heavenly and the earthly man, and would doubtless be tempted to identify their Lord with

There is a great difference between the man now formed [Gen 2:7] and the one first created in the image of God *(διαφορὰ παμμεγέθης ἐστὶ τοῦ τε νῦν πλασθέντος ἀνθρώπου καὶ τοῦ κατὰ εἰκόνα θεοῦ γεγονότος πρότερον)*. Indeed, the formed one is endowed with senses and participates in a certain quality, composed of body and soul, man or woman, of mortal nature. But the one in the image (of God) is an idea or kind or seal, intelligible, incorporeal, neither male nor female, of immortal nature (*Opif. mund.* 134).

Certain authors, despite the relationship *πρότερον-νῦν,* "first/now," maintain that here Philo means a pure ideal hierarchy, a logical and not temporal succession.[23] But Philo does not divide present human beings two ways, heavenly-earthly; furthermore, though considering the celestial as a Platonic idea with exemplary value, we must recognize that the earthly would be a pretty poor copy, since the qualities are antithetical. The problem is complex (e.g.: Is the origin of this conception Platonic or Jewish?), and it is not up to us to resolve it.[24] For us now it is enough to note that in Philo there is a distinction between the two types, and that the mention of the heavenly always precedes that of the earthly.

Gnosticism for its part is more insistent on the temporal succession. We cannot here plunge into the question of Gnostic origins. Here it is enough to note that objectively the polemic of 1 Cor 15:46 *can* be pertinent to certain Gnostic texts, and that consequently the existence at Corinth of certain similar positions was possible; if, then, the literary texts of Gnosticism are later than the Pauline correspondence, this is of appropriate interest, since the Apostle's polemic actually may have had in mind certain preliterary contents. Characteristic of these circles are the various speculations about the figure of a divine *"Ἄνθρωπος- Urmensch-*"primal man," who is prior to the earthly man, into whom he fell.[25] We refer hcrc to two types of text.

First of all, the *Corpus Hermeticum* offers us a type of gnosis, as yet completely un-Christianized. Especially characteristic is the anthropology

the former, in an attempt to accommodate their faith to contemporary thought" (W. D. Davies, op. cit., 52); contra H. Conzelmann, op. cit., 287.

23. See R. Scroggs, op. cit., 115–122; J. P. Versteeg, op. cit., 73; R. Morissette, "L'antithèse," 119. "The whole exposition of Philo on Genesis 1 and 2 is characterized by a de-historicization" (J. Jervell, op. cit., 66). See also A. J. M. Wedderburn, "Philo's 'Heavenly Man,' " NT 15 (1973) 301–326, esp. 303–306.

24. See also E. Bréhier, *Les Idées philosophiques et religieuses de Philon d'Alexandrie* (Paris, 1925²) 121–126.

25. But see the brief critical observations on the configuration of this myth in H. Conzelmann, op. cit., 284–286. See also B. A. Pearson, *The Pneumatikos-psychikos Terminology in 1 Cor. A Study in the Theology of the Corinthian Opponents of Paul and Its Relation to Gnosticism,* dissertation, Harvard University, 1968 (see HThR 61 [1968] 646f.).

of *Poimandres* 12-23, where the archetype-Man, by uniting himself to nature, gives origin to the present actual man:

> Nature received the *breath* (*τὸ πνεῦμα:* in a cosmological sense) from the ether and produced the bodies according to the human form. And thus *the Man, from life and light became soul and intellect (ὁ δὲ Ἄνθρωπος ἐκ ζωῆς καὶ φωτὸς ἐγένετο εἰς ψυχὴν καὶ νοῦν) (Corp. Herm.* 1:17).

> It is because of this that, alone among the living beings on earth, man is twofold: mortal as to the body, but immortal *as to the essential Man (διὰ τὸν οὐσιώδη ἄνθρωπον)* (1:15).

The literary affinity of the Greek text *Corp. Herm.* 1:17 with 1 Cor 15:45a is striking.[26] But significantly characteristic of the Pauline text is the absence of the stage before the *ἐγένετο,* ''became,'' i.e., the state of *ζωὴ καὶ φῶς,* ''life and light,'' from which man would have fallen; on the contrary, for the biblical text ''life'' is combined simultaneously with ''soul'' (note the *ψυχὴ ζῶσα,* ''living soul''). This all depends on the fact that for Paul the speech is historicizing, while in the *Corp. Herm.* it is mythologizing (see below).

In the second place, we quote from the *Book of the Naasenes* (Hippolytus, *Confut.* V. 7:2–9:9), in which Gnostic speculation explicitly uses Judeo-Christian data.[27] In 7:7 we read:

> In order that *the great man from above (ὁ μέγας ἄνθρωπος ἄνωθεν)* be completely reduced to servitude . . . he was also given a soul *in order that by means of the soul he should suffer (ἵνα διὰ τῆς ψυχῆς πάσχῃ),* and that the creature of the great, most beautiful, perfect man be punished in servitude;

and thus man finds himself ''cast down from the first-born superior Adamas . . . *into an earthly work of oblivion (εἰς πλάσμα τῆς λήθης, τὸ χοϊκόν—* 7:36); so the necessity of *a superior heavenly spiritual generation (ἡ γένεσις*

---

26. Their comparison suggests the following parallelism:

1 Cor 15:45a	Corp. Herm. 1:17
ἐκ ζωῆς καὶ φωτὸς	
ἐγένετο	ἐγένετο
ὁ πρῶτος ἄνθρωπος Ἀδὰμ	ὁ Ἄνθρωπος
εἰς ψυχὴν ζῶσαν.	εἰς ψυχὴν καὶ νοῦν.
From life and light	
The first man, Adam,	the Man
became	became
a living soul.	soul and intellect.

27. See the commentated edition in *Testi gnostici cristiani,* ed. M. Simonetti (Bari, 1970) 29–50 [also W. Scott, *Hermetica,* 4 vols. (Oxford, 1926–36)—T. P. W.].

ἡ πνευματιϰή, ἡ ἐπουράνιος, ἡ ἄνω) is justified'' (8:41). In this writing we find a much greater devaluation of human ψυχή, "soul," than in the *Corp. Herm.*[28] Still, the judgment on the "future" of man is identical; moreover, we meet the adjective τὸ χοϊϰόν "earthy," as in 1 Cor 15:47-49, but with the chronological order reversed. The theme of the original fall is evident, and this leads us to consider the Jewish background.

2) *Apocalyptic and rabbinic Judaism.* In Judaism the pattern that Paul opposes ("first the pneumatic, then the psychic") is still more clear because it is based on the biblical passage of original sin (see Gen 3). This has led in various circles to ever broader and more inquisitive speculations on the condition of the prelapsarian Adam compared with his state after the fall. For documentation on the subject, particularly pertinent are the following apocryphal texts: *Slav. Hen.* 30:8ff.; *Vita Ad.* 4:2; 12-17; *Jub.* 2:14; 3:15; *2 Bar.* 23:4; the same is true of certain rabbinic texts: *Gen. Rab.* 8:10; *Lev. Rab.* 20; *Sifr. Deut* 1:10; *TB Sanh.* 38a; *Baba Batra* 58a; *Pirq. R. Eliezer* 13; *Pesiq.* 36b, etc.[29] What appears from these texts we repeat in the words of W. D. Davies:[30]

> Adam as created by God was no ordinary man; he was of an enormous size extending from one end of the earth to the other, and from heaven to earth. At the fall he was reduced to 100 yards, the first authority to attribute this length to him being R. Meir (c. A.D. 150). Although there is nothing to that effect in Genesis, Adam was conceived as being created immortal, one day in his life might correspond to a thousand years. Adam was also possessed of a glory derived from God himself. There was an indescribable brightness in his face, the brightness of the sole of his foot darkened the Sun, how much brighter was his face! The light which he possessed enabled him to see throughout the world. His difference from ordinary mortals is emphasized by his bisexuality. Moreover Adam was worthy of the worship of angels. They had been "best-men" at his wedding and had served him at table. Finally, the wisdom of Adam was continually praised. His wisdom exceeded that of the angels in that he was able to name all the beasts of the earth, while the angels could not. The First Man was therefore altogether glorious; his fall was correspondingly disastrous.

28. See M. Simonetti, " 'Psyché' e 'psychikos' nella gnosi valentiniana," *RivStLettRel* 2 (1966) 1–47.

29. See H.-L. Strack and P. Billerbeck, *Kommentar zum Neuen Testament aus Talmud und Midrasch* (Munich, 1965⁴) II 702; III 325; IV 887, 940, 947.

30. Op. cit., 45–46. See also J. Jervell, op. cit., 96ff.; E. Brandenburger, op. cit., 135ff.

On this basis we understand the promise at Qumran of a reintegration of all the elect in "all the glory of Adam" (*kwl kbwd 'dm:* thus in *1 QS* 4:23; *1 QH* 17:15; *CD* 3:20; *4QpPs* 37 3:1f; *test. Lev.* 18:10-13; cf. Sir 49:16).[31]

On top of these conceptions we have the doctrine of the "two spirits" (see esp. *1QS* 3:13-4:26),[32] such as that of the two *yeṣer* = "inclinations" (see, e.g., *test. As.* 1; *Gen. Rab.* 9; *Tanh. ber 4b*).[33] It is sufficient for us here to simply note this thematic in order to say that following its lead certain Jewish circles sometimes arrive at exaggerated forms of moral determinism.[34]

III. The last Adam (becomes) life-giving spirit

The Pauline expression ὁ ἔσχατος Ἀδάμ, "the last Adam" (v. 45b), is certainly original and without comparison.[35] If the corresponding antithetical rabbinic expression *'adam hari'shôn* can also be translated "the first man," the Pauline expression cannot have a simple, vague anthropological meaning (see the expression of v. 47b: ὁ δεύτερος ἄνθρωπος, "the second man") nor all the less only futurological. It is true that in our whole passage the name of Christ never appears; however, the "last Adam" cannot but refer to him, and so have a characteristic Christological and hence historical dimension. Indeed, such a meaning is supported by the polemical intention of v. 46 (where the postposition of the "pneumatic" to the "psychic" can be understood only on the basis of faith in Christ), by the motif of the resurrection (which throughout chapter 15 begins with that

31. This line of speculation finds a continuation in the Christian (Judeo-Christian) world through the *Pseudo-Clementines*, where Adam also has a universal knowledge, is immortal, already has the "spirit of Christ" and every kind of material benefits (see *Hom.* 3:18, 20; 8:10).

32. See A. Dupont-Sommer, "L'instruction sur les deux Esprits dans le 'Manuel de Discipline,'" RHR 142 (1952) 5-35; J. Daniélou, "Une source de la spiritualité chrétienne dans les manuscrits de la Mer Morte: la doctrine des deux Esprits," *Dieu Vivant* 25 (1953) 127-136; M. Treves, "The Two Spirits of the Rule of the Community," RQ 3 (1961) 449-452; J. Light, "An Analysis of the Treatise of the Two Spirits in DSD," *Scripta Hierosolymitana* IV (Jerusalem, 1965²) 88-100.

33. See Strack-Billerbeck, op. cit. IV 466-483 (Excursus 19: "Der gute und der böse Treib"); G. F. Moore, *Judaism* 3 vols. (Oxford, 1927) 1:480ff.; W. D. Davies, op. cit., 20ff.

34. See J. Murphy-O'Connor, "La 'Vérité' chez Saint Paul et à Qumran," RB 72 (1965) 29-76, esp. 65-66 = "Truth: Paul and Qumran," in *Paul and Qumran* (London, 1968), reissued as *Paul and the Dead Sea Scrolls* (New York, 1990) 179-230, esp. 218-219. Concerning the *yeṣer harā'*, for example, apparently it was older in man than the *yeṣer tôb*: "The evil impulse is 13 years older than the good impulse: from the mother's bosom this grows little by little with man. . . . After 13 years the good impulse is born" (*Aboth* of R. Nathan 16); see also Sir 15:14. Still, aspects of optimism are found in 4 Esdr 4:30-31; *Sif. Lev.* 5:17.

35. See F. Schiele, "Die rabbinischen Parallelen zu I Kor 15:45-50," ZWTh 42 (1899) 20-31; Strack-Billerbeck, op. cit. III 477f. Alongside the frequent rabbinic expression *'adam hari'shôn* ("first Adam"), only later, in a medieval tractate, do we meet that Jewish opinion whereby the "Last Man/Adam" is the Messiah: *h'dm h'hrwn hw'hmshyh* (F. Schiele, art. cit., 29).

of Christ), and above all by the explicit contrast of v. 22 ("As in Adam all die, so also in Christ all will come to life"; cf. Rom 5:12-21).[36] Now, the identification of Christ as the "last Adam" or "second man" undoubtedly has repercussions on the conception of man. Precisely for that reason we must investigate the anthropological implications. But first we must study the identification in itself along with its pneumatic quality.

1) *The value of Gen 2:7 for "psychic-pneumatic" terminology.* The use of the adjective ψυχικός, "psychic," in the New Testament is not only rare but is proper to Pauline language: 1 Cor 2:14; 15:44 (twice), 46.[37] Moreover, the Apostle always contrasts the adjective with πνευματικός, "pneumatic." But the resulting antithesis is always different. In 1 Cor 2:14 ("The psychic man does not accept the things of the Spirit of God . . . but the pneumatic judges all things") we find opposition between two categories of persons existing simultaneously in the present and characterized by opposite attitudes toward divine revelation. But in 1 Cor 15:44, 46 the contrast is between two anthropological conditions that are successive rather than coexistent, so the ψυχικόν is now not a valid label for a grouping of part of humanity but is a universal description without exception. For this reason, too, we believe that our adjective does not have the whole pejorative sense here that it has in the first text (see below). Moreover, in 15:44, 46 the contrast seems to be conditioned by the character of commentary, and hence by the presence of the citation of Gen 2:7. We conclude this both from the impossibility of finding the origin of such terminology elsewhere[38] and from the particularly solemn formula οὕτως καὶ γέγραπται, "Thus also has it been written,"[39] which insists on the determining importance of the citation for the aims of the speech. In fact, Gen 2:7 (see the Greek text above) distinguishes the making of the man from earth

36. So just from this it would already appear that the expression of v. 47b ("the second man from heaven") cannot simply refer to a future coming of Christ like that of the Son of Man; contra C. K. Barrett, *The First Epistle to the Corinthians* (London, 1971²) ad loc.; K.-A. Bauer, *Leiblichkeit*, 101, n. 80. Better, H. Conzelmann, op. cit., ad loc.: in v. 47 "the antithesis is repeated in a varied form: ψυχικός is explained by χοικός, 'earth[l]y,' πνευματικός by ἐξ' οὐρανοῦ, 'from heaven.' " See also A. Vögtle, "Die Adam-Christus-Typologie und 'der Menschensohn,' " TrThZ 60 (1951) 309–328; O. Cullmann, *Christology of the New Testament* (Philadelphia, 1963) 167–168; F. Mussner, *Die Auferstehung Jesu* (Munich, 1969) 110f.

37. The other two occurrences (Jude 19; Jas 3:15) actually depend on the text of 1 Cor 2:14; see R. Morissette, "L'antithèse," 100.

38. See R. Morissette, art. cit., 103–106; the author takes account both of Philo ("Among all the exegeses proposed by the Alexandrine for Gen 2:7 or even 1:26, none contains either adjective *psychikos* or *pneumatikos*") and of the Gnostic writers of Nag-Hammadi, Valentinians and Naasenes ("historically later"; precisely then in *The Hypostasis of the Archontes* and *On the Origin of the World* the adjective "*psychikos* designates the final condition of the fully animate Adam, conformed to the image of God, i.e., in possession of the divine *pneuma*"!).

39. In the New Testament this recurs only in Matt 2:5 and Luke 24:46.

(v. 7a) from the breathing of the "breath of life" (v. 7b); this second act is commented on as follows in *Gen. Rab.* 14:

> This means that He (God) formed him as a lifeless mass, extending from heaven to earth, and only then breathed the soul into him. Therefore in this world man (has life) through breathing, while in the future aeon he will receive it as a gift, since it is written, "And I shall put my Spirit in you and you will live" (Ezek 37:14).

So even the midrash takes the *n^eshamah*, "soul," to be present in relation to the future *rûaḥ*, "spirit" (with the Ezekiel citation); but then even the *nefesh ḥayyâh (ψυχὴ ζῶσα)*, "living soul," is found in a situation of tension and of waiting for a new "pneumatic" mode of being, put into act by the eschatological intervention of God, which will repeat in a new and definitive form the creative action. The Genesis text is, then, decisive for the Pauline vocabulary in use here (note the chiastic sequence: v. 44, σῶμα ψυχικόν, "psychic body"; v. 45, ψυχὴ ζῶσα, "living soul"; v. 46, τὸ ψυχικόν, "what is psychic"). But if Paul adopts his adjectives in the light of the Genesis passage, that means that τὸ ψυχικόν identifies simply the creaturely man, who in relation to τὸ πνευματικόν, "what is spiritual," is judged not so much in terms of moral categories as simply in terms of levels of being.

2) Originality and meaning of the definition "life-giving spirit." Here we wish to ask ourselves how Paul could have come by such a bold and exceptional formula as that of v. 45b ("the last Adam became εἰς πνεῦμα ζῳοποιοῦν, "a life-giving spirit"). It is difficult to provide a single explanation; more probably various influences are at work here. A first reason may be the same text, Gen 2:7b ("and blew into his face *the breath of life,* πνοὴν ζωῆς"), especially since Paul has just cited Gen 2:7c in v. 45a, and in Philo we find the variant πνεῦμα "spirit," in place of πνοή, "breath" (see *Leg. all.* 1:42).[40] It is also possible that Paul is dependent on the Alexandrine Jewish wisdom tradition; indeed, wisdom is there defined as πνεῦμα (Wis 7:22 = 1 Cor 15:45b), and sent "from heaven" (Wis 9:10 = 1 Cor 15:47b), union with which produces "immortality" (Wis 8:17 = 1 Cor 15:42b, 53).[41] Finally, we must also not forget a similar definition given

---

40. Interesting in this regard is a text of the *Book of Baruch* of the Gnostic Justinus (= Hippolytus, *Confut.* V 26:36): "When the prophets say, 'Hear, O heavens, and incline the ear, O earth' (Isa 1:2), by 'heavens' they mean the Spirit that is in man (οὐρανὸν λέγει τὸ πνεῦμα τὸ ἐν τῷ ἀνθρώπῳ) and by 'earth' the soul that is in man with the Spirit (γῆν δὲ τὴν ψυχὴν τὴν ἐν τῷ ἀνθρώπῳ σὺν τῷ πνεύματι)." This witnesses, then, to a true pneumatological reading of Gen 2:7, just like that which Paul seems to have made.

41. In this direction see the position of A. Feuillet, *Le Christ sagesse de Dieu selon les Epîtres pauliniennes* (Paris, 1966) 330–333.

of Moses in the apocryphal *Ass. Mos.* 11:16: "a holy spirit worthy of the Lord, manifold and incomprehensible."[42]

In 1 Cor 15:45b, then, the boldest thing is not so much the apparent identification of Jesus Christ with the pneuma (cf. 6:17) as that he is called "ζῳοποιοῦν, "*life-giving* spirit." For the context indicates that the word "spirit" actually is not in opposition to "body," since the "life-giving spirit" (v. 45b) is parallel to "spiritual body" (v. 44): both expressions are meant to indicate the point of arrival of the resurrection (but with the difference that the former expression is used only of Christ, whereas the latter applies to anyone who rises).

Moreover, the lack of an article before πνεῦμα indicates that the last Adam, far from dissolving definitively into the anonymous sphere of the divine Spirit, has simply acquired a new mode of being, which, moreover, grammatically only has the function of predicate: "as the first Adam" does not disappear to leave room for the "living soul," but rather is himself realized as a living being, so the "last Adam" does not vanish into an impersonal life-giving spirit, but rather comes to realize himself as such. So the subject is always the same Christ, who has become once and for all "life-giving spirit," and only in that manner can actually be called the "last Adam." We must not forget that such a definition is not altogether new in the biblical tradition, since it is already found in connection with Zedekiah, king of Jerusalem: in Lam 4:20 he is actually called *rûaḥ 'appênû* ("breath/spirit of our nostrils," i.e., "spirit of life"). This expression can be considered synonymous with "life-giving spirit," granted that with that title the king is identified as dispenser and guarantor of the vitality of the whole people; the background of such language is in the set of royal and divine titles in ancient Egypt.[43]

42. The first edition of the text is in A. M. Ceriani, *Monumenta sacra et profana*, I (Milan, 1861) 61. Interesting, then, is the reference made by R. H. Charles (*The Apocrypha and Pseudepigrapha of the Old Testament*, II [Oxford, 1913], 423]) to πνεῦμα . . . ἅγιον . . . πολυμερές, "a holy . . . manifold . . . spirit" of Wis 7:22. Still on the subject of these bold definitions of Judaism contemporaneous with Paul, Philo of Alexandria himself writes that at his death Moses became εἰς νοῦν ἡλιοειδέστατον ("a mind bright as the sun": *Vit. Mois.* II 288; see also *Quaest. et solut. in Ex.* 11:29).

43. In ancient Egypt Pharaoh, as well as the deity, in the same way grants and maintains the life and well-being of his subjects; see J. Hehn, "Zum Problem des Geistes im Alten Orient und im Alten Testament," ZAW-NF 2 (1925) 210–225. For example, a courtier salutes Akhenaten with the title "Air for Every Nose," while a poem celebrates Sethi II as "King of Beauty, Who Gives Breath": see P. van Imschoot, "L'Esprit de Jahvé, source de vie, dans l'Ancien Testament," RB 44 (1935) 481–501; 493f. (with other texts); an inscription of Abydos makes this supplication to Ramses II: "Promise us, O King, the life you give, you who are the breath of our nostrils"; see J. de Savignac, "Théologie pharaonique et messianisme d'Israel," VT 7 (1957) 82–90. We also find similar terminology on the soil of Canaan in the El-Amarna period; here indeed the vassals of Egypt identify the Pharaoh as "breath of my

But what, then, is the meaning of ζῳοποιοῦν, "life-giving"? First of all, we note that such a participle has as subject the pneuma attributed to the last Adam (and not God), and that its active value is exercised outside the last Adam (and not upon him); we therefore reject the translation "a being spiritualized by a life-making Spirit."[44] Indeed, the opposition with the ψυχὴ ζῶσα, "living soul," of the first Adam is on two levels: in the first place, Christ becomes πνεῦμα (or even "pneumatic body," a title to which if anything the quoted translation could apply), and already that would be enough to differentiate the last Adam far, far from the first; but in the second place, Christ actually becomes the cause of life for others distinct from himself, capable, that is, of giving life to a new type of humanity in a different sense, but with the same power wherewith Yahweh in Gen 2:7b breathed the "breath of life" into the first man. In biblical tradition "giving life" is something proper and exclusive to God alone and to God's Spirit;[45] in particular the verb ζῳοποιέω, "give life" (like the synonym ζῳογονέω), regularly has God as subject: "You give life to all things" (σὺ ζῳοποιεῖς τὰ πάντα: Neh 9:6); "Am I perhaps God, that I can cause to die and cause to live?" (2 Kgs 5:7); "You it is who restore my life" (Ps 70:20); the same is also said of Wisdom: she "will give life to whoever is on her side" (ζῳοποιήσει τὸν παρ' αὐτῆς: Qoh 7:12). Now, the attribution of this verb and of this activity in a Christological sense to the last Adam makes of him a being set on a footing of equality with God himself, and it is here that there appears the incommensurable distance from the first man, the earthly one, who was and is only the passive recipient of life.

But how and when is the function of giving life exercised? In the New Testament this verb has a meaning related to that of ἐγείρειν, "raise up/resurrect." In fact, of the ten occurrences (John 5:21; 6:63; Rom 4:17; 8:11; 1 Cor 15:22, 36, 45; 2 Cor 3:6; Gal 3:21; 1 Pet 3:18), one establishes a relationship with the gift of the Spirit obtained by faith in the risen Christ (Gal 3:21 in reference to 3:14), while six others are evidently equivalent to "raise up" or provide a general definition of God (Rom 4:17) or refer to the seed that must first die (1 Cor 15:36) or allude to the eschatological

---

life" or "my vital breath"; see J. A. Knudtzon, *Die el-Amarna Tafeln,* I (Leipzig, 1915: letter 141:2, 6, 10, 13, 37, 43; 143:9, 15, 17; 144:2, 6, 7, 8; 281:3).

44. Contra B. Schneider, art. cit., 155.

45. See the following studies: G. von Rad, "Life and Death in the Old Testament," in the art. ζάω, TDNT 2:843–849; L. Dürr, *Die Wertung des Lebens im Alten Testament und im alten Orient* (Münster, 1926); E. Schmitt, *Leben in den Weisheitsbüchern Job, Sprüche und Jesus Sirach* (Freiburg in B., 1954); P. Grelot, *De la mort à la vie éternelle. Études de Théologie biblique* (Paris, 1971). See also the word "life" in the dictionaries of biblical theology of J. B. Baur and of X. Léon-Dufour; also J. Guillet, *Themes of the Bible* (Notre Dame, n.d., ca. 1960) 172ff.

resurrection, whether in a present sense (John 5:21) or even a future one (1 Cor 15:22; Rom 8:11).[46] The three remaining occurrences have ζῳοποιέω spoken of the spirit without object: thus 2 Cor 3:6 ("the letter kills, but the spirit gives life"); John 6:63 ("it is the spirit that gives life; the flesh profits nothing"); and our 1 Cor 15:45.

In our text, with the participle "life-giving" in the absolute state, with no determining object, we have the problem of identifying to what it refers.[47] It seems that first of all we must maintain the eschatological meaning of the verb. Its use in chapter 15 (vv. 22, 36) and the theme of the immediate context allude to the final general resurrection. Hence the affirmation of v. 45b refers above all to the future intervention of the last Adam, who will initiate the new creation by giving life to our mortal bodies, just as Yahweh initiated the first creation by breathing "a breath of life" into the man (Gen 2:7b); in the foreground, then, stands physical life.[48] This eschatological value of the "life-giving spirit" is confirmed by Phil 3:20-21: "We await as savior the Lord Jesus Christ, who will *transform (μετασχηματίσει) our humble body (τὸ σῶμα τῆς ταπεινώσεως ἡμῶν* = the "psychic body" of 1 Cor 15:44), configuring it *to his glorious body (τῷ σώματι τῆς δόξης αὐτοῦ* = the "pneumatic body" of ibid.) according to his power to subject all things to himself." And it is in this sense that we find precisely the future verb "we shall bear" (of 1 Cor 15:49).

46. In support of this conception there is also at least one Jewish inscription at Beth She'arim ("who promised to give life to the dead"), cited by F. Vattioni, "La resurrezione nel mondo giudaico," *Il Sangue della Redenz.* 58 (1972) 90–110, 107. See also *Exod. Rab.* 48, where God says to Israel: "In this world my spirit has placed the truth in you; but in the future it will give you life, as it is said: 'I shall place my spirit in you and you will live' (Ezek. 37:14)"; see 2 Macc 7:23.

47. Here the commentators are divided: H. Conzelmann does not decide; for the others, ζῳοποιοῦν would have "not a soteriological . . . but a speculative meaning" (Ph. Bachmann) or is equivalent to "the source and the author of all life on earth" (J. Weiss, who refers to 8:6; E. Walter), or it is "the source of eternal life" (J. Héring), or more generically it gives life (C. K. Barrett) at least to Christians (J. Sickenberger; F. F. Bruce) in the sense of Rom 1:4 (H. Lietzmann-W. G. Kümmel) with an eschatological nuance (J. Huby; C. Spicq). Others insist that "life-giving" is intended as a present gift of the Spirit (C. T. Craig; L. Morris) or that it gives to our bodies "an ever-new youth" (F. Godet). Only F. W. Grosheide, *Commentary on the First Epistle to the Corinthians* (Grand Rapids, 1954²) ad loc., gives the participle a clear eschatological significance: "In view of the fact that Paul speaks about the spiritual body which the believers receive at the resurrection, the term *life-giving* (unqualified) must be taken of the resurrection (cf. Rom. 8:11)." Meanwhile N. A. Dahl, *The Resurrection of the Body. A Study of I Corinthians 15* (London, 1962), seems to refer the verb to either the present or the future (see pp. 16 and 116). And J. P. Versteeg, *Christus en de Geest*, 43-67, does intend our expression in an eschatological sense, but in the direction of a "realized eschatology" (see 397f.: "In the risen Christ the end of time has become reality . . . and of this the Spirit is the great inaugurator").

48. Indeed, 1 Cor 15:36 reads thus: "What you sow *is not given life (οὐ ζῳοποιεῖται)* unless it first die"; this is certainly physical death, and it is from this that the last Adam gives life (against E. Larsson, *Christus als Vorbild* [Lund, 1962] 323, who speaks only of a sacramental death).

Only on a second level can our participle "also refer to the present"[49] and be understood in the sense of the sanctification of the Christian as a historical person (see below).

3) *The moment from which this definition is valid.* It is important for us now to determine when the truth of the pneumatological description of Christ comes into effect, and also to be able to distinguish two possible successive points in the arc of its existence. Indeed, that we must be dealing with a real existential distinction seems clear from the presence of the single aorist verb ἐγένετο, "became," governing two predicate complements introduced by εἰς, "unto" (hence, borrowed from a Semitic source); if this distinguishes two different conditions of the first Adam (i.e., the mere form of clay and the "living soul"), the same must happen in the last Adam. Thus a first interpretation is excluded that would attribute the description "life-giving spirit" to the preexistent Christ, thus interpreting it as something inhering in Christ considered in the abstract;[50] against such an explanation there also stands the accented chronological succession of "pneumatic" to "psychic" (v. 46), for which the "life-giving spirit" must also come after the "living soul."

So there remain two possibilities. Some few would refer the last Adam becoming a life-giving spirit to the moment of the incarnation, and so to the phase of his earthly life:[51] the earthly Jesus would already have possessed the life-giving spirit through his participation in the "divine being" (Allo) or "became such a Spirit through His entire work as Mediator" (Grosheide). Now, if we should read v. 45 with blinders, isolating it from the context, we could accept such an interpretation. But the whole of the discourse throughout chapter 15 goes in the direction of the resurrection.[52] Paul had actually begun the treatment with the kerygma of the resurrection of Christ (15:3ff.); Christ himself was identified as the "first of those who fall asleep" (v. 20) and instrumental cause of the general resurrection (v. 21f.)

49. R. Bultmann, art. ζωοποιέω, TDNT 2:875.

50. This is what J. Weiss thought, *Der erste Korintherbrief* (Göttingen, 1910⁹) ad loc., basing himself on the single ἐγένετο, "became," and so considering the two following complements to be contemporaneous; but we must note that v. 45a is a biblical citation, while v. 45b is Pauline and echoes the Genesis text only as an application to a new case, specifically that of the "last Adam" understood Christologically.

51. Thus E. B. Allo, *Première Épître aux Corinthiens* (Paris, 1934); F. W. Grosheide, op. cit., ad loc.

52. This can be called at present the *sententia communis* among exegetes. Thus, for instance, E. Schweizer, art. πνεῦμα, TDNT 6:420; I. Hermann, *Kyrios und Pneuma. Studien zur Christologie der paulinischen Hauptbriefen* (Munich, 1961) 62; H. Conzelmann, op. cit., ad loc.; J. P. Versteeg, op. cit., 57; K.-A. Bauer, op. cit., 100, etc.

In our pericope the Apostle wants to answer the question "How do the dead rise?" (v. 35), and the outcome of Jesus' experience is precisely for him something crucial, indeed a guarantee of the resurrection of Christians, so that already for him the identification of the "spiritual body" has an exemplary value.[53] We can therefore say that only with Easter does the last Adam reach his definitive stature; only the Risen One is "the second man" (v. 47b), that is, the truly new man who can finally act as counterpart to the first Adam. The two titles are, in fact, in opposition to Adam: first of all because Jesus becomes a life-giving spirit, i.e., active dispenser of life as was Yahweh at the beginning;[54] and in the second place because he becomes σῶμα πνευματικόν, "spiritual body," in a passive sense, thus showing what Paul was eager to show, i.e., that "it is not first the spiritual, but the psychic and then the spiritual" (v. 46). "This reduces the force of the mythology. Primal man and resurrection do not fit together."[55]

IV. Paul's optimistic anthropology

However original the Christology of 1 Cor 15:45-49, we must not forget that this does not constitute the real interest of the section. The central theme still remains the resurrection of human beings. Eschatology and Christology are presented so fused together as to be conditioned and clarified by experience: human future is bound to the experience of Christ; on the other hand, the newness of the risen Christ is understood only in relation to a definition of the basic human or Adamic condition.[56] But it is precisely the presence of these two themes that gives our passage a distinctly optimistic anthropological orientation that we would be hard pressed to find elsewhere in the Pauline correspondence. Here, for greater clarity, we shall successively distinguish the two components, extracting from each the deductions on the anthropological level. What we shall say is simply the conclusion to all we have thus far developed.

53. It is perfectly possible that behind the repetitive rhythmic antitheses of vv. 42b-44a there is concealed a fragment of a very ancient Christological hymn; see R. Morissette, "La condition de ressuscité," 226.
54. In this sense our text is related to the description "Son of God in power" of Rom 1:4, where the connection with the "resurrection from the dead" is explicit.
55. H. Conzelmann, op. cit., 287, n. 58.
56. This explains the recourse of many authors to the category of "corporate personality" to explain the function of the two Adams. But rather than actually resolving the data in question, this just repeats it in different terms, leaving everything quite unchanged. See C. K. Barrett, op. cit., 376: "Neither of the two men whom Paul has mentioned is simply a private individual; each was an *Adam*, a representative man; what each was, others became."

1) *The anthropological impact of eschatology.* We will not delay over this aspect, because it is characteristic of the whole of chapter 15, and so would presuppose a broader study than this. Suffice it to say that in Paul's vision, and in the Bible as a whole, the resurrection represents the total elevation of the whole human being, the bodily and spiritual element alike.[57]

Here it is that we encounter the first and decisive separation from Greek tradition, the interests of which were almost completely spiritual.[58] From this point of view, it cannot help but seem surprising that Paul terms the risen man σῶμα πνευματικόν, "spiritual body" (see the parallel σῶμα τῆς δόξης, "body of glory," in Phil 3:21). Without getting involved in all its implications, we want to study the importance attributed to human corporeality: if the quality of the ψυχικόν, "animal/psychic," must fall away to leave room for the πνευματικόν, "spiritual/pneumatic," that does not make his "somaticity" unimportant; on the contrary, the σῶμα, "body," becomes the factor that stabilizes the continuity between the present age and the future.

It follows, then, that the body, contrary to any pessimistic conception, plays the integrating role in the human person, revealing it in its relational aspect. And here it is that we perceive its radical difference from the concept of "flesh": "The *sôma* is fundamentally *for God*, while the *sarx* is fundamentally *distant from God.*"[59] The Pauline language presents no

---

57. On the biblical faith in the resurrection, see, for example, F. Nötscher, *Altorientalischer und Alttestamentlicher Auferstehungsglauben* (Würzburg, 1926; Darmstadt, 1970); H. Birkeland, *The Belief in the Resurrection of the Dead in the OT* (Lund, 1950); R. Martin-Achard, *De la mort à la résurrection d'après l'A.T.* (Neuchâtel, 1956); K. Schubert, "Die Entwicklung der Auferstehungslehre von der nachexilischen bis zur frührabbinischen Zeit," BZ NF 6 (1962) 177–214; P. Hoffmann, *Die Toten in Christus. Eine religionsgeschichtliche und exegetische Untersuchung zur paulinischen Eschatologie* (Münster, 1969²); P. Siber, *Mit Christus leben. Eine Studie zur paulinischen Auferstehungshoffnung* (Zurich, 1971); B. Rigaux, *Dieu l'a ressuscité* (Gembloux, 1973); C. Marcheselli-Casale, *Risorgeremo, ma come?* RivBibl Suppl. 18 (Bologna, 1988).

58. See Aeschylus, *Eumenides,* 646ff., where Apollo himself declares, "Zeus could undo shackles, such hurt can be made good, and there is every kind of way to get out. But once the dust has drained down all a man's blood, once the man has died, there is no raising him up again. This is a thing for which my father never made curative spells" (*Aeschylus I, Oresteia,* trans. R. Lattimore [New York, 1967]). On Greek anthropology, see, for example, J. Hessen, *Platonismus und Prophetismus* (Munich-Basel, 1955²) 98ff.; J. Pépin, *Idées grecques sur l'homme et sur Dieu* (Paris, 1971) 53ff. See the characteristic definition of Plato, *Alcibiades,* 130c: "Since the human being is neither body nor the body-soul complex (οὔτε τὸ σῶμα οὔτε τὸ συναμφότερόν ἐστιν ἄνθρωπος) . . . there is nothing else that the human being is but the soul (λείπεται μηδὲν ἄλλο τὸν ἄνθρωπον συμβαίνειν ἢ ψυχήν)"!

59. R. Morissette, "L'expression 'sôma,' " 234; see also R. Bultmann, *Theology of the New Testament* (New York, 1951) 192–203; K.-A. Bauer, *Leiblichkeit,* 103–105. See now on the Jewish background G. Stenberger, *Der Leib der Auferstehung. Studien zur Anthropologie und Eschatologie des palästinischen Judentums im neutestamentlichen Zeitalter (ca. 170 v. Chr.–100 n. Chr.)* (Rome, 1972).

contradiction[60] but rather emphasizes the fact that man can abandon his character of being "psychic" only through the intervention of the power of God, of God's spirit (which is Christ's spirit as well; cf. v. 45b). But the corporeal character of the risen man defines the divine intervention as a creative act.[61] On this rests the hope of a total salvation beyond death, when God will finally be shown as "savior" in the full sense.[62]

It thus already appears from these concepts that the truly antithetic terms are not $σῶμα$ and $ψυχή$, "body/psyche," but rather $ψυχή$ and $πνεῦμα$, "psyche/pneuma: soul/spirit," as identifying two different human conditions, both having reference to $σῶμα$ but chronologically successive. Can we conclude from this to a complete depreciation of the "psychic man"? Not exactly. We believe rather that the Apostle here reveals an interesting positive conception of the present human condition. And to demonstrate this we must consider the Christological component.

2) *The anthropological impact of Christology.* The comparison of the first Adam and the last Adam (which permits us to speak of an Adamic Christology) has in our text important anthropological implications concerning the exact understanding of the body or of the "psychic" man. To begin with, we note that this Pauline description is true for historical man and for each human being living in the history of Adam until the last human being, that is, before the final day and the transformation through the resurrection (see vv. 50-51). Now here is the question: What is Paul's conception of this historical condition of humanity in our text? Does the contrast between the "psychic body" and the "pneumatic body" devaluate the former? In what sense? It is not rare to find among the authors a clearly negative judgment of the "psychic man." For all these we may cite the opinion of R. Scroggs: "The $σῶμα$ $ψυχικόν$ ['psychic body'] is the distorted human existence of every man after the fall, even of the Christian."[63] But is this really the sense of our text? I believe we must attend to certain ele-

60. For a similar expression, cf. the Qumran phrase *rûaḥ baśar* = "spirit of flesh" ("man"): "But how can the spirit of flesh understand all this?" (1 QH 13:13; cf. 17:25). See also the expression $πνεῦμα$ $ψυχικόν$ = "psychic pneuma/breath of life" in Plutarch (H. G. Liddell, R. Scott, and H. S. Jones, *A Greek-English Lexicon* [Oxford, 1961⁹] s.v.).

61. See H. Schwantes, *Schöpfung der Endzeit. Ein Beitrag zum Verständnis der Auferweckung bei Paulus* (Stuttgart, 1962) 86.

62. It is interesting to note that the Pauline sense of salvation is clearly oriented in an eschatological direction: for the word "save" see Rom 5:9, 10; 8:24; 10:9; 11:26; 1 Cor 3:15; 5:5; 2 Thess 2:10; 2 Tim 4:18; for the title "savior" see Phil 3:20; 2 Tim 1:10; Titus 2:13; for the noun "salvation" see Rom 13:11; Phil 1:28, etc.

63. Op. cit., 85; see also K.-A. Bauer, op. cit., 103 (the "psychic body" is simultaneously equivalent to the $σῶμα$ $θνητόν$, "dead body," of Rom 8:11 and the $σῶμα$ $τῆς$ $ἁμαρτίας$, "body of sin," of Rom 6:6); R. Morissette, "L'antithèse," 101, passim; H. Conzelmann, *Outline of the Theology of the New Testament* (New York, 1969) 176-178.

ments of this passage to show that the anthropology of the Apostle has an optimistic nuance that would allow a much more benevolent conception of the present human condition.

a) First, we must reclaim for the adjective ψυχικόν, "psychic," a semantic character that is not at all negative. Of course, the contrast with πνευματικόν, "spiritual," places the present man in a situation of inferiority over against the resurrected; and this is witnessed in vv. 42b-43 by the synonymous parallelism with φθορά, "corruption," ἀτιμία, "dishonor," as ἀσθένεια, "weakness." But already the next parallelism, with the rare adjective χοϊκός (vv. 47-49: "earthly") softens the scornful connotation of the three nouns, inviting us to hear them simply on the level of creaturely "earthliness." Indeed, if the adjective "psychic" is here an allusion to the ψυχὴ ζῶσα, "living soul," of Gen 2:7 (see above), it becomes clear that it describes the human being only as a creature of God, and does so independently of sin.

Moreover, the Hebrew concept of the underlying nefesh, "soul," confirms us in the understanding of the human being considered primarily as "living creature, where in the foreground appears the idea of potentiality before God and dependence on him, whereas it would take the expression baśar to indicate the idea of distance from the Lord."[64] In fact, we must remember that Paul is setting up his opposition not between the πνεῦμα, "soul," and the σάρξ, "flesh,"[65] but rather between the πνεῦμα "spirit" and the ψυχή "soul"; so it is quite impossible for the adjective ψυχικός, "psychic," to have the same pejorative sense as the derivatives of σάρξ, "flesh." Nor, on the other hand, have we the right to apply to our text the same sense that the antithesis has in 1 Cor 2:14-15 (see above); indeed, in 15:44, 46 the application of ψυχικός is so universal as necessarily to include even the one who is there entitled πνευματικός. Hence the connotation of "psychic" is different here, i.e., on the level of creation, and consequently more positive.[66]

64. R. Morissette, art. cit., 115f.; see D. Lys, Nèphèsh. Histoire de l'âme dans la révélation d'Israël au sein des religions proche-orientales (Paris, 1959).
65. In this sense cf. the adjective σαρκικός, "fleshly" (1 Cor 9:11 = Rom 15:27f.), and especially σάρκινος, "fleshly" (Rom 7:14; 1 Cor 3:1), but also the modal expressions κατὰ σάρκα, "according to the flesh" (Rom 8:4-5), and ἐν σαρκί, "in the flesh" (Rom 8:8f.).
66. Nor does the LXX Bible reveal any pejorative sense for the adjective ψυχικός (4 Macc 1:32) or the adverb ψυχικῶς (2 Macc 2:24, 37). For a survival of the positive meaning of our adjective in some sections of ancient Gnosis, see M. Simonetti, art. cit., 20f., 28-36; for example, the Valentinians distinguish the hylic man, made in the image of God, from the psychic man, made in God's likeness, since in Gen 2:7 "his substance is called breath of life (πνεῦμα ζωῆς), in that it derives from spiritual emanation (ἐκ πνευματικῆς ἀπορροίας)"! (thus in Irenaeus, Adv. haer. 1:5:5). See also R. Bultmann, Theology of the New Testament, trans. K. Grobel, I (New York, 1951) 204-205.

b) In the second place, we notice the absence of hamartiological vocabulary. This fact is particularly eloquent if we compare our text with Rom 5:12-21, where the antithetic Adam-Christ is also found, but developed in a different direction. There the hamartiological language is varied and abundant: ἁμαρτία-ἁμαρτάνω-ἁμαρτωλός, "sin/sinner" (ten times); παράπτωμα, "transgression" (six times); κρίμα-κατάκριμα, "judgment" (three times); παράβασις, "transgression" (once); παρακοή, "disobedience" (once).

On the other hand, in 1 Cor 15:45-49 (but also in vv. 21-22) there is the most complete silence about these concepts, and indeed the terms παράπτωμα, κατάκριμα, παράβασις, παρακοή, are completely lacking throughout the letter. As for the derivatives of ἁμαρτ-, "sin-," the adjective is never found; the rare substantive ἁμάρτημα (6:18) occurs once in the indeterminate sense of "sinful action." Also, the verb (6:18; 7:28, 36; 8:12; 15:34) is always used with reference to concrete cases in life and with paraenetic intent; and as for the substantive ἁμαρτία, "sin," it occurs practically always in the plural in the context of the confession of faith in the death and resurrection of Christ (15:3, 17).[67] The only occurrence of ἁμαρτία, "sin," in the singular in 1 Corinthians is found in 15:56, so not far from our passage; but rather than making difficulties in relation to its immediate context,[68] v. 56 is already beyond the literary and thematic perspective of vv. 45-49. Thus it is quite clear that here the Adam opposite Christ is not sinner but rather created and mortal man; consequently, the same is true of the "earthly" persons who derive from him.

So in the foreground we find not sin but rather death, and that not in a spiritual sense (as in Rom 5-8, where it stands in opposition to the grace and the redemption of Christ),[69] but rather in a physical sense. This conclusion can already be drawn from the evidence in vv. 21f.: "Since through one man there is death, thus also through one man there will be resurrection of the dead; for as all die in Adam, so also in Christ all will be brought to life";[70] but see v. 36, which now governs our passage from closer: "Fool, what you plant does not come to life unless it first dies." The eschatological victory over death is the subject of vv. 26, 53-55, where we find the significant contrast τὸ θνητόν-ἀθανασία, "that which is

67. On the pre-Pauline origin of this plural, see, e.g., K. Lehmann, *Auferweckt am dritten Tag nach der Schrift* (Freiburg-Basel-Vienna, 1969²) 90-91.
68. Actually, v. 56 interrupts the line of thought and has every appearance of being "an interruption" (H. Lietzmann) or "a gloss" (H. Conzelmann).
69. In this sense, see P. Rossano, "Il concetto di 'hamartia' in Rom 5-8," RivBibl 6 (1958) 190-207; H. Conzelmann, *Theology*, 176.
70. Even so, the δι' ἀνθρώπου, "through a man," of v. 21 alludes to Adam as responsible for death; the allusion to sin is implicit. Thus we anticipate the theme of Rom 5:12-21, where, however, Adam is presented directly as the cause of sin and only indirectly as the cause of death.

mortal/immortality." All this leads us to maintain that the φθορά-ἀτιμία-ἀσθένεια, "destruction-dishonor-weakness" of vv. 42b-43 should also be interpreted in the same sense. Indeed, these three concepts (along with that of the 'psychic body') are in the last analysis linked only to the ψυχὴ ζῶσα, "living soul," of v. 45, which describes man without reference to sin.

c) We must not lose sight of an interesting parallel implicit in our passage between the earthly Jesus and every other historical human person. The equivalence emanates from the Christology developed here. As we have shown above, it is only with his resurrection that Jesus Christ became σῶμα πνευματικόν, "a spiritual body," as well as πνεῦμα ζωοποιοῦν, "life-giving spirit." The human stage that precedes this event, then, is also applicable to him, and all that is said to interpret an expression like σῶμα ψυχικόν, "psychic body," necessarily applies to the pre-paschal Jesus. In other words, even before becoming the antitype of Adam on a very different level, Jesus himself was participant with and heir to the first Adam, i.e., simple "living soul" or "psychic body." In light of this, it is hard to see the element of sin as an integral part of the definition of the "psychic body." Rather, referring to Heb 4:15 (where we read that Jesus was "tested like us in all things except sin"), we are inclined to perceive in the "psychic body" a character of the universal human condition prescinding from the degrading component of sin.[71]

From this point of view it can be interesting to cite a passage from the *Book of Baruch* by the Gnostic Justin (Hippolytus, *Confut.* V 25:32), where Jesus on the cross, "after having said, 'Woman, behold your son,' that is, the psychic man and the earthly man *(τὸν ψυχικόν ἄνθρωπον καὶ τὸν χοϊκόν)*, having commended the spirit into the hands of the Father, ascended to the Good." The text, which evidently refers to 1 Cor 15:46f. in the employment of vocabulary, nevertheless represents a clearly more negative language insofar as it reflects Gnostic usage.[72] Indeed, while in Paul the whole present human being is only "psychic" and the "pneumatic" refers only to the future, the Gnostic text offers us a dualistic anthropological vision that maintains the present coexistence of the two

71. At the same time the character of the "psychic man" represents a discrete but noteworthy allusion (something quite rare in Paul) to the full humanity of Jesus of Nazareth as yet not transfigured by the glory of the resurrection (see H. D. Wendland, "Paulus und der geschichtliche Jesus" in *Die Briefe an die Korinther* [Göttingen, 1968¹²] 203ff.). And similarly 1 Cor 15:36f. (cf. John 12:24) can be considered a tacit reference to this earthly life of Jesus as promise and condition of life in the resurrection; see H. Riesenfeld, "Das Wortbild vom Weizenkorn bei Paulus," in *Studien zum NT und Patristik*, Festschrift for E. Klostermann (Berlin, 1961) 43–55.

72. Thus, for instance, "at the moment of death, in the motif of the separation of the spirit of Jesus from the soul and body, [which would be] unworthy to ascend to heaven" (M. Simonetti, in *Testi gnostici cristiani* [Bari, 1970] 59, n. 100).

"psychic-pneumatic" principles (concerning "the spirit that is found in all human beings," see ibid., 25:21, 36, 37) opposed and in conflict with one another (ibid., 25:25). The result is definitively a less calm and more pessimistic conception of the human person.

d) A reliable illumination of the anthropology of our passage comes from the chronological succession "first/then." There actually emerges an original conception of the history of salvation, which is, however, systematically disregarded in the studies.[73] The πρῶτον-ἔπειτα, "first/then" (v. 46 = v. 47: πρῶτος-δεύτερος, "first/second") divides the discourse about time into two great sections: that of the first creation and that of the last creation, the one governed by the ψυχή, "soul," and the other by the πνεῦμα, "spirit." Excluding so much as a hint of allusion to Adam as sinner, and hence to human sin, the passage lacks that intermediate stage so heavily stressed in Rom 7, where three steps—paradise, sin, and redemption—impose themselves on us.[74]

The scheme of the history of salvation in 1 Cor 15:45-49 is binary rather than ternary. Moreover, the two times understood here are treated on two interdependent but distinct levels. First of all, in the Christological sense: the πρῶτον, "first," refers to Adam and the ἔπειτα, "then," to the risen Christ. Secondly, in the anthropological sense: the "first" is said of every historical person, and the "then" of the eschatological stage, of the general resurrection.[75] The relation between the two heads of families is the basis of the relationship of their adherents, who reproduce the "image" of each respectively (v. 49). We hence conclude that according to our text, a coexistence between "psychic" and "pneumatic" is quite impossible, since the latter overcomes the former and destroys it. But then are the two stages of the history of salvation so completely separated as to exclude any effect on each other? Does Paul perhaps think in the rabbinic terms of the two irreconcilable "eons," present and future?[76]

e) We are here aided by the πνεῦμα ζῳοποιοῦν of v. 45b, which recalls in 15:45-49 certain other decisive elements of Pauline theology. We have noted above the eschatological orientation of this expression. Even so, the

73. See esp. L. Goppelt, "Paulus und die Heilsgeschichte," NTS 13 (1966-67) 31-42; U. Luz, *Das Geschichtsverständnis des Paulus* (Munich, 1968): see the review by J. Cambier, Bib 51 (1970) 241-252; O. Cullmann, *Heil als Geschichte: Heilsgeschichtliche Existenz im Neuen Testament* (Tübingen, 1965) 225-245.
74. S. Lyonnet rightly clarifies this structure in his "L'histoire de la salut selon le chapitre VII de l'épitre aux Romains," Bib 43 (1962) 117-151.
75. So we must correct the exclusive anthropological reduction of v. 46 maintained by J. Jeremias, art. *Adam*, TDNT 1:143.
76. See H. Sasse, art. αἰών, TDNT 1: esp. 202-207.

existence of a certain thematic parallelism with Rom 1:4 ("constituted Son of God in *power* according to the Spirit of holiness of the resurrection of the dead") as well as the New Testament use of ζωοποιεῖν, "give life," along with an unmodified "pneuma" (2 Cor 3:6; John 6:63) would invite us to recognize also a reference to the present in the participle. Such an understanding is also recommended by the fact that the last Adam becomes εἰς πνεῦμα, "spirit," at the moment of the resurrection; as such, he cannot remain passive until the parousia and only then exercise his life-giving function. In fact, it belongs to the definition of pneuma to be bringer of life (besides Gen 2:7 see Ezek 37:1-14; Ps 104:29-30).

Therefore, if Christ became pneuma (acts through the Spirit) already with Easter, and if by nature the Spirit is life-giving, it follows that even the ζωοποιοῦν, "life-giving" of 1 Cor 15:45b cannot have only an eschatological dimension. Though this does remain primary, since even the aspect of giving life in the present acquires its true significance only in relation to its future consummation, still it is recognized that even the era of the σῶμα ψυχικόν, "psychic body," is under the influence of an intervention that is already salvific today. This intervention, then, according to the immediate context, seems not to be understood in a medicinal or healing sense (since there is no reference to particular infirm persons to be cured) so much as in the broad sense of raising another.

We therefore find here the fundamental Pauline thesis of a salvation already radically present with the acceptance of Christ's lordship (see 1 Cor 6:11; 2 Cor 5:17; Gal 1:4; Rom 5:2, 5; 8:2, etc.). We read in Rom 8:9, 11 precisely that "his" Spirit already "dwells" in the Christian, but this fact is also true in view of the eschatological future (cf. v. 11: "he will give life to your mortal bodies"). "To bear his image" in the future (1 Cor 15:49), then, will be made possible because the Spirit of Christ is already imprinting it powerfully on the present "psychic body" in order to transform it finally and totally into the "pneumatic."[77] In any case, eliminated is every kind of Gnosticizing mythology that would conceive of the spirit as a primary datum, and so as a natural component of the human being.[78]

V. Conclusion

The Christological originality of 1 Cor 15:45-49, along with the eschatogical orientation of the whole chapter, illuminates and corroborates a

---

77. It appears from this that οἱ ἐπουράνιοι, "those of heaven," of v. 48 cannot refer to the present (contra Eph 2:6) but constitutes an "enormous prolepsis" (J. Weiss, op. cit., 376), explicable through attraction by the singular ὁ ἐπουράνιος, "the heavenly one," referring to Christ. Actually the time is established by the future φορέσομεν, "we shall bear," of v. 49.

78. See J. P. Versteeg, *Christus en de Geest*, 96.

no less interesting aspect of Pauline anthropology. Above all, we find the exclusion of any Gnostic type of dualism, since the σῶμα ψυχικόν, "psychic body," describes every human being in history without exception. It likewise rules out Jewish pessimism, which, by accenting the consequences of Adam's fall, emphasizes a lost original, ideal paradisiac condition. Therefore, the redemption implied in the Pauline text consists not so much in the liberation from sin as in the promotion of the whole person from "psychic" to "pneumatic" and from "earthly" to "heavenly." As man is here considered only in his creaturely aspect (cf. the utilization of Gen 2:7), he appears above all to the eyes of the Apostle under the visual angle of his goodness, as a being coming forth from God's hand and so conformed to God's plan. There is no better context than this to remember Wis 11:26, which describes God as δεσπότης φιλόψυχος ("Lord, lover of ψυχή = life"): "Indeed, if you had hated something you would not have formed it" (v. 24)! The true turning point of salvation for every single person would seem to be deferred to the future resurrection. But the figure of Christ, already risen, as the "last Adam" already stands before each one as an image of the perfect man, who acts both as exemplary cause (cf. v. 48: οἷος . . . τοιοῦτοι, "as the one . . . so such ones") and as efficient cause (cf. v. 45b: πνεῦμα ζῳοποιοῦν, "life-giving spirit," primarily in the future without excluding an effective and determinative influence already in the present.

Comparing this passage to the Letter to the Romans, we observe certain basic differences: the theme of sin-death of Adam and of all human beings in the first place, as also the theme of the expiatory death of Christ, and the consequent theme of a radical newness of the Christian already in present history.[79]

We only wanted to call attention to a different aspect of Pauline anthropology. It is true that it will be integrated and transformed by successive developments of the Apostle's thought. Nevertheless, it remains in the canonical writings as a real and authoritative testimony to a pluralistic manner of approaching both the mystery of Christ and the mystery of humanity.

---

79. This thematic complex actually appears already with 2 Corinthians: see, for instance, 5:14-21.

Chapter 14

The Apostle's Sufferings:
Anthropology and Eschatology in 2 Corinthians 4:7–5:10

A survey evaluation of the history of the exegesis of 2 Cor 5:1-10 published in 1973 and treating a hundred fifty years of hermeneutics[1] concludes by substantially confirming what E. Allo had written in 1937 in his classic commentary on the letter: "Nothing in Paul's letters has, we believe, been so badly understood as this passage. . . . It is true that many verses here are obscure in themselves; but the critics, with their different interpretations, have obscured the meaning even more. Just as the best fishing is found in turbulent waters, each commentator has tried to extract from it confirmation of his own general system concerning the nature of Paulinism and particularly of eschatology."[2]

We will not attempt here to resolve all the problems connected with this text. Even in exegesis, especially Pauline exegesis, interventions with a magic wand belong only to fantasy or to credulity. Indeed, as we shall say, the mistake of the commentators has perhaps been to try to be clearer than Paul himself, without recognizing that in our passage the clearest thing is the very obscurity or at least the complexity of the Apostle's language. This must be understood as a sign of the intrinsic difficulty of the argument at hand, for which Paul does not offer dogmatic solutions but rather offers only certain suggestions, opens up certain ways of looking at it, confirms or excludes certain perspectives typical of Christian faith, but being careful always to look to "things invisible" (4:18).

Let us say from the beginning that we maintain that we need not dismember the section 4:7–5:10; on the contrary, in it we see a noteworthy homogeneity of theme, even though we can hardly deny a certain

1. F. G. Lang, *2 Korinther 5:1-10 in der neueren Forschung* (Tübingen, 1973).
2. E. B. Allo, *Seconde Épître aux Corinthiens* (Paris, 1937) 134 (1956²).

"growth" in the logic of the discourse. In what follows, then, after clearing the field of certain problems with a brief treatment of certain crucial points, we shall emphasize the three important concepts after which this chapter is named.

I. Facing certain current positions

a) The work of Baumert, published in 1973, represents the last and most respectable overall interpretation of the whole section.[3] The key to his reading could be defined as a "mystical character," since his whole study is meant to exclude from the foreground of the passage its traditional eschatological interpretation, which he replaces with one that we might call "presentialist," one of orientation to the present. Here are some of his significant exegetical choices. In 4:14b the futures "will raise" (ἐγερεῖ) and "will place beside" (παραστήσει) are explained with the category of the modal future (modality of "must") so as not to refer to the post-historic future but to present, powerful intra-historic action of God; the sense is: "God must raise us up and place us beside you," but now, today, whether in a sacramental or in an existential sense, not through the final resurrection.

What shall we say of this? It is certainly an ingenious discovery, but is hardly more than an expedient[4] that surely has the taste of originality but also of being forced. It doesn't really make sense to read in a modal significance here, when just before (in 4:14a) the aorist participle ὁ ἐγείρας, "who raised," refers to the effective divine intervention in the resurrection of Jesus; now if this is in the somatic order, how is it possible that the resurrection of the Apostle and of the Christian should be only in the spiritual-mystical order? The comparison would no longer be possible—a comparison that is indicated by the "and" καί comparativum that unites precisely v. 14a with v. 14b.

The trouble is that after this original choice, the whole interpretation of the following passage follows in the same direction. Thus in 4:16-18 the author reads only "a soteriological dualism between what is already redeemed in us and what is not yet so, and not the anthropological dual-

---

3. N. Baumert, *Täglich sterben und auferstehen. Der Literalsinn von 2 Kor 4,12–5,10* (Munich, 1973).

4. On the use of the modal future in the New Testament, see Blass-Debrunner, §362 (it corresponds to the "Gesetzsprache" of the Old Testament and is present in the Synoptics); see M. Zerwick, *Graecitas Biblica*, no. 276 (*sicut futurum semiticum quod saepe connotat aliquod posse*, "like a Semitic future, which often indicates some kind of possibility"). Also the review by H. Merklein in BZ 20 (1976) 137–140 calls this choice a *Verlegenheitslösung*, "solution [based on] awkwardness" (p. 140).

ism between body and soul";[5] thus the "glory" *(δόξα)* of v. 17 has not a future but a present meaning in reference to the apostolic ministry. However, the alternative between soteriological and anthropological dualism does not conform to the sense of the text, which is here established by the immediate context in the letter and by many parallelisms in the cultural environment in the realms of both Stoic philosophy (metaphysical; see Seneca, *Tranq. an.* 16:4; *Ep.* 58:20, 24) and Jewish apocalyptic (eschatological; see *Syr. Bar.* 15:8; 48:50; 4 Macc 17:12).

The author admits that 5:1 deals with what follows earthly life, but only through the identity of the future glory with that of the present. Consequently, in v. 2 the reference to being "clothed over" refers not to the end of this life but rather to the present historical time. Thus, the present participle *βαρούμενοι*, "weighed down," of v. 4 should not be understood in a Platonic-anthropological sense (in conformity with Wis 9:15), but refers to the burden of the apostolic ministry. Even if this last item is granted, it is simplistic and preconceived to reduce the whole metaphor of "clothe/clothe over" of vv. 2-4 to what already exists of the "himmlisches" in the Christian rather than the earthly body,[6] whereas the image is used anthropologically in the Greek and the Jewish environment alike (see below). Consequently, for Baumert the correlative concepts of "exile/native land" in vv. 6-9 define only "two present and contemporaneous modes of existence." Not only that, but the "tribunal of Christ" *(βῆμα τοῦ Χριστοῦ)* in 5:10 is read not in reference to the scene of the Last Day, since it is the entire present life that takes place "before the glorious Lord as its present judge."[7]

We cannot but admire the absolute consistency of this interpretation. But what is surprising is not so much its complete overturning of the traditional hermeneutic as the complete failure of its basic grounds to be convincing—they smell strongly of prejudgment. Besides, the work unacceptably undervalues the abundant comparative material; to close one's eyes to it is to act like an ostrich.

b) The Christological interpretation of 5:1b *(οἰκοδομὴν ἐκ θεοῦ ἔχομεν, οἰκίαν ἀχειροποίητον αἰώνιον ἐν τοῖς οὐρανοῖς,* "We have a dwelling-place from God, a house not made by hands, eternal in the heavens")[8] has been ad-

---

5. N. Baumert, *Täglich sterben und auferstehen,* 123.

6. Ibid., 197.

7. Ibid., 249.

8. We simply mention that according to G. Wagner, "Le tabernacle et la vie 'en Christ.' Exégèse de 2 Corinthiens 5:1 à 10," RHPhR 41 (1961) 379–393, even the *οἰκία τοῦ σκήνους,* "house of the tent," of v. 1a would have a Christological sense, referring not to the simple mortal human body but to a way of being, that is, to the Christian's pilgrimage here below; then

vanced by J. A. T. Robinson.[9] But he means substantially the "dwelling-place in heaven" in not so much an individual as a collective and ecclesiological sense, or better as a tension between individuality and solidarity (Christ/Church), and hence as a factor of participation.[10] Now, the most properly Christological interpretation of the text has been done by A. Feuillet[11] and by J. F. Collange,[12] followed by other, especially French-speaking, scholars.[13] These authors readily appeal to Mark 14:58: "We have heard him say that ὅτι ἐγὼ καταλύσω τὸν ναὸν τοῦτον τὸν χειροποίητον, (I shall destroy this temple made by hands) and in three days ἄλλον ἀχειροποίητον οἰκοδομήσω (I shall build another not made by hands)," maintaining a possible dependence of the Pauline passage upon this Gospel logion. But it is pretty hard to avoid the insistent impression here of a biblizistisches Kombinazionsverfahren, a "biblicist procedure of combination."[14] For the verb οἴδαμεν, "we know," of v. 1 seems too weak to introduce a saying referred to Jesus (cf. the participle εἰδότες "knowing" in the context: 4:14; 5:6, 11).

Moreover, the Pauline text lacks the specific term ναός, which would be more appropriately referred to Christ (cf. John 2:19-22); on the contrary, the nouns used have no Christological correspondence, neither οἰκοδομή, "dwelling-place" (which if anything is found in Paul with an ecclesiological sense and alluding to a construction as an activity in progress); nor οἰκία, "house" (whereas the use of this word is attested anthropologically in Plato, Apol. 40c and in Cicero, Tusc. I 22:51); nor οἰκητήριον ἡμῶν, "our dwelling," of the following v. 2 (where the possessive pronoun assimilates it to the ἐπίγειος ἡμῶν οἰκία, "our earthly home," of v. 1). As for the present ἔχομεν, this can very well be equivalent to a fu-

---

ἐν τῷ σκήνει, "in the tent," of v. 4 would be equivalent to ἐν τῷ Χριστῷ, "in Christ." This curious interpretation has justly failed to be accepted, devoid as it is of a solid basis. For the Christological meaning of "tent" (but in Heb 9:11), see A. Vanhoye, "Par la tente plus grande et plus parfait . . . (Héb 9,11)," Bib 46 (1965) 1-28.

9. The Body: A Study in Pauline Theology (Philadelphia, 1977 = 1952) 76-78.

10. The ecclesiological interpretation of 5:1b has been emphasized by E. E. Ellis, "2 Corinthians 5:1-10 in Pauline Eschatology," NTS 6 (1959-60) 211-224, understanding even the οἰκία τοῦ σκήνους, "house of the tent," of v. 1a as the whole of humanity placed under the sign of death in Adam. For a criticism see D. E. H. Whiteley, The Theology of St. Paul (Oxford, 1964) 255-256.

11. "La demeure céleste et la destinée des chrétiens. Exégèse de II Cor., v,1-10," RechSR 44 (1956) 161-192, 360-402.

12. Énigmes de la Deuxième Épître aux Corinthiens. Étude exégètique de 2 Cor 2:14-7:4 (Cambridge, 1972) 171-174.

13. E.g., P. Grelot, De la mort à la vie éternelle, LD 67 (Paris, 1971) 98; P. Benoit, "L'évolution du langage apocalyptique dans le Corpus paulinien," in auct. var., Apocalypses et théologie de l'espérance, LD 95 (Paris, 1977) 299-335, esp. 319-325 (note p. 324: "I have said that Paul 'suspects'; indeed the whole passage gives the impression that he does not clearly conceive the solution to the problem that distresses him"); X. Léon-Dufour, Face à la mort: Jésus et Paul (Paris, 1979) 266f. (without discussion).

14. F. G. Lang, 2 Korinther 5,1-10, 185, n. 347.

ture (Blass-Debrunner, par. 323) to express present certainty about something that will surely take place in the future (Windisch, ad. loc., *"Präsens des dogmatischen Lehrsatzes und der religiösen Gewissheit"*; thus also Allo, Lietzmann, and more recently Barrett and Bultmann), all the more legitimate in an eschatological context (cf. the ἔστιν, "is," of 1 Cor 15:44b concerning the "pneumatic soma").

Moreover, when the Pauline correspondence speaks of "putting on Christ" (Rom 13:14; Gal 3:27; Eph 4:24; Col 3:10), it does so without ambiguity, with clearly explicit reference to Christ, whereas here the language would be too obscure, understandable only on the basis of an exegetical effort of considerable good will, not to mention that the same verb was already used in 1 Cor 15:53 in a sense that is not at all Christological. In sum, the whole context of 5:1 gives no reason to suggest a Christological sense for the "heavenly dwelling." The only and closest mentions of Christ are in 4:14 and 5:10; the former comparing the resurrection of the Christian with that of Christ, but the καί, "and," says clearly that we are dealing with two different events, while the σὺν Ἰησοῦ, "with Jesus" (cf. σὺν ὑμῖν, "with you") of v. 14b indicates simply an association of destiny;[15] the second mention concerns precisely the appearance "before the judgment seat of Christ," which therefore excludes any confusion of roles.

c) Another position would perceive in 5:1-10 a polemic intention of Paul against his Gnosticizing opponents in Corinth. Thus Bultmann, and especially Schmithals and Hoffmann.[16] These interpret everything that could be a reference to a possible "intermediate state" (especially vv. 3 and 8) as an allusion to the terminology of his adversaries, taken up to deny their doctrine; this would be true especially for the concept of γυμνότης, "nakedness" (v. 3), and ἐκδημῆσαι ἐκ τοῦ σώματος, "be absent from the body" (v. 8). Here Paul would want to combat the Greco-Gnostic theory of a purely spiritual (naked) existence after death, and hence a theory of redemption as liberation from the body. But we must concede that these authors honestly recognize their conclusion about such a polemic to be a mere theory, and in their exegesis they are generous with *maybe's* and *apparently's*.

15. According to R. C. Tannehill (*Dying and Rising with Christ: A Study in Pauline Theology* [Berlin, 1967] 88), "rising with Christ" and Christ as "the first fruits of those who have fallen asleep" in 1 Cor 15:21 come down to the same thing.

16. R. Bultmann, *Exegetische Probleme des zweiten Korintherbriefes* (Darmstadt, 1963 [1947¹]) 4f.; W. Schmithals, *Wisdom in Corinth*, trans. J. E. Steely (Nashville, 1971) 260f. = *Die Gnosis in Korinth* (Göttingen, 1965²) 246f.; P. Hoffmann, *Die Toten in Christus. Eine religionsgeschichtliche und exegetische Untersuchung zur paulinischen Eschatologie* (Münster, 1978³) 267f. See also R. Jewett, *Paul's Anthropological Terms: A Study of Their Use in Conflict Settings* (Leiden, 1971) 274–277.

The text actually makes no mention of combative intentions on Paul's part, whereas elsewhere in the letter they are manifest and even explosive (and not only in chapters 10–13; see also 2:17; 3:1; 4:2); at least in 5:5 these authors do not perceive any shadow of polemic. We get the clear impression that in 5:1-10 Paul proceeds with a peaceful expository tone, his eyes not on external opponents but on the experience of his own internal suffering. That he uses dualistic terminology that is Greek and in part also Jewish (see below) does not necessarily mean that he is combating it—or must we discover behind every word of Paul a concealed polemic intent, so that every term ipso facto reveals an adversary in ambush? Apart from everything else, it would be a remarkable sign of pessimism to maintain that whenever Paul thinks or writes, he is always doing so against someone. And then, why does Paul not appeal to the convincing theme of the resurrection, as in 1 Cor 15? He could thus really have taken on his supposed adversaries.

The exegesis of Schmithals and Hoffmann on vv. 3 and 8 ends up looking too much like pigheaded argumentation; the former actually admitting that Paul misunderstands the position of his opponents (Schmithals, 251). I should think that this technique contributes more to complicate the meaning of the text than to clarify it.[17]

II. Thematic analysis of the passage:
the Apostle's sufferings between faith and hope

The passage 2 Cor 4:7–5:10 is very rich in both the concepts and the language it displays. The images intertwine and are all of anthropological significance: the relationship between treasure and vessels (4:7), between the outer and the inner man (4:16), the figure of the house (5:1-2a), of the clothing (5:2b-4), and of exile (5:6-9). To this we add the rare expression about the "nekrosis, 'dying,' of Jesus" (4:10); the χάρις πλεονάσασα, "grace increasing" (4:15); the βάρος δόξης, "weight of glory" (4:17); the abstract and proverb-like statement of 4:18, οἰκία τοῦ σκήνους, "tent house," contrasted with that "not made by hands" (5:1); the adjective γυμνοί, "naked" (5:3); the interruption of 5:7 between vv. 6 and 8; the Christological meaning of "judgment seat" in 5:10.

The discourse is very personal. What emerges in the foreground is an experience of life, something that touches the Apostle in his living flesh. Especially striking is the insistence on his own physical diminution,

---

17. Against the hypothesis of Gnostic opponents, see also the competent and sharp judgment of H.-M. Schenke and K.-M. Fischer, *Einleitung in die Schriften des NT—I. Die Briefe des Paulus und Schriften des Paulinismus* (East Berlin, 1978) 104–105.

which betrays his preoccupation with νέϰρωσις, that is, with death's assertion of itself. Many are the expressions of this type: already each of the four antitheses of 4:8-9 begins with a negative term (θλιβόμενοι, ἀπορούμενοι, διωϰόμενοι, ϰαταβαλλόμενοι, "afflicted, perplexed, persecuted, struck down"), even though the emphasis falls on the second member, the positive character of which, however, comes only from the repetition of the negative οὐϰ, "not," with an even more negative term (namely, στενοχωρούμενοι, ἐξαπορούμενοι, ἐγϰαταλειπόμενοι, ἀπολλύμενοι, "crushed, utterly confounded, abandoned, destroyed"). The present participle περιφέροντες, "carry about," of v. 10 taking νέϰρωσις as its object suggests the idea of something one cannot get rid of, something inherent, which is therefore present always and everywhere; and this is confirmed by the expression of the following v. 11: "we are always exposed to death" (also "our mortal flesh"). Similarly, the verb διαφθείρεται, "decays," in 4:16; the mention of θλῖψις, "affliction," in 4:17; the verb ϰαταλυθῇ, "has been destroyed," in 5:1, referring to the "earthly" house/tent; the verb στενάζομεν, "groan," repeated in 5:2, 4; the probable component of fear in 5:3 of being found "naked" (dying before the parousia); the substantival adjective τὸ θνητόν, "that which is mortal," in 5:4; the concept of ἐϰδημεῖν, "be exiled," in 5:6, 8, 9, with the instability and precariousness this suggests; and even the concept of "faith" in 5:7, which by its contrast with "vision" takes on a connotation of obscurity and imperfection.

The allusion to the tribulations of Paul's ministry is evident, and these derive not only from the objective and inevitable difficulties and hardships of travel and lodging, the burden of manual labor (cf. Acts 18:3; 20:34), or even from the sickness that afflicted him (cf. 2 Cor 12:7; Gal 4:13). Even more so (as 2 Corinthians alone amply documents), not only was his life already exposed in Asia to a "sentence of death" (1:8-9), which we cannot better define, but it is constantly, in various ways, put to the test "in tribulations, in necessity, in anguish, in beatings, in prisons, in riots, in toil, in sleeplessness, in fasts" (6:4-5; cf. 1 Cor 4:9-13; esp. 2 Cor 11:23f.)

Still, all these experiences of limitation and pain did not lead Paul to depression or self-pity. That he was "satisfied [εὐδοϰῶ] with infirmities, insults, deprivations, persecutions, anguish suffered for Christ" (12:10) should not be understood too psychologically and somewhat masochistically, as suggested by the Vulgate *placeo mihi* ("I like"): both because the context of the statement is theological and because the same verb εὐδοϰέω is better translated "accept, approve" and precisely, "say yes" (thus Bultmann, ad loc.: "Deshalb sage ich Ja zu . . .").

In our passage 4:7–5:10, what moves Paul "not to lose heart" (4:16: οὐϰ ἐγϰαϰοῦμεν; cf. 4:6) and to "be of good courage" (5:6: θαρροῦντες; cf.

5:8) depends on two basic reasons: faith in Christ and eschatological hope. Between these two poles runs his existence, and thus are his tribulations alleviated.

In the first place, it is the typical Christian faith that strengthens the whole apostolic behavior from within. A little later in 5:14 Paul will say that Christ and his agape συνέχει ἡμᾶς, that is, "contains us," in the sense of "sustaining us, keeping us steady, binding us," or "dominating us" (Bultmann: "beherrschen") and "holding us in his power," like "having us in his hand" (Wendland: "hält uns in ihrer Gewalt"; less happily Barrett: "controls our action"). Paul, indeed, though humanly comparable to a "vessel of clay," is fully conscious of guarding and handling a "treasure" (4:7a); he knows well that he must leave room for God's power (4:7b), which proves itself in weakness (13:4; cf. 1 Cor 2:3-5; 2 Cor 12:9).[18] The affirmation of death in himself is always related to Jesus, so that the sufferings experienced have not only a human explanation but by faith represent a participation in those of Christ (1:5; cf. esp. Phil 3:10; Col 1:24). In 4:10-14, in fact, there emerges the typical paschal pattern of the life/death dialectic, which not only from the outside makes sense of the apostolic service but inheres from within, giving him the very rhythm of the paschal mystery: "So that death is at work in us, but life in you" (v. 12). This refers to the same fertility as that of the "blood poured out" (Mark 14:24) and of the "grain of wheat that dies" (John 12:24; 1 Cor 15:36). To this extent the thesis of Baumert examined above is justified, i.e., insofar as the apostolic existence, according to the book's title, is truly "a daily dying and rising."[19] The text of 4:13 (citing Ps 115:1 LXX) then makes explicit reference to πίστις, "faith" (in a more positive sense than 5:7) as moving almost irresistibly to the task of evangelization. This impulse to engage in the preaching Paul gets not only from his "mystical" union with Christ but even more basically from the encounter he had with him when there shone in his heart the light of God, which revealed to him the knowledge of the divine glory that shines in the face of Jesus Christ (4:6; cf. Gal 1:16), in which it can be seen as in a mirror (3:18).

---

18. For bibliography on this theme, see P. Bonnard, "Faiblesse et puissance selon St. Paul," EThL 33 (1958) 61-82; E. Güttgemanns, Der leidende Apostel und sein Herr (Göttingen, 1966); Ph. Seidensticker, Paulus, der verfolgte Apostel Jesu Christi (Stuttgart, 1965); E. Kamlah, "Wie beurteilt Paulus sein Leiden? Ein Beitrag zur Untersuchung seiner Denkstruktur," ZNW 54 (1963) 217-232; G. G. O'Collins, "Power Made Perfect in Weakness: 2 Cor 12:9-10," CBQ 33 (1971) 528-537. See also P. Iovino, Chiesa e tribolazione. Il tema della θλῖψις nelle lettere di S. Paolo, Fac. Theol. di Sicilia, Studi 1 (Palermo, 1985).

19. On the theme see also R. C. Tannehill, Dying and Rising with Christ; E. Schweizer, "Die 'Mystik' des Sterbens und Auferstehens mit Christus bei Paulus," Beiträge zur Theologie des NT (Zurich, 1970) 182-203.

In the second place, the eschatological orientation of the apostolic tribulations also gives them value and makes them bearable. Already the concept of ζωή, "life," in 4:10-11 indicates that the νέκρωσις has precisely life "in our body" and "in our mortal flesh" as its fruit, so that even the body has its share in the whole life.[20] In 4:14 the explicit concept of resurrection appears through a parallelism and hence a comparison of destiny between that of Christ and that of Paul and Christians generally. The "eternal weight of glory" in 14:17 must also be read in this perspective because of its apocalyptic parallels (e.g., in Syr. Bar. 15:18; 48:50; 51:12; cf. 4 Macc 17:12; see also Seneca, Tranq. an. 16:4). Then even the statement of 4:18, "The things that are invisible are eternal," does not retain the spiritual/ metaphysical meaning of the parallels in Greek literature in the sense of something "beyond" the material things (e.g., Plato, Phaed. 79a; Seneca, Ep. 58:27; Corp. Herm. 7:1-2), but acquires a clearer eschatological reference to what is to come, and hence a more Jewish timbre (cf. Syr. Bar. 52:7; 4 Esdr 7:16: "Why have you not accepted in your heart what is future but what is in the present?"). In 5:1-10 the attention of Paul to "the things that are unseen" becomes still more insistent, though he relies on the help of various images and his syntax grows heavier (note the repetition of v. 2 in v. 4 and of v. 6 in v. 8), an evident sign not of a wavering hope but only of the inadequacy of language to describe these things that are unseen. The present "we have" of v. 1 already expresses the solid certainty already possessed of a new dwelling beyond history "in the heavens." The repetition of the present indicative "we groan" or "we sigh" in vv. 2 and 4 indicates precisely the sighs and groans of waiting, a component of "intensely desiring" expressed by the present participle ἐπιποθοῦντες of v. 2. This straining toward what must come manifests itself in v. 3 with the future passive indicative εὑρεθησόμεθα, "we shall be found," indicating the ineluctability of an encounter, the determination of which does not depend on us; even the conjunction εἴ γε καί, "whether indeed . . .," moves toward an orientation toward a future anthropologically open to the alternative between being "clothed" or being "naked."[21]

20. Here should be noted the difference of the Platonic conception, according to which the ideal life is obtained by the liberation of the psyche from the body: Plato, Phaed. 66e–67a ("as long as we are in life, we will be nearer to knowledge the less we have to do with the body . . . until the god chooses to come to deliver us from all"; see 67e: philosophers are out of harmony with their own bodies and so have no fear of death). Thus Philo of Alexandria, De gig. 14: true philosophers urge themselves "to die to the bodily life" (τὸν μετὰ σωμάτων ἀποθνῄσκειν βίον) to participate in "incorporeal and incorruptible life" (τῆς ἀσωμάτου καὶ ἀφθάρτου); see Quod det. pot. ins. 49.

21. The translation of v. 3 (εἴ γε καὶ ἐνδυσάμενοι οὐ γυμνοὶ εὑρεθησόμεθα, "if, indeed, we shall be found having been clothed, not naked") is as difficult as it is important for the interpretation of the whole pericope. Here it is not a matter of fully discussing the text and grammar

The image of "being clothed over" (vv. 2, 4b) is quite understandable in an eschatological context, as already in 1 Cor 15:53-54, a passage that does explain 2 Cor 5:4c. Furthermore, in v. 5 the pneumatological concept of ἀρραβών, "down payment" (cf. 1:22; Eph 1:14; also the ἀπαρχή, "first-fruits," in Rom 8:23), orients the one who possesses it to a later and perfect completion. In vv. 6-9 the typical concept of exile and of "journey" (v. 7) πρὸς τὸν κύριον, "with the Lord" (v. 8), clearly reveals the dynamic and goal-oriented dimension of apostolic and Christian life (cf. Phil 3:13-14). Finally, in v. 10 the "judgment seat of Christ" describes the place of a universal and definitive summons to judgment and indicates the final end point of all human existence (cf. 1 Hen 61:8: "And the Lord of the Spirits placed the Chosen One on the throne of glory; and he will judge all the saints on high in heaven, and all their actions will be weighed in the balance"; see 45:3; 51:3; 62:2).

In conclusion, we could describe the whole section as standing between two extremities: the beginning (4:6) alludes discreetly to the moment of Paul's conversion, and so to the absolute beginning of his Christian/apostolic existence. The end (5:10) looks forward to the final, eschatologi-

---

of the phrase. I think, however, that we should reject Bultmann's version, ad loc., reading ἐκδυσάμενοι, "unclothed," rather than "clothed" (thus also against Nestle and Merk, the critical edition of K. Aland, who, however, does not provide justification in the critical apparatus; it is a "Western" reading: D, Marcion, Tertullian, a correction in Ambrosiaster): Paul, against Gnostic opponents, would be expressing the hope that despite having "taken off" the earthly body, he will not be "naked," because there will be a Himmelsgewand, "heavenly raiment," in the parousia, not for the damned but for Christians. Thus the position of Collange (210–218) seems wrong: he separates the καί from the εἴ γε (contra Gal 3:4) and interprets both the aorist participle and the adjective Christologically: "to be naked" would mean being separated from Christ after having put him on in baptism, having rejected him as one would cast aside a garment; but the language of "nakedness" in this sense is not Pauline; rather, Paul would speak of the "old man" or of returning to the "flesh" (see 2 Cor 5:16-17; Gal 3:3).

The recent Italian ecumenical translation distorts the sense of the aorist and especially of the conjunction, reading "We thus hope to be clothed in it and not to be found naked" (echoing the version of J. Héring, ad loc., "Afin que l'ayant revêtu nous ne soyons pas trouvés nus," and especially of C. K. Barrett, ad loc.: "in the hope that, when we have put it on, we shall not be discovered to be naked"; but the εἴ γε καί, "if indeed," does not introduce a final clause, nor does it express hope, since the γε is added "simply to lay stress on the condition": Liddell-Scott-Jones, s.v.; Blass-Debrunner 439.2).

The solution, I should think, consists in referring the aorist participle, not to the heavenly future body (with which we shall be clothed), but to the present, earthly body (with which we are or shall have been clothed). There will thus not be a true coordination between the aorist participle and the adjective as predicates of the passive future indicative, for the objection is valid (advanced for example by Collange, 212) according to which in order to be coordinate with the second the first ought rather to be a perfect participle, ἐνδεδυμένοι, "having been [and remaining] clothed" (even though an argument based on the asyndetic structure of the antithesis would not be decisive given such a construction in v. 7). The aorist participle is better considered separately as appropriately signifying a past situation in respect to the future "we shall be found." Thus the sentence could be translated: "provided that having earlier been wearing clothes, we shall not be found naked."

242 History and Exegesis

cal outcome of the whole process of the development of his ministerial task. Between these two extremes runs the whole life of the Apostle, of which the dramatic dimension of suffering between faith and hope re-echoes in this passage.

III. An evasive anthropology

Underlying the whole of 4:7–5:10 is an anthropological conception that is evident, but at the same time difficult to grasp on its exact semantic level.

We begin by considering the terminology. The problematic expressions are the following: "in vessels of clay" (ἐν ὀστρακίνοις σκεύεσιν: 4:7); "in the [our] body" (ἐν τῷ σώματι [ἡμῶν]: 4:10 [twice]); "in our mortal flesh" (ἐν τῇ θνητῇ σαρκὶ ἡμῶν: 4:11); "will raise us up" (ἡμᾶς . . . ἐγερεῖ: 4:14); "our outer" and "our inner man" (ὁ ἔξω ἡμῶν ἄνθρωπος and ὁ ἔσω ἡμῶν: 4:16); "the tent of our earthly dwelling" (ἡ ἐπίγειος ἡμῶν οἰκία τοῦ σκήνους: 5:1a), with which is found an antithetic or climactic parallel "the dwelling from God not made by hands" (οἰκοδομὴν ἐκ θεοῦ . . . ἀχειροποίητον: 5:1b) and "our dwelling" (τὸ οἰκητήριον ἡμῶν: 5:2); "in the tent" and "what is mortal" (ἐν τῷ σκήνει and θνητόν: 5:4); "in the body" (ἐν τῷ σώματι: 5:6); "out of the body" (ἐκ τοῦ σώματος: 5:8); "through the body" (διὰ τοῦ σώματος: 5:10). To these expressions must be added the images of clothing (5:2-4) and of exile (5:6, 8-9). Moreover, the first person plural pronoun (ἡμῶν, ἡμῖν, ἡμᾶς, "our, to us, us") recurs sixteen times, and the distributive pronoun ἕκαστος, "each one," once (5:10). As we see, in a few verses there occur some fifteen expressions that make the passage remarkably rich anthropologically. And this is strictly connected with the theme of apostolic sufferings, which find their material precisely in the bodily and historical dimension (cf. the ἐπίγειος, "earthly," of 5:1a) of the Apostle/Christian.

Precisely here there arises a problem: How must we understand the anthropology that emerges here? We cannot answer this without simultaneously passing judgment on the language in which it is expressed—is it characteristically Greek or Jewish? And hence, is the language here present dualistic or holistic in nature? The opinions of the authors diverge, even to an extreme degree, on the issue of whether it is Greek or Jewish, or even exclusively Christian.[22] Others recognize, more correctly I believe,

22. For instance, the Greek background is championed by C. Clemen, *Religionsgeschichtliche Erklärung des NT* (Berlin-New York, 1973 [Giessen, 1924²]) 334-335, where parallels are derived only from the pagan milieu; but for the "Jewish" reading, see W. D. Davies, *Paul and Rabbinic Judaism* (London, 1965³ [1948]) 314: "The language of Paul can be explained without recourse to Hellenistic sources." For the "Christian" reading, see J.-F. Collange, op. cit., 170-243. More recently R. H. Gundry, *"Sōma" in Biblical Theology with Emphasis on Pauline Anthropology* (Cambridge, 1976), but without emphasizing parallels of the milieu, and oppos-

the actual complexity and lack of system of Paul's thought in our pericope.[23] We must not, of course, ignore a decisive Jewish component, but we must also honestly admit a real Hellenizing language, with the necessary specification that both have undergone in the new Christian perspective. Indeed, it is this that is in the last analysis determinative, for even if certain Greek and Jewish concepts are here merged in the Christian synthesis, there are still certain ideas that remain exclusively Christian, with no possibility of possible parallels (as in 4:10-12: participation in the paschal mystery; in 4:14: the resurrection of Christ; in 5:5: the gift of the Spirit as down payment).

On the other hand, the passage that could apparently still stand up, even if separated from a context of Christian faith, is surely 4:16-18, of which Windisch correctly says that "it could just as well stand unaltered in a Jewish apocalypse or a letter of Seneca" (ad loc.), while according to J. Héring these verses "could have been written by Philo or another Platonic author" (ad loc.) But then, our passage contains such a fusion of elements that a semantic autopsy of the various phases would reveal many cultural links, though we know that the individual pieces alone simply cannot provide the full meaning of the whole sentence. We now will give some examples.

First of all, the text of 4:7 (literally: "We have this treasure in vessels of clay, in order that the superabundance of power be God's and not from us"). Verse 7a shows a strident opposition between "treasure" and "vessels of clay," which v. 7b interprets nonmetaphorically as the relationship between the saving power of God and the feebleness of the Apostle as God's instrument (cf. 1 Cor 2:3-5; 2 Cor 12:9-10). Now, the anthropological use of the image of the "vessel" is at home in the Greco-Roman world; the best known text is Cicero's "The body is a vessel or a type of receptacle of the soul" (*Tusc.* I 22:52; but cf. Lucretius, *Rer. nat.* III 440 and 555);[24] even so, the precise term σκεῦος, "vessel," in an anthropological use is unattested in Greek literature except in Scripture (cf. in LXX: Ps 31 [30]:12; Jer 22:28). This is based on the comparison of God/the Creator to a potter (Lam 4:2; Isa 64:8; Gen 2:7; Rom 9:20-23); and thus

---

ing the Bultmannian holistic interpretation, has strongly defended anthropological dualism in the Pauline correspondence; on 2 Cor 4:16 and 5:1-10, see pp. 135–137 and 149–154.

23. See esp. H. Windisch, *Der zweite Korintherbrief* (Göttingen, 1924⁹ [1970]), which is the work richest in documentation on parallels in the milieu; also J. Dupont, *Syn Christôi. L'union avec le Christ suivant St. Paul* (Bruges, 1952) 164–170. Also basically respectful of Paul's complexity are the commentaries of C. K. Barrett (London, 1976²) and R. Bultmann (posthumously edited by E. Dinkler: Göttingen, 1976); very reserved is H. D. Wendland (Göttingen, 1968), who is quite noncommittal.

24. See also J. Pépin, *Idées grecques sur l'homme et sur Dieu* (Paris, 1971) 122f., n. 3.

244 *History and Exegesis*

certain rabbinic texts document the same metaphor as Paul's (e.g., *Sifr. Deut.* 11:22 par. 48).[25] The term, therefore, means specifically "vessel" and has a clear anthropological value; it is, then, not equivalent to the generic Hebrew *kᵉlî* in the broad meaning of "instrument," also because our text is specified with the adjective ὀστϱάκινος, which specifically indicates a "clay" vessel.[26]

But not only is the use of the word here metaphorical, it is foreign to a dualistic perspective. Indeed, it is not contrasted with ψυχή, "soul" which is correctly avoided in the context (the term is found in 2 Corinthians only in 4:23, 12:15, and then with a Semitic connotation).[27] The antithesis is, rather, with θησαυϱός, "treasure," which, specified as it is by the demonstrative adjective οὗτος, "this," refers to what immediately precedes; therefore the treasure is not the soul but rather either "the illumination of the knowledge of God's glory in our hearts" (4:6) or else the apostolic διακονία, "service," itself (4:1) as ministry of the new covenant (cf. 3:5-11). At question, then, is not the opposition of soul and body but rather the opposition between the message of the gospel and the whole human being as its fragile guard and bearer. But in this view, σκεῦος, "vessel," does also include the human body; indeed a particular emphasis falls on the body, since a little later Paul speaks of "carrying the death of Jesus in our *body*" (v. 10), which, although destined to receive in itself also the life of Jesus (v. 11), is at the center of the Apostle's experience of suffering. In any case, as we see, there is a certain wavering between a holistic anthropological conception and one that is not clearly dualistic but tends to emphasize the bodily dimension of the human person.

In the second place we consider 4:16 and the opposition contained there between ὁ ἔξω ἡμῶν ἄνθϱωπος and ὁ ἔσω ἡμῶν "our outer / our inner man." The terminology is clearly derived from Greek philosophy. Of the various parallels in the milieu we note only the principal ones: Plato, *Rep.* IX 589a; Philo, *Det. pot. ins.* 22f;[28] Epictetus, *Diatr.* III 3:13, II 7:3; 8:14; *Corpus Herm.* I 15; XIII 7f.; Plotinus, *Enn.* III 2:15. In all these cases the "outer man" refers to the human body, and hence to the material aspect. Paul, too, moves in this direction; if there is a difference it concerns his specific point of view: for him the outer man is understood not in the sense of the human senses and passions as a source of human slavery; rather, it

25. See Strack-Billerbeck, III 516.
26. Against J.-F. Collange, op. cit., 146.
27. Therefore the Liddell-Scott-Jones Lexicon (Oxford, 1961) should be considered out of order when it offers as a secondary meaning of σκεῦος: "the *body*, as *vessel* of the soul," a metaph. clearly expressed in 2 Ep. Cor. 4.7"! See, rather, C. Maurer, art. σκεῦος, TDNT 7:365.
28. See also *Agr.* 8 and 108; *Plant.* 42; *Conf. ling.* 24; *Rer. div. her.* 231; *Congr.* 97; *Fug.* 71; *Somn.* II 207; *Omn. prob. lib.* 111; *Quaest. Gen.* I 94.

is seen as another way of indicating, without disparagement, the simple "mortal flesh" of v. 11 and therefore, given the context, the possibility of undergoing the various apostolic sufferings in this "visible" world (v. 18) but with the prospect of the resurrection (v. 14). In any case, the expression alludes clearly enough to the bodily dimension of the human person. But Paul seems to differentiate himself more from the surrounding culture in the conception of the "inner man." Actually, for the Greek tradition this was simply equivalent to the ψυχή, "soul,"[29] or the νοῦς, "mind,"[30] or else to the "demon within,"[31] not to speak of the divine spark in Gnosticism. In all these cases the anthropological dualism is so deeply rooted that the various ancient writers use images of a strongly extrinsic flavor.[32]

The expression "the inner man" recurs in Rom 7:22 and Eph 3:16, and we need not always read the same meaning into it.[33] But certainly by it Paul intends the deepest human inwardness (cf. Rom 12:2; Eph 4:23). Still, the text 2 Cor 4:16 seems not to stop with this neutral, unspecified anthropological conception. Without reaching M. Barth's extreme, which actually sees a Christological title in the expression,[34] it would seem we cannot limit the expression to its originally purely psychological meaning. Indeed, its immediate context is dense with allusions to the new Christian realities, which condition it: note the allusion to the "life of Jesus" in vv. 10-11, the "spirit of faith" in v. 13, "grace" in 15, and then the "down payment of the Spirit" in 5:5 and the "new creation" in 5:17.

All these ideas surely fill the expression "inner man" with a new meaning. But here we must ask, Do they perhaps change it completely? Indeed, several scholars interpret it as equivalent to the new Adam, the man of the Age to Come, the "new creation" itself (5:17); according to Lietzmann it "indicates the pneumatic possession of the Christian, the same thing that in 5:5 is called ἀρραβὼν τοῦ πνεύματος, 'the down payment of the Spirit': it is the seed of the 'new creation' that little by little keeps developing, it is the Christ who is formed in the Christian, according to Gal 2:20;

29. See Plato, *I Alc.* 130c; *Leg.* XII 959a-b; *Rep.* IV 430e-431a.
30. See, e.g., Philo, *Congr.* 97: "The intellect is properly the man of man, the stronger in the weaker, the immortal in the mortal"; see *Quaest. Gen.* I 79.
31. Thus Marcus Aurelius, *Medit.* II 13 and 17; III 5; V 27; see also III 3; VIII 40.
32. E.g., for Plato the body is "prison" of the soul (*Phaed.* 62b; *Ax.* 365e) and even "tomb" (*Crat.* 400c; thus Philo, *Quaest. Gen.* I 70; see 93); for Plutarch it is a horse that carries the rider (*Adv. Colot.* 21:1119A); according to Epictetus, it is "by nature a corpse" (*Diatr.* III 10:15); for Marcus Aurelius, "that which is hidden within you . . . mind you do not think of it as a single whole with that other which surrounds it" (*Medit.* X 38).
33. See R. Bultmann, ad loc.; M. Barth, *Ephesians I-II* (Garden City, N.Y., 1974) I, 389-392.
34. Ibid., 391f. [in reference to the usage in Ephesians—T. P. W.].

4:19."[35] That there is here an intimate connection with these realities is beyond doubt. But the idea expressed by the verb ἀνακαινοῦται, "is renewed," distinguishes the subject (specifically, the "inner man") from that with which some would want to identify it (i.e., the Spirit or Christ within us): if the "inner man" is already the "new creation," how can it "be renewed"? It would be better to say that the daily renewal of the "inner man" comes *through* the Spirit given to us by God as a down payment (5:5) and that the "new creation" (5:17) exists at a level deeper and higher than the simple "inner man," which it includes but does not replace.[36]

In short, we should acknowledge in the expression the anthropological sense with a Greek nuance, but well integrated into the Christian newness; and it is of course this latter that we must grasp to enrich a purely philosophical expression (and it seems not even Saint Thomas, ad loc., does so adequately when he defines the inner man as "mind or reason, furnished with the hope of the future reward and strengthened by the protection of faith"). In each case there remains in the background an anthropological dualism that is not between "mortal body" and "Christ within," but between "mortal body" and "human spirit renewed by the divine Spirit."[37] In the first case, indeed, in the strict sense of the term the "outer man" should approximate the "old man" in the hamartiological sense as well, but that would already put us on the threshold of Gnosticism.

In the third place, it is useful to seek the sense of the image of the "house" in 5:1-2a, which Paul expresses with several expressions (οἰκία τοῦ σκήνους, οἰκοδομή, οἰκία, οἰκητήριον, "house of the tent, building, house, dwelling"). That this is an anthropological metaphor is certain. Even so, the terms οἰκία/*domus*/house in Greco-Roman literature are not much used in this sense. At the most it seems to be only Plato (*Apol.* 40c) who speaks

35. H. Lietzmann, *An die Korinther I.II* (Tübingen, 1949⁴) 117. The same direction is represented in the commentaries of Héring, Wendland, Barrett, Bultmann. Disagreeing are Allo, Collange, and S. Cipriani (*Le Lettere di S. Paolo* [Assisi, 1974⁶] ad loc.: "Man in his part that is the more noble, illuminated, and guided by the Spirit of God").

36. Correctly J.-F. Collange, op. cit., 175, citing B. Rey, *Créés dans le Christ Jésus. La création nouvelle selon St. Paul* (Paris, 1966) 147–156, distinguishes between the "inner man" and the "new man": only the latter is the one reborn in baptism, while the former is only man as a conscious being. But as said above (see the preceding note), we must distinguish the different occurrences; in our text, then, the mention of the "inner man" is properly associated with the idea of renewal. But the distinction between the two is valid; Paul never speaks of "putting on the interior man" but "the new man"!

37. See R. H. Gundry, "*Sōma*" in *Biblical Theology*, 136f. C. F. D. Moule offers a strong presentation of the Pneuma as so transforming man as to lead him little by little to his eschatological maturity even on the physical level ("St. Paul and Dualism: The Pauline Conception of Resurrection," NTS 12 [1965–66] 106–123).

of death as a μετοίκησις, "change of residence." Rather, the opposite idea is present, that the body is not a true "home" (understanding "worthy of the soul"); it is only a *hospitium*, "guest house" (Cicero, *Senect.* 23:84: "Ita discedo tamquam ex hospitio, non tamquam ex domo"); a *deversorium*, "inn" (ibid.); an *aliena domus*, "someone else's house" (idem, *Tusc.* I 22:51); at the most an *obnoxium domicilium*, "slave quarters" (Seneca, *Ep.* 65:21). Rather, the true *domus* is heaven after death (Cicero, *Tusc.* I 22:51; *Divin.* I 25:53). The Bible makes little use of Hebrew *byt*, "house," anthropologically (see Job 4:19); the Rabbis even less. However, Philo returns several times precisely to οἰκία, "house," to indicate the body as dwelling of the soul: *Det. pot. ins.* 33; *Praem.* 120; *Omn. prob.* 111 (see *Virt.* 77: death = ἀποικία, "absence from home").

But more frequent is the concept of σκῆνος, "tent"; precisely "the normal use" of this Greek term "is the transf. one for a body";[38] see Ps.-Plat., *Ax.* 365e-366a; Philo, *Quaest. in Gen.* 1:28; *Corp. Herm.* 13:15; Wis 9:15.

In the New Testament the expression is found only in our passage, 2 Cor 5:1, 4 (see also σκήνωμα, "tent-dwelling," in 2 Pet 1:13f.). The expression οἰκία τοῦ σκήνους, "house of the tent," of 5:1 should be understood as a genitive of specification (if not epexegetical), so that the second term specifies the first more exactly and takes the accent on itself; and thus in 5:4 it is repeated by itself. Paul says: Our house on this earth is like a tent, that is, provisional and fragile, and this tent is our body, destined sooner or later to be "dissolved/knocked down/destroyed" (καταλυθῇ).

Still, it is important to note that Paul does not mention "soul" (ψυχή). This shows that his interest does not turn on dualism as such. He does presuppose a duality, but the attention of his speech is on the one hand wholly concentrated on what we would call the material component of the person; on the other hand, with Greek logic we would expect that he would affirm the pure immortality of the soul separated from the body. But in fact the speech about the future after death is concerned with the total person, as the personal pronoun ἡμᾶς, "us," of v. 5 suggests (see below).

To this image of the home belongs also the metaphorical terminology of exile in vv. 6, 8, 9, with the verbs ἐνδημέω/ἐκδημέω, "be at home/be absent." The true home, indeed, and hence the native land is that of the

38. See W. Michaelis, art. σκῆνος, TDNT 7:381. [In Par. Jer. (composed between 70 and 130 A.D.) 6:1 we read: "Prepare yourself, O my heart; rejoice and exult in your *tent* (σκηνωμα), that is, in your *house of flesh* (σαρκικος οικος), for your suffering has been changed into joy. Indeed the Powerful One comes and will take you 'from your tent *(εκ του σκηνηματος σου)*.' "—Addition by author. T. P. W., trans.]

248 *History and Exegesis*

future (see above). Already Socrates in Plato, *Phaed.* 67, spoke of his own life as an "emigration" *(ἀποδημία)*; cf. 61e; *Apol.* 40c. But it is especially Philo of Alexandria who insists repeatedly on this theme: "The whole of life in the body is exile" (*Rer. div. her.* 82; cf. 276; *Somn.* 1:180-181: *Conf. ling.* 76-82; but see Plutarch, *De facie* 943c). Even here the two expressions in antithetic parallelism, "to dwell on in the flesh" (v. 6) and "to be exiled from the body" (v. 8), suggest the dualistic anthropology.[39] Still, there is never any allusion to the "soul." We must therefore conclude that the mention of the σῶμα, "body," according to the whole context, always refers to "our mortal flesh" (4:11) as that which mediates νέκρωσις, "dying" (4:10), which the Apostle experiences daily; it is our actual historical body, subject to suffering and death, but which does not therefore exclude another somatic form (namely, that of the "pneumatic body" of 1 Cor 14:44).

Precisely this context of the Apostle's suffering, fruitful as it is for life (see above), distances Paul's anthropology from that of the Greco-Roman milieu, to which certain expressions would seem to assimilate it: nothing here of the disparaging of life, which Seneca defines as "useless meat and fluid, useful only for receiving food, [. . .] an idle and dissipated animal" (*Ep.* 92:10), and Chrysippus calls "a 'nothing' for us, like fingernails and hair" (*SVF* III 752, p. 187).[40] Both Semitic anthropology and Christological faith in the paschal mystery have a determinative influence on Paul's discourse.

Finally, we must briefly consider the dialectical image "clothed"/"naked" of 5:2b-4. The idea of the flesh as *clothing* is already found in Empedocles (Diels, fr. 126), but becomes conspicuous in Plato (*Gorg.* 523c-d) and is present again in Seneca (*Ep.* 92:13; 102:25; *Ad Marc.* 25:1) and in the *Corpus Hermeticum* (7:2; 10:17-18). This is particularly developed in the late apocryphal *Asc. Is.* (7:22; 8:26; 9:2, 8, 9, 17; cf. 4 Esdr 14:14). As for the correlative idea of *nakedness*, we find it in Plato (*Gorg.* 523e, 524d; *Crat.* 403b; clearly expressed of the ψυχὴ γυμνὴ τοῦ σώματος, "soul stripped of the body"), in Plutarch (*De sera* 26), in Philo (*Virt.* 76; cf. *Leg. alleg.* II 55-59: "The soul that loves God strips itself of the body"), in Hadrian (*Hist. Aug.* I 25), in the *Corpus Hermeticum* (10:17).[41]

39. The position of R. Jewett is scarcely worth noting, that in 2 Cor 5:6-8 Paul would simply be quoting a phrase of his Gnostic adversaries depreciating the body, in order to Christianize it with his own concept of a relational and eschatological reality (op. cit., 276); but this is just a pure hypothesis useful for the author's thesis.
40. See also n. 32. Another current of opinion maintained the death of the soul as well, since it is subject to suffering, and especially to birth (thus Panaetius and Epicurus; see Aristotle's principle, "Whatever is born is destined to perish"); hence the Platonic, Pythagorean, and Stoic principle of metensomatosis, i.e., the preexistence of the soul, which passes into the body without really being born. On all this see J. Pépin, op. cit., esp. 145-160.
41. For the Gnostics, see Irenaeus (*Adv. haer.* I:5:5), Clement of Alexandria (*Exc. ex Theod.* 55), Hippolytus (*Ref.* V 8:44). On the mystery religions, see F. Cumont, *The Oriental Religions*

In Paul's text we should note these elements of expression: he twice uses the verb ἐπενδύσασθαι (vv. 2b, 4b), which literally means "put on over"[42] and indicates in no wise stripping but adding another bodily "garment" to that with which one is presently clothed; this is reinforced by the participle ἐπιποθοῦντες (v. 2), which explicitly indicates "desiring" so to do; moreover, v. 4b emphasizes that "we do not want to strip." This strong sense of attachment to the "garment"/body, which now appears alone in strident opposition to the dominant surrounding culture, stands out all the more because of the groan mentioned in v. 4a (cf. v. 2a). It is to be explained not as terror of the total death of the individual, which is completely outside Paul's Christian perspective (see below), but only as repugnance for physical death, which contrasts with the definitive anthropological perfection to be realized in the parousia. Hence a text of such Hellenistic flavor as Wis 9:15 (φθαρτὸν γὰρ σῶμα βαρύνει ψυχήν, "for the perishable body weighs down the soul") cannot be considered parallel to this one, both because the identical verb has a different meaning[43] and because there is here no allusion to the "soul" in itself. We should add that in v. 3 the prospect of "being found naked" (i.e., stripped of the body) is considered in the form of a negative conditional, a signal that Paul is not enthusiastic about it (and that as regards the *terminus a quo* of the anthropological condition rather than the *terminus ad quem* of communion with the Lord).

As we see, there is agreement with Greco-Roman culture, but it is rather superficial, limited to terminology. Paul remains at a distance in two ways:[44] first of all, he does not consider it desirable to be found naked, i.e., he does not like death as physical dissolution (unlike Plato, *Phaed.* 67d-e); then at the center of his message there is not the body/soul contrast but only that of the anthropological present and of the future, understood globally. It is not clear "how he understood life after death. . . .

---

in *Roman Paganism* (New York, 1954 = 1911) 125–126, 269, n. 54 = *Les religions orientales dans le paganisme romain* (Paris, 1963⁴ [1929]), 117, 217 n. 36, 282 n. 69).

42. Liddell-Scott-Jones, s.v., with documentation.

43. The present participle βαρούμενοι, "weighed down," in 2 Cor 5:4 can in principle have two meanings: either psychological in the sense of "anguished," more likely so because of the immediately following ἐπ᾽ ᾧ, "in that . . .," which gives the reasons for the existential anguish; or else physical in the sense of "weighted down," i.e., by the body/tent (this meaning is more attested in Greek literature, with reference to wine, sleep, trouble). The latter would harmonize more with Wis 9:15, but only in the letter, for this would at any rate contrast with the desire "not to be stripped," of which Wisdom certainly does not speak (see also Philo, *Migr. Abr.* 204; Epictetus, *Diatr.* I:1:15; 9:14f.). It is not impossible that the Pauline στενάζομεν βαρούμενοι, "we groan being weighed down," switches the grammatical value of the terms, which would read more smoothly βαρούμεθα στενάζοντες, "we are weighed down groaning," giving the participle the value of a principal verb, which fits it better.

44. Thus correctly J. N. Sevenster, "Some Remarks on the γυμνός in II Cor V 3," *Studia Paulina in honorem J De Zwaan* (Haarlem, 1953) 202–214, esp. 208f.

When his hope has its center in the question: 'being away from the Lord' or 'being with Christ,' the other one: 'which part of man will live after death?' must lose much of its importance."[45]

IV. An essential but unsystematic eschatology

The particular level of eschatological discourse in 2 Cor 4:7–5:10 still remains surprising. Not only is it not systematic, but it is not very clear, departing considerably from the evident themes of 1 Cor 15. Indeed, our pericope is missing a number of typical Pauline terms that carry key ideas. Not only is there not a single element of the traditional apocalyptic scenario (cf. at least the fragments of 1 Cor 15:52; 1 Thess 4:16), but not even the word *parousia* appears, even though it seems reasonable to see it suggested in 5:3, 10.

Even the idea of resurrection makes only a timid appearance in 4:14, where, however, the element of eschatological hope is actually lumped together with confession of Christological faith. In a parallel way, the repeated mention of the σῶμα, "body," is practically always related to the present historical, suffering body, from which a future separation is foreseen, rather than to the risen and pneumatic body, to which he alludes, if at all, with such a paraphrase as 4:10-11; 5:4c or with veiled images as in 5:1b, 2, 4b.

So it is hardly surprising that the attempt should be made to interpret the whole passage in a present sense.[46] But the enterprise is surely forced, for there are elements that certainly are oriented to an eschatological future, the strongest of which is precisely the affirmation of the resurrection in 4:14, and the simplest, the conditional sentence in 5:1.

What could explain the level of Paul's discourse seems to be the general framework of its context, decisively provided by the theme of suffering. Here, in fact, it is possible to recognize the permanence of a certain typical Jewish pattern proper to apocalyptic, which establishes a contrast *from the lesser to the greater* between the trials of the present life and the glory to come. We have already identified certain such texts above (see section II). We can also add 4 Esdr 7:3-25, where, in terms of the opposition between the restriction of the present world and the expansiveness of the world to come (vv. 10-16), the destiny of Israel is compared to one who must reach the open space of the sea by sailing down a narrow river, or of a city by traveling a single road (vv. 3-9; v. 5b: "if one does not pass

---

45. Ibid., 212.
46. Thus N. Baumert, op. cit. (see above, I-a); but he recognizes that here the theme of the final completion "is never lost from view, but is always understood" (264).

through the narrow space, how is one to reach what is open?"). That is why one must concentrate not on what one is now experiencing but rather on what is to come in the future (v. 16). Hence the axiom of 4 Esdr 7:18: "The just shall bear constraints hoping for the free spaces"!

In this perspective we recognize a central role for 2 Cor 4:17, where a clear opposition is set up between "the brief and light sufferings" and "an extraordinary eternal weight of glory," confirmed by the parallel of Rom 8:18. This also explains the different eschatological point of view of our passage over against 1 Cor 15, where precisely the theme of suffering is not central but is only touched marginally in vv. 30-32; there, in fact, the point of departure of the whole discourse consists not in the apostolic tribulations but in the confession of Christ's resurrection (vv. 1f.) and the desire to know how the dead rise (vv. 35f.) The difference of viewpoint is confirmed in that there no mention is made of the eschatological judgment, whereas here the whole section ends precisely with this perspective in 5:10. And this is typical of Jewish apocalyptic in the course of discourse on the sufferings and the final reward of the just or of the entire people (thus from Dan 7 on).[47]

This said, let us try to inspect the major eschatological elements offered by our text. Those we treat will not be many nor will they be all, but they will be essential.

a) First of all we note the presence of the clear perspective of death burdening the Apostle's existence, not only in the sense of the common, universal ultimate fate of creatures but also as the daily diminishment and dissolution of earthly dwelling on account of the many sufferings (5:1 and 4:16a; cf. 4:11: "We are handed over to death"). Even so, this experience is not played in the key of Stoicism natural, after the "We die daily" of Seneca.[48] Paul's viewpoint is rather simultaneously that of the paschal mystery in its ecclesial reflections, of supernatural anthropology, and of an eschatological openness. This last component is particularly characteristic of our passage in comparison with the parallel in Rom 8:36: "Through you we are put to death daily" (Ps 43:23), where in the context the per-

---

47. On the apocalyptic theme of the increase of suffering upon the vigil of the Messiah's coming, see, e.g., P. Volz, *Die Eschatologie des jüdischen Gemeinde* (Hildesheim, 1966 [Tübingen, 1934]) 158-163; D. S. Russell, *The Method and Message of Jewish Apocalyptic* (London, 1964) 271f. It is not impossible, but requires more study, that behind 2 Cor 4:7-5:10 the theme of the "righteous sufferer" is also to be found; concerning the identification of the motif in the Jewish background, see L. Ruppert, *Der leidende Gerechte. Eine motif-geschichtliche Untersuchung zum AT und zwischentestamentlichen Judentum* (Würzburg 1972); *Der leidende Gerechte und seine Feinde. Eine Wortfelduntersuchung* (Würzburg, 1973).

48. *Ep.* 24:1920; see ibid., 26:8-10: " 'Meditate on death.' The one who speaks thus, calls for meditation on liberty."

spective is not so much eschatological as existential. Moreover, we must emphasize that in 2 Cor 4:7–5:10 death comes about through the loss of our present historical body; this is compared to a vessel of fragile, and hence easily broken, clay (4:7); is subject to corruption (4:16); is destined to be replaced (5:1), being transformed into another "garment" (5:2-4); and from it we will have to be exiled (5:6, 8).

b) After death Paul foresees a permanent bodily dimension different from the present one. The very fact that in this passage the term "soul" (ψυχή) never occurs would by itself lead us to believe that Paul's perspective is not strictly that of Platonic anthropological dualism. Paul has the entire person in mind. According to 4:10f., "the life of Jesus" must show itself "in our body" (even though this may have a reference to the apostolic present, as in 6:9b); in any case, the "extraordinary weight of glory" (4:17) regards our somatic dimension as well. In 5:12 we have several expressions in this direction: "dwelling of God," "eternal house in heaven, not made by hands," "our dwelling from heaven," and then also the "put on over"—how else to understand it except as a reference to a new σῶμα? Another understanding would be simply that of the "afterlife," presented under the image of a *locus aliquis*, "a certain place" (thus Seneca, *Ep.* 36:16).[49] But it is precisely the image of "clothing" (see above) that leads us to think of something more personal, something that belongs to one in an individual sense, and not just a place of sojourn. Besides, the belief of the Pharisees (whence comes Paul) was that the soul passes εἰς ἕτερον σῶμα, i.e., "to another [form of] body."[50]

c) But Paul's perspective is not that of the eschatological resurrection, as is 1 Cor 15. His thought rather concerns what is to happen immedi-

49. In antiquity the term *domus aeterna*/οἶκος αἰώνιος/*byt 'wlm* ("eternal home") designated simply the grave. The usage goes back to ancient Egypt, whence it passed especially into the Greek and Latin funerary inscriptions, both pagan and Jewish, and also Christian (see already Ps 48:12; Tob 3:6; Qoh 12:5); see, for example, Stommel, "Domus aeterna," RAC IV, 109–128; F. Cumont, *Oriental Religions*, 240, n. 91 = *Les religions orientales*, 247f.; see also the essential bibliography and a brief documentation in P. W. van der Horst, *The Sentences of Pseudo-Phocylides* (Leiden, 1978), commentary on vv. 112–113. But is it not perhaps an allegorical usage, and almost a synecdoche? For instance, in the text cited from Pseudo-Phocylides, it is Hades as a whole that is called "common eternal home and fatherland, a common place for all, poor and kings" (κοινὰ μέλαθρα δόμων αἰώνια καὶ πατρὶς ῞Αιδης, ξυνὸς χῶρος ἅπασι, πεγηοί τε καὶ βασιλεῦσιν). Cf. also the "treasury of life" (*biṣrôr haḥayyîm* in MT; *gnz ḥyy 'wlm* in Targum Jonathan) for the soul of David in 1 Sam 25:29. See also the *Martyrdom of St. Polycarp* II, concerning martyrs: "They wanted to be stripped of life to pass at God's call to the shining dwellings of salvation. . . . There is prepared for them with the martyrdom of one hour, an indestructible and imperishable joy" (where we sense the clear echo of 2 Cor 5:1-2 and 4:17).

50. Fl. Josephus, *Bell. jud.* II 8:14:163; but this text, unlike 2 Corinthians, is expressed in explicitly dualistic terms, ψυχή + σῶμα, "soul/body," and further attributes the "other body" to the good alone.

ately at the end of the Christian's life. On this question our text refers to one (or more) of three possibilities: either the parousia takes place soon, bringing about the end of the present experience of history (and the desire to be clothed over [5:2-4] makes sense in this direction); or at one's own individual death one already experiences a new bodily dimension (but the heavenly dwelling in 5:1 probably refers as well to the moment of an approaching parousia that is foreseen; indeed, in 5:2a the image of the house merges with that of clothing, and Paul specifically desires to be "clothed over"); or else there is an intermediate provisional and imperfect state between death and the parousia. In fact, the image of "nakedness" in 5:3 seems to go in this direction (see also Lietzmann and Barrett).[51]

As for this γυμνότης, "nakedness," as we have already mentioned more than once, three interpretations have been proposed. One, proposed by certain Protestant authors, sees the nakedness as eternal damnation consisting precisely in the fact that in the last days the reprobate will not rise again, nor will they be clothed in a heavenly body;[52] but the Jewish authors cited in support of the thesis are too few and not really representative. A second solution would understand the nakedness as a state of separation from Christ/"garment" feared at the moment of death (thus Collange), but this seems to have no Pauline foundation (see above). The third interpretation reads the adjective γυμνοί, "naked," as an echo of Greek anthropology—or at least of Greek anthropological terminology. We have already reported above several parallels to this. Nor should we be astonished at a possible "Platonizing" component in Paul's eschatology. After all, he comes from Judaism, where the eschatological ideas leave room for some form of survival between death and resurrection,[53] with this either reflecting Greek influence, or perhaps better, representing a logical development of earlier biblical elements (like *sheôl*).

We should simply admit that Judaism does not provide a systematic vision of the question; between 100 B.C. and 100 of the present era "there is obviously no single Jewish doctrine about life after death in the period under consideration; there is rather a great variety and a pluralism of ideas both about the end of world history and about death and about that which follows the death of the individual person."[54] For example, Pseudo-

---

51. On the translation of the difficult v. 3, see above, n. 21.
52. See A. Oepke, in TDNT 2:774-775; R. Bultmann, ad loc.
53. See P. Volz, *Die Eschatologie*, 256-272; D. S. Russell, *The Method and Message*, 353-366 and 401; C. Marcheselli-Casale, *Risorgeremo*, passim.
54. Thus concludes C. C. Cavallin, *Life after Death: Paul's Argument for the Resurrection of the Dead in 1 Cor 15—Part I. An Enquiry into the Jewish Background* (Lund, 1974) 199; and on p. 212 he adds: "No common anthropology, at least no common view on the relation between the body and the soul has been found. . . . In the same writings, and even the same

Phocylides, an anonymous Hellenistic Jew who wrote in Alexandria between 30 and 40 A.D.,[55] simply juxtaposes apparently contradictory ideas, such as the bodily resurrection of the dead (v. 103f.: "In fact, we hope that the remains of the departed will soon come to the light again out of the earth": καὶ τάχα δ' ἐκ γαίης ἐλπίζομεν ἐς φάος ἐλθεῖν / λείψαν' ἀποιχομένων) and the immortality of the soul (v. 115: "but our soul is immortal and lives ageless forever": ψυχὴ δ' ἀθάνατος καὶ ἀγήρως ζῇ διὰ παντός).

Therefore we should not be surprised if Paul, too, whose cultural roots are sunk deeply in the same soil, without any systematic preoccupation refers to different eschatological solutions, expressed with the contrasting images of clothing over and of nakedness. Paul believes in or at least foresees the possibility of an "intermediate state," but its details hold not the slightest interest for him.[56] Of course, it is particularly difficult to imagine a person either without a material body or with a body different from the present one, but this is precisely why Paul has recourse to various images.[57] But we must observe in the first place that in Paul's wishes there is not the nakedness, which he indeed seems to fear (contrary to Socrates' desire for death as expressed by Plato, *Phaed.* 67d-68c), but rather the typically Jewish perspective of taking on a new bodily form. This is so at least in 5:1-4. But probably in the following 5:6-8 the possibility begins to rise, and so would Paul's inclination toward a separation from the body.

Evidently as a result of the effect of his whole correspondence, Paul must have experienced an evolution in the issue of eschatology, even though this is no place to discuss it.[58] The "sentence of death," received in Asia (1:8-9: ἀπόκριμα τοῦ θανάτου) must have already oriented him to count on the real possibility of dying before the parousia.

d) The determining function of the Pneuma. In our passage the affirmation of 5:5 ("Now, God is the one who has made us for this destiny, in giving us the down payment of the Spirit")[59] would seem at first sight

---

passages, concepts and symbols from widely differing anthropologies are used in order to express the hope of personal survival of death: immortality of the soul or resurrection of the body. The writers intend to state that the *personality survives.*" See also M. Hengel, *Judentum und Hellenismus* (Tübingen, 1969) 362; U. Fischer, *Eschatologie und Jenseitserwartung im hellenistischen Diasporajudentum* (Berlin and New York, 1978). Hence the conclusions of P. Benoit, "L'évolution du langage apocalyptique," 320, are hasty and sketchy.

55. Thus according to P. W. van der Horst, *The Sentences.*

56. See R. H. Gundry, op. cit., 152 and 154. See also L. Cranford, "A New Look at 2 Corinthians 5,1-10," *Southwestern Journal of Theology* 19 (1976) 95-100.

57. See W. Lillie, "An Approach to II Corinthians 4,1-10," *ScottJournTheol*, 30 (1977) 59-70.

58. See P. Benoit, already cited, "L'évolution du langage apocalyptique."

59. Verse 5 is structured in two phrases characterized by two aorist participles used as substantives and joined by the single subject θεός (ὁ δὲ κατεργασάμενος . . . ὁ δούς), "God (who has destined . . . who has given . . .)." But the second phrase must be considered as in

to be out of place. It actually recalls 1:22 and looks like a sacramental reference in a context that rather is eschatological. But in fact v. 5, with its phrase εἰς αὐτὸ τοῦτο, "for this very thing," refers us back to what has been said just before (v. 4c: "in order that what is mortal may be absorbed by life"). Hence the relationship becomes clear enough between the Spirit received today in history and that which will be verified in the Christian eschatologically.

The Pneuma is not just a mystical reality, valid for the present. It is dynamic by nature, and indicates a tension toward a future completion, as is also suggested by the idea of the "first payment," which orients the whole Christian life toward a complete settlement which is still to come but which is of the same nature as that which one already possesses. In this sense there are two parallel texts semantically closer to ours: Rom 8:11 and Eph 1:14 (and 4:30). The former directly relates the Spirit to the resurrection of the body, of which this Spirit becomes a guarantee precisely because it "dwells in" the Christian. Besides, in Rom 8:23 we find the same verb στενάζειν, "groan," present in 2 Cor 5:2, 4, but explicitly connected with the Spirit. The latter, more in a communal than an individual sense, makes of the Pneuma an anticipation and a pledge "of the inheritance for the total remittance of the property" of God, i.e., of God's people.

Thus there is a causal relation between the Spirit and the resurrection, as we also see in other biblical texts (cf. Ezek 37:5, 6, 10, 14; Ps 104:30; 1 Cor 15:44f.; Rom 1:4; Rev 11:11).[60] "Such is Paul's last word on the Spirit: it is the divine power of life and resurrection, which now accomplishes its purpose in us through Christ, and will be fully unfolded in the resurrection and the transformation of our mortal bodies."[61] The conclusion then is: What has already been begun today in Christ and in the Spirit is destined not to die but to grow, be affirmed, flourish, and mature fully.

---

apposition to the whole first phrase and not just the word "God" (in fact, there is no καί, "and," as in 1:22), and hence its sense is adverbial rather than relative; therefore the giving of the Spirit is not an act standing on its own but is simply an explanation of how it is that God has prepared us for new bodily life. That is why in the translation we correlate the two participles, making the second simultaneous with the first.

60. See also the Mishna, Sot. 9:5 at the end: "Rabbi Pinchas ben Jair used to say: Diligence leads to innocence . . .; piety leads to the Holy Spirit, and the Holy Spirit makes us worthy of the resurrection of the dead" (after V. Castiglioni [Rome, 1962]).

61. W. Pfister, Das Leben im Geiste nach Paulus. Der Geist als Anfang und Vollendung des christlichen Lebens (Fribourg, 1963). On the same theme see E. Sokolowski, Die Begriffe Geist und Leben bei Paulus in ihren Beziehungen zu einander (Göttingen, 1903); W. Deissner, Auferstehungshoffnung und Pneumagedanke bei Paulus (Leipzig, 1912); P. Siber, Mit Christus leben. Eine Studie zur paulinischen Auferstehungshoffnung (Zurich, 1971); E. Schweizer, Heiliger Geist (Stuttgart and Berlin, 1978) 153–159 and 167f.

Such is the "new creation (or creature)," of which Paul writes a little further on in 2 Cor 5:17.

Now, would God choose to discontinue what he himself has begun in such an original, committed, and promising manner? But it is precisely this that shows us that if we must speak of immortality, it is founded more on grace than on nature. Paul's viewpoint is theological rather than philosophical: for him what counts is the immortality of the new life in Christ, obviously not alone, but insofar as it touches our humanity.[62] The Pneuma itself seems to be the guarantee of a permanence of the individual personality after death, even if for us this is difficult to imagine, prescinding from the present historical body. But the fact that in our passage Paul never mentions the ψυχή, "soul," and uses only the personal pronoun "we" gives us to understand that he is thinking not of a purely spiritual survival (which would no longer be "personal," at least according to Aristotelian and Thomistic philosophy) but rather a *personal* permanence. Now if the language of our own day uses the word "soul" to designate such a subsistence of the human *I*, this is simply because it is a term that has been long in use, and because somehow "a verbal instrument is absolutely indispensable."[63]

V. Conclusion

Second Corinthians 4:7–5:10 is substantially a single unit. The basic theme is provided by a reflection on the Apostle's sufferings, which are

62. E. Schweizer, *Heiliger Geist*, writes on p. 158: with the Spirit in us "something has begun that will not end, even if the person, with the body and the soul, dies." This statement reveals a supernatural anthropology too dualistic. To say that only the Holy Spirit survives means that the Spirit's presence in the Christian is only extrinsic; but if the Pneuma does not somehow implicate the human *I*, what good does it do? Would the human person then be a "new creation"? Here too the author reveals the typical Lutheran roots of a justification that is only forensic.

63. Thus says fairly enough the "Letter on Certain Questions Regarding Eschatology" (published by the Sacred Congregation for the Doctrine of the Faith, 17 May 1979) n. 3. This document somewhat later continues, "Neither Scripture nor theology provides us with sufficient light for a representation of the afterlife. The Christian must firmly retain two essential points: one must on the one hand believe in the fundamental continuity that exists, through the power of the Holy Spirit, between the present life in Christ and the future one . . .; but on the other hand, the Christian must discern the radical rupture between the present and the future in that the order of faith is replaced by that of full light."

We here leave aside the problem posed by 5:10, i.e., the relationship between the affirmation of a future judgment based on works done in this life and the Pauline principle of justification by faith without works; concerning this, besides the commentaries, see, e.g., K. P. Donfried, "Justification and Last Judgment in Paul," Int 30 (1976) 140–152; E. Synofzik, *Die Gerichts- und Vergeltungsaussagen bei Paulus. Eine traditionsgeschichtliche Untersuchung* (Göttingen, 1977); M. Wolter, *Rechtfertigung und zukünftiges Heil. Untersuchungen zu Röm 5,1-11* (Berlin, 1978); S. H. Travis, *Christ and the Judgment of God. Divine Retribution in the New Testament* (Southampton, 1986).

disproportionate both to the "treasure" of the mission to evangelize and to the future "weight of glory." If the logical point of departure is the present sufferings, the final point of arrival is the life to come with the Lord, and so the discourse naturally evolves according to an eschatological dimension. In that sense, the text of 4:17 represents the point of contact of both aspects, which here meet not just as successive events but with some kind of relationship of cause and effect. Between the two components there comes a third factor, a specific anthropological factor underlying the whole pericope.

1) The speech about the sufferings is framed within an entire thematic complex typical of 2 Corinthians, where these are understood as a distinctive sign of the Apostle (already in 1:8-9, then in 6:4-10; and especially in 10–13). In our text the motif begins with the metaphorical allusion to the "vessels of clay" in 4:7; it is brought into focus through the paschal hermeneutical pattern in 4:10-12 (with the mutual relationship between the "dying," νέκρωσις, and the "life," ζωή, "of Jesus"/"in our body"); and it culminates in the eschatological perspective of 4:17-18. In 5:1-10 there is no explicit reference at all to the sufferings (unless cryptically in the "earthly" dwelling of 5:1; in the adjectival substantive το θνητόν, "the mortal," in 5:4; in the desire to be exiled from the body in 5:6, 8; in the contrast between faith and vision in 5:6). This probably indicates precisely that these have served to prepare for the treatment of what happens after death, and that they have a close connection to this latter. And this connection is quite understandable against the background of reflection that is characteristic of apocalyptic literature.

2) The anthropology of our passage is distinguished by a particular insistence on the somatic aspect of the human person, witnessed especially by the frequent recurrence of the term σῶμα, by similar expressions (like "our mortal flesh" in 4:11 and "the outer man" in 4:16), and by multiple images such as "vessels of clay" (4:7), the "house" and the "clothing" (in 5:1-4), "exile" (in 5:6-9). It would seem to be treated from the point of view of a dualistic anthropology, especially because it is just here that we can perceive the echo of certain concepts of Greek and Judeo-Hellenistic philosophy. But the absolute absence of the term ψυχή, "soul," when this would have been very useful and illuminating, must set us on guard against hasty conclusions. Now, the reference to the "inner man" would seem to indicate a "spiritualistic" sense (4:16), but we cannot forget that the context (especially the decisive allusion to the divine Pneuma in 5:5) orients us toward an explanation of this expression that actually takes the

Holy Spirit into account. There is, thus, also in the text a supernatural anthropology that surpasses and integrates the natural, and could thus be said to be holistic in character (also because of the recurring use of the simple personal pronoun "we"). But Paul is clearly not speaking as a philosopher nor as a theologian presiding from his chair. His certainties are few: this body is destined to die, but with its dissolution the personal existence of the Christian does not diminish. This is the equivalent of saying that his anthropology is all eschatologically oriented.

3) In fact, the passage culminates logically as well as literarily on an eschatological horizon. By saying so, we oppose the "presentialist" thesis of Baumert, and as we explain it, it seems to us that we cannot accept the Christological interpretation of the "eternal dwelling" (5:1) of Feuillet, Collange, and others. The perspective is rather that of the survival of the Christian; but the description of this survival oscillates between a new corporeal existence and a condition of "nakedness" (5:3), which then seems to prevail with the image of "exile" in 5:6-9. The lack of a systematic treatment by the Apostle fits well into the Jewish background of the time, which often enough presents contradictory phenomena (cf. Pseudo-Phocylides).

The immediate but veiled desire of Paul is to be present at the parousia; perhaps that is why he is very reticent on the theme of the resurrection. The alternative is a presence "with the Lord" (5:8) immediately after death. Paul has one fundamental certainty: the "new creation" (5:17) cannot die, since the baptismal Spirit has been given to the Christian as a "first payment" (5:5) of an assured full settlement to come. Union with the Lord does not fail; "therefore we strive, whether living in the body or exiled from it, to be pleasing to him" (5:9; cf. Phil 1:23; 1 Thess 5:9-10; Rom 14:8-9).

Chapter 15

The Presence of Paul's Opponents in 2 Corinthians 10-13: Literary Examination

Any researcher today who approaches the theme of the opponents of Paul in 2 Cor 10-13[1] takes a very concrete risk: "inventing hot water," i.e., repeating what others have already said. Barrett clearly admitted as much many years ago, noting that it can seem quite impossible to add anything to what has already been said on the subject.[2] To attempt originality, then, is truly a hopeless enterprise. On the other hand, to resign oneself to a simple *status quaestionis* seems to me inadequate for research.[3]

So at the cost of disappointing the reader I shall for the most part avoid going further along the path of attempting to identify the opponents theologically and ecclesially, since this is precisely where all possible proposals and counterproposals have already been advanced. Obviously, in the following presentation I will inevitably have to refer to some of these positions to accept or reject them.

1. We believe that these chapters represent at least part of the so-called letter of many tears (cf. 2 Cor 2:4), and therefore refer to a situation earlier than 2 Cor 1-9 (although the "opponents" mentioned in the two sections could be related, if not the same). See esp. F. Watson, "2 Cor x-xiii and Paul's Painful Letter to the Corinthians," JTSt 35 (1984) 324-346; L. Aejmelaeus, *Streit und Versöhnung. Das Problem des 2. Korintherbriefes* (Helsinki, 1987); G. Dautzenberg, "Der zweite Korintherbrief als Briefsammlung," in W. Haase and H. Temporini, eds., ANRW II/25.4 (Berlin and New York, 1987) 3045-3066, 3052-3055.

2. C. K. Barrett, "ψευδαπόστολοι (2 Cor 11.13)," *Mélanges Bibliques Béda Rigaux* (Gembloux, 1970) 377-396, at 377.

3. For a *status quaestionis* see most recently R. P. Martin, "The Opponents of Paul in 2 Corinthians: An Old Issue Revisited," in G. F. Hawthorne and O. Betz, eds., *Tradition and Interpretation in the New Testament* (Grand Rapids and Tübingen, 1987) 279-289; C. Ginami, "Gli 'pseudo-apostoli' in 2 Cor," in R. Penna, ed., *Antipaolinismo: Reazioni a Paolo tra il I e il II secolo*, RSR 2 (Bologna, 1989) 55-64; J. L. Summey, *Identifying Paul's Opponents: The Question of Method in 2 Corinthians* (Sheffield, 1990).

I. Preliminaries

1) *The quality of the sources*

First of all, we must very clearly establish the quality of the sources we have available. It is only too clear that the writer of 2 Cor 10–13 is not one of the opponents, and therefore does not give us directly firsthand testimony regarding their specific pattern of belief. Not only are they presented indirectly, through the pen of another writer, but they reach us partially distorted by the apologetic and polemical genres that characterize Paul's text.[4] Therefore we can make them out only through their reflection, as if through a mirror, and moreover a mirror like the ancient ones, which show the images only obscurely, *in aenigmate.*

We are facing one of the most delicate critical undertakings methodologically speaking, yet one that is of considerable importance in understanding one aspect of Christian origins. All we can do is to use a partisan text to reconstruct the appearance of the person addressed, rather like a police artist attempting to sketch a face from the description of witnesses. Evidently it is easy to misunderstand, as demonstrated by the diversity and contrasts in the "artist's reconstructions" scholars have given us. As was said some years ago, reading the text is like "the incidental overhearing of one end of a telephone conversation," the other end of which we attempt to reconstruct.[5] This situation is proper to the genre of the letter as such; the letter, as the ancient letter writer Demetrius put it, is simply "half of a conversation."[6]

But what complicates our case is that the persons who interest us, Paul's opponents, are not even at the other end of the line—at least they are not the only ones there (see below); they are rather a *tertium quid,* an object of the conversation between Paul and the Corinthians, whom he is addressing. Our work is all the harder, then, since we are supposed to recognize the profile not of the direct interlocutors but of persons who are in

---

4. On the literary genre of 2 Cor 10–13, see the commentaries, and especially H. D. Betz, *Der Apostel Paulus und die sokratische Tradition. Eine exegetische Untersuchung zu seiner "Apologie" 2 Korinther 10–13,* BhTh 45 (Tübingen, 1972) esp. 13–42. See especially the study of J. P. Sampley, "Paul, His Opponents in 2 Corinthians 10–13, and the Rhetorical Handbooks," in J. Neusner et al., eds., *The Social World of Formative Christianity and Judaism* (Philadelphia, 1988) 162–177: Paul follows—with a certain liberty, indeed—the procedures of the rhetoric of the manuals, represented, for instance, by M. T. Cicero, *De inventione,* which enumerate four ways of obtaining the *benevolentia* of the audience in arguing one's own case: by avoiding arrogance in the presentation, by putting the opponents in a bad light, by showing consideration for the hearers, and by skill in the presentation of the case itself.

5. See M. D. Hooker, "Were There False Teachers in Colossae?" in B. Lindars and S. Smalley, eds., *Christ and the Spirit in the New Testament: Essays in Honour of C. F. D. Moule* (Cambridge, 1973) 315–331, at 315.

6. "De Elocutione," in R. Hercher, ed., *Epistolographi Graeci* (Paris, 1871) 13.

among them and are not the essential part of the problems between the Corinthian Church and its founder. If we had a letter addressed directly by Paul to his opponents, it would be much more simple, and we could easily reconstruct their distinctive features; as in Origen's *Contra Celsum*, one can work back quite well to the "true doctrine" of the opposing philosopher. But we must be satisfied with the procedure known as "mirror reading," as in many other instances in the New Testament, especially in Galatians.[7]

This is the question we want to answer, considering that Paul speaks *about* his enemies, not *to* them: In 2 Cor 10–13, when do we have a right to perceive a direct reference to them? Recently five principal (and two secondary) criteria have been proposed: the type of affirmation (i.e., either assertion or negation, command or prohibition, can suggest a polemic reference); the tone (since the emphasis indicates the importance of the theme); frequency (or repetition of a theme); clarity (which by its nature excludes ambiguity); the unusual argument (what is not common to Paul's theology can indicate a specific precise situation).[8]

This criteriological classification is surely useful. However, besides being developed only for the reading of polemic rather than apologetic texts, its whole perspective seems rather abstract to me. In our case there are at least two other dimensions we must consider. In the first place, the apologetic tone of the chapters should lead us to take seriously the emergence of the first person of the writer: every autobiographical allusion may indicate a self-defense, and behind every self-defense there is surely an accusation and therefore an accuser, an opponent. In the second place, we must emphasize the importance of direct or explicit references to possible opponents, who, though never named,[9] can be referred to in

7. See J. M. G. Barclay, "Mirror-reading a Polemical Letter: Galatians as a Test Case," JSNT 31 (1987) 73–93, who does not accept the criticisms of the method proposed by G. Lyons, *Pauline Autobiography: Toward a New Understanding* (Atlanta, 1985) 9, according to whom Gal 1–2 would not be apologetic in intent but would rather simply be attempting to present a lived paradigm of Christian freedom.

8. See J. G. M. Barclay, "Mirror-reading," 84–85; the author also adds coherence (whether the above criteria can lead to a coherent picture of the opponents) and historical plausibility (whether the results can be inserted into the historical moment without anachronism). Regarding the criteriology to be used in such cases, a much broader and more convincing (and also one more convincing), and valid for the New Testament in general, is represented by K. Berger, "Die impliziten Gegner. Zur Methode des Erschliessens von 'Gegnern' in neutestamentlichen Texten," in D. Lührmann and G. Strecker, eds., *Kirche. Festschrift G. Bornkamm* (Tübingen, 1980) 373–400.

9. The fact that Paul never speaks openly of his opponents, never calling them by name or identifying them by any religious or ecclesial designation, should surely not be understood as a sign of respect toward them (considering how tough, and consequently disrespectful, his tone is) nor as a sign of their being negligible in number, but rather as an indication of a scornful attitude toward persons "who do not deserve to be drawn out of anonymity" (F. Mussner, *Der Galaterbrief*, HThKNT IX [Freiburg-Basel-Vienna, 1981⁴] 11).

various ways: with indefinite pronouns, with participial forms, with metaphors, and with periphrastic designations, etc. And then there are implicit references, surely numerous, in various kinds of literary expressions, as in antithetic or concessive phrases, etc. Moreover, we must distinguish carefully whether these persons are really from outside or if they are simply some of the addressees.

2) *Three groups of addressees*

When we speak of 2 Cor 10–13, we must distinguish at least three different groups of persons to whom Paul intends to address himself.[10] In the first place there is the Corinthian community in general. Its presence is attested by the many second person plural pronouns ("you, yours")[11] as well as verbs in the second person plural, irregular though their frequency may be.[12] But we must note that the community is not in the foreground of the writer's interest, considering the scarcity of verbs and pronouns referring to it[13] and the practical absence of any participles or adjectives that describe what it is like or what it does (except for the predicative in 11:19 and two adverbs in 11:4, 19).[14] We get the definite impression that the writer speaks *with* the community, but not so much *about* it as about other persons.

In the second place we can isolate within the community the group of sinners referred to in 12:20-21; 13:2. Here we pass from a general situation (ὑμᾶς, "you") described in the "Lasterkatalog" of 12:20b to a spe-

---

10. See K. Prümm, *Diakonia Pneumatos. Der zweite Korintherbrief als Zugang zur apostolischen Botschaft. Auslegung und Theologie*, II/2 (Rome-Freiburg-Vienna, 1967) 87; J. Zmijewski, *Der Stil der paulinischen "Narrenrede." Analyse der Sprachgestaltung in 2. Kor 11,1–12,10 als Beitrag zur Methodik von Stiluntersuchungen neutestamentlicher Texte*, BBB 52 (Bonn, 1978) 413.

11. Nominative ὑμεῖς (11:7; 12:11; 13:7, 9); genitive ὑμῶν (10:6, 8, 13, 14, 15, 16; 11:3, 8; 12:11, 13, 14, 15, 19; 13:9, 11, 13); dative ὑμῖν (10:1, 15; 11:7, 9; 12:12, 19, 20; 13:3, 5); and accusative ὑμᾶς (10:1 [twice], 9, 14; 11:2 [twice], 6, 9, 11, 20 [twice]; 12:14 [twice], 15, 16 [twice], 17 [twice], 18, 20, 21; 13:1, 3, 4, 7, 12).

12. In chapters 10–12, where Paul confronts the opponents, the second person plural of the verb is rather rare: only in 10:7; 11:1, 4, 7, 16, 19, 20; 12:11, 13, 19, 20 (with sixteen verbs, of which one, ἀνέχομαι, "put up with," is repeated five times; only once is it accompanied by a participle: 11:19), while the first person is very frequent both in the singular (eighty-three times, plus six participles in the nominative singular) and in the plural (eleven times plus eleven nominative plural participles); but the second plural is abundant in chapter 13 (fifteen verbs), where the discourse to the addressees becomes more direct.

13. For the verb see the preceding note; for the pronouns (see n. 11) we must note that of the fifty-five occurrences, only four are in the nominative. In the other cases the "you" is only the direct or indirect object of the action of someone else, whether of Paul or of the opponents (this is true of the accusatives and datives, while the genitive is a possessive pronoun ten out of sixteen times).

14. Things change a bit in chapter 13, where the tone of the letter becomes more direct and familiar (see 13:2, 5, 9; here we also have a case of a second person plural verb governing a declarative clause: 13:6).

cific group of Corinthians (πολλούς, "many") "who have continued in their earlier sins and have not turned from impurity and fornication and debauchery" in 12:21; for these Paul in 13:2 no longer envisages any pardon, again broadening his view to the entire community (καὶ τοῖς λοιποῖς πᾶσιν, "and to all the rest"). It is to the whole Church of Corinth that Paul speaks of this group, whose sexual liberty must be understood in the light of previous admonitions (cf. 1 Cor 5:1-13; 6:9, 13b-18; 7:2; 10:8), even if this is the only place in 2 Corinthians where he speaks of it.[15] So I do not consider pertinent an interpretation that would identify as Paul's opponents Judeo-Hellenistic Christians who would not have emphasized the moral implications of the gospel.[16] This possibility does not fit either the isolation of the admonition or its placement toward the end of the section, where the tone of the letter grows more conclusive and direct.[17]

In the third place we have the group, difficult to describe, of the specific opponents of Paul, with whom he is indirectly dialoguing in chapters 10–12. It is to these, who make up precisely the principal interest of our chapter, that we dedicate the following paragraphs, distinguishing between explicit and implicit references.

II. Identification of a third party between writer and recipients

We will work here on certain passages that will let us gather the literary evidence about Paul's opponents, that is, to determine to what extent these opponents are actually present in 2 Cor 10–13, and hence in its basic intentions.

1) Vocabulary and grammar: direct references to the opponents

First of all, we must clear up a text-critical question concerning the reading of 10:12-13. Here it is actually possible, depending on how one judges the variants, to refer the passage to the writer or to his opponents, with

15. The perfect participle προημαρτηκότων (12:21) and προημαρτηκόσιν (13:2), as V. P. Furnish correctly notes, *II Corinthians*, Anchor Bible 32A (Garden City, N.Y., 1984) 526 (referring back to A. Plummer), does not mean "those who have sinned in the past," as it is commonly translated (RSV, NAB, NRSV), but implies a present persistence in the earlier sin: "those who have continued in their former sinning."

16. Thus D. Georgi, *Die Gegner des Paulus im 2. Korintherbrief. Studien zur religiösen Propaganda der Spätantike*, WMANT 11 (Neukirchen-Vluyn, 1964) 233–234 (see also the English edition [Philadelphia, 1986] with an "Epilogue," 333–450).

17. This is confirmed by the fact that in 12:21 we have the only two participles (προημαρτηκότων, "who have been sinning," and μετανοησάντων, "who have repented," the first of which is repeated in 13:2) in our section that describe the recipients (except the copulative φρόνιμοι ὄντες, "being clever," in 11:19), a sign that the reference is only to some, as is evidenced also by the use of the article.

a not inconsiderable difference in the understanding of the passage. The question has been treated well by some recent commentators,[18] and here we will be satisfied with the essential.

The problem is over the four words οὐ συνιᾶσιν. Ἡμεῖς δέ, "they do not understand. But we . . .," which conclude v. 12 and begin v. 13. If these are accepted as an integral part of the text, the pronoun αὐτοί, "self" [the import of this Greek word is very ambiguous], of v. 12b means "they" and is subject of a sentence (finished in verse 12) that describes the characteristics of the opponents; but if they are expunged as inauthentic, the same pronoun αὐτοί comes to signify "we," and the phrase of which it is subject continues through v. 13 and describes Paul's behavior.

We maintain that the longer reading must be preferred. We don't want to deny that the shorter reading makes sense; indeed, it would give a very good construction, well balanced on the antithesis οὐ . . . ἀλλά, "not . . . but," of v. 12, referred precisely to the person of the sender, who would be subject of the whole v. 13 as well. But the very fact that the longer text is more difficult provides a reason to prefer it,[19] apart from the fact that the overwhelming majority in the manuscript tradition favor it (including P[46] and Codex B).[20] For the rest, Paul would be contradicting himself if, after distancing himself in v. 12a from those who commend themselves, he were then to say in v. 12b that he measures himself and compares himself with himself; on the contrary, he boasts "according to the norm of the measure"[21] assigned to him by God. This is something others do not do, nor can they do it because they have not founded the Church of

---

18. See esp. V. P. Furnish, *II Corinthians*, 470–471; to the authors cited there we should add: for the short reading J. Sánchez Bosch, "'Gloriarse' *según San Pablo. Sentido y teología de* κανχάομαι, AB 40 (Rome, 1970) 212f., and R. P. Martin, *2 Corinthians*, WBC (Waco, Tex., 1986) 315; for the longer reading M. Carrez, *La deuxième épître de Saint Paul aux Corinthiens*, CNT VIII (Geneva, 1986) 205; F. Lang, *Die Briefe an die Korinther*, NTD 7 (Göttingen, 1986) 333; H.-J. Klauck, *2. Korintherbrief*, Neue Echter Bibel 8 (Würzburg, 1986) 80.

19. See H. D. Betz, *Der Apostel Paulus* 119, n. 558.

20. This is true not only of the critical editions of Aland-Black-Martini-Metzger-Wikgren, Nestle-Aland, and Merk but also in the case of the two variants of the verb "understand," συνιᾶσιν, read occasionally συνίουσιν and συνίσασιν but with the same meaning. The other two readings (omission of all four words and omission of only the first two) are meagerly attested (see the critical apparatus of Aland-Black-Martini-Metzger-Wikgren).

21. On the idea of κάνων as "ambit, area, sphere" in a geographical sense, see the inscription from Pisidia published by S. Mitchell, "Requisitioned Transport in the Roman Empire: A New Inscription from Pisidia," *Journal of Roman Studies* 66 (1976) 106–131, and E. A. Judge, *New Documents Illustrating Early Christianity, 1977* (North Ryde, 1981) 36–45. But the commentators translate "the province" (C. K. Barrett), "Massstab, scil. Missionsgebiet" (R. Bultmann), "the jurisdiction" (V. P. Furnish), "the sphere of service" (R. P. Martin), "le cahier de charges" (M. Carrez), to say that the measure of Paul is the recognized division of missionary responsibility on which agreement was reached at Jerusalem (Gal 2:9); thus also decisively H.-J. Klauck, *2. Korintherbrief*, 11 and 80–81.

Corinth. Still, v. 12b is one of those passages that offer material to give us an idea not of Paul's answer but of the position of the opponents.

Here we want to pass in review all the lexical and grammatical forms used in 2 Cor 10–12 to indicate the opponents of Paul's person and ministry.

1) Much used is the *indefinite masculine pronoun* τις, "someone" (10:7; 11:20 [five times], 21); τινες "some" (10:2, 12).[22] The prevalence of the singular pronoun over the plural does not constitute a problem, both because it does not so much have the individual sense of "someone in particular" as the extensive sense of "anyone," which could cover several individuals,[23] and because the phenomenon is more material than formal (in fact, establishing 11:20-21 as a single context); and this is confirmed by the fact that the plural in 10:2 represents the first specific reference to the opponents in our chapters. From time to time the pronoun represents the subject of a verb either in participial or especially in finite form:

10:2: τινας τοὺς λογιζομένους ἡμᾶς ὡς κατὰ σάρκα περιπατοῦντας, "some who esteem us as walking according to the flesh"

10:7: εἴ τις πέποιθεν ἑαυτῷ Χριστοῦ εἶναι, "If someone is self-assured of belonging to Christ"

10:12: τισιν τῶν ἑαυτοὺς συνιστανόντων, "to some of those who commend themselves"

11:20: εἴ τις ὑμᾶς καταδουλοῖ, εἴ τις κατεσθίει, εἴ τις λαμβάνει, εἴ τις ἐπαίρεται, εἴ τις εἰς πρόσωπον ὑμᾶς δέρει, "If someone makes you a slave, if someone devours you, if someone takes advantage of you, if someone is presumptuous, if someone strikes you in the face"

11:21: ἄν τις τολμᾷ, "if someone dares"

These occurrences do not all have the same narrative or biographical sense; specifically, the five recurrences of the pronoun in 11:20 suggest a picture of the enemies that is not realistic but rather ironic and caricatur-

22. Because they do not refer to the opponent, we do not count the occurrences in 11:16 and 12:6 (which refers to the effect Paul's "boasting" could have on the community); 12:17 (an allusion to "one" of those sent by Paul). Nor does 11:29 (twice) fit our case. However, M. L. Barré thinks otherwise in "Paul as 'Eschatological Person': A New Look at 2 Cor 11:29," CBQ 37 (1975) 500–526; according to him, we would have here a resumption of the τις, "someone," of 11:21b, indicating the opponents as overcome by the forces of evil in the eschatological conflict—but such a perspective is foreign to our chapters.

23. This is quite unlike 2:5, where the τις alludes to a specific, even though unnamed, individual, who becomes the object of the discourse in 2:5-8 with a series of verbs and other pronouns describing him. Even in 10:7 C. K. Barrett, 2 Corinthians, 256, believes that we have here not a generalization but reference to a specific individual; but V. P. Furnish, 2 Corinthians, 466, observes that the phrase εἴ τις, "if someone," usually has a general sense in the Pauline letters (see Rom 8:9b; 1 Cor 3:12; Phil 3:4, etc.).

ing, as the rhetorical effect would indicate.[24] Here Paul wants to show that they are acting not for the Corinthians but against them, whereas he is willing to give all of himself for them. So the opponents seem well enough sketched out; in their audacity they are presented as personally opposed to Paul, and with presumptuous titles of self-recommendation.

2) The third person *personal pronoun* occurs only once in the singular and once in the plural:

10:7: καθὼς αὐτὸς Χριστοῦ, "that he is of Christ";
10:12: αὐτοὶ ἐν ἑαυτοῖς ἑαυτοὺς μετροῦντες καὶ συγκρίνοντες ἑαυτοὺς ἑαυτοῖς, "they, measuring themselves by themselves [or one another] and comparing themselves to themselves."

In this case, strengthened by the use of the reflexive pronoun, the individuation is more clear, but these personal pronouns, being so scarce, add very little to the indefinite pronoun—also because in each case the personal pronoun has a τις, "someone," or τισιν, "some," as antecedent. And in any case he is refuting a claim of the opponents that they have a special relationship to Christ, showing that they have only themselves to compare themselves with, finding the standard to measure their own behavior only in themselves and desiring to compare others only with themselves.[25]

3) Twice Paul uses the *demonstrative pronoun* to indicate the opponents, once the singular τοιοῦτος, "such a one," and once the plural τοιοῦτοι, "such":

10:11: τοῦτο λογιζέσθω ὁ τοιοῦτος ὅτι . . ., "Let such a one consider this";
11:13: οἱ γὰρ τοιοῦτοι, "for such persons . . ."

The use of the article in these cases is anaphoric, indicating reference to persons already mentioned. In 10:11 it is referring to 10:10, where someone is quoted as saying that Paul is strong only in his letters, while he is weak when present. Here the verb φησίν, "he says," in the singular[26]

24. See H. Lausberg, *Handbuch der literarischen Rhetorik*, I (Munich, 1960) §259, concerning the technique of αὔξησις or *amplificatio*, "exaggeration," as an instrument of partisan argument.
25. On the (also rhetorical) Greek concepts of σύγκρισις and μέτρος, "comparison" and "measure," see H. D. Betz, *Der Apostel Paulus*, 119ff.; worthy of note is the anti-Sophist position of Plato, *Leg.* 716C: "For us God is the greatest measure of all things, much more so than a human person could be, as some say."
26. The plural φασίν, "they say," is attested only in Codex B and the Latin and Syriac versions.

can be equivalent simply to the impersonal "it is said,"[27] and hence the demonstrative ὁ τοιοῦτος, "such a one," actually is of uncertain meaning.[28] In 11:13 the plural refers to "those who seek a pretext" (11:12) and governs a series of three predicates, to which we will return; in the context, the pretext sought by the rivals is that Paul also accepts financial support from the community, "pour être trouvés nos pareils sur le point où ils se vantent" (BJ). The refusal of such support by Paul (cf. 11:7-12) unmasks their πλεονεξία, "greed" (cf. 12:17, 18), and the community can easily see the difference. In this regard, we must note the contrast between the end of v. 12e and the beginning of v. 13: ἡμεῖς. οἱ γὰρ τοιοῦτοι . . ., "we . . . For such persons . . ." The two are clearly contrasted.

4) *The plural adjective of quantity* πολλοί, "many," occurs once in 11:18:[29] πολλοὶ καυχῶνται κατὰ σάρκα, "many boast according to the flesh." The mention of these "many," which functions as an introduction to the immediately following phrase, κἀγὼ καυχήσομαι, "I too shall boast," is supposed to provide some justification for the boastful attitude Paul is assuming (who recognizes in 11:17 that what he says is not according to the Lord, but foolish: in the genre of "Narrenrede"). We are probably dealing, then, with a rhetorical exaggeration, and even though the adjective by its nature indicates a good number of persons, we do not actually have to think of a multitude; it is enough to think of a few rivals, a small group of a few persons (even only three or four; cf. the pronoun τινες, "some").

5) *Qualifying adjectives* used by Paul to describe his opponents are extremely rare. Apart from 11:13, where the adjective δόλιοι, "deceitful," modifies a substantive (see below, no. 7), we have only 11:19: ἀνέχεσθε τῶν ἀφρόνων, "you put up with fools." Here the adjective is used as a substantive, and the clause does not imply an exclusive reference to the opponents of Paul but to the class of fools in general. It is true that the article could be meant to refer to the category mentioned in the preceding verse (πολλοὶ καυχῶνται κατὰ σάρκα, "many boast according to the flesh"). But

27. See Blass-Debrunner-Rehkopf, §130.3: " 'The (imaginary) opponent says' as in the diatribe." For this opinion V. P. Furnish, *II Corinthians*, 468, refers to Epictetus, *Diatr.* III 9:15; IV 1:11, 151, 158; 9:6, 7; see other references in W. Bauer, *Wörterbuch* (and in Arndt-Gingrich, eds., *A Greek-English Lexicon*) s.v. φημί. C. K. Barrett, *2 Corinthians*, 260, thinks of a single individual; but the use of φησίν, "says," after a plural is attested in Libanius, *Or.* 52:39 (cited in Liddell-Scott-Jones, *Lexicon*, s.v.).
28. See M. Carrez, *Deuxième épître*, 203: "His opponents are reduced to a singular interlocutor"; H. Lietzmann, *Korinther I–II*, 142: "such people"; R. Bultmann, *Zweiter Korintherbrief*, 192: "one who says such a thing"; V. P. Furnish, *II Corinthians*, 469: "Such a person: that is, whoever would criticize Paul."
29. From this text we distinguish the occurrence in 12:21, where, as we have said, the reference is to a group of sinners.

on the one hand we have seen that πολλοί, "many," should not be taken literally, and especially on the other, the root of ἄφρων/ἀφροσύνη, "fool/ foolishness," in 2 Cor 10–13 is used elsewhere only in reference to Paul (cf. the substantive in 11:1, 17, 21, and the adjective in 11:16 [twice]; 12:6, 11). Hence the phrase in 11:19 is universal in sense and includes Paul himself, though purely ironically.

This lack of adjectives tells us that Paul does not bother to reflect on the nature of his opponents; rather, in Semitic fashion, he uses nouns (see below). But especially he considers actions, using various words to indicate what they do.

6) The function of *verbs*, indeed, is to indicate the action, becoming, or even state of specific subjects which, thanks to the verbs, come to be better described in their concrete identity.

Before listing them we note that the text alternates between the singular and plural of the third person in the finite tenses, and between singular and plural in the participles. We will not distinguish this use of number, since the singular is explained by the use of the indefinite pronominal subject τις, "someone" (see above). The verbs employed[30] are nineteen in all, one of which (καυχῶνται, "boast") is repeated twice for a total of twenty occurrences. They all occur only in chapters 10–11:

> 10:2: τοὺς λογιζομένους, "those who consider"
> 10:7: πέποιθεν, "have been confident"
> 10:10: φησίν, "says"
> 10:12: τῶν ἑαυτοὺς συνιστανόντων . . . μετροῦντες καὶ συγκρίνοντες . . . οὐ συνιᾶσιν, "who commend themselves . . . who measure and compare . . . they do not understand"
> 11:4: ὁ ἐρχόμενος . . . κηρύσσει, "the one who comes . . . announces"
> 11:12: τῶν θελόντων . . . καυκῶνται εὑρεθῶσιν, "those who want . . . boast . . . be found"
> 11:13: μετασχηματιζόμενοι, "disguising themselves"
> 11:18: καυχῶνται, "boast"
> 11:20: καταδουλοῖ . . . κατεσθίει . . . λαμβάνει . . . ἐπαίρεται . . . δέρει, "enslaves . . . devours . . . takes advantage . . . is presumptuous . . . strikes"
> 11:21: τολμᾷ, "dares"

---

30. Obviously we do not include the form εἰσιν, "are," which occurs four times in 11:22f., since its verbal character is annulled by its copulative function, i.e., by simply joining a subject ("they" is understood in the verb form) and four nouns used as predicates.

From all these verbs we can extract a certain picture of the opponents.

a) The participial substantive ὁ ἐρχόμενος, "the one who comes" (11:4), says that at least some of them (see below) come from outside, and hence are intruders. Evidently we understand the use of the singular in a collective or generalizing sense.[31] At most we would think of a leader of the opponents as an exponent of their case, but not to be identified with the offender of 2:5-11; 7:12,[32] precisely because he comes from outside the community.

b) Not only do these have opinions (cf. λογιζομένους, "consider") and personal convictions (cf. πέποιθεν, "have been confident") on their belonging to Christ (10:7)[33] as well as about the purely human motives for Paul's behavior (10:2), but also:

c) they actively "preach" (cf. 11:4: κηρύσσει) and tailor their message quite differently from that of Paul. With regard to this, what we read of "another Jesus . . . another pneuma . . . another gospel"[34] would seem to give us the theological identity of the opponents in comprehensive terms. But in reality we must be very prudent because the terms are quite general and so have lent themselves to very different interpretations by exegetes. Not only is the association Jesus/pneuma/gospel unparalleled in its comprehensiveness, but some of its components are also unusual: thus in chapters 10–13 there is no other mention of the Spirit in relation to Christian identity[35] nor to the gospel in reference to its content, but only

31. Thus also Gal 5:10 compared with 1:7; and in 2 Cor 11:4 the singular may be influenced by the reference to ὁ ὄφις, "the serpent," in 11:3 (see J. Zmijewski, *Der Stil,* 99).

32. Whereas this seems to be the meaning toward which C. K. Barrett leans, *2 Corinthians,* 275; but R. P. Martin, *2 Corinthians,* 335, speaks only of a "ringleader . . . spokesperson." Meanwhile E. Käsemann, "Die Legitimität des Apostels. Eine Untersuchung zu II Korinther 10–13," ZNW 41 (1942) 33–71, criticizes the old thesis of A. Hausrath and A. Schlatter, according to which the singular would refer to someone sent from the Jerusalem Church (Peter) who must have come to Corinth to judge the situation (see p. 38: "an almost novelistic expansion").

33. I believe we must exclude a reference to the Corinthian faction mentioned in 1 Cor 1:12 (against W. Schmithals, *Gnosis in Corinth,* trans. J. E. Steely [Nashville, 1971] 197–199 = *Die Gnosis in Korinth. Eine Untersuchung zu den Korintherbriefen,* FRLANT 66 [Göttingen, 1965²] 186–188) on the basis of the coming dispute in 2 Cor 10–13, where the supposed special relationship of the opponents with Christ is especially associated with their apostolate (see 11:13, 23).

34. There is probably no difference between the variation between ἄλλος, "other," and ἕτερος, "other": 1 Cor 12:9, 10; Gal 1:6-7 (against W. Schmithals, *Die Gnosis,* 134–136: Gnostic conceptions of the Spirit).

35. The use in 12:18 is in a different kind of context. As for the rest, H. Windisch, *Der zweite Korintherbrief,* Meyer Kommentar (Göttingen, 1924) 328, had already shown that in chapters 1–9, where it speaks of the Spirit with tacit reference to the opponents, they do not teach "another" Spirit but simply leave no room for it (see 3:3, 6ff. and also 1:22; 4:13; 5:5; 6:6).

to the vindication of Paul's jurisdiction (see 10:14, 16) and to his preaching it free (11:7). These things, then, were not a matter of controversy except insofar as the very presence of the opponents at Corinth was a general danger in that they opposed Paul's apostolic authority.[36] Now, all this must have implied doctrinal differences (see 11:3), but these are not perceptible with sufficient clarity. Indeed, we cannot exclude the possibility that the list of v. 4 has essentially a rhetorical function for the Corinthian community, whom Paul asks to be just as receptive to him (11:1: ἀνέχεσθέ μου, "put up with me") as they are toward others (11:4 καλῶς ἀνέχεσθε, "well do you put up with").[37]

d) On the other hand, their practical behavior toward the Corinthian Christians is clear: the five verbs in 11:20 describe the opponents as persons who take advantage of the community, eager "to enslave, to devour, to take (into their own control), to exalt themselves (over others), strike in the face." This accumulation of verbs indicates an evident polemic intent and a sure rhetorical effect. Paul's irony here reaches the genre of "groteske Parodie."[38] The verse, therefore, tells us little about the objective identity of Paul's adversaries. Again, this is evidence of Paul's preoccupation before the ingenuousness of the Corinthians, who do not recognize those who are twisting the gospel to their own personal purposes (see 2:17; 5:5).

e) A series of verbs (10:12) presents them as devoid of any guarantee or recommendation and hence presumptuous, conceited, deceitful, and unintelligent. The objective foundation of this accusation is that they lack σύστασις, μέτρον, and σύγκρισις. The three concepts are interrelated, and all three involve an external reference or support, understood in turn as "recommendation," objective "measure," and "point of comparison." What Paul intends is not just specific letters of recommendation (see 3:1)

36. See the good exegesis of V. P. Furnish, *II Corinthians*, 500, 502, criticizing the repeated affirmation of D. Georgi, *Die Gegner*, 284–285, that it is Christology of all things that is the issue between Paul and his adversaries (thus also R. P. Martin, *2 Corinthians*, 336, 339). Furnish rightly observes that "nowhere in 2 Cor is Christology taken up in and for itself" (p. 501); also W. Oostendorp, *Another Jesus: A Gospel of Jewish-Christian Superiority in II Corinthians* (Kampen, 1967), notes that "Paul does not here discuss those very points which he seemingly would have to discuss if either a Judaistic or pneumatic falsification of the gospel was at stake" (p. 15).

37. See H. Windisch, *Zweiter Korintherbrief*, 325; J. Zmijewski, *Der Stil*, 98. C. K. Barrett, "Paul's Opponents in II Corinthians," NTS 17 (1971) 233–275, writes very well that "the Corinthians do not examine the content of what is preached to them, but consider only the manner, and perhaps the credentials, of the preacher"; and that "in this verse Paul is attacking the Corinthians' gullibility more than the intruders" (p. 242).

38. J. Zmijewski, *Der Stil*, 230.

but the approval of the Lord. For "it is not one's own approval of self that makes one acceptable, but God's approval" (10:18; cf. 6:4; 4:2), as we read in 10:13 as well. This statement implies that Paul's opponents at Corinth based their claims rather worldlily by putting the emphasis on their own exploits, their own performances, which the Apostle considers completely irrelevant. Nor can we exclude the possibility that 10:13-16 contains a reference to the Jerusalem meeting (cf. Gal 2:6-10), which recognized Paul's missionary authority among the gentiles, an authority that the opponents did not have. He can therefore claim that they "boast" audaciously (καυχῶνται: 11:12, 18; τολμᾷ, "dare to": 11:21), they are crafty in their own interests (θελόντων ἀφορμήν, "desiring a pretext": 11:12; μετασχηματιζόμενοι, "disguising themselves": 11:13) and in short have no missionary or pastoral understanding, or even good sense (οὐ συνιᾶσιν, "they do not understand": 10:12).[39]

To sum all this up, we see that the presentation of the opponents on the basis of the verbs is strongly conditioned by Paul's negative judgment. What is more objective and can perhaps be used for our artist's reconstruction of the opponents' features is that they boast ἐν ἀλλοτρίοις κόποις, "in another's labors" (10:15), (ἐν ἀλλοτρίῳ κανόνι, "in another's area") (10:16), taking advantage of Paul's apostolic work to the detriment of Paul himself, something that he would never do (cf. Rom 15:20).

7) The *designation* of the opponents *with substantives* is rather rare in 2 Cor 10-13, but hence all the more significant. Besides the series of four descriptions in 11:22 (ἑβραῖοι, ἰσραηλῖται, σπέρμα 'Αβραάμ, διάκονοι Χριστοῦ, "Hebrews, Israelites, offspring of Abraham, ministers of Christ"), they are twice referred to as τῶν ὑπερλίαν ἀποστόλων, "the superapostles" (11:5; 12:11), while once they are dubbed ψευδαπόστολοι, ἐργάται δόλιοι, "false apostles, deceitful workers" (11:13), to which we must also somehow relate the ψευδάδελφοι, "false brethren," of 11:26 (cf. Gal 2:4). Actually, certain authors have wanted to see in these expressions reference to two different categories of persons:[40] only 11:13 would designate Paul's concrete opponents at Corinth, while 11:5 and 12:11 would allude to Peter and the other apostles of Jerusalem (in conformity with the mild irony of

---

39. It is not impossible that the basis of this antithesis is the Pauline opposition between boasting of one's deeds and relying only on faith: see the same citation of Jer 9:22, 23 in 2 Cor 10:17 and 1 Cor 1:31 (this may also be resonating in Rom 5:11; Gal 6:14; Phil 3:3); see V. P. Furnish, *II Corinthians*, 482f.

40. See E. Käsemann, "Die Legitimität," 41–48; C. K. Barrett, *2 Corinthians*, 287; "Paul's Opponents," 242–244, 249–253; M. E. Thrall, "Super-Apostles, Servants of Christ, and Servants of Satan," JSNT 6 (1980) 42–57; R. P. Martin, *2 Corinthians*, 342; R. P. Martin, "The Opponents," 285–286.

Gal 2:9: "those who seemed to be the pillars"), of whom Paul's direct rivals may have been emissaries.

We begin our brief analysis on the subject with 11:13 (and 15), the meaning of which is very clear. Here the polemic becomes more explicit and more severe, without any indulgent attenuation. The term ψευδαπόστολοι, "false apostles," is a neologism that may have been coined by Paul himself,[41] picking up on an accusation of these same opponents against him.[42] The sense is very much similar to that of ψευδοπροφῆται, "false prophets,"[43] witnessed to in the LXX (see esp. Jer 36:8 = MT 29:8), in Flavius Josephus (*Ant.* 10:111) and in the New Testament (see 2 Pet 2:1: false prophets and false teachers), and indicates prophets who are not sent by the Lord and are not conformed to God's will. Also, the ἐργάται δόλιοι, "deceitful workers," moves in this direction, for while the noun possibly derives from the missionary speech of the early Church,[44] the adjective describes their activity as insidious and deceitful. The expression is just like κακοὶ ἐργάται, "evil workers, in Phil 3:2, the negative sense of which is evident, even though it says nothing of the content of their preaching.

But there is something that can be deduced from our context about the character of their enterprise at Corinth. From 11:7-11 we recognize indirectly, from the fact that Paul notes that he preached the gospel free, that the rivals on the contrary accepted sustenance (and perhaps also financial support: cf. 12:14b-18) from the community. But this fact alone does not justify Paul's accusation, since the maintenance of the preacher was a missionary rule that the tradition traced back to Jesus, as even Paul recognizes elsewhere (1 Cor 9:7-14, where in v. 14 specific reference is made to a precept of the Lord witnessed by Luke 10:7 = Matt 10:10; 1 Tim 5:18; *Did.* 13:2), even though this is refused by the Apostle in his personal missionary style (1 Cor 9:15-18).

The accusation of "false apostles" must allude to something more, which we can conjecture on the basis of *Did.* 11:4-6. Here the difference between ἀπόστολος, "apostle," and ψευδοπροφήτης, "false prophet," is indicated twice: the latter label is given to the apostle who claims the right to stay more than two days at the expense of the community, or else who upon leaving demands money in addition to the bread for the journey. Probably, then, the pseudapostolicity in this case consists at least in part in their opportunistic and self-interested, if not exploitative (cf. 11:20),

---

41. Thus W. G. Kümmel in the "Anhang" to H. Lietzmann, *An die Korinther*, 211; also R. P. Martin, *2 Corinthians*, 350.

42. Thus C. K. Barrett, "ψευδαπόστολοι," 390–391.

43. See H. Windisch, *Zweite Korintherbrief*, 341.

44. See Matt 9:37-38 (par. Luke 10:2); 10:10 (par. Luke 10:7; resumed in 1 Tim 5:18; *Did.* 13:2); 2 Tim 2:15.

behavior (see 11:20);[45] it is against such persons that Paul wants to put his addressees on guard.

The accusation "ministers of Satan" (11:14-15) is metaphorical (see below, Rhetorical figures (e), metaphor, pp. 281–82); it raises the stakes and becomes quite an insult, tending to present the rivals as opponents not just of Paul but even of God and of the gospel.[46] Associating them with Satan, then, perhaps implies an allusion to the content of their preaching or rather to their apparent (note the use of the verb μετασχηματίζειν, "disguise oneself") behavior with regard to the gospel, and to their realization of the "signs of the apostle," which in 12:12 Paul will also claim for himself. They must have been showing off "signs, wonders, and mighty deeds," not in the service of the gospel, the risen Lord and his Spirit,[47] but as endorsement of themselves, or at any rate in such a way as to draw the Corinthians away from the gospel of the Cross. In fact, these things can belong to the manifestation of the anti-Christ, as we read in 2 Thess 2:9; Did. 16:4; Hippolytus, De antichristo 6.[48] Therefore, Paul does not insist that he has accomplished such deeds in his own ministry, but he certainly attributes them to his rivals, thus inciting the Corinthians to go beyond appearances.

Now, as for the identification of the ὑπερλίαν ἀπόστολοι, "superapostles," the reasons given to consider them distinct from the "pseudo-apostles"

45. These considerations do not touch the problem of the negative reaction of the Corinthians to Paul but not to his rivals. It was probably a series of factors that put Paul on the defensive (see the good treatment in V. P. Furnish, II Corinthians, 506–509).

46. See the texts Apoc. Mos. 17:1-2; Vit. Ad. Latin 9:1, Slavic 38:1; 1QS 3:21. The opinion of M. E. Thrall, "Super-Apostles," 50–56, who would see here an allusion to Matt 16:23 (ὕπαγε ὀπίσω μου, σατανᾶ, "get behind me, satan") because the opponents claimed to represent Peter, seems to me to be stretching things; the terms are, after all, too generic to allow us to say that Paul is acquainted with this tradition.

47. Such would be the meaning of the promises of Jesus in Matt 10:1, 8; Mark 16:17-18. And such also the intention of Paul in Rom 15:18-19; Gal 3:1-5; and also in 2 Cor 12:12 the allusion to ὑπομονή, "endurance," links his ministry to a context of trials, difficulties, and afflictions that would make the power of the gospel derive more from the weakness of the Cross than from some triumphalistic ostentation. See E. Käsemann, "Die Legitimität," 61–71; H. K. Nielsen, "Paulus Verwendung des Begriffes Δύναμις. Eine Replik zur Kreuzestheologie," in S. Pedersen, ed., Die paulinische Literatur und Theologie, Teologiske Studier 7 (Arhus-Göttingen, 1980) 137–158, esp. 152–154.

48. Here are the texts: 2 Thess 2:9: ὁ ἄνομος . . . οὗ ἐστιν ἡ παρουσία κατ᾽ ἐνέργειαν τοῦ σατανᾶ ἐν πάσῃ δυνάμει καὶ σημείοις καὶ τέρασιν ψεύδους, "The lawless one, whose coming is by the work of Satan with all power and false signs and wonders." Did. 16:4: καὶ τότε φανήσεται ὁ κοσμοπλανὴς ὡς υἱὸς θεοῦ καὶ ποιήσει σημεῖα καὶ τέρατα, "Then the deceiver of the world will appear as the Son of God and will do signs and wonders." Hippolytus, De antichristo 6: ἀπέστειλεν ὁ κύριος τοὺς ἀποστόλους εἰς πάντα τὰ ἔθνη, καὶ αὐτὸς ὁμοίως πέμψει ψευδαποστόλους, "The Lord sent apostles to all nations, and so likewise will this one send false apostles." See E. Ernst, Die eschatalogischen Gegenspieler in den Schriften des Neuen Testamentes, Biblische Untersuchungen 3 (Regensburg, 1967) 41–44, which also quotes the Apocalypse of Elijah 33:1-3, where the anti-Christ is described as able to make the lame walk and the mute speak, to give sight to the blind and to cleanse the lepers.

seem unconvincing to me.[49] The following observations would seem to refute these reasons.[50]

a) The comparison with the other apostles that Paul establishes elsewhere (cf. 1 Cor 9; 15; Gal 2) is always described circumstantially, even citing their names; here, on the other hand, the "superapostles" are treated so generically that we have no reason to seek their identity outside the immediate context, which is treating precisely the concrete opponents in Corinth.

b) Consequently, the transition from 11:1-4 to 11:5 does not in the least suggest a change of reference in regard to the third parties who stand between the sender and the recipients of the letter; indeed, the coordinating particle γάρ, "for," implies an explicative nexus with what has just been said.

c) The concession Paul makes in 11:6a, εἰ δὲ καὶ ἰδιώτης τῷ λόγῳ, "but if unskilled in speech," thus acknowledging a difference from the "superapostles" would be superfluous if this implied a comparison with the apostles of the Church of Jerusalem, who in Acts 4:13 are described as ἄνθρωποι ἀγράμματοι καὶ ἰδιῶται, "unlearned and unskilled men."

d) The fact that Paul is compared with the false prophets and not with the true, great apostles is well explained in the context. It is actually they who have compared him unfavorably with themselves, and even though he would rather not do so (10:12), he admits to speaking as a fool (see the "Narrenrede" in 11:16–12:10). The compound adverb ὑπερλίαν, "beyond measure," implies a stronger irony than Gal 2:9 and is comparable to similar polemical or satirical expressions attested to in the Greek world;[51] this is, then, not some sort of respectful discourse. So the expression may

49. The authors who maintain this (see above, n. 40) emphasize these observations: (1) the tone with which Paul speaks of the "superapostles" is more respectful than when he speaks of the "pseudo-apostles"; (2) Paul would not easily compare himself with the false apostles, whereas he has already in 1 Cor 15:9 (cf. 2 Cor 12:11b) compared himself with the major apostles; (3) after each of the two occurrences of "superapostles," Paul speaks of financial support (in 11:7-11 and 12:13-18), and that is in conformity with the comparison already made with the great apostles in 1 Cor 9: "The other apostles and the brothers of the Lord and Cephas"; (4) the irony in the expression "superapostles" is similar to that contained in Gal 2:9, where James, Cephas, and John are identified as "those who are considered pillars."

50. Some of these are well expressed by V. P. Furnish, *II Corinthians*, 503–504; see also S. E. McClelland, " 'Super-Apostles, Servants of Christ, Servants of Satan.' A Response" [to M. E. Thrall], JSNT 14 (1982) 82–87.

51. See H. D. Betz, *Der Apostel Paulus*, 121, n. 570, with citations from Plato and Lucian: πάσσοφοι, ὑπεράνθρωπος, ὑπερνέφελος, τρισόλβιος "all-wise, superhuman, above the clouds, thrice lucky," etc. H.-J. Klauck, *2. Korintherbrief*, 83, also maintains that we have here "sarcastic labeling."

refer to excessive claims made by the opponents in the Corinthian community, but it is certainly a polemic designation, expressing even more the personal attitude of Paul, who intends to make them ridiculous in the eyes of his readers.

In any case, the Apostle acknowledges that they are "Hebrews . . . Israelites . . . seed of Abraham . . . servants of Christ."[52] Their Jewish origin is, then, certain, not only ethnically but religiously. But the same cannot be said for their Palestinian origin nor their association with the Church of Jerusalem. Rather, the allusions to their oratorical skill (10:10; 11:6) and ecstatic experiences (12:1-10) and the demonstration of extraordinary powers (12:12; 13:3) would point us toward Hellenistic Judaism,[53] but still recognizing their adherence to Christ. To go beyond this and claim that they represent the Hellenistic type of the *theios aner*, "divine man,"[54] seems excessive to me, both because this cultural category is a modern construction and because the elements offered in our chapters are too vague and indirect, and are too much characterized by Paul's polemic to permit such a conclusion.[55]

2) Rhetorical figures: indirect allusions to the opponents

After the direct allusions in 2 Cor 10–13, we can also perceive the third parties between writer and recipients on the basis of indirect and allusive references. Here the task grows more delicate, and so discretion is necessary to avoid the risk of espying an opponent behind Paul's every word or phrase. But I should think that certain literary procedures by their nature conceal a reference to a third party. These are what classical rhetoric calls *figurae sententiae*, and they belong to the *ornatus locutionis*.[56] Certain of these can be profitably pursued in our research.

52. See a good discussion of these terms in D. Georgi, *Die Gegner*, in turn: 51–60, 60–63, 63–82, 31–38.

53. See V. P. Furnish, *II Corinthians*, 53. But it does not seem to me that this is the sense of the expression "seed of Abraham" (as D. Georgi, *Die Gegner*, 63–82, would have it; V. P. Furnish, *II Corinthians*, 534f.), since Paul regularly treats Abraham from the point of view not of cultural identity but of the model of faith (see Rom 4:1-18; 9:6-8; Gal 3:6-29; 4:22ff.), or at most, of belonging to the nation (see Rom 11:1).

54. Thus D. Georgi, *Die Gegner*, 299–300.

55. See also C. R. Holladay, *Theios Aner in Hellenistic Judaism: A Critique of the Use of This Category in New Testament Christology*, SBL DS 40 (Missoula, Mont., 1977); the critique of this author is attenuated by G. P. Corrington, *The "Divine Man." His Origin and Function in Hellenistic Popular Religion*, American University Studies, Ser. 7: Theology and Religion 17 (New York-Bern-Frankfurt, 1986).

56. See H. Lausberg, *Handbuch*, §§755–910. [The technicality of the rhetorical vocabulary often makes translation of the Latin or Greek terms into English impossible or almost meaningless. I shall attempt a rough rendering when this seems possible.—T. P. W.] "Ironia" also belongs to *ornatus locutionis*. This is expressed both *in verbis singulis*, "in single words," and

a) *Antithesis* in itself expresses an opposition and can be employed on various levels (in describing just one person or thing among many), thus revealing the complexity of the datum.[57] Chapters 10–13 open at once with an antithesis in 10:1, where Paul presents himself to the addressees as κατὰ πρόσωπον μὲν ταπεινὸς ἐν ὑμῖν, ἀπὼν δὲ θαρρῶ εἰς ὑμᾶς, "meek among you to the face, but bold when absent." The antithesis between humility and boldness is found in 10:10: αἱ ἐπιστολαί . . . βαρεῖαι καὶ ἰσχυραί, ἡ δὲ παρουσία τοῦ σώματος ἀσθενὴς καὶ ὁ λόγος ἐξουθενημένος, "the letters . . . are weighty and strong, but the bodily presence is weak and the speech contemptible." In this second text the antithesis is clearly formulated by the opponents, who are explicitly quoted with the verb φησίν, "he says" (see above); and so this reveals a major stand against Paul, who is supposed to be discredited before the Corinthians as a weak and timid person. But with 10:1 it is more plausible that it is Paul himself who coined the terms of the antithesis ταπεινός/θαρρεῖν, "meek/bold," as an anticipatory reformulation of the accusation quoted in 10:10, since this vocabulary is not repeated there.[58] In substance, however, this reflects the opinion of the opponents.

Much the same could be said of 10:3-4, 6, where the following oppositions recur: ἐν σαρκί . . . οὐ κατὰ σάρκα, "in the flesh . . . not according to the flesh" (v. 3); τὰ γὰρ ὅπλα . . . ἡμῶν οὐ σαρκικὰ ἀλλὰ δυνατά, "for our arms . . . are not fleshly but powerful" (v. 4); παρακοήν . . . ὑπακοή, "disobedience . . . obedience" (v. 6). We can here read an implicit reference to the opponents, who drive Paul to the defensive. These expressions reflect the offense, that is, the accusation against Paul that he acts weakly, in too human a manner, without the force needed to gain respect and capable of manifesting God's power.

In 10:18 we read another antithesis: οὐ γὰρ ὁ ἑαυτὸν συνιστάνων . . . ἀλλὰ ὃν ὁ κύριος συνίστησιν, "not who commends self but whom the Lord commends." Its formulation generally resumes the concrete case presented in 10:12 in abstract and universal terms: οὐ γὰρ τολμῶμεν . . . ἀλλὰ αὐτοί, "not we . . . but they . . ." (see above). Verse 10:13 runs in the same

---

in verbis conjunctis, "in phrases and sentences": as such (i.e., as a trope of speech and of thought), irony affects the whole text and is scattered throughout 2 Cor 10–13. For that reason we do not treat it as a *figura* by itself. For its use in ancient rhetoric, see C. Forbes, "Comparison, Self-Praise and Irony: Paul's Boasting and the Conventions of Hellenistic Rhetoric," NTS 32 (1986) 1–30, 10–13. In general, see also the study of J. Sampley cited above at n. 4.

57. See also N. Schneider, *Die rhetorische Eigenart der paulinischen Antithese*, HUTh 11 (Tübingen, 1970). The author wants ultimately to distinguish between *Antithese* and *Gegensatz* ("antithesis" and "opposition"; see pp. 15f.). The texts that we will consider are surely antitheses properly speaking (see ibid., p. 62).

58. Hence it is probable that 10:1 already implies an irony toward the opponents and that Paul is already mustering his defense: see H. D. Betz, *Der Apostel Paulus*, 52.

direction: οὐκ εἰς τὰ ἄμετρα καυχησόμεθα, ἀλλὰ κατὰ τὸ μέτρον τοῦ κάνονος . . ., "We shall not boast beyond measure but according to the measure apportioned," demonstrating again the opposition between Paul and his rivals (see above).[59]

b) Also certain *negations* can indicate a contrast with certain accusers, even though they are not directly quoted. This is the case, according to the immediate context, of 10:14 (οὐ γὰρ ὡς μὴ ἐφικνούμενοι εἰς ὑμᾶς, "not as if we did not reach you"); 10:15 (οὐκ εἰς τὰ ἄμετρα καυχώμενοι, "we shall not boast beyond measure"); 10:16 (οὐκ ἐν ἀλλοτρίῳ κανόνι, "not in another's area"), which we have already encountered above. But even the negative phrase in 11:5, λογίζομαι γὰρ μηδὲν ὑστερηκέναι, "I consider myself not at all inferior" (repeated in 12:11b: οὐδὲν γὰρ ὑστέρησα, "I was not at all inferior") conceals a possible reproof leveled at Paul for not being on a par with the "superapostles," i.e., being behind them and hence inferior, not having reached their level.[60]

c) In some cases we have the *question* used rhetorically as a syntactic *immutatio*, "transformation," in which an affirmative sentence is transformed into an interrogative, thus becoming similar to an *exclamatio*.[61] Thus in 11:7: "Have I perhaps sinned by humbling myself that you might be exalted?"; 11:11: "Because I don't love you?"; 12:13a: "How have you been inferior to other Churches, except in that I have not been a burden to you?" The acute irony in each of these questions could presuppose an accusation made against the questioner. This is all the more likely in that all three questions turn on an identical theme: the fact that Paul has not accepted sustenance from the Corinthians. But Paul turns the criticisms leveled against him into evidence for his affection for them and grounds for his own boasting.

Moreover, the simple questions of 11:22f. in fact overtly describe the opponents (see above).[62]

d) *Repetition* also (or *commoratio in una re*, "dwelling on one thing") betrays a reference to an accusation. For the accentuation of an argument at least shows that the writer is anxious to note it particularly and affirm it vigorously. It presupposes, then, that the recipients are likely to forget it or to think the opposite, or perhaps to be led by others not to attend

59. But other antitheses are Pauline in origin, belonging to his reply, above all between "weakness" and "power" with a Christological content (12:9-10; 13:3b-4).
60. But most of the negations in 2 Cor 10–13 most likely belong to Paul's reply: see 11:4, 6, 9 (parallels 12:13, 14 [thrice], 16), 10, 11, 15, 17, 29; 12:1, 2, 3, 4, 5, 6, 7, 18, 20.
61. See H. Lausberg, *Elemente der literarischen Rhetorik* (Munich, 1967 [1949]) §§428,1 and 445.
62. Other questions belong rather to Paul's response: 11:29; 12:15, 17, 18.

to it. What we find most important here is not the repetition of a specific word[63] but the repetition of an idea in various forms. In this regard we can discern three principal centers of interest.

In the first place, let us consider 10:12-18. Here there is a notable emphasis on the idea of ''measure'' (recurring five times in the root μετρ-, ''measure''; three times in the noun κανών, ''area, field,'' once in the verb μερίζειν, ''apportion''). We can add to this the idea of ''boasting'' (four times), while the whole pericope is held together by the technique of *inclusio* between two recurrences of the verb συνιστάναι, ''recommend.'' What Paul is concerned to show clearly is that we can *not* (six negative sentences: 10:12, 13, 14, 15, 16, 18) glory in what God has not assigned to us, what does not, therefore, concern us. It is all too clear that this text is aimed at a contrary position. What is in question is a certain conception of the boundaries (territorial, or better, religious-cultural) of the apostolic ministry (see above).

In the second place, 11:7-12 also represents a literary unity well centered on one single theme, which furthermore itself returns in 12:13-18. It is Paul's justification of himself for having preached the gospel at Corinth free of charge, not accepting the sustenance offered by that community.[64] It is in view of this that we must understand the terms δωρεάν, ''gratis'' (11:7); ἐσύλησα . . . ὀψώνιον, ''plundered . . . support'' (11:8); οὐ κατενάρκησα, ''I did not burden'' (11:9; cf. 12:13); ἀβαρής, ''not burdensome'' (11:9; cf. 12:16: οὐ κατεβάρησα, ''I did not weigh down''); θησαυρίζειν, ''save up'' (12:14); δαπανάω, ''squander'' (12:15 twice); πλεονεκτέω ''take advantage'' (12:17, 18). With this varied vocabulary Paul defends himself

---

63. Nevertheless, note for instance the recurrence of the following words or roots: ἀσθεν-, ''weak-'' (10:10; 11:21, 29; 12:10; 13:3, 4, 9); καταναρκάω, ''burden'' (11:9; 12:13, 14; only occurrence in the New Testament); καυχ-, ''boast-'' (10:8, 13, 15, 16, 17; 11:10, 12, 16, 17, 18, 30; 12:1, 5, 6, 9); φρον-, ἀφρον-, ''clever, foolish'' (11:1, 16 [twice] 17, 19 [twice]), 21; 12:6, 11); ταπειν-, ''humble'' (10:1; 11:7; 12:21); ὑστερεῖν, ''be inferior'' (11:5; 12:11; cf. 11:8, 9), etc. On the other hand, it is surprising to note that other important words are completely or largely absent: thus ἁμαρτ-, ''sin-'' (only 12:21; in 11:7 it is irrelevant); γράμμα-γράπτειν-γραφή, ''write-''; ζωή, ''life'' (only ζάω, ''live,'' in 13:4 [twice]); νόμος, πιστ-, ''law, faith-'' (only 10:15; 13:5); πνεῦμα, ''spirit'' (only 11:4, except for the final salutation of the letter in 13:13), etc. The vocabulary can hardly be typified as theological.

64. We rely here on the thesis of P. Marshall, *Enmity in Corinth: Social Conventions in Paul's Relations with the Corinthians*, WUNT 2:23 (Tübingen, 1987), according to which Paul's use of the verb ἡττᾶσθαι, ''be inferior,'' in 12:13 suggests that Paul's opponents have persuaded the Corinthians that his refusal of their offer of help was best explained by the fact that he considered them inferior to the other Churches, while its acceptance by the rivals, in contrast, showed their affection and esteem (see p. 177). Less well established, however, seems to be the declaration that the offer had been made to Paul by the prosperous Christians of Corinth (see the ''hybrists'' of 1 Cor 4:6-21) as a proposal of friendship in order to attract Paul to their side, while his refusal would have been viewed as a serious affront to their position, and to the whole community, so that they then sided with the rival apostles (see pp. 214-217 and 232).

against the accusation, but moreover he is effecting a *captatio benevolentiae*, "ingratiation, by showing that the opposite behavior would have been burdensome, and so harmful to the community, as in fact that of his antagonists has been, as indicated by the verbs συλάω ("plunder"), καταναρκάω ("burden"), καταβαρέω ("weigh down"), δαπανάω ("squander"), πλεονεκτέω ("take advantage"), θησαυρίζω ("store up"). Thus his speech in turn becomes itself an accusation.

Finally we have the "Peristasenkatalog" in 11:23b-27.[65] Here also we encounter repetition. Indeed, it appears in both its forms: of word (in v. 26 the word κίνδυνος, "danger," occurs eight times; see also in vv. 23-25 the numerical succession: πολλάκις, πεντάκις, τρίς, ἅπαξ, τρίς, "oftentimes, five times, thrice, once, thrice") and especially of idea. The idea is to emphasize the superiority of Paul as minister of Christ in comparison with the opponents (cf. v. 23: ὑπὲρ ἐγώ, "I . . . more"; περισσοτέρως, "more so," twice; ὑπερβαλλόντως, "exceedingly"). The insistent enumeration of hardships he has borne (the series consists of a full twenty-eight *peristaseis*, "conditions") implies the contention that his opponents cannot produce a similar identity card. Behind the use of the comparative in v. 23 we can assume that they also claim something of the sort for themselves (cf. also 21b, "If anyone dares [to boast]"), and that hence in comparing Paul with them it is a question only of quantity. Even so, the main preoccupation of the Apostle is not so much to ascertain who has suffered the most for the gospel (though he does claim this for himself) as to make it perfectly clear that he will glory only in what appertains to his weakness (cf. 11:30; 12:5, 10) and that it is only in this series of manifold difficulties that he paradoxically acknowledges his own "cursus honorum."[66] The enemies, on the contrary, glory in their personal boldness (cf. 10:12-16), their missionary successes (ibid.), their eloquence (cf. 11:4-6), their ecstatic experiences (cf. 12:1-4), their ability to work wonders (cf. 12:11-12).

It is evident that in none of these matters are we dealing with decisive questions of high theology.

e) The figure of the *concession* "consists in admitting that the opponent is correct in one or the other argument. However, this admission generally is counterbalanced by more important reasons adduced by the speaker, so that the *concessio* refers to matters of little importance and so comes close to irony."[67]

65. See a bibliography on the issue in H. D. Betz, *Der Apostel Paulus*, 98, nn. 379 and 380; see also J. Zmijewski, *Der Stil*, 243-275.
66. A. Friedrichsen, "Zum Stil des paulinischen Peristasenkatalog 2 Cor 11:23ff," *Symbolae Osloenses* 7 (1928) 25-29, p. 26. See also D. Georgi, *Die Gegner*, 295; V. P. Furnish, *II Corinthians*, 535f.
67. H. Lausberg, *Elemente*, §437.

In our chapters we have especially two evident cases. In 11:6, with the protasis εἰ δὲ καὶ ἰδιώτης τῷ λόγῳ, "if indeed unskilled in speech," Paul concedes that he is not well versed in the art of oratory. Similar admissions are found in Dio of Prusa, who actually was very much skilled in it.[68] But in 2 Cor 11:6 it is not likely we are looking at a mere rhetorical device,[69] since an appropriate criticism is documented already in 10:10, where Paul quotes an accusation of the opponents (φησίν, "he says"), according to which ὁ λόγος, "the speech" (of Paul) ἐξουθενημένος, "is contemptible."

A different kind of concession typifies 12:1-10. The passage begins with a καυχᾶσθαι δεῖ, "boasting must be done," which is a repetitio (cf. 11:30; 11:18; 10:8).[70] This has every appearance of conceding to the rivals what they have reproached him for: that he cannot boast to the Corinthians of ὀπτασίας καὶ ἀποκαλύψεις κυρίου, "visions and revelations of the Lord."[71] But the concession that Paul makes is of a particular type: he does not admit the truth of the accusation (as in 11:6) but does admit that here there is something to boast about (even though it is not advantageous [οὐ συμφέρον δέ] to do so). Now, we can actually suspect that the pair of nouns "visions and revelations" goes back to the same opponents,[72] considering that neither the plural of either noun nor the conjunction of the two appears anywhere else in the New Testament (cf. also 12:7). Probably the description of the journey to the third heaven is also a concession to the desire of the Corinthian addressees precisely for the extraordinary.[73] But

---

68. See the texts cited in H. Windisch, Zweiter Korintherbrief, 332, of Dio Chrysostomus, Or. 12:15 ("You have been eager to hear a person who is neither handsome nor strong, with no ability at either rhetoric or flattery"); 35:1 ("I know that I am not well enough prepared to please you with my speeches. . . . Indeed, by nature I can speak only simply and poorly, and no better than anyone else"). See also Plato, Phaed. 236D, where Socrates exclaims: "I shall be ridiculous, being an amateur (ἰδιώτης) at improvising on these things in competition with a great artist."

69. Against H. D. Betz, Der Apostel Paulus, 59–66, who speaks of a simple topos of the Socratic tradition, used here as a means of self-defense; but the ancient writers cited are not responding in their texts to known accusations.

70. Many manuscripts, as well as the Vulgate, assimilate the phrase completely to 11:30a, preceding it with an εἰ, "if," while others change the verb δεῖ, "is necessary," to the particle δέ, "but," or else δή, "indeed," connecting the infinitive with the following οὐ συμφέρον, "boasting, however, is not fitting" (see the critical edition of Aland-Black-Martini-Metzger-Wikgren).

71. The plural without an article suggests that Paul intends to refer to a general topos without alluding to a number of visions he has had (thus R. Bultmann, 2 Corinthians, 219 = Zweiter Korintherbrief,) 220; V. P. Furnish, II Corinthians, 524. But R. P. Martin, 2 Corinthians, 396, is of the contrary opinion. Concretely, Paul here describes his own ecstatic experience of being rapt into the third heaven (see A. T. Lincoln, Paradise Now and Not Yet: Studies in the Role of the Heavenly Dimensions in Paul's Thought with Special Reference to His Eschatology, SNTS MS 43 [Cambridge, 1981] 71–86).

72. See J. Zmijewski, Der Stil, 329.

73. The fact that in 12:6a Paul emphasizes the truth of what he is saying (ἀλήθειαν γὰρ ἐρῶ, "I speak the truth") leads C. K. Barrett, 2 Corinthians, 312, to think that the opponents were actually boasting about visions they had never had, moved only by the needs of the Corinthians. But the phrase should not be emphasized too much (cf. also 11:8; 13:8).

in distinction to both opponents and Corinthians, Paul does not attach much importance to these things, and he shows this by using the generic third person singular (ἄνθρωπος, "a man") and also by returning so soon to the theme of boasting in weakness, which brackets our whole passage (see 11:30 and 12:10).

f) Paul also uses the *comparison* (in rhetorical terms: *simile*) in both its variant forms, the *exemplum* and the *similitudo*. We have the former in 11:3: "I fear that, just as *the serpent in its cunning misled Eve*, so your thoughts are led astray from their simplicity and purity with regard to Christ." Here we turn to a biblical fact (ὁ ὄφις ἐξηπάτησεν Εὔαν ἐν τῇ πανουργίᾳ αὐτοῦ), with which they are implicitly compared who would mislead the thoughts of the Corinthians. The allusion to Gen 3 is evident (cf. 3:13 LXX: ὁ ὄφις ἠπάτησέν με, "the serpent deceived me"), and the common element, the *tertium quid comparationis*, between this story and the Corinthian situation is the deception of simple persons, "virgins" (cf. 2 Cor 11:2). Indirectly, then, Paul likens the Corinthian intruders to the serpent of the earthly paradise, with which they share the same πανουργία, "cunning."[74] The fact that there is no specific subject to correspond to the ὄφις, "serpent," while in the second term of the comparison the verb appears only in the passive (φθαρῇ, "be led astray/seduced"), indicates that Paul is primarily preoccupied with the fate of the Corinthian Christians rather than those who correspond to the serpent. Even so, these latter are definitely present in his thought, and indeed the implicit comparison carries considerable weight.

The second comparison is in 12:14b: "For it is not the children who should save up for the parents, but the parents for the children." Here the reference is to a common situation of daily life, even to a law of nature.[75] But on the basis of the context, which deals with Paul's preaching free of charge at Corinth, we note an allusion to the fact that the opponents have subverted this relationship: these, who as preachers are comparable to parents (note this image applied by Paul to himself in 1 Cor 4:15; 2 Cor 6:13; Gal 4:19; 1 Thess 2:11), have reversed the situation and have only taken rather than given (cf. 11:20).

g) Finally, we note the recourse to *metaphor*, or better, *allegory* (as a continued metaphor), namely, the substitution of a different thought for the

---

74. Paul himself in 12:16 claims that he has himself won the Corinthians by "being cunning" (ὑπάρχων πανοῦργος), while attributing a positive and slightly ironic sense to the idea with regard to the free preaching of the gospel.

75. Thus Philo, *Vita Mos.* 2:245; see also Plutarch, *Cupid. div.* 526A (cited in H. Windisch, *Zweiter Korintherbrief*, 399). In 2 Cor 12:14b there is also actually the rhetorical device of the antithesis (see N. Schneider, *Die rhetorische*, 62).

282 History and Exegesis

one intended, to indicate some similarity or analogy. According to rhetoric this can be open *(permixta apertis allegoria)* or closed on itself *(tota allegoria)*. We see examples of each kind in 2 Cor 10–13.

We discover the first type in 11:14-15: "Even Satan adopts the disguise of an angel of light, so it is not a great thing if his ministers disguise themselves as ministers of righteousness; but their end will correspond to their deeds." The semantic key to the allegory is the word μετασχηματίζειν, "disguise," which had already been used in 11:13 concerning the "pseudo-apostles." The speech directly concerns Satan and Satan's ministers, according to a *topos* attested in intertestamental literature,[76] but in context this refers to the opponents, who "transform themselves into apostles of Christ." This metaphorical language is particularly effective, since the evocation of the satanic world identifies the persons in question unambiguously and immediately arouses a reaction of loathing.

The second type of allegory, known also as the *aenigma* because of its obscurity, appears in 12:7: "I was given a thorn in the flesh, an angel of Satan to keep striking me, so that I would not get puffed up." The metaphorical character of the language is given by the three different images employed, σκόλοψ, "thorn,"[77] ἄγγελος σατανᾶ, "messenger/angel of Satan," κολαφίζειν, "buffet," each of which is drawn from a different sphere of experience, but all three of which converge to designate a single reality. But they provide no semantic openings that would give a sure basis for a univocal interpretation, which is demonstrated by the variety of meanings proposed by exegetes.

We consider this text here because among the various hermeneutical positions taken,[78] there is one that would insist on a trial external to Paul

---

76. See *Apoc. Mos.* 17:1: "Then Satan came in the form of an angel and sang hymns to God as the angels" (trans. M. D. Johnson, in J. H. Charlesworth, ed., *The Old Testament Pseudepigrapha*, II [Garden City, N.Y., 1985] 277); *Vit. Ad.* 9:1: "Then Satan was angry and transformed himself into the brightness of angels" (ibid., 260). In 1QS 3:20-21 it distinguishes between "the angel of light" and "the angel of darkness."

77. Between the two possible meanings of this Greek term, "pointed stake" (see M. Park, "Paul's σκόλοψ τῇ σαρκί: Thorn or Stake? (2 Cor xii 7)," NT 22 [1980] 179-183) or "thorn, splinter," we prefer the latter (see G. Delling, in TDNT 7:409–413), especially because this is the meaning it always has in the LXX (Num 33:35; Sir 43:19; Ezek 28:24 as a synonym of ἄκανθα, "thistle"; Hos 2:6). Thus the dative τῇ σαρκί, "to the flesh," is understood not as a *dativum incommodi* ("for my flesh" as in 1 Cor 7:28) but as the equivalent of an adverbial phrase of place ("in my flesh" as in Num 33:55). Thus most commentators.

78. For a review of the interpretations see, e.g., E. B. Allo, *Saint Paul: Seconde épître aux Corinthiens*, EB (Paris, 1937) 313–323; K. Prümm, *Diakonia*, I, 660–664; and also K. L. Schmidt, in TDNT 3:819–821; specifically for patristics see E. Vallauri, "Lo 'stimulus' di Paolo nei Padri," in auct. var., *Gesù apostolo e sommo sacerdote. Studi biblici in memoria di P. Teodorico Ballarini* (Casale Monferrato, 1984) 203–212. Most scholars maintain that it is a question of trials arising from within Paul's own self, whether on the interior level (sexual temptations, sense of unworthiness, anguish over Jewish failure to believe, demoniacal opposition during the journey to the third heaven), or on the physical level (a malady diagnosed by various authors with very diverse hypotheses, from epilepsy to stammering).

himself and his ministry, namely, persecution by his opponents in general, and specifically those who have insinuated themselves into Corinth.[79] One thing seems clear from the context: the trial in question is presented as a consequence of, or at least an experience that comes after, the rapture into the third heaven.[80] The fourteen years mentioned in 12:2, in accordance with different chronologies adopted for the date of 2 Corinthians, lead us basically to the triennium from the year 40 to 42. If the trial follows this period, certain of the interpretations proposed become impossible, and there remain especially assured elements to take into account: the relatively limited time within which it could have begun and its duration. Two possibilities seem to fit this: we must think either of a malady contracted by Paul during his apostolic travels, or else of the difficulties that were presented to him by various kinds of rivals, especially by Judaizers.[81]

The latter interpretation is favored by various considerations:

a) The phrase τῇ σαρκί, "in the flesh," is the same in 1 Cor 7:28 (cf. Phil 1:24), where it refers not to the body but to human life in general, and so we should reject the comparison of our text to Gal 4:13, 14, where we find an illness ἐν τῇ σαρκί μου, "in my flesh."[82]

b) The term σκόλοψ, "thorn," is already used in the Greek of the LXX, Num 33:55 (in the plural; cf. Josh 23:13) and Ezek 28:24 (in the singular), referring to a group of enemies of Israel.

c) The expression ἄγγελος σατανᾶ, "angel of Satan," even though unknown elsewhere in this exact form, recalls the text of 11:14-15, where

79. Besides mention by certain fathers of the Church (see, for example, St. John Chrysostom, *In epist. II ad Cor. homil. XXVI* [PL 61:578], who refers the expression to Alexander the Coppersmith, Hymenaeus, and Philetus, mentioned in 1 Tim 1:20; 2 Tim 2:17; 4:14), the opinion is maintained by the following contemporary authors: T. Y. Mullins, "Paul's Thorn in the Flesh," JBL 76 (1957) 299–303; W. Bieder, "Paulus und seine Gegner in Korinth," ThZ 17 (1961) 319–333; J. J. Thierry, "Der Dorn im Fleische (2 Kor XII 7–9)," NT 5 (1962) 301–310; H. Binder, "Die angebliche Krankheit des Paulus," ThZ 32 (1976) 1–13; M. L. Barré, "Qumran and the Weakness of Paul," CBQ 42 (1980) 216–227; M. Carrez, *La deuxième épître*, 230f.; see also C. Forbes, "Comparison," 21. According to P. F. Beatrice, "Apollos of Alexandria and the Origins of Jewish-Christian Baptist Encratism," NTS 31 (1985) 294 (abridgment of a paper read at the S.N.T.S. at Basel in 1984; see also the same author, "Gli avversari di Paolo e il problema della gnosi a Corinto," *Cristianesimo nella Storia* 6 [1985] 1–25), the "thorn" would be Apollo of Alexandria. Recently J. W. McCant, "Paul's Thorn of Rejected Apostleship," NTS 34 (1988) 550–572, has maintained that it was the rejection of the legitimacy of Paul's apostleship, specifically by the Corinthians; this seems unlikely if for no other reason than that the trial to which Paul alludes is something that began much earlier (note 12:2), which cannot be linked with the problem to which 2 Corinthians attests.

80. The conjunction διό, "therefore," in 12:7 is not at all certain textually (note the critical apparatus of the Aland-Black-Martini-Metzger-Wikgren edition); but in any case the mention of the "thorn" is in direct consequential relation to the "greatness of the revelation."

81. See the earlier 1 Thess 2:15-16 and chapter 16 below.

82. See T. Y. Mullins, "Paul's Thorn," 300; J. W. McCant, "Paul's Thorn," 564f.

the phrase ὁ σατανᾶς μετασχηματίζεται εἰς ἄγγελον φωτός . . . καὶ οἱ διάκονοι αὐτοῦ, "Satan disguises himself as an angel of light . . . and his ministers," certainly alludes to the group of Paul's opponents, while the singular in 12:7 can be explained by the fact that it is in apposition to σκόλοψ, "thorn."

d) The only other occurrence of the verb ἀφιστάναι, "keep away," in Paul is 1 Cor 4:11, within the "Peristasenkatalog," and clearly refers to external trials suffered by Paul from his adversaries during his evangelizing ministry.

e) Also the expression κολαφίζειν, "buffet," in 12:8 confirms the interpretation as referring to persons, since this verb is almost always used of persons.[83]

f) The contextual subject of Paul's prayer and especially the assurance of the Lord's helping power (see 12:8-9) has a parallel in 1QH 2:21-26, where the petitioner gives thanks to Adonai for having saved him from the violent and from their arrows (hiṣṣîm), "manifesting your power in me."[84]

g) Both before (11:23-33) and after (12:10) our passage we have two lists of the various difficulties that Paul exhibited, and not only does neither speak of a σκόλοψ but they never so much as mention any malady. On the one hand, that confirms that the σκόλοψ is a simple metaphor (while in the "Peristasenkataloge" we may find the device of hyperbole but not of metaphor), and, on the other hand, that signifies that the image turns out to be precisely among the external difficulties listed there. Among these, the two lists find a point of contact in the διωγμοῖς, "persecutions" (12:10), to which correspond especially the κίνδυνοι ἐν ψευδαδέλφοις, "perils from false brethren," which represent the climax of a whole series of eight different "perils."[85] It would seem, then, that the σκόλοψ, "thorn," is part of that more general ἐπίστασις καθ᾽ ἡμέραν, ἡ μέριμνα πασῶν τῶν ἐκκλησιῶν,

83. See R. P. Martin, 2 Corinthians, 417. But we must be precise: it is thus used in all New Testament recurrences. But W. Bauer, Wörterbuch, s.v., cites certain passages from the Pastor of Hermes and from 1 Clement in which the word refers to abstract nouns (such as tribulation, life, understanding, justice and peace, wickedness, holy spirit and evil spirit). In Liddell-Scott-Jones, Lexicon, s.v., citations are found from Dioscurides and from Galen with reference to illnesses.

84. See M. L. Barré, "Qumran."

85. See J. Zmijewski, Der Stil, 258–259. More complicated is the explanation of M. L. Barré, "Paul as 'Eschatological Person,' " 505, according to which there would be an intricate chiastic structure in 11:26, alternating places and persons. We can perhaps better think of a series of four pairs of nouns, of which the two middle ones are antithetic (my people/pagans, city/desert), while the first and last (rivers/bandits, sea/false brethren) refer to experience dealing with the opponents.

"daily pressure, the concern for all the churches" (11:28), to which our 2 Cor 10–13 is passionate testimony.

3) *Convergence between outer and inner parties*

All we have said thus far leads to the clear conclusion that there was at Corinth a definite group of opponents of Paul coming from outside, and thus external to the community, as suggested by the image of the "serpent" (11:3); the explicit participle ὁ ἐρχόμενος, "the one who comes" (11:4); their identification as ἀπόστολοι, "apostles" (11:5, 13; 12:11); the theme of their being sustained by the community itself (11:7-12; 12:13ff.); probably also Paul's accusation of not acting according to the measure of the norm established by God; and perhaps also their designation as "Hebrews, Israelites, offspring of Abraham" (11:22).

Still, we must ask if the whole group of the opponents came from outside[86] or if they found allies in a preexisting internal party or indeed from one that they themselves rallied. The question is this: When engaging in polemics with the opponents, is Paul also addressing part of the Corinthian community, or does he just want to defend himself in order to put them on their guard against the influence of his rivals? Were there actually opponents of Paul within the Corinthian Church itself?

The answer definitely must be yes, even though it remains hard to reconstruct what the party consisted of. There was unquestionably a specific adversary at Corinth who caused Paul much trouble (see 2:5-8; 7:12).[87] But even though it is difficult to determine whether he came forth from the community itself or from without, still on the basis of 2:6 we can conclude that a minority of the Corinthians supported him, since it is only "a majority," ὑπὸ τῶν πλειόνων[88] that approved his condemnation. Now, the ironic use of the verbs λαμβάνετε, "take . . . in" (11:4), and ἀνέχεσθε, "put up with" (11:4, 19, 20), explicitly means that at least some of the recipients adopted a receptive attitude toward the superapostles and the false apostles who have come from outside.[89] The very fact that Paul has

86. This is what V. P. Furnish seems to think, *II Corinthians*, 52.
87. Besides the commentaries see C. K. Barrett, "ὁ ἀδικήσας (2 Cor 7.12)," in *Essays on Paul* (Philadelphia, 1982 = 1970), 108–117; P. F. Beatrice, "Apollos in Alexandria," 294.
88. The Greek πλείονες means "most, the majority" or a qualified representation (see also 4:15; 9:2; 1 Cor 9:19; 10:5; 15:6; Phil 1:14) and should not be confused with οἱ πολλοί, which even semantically can mean not only "the many" but "all, the whole" (see Rom 5:15, 19; 12:5; 1 Cor 10:17; see J. Jeremias in TDNT 6:536, 538f.). R. P. Martin, ad loc., mixes the terms, citing Dan 9:27; 11:33, 39; 12:3, since here the Hebrew *ha-rabbim* not only may not mean "all" but in the LXX and Theodotion is rendered as πολλοί rather than πλείονες.
89. Some would have it (see R. P. Martin, *2 Corinthians*, 307) that even in the phrase τὰ κατὰ πρόσωπον βλέπετε, "look at what is in front of you" (10:7), the verb would have an in-

to defend himself for not having accepted sustenance from the community (see esp. 12:13) betrays resentment on the part of the community or at least part of it. Finally, in 13:3 Paul clearly states that the addressees seek proof that Christ does speak in him, and at least in part they show that they have some difficulty in recognizing his apostolic legitimacy.

It is, then, rather hard to distinguish, in the passages examined above expressing the polemic with the opponents, when it is that Paul addresses the outside rivals and when he means to convince those who are members of the Corinthian Church. It is best to assume that they both formed one united party in Paul's eyes, even if within it the so-called superapostles performed a dominant function.[90]

In any case, then, in writing 2 Cor 10–13 Paul is not writing only about "third parties" but intends to include in his polemic at least a part of the community he addresses. Therefore the second person plural in 12:19a (πάλαι δοκεῖτε ὅτι ὑμῖν ἀπολογούμεθα, "Have you thought all this time that we are defending ourselves before you?") means to indicate the Corinthians not only as judges ("before you") of a case between two disputants (Paul and his opponents), but even in a certain way as accusers and so participants in his case ("by you"). His apparent renunciation, then, of any self-defense, as expressed here, actually means that Paul does not want to give too much weight to the contentions of his rivals, and is especially concerned not about his own benefit but about that which will build up the community (note 12:19b).[91]

For the rest, Paul openly states that he fears that when he comes to Corinth, he will not find the Corinthians "as I want." This indicates a gap between his positions and those of the addressees; it probably points back to the beginning of these chapters, where he declared himself "ready to punish any disobedience" (10:6), relying on the authority given him by the Lord "to build you up, not to destroy you" (10:8).

To sum it all up, as in the case of the Galatians, it is precisely the situation of the Corinthians that has driven Paul to write 2 Cor 10–13: not only the fact that certain outside preachers opposed to Paul have insinuated themselves at Corinth, and not only the theoretical risk of the Corinthians

---

dicative meaning, and so would imply a reproof to the addressees ("You see only the end of your nose": trans. J. A. T. Robinson, quoted ibid.); but by most it is understood as an imperative, since that is the thrust of the whole following sentence.

90. See C. Forbes, "Comparison," 15. See also the still good section in E.-B. Allo, *Seconde épître*, 269–274.

91. See H. Windisch, *Zweiter Korintherbrief*, 406. For his part, H. D. Betz, *Der Apostel Paulus*, 14–18, shows that a similar renunciation already belongs to the Socratic tradition of distinguishing between two modes of defense: one with the refined means of rhetoric, the other with a simple preoccupation for truth (see Plato, *Apol.* 17a-c).

themselves yielding, but the actual fact that they have already yielded in part and have embraced the opinions of the intruders, joining up in a single anti-Pauline party with them.

It remains that most of the responsibility for this opposition lies with the intruders, who have simply found favorable soil at Corinth for easy acceptance. It is these, then, who represent a really new element, not only within the Corinthian Church but within the early Church in general.

III. Conclusions

After all we have said, it is still difficult to draw a definitive, unequivocal artist's reconstruction of the faces of these opponents. What C. K. Barrett has said about the literary problem of 2 Corinthians, that the theories are more numerous than the facts and that the two are not always clearly distinguished,[92] applies to our argument as well. One author has tried to form a synthesis of all the typical elements of this group of rivals in order to paint a complete picture of them,[93] but in so doing he runs the risk of distinguishing aspects that are not distinctive among them or of overlooking important points or of simply repeating what is already clearly stated in Paul's text. But it is precisely this that must be interpreted, and such interpretation can be done only by adroitly evaluating its important components, but even more, its presuppositions, omissions, and allusions.

We cannot, of course, treat the question thoroughly here. But certain elementary considerations are necessary. We maintain that we can affirm four characteristics, perhaps minimal but still fundamental.

First of all, Paul's opponents are *Christians* (see 10:7; 11:4, 13, 23), not Jews or pagans. This historical-theological and ecclesial dignity should be restored to them and emphasized, overriding the simple, easy label of ''opponents,'' which has (beginning with Paul himself) polemically confined them in the limbo of the negative and of the losers. What is happening at Corinth is only an intra-ecclesial debate, and in their own way they are witnesses at least to a pluralism of missionary style, if not of different hermeneutics of the gospel. The fact that Paul can reason only in

92. *Second Epistle*, 5.
93. See M. Carrez, ''Réalité christologique et référence apostolique de l'Apôtre Paul en présence d'une église divisée (2 Cor 10–13),'' in A. Vanhoye, ed., *L'Apôtre Paul*, 163–183, esp. 164–174, where the author lists a series of nine characteristics: they are Judaizing; they possess *gnosis*; they make a display of extraordinary spiritual experiences; they attribute great importance to inspiration; they love signs, miracles, and prodigies; there is danger they will separate others from Christ; they have a special interest in the financial help of the community; they are treated as ''false apostles''; they preach another Jesus, another spirit, another gospel.

black and white,[94] and even tends to demonize the rivals (cf. 11:3, 13-15; 12:7),[95] hardly nullifies the rich historical and conceptual complexity of Christian origins or the fact that these very opponents of the Apostle are a legitimate, integral part thereof.

In the second place, it should be recognized that they are *itinerant preachers*, because they are presented as "apostles" (cf. 11:5, 13; 12:11; also 11:23: "ministers of Christ"),[96] because they devote themselves to the preaching of the gospel (11:4, 6), and because they go into a Church they have not founded (cf. 10:13-16; 11:4) and from which they accept or even claim the normal sustenance (see 11:7-12, 20; 12:13-18). In this respect they are clearly distinguished from Paul and his co-workers, who, although itinerants themselves, are rather founders of communities.[97]

A third characteristic is completely certain, concerning their *Jewish origin*, both ethnic and religious. The three designations found in the figure of "repetition" in 11:22 (Hebrews, Israelites, offspring of Abraham) underline this beyond question. They themselves had probably insisted on this characteristic, perhaps perceiving Paul as a Jew who has distanced himself from true Judaism.[98]

But precisely here we encounter certain historical uncertainties typical of 2 Cor 10-13, which we can reduce to two groups. The first group concerns the precise Jewish cultural matrix. Here the unanswered questions are these: Are the Jewish-Christian opponents Palestinian in origin or Hellenistic? Or can we hypothesize a mixed combination? The second group concerns their institutional placement: Do they have some link to the Jerusalem Church? Of what sort? Or are they autonomous? Or do they fit into a larger social-ecclesial phenomenon?

The fourth assured datum concerns the *conflict* between the two sides, since Paul's polemic against them was certainly preceded by a polemic of theirs against the Apostle. But now, though many elements of the conflict can easily be reconstructed (see above), its major contours escape us. Particularly the configuration of their beliefs is unclear: Do they promote

94. See E. P. Sanders, *Paul, the Law, and the Jewish People* (Philadelphia, 1983) 70 and 138.

95. The case is similar to that of 1 John: see J. Painter, "The 'Opponents' in I John," NTS 32 (1986) 48–71; H.-J. Klauck, "Internal Opponents: The Treatment of the Secessionists in the First Epistle of John," *Concilium: Truth and Its Victims* (Edinburgh, 1988) 55–65 (note p. 63: "If faith and love come into conflict, must love necessarily fall by the wayside?").

96. In 2 Cor 10-13 it is not certain that they exhibited letters of recommendation; indeed, 10:12 contrasts with 3:1. We can thus imagine different groups of adversaries.

97. See the stimulating study of G. Theissen, "Legitimation und Lebensunterhalt: ein Beitrag zur Soziologie urchristlicher Missionare," NTS 21 (1974–75) 192–221.

98. An article by C. Forbes, "Paul's Opponents in Corinth," *Buried History* 19 (1983) 19–23 (cited from *New Testament Abstracts* 28 [1984] n. 625) maintains that both the "superapostles" of Corinth and the Jewish agitators of Alexandria (see the Letter of Claudius in P. Lond. 1912) were manifestations of a resurgent Jewish national pride.

a legalistic interpretation of the gospel? Or are they rather pneumatic charismatics? Or do they simply not care much about doctrinal questions, and should we understand the conflict rather on a personal level?[99]

What our study at least shows, from the literary work we have done, is the notable presence of the opponents in 2 Cor 10–13 on both the grammatical and the rhetorical level. It is the Corinthians that Paul addresses, but always with these persons in mind. It is they who have provoked him to write in tones of evident preoccupation. And finally it is Paul alone who has saved their memory from historical oblivion.

---

99. In this latter sense, besides G. Theissen, "Legitimation und Lebensunterhaltung," NTS 21 (1974–75) 192–221, 205, and V. P. Furnish, *II Corinthians*, 53, see also J. A. Hickling, "Is the Second Epistle to the Corinthians a Source for Early Church History?" ZNW 66 (1975) 284–287.

Chapter 16

The Evolution of Paul's Attitude Toward the Jews

The problem of the relations of Paul to Judaism has usually been and continues to be approached from the point of view of systematic theology, which emphasizes their different ways of dealing with the great themes of law, grace, salvation in general, and the question of how the Old Testament is used.[1]

Less common is an approach to the question that would look first at the concrete relations of the Apostle with the historical Israelite people and, when appropriate, with the Jews of his day.[2] Sometimes, indeed, facile charges of Paul's supposed anti-Judaism are made.[3] What is important is, rather, to follow the evolution of attitude experienced by Paul in the course of his missionary enterprise in order to see whether everything is immutably fixed in his judgments of the Jews from beginning to end, or whether we can recognize variations conditioned by circumstances and by reflection, by way of a maturing in the subject. Our perspective is, then, quite practical and examines the relations between persons more than between ideas, even though a limited discussion of the latter is inevitable.

1. Here we will only mention a few representative studies: H. Windisch, *Paulus und das Judentum* (Stuttgart, 1935); W. D. Davies, *Paul and Rabbinic Judaism* (London, 1958²); "Paul and the People of Israel," NTS 24 (1977) 4-39; K. Stendahl, *Paul Among Jews and Gentiles, and Other Essays* (Philadelphia, 1976); M. Barth, "St. Paul—A Good Jew," *Horizons in Biblical Theology* 1 (1979) 7-45; E. P. Sanders, *Paul and Palestinian Judaism: A Comparison of Patterns of Religion* (London, 1977); *Paul, the Law, and the Jewish People* (Philadelphia, 1983); H. Räisänen, *Paul and the Law*, WUNT 29 (Tübingen, 1983). See also chapter 21 in the second volume of the present work.

2. See the bibliography used below. Such an approach typifies especially F. Watson, *Paul, Judaism and the Gentiles: A Sociological Approach*, SNTS MS 56 (Cambridge, 1986).

3. Even according to E. Käsemann ("Paul and Israel" [1961] in *New Testament Questions of Today* [Philadelphia, 1969] 183-187, at 184): "The Apostle's true adversary is the devout Jew" (quoted by M. Barth, "St. Paul—A Good Jew," 7). On a more popular level, see J. Holzner, *Rings um Paulus* (Munich, 1947): Paul "now sees that the Old Testament is not identified with Judaism, that Judaism is an infidelity, a defective development, a deviation, one expression, unilateral and limited to one nation, of the Old Testament."

The treatment of the theme requires a few preliminary methodological clarifications. The area of inquiry excludes the Book of the Acts of the Apostles and is limited to the firsthand Pauline documents, that is, the letters. Nor will we consider all the Pauline letters, but only those generally considered to be certainly authentic (omitting only Philemon, which has nothing pertinent to our question). At this point, of course, we must try to determine the precise chronological order of these writings. The main problem regards the dating of Philippians, which I think—admittedly with some hesitation—can be dated during a probable imprisonment of Paul at Ephesus during the so-called third missionary journey. I also accept methodologically the opinion of those who break up 2 Corinthians redactionally, setting a letter of chapters 10–13 ahead of that of chapters 1–9.[4] So we will follow this order of the epistles: 1 Thessalonians, 1 Corinthians, 2 Corinthians 10–13, Philippians, 2 Corinthians 1–9, Galatians, Romans.

I. The First Letter to the Thessalonians

In this first Pauline letter there is only one reference to the Jews, in 2:14-16. The passage is very limited and self-contained. But it is a very strong, almost violent text, without anything comparable in other letters. The Apostle lists a series of accusations against "the Jews," which can be listed in order:

1) they have brought sufferings on the Churches of God that are in Judea in Christ Jesus (2:14);
2) they have killed the Lord Jesus and the prophets (1:15a);
3) they have persecuted us (2:15b);
4) they are displeasing to God (2:15c);
5) they are opposed to all human beings (2:15d);
6) they prevent us from preaching to the gentiles that they might be saved (2:16a).

These six weighty accusations are followed by a logical conclusion in v. 16b: they "are always filling up the measure of their sins," to which another is then added, considering the matter not from the part of the guilty but from the part of God's punishing justice: "But wrath has come on them to the end" (16c: ἔφθασεν δὲ ἐπ᾽ αὐτοὺς ἡ ὀργὴ εἰς τέλος).[5] In the face

---

4. See the New Testament introductions, such as those of Feine-Behm-Kümmel, Wikenhauser-Schmid, George-Grelot, and commentaries on the epistles.

5. Who precisely are these "Jews"? They are introduced in connection with the "Churches of Judea"; thus we might think that it referred only to Palestinian Jews. But in fact this applies only to the first two accusations. But since the other four have a wider horizon, there

292 History and Exegesis

of unusual force of this anti-Jewish indictment, we may be tempted to embrace the hypothesis that this is a late, post-Pauline interpolation.[6] There are surely apparently valid reasons to accept this proposal. Actually, the first accusation seems to make no sense in the hand of Paul, who by his own admission had been a hard persecutor of the first Palestinian communities (cf. 1 Cor 15:9; Gal 1:13; Phil 3:6). The fourth and fifth would much better express the viewpoint of a pagan than of a Jew such as Paul elsewhere repeatedly acknowledges himself to be (see 2 Cor 11:22; Gal 1:14; Phil 3:5; Rom 9:3; 11:1);[7] moreover, the conclusion of v. 16c would be easily explicable if it were written after A.D. 70. Finally, this section contains certain *hapax legomena* for the whole New Testament (v. 14: συμφυλῆται, "compatriots"; v. 15: ἐκδιώκειν, "persecute harshly"; ἐναντίων, "opposed," applied to persons; v. 16: ἀναπληροῦν, in the sense of "fill," but in a metaphorical sense) or for Paul (v. 15a: ἀποκτείνω, "kill," in a physical sense, which recurs only in Rom 11:3 as a citation of 3 Kingdoms [1 Kings] 19:10 LXX).

Even so, given the lack of textual uncertainties in the Greek manuscript tradition,[8] before resorting to an extreme solution of hypothesizing an interpolation, we should see if we can explain the passage as an authentic expression of the letter's author. Now, the pericope actually does show certain features that make a Pauline paternity plausible. First of all, we can point to certain texts in Jewish tradition that speak openly of the sins of the people and God's wrath against them (see 2 Kgs 17:14-20; 2 Chr 36:16; Jub 1:12-13; 1QS 1:23; CD 20:29).[9] Moreover, we can trace certain

---

can be no doubt that as the speech continues, the Jews also include for Paul those of the diaspora, thus acquiring a far wider meaning.

6. Thus B. A. Pearson, "I Thessalonians 2:13-16: A Deutero-Pauline Interpolation," HThR 64 (1971) 79–94; D. Schmidt, "1 Thess. 2:13-16: Linguistic Evidence for an Interpolation," JBL 102 (1983) 269–279. On the other hand, K. P. Donfried clearly favors authenticity in "Paul and Judaism. I Thessalonians 2:13-16 as a Test Case," Int 38 (1984) 242–253.

7. The fifth accusation especially is typical of pagan anti-Semitism, as attested by Cicero, *De provinciis consularibus* 5:10; B.G.U. 1079 (of the year A.D. 41); P. Lond. 1912, lines 90 and 100 (letter of Claudius to the Alexandrians, in the same year); Pliny the Elder, *Hist. nat.* 13:4:46; Juvenal, *Sat.* 14:103-104; Tacitus, *Hist.* 5:4-5; Philostratus, *Vit. Apoll.* 5:33; the accusation is also attested by the Jew Flavius Josephus, *C. Ap.* 1:139 (attributed to a certain Lysimachus).

8. The only variants concern: the insertion of the adjective ἰδίους, "their own," in v. 15a between the article τούς, "the," and the noun προφήτας, "prophets"; the reading ἔφθακεν instead of ἔφθασεν [a difference of tenses] in v. 16c; the addition of the genitive τοῦ θεοῦ, "of God," to specify ἡ ὀργή, "the wrath," in the same verse. The Nestle-Aland critical edition (Stuttgart, 1981⁴) notes the existence of one lone Vulgate manuscript that omits the whole v. 16c.

9. See O. Michel, "Fragen zu 1. Thessaloniker 2,14-16: Antijüdische Polemik bei Paulus," in W. Eckert et al., eds., *Antijudaismus im Neuen Testament? Exegetische und systematische Beiträge* (Munich, 1967) 50–59. In v. 16b Paul uses phraseology against the Jews that is already biblical, even if it is there applied to pagans (see Gen 15:16; Dan 8:23; 2 Macc 6:14f.). Besides, v. 16c finds a surprising parallel in *Test. Lev.* 6:11 (ἔφθασεν δὲ αὐτοὺς ἡ ὀργὴ τοῦ θεοῦ εἰς τέλος, "the wrath of God came on them decisively," said of the Shechemites), which one could

elements that connect our text with pre-Synoptic tradition (as witnessed in Matt 23:29-38 with the terms ἀποκτείνειν, προφήτας, διώκειν, πληροῦν, "kill, prophets, persecute, fill up").[10] We could also associate v. 16c with certain historical facts injurious to the Jews before 70 (such as anti-Jewish persecutions under Caligula and Claudius; in ancient Jewish understanding, the suffering of martyrs is a sign of the approaching end).[11] The opinion has also been expressed that Paul is alluding only to a minority of Jews—those who according to Rom 2:28 are false Jews, signed with circumcision of the flesh but not of the heart.[12] Finally, we must recognize that Paul is writing 1 Thessalonians against a background of the imminently expected parousia, which leaves the Jews but little time for either rebellion or repentance.[13] Apart from anything else, it is always a sound hermeneutical principle not to try to harmonize an author's earlier writings with later ones at all costs, as if an evolution were impossible. In our case it would certainly be a preconception to deny the authenticity of 1 Thess 2:14-16 only because later in Rom 9:1-5 Paul expresses himself in quite different terms.

We can, then, make some observations about each of the accusations.

1) In the first accusation Paul seems to speak only in the third person about the Jews as persecuting the Churches of Judea, as though he had never taken part. The statement, lacking any autobiographical allusion, is found in a context of considerable warmth toward the Thessalonians, where Paul first reprovingly expatiates on his past disinterested and even maternal self-sacrifice for this community (2:1-12) and then on his ardent desire to see them again and return to their midst (2:17–3:10). Thus the recalling of his own past persecution of Christians would be out of place. Besides, the third person can also include Paul himself, but at a time when he speaks of events which belong to a remote past and which no longer characterize him, but only those who, compatriots and coreligionists though they be, have not joined him in his choice of Christianity. In any case, the facts mentioned refer only to "Judea," i.e., the whole of Palestine.[14] But nothing says that this refers to the period before Paul was Chris-

---

surely hypothesize to be dependent on the Pauline text (see B. Rigaux, *Saint Paul: Les épîtres aux Thessaloniciens* [Paris-Gembloux, 1956] 112-113, 455-456) or else suppose that the phrase was a stereotyped expression (see P. Sacchi, *Apocrifi dell'Antico Testamento* [Turin, 1981] 796).

10. See R. Schippers, "The Pre-Synoptic Tradition in I Thess. II 13-16," NT 8 (1966) 223-234.

11. See E. Bammel, "Judenverfolgung und Naherwartung. Zur Eschatologie des Ersten Thessalonikerbriefes," ZThK 56 (1959) 294-315.

12. See J. Coppens, "Une diatribe antijuive dans I Thess., II, 13-16," EThL 51 (1975) 90-95.

13. See G. E. Okeke, "I Thessalonians 2:13-16: The Fate of the Unbelieving Jews," NTS 27 (1980) 127-136.

14. This use of "Judea" in the broad sense is witnessed alike in the New Testament (see

tian, since from Acts 12 we know that under Herod Aggripa I (A.D. 41-44), the killing of James the Greater and the jailing of Peter took place. Perhaps it is these more recent events that best explain Paul's silence about his own activity in persecution, by now long past.

2) The second accusation attributes the killing of the Lord Jesus and the prophets to the Jews.[15] The association of the two terms, with the "Lord Jesus" preceding rather than following the "prophets," probably indicates that the fate of Jesus (upon which the accent falls) is deliberately inserted into the line about the customary treatment of the prophets by the Jews (see the parable of the murderous tenders of the vineyard in Mark 12:1-8 and parallels). And once again the third person speech suggests a denial of responsibility by Paul; but he does not so much insist on the event itself and its moral reprehensibility, but rather simply suggests its background in the history of salvation.[16]

3) The reproof regarding the persecution of Paul himself by Jews is extremely sober and brief. By the time he is writing 1 Thessalonians, if we follow the account of Acts, he has endured several violent reactions from his compatriots—first in Damascus (see Acts 9:23) and at Jerusalem (9:29); then at Pisidian Antioch (13:44-52), at Iconium (14:2), at Lystra (14:19), again at Thessalonica (17:5) and Beroea (17:13), while the Corinthian crisis was about to erupt (18:6, 12f.) It is, then, surprising that Paul, after all these events, limits himself to a simple allusion that fails to present the various abuses he himself has endured.

4) The affirmation that the Jews "do not please God" is formulated with a typical Pauline phrase (cf. 1 Thess 2:4; 4:1; 2 Cor 5:9; Rom 8:8; and also 1 Cor 7:32; Gal 1:10) that expresses the ideal of the apostolic task and of the simple Christian life as well. The verb ἀρέσκω, "to please," indicates not so much a state as a way of behaving made up of concrete acts, a specific conduct.[17] What we have in our passage, then, is not so much a negative labeling of the Jews with a mark of infamy as it is a way of point-

---

Luke 1:5; 4:44; 7:17; 23:5; Acts 10:37; 11:1, 29; 21:20), in Jewish writers (see *Letter of Aristeas* 4:12; Fl. Josephus, *Ant.* 1:160), and in pagan writers (Strabo 16:479f.; Tacitus, *Hist.* 5:9).

15. The expression καὶ τοὺς προφήτας, "and the prophets," could also be the direct object of the participle ἐκδιωξάντων, "who persecuted"; what leads us to associate it rather with the preceding participle ἀποκτεινάντων, "who killed," is the traditional nature of the theme of killing rather than persecuting the prophets: thus Jesus (Matt 21:31, 34, 37; Mark 12:5; Luke 13:34); Stephen (Acts 7:52); and Paul himself (Rom 11:3; 1 Kgs 19:10, 14).

16. In any case, the Apostle does not express himself absolutely in terms of "deicide," as will subsequently become common (see Melito of Sardis, *On Easter* 96).

17. See W. Foerster, ἀρέσκω, TDNT 1:455.

ing out their basic condition. All that the accusation says is that the anti-Christian deeds they have done cannot please God. In this Paul seems to resurrect the spirit, if not the letter, of the famous pronouncement of his master Rabbi Gamaliel, who warned his co-religionists not to become θεομάχοι, "fighters against God" (see Acts 5:38-39).

5) The fifth accusation is that which most reflects an extra-Judaic point of view (cf. Tacitus, *Hist.* 5:5: *adversus omnes alios hostile odium*, "hostile hatred of others"). Even so, the generalizing expression "all men," πάντες ἄνθρωποι, is clearly Pauline (cf. Rom 12:17-18; 1 Cor 7:7; 15:19; 2 Cor 3:2; Phil 4:5). But above all we must note that the reproach does not have an absolute meaning, since it is specified by the accusation that follows immediately (v. 16a), which is not separated from this one by a new καί, "and," as is the case with all that precede it, but begins with a κωλυόν-των, "preventing," that is simply in apposition to ἐναντίων, "opposed"; that is, v. 15d is now explained (and restricted) by v. 16a. It is as if to say that the opposition to "all men" is not actually racial or cultural but must be understood in a strictly apostolic perspective.

6) Verse 16a not only includes the last accusation but represents a climax, the goal of the long list that preceded. Even just on a literary level it is the most fully developed; introduced by a participle, it includes an infinitive phrase, which in turn is modified by a final clause: "They prevent us *from speaking* (infin.: λαλῆσαι) to the gentiles in order that they might be saved." It is finally here that we recognize the true reason for Paul's severe indictment: the climax of Israel's sins (v. 16b) is not the execution of Jesus but the obstacle set up against the missionary work.

At the beginning of the chapter Paul had already noted, "We have had the strength in our God *to proclaim* (λαλῆσαι) the gospel of God to you among many tribulations" (2:2). As we see, the verb λαλέω, "speak," has the strong sense of "announce" and in 2:16 of "evangelize," especially because it is followed by the noun ἔθνη, "nations," which indicates the classic addressees of Paul's mission (see Gal 1:16; 2:7-9). Now, "the fact that the Jews interfere with the realization of the new moment of God, and not just the attempts on the life of individuals, shows them to be enemies of God, and it is on these grounds, according to Paul, that one can take up current anti-Semitic opinions in a new theological sense."[18] But these, we repeat, contain nothing anti-racial. Still, they are weighty of course.

---

18. E. Bammel, "Judenverfolgung," 307.

However, Paul's tone here surely has something to do with his fiery temperament, which tends to exaggerate polemic as well as praise (see a little below: 2:19-20). His perspective is missionary.[19] We are, then, confronting not a global and theoretical judgment of the Jews but a position taken on the basis of historical circumstances. Moreover, they are introduced at the beginning of the pericope only as a point of comparison with the citizens of Thessalonica in their treatment of the Christians of the city, who have had to suffer *in imitation (μιμηταὶ ἐγενήθητε)* of the Christians of Judea. An implicit analogy, then, continues throughout the text between the non-Christian Thessalonians and the Jews, so that whatever is said of the latter is likewise somehow meant for the former.[20] Essentially, the sixth and last accusation is a development of the third, in the light of which we must read the fourth and fifth.

Verse 16c remains to be considered briefly. What is this wrath [of God], which is said to have already come on them εἰς τέλος, "to the end"? I think the commentary of B. Rigaux in 1956 had already indicated the right direction when he says that nothing in the text suggests an allusion to specific events, and would simply perceive "the change of God's attitude that has already taken place, the 'hardening,' " while the τέλος, "end," is "an indeterminate end, both temporal and eschatological, like the ὀργή, "wrath," that leads there.[21]

Enlarging on this suggestion, I think we can establish an analogy between our text and Rom 9:22, where the Israelites are described as "vessels of wrath, ready for destruction" *(σκεύη ὀργῆς, κατηρτισμένα εἰς ἀπώλειαν)*. Despite all the contextual differences (see below), we cannot help but note a parallelism at least of ideas if not of vocabulary. Besides the strict affinity between the two adverbial clauses εἰς τέλος, "to the end," and εἰς ἀπώλειαν, "for destruction," the statement that ἔφθασεν δὲ ἐπ' αὐτοὺς ἡ ὀργή, "but wrath has come upon them" (1 Thess 2:16c), is perfectly comparable not only to the image of "vessels of wrath" (Rom 9:22b) but especially to the almost adjoining declaration that "God wants to show his wrath" upon the Jews (Rom 9:22a: θέλων ὁ θεὸς ἐνδείξασθαι τὴν ὀργήν).[22]

19. H. Windisch, *Paulus und das Judentum*, 21, already realized that it was a matter of "a purely ecclesially, purely apostolically conceived anti-Semitism."

20. Συμφυλεταί, "compatriots," has a local rather than racial sense (*concives*, "fellow citizens": Ambrosiaster) and certainly includes the pagans of Thessalonica, while not excluding the Jews of the city as well, who have provoked the persecution (Acts 17:5). The two sources of the persecution there may be explained by the fact that these Christians came from both parts of the population.

21. B. Rigaux, *Les épîtres aux Thessaloniciens*, 454.

22. It is interesting to note that the term ὀργή, "wrath," recurs in the authentic Pauline letters only in 1 Thessalonians (1:10; 2:16; 5:9) and in Romans (1:18; 2:5, 8; 3:5; 4:15; 5:9; 9:22, twice; 12:19; 13:4, 5).

What is this "anger" in this perspective? In conformity with the preceding Rom 9:18 ("God shows pity to whom he wants and hardens whom he wants"), this is simply an actual and historical realization of the obstinacy of Israel in their failure to believe the gospel. "In the showing of wrath there is accomplished the predisposition to eschatological destruction."[23] The difference in Rom 9:22 is that there we find not only the wrath but also a magnanimous forbearance of God (in view of their conversion and final salvation).[24]

But the concept of God's wrath upon the children of Israel is also attested in intertestamental literature (see Jub. 15:34; Eth. Enoch 89:32-33; 2 Bar 64:4). Thus Paul's application of it to the Jews in 1 Thess 2:16c is not absolutely new; what is original is rather the implicit reference to the gospel, and to the obstacles they have placed to its dissemination. Paul's point of view is still that of the mission, not yet that of salvation history as in Rom 9-11. The Jews in 1 Thess 2:14-16 do not yet present a problem by the mystery of their unbelief, but rather by their active opposition to the Christian preaching. It is only this that explains the severity of Paul's stance.

II. The First Letter to the Corinthians

First Corinthians mentions the Jews at five different points, under five formal aspects.

—1:22, 23, 24: In the context of a reflection on the vanity of human wisdom in the face of the word of the Cross, Paul brings up the "Jews" three times by saying that they "seek signs" (v. 22) and that for them Christ is "a stumbling block" (v. 23: σκάνδαλον), but that he can become "the power of God" for those who are called (v. 24). But what surely must be noted is that all three times the Ἰουδαῖοι, "Jews," are paired up with the Ἕλληνες, "Greeks" (vv. 22, 24)/ἔθνη, "gentiles" (v. 23). We can, then, state that the Pauline perspective is universalistic in the sense that he treats Jews and gentiles on a basis of equality before the mystery of God's wisdom manifest in the Cross of Christ. Still, we should note that all three times the "Jews" are mentioned first; indeed, in v. 24 we first encounter the paired phrase Ἰουδαίοις τε καὶ Ἕλλησιν, "Jews and Greeks alike," which

23. U. Wilckens, *Der Brief an die Römer (Röm 6-11)*, EKK VI/2, (Zurich and Neukirchen-Vluyn, 1980) 203 (with citation of 1 Thess 2:16b!); also E. Käsemann, *Commentary on Romans* (Grand Rapids, Mich., 1980) 270 = *An Die Römer*, HzNT 8a (Tübingen, 1980⁴), 261, rightly refers to Rom 1:18-3:20 and to the theme of "the power of the final judge already manifested in the present."
24. See H. Schlier, *Der Römerbrief*, HThKNT VI (Freiburg-Basel-Vienna, 1977) 301ff.

will recur with slight variations throughout the Pauline letters, indicating the precedence of the Jews in the history of salvation as recipients of the gospel, and so of God's call.[25]

—9:20f.: The text is very irenic but expresses a genuine preoccupation of Paul's. To become a "Jew to the Jews" (v. 20), i.e., "like one who is under the Law with those who are under the Law" (v. 21), is an attitude called for more by the desire to spread the preaching of the gospel than by a formally positive judgment on Judaism itself, since this practice is paired up with the practice adopted for "those who do not have the Law" (v. 22: the gentiles). In any case, there is no polemic here, and if we should want to translate this principle into biographical terms, we should find material enough in the Acts of the Apostles (see 16:1-3: circumcision of Timothy; 18:19: discharging of a nazirite vow; 20:16: participating in the feast of Pentecost; 21:26: sponsoring a purification in the Jerusalem Temple). Nevertheless, this is not enough to maintain that Paul exercised a mission to the Jews equivalent to that to the gentiles; we probably have a rhetorical parallelism, for this is the only such statement in his letters.[26] At any rate, in 1 Cor 7:17 Paul had already written that everyone should live in the condition in which they were at the time God called them to Christian faith, whether circumcised or not. And we should always note, both here and in 9:20-22, that the Jews always are mentioned first in any example Paul provides.[27]

25. According to the exegesis of Chr. Senft, *La première épître de Saint Paul aux Corinthiens*, CNT VII (Neuchâtel, 1979) 40, after having said in v. 21 that the world has not known God, Paul in v. 22 will substitute the two terms "Jews and Greeks," treated with perfect equality, for the expression "the world." The statement ought to be much better nuanced. Actually the concepts of "wisdom" and "foolishness," which in vv. 18-21 described the world in general, are limited in vv. 22-23 to the "Greeks/gentiles," while the Jews are typified by a new vocabulary ("signs/scandal"). This is perhaps an indication that "Jews and Greeks" do not actualize the definition of "the world" in the same way!

26. Actually, the idea of a first mission of Paul to the Jews (thus J. Munck, *Paul and the Salvation of Mankind* [London, 1959] 119f., according to whom it was abandoned because of its failure, but against this see E. P. Sanders, *Paul, the Law*, 179–190) could also be confirmed by 1 Cor 1:22-24 (besides 1 Thess 2:15f.). But then, such a mission (related, let us note, to that among the gentiles) is best located in the phase before the Jerusalem council; and the division of spheres of competence that took place there, as attested by Gal 2:7-9, is best explained if such a meeting followed the mission to Corinth rather than preceded it, whether this should be dated in the traditional limits of 50–52 (thus R. Jewett, *A Chronology of Paul's Life* [Philadelphia, 1979]; J. Murphy O'Connor, "Pauline Missions Before the Jerusalem Conference," RB 89 [1982] 71–91) or set some ten years earlier (thus G. Lüdemann, *Paulus, der Heidenapostel—I. Probleme zur Chronologie*, FRLANT 123 [Göttingen, 1980] 79–86, 139–148).

27. The commentary of W. F. Orr and J. A. Walther, *I Corinthians*, Anchor Bible (Garden City, N.Y., 1976) 243, does not so much as mention the Jews but interprets the passage as vaguely as possible as apostolic dedication to "others." It seems to me that we thus lose the concrete cultural and historical intent of Paul.

—10:18: Here "Israel according to the flesh" (i.e., the historical Israel; see 2 Cor 5:16) is taken directly as an example for an instruction on the eucharistic meal and on the theme of communion with the "bread," but here it is a matter of "eating sacrificial victims." Paul refers to a cultic practice that "is unquestioningly recognized as valid."[28]

—10:32: "Do not be an obstacle either to Jews or to Greeks or to the Church of God." In a paraenetic framework this principle sets up a surprising and interesting ranking among three distinct and very different groups with which the Christian resorts in human, religious, and cultural relations. And it is the Jews who always take the first place, in this case preceding even the members of the Church, as well as the Greeks. It is they, then, that the Christians are invited to put in the first place in comparison to themselves. To them goes the first attention.

—12:13: We see again the formula εἴτε Ἰουδαῖοι εἴτε Ἕλληνες, "whether Jews or Greeks" (followed at once by the pair "slave and free"), to say that all without distinction have been baptized in one and the same Spirit to make up the one body (of Christ). This implies the idea that the body of Christ overcomes all religious and national distinctions. In it the Jews also are called to overcome their particularism. Christ is above every religious tradition, and also above the sum of all of them. But the fact remains that it is the Jews who are first destined to enter and become part of this body.

As we see, there is simply no polemic sense in Paul's perspective on the Jews in 1 Corinthians. What dominates is simply the Apostle's view of their summons to the gospel along with the gentiles, but with precedence over them.[29]

---

28. H. Conzelmann, *1 Corinthians*, Hermeneia, trans. J. W. Leitch (Philadelphia, 1975) 172 = *Der erste Brief an die Korinther*, Meyer Kommentar (Göttingen, 1969) 204.

29. The formula Ἀνάθεμα Ἰησοῦς, "Cursed be Jesus," in 1 Cor 12:3 has led to a whole line of interpretation that would see in it a curse required of Christians by the Jews as a condition for their participation in synagogal worship: see V. H. Neufeld, *The Earliest Christian Confessions* (Leiden, 1962) 64; J. D. M. Derrett, "Cursing Jesus (1 Cor. XIII.3): The Jews as Religious "Persecutors," NTS 21 (1974–75) 544–554; among the commentaries, see W. F. Orr and J. A. Walther (also O. Cullmann, *La foi et le culte de l'église primitive*, [Neuchâtel, 1963] 63, has maintained persecution as the *Sitz im Leben* without specifying whence it came). However, I think this hypothesis cannot be sustained for three reasons: (a) the supposed parallels are all late texts (see Pliny the Younger, *Epist.* 10:96, 5-6; *Mart. Polycarp.* 9:2f.); (b) Paul's formula in v. 3a can be explained as a simple literary expedient to emphasize the true confession of faith in v. 3b by way of contrast (see J. M. Bassler, "1 Cor 12:3—Curse and Confession in Context," JBL 101 [1982] 415–418); (c) the general context of 1 Corinthians gives no reason to understand an anti-Jewish polemic.

III. The intermediate letter to the Corinthians

We here adopt the hypothesis[30] that the four chapters 2 Cor 10–13 make up at least part of the letter written "with tears" (or the "Zwischenbrief"), mentioned in 2 Cor 2:4; 7:8. In them Paul makes an impassioned apology for his own behavior with regard to the Christians of Corinth accompanied by a violent polemic against the "superapostles,"[31] who have disturbed this community and opposed his apostolic ministry. In 11:22 he recognizes that they are "Hebrews," "Israelites," "offspring of Abraham" but then adds that they are also "ministers of Christ" (11:23). This description locates them clearly within the boundaries of Christianity, therefore Jewish Christians, and thus outside our specific enterprise. At most, we can deduce that to belong ethnically to the Jewish people provided grounds for honor and for boasting within the first Christian communities.[32]

We find the statement of 2 Cor 11:24 more interesting: "From the Jews I have five times received the forty strokes minus one." The practice to which Paul alludes is well documented in the Mishnah *Makkôt* 3:10 (cf. Deut 25:2-3). It is problematic to know to what occasions (five times!) in his life before this he refers, seeing that the Acts of the Apostles is completely silent about any such punishment, but there is no way to satisfy our curiosity. We cannot exclude the possibility that this is an "example of rhetorical exaggeration."[33] But the report is still important. On the one hand, it allows us to hypothesize plausibly that the beatings were administered to him in connection with his mission to the gentiles, which failed to call for full obedience to the Torah, and which specifically depreciated circumcision.[34] On the other hand, "the most important thing to be derived from 2 Cor 11:24 is that both Paul and the Jews who punished him regarded the Christian movement as falling within Judaism. . . .

30. See above, note 4. Also F. Watson, "2 Cor X–XIII and Paul's Painful Letter to the Corinthians," JThS 35 (1984) 324–346.
31. 2 Cor 11:5, 13; 12:11. See D. Kee, "Who Were the 'Super-Apostles' of 2 Corinthians 10–13?" RestorQuart 23 (1980) 65–76 (Hellenistic Jews with syncretistic-Gnostic principles); M. E. Thrall, "Super-Apostles, Servants of Christ, and Servants of Satan," JSNT 6 (1980) 42–57 (the apostles of Jerusalem, associated with Peter in his double role attested by the synoptic tradition); S. E. McClelland, " 'Super-Apostles, Servants of Christ, Servants of Satan': A Response," JSNT 14 (1982) 82–87 (it is not certain that they are Jewish Christians). See above, chap. 15.
32. See R. Bultmann, *The Second Letter to the Corinthians*, trans. R. A. Harrisville (Minneapolis, 1985) 214 = *Der zweite Brief an die Korinther*, ed. E. Dinkler, Meyer Kommentar (Göttingen, 1976) 215–216.
33. E. P. Sanders, *Paul, the Law, and the Jewish People* (Philadelphia, 1983) 190: "Paul depicts himself as in danger from all groups other than Pauline Christians in every conceivable place."
34. We know that from the third century on it was normal to administer a beating to a teacher who had deserved expulsion from the synagogue, in lieu of the expulsion itself (see Strack-Billerbeck, IV 318–320). It is possible that this happened even earlier, at least in isolated cases (see C. K. Barrett, *The Second Epistle to the Corinthians* [London, 1976²] 296).

Punishment implies *inclusion*. If Paul had considered that he had withdrawn from Judaism, he would not have attended synagogue. If the members of the synagogue had considered him an outsider, they would not have punished him."[35]

In any case, we must emphasize that in both 11:24 and 11:26 ("dangers from [my] people": κινδύνοι ἐκ γένους) the allusions to the difficulties suffered at the hands of the Jews are very sober—a sobriety that contrasts markedly with the bitterness of 1 Thess 2:14-16 (see above). These allusions are only a part of a much vaster autobiographical framework (see 11:22–12:10) that is in no way dominated by anti-Jewish polemic but rather by a defense before the Corinthians of a certain conception of the apostolic ministry, experienced under the paschal sign of weakness placed in the service of the power of God. Paul means to say that even the troubles encountered with the Jews, like all the other troubles, form part of his credentials as an apostle. The two allusions to his co-religionists leave the Jews still only at the periphery of Paul's attention. The facts they refer to are episodic and give no evidence of any particular problem in regard to this people.

IV. The Letter to the Philippians

In Phil 3:2 we read a threefold warning: "Beware the dogs, beware the evil workers, beware the mutilation!" The terms are severe, revealing turbulent feelings through the insistent repetition of the metaphorically used verb βλέπετε, "watch/beware," and the contemptuous images, the third of which treats circumcision with heavy sarcasm through the rhetorical figure of paronomasia (κατατομή, "mutilation," for περιτομή, "circumcision").

But who are these opponents to Paul's preaching and dangerous seducers of the Philippian Church? The three identifications most likely refer to a single group.[36] But there seems to be an ambiguity in the terms

---

35. E. P. Sanders, *Paul, the Law*, 192; "Paul's converts were taken seriously enough by synagogue authorities to lead them to discipline the one who had brought them into the people of God without requiring circumcision. Paul told them that they were heirs to the promises made to Abraham, and both he and non-Christian Jews regarded this as a serious issue. They punished Paul and he submitted to the punishment, because they all agreed that the question of who constitutes Israel was a matter of crucial importance."

36. Theoretically we could distinguish three different types of opponents: pagan agitators (in reference to whom the designation "dogs" is part of a customary Jewish terminology: see Strack-Billerbeck, I 724f.; III 621f.); Jewish-Christian missionaries (see the related expression ἐργάται δόλιοι, "deceitful workers," applied to the "false apostles" in 2 Cor 11:13); and Jewish propagandists (who because of their insistence on circumcision would be caustically labeled as proponents of a "mutilation" or "disfigurement"; on the necessity of circumci-

that should permit us to identify it: Is it simply Jewish,[37] or Jewish-Christian,[38] or none of the above? Actually, as J. Gnilka notes, the words used by Paul are more an invective than a description. But one thing is clear enough in Phil 3:2-5: they are very insistent in requiring circumcision. This is seen especially in v. 3 ("For it is we who are the circumcision, who worship in the spirit of God and glory in Christ Jesus, and do not trust in the flesh"), which has its parallel in Rom 2:28-29, where the distinction is made between the manifest Jew (circumcision of the flesh) and the hidden but true Jew (circumcision of the heart in the spirit).

But while Rom 2:28-29 certainly refers to the Jews, this does not mean that the same is already the case in Phil 3:2-3, where the idea of a spiritual circumcision arises for the first time, and that in terms which are not yet unequivocal, at least insofar as they refer to the rivals. The adversaries demand the observance of the Law, at least in general (3:5-9), while Paul insists on justification through faith in Christ. It is precisely here that the contrast between faith and Law appears for the first time, even if the terminology is not yet developed.

Moreover, I think it quite abnormal that Paul should apply such an insulting term as "dogs" to his fellow Jews, an insult inconceivable in reference to persons of his own stock (note 3:5).[39] The improbability of this is emphasized by the fact that the identification "dogs" is applied within primitive Christianity to the unbaptized in general, and specifically to heretics (cf. Rev 22:15; *Did.* 9:5; Ignatius, *Ad Eph.* 7:1; see also Matt 7:6; 2 Pet 2:22).

Furthermore, the list of grounds for praise in vv. 5-6 (proper circumcision on the eighth day, the stock of Israel, the tribe of Benjamin, Hebrew of Hebrews, adherence to Pharisaic law, persecutor of the Church, irreproachable in observance of the law), while having a Jewish stamp, do not really presuppose a Jewish counterpart, since it is explicitly said that they are "more" than what the rivals can boast of. The ἐγὼ μᾶλλον, "I more

---

sion see Fl. Josephus, *Ant.* 20:40-45 in reference to the conversion of Izates, king of Adiabene, to Judaism in the Claudian period). We do not here consider the "opponents" described in Phil 3:18-19, who seem to have nothing in common with extra-Christian Judaism; see R. Jewett, "Conflicting Movements in the Early Church as Reflected in Philippians," NT 12 (1970) 362–390, esp. 372–378.

37. Thus E. Lohmeyer, *Die Briefe an die Philipper, an die Kolosser und an Philemon*, Meyer Kommentar (Göttingen, 1964[13]) 124–126; P. Richardson, *Israel in the Apostolic Church*, SNTS MS 10 (New York-Cambridge, 1969) 113. See an overview of the various opinions in J. Heriban, "Retto φρονεῖν and κένωσις. Studio esegetico su Fil 2,1-5.6-11," BSR 51 (Rome, 1983) 43–44, n. 18.

38. Thus J. Gnilka, *Der Philipperbrief*, HThKNT X/3 (Freiburg-Basel-Vienna, 1976²) 211–218 (IV. Exkursus: "Die philippinischen Irrlehrer"); G. Lüdemann, *Paulus, der Heidenapostel—I. Antipaulinismus im frühen Christentum*, FRLANT 130 (Göttingen, 1983) 155.

39. See A. Suhl, *Paulus und seine Briefe. Ein Beitrag zur paulinischen Chronologie* (Gütersloh, 1975) 197 (with a reference to Rom 10:1f.).

so,'' of v. 4b says precisely that Paul could "glory in the flesh" much more than his opponents at Philippi. Therefore the list of reasons for boasting do describe him, but not them, who at most could boast of circumcision (but not on the eighth day!). It is a different situation, then, from 2 Cor 11:22, where being "Hebrew, Israelite, offspring of Abraham" is a common denominator between Paul and the (Judeo-Christian) "superapostles." Here, rather, Paul alludes to Christians of gentile origin. "What throws Paul into a rage must be precisely the fact that these as yet uncircumcised Christians of gentile origin were having themselves circumcised or wanted to do so.''[40]

In conclusion, then, Philippians is not actually a polemic against Jews. Though Paul does say that all that he first considered "a gain" *(κέρδη)* in his condition as a pious Jew has now become "a loss" *(ζημία)*, that is, now that he has encountered Christ. But the reasoning is concerned with two different forms of "justice" before God, through a confrontation that is not this time with Jewish opponents. We have the beginnings of a theological reflection rather than a mission-based contrast with the children of Israel.

V. The Second Letter to the Corinthians, chapter 3

In the rich but difficult text 2 Cor 3:4–4:6, Paul centers his discourse on the comparison and indeed the contrast of two διακονίαι, or ministries: that of Moses and that of the Christian apostle (see 3:4-17), even though this does seem then to become a contrast between Moses and Christ himself (see 3:18–4:6).[41] Paul is here doing a midrashic re-reading of Exod 34:29-35, using the rabbinic technique of *qal waḥomer* or passage *a minore ad maius* (especially evident in 3:8, 9, 11): If Moses had a shining face because of having spoken with God and had to cover himself with a veil (for fear

40. A. Suhl, *Paulus*, 198. Obviously, then, the expression κακοὶ ἐργάται, "evil workers," does not have a missionary sense (as in 2 Cor 11:13, where the adjective is different besides) but simply means that these Christians of Philippi "do evil, behave evilly" in adopting circumcision (from a linguistic viewpoint see 1 Macc 3:6: πάντες οἱ ἐργάται τῆς ἀνομίας, "all the workers of lawlessness"; Luke 13:27: πάντες ἐργάται ἀδικίας, "all workers of injustice"; Xenophon, *Memor.* 2:1:27: ἐργάτης τῶν καλῶν, "workers of good things"). Paul's intervention, albeit severe, is genuinely pastoral.

41. Concerning this pericope as a whole, besides our exegesis proposed in "Lo Spirito di Cristo. Cristologia e pneumatologia secondo un'originale formulazione paolina," RivBib Suppl. 7 (Brescia, 1976) 187-205, we cite some more recent studies: A. T. Hanson, "The Midrash in II Corinthians 3: A Reconsideration," JSNT 9 (1980) 2-28; P. von der Osten-Sacken, "Geist im Buchstaben. Vom Glanz des Mose und des Paulus," EvTh 41 (1981) 230-235; E. Richard, "Polemics, Old Testament, and Theology: A Study of II Cor., III,1-IV,6," RB 88 (1981) 340-367; J. A. Fitzmyer, "Glory Reflected in the Face of Christ (2 Cor 3:7-4:6) and a Palestinian Jewish Motif," ThSt 42 (1981) 630-644.

that the splendor should perish, and until he would return to speak with God in the tent), then all the more glorious is the apostolic ministry, because it has no need of a veil, since the "surpassing glory" (3:10) of the new ministry of the gospel is destined to remain intact through the unceasing face-to-face encounter with the glory of God, which shines on the face of Christ (see 3:4; 4:6), and through the life-giving function of the Spirit (see 3:6, 17f.)

In this perspective the comparison of the two covenants has a secondary role,[42] both because the whole general context (from 2:14 to 6:10) is only a reflection on the nature and function of the apostolic ministry, and because the explicit reference to the "new covenant" in 3:6 is still governed by the concept of διακονία (διακόνους καινῆς διαθήκης, "ministers of a new covenant") and, since it occurs without the article, would seem to be a new modality of the "old covenant" (v. 14: τῆς παλαιᾶς διαθήκης) rather than an alternative to it (in the same sense see Jer 38:31 LXX).[43]

At this point Paul's discourse takes a historically concrete turn: upon "the children of Israel" (v. 13) "until this very day this same veil remains upon the reading of the old covenant" (14b); "until today, whenever Moses is read a veil lies on their hearts" (v. 15). Paul is obviously passing judgment here on the Jews of his own time. And it is an essentially negative judgment. But actually we must distinguish between the conception Paul has of the "covenant" and what he thinks of the Jews whom he is facing.[44]

On the one hand, the covenant, while described as "old," still unquestionably conceals a component of "glory" (see vv. 7-11); and Paul recognizes that it must be read (vv. 14, 15), which in all probability reflects his own personal habit of reading and meditating on the ancient Scriptures, especially the Pentateuch (note v. 15: "when Moses is read"). But on the other hand, he indicates that the veil has passed from the "face" of Moses

42. Thus with W. D. Davies, "Paul and the People of Israel," 11f., against most studies (for example, most recently E. P. Sanders, *Paul, the Law*, 139).

43. The position of J. Carmignac is absolutely untenable, "II Corinthiens III.6,14 et le début de la formation du NT," NTS 24 (1978) 384–386, where the "new covenant" would have a literary sense and would already allude to 1-2 Thessalonians and 1 Corinthians, perhaps Galatians and Philippians, and even Mark and Matthew! Apart from any historical consideration, the meaning of the term "covenant" must be deduced only from biblical usage (see C. K. Barrett, *The Second Epistle to the Corinthians*, 112; E. Richard, "Polemics," would see the whole passage 2 Cor 3:4-18 as a commentary on Jer 38:31 LXX).

44. C. J. A. Hickling rightly observes, "The Sequence of Thought in II Corinthians, Chapter Three," NTS 21 (1975) 380–395, at 393: "The problem of Jewish failure to believe in Jesus, which is the subject of what amounts to an *excursus* from the main direction of Paul's thought in this chapter, was one sufficiently painful and urgent in Paul's mind to be raised almost automatically. . . . Paul's own failure to convert any significant number of his fellow-Jews may have been a particularly stinging part of his opponents' attack on his reputation as a public speaker."

to the "heart" of the Israelites, but with a quite different function: no longer to keep Moses from being seen but to keep from seeing, i.e., not to see that the old glory has now given way to something "surpassing" (v. 10). Paul uses the same verb ἐπωρώθησαν, "were hardened," that he will use again in Rom 11:7; but here he uses it in a general sense without any distinction, since the repeated pronoun αὐτῶν, "their" (vv. 14a, 15), refers globally to τοὺς υἱοὺς Ἰσραήλ, "the children of Israel" (v. 13), whereas there he will insist on a distinction concerning "Israel" (Rom 11:7a) between "the elect" (ibid., 11:7b: ἡ ἐκλογή) and "the others" (11:7c: οἱ δὲ λοιποὶ ἐπωρώθησαν), who "were hardened."

So here Paul does not nuance his own judgment. In all probability he is thinking of Sabbath worship of the synagogue, in which he normally takes part, where they do read the texts of the Old Testament, that is, where "Moses is always present";[45] and it is not unnatural to suppose that Paul is thinking of all the times, in various synagogues from Jerusalem to Corinth, that he has, with almost no success, maintained among his co-religionists the necessity of "reading Moses" with hearts unveiled through adherence to Christ (see Acts 9:22, 29; 13:5, 15f., etc.). And still we ought to note that he does not inveigh against them. He simply affirms that "the same veil . . . remains, it not being manifest [or: manifested] [understanding: to them] that in Christ it [the veil] can be removed" (2 Cor 3:14b).[46]

45. R. Bultmann, 2 Corinthians, 86 = Der zweite Brief an die Korinther, 89.
46. All in all, I find this translation the best: the comma after the main verb μένει, "remains," is required by the fact that the participle ἀνακαλυπτόμενον, "unveiled," is negated not by the objective negative οὐκ, "not" (which would have negated only the participle and referred it concretely to τὸ αὐτὸ κάλυμμα, "the same veil"), but by the subjective μή, "not" (which negates precisely a whole clause or phrase); see Blass-Debrunner-Rehkopf, 426. The participle, therefore, should be considered an accusative absolute. The objection of R. Bultmann is not valid; he maintains that the participle should in that case have been μὴ ἀποκαλυπτόμενον, "not revealed": Der zweite Brief, 90, because later, in 3:18, the same verb returns in the expression ἀνακεκαλυμμένῳ προσώπῳ, "with face unveiled." Above all, we must note that the unexpressed subject of the forceful verb καταργεῖται, "is finished," should be τὸ αὐτὸ κάλυμμα, "the same veil," and not the παλαιὰ διαθήκη, "the old covenant" (contra R. Bultmann, ibid.; I had maintained the same thing myself in "Lo Spirito di Cristo," 190, and "Atteggiamenti di Paolo verso l'Antico Testamento," RivBibl 32 [1984] 192).
It is true that the same verb (but as a participle) recurs with a different subject in vv. 7, 11, and 13 and that "the veil" is the subject of another verb in v. 16 (περιαιρεῖται, "will be taken away"), but: (a) the subject agreeing with the καταργούμενον, "finished," in vv. 7, 11, 13 cannot be the "old covenant" of v. 14 both because this expression appears only later and because in v. 7 the explicit subject is δόξα, "glory," while in vv. 11, 13 it is a generic neuter subject that could also refer to the ministry/διακονία of Moses, and not necessarily to the Law (contra E. P. Sanders, Paul, the Law, 139), which is not so much as named; (b) that the verb applied to the veil in v. 16 is a different one can be explained simply because it is a somewhat free quotation of Exod 34:34 LXX, as most scholars recognize. Moreover, a decisive argument is that it would be most surprising if Paul were to state "the old covenant" is being eliminated without further arguing this truly revolutionary (and Marcionite!) claim: (a) because the expression "old covenant" is a hapax legomenon in the whole New Testament;

What Paul is anxious to do is to say, not that the old covenant is being eliminated (something he never says anywhere else! cf., on the other hand, Heb 8:13; 7:18), but that through faith in Christ this covenant can be understood more deeply: in Christ and in the Spirit this faith can disclose to Jews new horizons in the history of salvation. This failure to understand the depths of the covenant Paul seems in a certain sense to remove from their personal responsibility, attributing it to "the god of this world," who "has blinded the minds of the unbelievers, that they might not see the splendor of the glorious gospel of Christ" (4:4; cf. Rom 15:31). It seems to be a sort of excuse to keep Paul from having to call his co-religionists directly to account; but the result is that he makes an altogether exceptional choice to borrow a motif from Gnostic apocalyptic (with a dualistic Iranian resonance), which actually ends up developing an anti-Jewish flavor (note 4:3: "Our gospel is veiled for those who are perishing").[47]

Paradoxically, what is most clear in this whole passage is its apparent obscurity, which derives from the complexity of the matter it treats, i.e., from the theological complexity of the Israelite people itself and its covenant with God, in its encounter with the "new covenant." From 2 Corinthians we see that the wine of Paul's Christian understanding of Israel has not yet finished its fermentation. Basically, the reason the Jews do not perceive the glory of Christ is that for them the only glory is in Moses and in his covenant. Now, this is a glory which Paul recognizes but which he judges incomplete, if not transient. They lack the extra that is of Christ and of the Spirit, which would make it possible for them to perceive a "much greater glory" (3:10). But the fact remains that 2 Cor 3 does represent the confrontation of Paul's apostolic and theological consciousness with the problem of Israel.

VI. The Letter to the Galatians

Even in his Letter to the Galatians, Paul does not yet demonstrate a thorough understanding of the problem of Israel's unbelief.

(b) because in Paul's usage elsewhere the concept of "covenant" is essentially positive (on Gal 4:24-31, see below); (c) because Heb 8:13 ("By saying 'new covenant' God has declared the first one obsolete") feels it necessary to set this declaration in the context of a much broader argument (Heb 8–9), such as is completely missing here. And after all, as W. D. Davies, "Paul and the People of Israel," 11, acutely observes, "The adjective *[new]* . . . can be applied to the new moon, which is simply the old moon in a new light"!

47. See also the exegesis of Ps.-Philo, LAB 12:1: "And it came to pass that when [Moses] went down to the children of Israel, they did not recognize him by sight. But when he spoke, then they knew him"; and he cites Gen 42:8: as in Egypt, when Joseph knew his brothers but they did not recognize him.

As far as vocabulary is concerned, apart from the two uses of the term Ἰουδαϊσμός, "Judaism," in 1:13, 14 in his autobiographical reports of his pre-Christian conduct, he uses the term Ἰουδαῖος, "Jew," four times: in the context of the incident in Antioch (2:13, 14: along with the adverb ἰουδαϊκῶς, "in a Jewish manner," and the verb ἰουδαΐζειν, "Judaize")' in designating himself and Peter (2:15); and alongside Ἕλλην, "Greek," to deny any separation in Christ (3:28). Such use reveals only an indirect, not a direct, interest in the Jews. But the term never has, any more than elsewhere, a contemptuous sense.

This is all the more evident in the autograph concluding blessing of 6:16: "And to all who follow this norm [of the καινὴ κτίσις, "new creation": v. 15], peace upon them and mercy, and upon the Israel of God." The final expression (καὶ ἐπὶ τὸν Ἰσραὴλ τοῦ θεοῦ, "and upon God's Israel") seems ambiguous at first glance. To whom does it refer? On the basis of the earlier thematic developments of the letter, it would seem to apply only to Christians, and to all of these, whether of Jewish or gentile origin, for they have been declared true offspring of Abraham on the basis of faith (see 3:29);[48] but apart from the presence of καί, "and," which suggests the distinguishing of a second group, the leap in Pauline language would be too great (even in relation to 1 Cor 10:18) and would have required a more developed explanation, since the term "Israel," both in the Bible and in extrabiblical literature, always indicates the Jewish people. Now, we can think of the Jewish people as a whole[49] or else of a part of it, i.e., of those Jews who have heard the gospel.[50] There is only limited validity to the objection of E. P. Sanders that "we can hardly think that he now includes his opponents as receiving the same blessing as those who walk by the rule that circumcision does not matter."[51] Indeed, Paul has just said that "it is neither circumcision that matters nor uncircumcision" (6:15). But it seems to me that in these last lines of the letter, written by Paul with his own hand (6:11), there comes to light a first stage

48. Thus, esp., E. P. Sanders, *Paul, the Law*, 173–174; see also the commentaries of H. Schlier, Meyer Kommentar VII (Tübingen, 1962³) ad loc.; P. Bonnard, CNT IX (Neuchâtel, 1972²) ad loc.
49. Thus, F. Mussner, *Der Galaterbrief*, HThKNT IX (Freiburg-Basel-Vienna, 1974) 417, n. 59, who identifies the expression of Gal 6:16 with the πᾶς Ἰσραήλ, "all Israel," of Rom 11:26; agreeing with him is also F. F. Bruce, *The Epistle to the Galatians*, NIGTC (Exeter, 1982) 275.
50. Thus already E. de Witt Burton, *A Critical and Exegetical Commentary on the Epistle to the Galatians*, ICC (Edinburgh, 1921) ad loc., who refers rather to the "remnant" (λεῖμμα) of Rom 11:5; see also P. Richardson, *Israel*, 74–84. Thus S. Lyonnet, who in "Die Israelfrage nach Röm 9–11," ed. L. De Lorenzi (Rome, 1977) 50, would like to correct the version offered in *La Bible de Jérusalem*. Similarly H. D. Betz, *Galatians* (Philadelphia, 1979), after a good discussion of the text, maintains that with this formula Paul "extends the blessing . . . to those Jewish-Christians who approve his κανών ("rule") in v 15" (p. 323); see also U. Borse, *Der Brief an die Galater*, RNT (Regensburg, 1984) 223.
51. *Paul, the Law*, 174.

of the problem soon to be treated more fully in Rom 9-11 (see, for example, 9:6b: "Not all the descendants of Israel are Israel"). We can, then, also imagine that Paul here understands the whole people of Israel, but considered under the precise formal aspect of the people of God, insofar as this is represented by those children of Israel who are revealed as true children of Abraham through faith in Christ.

In any case, the Letter to the Galatians is not written against the Jews[52] but against these Christians (who are especially of Jewish origin and inspiration) who wanted to attribute to the Mosaic Law (and more specifically to circumcision and the dietary and festal provisions; see 2:11-14; 4:10; 5:2) a determining function in justification (see 1:6: "another gospel"; 1:8-9: "a different gospel"; 2:4: "false brethren who had crept in to spy on the liberty we have in Christ Jesus, in order to enslave us"). The polemic of course involves an indirect reaction against Judaism. But this reaction never becomes the principal issue.[53]

I maintain that neither does the well-known, difficult passage about the two sons of Abraham (4:21-31) have a directly anti-Jewish intent.[54] Having said that the two mothers (Hagar and Sarah, the slave and the free in chronological succession) are equivalent to "two covenants" (4:24) and to two different kinds of Jerusalem (4:25-27: the one of "the present" and the other "on high"), the Apostle continues, "Now you, brothers, are children of the promise like Isaac; but just as then the one who was born according to the flesh persecuted the one born according to the Spirit, so it is now" (4:28-29). The reference to the actuality is explicit, so as to make us consider the Pauline re-reading of Gen 16:15; 21:1-3, 9-10 to be typological, despite Paul's reference to it as "allegory" (4:24).[55]

---

52. A broad convergence has been reached on this opinion: see G. Howard, *Paul: Crisis in Galatia. A Study in Early Christian Theology*, SNTS MS 35 (Cambridge, 1979) 1-19; F. Mussner, *Traktat über die Juden* (Munich, 1979) 227-228; E. P. Sanders, *Paul, the Law*, 18-19; G. Lüdemann, *Paulus—II*, 144-152. Of a different opinion is H. D. Betz, *Galatians*, 116. Meanwhile R. Jewett, "Agitators and the Galatian Congregation," NTS 17 (1970-71) 198-212, believes that these are Jewish-Christian missionaries coming from Jerusalem, driven by the climate developed in Palestine by the Zealots in the late 40s (agreeing with him is F. F. Bruce, *Galatians*, 31f., 224, 269); whereas W. Schmithals, "Judaisten in Galatien?" ZNW 74 (1983) 27-58, maintains that Paul's adversaries represent a Jewish or Jewish-Christian "enthusiasm" of Gnostic background (see his "Die Haeretiker in Galatien," ZNW 47 [1956] 26-27).

53. This remains true even if H. Räisänen is correct in "Galatians 2.16 and Paul's Break with Judaism," NTS 31 (1985) 543-553, where he claims that the rupture with Judaism was inevitable from the precise moment when Paul began to claim that faith in Christ was the *only* way of salvation (note p. 550).

54. Against H. D. Betz, *Galatians*, 246: "one of Paul's sharpest attacks upon the Jews."

55. Besides the commentaries, see A. T. Hanson, *Studies in Paul's Technique and Theology* (London, 1974) 94f.

But who today corresponds to the child according to the flesh, who persecutes his own brother?[56] Simply to say that it is the Jews[57] seems to me insufficiently nuanced; indeed, how can he state that the Jews should be driven out, excluded from any inheritance (4:30; Gen 21:10), and then a little later in Rom 11:25-32 maintain that they are destined for eschatological salvation?[58] From one letter to the next this would be not evolution but a complete reversal of thought, and the judgment passed in 4:30 would be most abnormal. Meanwhile, however, to recast the theory and say that it is rather a matter of gentiles who submit to and constrain others to circumcision, as has recently been maintained, seems to me quite unfounded;[59] paradoxically, according to this opinion to be Christians would be equivalent to being children of the "present Jerusalem," i.e., certainly children of Sarah, but just as are all the Jews in opposition to the gentile children of Hagar! But then where is the newness of Christianity, the καινὴ κτίσις, "the new creation"?

I think it much better to follow the theme of persecution present in 4:29, comparing it with 5:11 ("But as for me, brethren, if I still preach circumcision, why am I persecuted?") and with 6:12 ("They constrain you to be circumcised only so as not to be persecuted because of the Cross of Christ"). Well, in the whole letter (apart from the autobiographical notes in 1:13f., 23), the only logical context for persecution is represented by the Judeo-Christian opponents (see 1:7: οἱ ταράσσοντες ὑμᾶς, "those who disturb you"; 2:4: τοὺς παρεισάκτους ψευδαδέλφους . . . ἵνα ἡμᾶς καταδουλώσουσιν, "the false brethren brought in by stealth . . . to make slaves of you";

56. The Bible does not speak of a persecution of Isaac by Ishmael. Paul is using a Palestinian *haggadah*, which interpreted the Hebrew participle *m'ṣaḥēq* in Gen 21:9 (from *ṣḥq:* "laugh, make sport of") in a hostile sense: see the documentation of Strack-Billerbeck, III 575f. (Tos. *Sota* 6:6; *Gen. Rab.* 53:11); R. Le Déaut, "Traditions targumiques dans le Corpus Paulinum," *Bib* 42 (1961) 28–48, 37–43 (TgPs.-Jo on Gen 22:1).

57. See H. D. Betz, *Galatians*, 250; U. Borse, *Galater*, 175. (Worse yet is the expression of J. B. Lightfoot, *St. Paul's Epistle to the Galatians* [London, 1890]: "The apostle thus confidently sounds the death-knell of Judaism," 184!)

58. H. D. Betz, *Galatians*, 251, recognizes that there is here a "decisive difference" between Galatians and Romans; but F. Mussner, *Galaterbrief*, 332, n. 79, correctly counters that such a contradiction would indicate a "schizophrenia" in Paul, and adds that it would be an extraordinary insult to make the Jews Hagar's children!

59. Thus L. Gaston, "Israel's Enemies in Pauline Theology," *NTS* 28 (1982) 400–423: the author maintains that the very rare Greek verb συστοιχεῖ of Gal 4:25 (found elsewhere only in Polybius 10:23:7 as a present participle referring to horsemen in battle drawn up in an orderly line) means not "corresponds" but "opposes" (cf. the substantive συστοιχία in Aristotle, *Metaph.* 1:5; *Part. anim.* 3:7, said of Pythagoreans, who set up two opposing columns of conflicting ideas), and consequently, according to Paul, the association Sinai/Hagar (= gentiles) would be opposed to the present Jerusalem. But then, what would be the difference between ἡ νῦν, "the present," and ἡ ἄνω Ἰηρουσαλήμ, "the Jerusalem above," if the former no longer corresponds to Sinai/Hagar?

4:17: ζηλοῦσιν ὑμᾶς οὐ καλῶς, "they are zealous for you—but not well"; 5:10: ὁ δὲ ταράσσων ὑμᾶς βαστάσει τὸ κρίμα, ὅστις ἐὰν ᾖ, "the one that disturbs you, whoever it be, will undergo judgment"; 5:12: οἱ ἀναστατοῦντες ὑμᾶς, "those who unsettle you"). Since this is the case, it is permissible to conclude that the persecuting brother in 4:29 is not to be identified with the Jews but with the "false brothers" (2:4), i.e., with those Judaizing Christians who in anti-Pauline polemic insisted on imposing the yoke of the Mosaic Law on the baptized.[60]

In this perspective "the present Jerusalem" (4:25) is not so much that of the Jews as that of the Christian Mother Church; in fact, this is the only Jerusalem already mentioned at the beginning of the letter (1:18; 2:1). Of course, it was impossible for Paul to think only of a Jewish-Christian Jerusalem, since the city was still the *hieropolis* and *metropolis* of the Jews (see Philo, *Leg. ad C.* 281f.). Hence Judaism and Judeo-Christianity are here interrelated. Still, it is of the latter that Paul thinks with the greater uneasiness, since the former is obviously alien; and in 2:15 he seems to acknowledge a right to respect for those who are "by nature Jews" (φύσει Ἰουδαῖοι), among whom he counts himself and Peter. But "the present Jerusalem," which in its Judaizing attempts is an obstacle to the mission to the gentiles (see Ps. Sol. 17:22: the Messiah will purify Jerusalem of the gentiles who tread it underfoot), is henceforth, according to Paul, surpassed by the heavenly Jerusalem, which in contrast is free of the yoke of the Law, and to which the Christians (especially those who have come out of paganism) already belong.[61] And Paul, in accord with the agreements reached at the so-called apostolic council (cf. 2:7, 9), strenuously defends his own independent role as missionary to the gentiles; any other preachers in competition with "his gospel" have simply "crept in surreptitiously" (παρεισάκτους: 2:4), are anathematized by him (see 1:8-9), and should be rejected by the Galatians (ἔκβαλε, "cast out": 4:30; cf. Gen

60. Thus the commentaries of Th. Zahn, E. de Witt Burton, M.-J. Lagrange, H. Schlier, F. Mussner, F. F. Bruce (who, however, also hypothesizes the possibility that it does refer to the Jews if the letter was directed to the Churches of southern Galatia: see Acts 13:50; 14:2-5, 19).

61. See F. Mussner, *Galaterbrief,* 325; J. Bligh, *Galatians* (London, 1969) 390; and G. Howard, *Paul: Crisis,* 9–11. There never developed a particular theological theme of a "present Jerusalem" in intertestamental literature (see only *Baba Batra* 75b, where R. Johanan, who died in 279, speaks of the "Jerusalem of this world": Strack-Billerbeck, III 22). On the contrary, the "heavenly Jerusalem" is amply attested: see P. Volz, *Die Eschatologie der jüdischen Gemeinde im neutestamentlichen Zeitalter* (Hildesheim, 1966 = Tübingen, 1934) 371–376. This Jerusalem, according to Paul, "already has, so to speak, a bridgehead in this world" (W. D. Davies, *Paul and the People of Israel,* 10).

21:10).[62] The διώκομαι, "am persecuted," of 5:11 fits well into this framework.

In contrast, according to 6:12, Paul's opponents in Galatia want to avoid being persecuted. By whom? We can think here of no one but the Jews, who continued to think of Jewish Christians as members of the Synagogue.[63] And, as we have seen, the contemporaneous letter, 2 Cor 11:24, speaks of beatings inflicted on Paul himself by the Jews. But the persecution of Paul's opponents by the Jews is not a matter of concern for us now.

Therefore, we cannot deny that in Galatians, and particularly in 4:21-31, Judaism is present at least on the horizon of Paul's thought, and that he is therefore thinking at least indirectly of the Jews.[64] But his attitude toward them is determined precisely by the problem posed by the Christians of Jewish origin and observance, with whom he enters into polemic precisely insofar as they would impose their own soteriological and legalistic opinions on the gentiles, especially those of Paul's Churches. Paul, after all, is facing the fact that for many Christians Judaism retains a great power of attraction, doubtless a sign of its vitality and spiritual riches.[65] Still, the "Jewish question" at this point has not yet clearly emerged into the foreground in the framework of his reflection. It is only in the background, but it is there in force and is pressing to be taken directly into consideration.

VII. The Letter to the Romans

The letter to the Christians of Rome, which is probably the last written by Paul, signals the evident, and I might say insuppressible, emergence of the problem of the Jews in Paul's consciousness. In fact, while the Letter

---

62. We could think of a directly anti-Jewish intent in Paul only if we prescind from the concrete situation of the Churches of Galatia: "It is a question of driving the opponents out of the Galatian communities; it is not the Jews who are at issue, even if v. 25, with its 'present Jerusalem' may allude to Judaism, as most commentators believe, but which seems unlikely to us" (F. Mussner, *Galaterbrief,* 332). The opinion of C. K. Barrett seems quite theoretical in "The Allegory of Abraham, Sarah, and Hagar in the Argument of Galatians," in *Rechtfertigung. Festschrift für E. Käsemann* (Tübingen, 1975) 1–16, according to which the imperative in 4:30 would express "the command of God to his (angelic) agents" (p. 13).

63. E. de Witt Burton asserts correctly, *Galatians,* 349, that Paul's opponents are revealed as "members of the orthodox Jewish community, different from other Jews only in that they accepted Jesus as the expected Messiah, but they wish to remain in good standing in the Jewish community" (see Acts 8:1; 9:2, 13, 21). It is altogether improbable that the Galatian agitators feared persecution by the Christian community of Jerusalem.

64. According to W. D. Davies, "Paul and the People of Israel," 10, to want to distinguish "Jews from Jewish Christians here is to split hairs."

65. See F. Cipriani, " 'Illa quae sursum est Jerusalem . . .'. Esegesi e Teologia di un testo Paolino (Gal 4:25-27)," in *Gerusalemme, Atti della XXVI Settimana Biblica,* in onore di C. M. Martini (Brescia, 1982) 219–236, 233.

to the Galatians deals only with the question of the salvation of the gentiles, which Paul perceives in complete abstraction from the Law of Moses, and hence transcending pure Judaism, now the Letter to the Romans sees the inevitable full treatment, heretofore suppressed but now unavoidable, of the salvation of the Jews, or at least of their place in the divine plan of salvation. While writing the letter, Paul is aware that the mission (his mission) to the gentiles has been successful, whereas the mission (of Cephas) among the Jews has all but failed.[66] Hence derives the formulation of certain principal questions: What is the relative position of Jews and Gentiles before God as revealed in Christ? What value has the Law in respect to faith? How can one uphold God's faithfulness toward his people, considering that as a whole they have not accepted the gospel? Is there, or will there be salvation for Israel? When and to what extent?

It is interesting to note that these questions finally develop explicitly after the difficult encounter with the crisis in Galatia; but the present writing, while picking up the themes of the earlier letter, offers more reflective answers, better nuanced than those of the strongly polemic tone used with the Galatians. The changed historical situation of the Letter to the Romans doubtless contributed to this.[67] It was written just before Paul's fateful journey to Jerusalem to deliver a collection, and intends to gain the support of the Roman Christians, closely tied as they are to the Judeo-Christian Mother Church; to them he demonstrates in generous, irenic terms how much he is maturing with regard to the problem of the salvation of the Jews in relation to the gospel. To this is added the fact that he is writing (the only instance!) to a community almost completely unknown to him, and one definitely of Jewish origin,[68] if not also largely Jewish Christian in present character.[69]

Paul confronts the problem twice—at the beginning and the end of the principal body of the letter, specifically in chapters 1-4 (esp. 2-4) and chap-

66. For this claim see D. Zeller, *Juden und Heiden in der Mission des Paulus. Studien zum Römerbrief*, FzB 1 (Stuttgart, 1973, 1976²) 77 and 110; W. D. Davies, *Paul and the People of Israel*, 13 and 28; E. P. Sanders, *Paul, the Law*, 193.
67. See T. W. Manson, "St. Paul's Letter to the Romans, and Others," BJRL 21 (1948) 224–240; J. Jervell, "Der Brief nach Jerusalem. Über Veranlassung und Adresse des Römerbriefs," StTh 25 (1971) 61–73 (= "The Letter to Jerusalem," in *The Romans Debate*, ed. K. P. Donfried [Minneapolis, 1977] 61–74); G. Bornkamm, "Der Römerbrief als Testament des Paulus," in *Geschichte und Glaube. Gesammelte Aufsätze*, IV (Munich, 1971) 120–139; U. Borse, "Die geschichtliche und theologische Einordnung des Römerbriefs," BZ 16 (1972) 70–83; U. Wilckens, "Über Abfassungszweck und Aufbau des Römerbriefs," in *Rechtfertigung als Freiheit. Paulusstudien* (Neukirchen-Vluyn, 1974) 110–170. See also W. D. Davies, *Paul and the People of Israel*, 12f.; E. P. Sanders, *Paul and the Law*, 31.
68. See chap. 2 above.
69. See R. E. Brown and J. P. Meier, *Antioch and Rome. New Testament Cradles of Catholic Christianity* (New York, 1983) 105–183; see chap. 3 above.

ters 9–11. The mere quantitative extent of the discussion already indicates how close is the question to Paul's heart, as we could also deduce from the fact that Romans is the only writing of Paul's in which the "Jewish question" is debated not only so extensively but also in explicit, deliberate terms.[70]

In the section 1:18–5:21, the basic theme can be considered to be God's impartiality with regard to Jews and gentiles alike.[71] It recognizes certain priority for the Jews (note the adverb πρῶτον, "first") in the destination of the gospel (see 1:16), but also equality with the gentiles in infamy (see 2:9) and in honor (see 2:10), depending on whether they behave well or ill. And in 3:1-4 there already arises the subject of the special election of Israel, which will be resumed and developed only in chapters 9–11 (see above, chap. 4).[72]

But Paul's argumentation tends to show that before God all, Jews and gentiles, are alike in three ways: in the observance of the Law (1:18–2:29; note 2:11: "Indeed, before God there is no partiality");[73] in the universality of sin (3:9-20; cf. 3:23: "All indeed have sinned"); and in the one identical way of redemption, consisting in faith in Jesus Christ without reference to the works of the Law (3:21–5:21; note 3:22b: "Indeed, there is no difference"; 3:29: "Or is God the God of the Jews alone? Is he not also of the gentiles? Yes, of the gentiles as well!" 5:18: "To all, the justice that gives life").

70. In the first section the term Ἰουδαῖος "Jews" occurs nine times (1:16; 2:9, 10, 17, 28 twice; 3:1, 9, 29); in the second section we find the same noun twice (9:24; 10:12), Ἰσραηλίτης "Israelites" twice (9:4; 11:1) and the noun Ἰσραήλ "Israel" eleven times (9:6 twice, 27 twice, 31; 10:19, 21; 11:2, 7, 25, 26). These simple statistics (to which we can add the different way in which the Old Testament is used, more abundantly and with greater development in chapters 9–11) themselves indicate that the second section is more directly concerned with the theme.
71. This subject has been well treated by J. M. Bassler, *Divine Impartiality. Paul and a Theological Axiom*, SBL DS 59 (Chico, Calif., 1982: also on the background in the Old Testament and in extrabiblical Judaism).
72. Also, the adverbial phrase οὐ πάντως in 3:9 should probably be translated not as "not at all" but as "not completely," as maintained by A. Feuillet, "La situation privilégiée des Juifs d'après Rom 3,9. Comparaison avec Rom 1,16 et 3,1-2," NRTh 105 (1983) 33–46.
73. "It is nowhere unambiguously stated in 1:18–2:29 that all without exception have sinned, only that all without exception who commit sin will receive their just punishment" (J. M. Bassler, *Divine Impartiality*, 155). In fact, at the center of these first pages of Romans is not so much the theme of the condemnation of gentiles and Jews considered incapable of observing the Law, as it is rather the claim that the Jews have no privilege to boast about, since the gentiles also have their law, and all are called to observe it, because "that one is not a Jew who appears so outwardly . . . but the one who is so inwardly" (2:28-29). The difficulty of reconciling the thematic of this section with Paul's theology is partly resolved if one can see here the determining presence of homiletic material of hellenistic Judaism, as maintained by C. Bussmann, *Themen der paulinischen Missionspredigt auf dem Hintergrund der spätjüdisch-hellenistischen Missionsliteratur* (Frankfurt-Bern, 1971) esp. 108–122; E. P. Sanders, *Paul, the Law*, 123–135 (p. 129: on Rom 1:18–2:29 "Christians are not in mind, the Christian viewpoint plays no role, and the entire chapter is written from a Jewish perspective"). See above, chap. 6.

This particular insistence on the equality between Ἰουδαίους τε καὶ Ἕλληνας, "Jews and Greeks alike" (3:9), would at first sight seem to be a lessening of the dignity of the Jews and of their special place in the history of salvation. In reality, we must carefully clarify Paul's thought. On the one hand, he intends (even while affirming the existence of a περισσὸν τοῦ Ἰουδαίου, "advantage for the Jew," in 3:1, which he will, however, only develop in chapters 9–11) to exclude all "boasting" (καύχησις) before God (3:27f.)—not boasting about the observance of the Law as such, but that which consists in a simple presumption of a specially privileged right to salvation.[74] On the other hand, we must recognize that association of Jews and gentiles on a footing of equality is a form of response on Paul's part to the problem of their salvation. That is, the Apostle begins with the fact of the salvation of the gentiles as an incontestable and fruitful reality of his mission (see 1:13f.; 15:15-24): If God has revealed himself in Christ and if the gentiles have accepted this gospel of grace, that indicates that the Law is not an indispensable condition for *entering* into the people of God; and in the light of the paschal events and of personal apostolic experience, Paul also judges the place of the Jews.

Still, we must note that Paul's tone is neither that of attack[75] nor that of irony.[76] He simply recognizes the claims of the Jew to honor (2:17f.) but tries to demonstrate that these are of no value from the moral point of view if one does not observe the Law, nor from the theological point of view as soon as the Law itself is substituted for faith (see 3:27). But the style Paul adopts is not that of polemic but rather the lively and persuasive style of the diatribe. The study of S. K. Stowers on the subject[77] would lead us to conclude that the various direct addresses, objections, false conclusions, questions and responses that characterize the letter, enlivening the various passages (for this first section note: 2:1-5, 17f.; 3:1-9, 27–4:1), "should not be thought of as aimed at the Jews as opponents,

---

74. This distinction should be made against the Bultmannian school (see H. Hübner, *Das Gesetz bei Paulus. Ein Beitrag zum Werden der paulinischen Theologie*, FRLANT 119 [Göttingen, 1978, 1980²] 79–118), together with A. van Dülmen, *Die Theologie des Gesetzes bei Paulus*, SBM 5 (Stuttgart, 1968), and especially U. Wilckens, "Was heisst bei Paulus: 'Aus Werken des Gesetzes wird kein Mensch gerecht'?" in *Rechtfertigung im neuzeitlichen Lebenszusammenhang* (Gütersloh, 1974) 77–106; H. Räisänen, "Legalism and Salvation by the Law," in *Die paulinische Literatur und Theologie*, ed. S. Pedersen (Arhus-Göttingen, 1980) 63–83, esp. 68–72 (p. 68: "One gets the impression that [for Bultmann] zeal for the Law is more harmful than transgression"!); E. P. Sanders, *Paul, the Law*, 32–36, 103–104.

75. See E. Käsemann, *Romans*, 68f., 102 = *An die Römer*, 64 and 96 (the one on 2:17, the other on 3:27).

76. In 2:17, contrary to C. E. B. Cranfield, *The Epistle to the Romans*, ICC (Edinburgh, 1982 [1975]), I, 164, the commentaries of H. Schlier, *Der Römerbrief*, 82; U. Wilckens, *Brief an die Römer*, I, 148, do not recognize any element of irony.

77. *The Diatribe and Paul's Letter to the Romans*, SBL DS 57 (Chico, Calif., 1981).

but rather as addressed to the Roman Church in the modes of indictment or censure. Their intent is not polemical but pedagogical.''[78] Paul simply presents himself to the Romans as a teacher who simply wants to expound the truth, leading his hearers to it through his debate.

We find the same style again in chapters 9–11 (note 9:14, 19f., 30, 32; 10:14, 18, 19; 11:1, 7, 11, 19). But the argumentation is more complex. Here the question is no longer so much how to flee from the universal power of sin and obtain communion with God as it is to recognize who belongs to the true Israel, who is part of the people of the covenant, and just where Israel stands in relation to the gentiles for the purpose of eschatological salvation. In chapters 1–4 the soteriology was treated in a strictly theological perspective; here it is in a perspective of the history of salvation and of community. This means that "Israel" comes out into the foreground (and here alone is the proper name used: see footnote 70). Paul faces the question on the basis of a paradoxical observation: on the one hand, there is his practical experience of the refusal of the gospel by the majority of the Jews (see 9:31; 10:16, 20f.; 11:7-10); but on the other hand, there is the theoretical conviction of their divine election, which is irrevocable (9:4; 11:2, 28-29).

It is precisely this contrast that makes the interpretation of Rom 9–11 so difficult; and if their length and depth show how important the issue was for Paul, their relative obscurity shows how difficult it was for Paul himself to unravel the difficult question. This is confirmed by another paradox concerning the Jews: on the one hand, they are in no way different from the gentiles whether in sin or in the designs of God's mercy (see 10:12; 11:32); on the other hand, they differ greatly from them through certain incontestable titles to preeminence that clearly distinguish them.[79] And Paul here expresses himself with certain positive statements, which are something new and practically unique in his letters.

78. S. K. Stowers, *The Diatribe*, 153; cf. 174: "The interlocutor is not to be thought of as an opponent whom the author is polemicizing against, but rather as a student whom the author is trying to lead to truth by using the methods of indictment and protrepic"; see also 167, 177-183.

79. It seems exaggerated to me to maintain that in these chapters "the feelings which they convey—concern, anguish, and triumphant expectation, are far more important than the ideas which they contain" (E. P. Sanders, *Paul, the Law*, 193). Even so, rather than a logical structure of successive unrepetitive pericopes, it is perhaps better, or at any rate easier, to identify the thematic unities within the text; besides the couple of paradoxes we have noted they are the following: the hardening of Israel is explained with the affirmation of God's sovereign will (9:6-29); in any case, there is a "remnant" that God has reserved for himself (9:27, 29; 10:16a; 11:4-7); there exist two kinds of "justice," one based on the Law and the other based on faith in Christ: this latter, Israel has not recognized, and the former is not sufficient by itself (9:30-10:21); the rejection by Israel has providentially permitted the entry of the gentiles (9:24-25; 10:19; 11:11); Israel's jealousy will finally encourage their total readmission (10:19; 11:12-15, 23-27, 31); but still, all is left to the inscrutable wisdom of God (11:33-36).

These declarations are found at once in the beginning of the section, as if Paul cannot help but begin with what most clashed alongside the Jews' failure to believe: "They are Israelites, and theirs is the adoption as children, the glory, the covenants, the legislation, the cult, the promises, and the ancestors, and from them comes Christ according to the flesh" (9:4f.). It is a long list of titles to honor that Paul frankly acknowledges for his "brethren, kindred according to the flesh" (9:3). Precisely this objectively privileged status of theirs increases his "great sorrow and continual suffering," λύπη . . . μεγάλη καὶ ἀδιάλειπτος ὀδύνη (9:2), so much that he would even want to be "separated from Christ for [their] sake" (9:3). Paul plays with the idea of vicarious expiation for their salvation (cf. 10:1), both object and expression of a desire that is exceedingly intense, even if unrealizable.[80] "To be ready for this is for Christians the supreme proof of love for Israel."[81]

Paul, then, emphasizes the description of himself as Jewish, and repeats it in 11:1b ("I too am an Israelite, of the offspring of Abraham, of the tribe of Benjamin"). But here the tone is quite different from 2 Cor 11:22 and Phil 3:5, which are primarily polemical, confrontational, saying that his (Judaizing) opponents have nothing over him. But now his attitude is practically the opposite, and he comes to recognize that he has nothing more than they, the Jews, except for faith in Christ. The fact is that he actually does not consider them opponents but only bearers of a problem that clashes with the unfolding of the history of salvation and with the very concept of God in this history.

One could say that the Jews now acquire in Paul's eyes the dignity of a *locus theologicus*—the Jews, that is, of the Christian era, not those of the Old Testament! Rather than being bypassed, or worse vilified, they now occupy the center of his reflection, which finds itself bewildered by contrasting feelings of disappointment and veneration, of regret that crosses over into condemnation, and of burning desire for their eschatological salvation. Now, I should think we ought to emphasize that if even in 9:6–11:32 the name "Israel" had a theological value and was meant to designate not the historical people in its entirety but only Israel of election or the remnant faithful to God (both that of the Old Testament and the Christian remnant),[82] even so, in 9:4-5 Paul begins, so to speak, in

80. On the value of ηὐχόμην, see C. E. B. Cranfield, *Romans*, II, 454–457 ("I would pray"). Certainly Paul's attitude goes beyond simple prophetic intercession like that of Moses in Exod 32:31-32 (see U. Wilckens, *Römer*, II, 187).

81. E. Käsemann, *Romans*, 258 = *An die Römer*, 248. "We must think of this when Paul speaks harsh words concerning Israel" (H. Schlier, *Römerbrief*, 284).

82. This is the central thesis of F. Refoulé, ". . . *Et ainsi tout Israël sera sauvé*": *Romains 11:25-32*, LD 117 (Paris, 1984); see also N. Ponsot, " 'et ainsi tout Israël sera sauvé': Rom.,

a roundabout way, considering the whole of the historical Israel (κατὰ σάρκα, "according to the flesh," vv. 4-5), of which he enumerates a whole series of objective privileges, which do not, however, include election by God nor the response of adherence by the people.[83] Now, they are privileges oriented to Christ (note 9:31; 10:4) and hence cannot be considered a basis for boasting.

Nevertheless, even before going on to speak of the "remnant" (9:6-29: v. 27; and then 11:2-6: v. 5) and of "election" (11:7), Paul speaks simply of the Ἰσραηλῖται, "Israelites" (9:4), as "brethren" (9:3). Normally he uses this expression only as a designation of Christians, and as such it recurs in 10:1 and in 11:25. But uniquely in 9:3 he extends it to indicate the members of the chosen people, though with the specification "my kindred according to the flesh." But here the final modifying phrase does not represent only a limiting explanation, since again in 11:14 he defines unbelieving Israel as μου τὴν σάρκα, "my flesh/my carnal relatives."[84] And even if in 11:28 the non-Christian Jews are identified as "enemies" (ἐχθροί), it is a matter of a description that has a theological rather than social sense; indeed, the logical context and the strict parallelism with the following ἀγαπητοί, "beloved," would witness rather to a relationship not between Jews and Christians but between unbelieving Jews and God (see 9:13; 11:21a).[85]

XI,26a," RB 89 (1982) 406–417. Among the various positions that we are opposing in this study, we note that of F. Mussner, *Traktat*, 52–67, according to whom the "mystery" announced by Paul in 11:25 would be explained only in 11:26b-27 and would consist in the salvation accomplished by the eschatological ῥυόμενος, "deliverer" (= Isa 59:20 = God through Christ) in favor of the whole historical Israel, without foreseeing an acceptance by them of faith in Christ; see also K. Stendahl, *Paul Among Jews and Gentiles*, 40. Against this theory of the two ways of salvation, one for gentiles (faith in Christ) and one for Jews (eschatological intervention), we find E. P. Sanders declaring himself decisively, *Paul, the Law*, 194–195. F. Refoulé correctly notes that for Paul there is no salvation prescinding from faith in Christ (see 9:30–10:13!), but his limitation of the μυστήριον, "mystery," only to the remnant is beside the point, since the "remnant" implies the "hardening" (πώρωσις) of Israel—and its temporary character, until the conversion of the gentiles (see C. E. B. Cranfield, *Romans*, II, 574–577)—as well as the reversal of the Jewish expectations, according to which the restoration of Israel would have preceded the entrance of the gentiles (see E. Käsemann, *Romans*, 312–313 = *An die Römer*, 302–303).

83. Against F. Refoulé, ". . . *Et ainsi*," 167–176, but in agreement with F. Dreyfus, "Le passé et le présent d'Israël (9:1-5; 11:1-24)," in *Die Israelfrage nach Röm 9–11*, ed. L. De Lorenzi (Rome, 1977) 131–151, esp. 132–139. Still, as F. Mussner correctly points out, *Traktat*, 46 (contra H. Schlier, *Römerbrief*, 286f.), these privileges are proper to Israel and remain so, since Paul never says that they have passed from Israel to the Church.

84. Still, the salvation of "some" of them, which Paul hopes for in 11:14, should be understood not as a result of a direct mission of his among the Jews but according to the context as a result of his normal mission among the gentiles (11:13), insofar as this is destined to "rouse their jealousy" (note the verb παραζηλόω in 10:19; 11:11, 14).

85. See Cranfield, II, 580; Käsemann, 315 = 305; Wilckens, II, 257 n. 1160; Schlier 341f. Of these commentators, only Schlier understands ἐχθροί, "enemies," in an active sense (the

Paul all but concludes the pericope of Rom 9–11 with the prospect of the eschatological salvation even of Israel, which today is unbelieving, and that is of "all Israel," πᾶς 'Ισραὴλ σωθήσεται, "all Israel will be saved" (11:26).[86]

As far as the actual concrete behavior of other Christians is concerned, especially of those of gentile origin, in the face of unbelieving Israel, even before their reintegration comes, Paul insistently exhorts them to guard against dishonorable anti-Jewish attitude or behavior, some forms of which were evidently beginning to develop (cf. 11:18: "Do not boast: it is not you that bear the root, but the root bears you"; 11:20b: "Do not rise up in pride, but fear"; cf. 11:29). He, therefore, does not just resign himself to the inscrutable ways of God's wisdom (see 11:33-36) but also requires of his readers a concrete attitude going beyond his personal example of prayer (cf. 9:3; 10:1) and tends to stimulate concrete relations of extreme respect and honor. From a Christian point of view, could one in the first century have said more?

VIII. Conclusion

Having examined all the texts concerning our subject, we must honestly recognize that it is not easy to trace a really proper line of evolution composed of successive steps. The clearest datum is the great distance separating the two passages, 1 Thess 2:14-16 and Rom 9–11. These, which are

---

Jews themselves are enemies of God; the alternative is that God "hates" them, making them enemies). F. Refoulé also seems to lean toward the passive sense, *"Et ainsi . . .,"* 197–199.

86. There are three reasons that keep me from accepting the limiting interpretation of "all Israel" proposed by F. Refoulé: (a) the idea of "Remnant," I should think, must refer only to Christians of Jewish origin rather than to the "just" Israel, even though that be what is prefigured by the corresponding Old Testament theme, since Paul's Christian logic does not begin with the Old Testament but with the experience of post-Easter faith; (b) unlike *Sanh.* 10:1-4, Paul is not preoccupied with enumerating exceptions, but rather his interest is concerned with how and when οἱ λοιποί, "the rest," i.e., the non-elect (11:7) can be saved, or grafted again onto the trunk of the good olive tree (Christian Judaism); (c) the πᾶς 'Ισραὴλ, "all Israel," of 11:26a is a chiastic reflection of πάντες οἱ ἐκ 'Ισραήλ, "all who descend from Israel," of 9:6b, concerning whom the intervening reasoning says precisely that unfortunately not all have shown themselves true children of Abraham by accepting faith in Christ. Hence it is better to understand the πᾶς, "all," in a global sense: *Non particulariter sicut modo, sed universaliter omnes*, "Not individually like here [in 9:16], but globally" (Saint Thomas Aquinas, *Ad Rom.*, 9:16). See A. Feuillet, *L'espérance de la conversion d'Israël en Rm XI,25-32: L'interprétation des versets 26 et 31*, in *De la Torah au Messie*, Mélanges H. Cazelles (Paris, 1981) 483-494, 492: "The Apostle thinks of the whole of Israel, though without excluding certain exceptions, which are always possible; what he means to say is that the abnormal situation of the present moment will cease, where the Jews who have become Christian remain the exception"; see also P. Schneider, "The Meaning of 'Israel' in the Writings of St. Paul," *Face to Face* 10 (1983) 12-16; D. G. Johnson, "The Structure and Meaning of Romans 11," *CBQ* 46 (1984) 91-103.

the first and the last in the authentic Pauline correspondence, represent two extremes, the two points of greatest divergence. The comparison is valid, obviously, if, as we have done, one rejects the hypothesis of the inauthenticity of 1 Thess 2:14-16. We see then that, as they say, a lot of water has gone under the bridge! The pitiless accusations of the former letter have given way to grieving feelings of the latter, and the sentence of condemnation to a consuming desire for salvation.

The best explanation for this kind of an about-face is found in the facts themselves, that is, the different roles occupied by the Jews in relation to Paul's mission to the pagans. At first he perceived them only as opponents of his apostolic enterprise among the gentiles, an obstacle to his mission. At the end they have become a theological problem. Precisely their continuing rejection of the gospel has induced the Apostle to re-evaluate them in a different light: paradoxically no longer under the negative aspect of simple opponents of the word of God (see 1 Thess 2:13, 16a), but from a more positive viewpoint, or at least a more problematic question: who is this people that calls into question the validity of the word of God with their own behavior (see Rom 9:6a) but is still destined for salvation (see Rom 9:27; 10:13; 11:14, 23, 24, 26)? At the beginning they are a contradiction, at the end a mystery. In any case, it is vitally important, and instructive, that the change of Paul's attitude did not develop in the opposite direction!

But what has been Paul's attitude between these two extreme stages? Since we have excluded mention of the Jews in Philippians,[87] there remain 1 Corinthians, 2 Corinthians, and Galatians. We note here that for the most part Jews are at the periphery of Paul's apostolic experience and marginal to his thought. He is the apostle of the gentiles, not of the circumcised (see Gal 2:7-9).[88] His conversation is at most with Jewish Christians, and always indirect at that. But precisely these, who were always a real thorn in his side, play a mediating role in the development in Paul of the problem raised by Israel's lack of faith. The faithfulness to the Law of Moses on the part of these Jewish Christians finally draws the others fully into the field of vision of Paul's theology. Evidently he was expecting the acceptance of the Christian faith *en masse* by those who not only were his kindred and co-religionists but also had always been those first addressed by the gospel (see Rom 1:16; and every time they are associated with the "Greeks" or the "gentiles," the "Jews" are named first). What a searing disappointment their refusal must have been (see Rom 9:3f.)!

87. Which is the only letter in which "Jew" and "Israel" do not appear as terms of conflict: for 3:5 is actually autobiographical.
88. See above, note 26.

Ultimately, the basic question that takes shape in Paul's consciousness is this: How is it possible that the Torah can not only co-exist with faith in Christ but can also impede its acceptance—in other words, why does Israel prefer Moses to Abraham? And since this is nevertheless the people irrevocably called by God, what will be their final outcome in relation to the believing gentiles?

This theme is first observed in 2 Cor 3 and in Galatians, in connection with the disturbing experience of the "false apostles" entering the Church of Corinth, and especially of the Judaizing "false brethren" who have crept into the Church of Galatia to win them to their cause. From this also we understand the place of Rom 1-4 as an earlier step to Rom 9-11. Hence this intermediate group of writings can be considered to provide a kind of connection, since they provide some distance from the violent tones of 1 Thessalonians and prepare for the more irenic character of Romans. This, in turn, will be followed by the deutero-Pauline Letter to the Ephesians, which will further develop the gains of Romans, applying them to the life of the Church.[89]

The fact of Paul's basic respect for Judaism remains. Even if in Gal 3 and Rom 9:6-29 he states that "not all of Abraham's descendants are his children" (Rom 9:7), he never goes so far as to speak of the Church as the "true" or "new Israel," or at least does not tend to give any such idea substitutive meaning or polemical weight.[90] Indeed, even if his Christian faith emphasizes its newness in relation to the historic Israel more than we see at Qumran, which actually considered itself the community of the "New Covenant" (CD 9:19; 8:21; 19:33-34), he never goes so far as to wish that "the wicked of Israel will be smashed, and destroyed forever" (4QpPs 37, III 12f.; cf. 1QM 1,2); and if some such idea is concealed in 1 Thess 2:16 (where the verb is, however, in the aorist rather than the future), the later writings move far beyond this.

In conclusion, I think one could say that if Paul has something to teach twentieth-century Christians, it is that we should set aside all disparagement of, or worse all hostility toward, the Jews, passing on to an attitude of appreciation and a serious theological discussion; it is necessary to honor at least the fact that "from them comes the Christ according to the flesh"

89. See K. M. Fischer, *Tendenz und Absicht des Epheserbriefes*, FRLANT 111 (Göttingen, 1973) 79-94; M. Rese, "Die Vorzüge Israels in Röm 9,4f.-Eph 2,12," ThZ 31 (1975) 211-222; R. Penna, *La lettera agli Efesini*, Scritti delle Origini Cristiane 10 (Bologna, 1988) 55-56 and 134ff.

90. See W. D. Davies, *Paul and the People of Israel*, 19; E. P. Sanders, *Paul, the Law, and the Jewish People*, 171-179. It will only be from the late second century that the name of Israel will begin to be transferred to the Church: Justin, *Dial.* 11:5 (cf. also the "new people" in *Barn.* 5:7; 7:5); see P. Richardson, *Israel in the Apostolic Church*, SNTS MS 10 (New York-Cambridge, 1969) 9.

(Rom 9:5) and that we are all therefore debtors to their history and to their religious identity. Only on the basis of the awareness that what there is between Christians and Jews is a "familial" debate[91] will it be possible to demonstrate that the gospel, rather than undermining the old trunk of Israel, is solidly grafted into it and moreover provides it with a new sap of life.

---

91. W. D. Davies, *Paul and the People of Israel*, 37; the greatest difference in our historical situation from that of Paul, as Davies points out, is the effect of the rabbinic synod of Jamnia, which forms something of a watershed between two different configurations of Judaism. Nevertheless, we must be able to hope for another change again, since " 'he who is wedded to the present will soon be widowed' " (p. 36)!

Index of Subjects

Abraham, testing of. *See Aqedah*
Adamic Christology, 216–223
Agape
  Christian reading of, 199–205
  exercised within Church, 203–204
  in 1 Cor 13, 196–205
  various meanings of, 196–198
Ἁμαρτία. *See* Sin
Aqedah
  biblical tradition of, 144–147
  formation of the theologoumenon of, 152–158
  rabbinic tradition of, 147–152
  in Romans 8:32, 161–168

Baptism. *See also* Death of Christ
  subsidiary to the death of Christ, 130–133, 141
  mediation between the Christ-event and the believer, 137
Body, soul, spirit, 225–226

Cicero (M. Tullius Cicero), 23, 34. *See also* Jewish Communities of Rome
Clement's letter, 57–59

Death, 128–129
  in 1 Cor 15, 227–228
Death of Christ. *See also Aqedah;* Suffering Servant
  expiatory value of, 164–165, 167–168
  preceding, establishing, giving meaning to baptism, 132

Dio Cassius, 25, 35
Diogenes the Cynic and 1 Cor 7:29b-31a, 181–190
Δύναμις. *See* Power

Faith, 179, 191

Gnostic anthropology, 213–215, 228–229

Hebrews, Letter to the, 56
Horace (Q. Horatius Flaccus), 23

Jewish Communities of Rome
  Augustus and, 23
  Cicero's direct reference to, 23–24
  Claudius' expulsion of, 35, 50
  Julius Caesar and, 35
  Nero and, 36
  organization of, 32–33
  Tiberius and, 35
Jewish war, 21–22
Jews. *See* Paul's attitude toward the Jews
Josephus (Flavius Josephus), 25, 35, 155–156
Juvenal (D. Junius Juvenal), 24, 30, 39, 40

Life, 129–130
Likeness, 135. *See also* Baptism

Martial (M. Valerius Martialis), 24, 39
Monteverde Catacomb, 26–27, 31, 37, 42–44

'Ομοίωμα. *See* Likeness
Ovid (P. Ovidius Naso), 23

Paul
    anthropology of, 223–231, 258
    autobiography of, 96–97,
        237–238
    detractors of, in Romans, 119,
        123
    opponents of, in 2 Cor 10–13,
        269, 285–289. *See also*
        Rhetorical figures
    sufferings of, 237–242
Paulinism, 8–13
Paul's attitude toward the Jews
    fixed or evolutionary? 290–291,
        318
    in 1 Corinthians, 297–299
    in 2 Corinthians 3, 303–306
    in Galatians, 306–311
    in Philippians 3:2, 301–303
    in Romans, 311–318
    in 1 Thessalonians 2:14-16
Persius (A. Persius Flaccus), 24
Peter, First Letter of, 54–55
Petronius Arbiter, 24
Philo of Alexandria
    and the *Aqedah*, 155
    anthropology of, 212–213
    mention of Roman Jews by, 38
    travel to Rome of, 23
Pneuma in 1 Cor 15:45, 255–256
Poppaea, 25, 36

Power
    in the Greek world, 170–173
    of God and of Christ, 172–180

Quintilian, 24

Resurrection. *See also*
    Monteverde Catacomb
    in Judaism, 253–254
    in Roman Jewish communities, 44
Rhetorical figures in 2 Cor 10:13,
    275–285. *See also* Paul's
    opponents
Roman Church
    by whom founded, 49–50
    its structures in the first
        century, 48–60
Romans, Letter to the, 93–102

Seneca (L. Annaeus Seneca), 23
Sin, 127–128
Suetonius (C. Suetonius
    Tranquillus), 46, 50
Suffering Servant in Romans 8:32,
    163, 167–168. *See also* Death
    of Christ
Σῶμα, Ψυχή, Πνεῦμα. *See* Body,
    soul, spirit

Tacitus (Cornelius Tacitus), 25
"Thorn in the flesh," 283–285

Valerius Maximus, 23

Index of Scriptural Texts

Romans
1:16   169
1:18–5:21   313–315
1:18–2:29   103–110
1:21-22   169
3:1-4   75–76
3:5-8   76–77
3:8   111–119
3:9-20   77–79
3:21–5:21   79–82
6–8   82–85
6:1-11   124–141
6:3   140–141
8:32   158–168
9–11   85–88, 315

1 Corinthians
1:18-25   169–180
1:18   169, 175
1:21   169
1:22, 23, 24   297
1:23-24   175

7:29b-31a   189–190
9:20   298
10:18   299
10:32   299
12:13   299
13   191–205
15:45-49   206–231

2 Corinthians
3:4–4:6   303–306
4:7–5:10   232
10–13   260–289

Galatians
3:27   140–141
4:21-31   308–311

Philippians
3:2   301–303

1 Thessalonians
2:14-16   291–297

227.066
P412
v. 1

97001